Poetry Focus 2026

Leaving Certificate poems and notes for **English Higher Level**

Martin Kieran & Frances Rocks

GILL EDUCATION

Gill Education
Hume Avenue
Park West
Dublin 12
www.gilleducation.ie

Gill Education is an imprint of M.H. Gill & Co.

© Martin Kieran & Frances Rocks 2024

ISBN: 978-0-7171-99426

All rights reserved. No part of this publication may be copied, reproduced or transmitted in any form or by any means without written permission of the publishers or else under the terms of any licence permitting limited copying issued by the Irish Copyright Licensing Agency.

Design: Graham Thew
Print origination: Carole Lynch

At the time of going to press, all web addresses were active and contained information relevant to the topics in this book. Gill Education does not, however, accept responsibility for the content or views contained on these websites. Content, views and addresses may change beyond the publisher or author's control. Students should always be supervised when reviewing websites.

For permission to reproduce photographs, the authors and publisher gratefully acknowledge the following:

© Adobe Stock: 380, 383, 415, 416, 417; © Alamy: 10, 18, 21, 34, 60, 112, 136, 139, 142, 144, 145, 147, 149, 156, 159, 166, 168, 171, 177, 180, 182, 198, 201, 209, 230, 233, 236, 249, 251, 257, 261, 264, 309, 310, 319, 370, 409, 426, 428, 435, 438, 439, 442, 448, 450, 451, 461, 464, 471, 474; © Antonio da Correggio, via Wikimedia Commons (CC BY-SA 4.0): 305, 307; © Bridgeman Images: 72, 76, 85, 87, 93, 334, 337, 338, 342, 365; © Collins Photo Agency: 324; © Derek Speirs: 245; © Getty Images: 38, 41, 49, 89, 91, 97, 98, 99, 101, 213, 215, 252, 254, 288, 290, 293, 297, 299, 314, 317, 350, 385, 390, 431, 432, 445, 457, 460; © iStock/Getty Premium: 5, 7, 15, 16, 17, 23, 27, 29, 32, 43, 46, 63, 65, 67, 70, 81, 83, 125, 129, 172, 190, 205, 208, 271, 301, 304, 328, 330, 353, 391, 392, 393, 397, 453, 475, 484; ©The Permissions Company, on behalf of Graywolf Press: 375; © PD Smith: 468, 470; © Rolling News: 266; © RTÉ Archives: 286; © Saint Patrick's Cathedral: 465; © Shutterstock: 119, 121, 130, 151, 154, 202, 204, 359, 363; © Stephanie Joy Photography: 228; ©The Josef and Yaye Breitenbach Charitable Foundation, photograph by Josef Breitenbach: 2; ©TopFoto: 186, 194, 195, 217; ©Wikimedia Commons: 275, 403.

The authors and publisher have made every effort to trace all copyright holders. If, however, any have been inadvertently overlooked, we would be pleased to make the necessary arrangement at the first opportunity.

Contents

Introduction v

Elizabeth Bishop
- 'The Fish' (OL) — 4
- 'The Bight' — 9
- 'At the Fishhouses' — 13
- 'The Prodigal' (OL) — 18
- 'Questions of Travel' — 22
- 'The Armadillo' — 28
- 'Sestina' — 33
- 'First Death in Nova Scotia' — 37
- 'Filling Station' (OL) — 42
- 'In the Waiting Room' — 47
- Sample Questions and Essay Material — 53
- Revision Overview — 59

John Donne
- A Note on Metaphysical Poetry — 62
- 'The Sun Rising' — 63
- 'Song (Go, And Catch A Falling Star)' (OL) — 67
- 'The Anniversary' — 71
- 'Song (Sweetest Love, I Do Not Go)' — 75
- 'A Valediction: Forbidding Mourning' — 80
- 'The Dream' — 85
- 'The Flea' (OL) — 89
- 'At the Round Earth's Imagined Corners' — 93
- 'Thou Hast Made Me, and Shall Thy Work Decay?' — 97
- 'Batter My Heart, Three-Personed God' — 101
- Sample Questions and Essay Material — 105
- Revision Overview — 111

T. S. Eliot
- 'The Love Song of J. Alfred Prufrock' — 114
- 'Preludes' (OL) — 124
- 'Aunt Helen' (OL) — 130
- from 'The Waste Land': 'II. A Game of Chess' — 134
- 'Journey of the Magi' — 141
- from 'Landscapes': 'III. Usk' — 147
- from 'Landscapes': 'IV. Rannoch, by Glencoe' — 151
- from 'Four Quartets': 'East Coker IV' — 155
- Sample Questions and Essay Material — 160
- Revision Overview — 165

Seamus Heaney
- 'The Forge' — 168
- 'Bogland' — 172
- 'The Tollund Man' — 176
- 'Mossbawn: Sunlight' — 181
- 'A Constable Calls' (OL) — 185
- 'The Skunk' — 190
- 'The Harvest Bow' — 194
- 'The Underground' (OL) — 198
- 'Postscript' — 202
- 'A Call' (OL) — 205
- 'Tate's Avenue' — 209
- 'The Pitchfork' — 213
- 'Lightenings viii' — 217
- Sample Questions and Essay Material — 221
- Revision Overview — 227

Paula Meehan
- 'Buying Winkles' (OL) — 230
- 'The Pattern' — 234
- 'The Statue of the Virgin at Granard Speaks' — 241
- 'Cora, Auntie' — 247
- 'The Exact Moment I Became a Poet' — 252
- 'My Father Perceived as a Vision of St Francis' — 256
- 'Hearth Lesson' (OL) — 260
- 'Prayer for the Children of Longing' (OL) — 265

(OL) indicates poems that are also prescribed for the Ordinary Level course.

- 'Death of a Field' — 270
- 'Them Ducks Died for Ireland' — 275
- Sample Questions and Essay Material — 279
- Revision Overview — 285

Eiléan Ní Chuilleanáin

- 'Lucina Schynning in Silence of the Nicht' — 288
- 'The Second Voyage' — 292
- 'Deaths and Engines' — 297
- 'Street' (OL) — 301
- 'Fireman's Lift' — 305
- 'All for You' — 309
- 'Following' — 313
- 'Kilcash' — 318
- 'Translation' — 323
- 'The Bend in the Road' — 328
- 'On Lacking the Killer Instinct' — 333
- 'To Niall Woods and Xenya Ostrovskaia, married in Dublin on 9 September 2009' (OL) — 338
- Sample Questions and Essay Material — 343
- Revision Overview — 349

Tracy K. Smith

- 'Joy' — 352
- 'Dominion over the Beasts of the Earth' — 357
- 'The Searchers' (OL) — 364
- 'Letter to a Photojournalist Going-In' — 369
- 'The Universe is a House Party' — 374
- 'The Museum of Obsolescence' — 379
- 'Don't You Wonder, Sometimes?' — 384
- 'It's Not' (OL) — 391
- 'The Universe as Primal Scream' — 395
- 'The Greatest Personal Privation' (OL) — 401
- 'I am 60 odd years of age' — 407
- 'Ghazal' — 414
- Sample Questions and Essay Material — 419
- Revision Overview — 425

W. B. Yeats

- 'The Lake Isle of Innisfree' (OL) — 428
- 'September 1913' — 431
- 'The Wild Swans at Coole' (OL) — 435
- 'An Irish Airman Foresees His Death' (OL) — 439
- 'Easter, 1916' — 443
- 'The Second Coming' — 448
- 'Sailing to Byzantium' — 452
- from 'Meditations in Time of Civil War': 'The Stare's Nest by My Window' — 457
- 'In Memory of Eva Gore-Booth and Con Markiewicz' — 461
- 'Swift's Epitaph' — 465
- 'An Acre of Grass' — 468
- from 'Under Ben Bulben' — 471
- 'Politics' — 475
- Sample Questions and Essay Material — 478
- Revision Overview — 483

The Unseen Poem

- 'Autumn' — 486
- 'Roller-Skaters' — 489
- 'At Cider Mill Farm' — 492
- 'Lipstick' — 495
- 'Stalled Train' — 498

Acknowledgements — Inside back cover

(OL) indicates poems that are also prescribed for the Ordinary Level course.

Introduction

Poetry Focus is a modern poetry textbook for Leaving Certificate Higher Level English. It includes all the prescribed poems for the 2026 exam as well as succinct commentaries on each one. Well-organised study notes allow students to develop their own individual responses and enhance their skills in critical literacy. **There is no single 'correct' approach to answering the poetry question.** Candidates are free to respond in any appropriate way that shows good knowledge of and engagement with the prescribed poems.

- **Concise poet biographies** provide context for the poems.
- **List of prescribed poems** gives a brief introduction to each poem.
- **Personal response** questions follow the text of each poem. These allow students to consider their first impressions before any in-depth study or analysis. These questions provide a good opportunity for written and/or oral exercises.
- **Critical literacy** highlights the main features of the poet's subject matter and style. These discussion notes will enhance the student's own critical appreciation through focused group work and/or written exercises. Analytical skills are developed in a coherent, practical way to give students confidence in articulating their own personal responses.
- **Analysis (writing about the poem) is provided using graded sample paragraphs** which aid students in fluently structuring and developing valid points, using fresh and varied expression. These model paragraphs also illustrate effective use of relevant quotations and reference.
- **Class/homework exercises** for each poem provide focused practice in writing personal responses to examination-style questions.
- **Points to consider** provide a memorable snapshot of the key aspects to remember about each poem.
- **Full sample Leaving Certificate essays** are accompanied by marking-scheme guidelines and examiner's comments. These show the student exactly what is required to achieve a successful top grade in the Leaving Cert. The examiner's comments illustrate the use of the PCLM marking scheme and are an invaluable aid for the ambitious student.
- **Sample essay plans** on each poet's work illustrate how to interpret a question and recognise the particular nuances of key words in examination questions. Student evaluation of these essay plans increases confidence in developing and organising clear responses to exam questions.
- **Sample Leaving Cert questions** on each poet are given at the end of their particular section.
- **Revision overviews** provide a concise and visual summary of each poet's work, through highlighting and interlinking relevant themes.
- **Unseen poetry** provides guidelines for this 20-mark section of the paper. Included are numerous sample questions and answers, which allow students to practise exam-style answers.

 The FREE eBook contains:

- **Investigate Further** sections, which contain **useful weblinks** should you want to learn more.
- **Pop-up key quotes** to encourage students to select their own individual combination of references from a poem and to write brief commentaries on specific quotations.
- Additional sample graded paragraphs called '**Developing your personal response**'.
- Audio of a selection of the poetry read by the poets, including Seamus Heaney, Paula Meehan and Eiléan Ní Chuilleanáin.

Further material can also be found on GillExplore.ie:

- **A glossary of common literary terms** provides an easy reference when answering questions.
- **A critical analysis checklist** offers useful hints and tips on how to show genuine engagement with the poetry.

How is the Prescribed Poetry Question Marked?

The Prescribed Poetry Question is marked out of 50 marks by reference to the PCLM assessment criteria:

- Clarity of purpose (P): 30% of the total (15 marks)
- Coherence of delivery (C): 30% of the total (15 marks)
- Efficiency of language use (L): 30% of the total (15 marks)
- Accuracy of mechanics (M): 10% of the total (5 marks)

Each answer will be in the form of a response to a specific task requiring candidates to:

- Display a clear and purposeful engagement with the set task (P)
- Sustain the response in an appropriate manner over the entire answer (C)
- Manage and control language appropriate to the task (L)
- Display levels of accuracy in spelling and grammar appropriate to the required/chosen register (M)

General

'Students at Higher Level will be required to study a representative selection from the work of eight poets: a representative selection would seek to reflect the range of a poet's themes and interests and exhibit his/her characteristic style and viewpoint. Normally the study of at least six poems by each poet would be expected.' (DES English Syllabus, 6.3)

The marking scheme guidelines from the State Examinations Commission state that in the case of each poet, the candidates have **freedom of choice** in relation to the poems studied. In addition, there is **not a finite list of any 'poet's themes and interests'**.

Note that in responding to the question set on any given poet, the candidates must refer to the poem(s) they have studied but are not required to refer to **any specific poem(s), nor are they expected to discuss or refer to all the poems they have chosen to study**.

In each of the questions in **Prescribed Poetry**, the underlying nature of the task is the invitation to the candidates to **engage with the poems themselves**.

Exam Advice

- **You are not expected to write about any set number of poems** in the examination. You might decide to focus in detail on a small number of poems, or you could choose to write in a more general way on several poems.
- Most candidates write one or two well-developed **paragraphs** on each of the poems they have chosen for discussion. In other cases, a paragraph will focus on one specific aspect of the poet's work. When discussing recurring themes or features of style, appropriate cross-references to other poems may be useful.
- Reflect on central **themes** and viewpoints in the poems you discuss. Comment also on the use of language and the poet's distinctive **style**. Examine imagery, tone, structure, rhythm and rhyme. Be careful not to simply list aspects of style, such as alliteration or repetition. There's little point in mentioning that a poet uses sound effects or metaphors without discussing the effectiveness of such characteristics.
- Focus on **the task** you have been given in the poetry question. Identify the key terms in the wording of the question and think of similar words for these terms. This will help you develop a relevant and coherent personal response in keeping with the PCLM marking scheme criteria.
- Always root your answers in the text of the poems. Support the points you make with **relevant reference and quotation**. Make sure your own expression is fresh and lively. Avoid awkward expressions, such as 'It says in the poem that …'. Look for alternatives: 'There is a sense of …', 'The tone seems to suggest …', 'It's evident that …', etc.
- Neat, **legible handwriting** will help to make a positive impression on examiners. Corrections should be made by simply drawing a line through the mistake. Scored-out words distract attention from the content of your work.
- Keep the emphasis on why particular poets **appeal to you**. Consider the continuing relevance or significance of a poet's work. Perhaps you have shared some of the feelings or experiences expressed in the poems. Avoid starting answers with prepared biographical sketches. Brief reference to a poet's life is better used when discussing how the poems themselves were shaped by their experiences.
- Remember that the examination encourages **individual engagement** with the prescribed poems. Poetry can make us think and feel and imagine. It opens our minds to the wonderful possibilities of language and ideas. Your interaction with the poems is what matters most. **Commentary notes and critical interpretations are all there to be challenged.** Read the poems carefully and have confidence in expressing your own personal response.

POETRY FOCUS

Elizabeth Bishop
1911–1979

'The armored cars of dreams, contrived to let us do so many a dangerous thing.'

Elizabeth Bishop was born in Worcester, Massachusetts in 1911. She spent part of her childhood with her Canadian grandparents following her father's death and mother's hospitalisation. She then lived with various relatives who, according to Bishop, took care of her because they felt sorry for her. These unsettling events, along with the memories of her youth, inspired her to read poetry – and eventually to write it. After studying English at university, she travelled extensively and lived in New York, Florida and, for 17 years, Brazil. She also taught at several American colleges. Throughout her life she suffered from ill health and depression. As a poet, she wrote sparingly, publishing only five slim volumes in 35 years. However, her work received high acclaim. 'I think geography comes first in my work,' she told an interviewer, 'and then animals. But I like people, too. I've written a few poems about people.' Bishop died suddenly in her Boston apartment on 6 October 1979. She was 68 years old. Her poetry continues to gain widespread recognition and study.

Investigate Further

To find out more about Elizabeth Bishop, or to hear readings of her poems, you could search some useful websites, such as YouTube, BBC Poetry, poetryfoundation.org and poetryarchive.org, or access additional material on this page of your eBook.

Prescribed Poems

Note that Bishop uses American spellings and punctuation in her work.

◯ 1 'The Fish' (OL)
Based on an actual experience from her time in Florida during the 1930s, the central notion of the poem is that both nature and human nature share admirable qualities of strength and endurance. **Page 4**

◯ 2 'The Bight'
In describing the small, untidy bight (bay), the poet displays a naturally keen observation and an expert use of metaphor. **Page 9**

◯ 3 'At the Fishhouses'
Bishop travels back to her childhood home in Nova Scotia and notes some of the changes that have taken place. Detailed description leads to intense reflection and introspection. **Page 13**

◯ 4 'The Prodigal' (OL)
This poem is based on the biblical parable of the Prodigal Son. Bishop imagines the squalor and degradation brought about by alcoholism. However, determination, hope and human resilience eventually triumph. **Page 18**

◯ 5 'Questions of Travel'
The striking Brazilian landscape encourages the poet to consider people's interest in foreign places. **Page 22**

◯ 6 'The Armadillo'
Bishop describes the beautiful – but dangerous – fire balloons that light up the darkness during an annual religious festival in Rio de Janeiro. **Page 28**

◯ 7 'Sestina'
In this deeply personal poem, Bishop remembers a painful childhood. Faced with her grandmother's sadness, she retreats to the kitchen of her family home and its familiar comforts. **Page 33**

◯ 8 'First Death in Nova Scotia'
Vividly recalling the death of her young cousin Arthur, the poet explores the innocence and bewilderment of childhood. Many of her memories are dominated by the Canadian winter landscape. **Page 37**

◯ 9 'Filling Station' (OL)
The description of a run-down filling station leads to other discoveries. Despite the grease and oily dirt, Bishop finds signs of family love and beauty in this unlikely place. Some critics see the poem as an allegory of all human life. **Page 42**

◯ 10 'In the Waiting Room'
Set in Worcester, Massachusetts in 1918, the poet returns to the theme of childhood and the loss of innocence. **Page 47**

(OL) indicates poems that are also prescribed for the Ordinary Level course.

1 The Fish

I caught a tremendous fish
and held him beside the boat
half out of water, with my hook
fast in a corner of his mouth.
He didn't fight. 5
He hadn't fought at all.
He hung a grunting weight,
battered and venerable
and homely. Here and there
his brown skin hung in strips 10
like ancient wallpaper,
and its pattern of darker brown
was like wallpaper:
shapes like full-blown roses
stained and lost through age. 15
He was speckled with barnacles,
fine rosettes of lime,
and infested
with tiny white sea-lice,
and underneath two or three 20
rags of green weed hung down.
While his gills were breathing in
the terrible oxygen
—the frightening gills,
fresh and crisp with blood, 25
that can cut so badly—
I thought of the coarse white flesh
packed in like feathers,
the big bones and the little bones,
the dramatic reds and blacks 30
of his shiny entrails,
and the pink swim-bladder
like a big peony.
I looked into his eyes
which were far larger than mine 35
but shallower, and yellowed,
the irises backed and packed
with tarnished tinfoil
seen through the lenses
of old scratched isinglass. 40

tremendous: huge, startling, fearsome.

venerable: ancient, worthy of respect.
homely: unattractive, plain.

rosettes: rose-shaped decorations made of ribbon, often awarded as prizes.
sea-lice: small parasites that live on the skin of fish.

gills: breathing organs of fish.

entrails: internal organs.

peony: large, flamboyant flower, usually pink.

irises: coloured parts of an eye.

isinglass: gelatine-like, opaque substance obtained from the bodies of fish.

ELIZABETH BISHOP

They shifted a little, but not
to return my stare.
—It was more like the tipping
of an object toward the light.
I admired his sullen face, 45
the mechanism of his jaw,
and then I saw
that from his lower lip
—if you could call it a lip—
grim, wet, and weaponlike, 50
hung five old pieces of fish-line,
or four and a wire leader
with the swivel still attached,
with all their five big hooks
grown firmly in his mouth. 55
A green line, frayed at the end
where he broke it, two heavier lines,
and a fine black thread
still crimped from the strain and snap
when it broke and he got away. 60
Like medals with their ribbons
frayed and wavering,
a five-haired beard of wisdom
trailing from his aching jaw.
I stared and stared 65
and victory filled up
the little rented boat,
from the pool of bilge
where oil had spread a rainbow
around the rusted engine 70
to the bailer rusted orange,
the sun-cracked thwarts,
the oarlocks on their strings,
the gunnels—until everything
was rainbow, rainbow, rainbow! 75
And I let the fish go.

sullen: bad-tempered, sulky.
mechanism: workings.

leader: wire connecting fishhook and line.

crimped: pressed into ridges.

frayed: unravelled, worn.

bilge: dirty water that collects in the bottom of a boat.

bailer: bucket used to scoop water out of a boat.
thwarts: rowers' benches.
oarlocks: metal devices for holding oars.
gunnels: upper edges of the side of a boat.

'He hung a grunting weight'

👤 Personal Response

1. Bishop uses vivid similes (lines 9–15) to describe the fish. What impact did this close examination of the fish make on you? Give reasons for your answer, using textual support.
2. What is the poet's attitude towards the fish? Where does it change as the poem progresses? Give a reason for this change. Refer closely to the poem in your response.
3. Who had the 'victory' in this situation – the fish or Bishop? Why did you come to this conclusion? Support your discussion with clear references to the poem.

👁 Critical Literacy

'The Fish' is from Elizabeth Bishop's first published collection, *North and South* (1946). She lived in Florida during the 1930s and the poem is based on her experience of catching a large jewfish at Key West. Bishop once said, 'I like painting probably better than I like poetry' and 'The Fish' is certainly a very visual poem. Bishop uses the fish as a way of exploring a 'green' awareness, the respect for nature and all living things.

The poem's opening line is direct and forceful ('I caught a tremendous fish'). Bishop's use of the personal pronoun 'I' gives a sense of immediacy and intimacy. The adjective 'tremendous' reflects the **poet's breathless excitement and awe at this magnificent specimen of a fish**. The act of catching the fish is described in a personal, down-to-earth way. Bishop once said, 'I always tell the truth in my poems … that's exactly how it happened.' The fish is 'half out of water', no longer in its natural habitat.

In line 5, the focus shifts from the person who caught the fish to the fish itself. **It is now given a personality**: 'He didn't fight.' The onomatopoeic 'grunting' allows us to be part of this scene, as we hear the distressed noises from the gasping, ugly ('homely'), exhausted ('battered') fish. Then another aspect of the fish is presented to us: it is 'venerable', ancient and worthy of reverence. Bishop the participant is giving way to Bishop the observer. She was influenced by the poetic movement known as Imagism, which emphasised the accurate description of a particular thing. The poet's precise similes, 'his brown skin hung in strips/like ancient wallpaper', use clear, sharp language.

The surface **detail is painstakingly and imaginatively described** ('like full-blown roses'). There seems to be an attempt to domesticate the creature, but the sordid reality of the blotches on the skin is also noted ('stained and lost through age'). The texture of the fish is described graphically, as if we were examining the skin under a microscope: 'speckled', 'infested', 'rags'. Colours ('lime', 'white' and 'green') help convey this vivid picture. Detailed phrasing captures the wildness of the creature, 'frightening gills,/fresh and crisp with blood' (lines 24–25). Its interior is also imagined

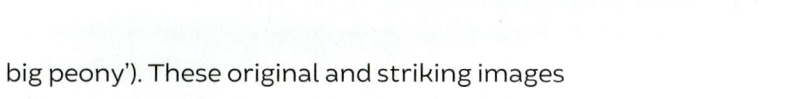

('pink swim-bladder/like a big peony'). These original and striking images appeal to both our visual and tactile senses.

Bishop's delight in catching this fine specimen soon gives way to an **emotional involvement with the fish** and his struggle for survival (line 34). She compares his eyes to her own ('far larger'). She notes the wear and tear from a long, hard life ('yellowed'). Alliteration and assonance create a lifeless image, 'the irises backed and packed/with tarnished tinfoil'. The unresponsive eyes suggest a lack of connection between creature and poet. This suggests both the independence and the vulnerability of the fish.

Progression in the poem is shown in the verbs: 'I caught', 'I thought', 'I looked' and, in line 45, 'I admired'. The **poet admires the resolute nature of the fish** ('his sullen face'). This fish has survived previous battles ('five big hooks/grown firmly in his mouth'). Precise detail emphasises the severity of these battles ('A green line, frayed at the end/where he broke it'). Military language highlights the effort the fish has made to survive: 'weaponlike', 'medals'. Bishop's sympathy is clear as she notes the fish's 'aching jaw'. For the fish, it is clear that the pain of battle remains.

Line 65 shows the poet transfixed ('I stared and stared'). Now the scene expands from a single fisher in a 'little rented boat' to something of **universal significance** ('victory' fills up the boat). Ordinary details (the 'bilge', the 'thwarts' and the 'gunnels') are transformed. The oil has 'spread a rainbow'. Everything is coloured and Bishop's relationship with the fish changes. She exercises mercy. A moment of epiphany occurs and she lets 'the fish go'. All the tension in the poem is finally released. The underlying drama contained between the opening line ('I caught a tremendous fish') and the closing line ('And I let the fish go.') has been resolved. **Victory belongs to both the poet and the fish**. The fish is free; the poet has seen and understood.

This poem is a long narrative with a clear beginning, middle and end. Bishop has chosen a suitably unrhymed form. The metre is appropriate for the speaking voice: dimeter (two stresses) and trimeter (three stresses). Short run-on lines suggest the poet excitedly examining her catch and the recurring use of dashes indicates her thought process as she moves from delight to wonder, empathy and, finally, comprehension. The concluding rhyming couplet brings a definite and satisfying resolution to the dramatic tension.

✒ Writing About the Poem

Elizabeth Bishop has been praised for her 'painterly eye'. Discuss this aspect of her style in 'The Fish'. Support your views with close reference to the poem.

Sample Paragraph

Elizabeth Bishop's painterly eye is evident throughout her poem 'The Fish'. The poet looks at the event ('I caught a tremendous fish') and then moves to describe the fish, using striking images ('brown skin hung in strips/like ancient wallpaper'). Like a camera, she pans this way and that, making us see also 'its pattern of darker brown' with 'shapes like full-blown roses'. She leads us to imagine the interior of the fish, its 'coarse white flesh/packed in like feathers'. If Bishop were painting this fish, I could imagine it in glistening colours. In her poem, she paints with words: 'the pink swim bladder'. She acknowledges this veteran as she notes the 'five big hooks/grown firmly in his mouth'. The poem concludes with a burst of colour ('rainbow, rainbow, rainbow!'). The rainbow from the oil-soaked bilge water has transformed the poet's relationship with the fish.

EXAMINER'S COMMENT

A mature and interesting interpretation of the question. This top-grade response is very well focused and there is a sustained personal perspective throughout. Effective use of quotations rounds off the answer. These are very well integrated into the commentary. Expression is fluent and assured.

Class/Homework Exercises

1. Bishop often structures her poems like a mini-drama. Examine the poem 'The Fish' and comment on how a dramatic effect is achieved. Consider setting, characterisation, conflict, the interior debate, tension building to climax and resolution. Refer closely to the text of the poem in your response.
2. 'Elizabeth Bishop has commented that she simply tried "to see things afresh" in her poetry.' To what extent is this true of her poem 'The Fish'? Support your answer with reference to the text.

Points to Consider

- **Themes include endurance and the relationship between nature and human nature.**
- **Observational details, vibrant language, personification, striking comparisons.**
- **Engaging first person narrative voice.**
- **Varying tones: joyful, admiring, celebratory.**
- **Memorable sound effects: assonance, alliteration, sibilance, repetition.**
- **Dramatic development that ends in a moment of insight.**

2 The Bight

On my birthday

At low tide like this how sheer the water is.
White, crumbling ribs of marl protrude and glare
and the boats are dry, the pilings dry as matches.
Absorbing, rather than being absorbed,
the water in the bight doesn't wet anything, 5
the color of the gas flame turned as low as possible.
One can smell it turning to gas; if one were Baudelaire
one could probably hear it turning to marimba music.
The little ocher dredge at work off the end of the dock
already plays the dry perfectly off-beat claves. 10
The birds are outsize. Pelicans crash
into this peculiar gas unnecessarily hard,
it seems to me, like pickaxes,
rarely coming up with anything to show for it,
and going off with humorous elbowings. 15
Black-and-white man-of-war birds soar
on impalpable drafts
and open their tails like scissors on the curves
or tense them like wishbones, till they tremble.
The frowsy sponge boats keep coming in 20
with the obliging air of retrievers,
bristling with jackstraw gaffs and hooks
and decorated with bobbles of sponges.
There is a fence of chicken wire along the dock
where, glinting like little plowshares, 25
the blue-gray shark tails are hung up to dry
for the Chinese-restaurant trade.
Some of the little white boats are still piled up
against each other, or lie on their sides, stove in,
and not yet salvaged, if they ever will be, from the last bad storm, 30
like torn-open, unanswered letters.
The bight is littered with old correspondences.
Click. Click. Goes the dredge,
and brings up a dripping jawful of marl.
All the untidy activity continues, 35
awful but cheerful.

Title: refers to a wide bay or inlet.

marl: rich clay soil.

pilings: heavy beams supporting a jetty.

Baudelaire: Charles Baudelaire (1821-1867), French symbolist poet.

marimba: wooden instrument similar to a xylophone, played by African and Central American jazz musicians.

ocher: ochre; orange-brown colour.

claves: clefs; musical keys.

impalpable drafts: slight air currents.

frowsy: shabby, foul-smelling.
retrievers: gundogs.
bristling: shining.
jackstraw gaffs: jagged criss-crossed sticks arranged to catch fish.
bobbles: trimmings.
plowshares: ploughing blades.

stove in: storm-damaged.
salvaged: repaired.

dredge: a machine for digging under water.

ELIZABETH BISHOP

POETRY FOCUS

'and the boats are dry'

👤 Personal Response

1. An unsettling, disturbing atmosphere is established in the first six lines. Choose two details which you consider particularly effective in creating this mood and discuss their impact on you.
2. Choose one simile that you think is particularly effective in the poem. Briefly explain your choice.
3. Although the poem is not directly personal, what does it suggest to you about Elizabeth Bishop herself? Refer to the text in your answer.

👁 Critical Literacy

'The Bight' shows Elizabeth Bishop's aesthetic appreciation of the world around her. The setting for this poem is Garrison Bight in Florida. In describing the small, untidy harbour, Bishop displays a characteristically keen eye for observation and an expert use of metaphor. The subtitle, 'On my birthday', suggests a special occasion and, perhaps, a time for reflection and reappraisal of life.

ELIZABETH BISHOP

The poem begins with an introduction to the bight at 'low tide' and gradually constructs a **vivid picture of an uninviting place**: 'White, crumbling ribs of marl protrude and glare'. Grim personification and a sharp 'r' sound emphasise the unsettling atmosphere. There is a sense of unreality about sea water that 'doesn't wet anything'. The description in these opening lines is typically detailed, sensual and precise – all carefully shaped by the poet's own personal vision of the world. References to 'the pilings dry as matches' and the 'gas flame' water are disturbing, implying that something dangerous might be about to happen.

Bishop echoes the French poet Baudelaire (line 7), who believed in expressing human experience through the objects and places around us. The water would then be heard 'turning to marimba music', dark and deep. She also finds an unexpected jazz rhythm ('perfectly off-beat claves') coming from the machine that is dredging 'off the end of the dock'. In lines 11–19, Bishop depicts the 'outsize' birds through a series of vigorous images. They seem awkward and out of place in this busy, built-up location. **Vivid descriptive language illustrates their mechanical movements**: pelicans 'crash' into the sea 'like pickaxes', while man-of-war birds 'open their tails like scissors'. An underlying sense of disquiet can be found in the detailed observations of these 'tense' birds as they 'tremble' in flight.

The poet's portrayal of the bight is quite realistic: 'frowsy sponge boats keep coming in' to harbour. With ironic humour, she acknowledges their unlikely beauty, 'bristling with jackstraw gaffs' and 'decorated with bobbles of sponges'. The cluttered dockside is a busy working environment where 'blue-gray shark tails are hung up to dry' (line 26). The 'little white boats' are a reminder of the local fishing community and its dependence on the sea. Bishop compares the small fishing boats to 'torn-open, unanswered letters'. The bight suddenly reminds her of a cluttered writing-desk – her own, presumably – 'littered with old correspondences'.

This metaphor is developed in lines 33–36. Bishop returns to sharp sounds: the 'Click. Click.' noise of the dredger (compared to an animal unearthing the wet clay) as it 'brings up a dripping jawful of marl'. The ending is highly symbolic of the poet's own impulse to dig deep into personal memories. Drawing a close comparison between her own life and the 'untidy activity' of the bight, she concludes that both are 'awful but cheerful'. **The matter-of-fact tone of these closing lines is good-humoured**. It reflects her realistic approach to the highs and lows of human experience – and the thoughts that are likely to have crossed her mind as she celebrated yet another birthday.

POETRY FOCUS

✒ Writing About the Poem

'Closely observed description and vivid imagery are striking features of Elizabeth Bishop's poems.' Discuss this statement in relation to 'The Bight'. Refer to the poem in support of your views.

Sample Paragraph

'The Bight' is a good example of how Bishop builds up a picture of a fairly inhospitable place. At first, she describes the 'crumbling ribs of marl', personifying the soil as an emaciated body. We get a sense of the sounds she hears – the 'dredge at work' pounding away in the background. Bishop uses imagery to bring the birds to life – particularly the vicious man-of-war birds whose tails are 'like scissors'. We also see the poet's eye for detail in her description of the damaged boats on the shore 'like torn-open, unanswered letters'. Bishop uses colour imagery effectively – 'blue-gray shark tails' are hanging out to dry. The poem ends with the rasping sound of the dredger – 'Click. Click' digging up 'a dripping jawful of marl'. This suggests how the bight keeps bringing back memories, both pleasant and unpleasant.

> **EXAMINER'S COMMENT**
>
> *A very well-focused, top-grade response, making excellent use of numerous accurate quotations. The various elements of the question are addressed and there is evidence of good personal engagement with the text. Expression throughout is also fluent and controlled.*

✍ Class/Homework Exercises

1. 'Elizabeth Bishop's poetry is both sensuous and reflective.' To what extent is this true of 'The Bight'? Support the points you make with suitable reference to the text of the poem.
2. 'In many of her poems, Elizabeth Bishop begins with vivid visual and aural details which lead to moments of intense understanding.' Discuss this statement with reference to 'The Bight'.

◎ Points to Consider

- Descriptive details give a clear picture of the littered bay at low tide.
- Enduring personal upheavals and disappointments are central themes.
- Bishop relates to the untidy location as she reappraises her own disorderly life.
- Striking metaphorical language, memorable patterns of unusual imagery.
- Contrasting tones: pessimistic, reflective, insightful, upbeat.

At the Fishhouses

ELIZABETH BISHOP

Although it is a cold evening,
down by one of the fishhouses
an old man sits netting,
his net, in the gloaming almost invisible,
a dark purple-brown,   5
and his shuttle worn and polished.
The air smells so strong of codfish
it makes one's nose run and one's eyes water.
The five fishhouses have steeply peaked roofs
and narrow, cleated gangplanks slant up   10
to storerooms in the gables
for the wheelbarrows to be pushed up and down on.
All is silver: the heavy surface of the sea,
swelling slowly as if considering spilling over,
is opaque, but the silver of the benches,   15
the lobster pots, and masts, scattered
among the wild jagged rocks,
is of an apparent translucence
like the small old buildings with an emerald moss
growing on their shoreward walls.   20
The big fish tubs are completely lined
with layers of beautiful herring scales
and the wheelbarrows are similarly plastered
with creamy iridescent coats of mail,
with small iridescent flies crawling on them.   25
Up on the little slope behind the houses,
set in the sparse bright sprinkle of grass,
is an ancient wooden capstan,
cracked, with two long bleached handles
and some melancholy stains, like dried blood,   30
where the ironwork has rusted.
The old man accepts a Lucky Strike.
He was a friend of my grandfather.
We talk of the decline in the population
and of codfish and herring   35
while he waits for a herring boat to come in.
There are sequins on his vest and on his thumb.
He has scraped the scales, the principal beauty,
from unnumbered fish with that black old knife,
the blade of which is almost worn away.   40

gloaming: twilight, evening.

shuttle: tool used for weaving and mending fishing nets.

cleated: wooden projections nailed to a ladder to prevent slipping.
gangplanks: removable ramps used for boarding or leaving boats.

opaque: murky, dark; difficult to see through.

translucence: semi-transparent, light shining partially through.

iridescent: glittering, changing colours.
coats of mail: armour made of metal rings.

capstan: round machine used for winding or hauling rope.

Lucky Strike: American cigarette.

sequins: small, shiny discs used for decorating clothes.

POETRY FOCUS

Down at the water's edge, at the place
where they haul up the boats, up the long ramp
descending into the water, thin silver
tree trunks are laid horizontally
across the gray stones, down and down   45
at intervals of four or five feet.

Cold dark deep and absolutely clear,
element bearable to no mortal,
to fish and to seals . . . One seal particularly
I have seen here evening after evening.   50
He was curious about me. He was interested in music;
like me a believer in total immersion,
so I used to sing him Baptist hymns.
I also sang 'A Mighty Fortress Is Our God.'
He stood up in the water and regarded me   55
steadily, moving his head a little.
Then he would disappear, then suddenly emerge
almost in the same spot, with a sort of shrug
as if it were against his better judgment.
Cold dark deep and absolutely clear,   60
the clear gray icy water . . . Back, behind us,
the dignified tall firs begin.
Bluish, associating with their shadows,
a million Christmas trees stand
waiting for Christmas. The water seems suspended   65
above the rounded gray and blue-gray stones.
I have seen it over and over, the same sea, the same,
slightly, indifferently swinging above the stones,
icily free above the stones,
above the stones and then the world.   70
If you should dip your hand in,
your wrist would ache immediately,
your bones would begin to ache and your hand would burn
as if the water were a transmutation of fire
that feeds on stones and burns with a dark gray flame.   75
If you tasted it, it would first taste bitter,
then briny, then surely burn your tongue.
It is like what we imagine knowledge to be:
dark, salt, clear, moving, utterly free,
drawn from the cold hard mouth   80
of the world, derived from the rocky breasts
forever, flowing and drawn, and since
our knowledge is historical, flowing, and flown.

total immersion: completely covered in liquid; a form of baptism.

associating: linking.

transmutation: changing shape.

briny: very salty.

'in the gloaming'

👤 Personal Response

1. In your opinion, what is the role of the old fisherman in the poem? Is he a link with the past, a person in harmony with his environment or something else? Refer closely to the text in your response.
2. Bishop uses a chilling maternal image at the conclusion of the poem. What effect has this startling metaphor on the poem's tone? Support your discussion with clear references from the text.
3. The poem provides an insight into 'what we imagine knowledge to be'. What lesson about knowledge did you draw from the poem's ending?

👁 Critical Literacy

'At the Fishhouses' comes from Elizabeth Bishop's award-winning second collection, *A Cold Spring* (1965). What Bishop sees is never quite what the rest of us see. She challenges us to look again. She gives us poetry as 'normal as sight ... as artificial as a glass eye'. An ordinary sight of an old fisherman 'in the gloaming' mending nets in Nova Scotia becomes a strange, exact hallucination examining the essence of knowledge. Bishop saw; now we see. She changes the view.

The poem's opening section (lines 1–40) gives us a **detailed, sensuous description** of a scene from Nova Scotia. Bishop has a clear sense of place. The fishhouses are described so vividly that we can almost smell the fish ('it makes one's nose run and one's eyes water'), see the fish tubs ('completely lined/with layers of beautiful herring scales') and hear the sea ('swelling slowly as if considering spilling over'). The poet draws us right into the scene with microscopic detail, making us pore over the surface of 'benches', 'lobster pots' and 'masts'. We experience the 'apparent translucence' of the weathered, silvered wood, which matches the cold, opaque, silver sea. Musical language lends beauty to this timeless scene. The long 'o' sound in 'Although' (in the opening line) is echoed in 'cold', 'old' and 'gloaming'. All is harmonious. The colours of the fisherman's net, 'dark purple-brown', become 'almost invisible'. Nothing jars. The rhythmic work is conveyed in the pulsating phrase 'for the wheelbarrows to be pushed up and down on'. Physical effort is suggested by the assonance of 'u' and 'o'. In lines 23–25, the wheelbarrows are described in minute detail ('plastered/with creamy iridescent coats of mail'). The small, circular fish scales are like the metal

ELIZABETH BISHOP

rings on a medieval knight's coat of armour. Bishop moves in closer to show us similarly coloured little flies, also 'iridescent', moving on the scales.

The poet's eye focuses on 'the little slope behind the houses' and an 'ancient wooden capstan'. Here is a **reminder of the tough physical work** of the past. The discarded cylinder is 'cracked' and has 'melancholy stains, like dried blood'; the ironwork has also 'rusted'. In line 32, a human connection is made when the 'old man accepts a Lucky Strike' cigarette. The personal detail ('a friend of my grandfather') gives a surface intimacy to this chilling poem. But there are hidden depths. The man is described as having 'sequins on his vest and on his thumb'. This decorative detail is more usually associated with glamorous ball gowns than an old fisherman's jersey. Has he destroyed the fish's 'principal beauty'? Does the image of the man's black knife, 'almost worn away', suggest a fading life?

In the poem's short second section (lines 41–46), we are at the water's edge and the repetition of 'down' draws us nearer the element of water as we note the 'long ramp/descending'. **The movement seems symbolic of Bishop's own descent into her subconscious mind**, 'down and down'.

The third section (lines 47–83) **changes the view**. We are now not merely looking, but seeing. We are **entering the interior**. We journey with Bishop to examine an element that is 'bearable to no mortal', yet is home 'to fish and to seals'. No human can survive in the icy waters of the North Atlantic Ocean: 'Cold dark deep and absolutely clear'. Another figure, a seal, appears in this bleak, surreal sequence. In this compelling episode, seal and poet are linked by a shared belief in 'total immersion'. For the seal, this is into water. Is it some form of baptism for Bishop? The poet, however, finds no comfort in religion, despite singing hymns for the seal ('A Mighty Fortress Is Our God'). Religion, like the distant fir trees, is behind her, waiting to be cut down.

The sea now takes on a nightmarish aspect as Bishop describes it 'indifferently swinging above the stones' (line 68). It is becoming a sea of knowledge. The poet warns us against it, telling us that we will be hurt if we dive in: wrists 'would ache immediately' and hands 'would burn'. Just as in the Garden of Eden, knowledge came with a terrible price. Mother Nature is depicted with a 'cold hard mouth' and 'rocky breasts'. This is no warm, comforting, maternal presence. Instead, Bishop's own dark life is suggested. These final lines – filled with harsh sea imagery – are insightful. Place has retreated and insight is present. We, together with the poet, realise that knowledge is like water ('flowing'). It is also 'drawn', just like waves are moved by the power of the moon. As we recognise that the mysterious waves slide into the past, so we realise that knowledge is 'historical' and ends up 'flown'. **All are part of the continuous change of nature**. In the end, Bishop seems to accept that the vast ocean – like life itself – defies understanding.

✒ Writing About the Poem

'Bishop gives us facts and minute details, sinking or sliding giddily off into the unknown.' Discuss this statement with reference to the poem 'At the Fishhouses'. Support your views with close reference to the text.

Sample Paragraph

I agree that Bishop gives us 'facts and minute details'. The 'five fishhouses' are clearly described, with their 'steeply peaked roofs'. The exchange between the poet and the old man is realistically shown, with even the brand of cigarette identified ('Lucky Strike'). We not only see the fish scales, 'coats of mail', but we also note the 'crawling' flies on the wheelbarrows. Then the poem turns to meditation. Here, the poet is 'sliding giddily off into the unknown'. From observing the Atlantic Ocean ('Cold dark deep and absolutely clear'), Bishop starts to explore the essence of knowledge – and even of life itself. Knowledge is not comfortable; the world is not a nice place, with its 'cold hard mouth'. The last two lines are dreamlike. I imagine a sea of knowledge that has been always changing and 'flowing' as new discoveries are made.

EXAMINER'S COMMENT

A precise discussion that deals directly with both aspects of the statement: 'facts and minute details' and 'sliding ... into the unknown'. Some good personal engagement and a clear understanding of the poem are evident in this top-grade response. There is also effective use of apt quotation.

✎ Class/Homework Exercises

1. How does Bishop's style contribute to the communication of her themes? Refer to two literary techniques used by the poet in 'At the Fishhouses' and comment on their effectiveness in each case. Refer closely to the text in your response.
2. 'Elizabeth Bishop is known for her skill at creating an authentic sense of place.' To what extent is this true of her poem 'At the Fishhouses'? Support your answer with reference to the text.

⊙ Points to Consider

- Poet's return to her childhood home allows Bishop to reflect on life.
- Conversational language, descriptive details and sensuous imagery add authenticity.
- Assonant effects echo the deeply reflective mood.
- Alliterative and sibilant sounds evoke a realistic sense of the sea.
- Surreal, nightmarish view of nature.
- Visionary conclusion that the ocean – like life itself – is beyond understanding.

4 The Prodigal

Title: the biblical parable of the Prodigal Son is about a young man who wasted his inheritance on drunkenness and ended up working as a swineherd. The word 'prodigal' refers to a spendthrift or wastrel.

The brown enormous odor he lived by
was too close, with its breathing and thick hair,
for him to judge. The floor was rotten; the sty
was plastered halfway up with glass-smooth dung.
Light-lashed, self-righteous, above moving snouts,   5
the pigs' eyes followed him, a cheerful stare—
even to the sow that always ate her young—
till, sickening, he leaned to scratch her head.
But sometimes mornings after drinking bouts
(he hid the pints behind a two-by-four),   10
the sunrise glazed the barnyard mud with red;
the burning puddles seemed to reassure.
And then he thought he almost might endure
his exile yet another year or more.

But evenings the first star came to warn.   15
The farmer whom he worked for came at dark
to shut the cows and horses in the barn
beneath their overhanging clouds of hay,
with pitchforks, faint forked lightnings, catching light,
safe and companionable as in the Ark.   20
The pigs stuck out their little feet and snored.
The lantern—like the sun, going away—
laid on the mud a pacing aureole.
Carrying a bucket along a slimy board,
he felt the bats' uncertain staggering flight,   25
his shuddering insights, beyond his control,
touching him. But it took him a long time
finally to make his mind up to go home.

odor: odour, smell.

sty: pig-shed.

snouts: pigs' noses.

bouts: sessions.

companionable: comfortable.

the Ark: Noah's Ark. In the Bible story, Noah built a boat to save animals from a great flood.

aureole: circle of light.

'the pigs' eyes followed him'

👤 Personal Response

1. In your opinion, is Elizabeth Bishop sympathetic to the central character in this poem? Give reasons for your answer, using close reference to the text.
2. Choose two images that you found particularly memorable in the poem. Comment briefly on the effectiveness of each.
3. The poet effectively juxtaposes the squalor of the prodigal's life with hope for the future. To what extent do you agree? Support your answer with close reference to the poem.

👁 Critical Literacy

ELIZABETH BISHOP

In 'The Prodigal', published in 1951, Elizabeth Bishop returns to the well-known Bible parable of the Prodigal Son. She imagines the squalor and humiliation this headstrong youth endured when he was forced to live among the pigs he looked after. The poet herself had experienced depression and alcoholism in her own life and could identify with the poem's excluded central figure. Bishop uses a double-sonnet form to trace the prodigal's struggle from wretchedness to eventual recovery.

The poem's opening lines present the revolting living conditions of the exiled prodigal's everyday life: 'The brown enormous odor' engulfs him. The disgusting stench and filth of the pig-sty is the only life he knows. Immersed in this animal-like state, he has lost all sense of judgement. Even the odour, 'with its breathing and thick hair', is beyond his notice. **Bishop's graphic imagery is typically precise**, describing the foul-smelling sty's shiny walls as 'plastered halfway up with glass-smooth dung'.

In lines 5–8, the 'Light-lashed' pigs are given human traits ('self-righteous', 'a cheerful stare'). The poet conveys a **disturbing sense of the young man's confused and drunken grasp on reality**. In his sub-human state, overwhelmed by nausea and isolation, he now seems almost at home among the pigs. Although he is 'sickening', he can still show odd gestures of affection towards them – 'even to the sow that always ate her young'.

Bishop explores the alcoholic's secretive world in lines 9–14. Ironically, the morning hangovers are not entirely without their compensations: 'burning puddles seemed to reassure'. Despite the ugliness and deprivation of his diminished existence, **he can occasionally recognise unexpected beauty in nature**, such as when 'the sunrise glazed the barnyard mud with red'. It is enough to give him hope: 'then he thought he almost might endure/his exile'. Emphatic broad vowel sounds add poignancy to this line.

19

POETRY FOCUS

The poem's <mark>second section</mark> begins on a more startling note: 'But evenings the first star came to warn' (<mark>line 15</mark>). There is a suggestion that the **prodigal is finally confronting his personal demons**. For the first time, he seems to realise that he is out of place in the orderly routine of farm work that is going on around him. Unlike the sleeping animals ('safe and companionable as in the Ark'), the unfortunate young man is now intensely aware of his alienation. He is poised on the brink of coming to his senses.

A turning point for the prodigal occurs when he finally separates himself from the snoring pigs. Yet ironically, it seems as though he almost envies their simple comfort and security 'beneath their overhanging clouds of hay'. Vivid images of routine farm life, such as 'The lantern – like the sun, going away' (<mark>line 22</mark>), take on a new symbolic significance for the unhappy exile. Is he finally considering the transience of life? Is there still a possibility of regaining his humanity? For an instant, **the young man seems to find a vague kind of hope** in the beautiful 'pacing aureole' of lamplight reflected on the mud.

A renewed vigour and purpose mark the poem's <mark>final lines</mark>. Bishop identifies exactly when the prodigal experiences 'shuddering insights'. This defining instant is symbolised by his acute awareness of 'the bats' uncertain staggering flight'. Taking his cue from nature, **he slowly accepts responsibility for his own destiny**: 'But it took him a long time/finally to make his mind up to go home'. This crucial decision to return from exile is a powerful illustration of human resilience. The poem's affirmative ending is emphasised by the importance placed on 'home' (the only unrhymed end word in the poem). Bishop's reworking of the well-known biblical tale carries a universal message of hope, offering the prospect of recovery not just from alcoholism, but from any form of human shame.

✒ Writing About the Poem

'Elizabeth Bishop's mood can vary greatly – from deep depression to quiet optimism.' Discuss this statement, with particular reference to 'The Prodigal'.

Sample Paragraph

'The Prodigal' is extremely grim. The early mood, describing the 'brown enormous odor', is meant to capture the terrible living conditions of the young alcoholic who had left his home, partied non-stop and fallen on hard times. The description of the outhouse is extremely repulsive. The prodigal has fallen low, living among the pigs. The images are negative – 'rotten', 'sickening'. But the mood changes when the alcoholic dares to hope that he will get it together and return to a decent life. Images of light and beauty suggest this – 'catching light', 'a pacing aureole'. The turning point is when the prodigal stumbles on 'shuddering insights' – his belief that he can regain his dignity. Although this is extremely difficult, he succeeds in the end.

EXAMINER'S COMMENT

A well-focused response that addresses the question. Effective use of accurate quotation throughout. The answer would have benefited from some discussion on the restrained ('quiet') nature of the final optimism. Expression is weakened by slang and overuse of the word 'extremely', which leaves it just below top-grade standard.

ELIZABETH BISHOP

✒ Class/Homework Exercises

1. 'Bishop's poetry often goes beyond description to reveal valuable insights about people's courage and resilience.' Discuss this statement with particular reference to 'The Prodigal'. Refer to the poem in your response.
2. 'While Elizabeth Bishop's poems can appear deceptively simple, they often contain underlying themes of universal significance.' Discuss this view with close reference to 'The Prodigal'.

◎ Points to Consider

- **Themes include the alcoholic's alienation, human determination and resilience.**
- **Odd glimpses of beauty exist in the most unexpected of circumstances.**
- **Effective descriptive details, personification and startling metaphorical language.**
- **Vivid picture of the prodigal's unhappy life and living conditions.**
- **Striking images of light and darkness.**
- **Varying tones, contrasting moods – despair and hope.**

5 Questions of Travel

There are too many waterfalls here; the crowded streams
hurry too rapidly down to the sea,
and the pressure of so many clouds on the mountaintops
makes them spill over the sides in soft slow-motion,
turning to waterfalls under our very eyes.   5
—For if those streaks, those mile-long, shiny, tearstains,
aren't waterfalls yet,
in a quick age or so, as ages go here,
they probably will be.
But if the streams and clouds keep travelling, travelling,   10
the mountains look like the hulls of capsized ships,
slime-hung and barnacled.

Think of the long trip home.
Should we have stayed at home and thought of here?
Where should we be today?   15
Is it right to be watching strangers in a play
in this strangest of theatres?
What childishness is it that while there's a breath of life
in our bodies, we are determined to rush
to see the sun the other way around?   20
The tiniest green hummingbird in the world?
To stare at some inexplicable old stonework,
inexplicable and impenetrable,
at any view,
instantly seen and always, always delightful?   25
Oh, must we dream our dreams
and have them, too?
And have we room
for one more folded sunset, still quite warm?

But surely it would have been a pity   30
not to have seen the trees along this road,
really exaggerated in their beauty,
not to have seen them gesturing
like noble pantomimists, robed in pink.
—Not to have had to stop for gas and heard   35
the sad, two-noted, wooden tune

here: Brazil.

hulls: main sections of ships.
capsized: overturned in the water.
barnacled: covered with small shellfish.

the sun the other way around: the view of the sun in the southern hemisphere.

inexplicable: incomprehensible; mysterious.

pantomimists: people taking part in a pantomime, a slapstick comedy.

ELIZABETH BISHOP

of disparate wooden clogs
carelessly clacking over
a grease-stained filling-station floor.
(In another country the clogs would all be tested.   40
Each pair there would have identical pitch.)
—A pity not to have heard
the other, less primitive music of the fat brown bird
who sings above the broken gasoline pump
in a bamboo church of Jesuit baroque: 45
three towers, five silver crosses.

—Yes, a pity not to have pondered,
blurr'dly and inconclusively,
on what connection can exist for centuries
between the crudest wooden footwear   50
and, careful and finicky,
the whittled fantasies of wooden cages.
—Never to have studied history in
the weak calligraphy of songbirds' cages.
—And never to have had to listen to rain   55
so much like politicians' speeches:
two hours of unrelenting oratory
and then a sudden golden silence
in which the traveller takes a notebook, writes:

'Is it lack of imagination that makes us come   60
to imagined places, not just stay at home?
Or could Pascal have been not entirely right
about just sitting quietly in one's room?

Continent, city, country, society:
the choice is never wide and never free.   65
And here, or there ... No. Should we have stayed at home,
wherever that may be?'

disparate: very different, separate.

church of Jesuit baroque: ornately decorated 17th-century churches, often found in Brazil.

finicky: excessively detailed, elaborate.
whittled: carved.
fantasies: amazing creations.
calligraphy: decorative handwriting (in this case, the swirling design of the carved birdcages).
unrelenting: never stopping, endless.

Pascal: Blaise Pascal, a 17th-century mathematician and philosopher who wrote that 'man's misfortunes spring from the single cause that he is unable to stay quietly in his room'.

'the pressure of so many clouds on the mountaintops'

POETRY FOCUS

👤 Personal Response

1. From your reading of lines 1–12, describe Bishop's reaction to the landscape. How does she feel about this abundance of nature? Is she delighted, unhappy, awestruck? Support your response with quotation from the text.
2. Choose one example of repetition in the poem and briefly explain what it adds to Bishop's treatment of the poem's theme.
3. The ending of the poem challenges the reader to consider the morality of travel. What lessons did you draw about travel and tourism from this poem? Support your answer with reference to the text.

👁 Critical Literacy

This is the title poem of Elizabeth Bishop's 1965 collection *Questions of Travel*. Bishop herself was a great traveller, aided by an inheritance from her father. In this poem, she questions the need for travel and the desire that people have to see the world for themselves. The poet provokes the reader by posing a series of questions about the ethics of travel. She places her original observations of Brazil before us and wonders whether it would be better if we simply imagined these places while sitting at home. Finally, she challenges us to consider where our 'home' is.

The poem's ==opening line== is an **irritable complaint** about Brazil: 'There are too many waterfalls here'. In the first section (==lines 1–12==), Bishop observes the luxuriant, fertile landscape spread out before her. She finds fault with the 'crowded streams' that 'hurry too rapidly' and the 'pressure of so many clouds'. The richness of the misty equatorial landscape is caught in a series of soft sibilant 's' sounds ('spill', 'sides', 'soft slow-motion'). Clouds melt into the 'mile-long, shiny, tearstains'. Everything is on the move, changing position and shape. Both Bishop and the water are 'travelling, travelling'. **Repetition emphasises this restless movement**. The circular motion suggests that neither traveller nor clouds have any real purpose or direction. An original and striking image of a mountain range ('like the hulls of capsized ships') catches our attention. The vegetation is 'slime-hung'; the outcrops of rocks are like the shells of crustaceans ('barnacled'). As always, the poet's interest lies in the shape and texture of the words.

A more **reflective mood is found in the poem's second section** (==lines 13–29==). Bishop presents readers with a **series of challenging questions** for consideration. In all, eight 'questions of travel' are posed. Should we remain 'at home' and imagine 'here'? Bishop is uneasy at the intrusion of tourists 'watching strangers in a play'. She is aware that this is how people live; it is not a performance for public consumption. The emphasis here is on the 'childishness' of the tourists as they rush around, greedily consuming sights, viewing the sun from its other side in southern countries, such as Brazil. But

as far as Bishop is concerned, historic ruins and 'old stonework' do not speak to the visitor. The repetition of 'inexplicable' stresses the difficulties of understanding foreign cultures. The unknowing response of tourists is captured in the conversational phrase 'always delightful'. Their selfish desire for more and more experiences is vividly shown in the image of the traveller coolly packing views, as if they were clothes or souvenirs being placed in a bag at the end of a trip: 'And have we room/for one more folded sunset, still quite warm?' Perhaps Bishop is asking whether any famous sight ever actually touched the traveller, or was it skimmed over in a rush to pack in as much as possible?

Justification for travel is the dominant theme of the third section (lines 30–59): 'But surely it would have been a pity/not to have seen'; '– A pity not to have heard'; 'a pity not to have pondered'; '– Never to have studied'; 'never to have had to listen'. The repetition of 'pity' beats out a tense rhythm as the poet seeks to approve travel. Bishop's well-known 'painterly eye' provides the evidence, as she presents a series of fresh, first-hand illustrations, e.g. the trees 'gesturing/like noble pantomimists, robed in pink'. The flowing movement of the trees, their flamboyant colour and their suggestion of Brazil's mime plays would be hard to imagine if not really experienced. The sound of this easy-going, carefree society is conveyed in the hard 'c' sound of 'carelessly clacking', which evokes the slovenly walk of local peasants. The Brazilian love of music is evident in 'clacking', a sound usually associated with the rhythmic castanets. The difference in cultures is noted: 'In another country the clogs would all be tested./Each pair there would have identical pitch.' Elsewhere, all would be sterile sameness.

Are these the experiences the traveller would miss by not being in another country? The locals' casual attitude to the usefulness of an object is shown in the contrasting images of the 'broken gasoline pump' and the intricate construction of a 'bamboo church' with 'three towers, five silver crosses'. **The spirit of the people soars in 'Jesuit baroque'**. A similar contrast is seen in wooden carving – the 'crudest wooden footwear' does not have the same importance for these free-spirited people as the 'careful and finicky ... fantasies of wooden cages' (lines 51–52). Another unstoppable force, that of equatorial rainstorms, is likened to the endless rant of a politician bellowing out his 'unrelenting oratory'. Could any of this be imagined from afar?

Lines 58–67 begin in 'golden silence', as Bishop attempts to clarify her own thinking on the value of travel. In the final lines, she **wonders if we travel because we lack the imagination to visualise these places**. However, in the previous section, the poet has graphically shown that nothing can surpass a person **actually hearing and seeing** a place and its people. A reference is made to the 17th-century philosopher Blaise Pascal, who preferred to remain at home. The poet feels that he was not '*entirely right*' about this,

and by sharing her playful images of Brazil with us, she has led us to agree with her. Another interesting question is posed: How free are we to go where we wish? Bishop states that the choices are '*never wide and never free*'; there are always checks on the traveller. But an emphatic '*No*' tells us that this does not take away from the authenticity of the experience.

In the poem's concluding lines, Bishop returns to the question of whether or not people should stay at home. She then teases the reader with the follow-up, '*wherever that may be*?' (line 67). This is a much deeper, philosophical reflection, which echoes in our minds. **Home is a place of belonging**, from which travellers set out and to which they return. The visited countries are not secure bases; the tourist does not belong there, but is merely a visitor en route to somewhere else. In short, the traveller's role is one of an outsider – observing, but not participating or belonging. Bishop's own life experience is revealed here. Perhaps she travelled so extensively because she never felt truly at home in any single place.

Writing About the Poem

'Elizabeth Bishop's poems are not only delightful observations, but are also considered meditations on human issues.' Discuss this statement with reference to the poem 'Questions of Travel'. Support your views with close reference to the text.

Sample Paragraph

Bishop was a tireless traveller and in 'Questions of Travel', she presents images from the equatorial landscape of Brazil, where clouds 'spill over the sides' of mountains. The mountain ranges are imaginatively compared to upturned ships. The sounds of the people intrude – 'carelessly clacking'. No detail is too minute to escape her famous 'painterly eye': 'the broken gasoline pump', 'the 'three towers' and 'five silver crosses' of the small bamboo church. But the poet also addresses moral questions surrounding travel. What right have we to watch people's private lives? Why do we not 'just stay at home'? The poem concludes with a curious question on the meaning of 'home'. Bishop asks us to consider where it is ('home,/wherever that may be'). Suddenly an accepted certainty becomes as hard to define as the clouds at the start of the poem.

EXAMINER'S COMMENT

An insightful top-grade examination of both parts of the statement – the poet's 'delightful observations' and her treatment of issues – is presented in this assured response. The thoughtful approach is referenced accurately with pertinent quotations from the poem.

✒ Class/Homework Exercises

1. Comment on the different tones in 'Questions of Travel'. Refer closely to the text in your response.
2. 'Elizabeth Bishop's poetry explores interesting aspects of home and belonging.' To what extent do you agree with this statement? Support your answer with suitable reference to 'Questions of Travel'.

◎ Points to Consider

- The stunning Brazilian landscape prompts Bishop to reconsider the value of travel.
- Other themes include the natural world, home, and the creative imagination.
- Memorable onomatopoeic effects – assonance, alliteration, sibilance.
- Descriptive language, effective use of powerful metaphors and similes.
- Reflective, philosophical tone; inconclusive ending.

The Armadillo

For Robert Lowell

This is the time of year
when almost every night
the frail, illegal fire balloons appear.
Climbing the mountain height,

rising toward a saint   5
still honored in these parts,
the paper chambers flush and fill with light
that comes and goes, like hearts.

Once up against the sky it's hard
to tell them from the stars—   10
planets, that is—the tinted ones:
Venus going down, or Mars,

or the pale green one. With a wind,
they flare and falter, wobble and toss;
but if it's still they steer between   15
the kite sticks of the Southern Cross,

receding, dwindling, solemnly
and steadily forsaking us,
or, in the downdraft from a peak,
suddenly turning dangerous.   20

Last night another big one fell.
It splattered like an egg of fire
against the cliff behind the house.
The flame ran down. We saw the pair

of owls who nest there flying up   25
and up, their whirling black-and-white
stained bright pink underneath, until
they shrieked up out of sight.

Title: an armadillo is a nocturnal burrowing creature found mainly in South America. It rolls up into a ball to protect itself from danger.

Dedication: Elizabeth Bishop dedicated 'The Armadillo' to her friend and fellow poet Robert Lowell.

time of year: St John's Day (24 June).

fire balloons: helium-filled balloons carrying colourful paper boxes.

a saint: St John.

these parts: Rio de Janeiro, Brazil.

chambers: hollow boxes.

tinted: shaded.

the pale green one: probably the planet Uranus.

kite sticks of the Southern Cross: cross-shaped constellation of stars.

ELIZABETH BISHOP

The ancient owls' nest must have burned.
Hastily, all alone,   30
a glistening armadillo left the scene,
rose-flecked, head down, tail down,

and then a baby rabbit jumped out,
short-eared, to our surprise.
So soft! – a handful of intangible ash   35
with fixed, ignited eyes.

Too pretty, dreamlike mimicry!
O falling fire and piercing cry
and panic, and a weak mailed fist
clenched ignorant against the sky!   40

intangible: flimsy, insubstantial.
ignited: lit up.

mimicry: imitation.

weak mailed fist: the animal's bony armour (defenceless against fire).

'chambers flush and fill with light'

POETRY FOCUS

👤 Personal Response

1. Based on your reading of the first four stanzas, how does the poet present the fire balloons? Are they mysterious, beautiful, threatening? Refer to the text in your answer.
2. Choose one verb which you consider is particularly effective in suggesting danger. Give a reason for your choice.
3. In your view, is this an optimistic or pessimistic poem? Give reasons for your response.

👁 Critical Literacy

'The Armadillo' describes St John's Day (24 June) in Brazil, where Elizabeth Bishop lived for more than 15 years. On this annual feast day, local people would celebrate by lighting fire balloons and releasing them into the night sky. Although this custom was illegal – because of the fire hazard – it still occurred widely.

The opening lines introduce us to an exotic, night-time scene. The sense of drama and excitement is evident as Bishop observes these 'illegal' balloons 'rising toward a saint'. They are also presented as fragile ('frail') but beautiful: 'the paper chambers flush and fill with light'. There is something magical and majestic about their ascent towards the heavens. **The language is simple and conversational**, reflecting the religious faith of the local people. Bishop compares the flickering light of the 'paper chambers' to 'hearts', perhaps suggesting the unpredictability of human feelings and even life itself.

Lines 9–20 associate the drifting balloons with distant planets, adding to their romantic air of mystery. The unsteady rhythm and alliterative description ('With a wind,/they flare and falter') suggest an irregular movement. The poet is **increasingly intrigued by the fire balloons** as they 'wobble' out of sight. She notes that they sometimes 'steer between' the stars. Although she appears to be disappointed that the balloons are 'steadily forsaking us', she also worries about them 'suddenly turning dangerous' as a result of air currents buffeting and igniting them.

The tone changes dramatically in line 21, as Bishop recalls the destructive force of one exploding balloon that fell to earth near her house: 'It splattered like an egg of fire'. This stirring simile and the onomatopoeic verb highlight the sense of unexpected destruction. The shock is immediately felt by humans and animals alike. Terrified owls – desperate to escape the descending flames – 'shrieked up out of sight' (line 28). Contrasting **colour images emphasise the gaudy chaos**: the 'whirling black-and-white' bodies of the owls are 'stained bright pink underneath'.

| 30

ELIZABETH BISHOP

The poet suddenly notices 'a glistening armadillo', isolated and alarmed. Determined to escape the fire, it scurries away: 'rose-flecked, head down, tail down' (line 32). Amid the chaos, a baby rabbit 'jumped out', its urgent movement reflecting the lethal atmosphere. Bishop expresses her intense shock at seeing its burnt ears: 'So soft! – a handful of intangible ash'. **This graphic metaphor emphasises the animal's weakness and suffering.**

Bishop's emotive voice emerges forcefully in the poem's closing lines. She rejects her earlier description of the elegant fire balloons as being '*Too pretty*'. Having witnessed the horrifying reality of the tormented animals, she condemns all her earlier romantic notions about the colourful festivities. Such thoughts are suddenly seen as '*dreamlike mimicry*'. **The final image of the trapped armadillo is highly dramatic.** Its '*piercing cry*' is harrowing. Bishop imagines the terrified creature in human terms ('*a weak mailed fist*'). Although the armadillo's helpless body is '*clenched ignorant against the sky*', it is unlikely that its coat of armour will save it from fire. The irony of this small creature's last hopeless act is pitiful. Despite its brave defiance, the armadillo is doomed.

Some critics have commented on the **symbolism** in the poem, seeing the victimised creatures as symbols for powerless and marginalised people everywhere. It has been said that the careless fire balloons signify warfare, mindless violence and ignorant destruction. Is Bishop indicating that people's fate is beyond their control? It has also been suggested that the fire balloons signify love ('that comes and goes, like hearts') or even the creative impulse itself – beautiful, elusive and sometimes tragic. As with all poems, readers must decide for themselves.

Writing About the Poem

Describe the tone in 'The Armadillo'. Does it change during the course of the poem? Refer to the text in your answer.

Sample Paragraph

The opening of 'The Armadillo' is filled with anticipation. Bishop sets the scene during the festival to honour St John. 'This is the time of year' suggests a special occasion. The tone is celebratory as the local community release countless 'illegal fire balloons' which light up the skies. The poet seems in awe of the spectacle, watching the 'paper chambers flush and fill with light'. The tone changes to sadness as she watches the balloons disappear, 'steadily forsaking us'. A dramatic transformation occurs when the exploding balloons start

EXAMINER'S COMMENT

A focused top-grade response that traces the development of tone in the poem. There is a real sense of well-informed engagement with the text. Short, accurate quotations are used effectively to illustrate the different changes in tone. The expression is clear, varied and controlled throughout.

'turning dangerous'. Terrified owls 'shrieked', a young rabbit is burnt to 'intangible ash' and the armadillo is reduced to 'panic'. Bishop's personal voice is filled with anger as she rages against the 'falling fire'.

✒ Class/Homework Exercises

1. 'In reading the poetry of Elizabeth Bishop, readers can discover moments of quiet reflection and shocking truth.' Discuss this statement in relation to 'The Armadillo', supporting the points you make with reference to the poem.
2. 'In her poems, Elizabeth Bishop often connects the twin themes of cruelty and vulnerability.' Discuss this view with suitable reference to 'The Armadillo'.

⊙ Points to Consider

- Both humans and animals are victims of humankind's thoughtless actions.
- Precise sense of place, detailed description of exotic atmospheres and experiences.
- Reflective tone reveals the poet's personal feelings and attitudes.
- Lack of judgemental comment allows us to find our own interpretation.
- Rich visual imagery, striking metaphors, onomatopoeia and end rhyme.

7 Sestina

ELIZABETH BISHOP

September rain falls on the house.
In the failing light, the old grandmother
sits in the kitchen with the child
beside the Little Marvel Stove,
reading the jokes from the almanac,   5
laughing and talking to hide her tears.

She thinks that her equinoctial tears
and the rain that beats on the roof of the house
were both foretold by the almanac,
but only known to a grandmother.   10
The iron kettle sings on the stove.
She cuts some bread and says to the child,

It's time for tea now; but the child
is watching the teakettle's small hard tears
dance like mad on the hot black stove,   15
the way the rain must dance on the house.
Tidying up, the old grandmother
hangs up the clever almanac

on its string. Birdlike, the almanac
hovers half open above the child,   20
hovers above the old grandmother
and her teacup full of dark brown tears.
She shivers and says she thinks the house
feels chilly, and puts more wood in the stove.

It was to be, says the Marvel Stove.   25
I know what I know, says the almanac.
With crayons the child draws a rigid house
and a winding pathway. Then the child
puts in a man with buttons like tears
and shows it proudly to the grandmother.   30

But secretly, while the grandmother
busies herself about the stove,
the little moons fall down like tears
from between the pages of the almanac
into the flower bed the child   35
has carefully placed in the front of the house.

Title: a sestina is a traditional poetic form of six six-line stanzas followed by a final stanza of three lines. In Bishop's 'Sestina', the same six words recur at the ends of lines in each stanza: tears, child, almanac, stove, grandmother, house. The final three-line stanza contains all six words.

the Little Marvel Stove: a heater or cooker that burns wood or coal.

almanac: calendar giving important dates, information and predictions.

equinoctial: the time when day and night are of equal length (usually around 22 September, 20 March).

Time to plant tears, says the almanac.
The grandmother sings to the marvellous stove
and the child draws another inscrutable house.

inscrutable: secret; impossible to understand or interpret.

POETRY FOCUS

'the child draws a rigid house'

👤 Personal Response

1. Describe the atmosphere in the house. Is it happy, unhappy, relaxed, secretive? Support your response with quotation from the text.
2. Choose one image that you find particularly interesting and effective in the poem. Briefly explain your choice.
3. Do the final three lines promise an optimistic or alarming future for the child? Refer closely to the text in support of your opinion.

👁 Critical Literacy

'Sestina' was written between 1960 and 1965. For Elizabeth Bishop, the creative act of writing brought shape and order to experience. This poem is autobiographical, as it tells of a home without a mother or father. It is one of Bishop's first poems about her childhood and she was in her fifties, living in Brazil, when she wrote it. The complicated structure of the poem can be seen as the poet's attempt to put order on her early childhood trauma.

The poem's opening stanza paints a domestic scene, which at first seems cosy and secure. The child and her grandmother sit in the evening light beside a stove. They are reading 'jokes from the almanac' and 'laughing and talking'. However, on closer observation, sadness is layered onto the scene with certain details: 'September rain', 'failing light' and the old grandmother hiding 'her tears'. Bishop adopts the point of view of adult recollection. She is an observer of her own childhood and the poem's **tone is disturbing and challenging**. We are introduced to someone who is concealing deeply rooted feelings of sorrow. The six end-words echo ('grandmother', 'stove', 'tears', 'almanac', 'child', 'house') alarmingly throughout the poem.

In **stanza two** the grandmother believes that her autumn tears and the rain were 'foretold by the almanac'. There is a sense of inevitability and tired resignation in the opening lines. But normal life resumes: 'The iron kettle sings on the stove'. The grandmother cuts some bread and says to the child: '*It's time for tea now*'. **Bishop suddenly switches from being an observer to being an interpreter**, as she lets the reader see the workings of the child's mind in the **third stanza**: 'but the child/is watching the teakettle's small hard tears'. The child interprets sorrow everywhere; even droplets of steam from a kettle are transformed into the unwept tears of the grandmother. The phrase 'dance like mad' strikes a poignant note as we remember that Bishop's own mother was committed to a psychiatric hospital when Bishop was just five years old; they never met again. A cartoon-like image of the almanac ends this stanza. We view it through the child's eyes, as 'the clever almanac'.

Stanza four focuses closely on the almanac. It is a **sinister presence**, personified as a bird of ill-omen: 'Birdlike' it hovers, suspended 'half open'. This mood of anxiety is heightened when we are told that the grandmother's cup is not full of tea, but of 'dark brown tears'. However, normality asserts itself again – the grandmother 'shivers' and puts wood on the fire.

Stanza five opens with the eerie personification of the Marvel Stove and the almanac. A **sense of inevitability** ('*It was to be*') and hidden secrets ('*I know what I know*') is absorbed by the child. Just as the older Bishop puts order on her traumatic childhood experiences by arranging them into the tightly knit form of the sestina, the child in the poem attempts to order her experiences by drawing houses. But the house is tense, 'rigid', inflexible. The unhappy history of this childhood cannot be changed; the situation was as it was. This house can only be reached by a 'winding pathway'. Does this echo Bishop's later travels, as she searches for home? The sadness of Bishop's situation focuses on the drawing now, as the child sketches a man with 'buttons like tears'.

In **stanza six**, the tears continue to fall, now 'into the flower bed' in the child's drawing. **Fantasy and reality are mixed** in the innocent awareness of the child, who feels but does not understand. The **final three lines** contain all six key words as the almanac instructs that it is '*Time to plant tears*'. Is the time for regret over? Is the child planting tears that will be wept in the future? Should the grandmother and child be shedding tears now? The 'child draws another inscrutable house'. The secrecy continues. Nothing is as it seems. The future looks chilling.

✒ Writing About the Poem

'Elizabeth Bishop's poetry is an emotional journey.' To what extent do you agree with this? Support your views with close reference to 'Sestina'.

Sample Paragraph

I agree that the reader goes on an emotional journey in 'Sestina' as Bishop struggles to come to terms with her traumatic childhood. Our hearts go out to the little girl, caught in an almost nightmare scenario. Bishop allows us to see the workings of the little mind as the child blends reality and fantasy, imagining that stoves and books talk. The chaotic experiences of Bishop's childhood are strictly contained in the structure of the sestina, with six stanzas, each of six lines ending with the same six end-words: house, grandmother, child, stove, almanac and tears. This mirrors the 'rigid' house of the little girl's drawings. Both the older and the younger Bishop are trying to put order on this overwhelming situation. The reader experiences the poignancy through the details of 'the rain that beats on the roof' and the teacup 'full of dark brown tears'.

> **EXAMINER'S COMMENT**
> A top-grade, insightful answer focusing on the emotional journey undertaken by both the poet and reader. There is a clear sense of engagement with the poem. Quotations are used effectively throughout.

✒ Class/Homework Exercises

1. Some critics have said that 'Sestina' is a sentimental poem. To what extent do you agree with this? Support your views with close reference to the poem.
2. 'Elizabeth Bishop's most compelling poems often address painful memories of the poet's childhood.' To what extent is this true of her poem 'Sestina'? Support your answer with reference to the text.

◎ Points to Consider

- Adult poet reflects on troubled childhood and the desire for security of home.
- Disturbing sinister tone, sense of inevitability.
- Ominous personification and surreal imagery blur reality.
- Tear imagery patterns emphasise sorrow-filled scene.
- Strict form of sestina contains and controls overflowing emotions.
- Vivid imagery, powerful metaphorical language.

8 First Death in Nova Scotia

ELIZABETH BISHOP

In the cold, cold parlor
my mother laid out Arthur
beneath the chromographs:
Edward, Prince of Wales,
with Princess Alexandra,   5
and King George with Queen Mary.
Below them on the table
stood a stuffed loon
shot and stuffed by Uncle
Arthur, Arthur's father.   10

Since Uncle Arthur fired
a bullet into him,
he hadn't said a word.
He kept his own counsel
on his white, frozen lake,   15
the marble-topped table.
His breast was deep and white,
cold and caressable;
his eyes were red glass,
much to be desired.   20

'Come,' said my mother,
'Come and say good-bye
to your little cousin Arthur.'
I was lifted up and given
one lily of the valley   25
to put in Arthur's hand.
Arthur's coffin was
a little frosted cake,
and the red-eyed loon eyed it
from his white, frozen lake.   30

Arthur was very small.
He was all white, like a doll
that hadn't been painted yet.
Jack Frost had started to paint him
the way he always painted   35

parlor: room set aside for entertaining guests.

chromographs: coloured copies of pictures.
Edward: British king, Edward VII (1841-1910).
Alexandra: Edward's wife (1844-1925).
King George: King George V (1865-1936).
Queen Mary: wife of King George V (1867-1953).
loon: an aquatic diving bird.

counsel: opinion.

frosted: iced.

the Maple Leaf (Forever).
He had just begun on his hair,
a few red strokes, and then
Jack Frost had dropped the brush
and left him white, forever. 40

The gracious royal couples
were warm in red and ermine;
their feet were well wrapped up
in the ladies' ermine trains.
They invited Arthur to be 45
the smallest page at court.
But how could Arthur go,
clutching his tiny lily,
with his eyes shut up so tight
and the roads deep in snow? 50

the Maple Leaf: Canadian national emblem.

ermine: white fur.

page: boy attendant.

'the roads deep in snow'

👤 Personal Response

1. With reference to lines 1–20 of the poem, describe the mood and atmosphere in the 'parlor'.
2. The poet uses several comparisons in this poem. Select one that you found particularly interesting and comment on its effectiveness.
3. The poem ends with a rhetorical question. In your opinion, how does this heighten the poem's mood of uncertainty?

👁 Critical Literacy

'First Death in Nova Scotia' was published when Elizabeth Bishop was in her early fifties. Written entirely in the past tense, it is an extraordinarily vivid memory of a disturbing experience. In the poem, Bishop's young narrator recounts the circumstances of an even younger cousin's death.

From the outset, we visualise Cousin Arthur's wake through a child's eyes. Characteristically, Bishop sets the scene in stanza one using **carefully chosen** descriptive details. It is winter in Nova Scotia. The dead child has been laid out in a 'cold, cold parlor'. Above the coffin are old photographs of two royal couples. Fragmented memories of unfamiliar objects add to the dreamlike atmosphere. A stuffed loon sits on the marble-topped table. The young girl is suddenly confronted with strange signs of life and death.

The dead boy and the 'dead' room soon become real for the reader, as does the dilemma faced by the **living child, who seems increasingly unsettled**. Stanza two focuses on the young narrator's obsession with the stuffed bird. By thinking hard about the death of this 'cold and caressable' loon, she is trying to find a possible explanation for death. The bird's spellbinding 'red glass' eyes fascinate the young girl and provide an escape from the sight of her cousin's body in the casket. Suddenly, somewhere in the child's imagination, Cousin Arthur and the personified bird become closely associated. Both share an unyielding cold stillness, suggested by the 'marble-topped table', which is compared to a 'white, frozen lake'.

In stanza three the child's mother lifts her up to the coffin so that she can place a lily of the valley in the dead boy's hand. Her mother's insistent invitation ('Come and say good-bye') is chillingly remote. We sense the young girl's vulnerability ('I was lifted up') as she is forced to place the flower in Arthur's hand. In a poignantly childlike image, she compares her cousin's white coffin to 'a little frosted cake'. **The mood turns increasingly strange and surreal** when the nervous narrator imagines the stuffed bird as a predator ('the red-eyed loon eyed it').

Bishop continues to explore childhood innocence in **stanza four**. Using the simplest of language, the child narrator describes her dead cousin: 'He was all white, like a doll'. In a renewed burst of imagination, she creates her own 'story' to explain what has happened to Arthur. His death must have been caused by the winter frost that 'paints' the autumn leaves, including the familiar maple leaf. This thought immediately brings to mind the Canadian song 'The Maple Leaf Forever'. To the child, it seems that Jack Frost started to paint Arthur, but 'dropped the brush/and left him white, forever'. This creative **stream of consciousness highlights the child's efforts to make sense of death's mysterious reality**.

The imagery of childhood fairytales continues in **stanza five** when the narrator pictures Arthur in the company of the royal families whose pictures hang on the parlour walls. He is now 'the smallest page at court'. For the first time, the cold has disappeared and the royals are 'warm in red and ermine'. This fantasy, however, is short-lived. Still shaken by the strangeness of the occasion, the young narrator questions how this could have happened – especially as Arthur could not travel anywhere 'with his eyes shut up so tight/and the roads deep in snow'. The poem's final, tender image reflects both the child's naivety and a genuine concern for her cousin. Ironically, all around are symbols of immortality – the heavenly royal images of Arthur's entrance into a new, more glorious life. But the narrator's **uncertainty remains central to the poem**.

✒ Writing About the Poem

'The unknowable nature of life and death is a central concern of Elizabeth Bishop's poetry.' Discuss this statement with reference to 'First Death in Nova Scotia'. Support the points you make by referring to the poem.

Sample Paragraph

In several poems I have studied, it's clear that Bishop addresses life's mysteries. Sometimes she does this through the eyes of a child, as in 'First Death in Nova Scotia'. It is an elegy for her young cousin, Arthur, and Bishop's memories of his funeral are extraordinarily clear. Everything about it confuses her. The formal setting is uninviting – a 'cold, cold parlor' has strange chromographs of the British Royal Family on the walls. Nothing is explained to her and she escapes into her own imaginary world, comparing Arthur's casket to 'a little frosted cake'. In the last verse, she imagines her dead cousin in an afterlife – in a magical royal castle, 'the smallest page at court'. However, the young Elizabeth is caught

EXAMINER'S COMMENT

A focused and sustained answer, showing good engagement with the text. Starting with a succinct overview, the paragraph traces the progress of thought through the poem, using apt and accurate quotations effectively. Clear expression and a convincing personal approach also contribute to this top-grade response.

between make-believe and reason. I thought Bishop really captured the uncertainty of a young child's mind in this poem.

✒ Class/Homework Exercises

1. In your opinion, does 'First Death in Nova Scotia' present a realistic view of death? Support your argument with reference to the text of the poem.
2. 'Elizabeth Bishop often makes effective use of simple language and child-like images to convey disturbing childhood experiences.' Discuss this statement with close reference to 'First Death in Nova Scotia'.

⊙ Points to Consider

- Cousin Arthur's death and wake is seen from the point of view of a child.
- Elegy based on vivid memories expressed in simple language.
- Surreal imagery emphasises the deathly cold atmosphere.
- Fairytale element conveys child's attempt to understand the finality of death.
- Effective use of colour, assonance, repetition.

9 Filling Station

Oh, but it is dirty!
– this little filling station,
oil-soaked, oil-permeated
to a disturbing, over-all
black translucency.   5
Be careful with that match!

Father wears a dirty,
oil-soaked monkey suit
that cuts him under the arms,
and several quick and saucy   10
and greasy sons assist him
(it's a family filling station),
all quite thoroughly dirty.

Do they live in the station?
It has a cement porch   15
behind the pumps, and on it
a set of crushed and grease-
impregnated wickerwork;
on the wicker sofa
a dirty dog, quite comfy.   20

Some comic books provide
the only note of color –
of certain color. They lie
upon a big dim doily
draping a taboret   25
(part of the set), beside
a big hirsute begonia.

Why the extraneous plant?
Why the taboret?
Why, oh why, the doily?   30
(Embroidered in daisy stitch
with marguerites, I think,
and heavy with gray crochet.)

oil-permeated: soaked through with oil.

translucency: shine, glow.

monkey suit: dungarees; all-in-one working clothes.

saucy: cheeky, insolent.

impregnated: saturated.

doily: ornamental napkin.

taboret: drum-shaped low seat; a stool or stand.

hirsute: hairy.

begonia: house plant with large multicoloured leaves.

extraneous: unnecessary, inappropriate.

daisy stitch: stitch pattern used in embroidery.

marguerites: daisies.

crochet: intricate knitting patterns.

Somebody embroidered the doily.
Somebody waters the plant,   35
or oils it, maybe. Somebody
arranges the rows of cans
so that they softly say:
ESSO—SO—SO—SO
to high-strung automobiles.   40
Somebody loves us all.

ESSO–SO–SO: Esso is a brand of oil; reference to the careful arrangement of oil cans.

👤 Personal Response

1. In your opinion, how does Bishop make the opening two stanzas of this poem dynamic and interesting? Comment on her use of punctuation, direct speech and compound words, which draw us into the world of the poem.
2. Trace the development of the poet's attitude to the filling station throughout the poem. Does it change from being critical to being more positive? Illustrate your answer with close reference to the text.
3. Comment on the effectiveness of Bishop's use of repetition in lines 34–41. Refer to the text in your response.

👁 Critical Literacy

Elizabeth Bishop was strongly influenced by a poetic movement called Imagism, which was concerned with the accurate description of a particular thing. In this poem, she gives us a recognisable description of a familiar American scene, the small-town gas station. Bishop found the new culture in 1960s California bewildering and it is interesting that the voice in this poem is that of an outsider trying to make sense of what is observed.

'it's a family filling station'

POETRY FOCUS

The matter-of-fact title of the poem sets the mood for this commonplace scene. The poem opens with a **highly strung comment, ridiculing the lack of hygiene** at the little station: 'Oh, but it is dirty!' The compound words ('oil-soaked', 'oil-permeated') suggest that everything is covered in a fine film of grease. This 'black translucency' has its own particular glow. Bishop's tense, dismissive tone creates an uneasy atmosphere. Another voice interrupts her thoughts: 'Be careful with that match!' In a few lines, the poet has set the scene, established the mood and introduced her characters. She uses a series of intensely descriptive lines that gives the poem a cinematic quality as we observe the details, like close-ups on a big screen.

The busy little station is captured in the second stanza through the poet's critical observations as she watches the family go about their business. The father is wearing a 'dirty,/oil-soaked monkey suit' that is too small for him ('cuts him under the arms'). The sons are described using alliteration of the letter 's', which suggests their fluid movements as well as their oily appearance ('several quick and saucy/and greasy sons assist'). Like the poet, we also become fascinated by this unremarkable spot. Bishop's critical tone becomes more harsh as she comments on the sons' insolence ('saucy') and their lack of hygiene ('all quite thoroughly dirty'). **We can hear the contempt in her voice**.

The third stanza questions, in a disbelieving tone, whether anyone could actually reside in such an awful place: 'Do they live in the station?' The poet's eye seems to pan around her surroundings **like a camera, picking up on small details** as she tries to piece the scene into some kind of order. She lingers on the porch and its set of 'crushed and grease-/impregnated wickerwork'. Her disdain is obvious to the reader. The dog is described as a 'dirty dog' – it is almost as if it, too, has been smeared in oil. The general untidiness is highlighted by the alliterative 'd' sound. Then, suddenly, the poem turns on the homely word 'comfy'. The poet is surprised to note that the dog is quite content here. We are reminded that because of the distressing circumstances of her own childhood, Bishop never fully knew what home was; we are left wondering if she longed to be 'comfy' too.

In stanzas four and five, she begins to notice evidence of a woman's hand in this place, particularly 'a big dim doily' on the 'taboret'. She notes the colourful 'comic books' and her eye is caught by the contradictory sight of 'a big hirsute begonia'. Even the plant has masculine qualities, being big and hairy. Bishop is observing the extraordinary in the ordinary; **in the most unlikely places, there is beauty and love**. We understand her puzzlement as she reflects, almost in exasperation: 'Why, oh why, the doily?' We, like the narrator, have to reassess our initial view of this cluttered gas station. On closer observation, there is care and attention to detail, including artistic embroidery, the lovely 'daisy stitch'. The critical, conversational tone of the

poem clearly belongs to someone who is an observer, someone who does not belong. Is this the role Bishop was forced to adopt in her own life?

The poet's disturbed tone gives way in the final stanzas to one of comfort. The lines whisper softly with sibilant 's' sounds. 'Somebody' cares for things, arranging the cans in order 'so that they softly say:/ESSO–SO–SO–SO'. Bishop commented that 'so–so–so' was a phrase used to calm highly strung horses. It is used here to calm herself, just as the oil in the cans is used to make the engines of 'high-strung automobiles' run smoothly. The tone relaxes and a touch of humour creeps in: she notes that 'Somebody waters the plant,/or oils it, maybe'. Repetition soothes. Bishop and her readers come to realise that there is 'Somebody' who cares. **The poem concludes on a quiet note of assurance that everybody gets love from somewhere: 'Somebody loves us all'**. This is a particularly poignant ending when we consider that Elizabeth Bishop's parents were both absent from her childhood.

Writing About the Poem

'Elizabeth Bishop's poems are often described as deceptively casual.' Discuss this view of the poet's work, with particular reference to 'Filling Station'. Support your response with close reference to the text.

Sample Paragraph

'Filling Station' deals with the need to feel cared for. Bishop adopts a casual tone: 'Oh, but it is dirty!' However, the phrases ('oil-soaked, oil-permeated') show a carefully crafted poem. The repetition of 'why' to suggest the puzzlement of the poet as she tries to make sense of this scene also convinces me that Bishop is a craftsperson. Similarly, the repetition of 'Somebody' leaves a sense of reassurance, as the poet states that 'Somebody loves us all'. The word 'comfy' is also casual as, suddenly, the tone changes when the poet realises that the dog is content to be living there. Bishop shows her skill in the use of the sibilant 's'. Just as the oil stops the gears in a car making noise, the carefully arranged oil cans send their message of comfort: 'Somebody loves us all'.

EXAMINER'S COMMENT

This is a solid mid-grade answer, which competently addresses the question. There is some good engagement with the poem and effective use is made of apt references. The expression is reasonably well controlled, although slightly repetitive at times, leaving this short of being a high-grade standard.

POETRY FOCUS

✒ Class/Homework Exercises

1. 'A sense of homelessness pervades Bishop's poetry'. Comment on this statement, referring to both the content and stylistic techniques used in 'Filling Station'. Support your discussion with reference to the poem.
2. 'Elizabeth Bishop succeeds in conveying her themes through effective use of striking visual imagery and powerful aural effects.' Discuss this view with reference to 'Filling Station'.

⊙ Points to Consider

- **Bishop attempts to comprehend the significance of a run-down filling station.**
- **Vivid picture of homely petrol station through closely observed visual detail.**
- **Cinematic techniques, conversational and colloquial language, flashes of humour.**
- **Contemptuous tone gives way to a concluding note of reassurance.**
- **Realisation that love and beauty can be found anywhere.**

10 In the Waiting Room

ELIZABETH BISHOP

In Worcester, Massachusetts,
I went with Aunt Consuelo
to keep her dentist's appointment
and sat and waited for her
in the dentist's waiting room.   5
It was winter. It got dark
early. The waiting room
was full of grown-up people,
arctics and overcoats,
lamps and magazines.   10
My aunt was inside
what seemed like a long time
and while I waited I read
the *National Geographic*
(I could read) and carefully   15
studied the photographs:
the inside of a volcano,
black, and full of ashes;
then it was spilling over
in rivulets of fire.   20
Osa and Martin Johnson
dressed in riding breeches,
laced boots, and pith helmets.
A dead man slung on a pole
—'Long Pig,' the caption said.   25
Babies with pointed heads
wound round and round with string;
black, naked women with necks
wound round and round with wire
like the necks of light bulbs.   30
Their breasts were horrifying.
I read it right straight through.
I was too shy to stop.
And then I looked at the cover:
the yellow margins, the date.   35
Suddenly, from inside,
came an *oh!* of pain
—Aunt Consuelo's voice—
not very loud or long.
I wasn't at all surprised;   40

Worcester: much of the poet's childhood was spent here.

arctics: waterproof overshoes.

National Geographic: international geography magazine.

Osa and Martin Johnson: well-known American explorers.
pith helmets: sun helmets made from dried jungle plants.
'Long Pig': term used by Polynesian cannibals for human flesh.

POETRY FOCUS

even then I knew she was
a foolish, timid woman.
I might have been embarrassed,
but wasn't. What took me
completely by surprise 45
was that it was *me*:
my voice, in my mouth.
Without thinking at all
I was my foolish aunt,
I—we—were falling, falling, 50
our eyes glued to the cover
of the *National Geographic*,
February, 1918.

I said to myself: three days
and you'll be seven years old. 55
I was saying it to stop
the sensation of falling off
the round, turning world
into cold, blue-black space.
But I felt: you are an *I*, 60
you are an *Elizabeth*,
you are one of *them*.
Why should you be one, too?
I scarcely dared to look
to see what it was I was. 65
I gave a sidelong glance
—I couldn't look any higher—
at shadowy gray knees,
trousers and skirts and boots
and different pairs of hands 70
lying under the lamps.
I knew that nothing stranger
had ever happened, that nothing
stranger could ever happen.

Why should I be my aunt, 75
or me, or anyone?
What similarities—
boots, hands, the family voice
I felt in my throat, or even
the *National Geographic* 80
and those awful hanging breasts –
held us all together
or made us all just one?
How—I didn't know any
word for it—how 'unlikely' ... 85

Elizabeth: the poet is addressing herself.

How had I come to be here,
like them, and overhear
a cry of pain that could have
got loud and worse but hadn't?

The waiting room was bright   90
and too hot. It was sliding
beneath a big black wave,
another, and another.

Then I was back in it.
The War was on. Outside,   95
in Worcester, Massachusetts,
were night and slush and cold,
and it was still the fifth
of February, 1918.

The War: World War I (1914–1918).

ELIZABETH BISHOP

'then it was spilling over'

POETRY FOCUS

👤 Personal Response

1. In your view, what image of women is presented in the poem? Support your answer with reference to the text.
2. Select two images that have a surreal or dream-like impact in the poem. Comment on the effectiveness of each image.
3. The unsettling experience of the transition from innocent child to an awareness of a unique self is conveyed through disturbing events in the poem. Comment on one such event that you considered effective.

👁 Critical Literacy

'In the Waiting Room' describes a defining coming-of-age experience for the poet when she was just six years old. While her aunt receives dental treatment, the child narrator looks through the pages of a *National Geographic* magazine and observes what is happening around her. In the powerful and provocative moments that follow, she begins to acknowledge her individual sense of being female.

The poem opens with a specific setting recalled in vivid detail by the child narrator. She flicks through a *National Geographic* magazine in the dentist's office while her aunt is in the dentist's surgery. Familiar images of 'grown-up people,/arctics and overcoats' seem to convey a sense of wellbeing. It is the winter of 1918 in Worcester, Massachusetts. Direct, simple language conveys the candid observations of the young girl, seen from the adult poet's perspective. Short sentences establish the fragmented flashback, allowing the reader to identify immediately with the narrative: 'It was winter. It got dark/early'.

The mood changes from line 18 onwards, as the young girl studies the dramatic magazine photographs of an active volcano 'spilling over/in rivulets of fire'. For the first time, **she recognises the earth's destructive force**. In contrast to the earlier feeling of security in the waiting room, the atmosphere becomes uneasy. Disturbing pictures ('A dead man slung on a pole', 'Babies with pointed heads') shock and fascinate. The child is drawn further into an astonishingly exotic scene of cannibalism and violence. Graphic images of disfigurement seem horrifying: 'naked women with necks/wound round and round with wire'. The repetition of 'round and round' emphasises the young girl's spiralling descent into an enthralling world. Caught between fascination, repulsion and embarrassment ('too shy to stop'), she concentrates on the magazine's cover in an effort to regain control of her feelings.

The child is unexpectedly startled by a voice 'from inside' (line 36). At first, she assumes that the sound ('an *oh!* of pain') has been made by her aunt. But then something extraordinary happens and she realises that she has made the sound herself: 'it was *me*'. This sudden awareness that the cry has come from within herself prompts a **strange, visionary experience** in which she identifies closely with her 'foolish aunt'. The scene is dramatic and dreamlike: 'I – we – were falling, falling'.

In the surreal sequence that follows, the child focuses on her approaching birthday as she tries to resist the sensation of fainting: 'three days/and you'll be seven years old' (lines 54–55). Ironically, it is at this crucial point (on the edge of 'cold, blue-black space') that she gains an astonishing insight into her own sense of self: 'you are an *Elizabeth,*/you are one of *them*'. The idea of sharing a common female identity with her aunt and the unfamiliar women in the magazine is overwhelming: 'nothing stranger/had ever happened' (lines 72–73). It seems as though **all women have lost their individuality and have merged into a single female identity**. Although she attempts to stay calm, she is plagued by recurring questions and confusion: 'Why should I be my aunt,/or me, or anyone?' The young Elizabeth's awakening to adulthood is obviously painful. In attempting to come to terms with her destiny as both an individual and also as part of a unified female gender, she makes this hesitant statement: 'How – I didn't know any/word for it – how "unlikely" …'.

Before she can return to reality, the young girl must endure further discomfort. Her surroundings feel 'bright/and too hot' (lines 90–91) and she imagines being submerged 'beneath a big black wave', a startling metaphor for helplessness and disorientation. In the final stanza, she regains her composure in the waiting room's apparent safety, where she lists the certainties of place and time. But there is a distinct sense of life's harshness: 'The War was on' and Massachusetts is experiencing 'slush and cold' (line 97). Such **symbols are central to our understanding of this deeply personal poem**. Just as the image of the erupting volcano seemed to signify Bishop's development, the waiting room itself marks a transition point in her self-awareness.

> ## 🖋 Writing About the Poem
>
> **'An unsettling sense of not being fully in control is a central theme in the poetry of Elizabeth Bishop.' To what extent is this true of 'In the Waiting Room'? Support your answer with reference to the text of the poem.**

Sample Paragraph

The theme of growing up is central to 'In the Waiting Room'. It's unlike nostalgic poems. They describe childhood in a sentimental way. The atmosphere is relaxed as the child relaxes. However, photographs of a dead man ('Long Pig') are upsetting. Photographs of native women terrify the child as some wear wire necklaces. The poet compares them to 'light bulbs' – an image which frightens her. The outside world is so violent she goes into a trance. However, what really unsettles her is the realisation that she is a young woman and she shares this with every other female. Her feelings are summed up when she describes being overcome, 'beneath a big black wave'. This leaves me feeling sympathy for this girl.

> **EXAMINER'S COMMENT**
>
> *A reasonably focused and sustained mid-grade response, which addresses the question competently. Good use is made of quotations. The expression could be more controlled in places, particularly in the opening section.*

Class/Homework Exercises

1. 'Bishop's reflective poems combine precise observation with striking imagery.' Discuss this view with reference to 'In the Waiting Room'.
2. 'In many of her poems, Elizabeth Bishop offers interesting insights into how children struggle to make sense of the adult world.' Discuss this statement with reference to 'In the Waiting Room'.

Points to Consider

- **Themes include loss of innocence, coming-of-age experience, lack of belonging.**
- **Realisation of unique individuality and common female identity.**
- **Conversational language relays candid observations of young girl.**
- **Contrasting tones of alarm, dismay and disgust.**
- **Unnerving imagery used to explore comprehension of the wider world.**
- **Dream-like atmosphere – surreal, nightmarish.**

Sample Leaving Cert Questions on Bishop's Poetry

1. 'Bishop's reflective poetry is defined largely by quiet observation, precise descriptive language and deep compassion.' Discuss this view, supporting your answer with reference to both the thematic concerns and poetic style in the poetry of Elizabeth Bishop on your course.
2. 'Bishop's powerful portrayal of the world of nature is conveyed through vibrant imagery and energetic expression.' To what extent do you agree or disagree with this view? Develop your answer with reference to Bishop's subject matter and writing style in her prescribed poems.
3. From your study of the poetry of Elizabeth Bishop on your course, select the poems that, in your opinion, best show her effective use of specific places to communicate a sense of separation and loss. Justify your selection by showing how Bishop's effective use of specific places communicates a sense of separation and loss.

How do I organise my answer?

(Sample question 1)

'Bishop's reflective poetry is defined largely by quiet observation, precise descriptive language and deep compassion.' Discuss this view, supporting your answer with reference to both the thematic concerns and poetic style of the poetry of Elizabeth Bishop on your course.

Sample Plan 1

Intro: (*Stance: agree with viewpoint in the question*) Bishop's poetry is distinguished by her position as the outsider. Poems thinly conceal her estrangement as orphan, woman and troubled adult. Recurring themes of identity, endurance and humankind's relationship with nature explored through detailed language and tones of care and concern.

Point 1: (*Endurance/epiphany – visual details*) 'The Fish' explores themes of endurance and hope through the precise description of a caught fish. Striking imagery conveys the unique wonder of the fish ('brown skin hung in strips', 'pink swim-bladder'). Details reveal the fish's astonishing beauty and tenacity, which compel compassion from poet and reader.

Understanding the Prescribed Poetry Question

Marks are awarded using the PCLM Marking Scheme: P = 15; C = 15; L = 15; M = 5 Total = 50

- **P** (Purpose = 15 marks) refers to the set question and is the launch pad for the answer. This involves engaging with all aspects of the question. Both theme and language must be addressed, although not necessarily equally.
- **C** (Coherence = 15 marks) refers to the organisation of the developed response and the use of accurate, relevant quotation. Paragraphing is essential.
- **L** (Language = 15 marks) refers to the student's skill in controlling language throughout the answer.
- **M** (Mechanics = 5 marks) refers to spelling and grammar.
- Although no specific number of poems is required, students usually discuss at least 3 or 4 in their written responses.
- Aim for at least 800 words, to be completed within 45–50 minutes.

NOTE

In keeping with the PCLM approach, the student has to take a stance – agreeing, disagreeing or partially agreeing – with the statement that:

– **Bishop's reflective poetry** (childhood, loss of innocence, coming-of-age experiences, belonging/alienation, endurance, man's relationship with nature, etc.)

… is defined through:

– **quiet observation, precise descriptive language and deep compassion** (observational detail, startling personification, striking comparisons, surreal imagery, sound effects, sympathetic tones, etc.)

Point 2: (*Alienation – comparisons*) 'The Prodigal' captures squalor ('enormous odor'). Unexpected beauty in nature ('the sunrise glazed the barnyard mud'). Sense of empathy towards central character in this dehumanised setting ('companionable as in the Ark').

Point 3: (*Childhood experience – striking imagery*) 'First Death in Nova Scotia' is a powerful observation of coming of age. Startling dreamlike imagery ('Arthur's coffin was/a little frosted cake') and fairytale language suggest an understanding of the child's terrifying experience ('Jack Frost had dropped the brush/and left him white, forever').

Point 4: (*Identity – surreal imagery*) 'In the Waiting Room' also uses bizarre imagery ('Babies with pointed heads') to show a child's struggle with nature's destructive forces. Dramatic otherworldly sequence signals the end of childhood. Sensitive tone, realisation of common identity ('you are one of *them*').

Conclusion: Poems reveal hidden beauty found in ordinary places. Bishop succeeds in 'making the familiar strange' through her carefully crafted poetry and sympathetic point of view.

Sample Paragraph: Point 1

'The Fish' is a detailed description of a close encounter between man and nature. It is full of vivid imagery. Through her language, the poet conveys the patterns on the fish's skin, 'shapes like full-blown roses'. The fish's admirable endurance is detailed, 'five big hooks grown firmly in his mouth'. Bishop's compassionate eye notes his 'aching jaw'. We share the poet's reflective moment of heightened awareness with the description of the symbol of hope, 'a rainbow'. The excitement is captured in short run-on lines. However, the rhyming couplet brings the poem to a happier conclusion – a respectful relationship between human beings and nature is expressed in the final line, 'And I let the fish go'.

> **EXAMINER'S COMMENT**
>
> *This well-written top-grade response carefully considers all the main aspects of the question. There is a clear sense of engagement with the poem, particularly in the succinct analysis of how Bishop's themes are communicated through stylistic features, such as the first person narrative, vivid imagery and sound effects. Textual support is excellent throughout and the final point is impressive.*

(Sample question 2)

'Bishop's powerful portrayal of the world of nature is conveyed through vibrant imagery and energetic expression.' To what extent do you agree or disagree with this view? Support your answer with reference to Bishop's subject matter and writing style in her prescribed poems.

NOTE

In keeping with the PCLM approach, the student has to take a stance by agreeing and/or disagreeing that Bishop's poetry conveys:

- **a powerful portrayal of the world of nature** (relationship between nature and human nature, beauty, power, vulnerability of nature, etc.)

... through:

- **vibrant imagery and energetic expression** (vivid details, sensuous imagery, striking comparisons, strong verbs, energetic sound effects, dramatic encounters, engaging conversational language, evocative tones, etc.)

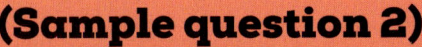

ELIZABETH BISHOP

Sample Plan 2

Intro: (*Stance: partially agree with viewpoint in the question*) Bishop not only provides a powerful portrayal of nature, but also examines people and their circumstances through vigorous imagery and lively language.

Point 1: (*Nature – coastal scene at low tide*) 'The Bight' gives a vivid view of a compelling scene that stimulates Bishop's imagination. Vibrant details and rich metaphors describe the small coastal bay's dilapidated scenery ('crumbling ribs of marl', 'frowsy sponge boats').

Point 2: (*Human nature – child, grandmother*) 'Sestina' examines childhood trauma through ominous personification ('Birdlike, the almanac/hovers') and surreal imagery ('a man with buttons like tears'). Poem's structure mirrors child's drawing of 'rigid' house, both trying to contain tremendous grief.

Point 3: (*Nature – Brazilian landscape*) 'Questions of Travel' is a painterly description of the luxuriant equatorial landscape. Bishop wonders why people are so interested in foreign places. Effective use of emphatic verbs ('hurry', 'spill'), surreal simile of exotic trees ('gesturing/like noble pantomimists, robed in pink').

Point 4: (*Nature – environment, animals*) 'The Armadillo' details the tragic consequences for nature of humankind's unthinking actions. Aural and visual imagery reflect the poet's frustration and compassion ('*piercing cry/and panic*').

Conclusion: Bishop makes 'the familiar strange' in her portrayals of both people and nature through her 'forever flowing' precise imagery and powerful language use.

Sample Paragraph: Point 4

Bishop's dramatic portrayal of nature is vivid and precise. 'The Armadillo' highlights the tragic consequences of people's thoughtless actions. The damaging effects of the 'fragile' fire balloons are shown through a powerful simile – one balloon 'splattered like an egg of fire'. The rabbit is described in the sibilant phrase, 'so soft'. The poet is urging us to be aware of the unique beauty under threat. The rabbit has been 'ignited' into 'intangible ash', only its eyes remain, red and fixed. The horrific danger of the lanterns is depicted in the alliterative phrase, 'falling fire'. This results in the 'glistening' armadillo scurrying 'head down, tail down' to find safety. The concluding lines force us to see just how vulnerable nature is – its 'weak mailed fist' raised against destruction.

EXAMINER'S COMMENT

Excellent response that focuses on all elements of the question. The 'powerful portrayal' aspect is effectively tackled ('dramatic', 'highlights', 'force us'). Informed and insightful views are presented in an argument seamlessly interwoven with textual support, making use of critical terms with skill. Impressive expression throughout. Top-grade standard.

MARKING SCHEME GUIDELINES

Candidates are free to agree and/or disagree with the statement, but they should engage with how various stylistic features effectively communicate compelling insights into the harshness and cruelty of life. Reward responses that include clear analysis of both themes and language use (though not necessarily equally) in Bishop's poetry.

INDICATIVE MATERIAL

- **Bishop uses a range of stylistic features** (dramatic settings, precise detail, vivid contrasts, diverse poetic forms, powerful imagery, striking aural effects, evocative tones, energetic language, etc.)

… to confront:

- **uncertainties and harsh realities of life** (alienation, grief, death, violence, addiction, suffering, troubling rites of passage, thought-provoking moments of epiphany, etc.)

Leaving Cert Sample Essay

'Elizabeth Bishop uses a range of stylistic features to confront the uncertainties and harsh realities of life.' To what extent do you agree or disagree with this view? Support your answer with reference to the poetry of Bishop on your course.

Sample Essay

1. Elizabeth Bishop often brings order to the chaotic experiences of life. In 'The Prodigal', the issue of addiction is addressed through vivid imagery. Elsewhere, the poet uses her controlled writing skill using the sestina form in the poem of the same name to discuss loss. She examines the disturbing subject of death in 'First Death in Nova Scotia' through the perspective of a child. Bishop can be a sympathetic observer who quietly gets our attention while she confronts the uncertainties and challenges of life.

2. 'Filling Station' is a graphic description of a run-down garage in which loneliness and belonging are explored. A driver observes a greasy station, irritated by its 'oil-soaked, oil-permeated' atmosphere which she dismisses with a patronising comment, 'Oh, but it is dirty!' Sibilant sound effects portray the owner in his 'dirty oil-soaked monkey suit' accompanied by his 'several quick and saucy and greasy sons'. The lady's contemptuous tone is very evident. But Bishop notices 'a dirty dog, quite comfy'. A moment of epiphany occurs. This is an environment of

nurturing and belonging, 'Somebody waters the plant'. The driver has discovered that love and happiness exist even in the most run-down places.

3. In 'Sestina', the adult poet examines the searing loss of her painful childhood. A cosy, domestic scene, a grandmother making tea, her granddaughter drawing, is filled with surreal imagery. Not everything is as it seems. The almanac book, with its facts about the cycles of the moon, transforms into a kind of mystery movie – 'Birdlike, the almanac/ hovers half open above the child'. The buttons in the child's drawing become 'like tears' and the 'little moons fall down like tears' into the flowerbed. Magic realism has steeped the scene with sadness. The young child is trying to create order with the 'carefully placed' flowerbed in her drawing. But the almanac suggests that life is hard, 'Time to plant tears'. The poem concludes with the child drawing 'another inscrutable house'. Life's uncertainties and harshness will not disappear.

4. The poet herself also attempts to control the painful memories of childhood herself by using the strict form of the sestina. The child's pencil drawing of an inflexible house mirrors this rigid structure of six 6-line stanzas, all with the same end words, 'house', 'grandmother', 'child', 'stove', 'almanac' and 'tears'. Unlike 'Filling Station', this poem does not end on a reassuring note. Instead, it ends in a worried tone and points towards a troubling time ahead, 'Time to plant tears'. Bishop faces up to the confusion and harshness of real life.

5. 'First Death in Nova Scotia' also uses the perspective of a child, rather than that of an adult, to tackle loss and death. Childlike language, 'In the cold, cold parlor' is used to bring us inside the innocent mind. She regards her dead cousin Arthur's coffin as 'a little frosted cake' and Arthur as 'a doll that hadn't been painted yet'. The child's attempt to grasp the reality of death is portrayed through a vivid stream of consciousness, 'Jack Frost had dropped the brush and left him white, forever'. The child retreats into the comforting world of fairy tales, imagining her little cousin as 'the smallest page at court'. But the fantasy is disrupted by the final question. How could he go 'with his eyes shut up so tight and the roads deep in snow?' Bishop accepts the uncertainty of death, leaving the unanswered question. Is there a possibility of an afterlife or not?

6. The bleak topic of alcohol addiction is addressed in 'The Prodigal' through a retelling of the Biblical story. Detailed description sets the degrading farmyard scene where the unhappy youth is living with the pigs. Broad assonant sounds emphasise the stench, 'The brown enormous odor he lived by/was too close'. His shame is evoked by the telling detail that 'he hid the pints behind a two-by-four'. However, the poet then

EXAM FOCUS

- As you may not be familiar with some of the poems referred to in the sample plans, substitute poems that you have studied closely.
- Key points about a particular poem can be developed over more than one paragraph.
- Paragraphs may also include cross-referencing and discussion of more than one poem.
- Remember that there is no single 'correct' answer to poetry questions, so always be confident in expressing your own considered response.

ELIZABETH BISHOP

changes the viewpoint. The alcoholic can still recognise a flash of beauty, 'sunrise glazed the barnyard mud with red'. He has not become completely dehumanised. There is a possibility of redemption from life with the pigs 'safe and companionable as in the Ark'. He is starting to realise, 'shuddering insights', that he can regain his humanity, but only if he wants to. Redemption is possible, although it won't be easy, 'But it took him a long time/finally to make his mind up to go home'.

7. Bishop is a poet who succeeds in making the familiar strange. She uses a greasy filling station, a homely domestic scene, a family ritual and a squalid farmyard to confront bitter aspects of life. The meticulous attention to detail in her imagery, use of tone, poetic form and aural effects slowly alters our perception of reality so that we too can face the unpredictable and difficult realities of life.

(800 words)

EXAMINER'S COMMENT

A confident critical response to the question, showing good engagement with Bishop's poetry – both subject matter and style (especially sound effects, tone and imagery). Focused discussion supported by accurate quotation ranges widely over several key poems. A little more emphasis on how the poet 'confronts' harsh truths would have secured full marks. Overall, however, points are generally well developed – despite some repetition in paragraph 4. Expression is clear and varied, adding to the essay's top-grade standard.

GRADE: H1
P = 14/15
C = 13/15
L = 14/15
M = 5/5
Total = 46/50

👀 Revision Overview

'The Fish' (OL)
Nature is a central theme. After surviving previous struggles against adversity, the fish gains Bishop's respect.
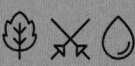

'The Bight'
A beautifully conceived poem that reflects on the chaotic nature of everyday existence.

'At the Fishhouses'
Detailed observation of the relationship between people and nature leads to insight and a sense of belonging.

'The Prodigal' (OL)
Compelling presentation of the power of the human spirit to endure hardship and to retain hope.

'Questions of Travel'
Reflective poem raises issues about the meaning and necessity of travel – and the morality of tourism.

'The Armadillo'
Powerful depiction of man-made disasters and careless violence signified by the suffering of defenceless animals.

'Sestina'
Unsettling story of a grandmother and a child living with loss addresses poignant themes of grief and coming of age.

'First Death in Nova Scotia'
In this recollection of childhood and loss of innocence, Bishop transforms the child's uncertainty into a dynamic poetic vision.

'Filling Station' (OL)
Closely observed description of a small family filling station where the nurturing influence of women is evident.

'In the Waiting Room'
Recalls a dramatic scene that highlights the difficult transition from childhood to adulthood.

💬 Last Words

'Bishop was spectacular at being unspectacular.'
Marianne Moore

'Bishop disliked the swagger and visibility of literary life.'
Eavan Boland

'The sun set in the sea ... and there was one of it and one of me.'
Elizabeth Bishop

 NATURE  TRAVEL/JOURNEYS   IDENTITY   MEANING OF LIFE   CONFLICT   SUFFERING   HISTORY/MEMORY   DEATH   LOVE   BEAUTY

John Donne
1572–1631

'Be thine own palace, or the world's thy jail.'

John Donne was born in London in 1572 into a prominent Roman Catholic family (his mother was a relation of the martyr Sir Thomas More). Donne was educated at home by Catholic tutors before attending university, where he trained as a lawyer. He converted to the Church of England during the 1590s.

After several appointments and trips abroad, he secretly married 17-year-old Anne More in 1601 and was briefly imprisoned as a result of her father's objection. The poet once wrote about the experience: 'John Donne – Anne Donne – Undone'. However, the marriage was a happy one, although the family struggled financially at times. His wife died in 1617, aged 33, after giving birth to their twelfth child.

In 1615, Donne had been ordained as an Anglican priest and he was later appointed Dean of St Paul's Cathedral, where he became famous for his spellbinding sermons. He also made his name as a highly original love poet. In his later years, Donne turned his talents to religious poetry, hymns and sermons. Whatever the subject, his writing reveals the same characteristics that typified the work of the greatest metaphysical poets: dazzling wordplay; subtle argument; surprising contrasts; intricate analysis; and striking imagery selected from law, medicine, geography, science and mathematics. His most prominent themes include love – romantic and spiritual, time, and death. Donne is now considered the most outstanding of all the English metaphysical poets.

Investigate Further

To find out more about John Donne, or to hear readings of his poems, you could search some useful websites, such as YouTube, BBC Poetry, poetryfoundation.org and poetryarchive.org, or access additional material on this page of your eBook.

Prescribed Poems

○ 1 'The Sun Rising'
Donne's lively love poem celebrates the joys of youthful romance. The dramatic opening where the poet ridicules the sun ('Busy old fool') for interrupting the couple is typically playful.
Page 63

○ 2 'Song (Go, And Catch A Falling Star)' (OL)
In this unusual love poem, Donne appears to argue that it is impossible to find a really beautiful and true woman. But while he is making fun of conventional love poetry, he actually succeeds in conveying the enduring nature of true love.
Page 67

○ 3 'The Anniversary'
This is a well-known poem about a couple celebrating their first year together. Using an extended metaphor (of the lovers as royalty), Donne argues passionately that the power of love can transcend time.
Page 71

○ 4 'Song (Sweetest Love, I Do Not Go)'
Another eloquent love poem on the theme of separation. Donne's affectionate tone gives readers an idealised view of romantic love. The poem ends with the reassurance that true lovers will 'ne'er parted be'.
Page 75

○ 5 'A Valediction: Forbidding Mourning'
Donne breathes new life into the traditional subject of lovers parting by using a series of ingenious metaphors and comparisons. These provide fresh ways of looking at separation which will help the couple.
Page 80

○ 6 'The Dream'
The poet awakens to find the woman he has been dreaming about standing at his bedside. In the course of this optimistic and sensual love poem, Donne touches on some fascinating aspects of dreams, desire and truth.
Page 85

○ 7 'The Flea' (OL)
This humorously erotic poem makes full use of the conceit (extended image) of a flea to explore Donne's relationship with the woman he loves. Characteristically, the poet advances a series of imaginative reasons to impress his lover.
Page 89

○ 8 'At The Round Earth's Imagined Corners'
Donne's Holy Sonnet is set against the dramatic backdrop of Judgement Day. What gives this powerful poem its universal significance is that the poet confronts the certainty of death, which all humans must face.
Page 93

○ 9 'Thou Hast Made Me, and Shall Thy Work Decay?'
In this deeply felt religious poem, Donne focuses on the intense spiritual struggle which preoccupied him. The sonnet reveals his passionate relationship with God as he meditates on the reality of life and death.
Page 97

○ 10 'Batter My Heart, Three-Personed God'
The poet is again deeply divided between his desire for spiritual salvation and his own sinful nature. Using violent imagery and the powerful language of secular love poetry, he urges God to enslave his soul.
Page 101

(OL) indicates poems that are also prescribed for the Ordinary Level course.

A Note on Metaphysical Poetry

Metaphysics is usually defined as a branch of philosophy concerned with explaining **the fundamental nature of existence**. 'Meta' means beyond, so metaphysical poems deal with philsophical subjects, such as religion, love and beauty.

Metaphysical poetry is a term used to describe the work of a group of British lyric poets who lived in England between 1590 and 1680. Among them were John Donne, George Herbert and Andrew Marvell. They did not call themselves Metaphysicals but were given this name by later writers because their poetry dealt with **philosophical speculation and abstract ideas**.

Their work was characterised by inventiveness of metaphor (often involving unusual and dissimilar images known as conceits). Such **witty and complex poetry** was influenced greatly by the changing times, new sciences and the newfound liberal behaviour of the 17th century.

Intellect and wit blending with strong feelings typify metaphysical poetry, especially that of John Donne. Indeed, Donne represents very well the school of poetry which is still somewhat vaguely called 'Metaphysical'. He brought the **whole of his experience** into his poetry.

Donne's writing is full of far-fetched imagery and allusions borrowed from various branches of learning. He often makes use of ideas and experience – and the most startling connections are discovered between them. The hallmark of Donne's metaphysical poetry is **passionate feeling and forceful argument**.

During the 18th century, many critics believed that the metaphysical poets only wanted to show off their learning. However, their work had a significant influence on leading 20th-century poets, such as T. S. Eliot, who promoted its **innovative and intellectual qualities**, and helped bring the poetry of John Donne back into favour with readers.

1 The Sun Rising

JOHN DONNE

    Busy old fool, unruly sun,
      Why dost thou thus,
Through windows, and through curtains call on us?
Must to thy motions lovers' seasons run?
    Saucy pedantic wretch, go chide   5
    Late school boys and sour prentices,
Go tell court huntsmen that the King will ride,
Call country ants to harvest offices;
Love, all alike, no season knows nor clime,
Nor hours, days, months, which are the rags of time. 10

    Thy beams, so reverend and strong
      Why shouldst thou think?
I could eclipse and cloud them with a wink,
But that I would not lose her sight so long;
    If her eyes have not blinded thine,   15
    Look, and tomorrow late, tell me,
Whether both th' Indias of spice and mine
Be where thou leftst them, or lie here with me.
Ask for those kings whom thou saw'st yesterday,
And thou shalt hear, All here in one bed lay. 20

    She's all states, and all princes I,
      Nothing else is.
Princes do but play us; compared to this,
All honour's mimic, all wealth alchemy.
    Thou, Sun, art half as happy as we,   25
    In that the world's contracted thus.
    Thine age asks ease, and since thy duties be
    To warm the world, that's done in warming us.
Shine here to us, and thou art everywhere;
This bed thy centre is, these walls thy sphere. 30

Saucy: impertinent, brazen.
pedantic: particular, fussy.
chide: scold.

court huntsmen: opportunistic courtiers.
country ants/harvest offices: probably a comic reference to farmers, telling them to get on with their work.
clime: climate.
rags: divisions.

eclipse and cloud: blot out, hide.

both th' Indias: East Indies (South Asia) and West Indies, famous respectively for spice and gold.

play: imitate.
all honour's mimic: everything which is held in high esteem is only an impersonation of the lovers.
alchemy: false gold, pretence.

sphere: world, universe.

'so reverend and strong'

👤 Personal Response

1. Describe Donne's attitude to the sun in the opening four lines of this poem. How is this reaction established?
2. Describe the poet's tone throughout stanza two. Is it respectful and realistic? Or exaggerated and mocking? Briefly explain your response.
3. Based on your reading of the poem, has Donne convinced you that true love is an all-conquering power? Give a reason for your answer.

👁 Critical Literacy

'The Sun Rising' (written in 1605) is one of Donne's most charming and successful metaphysical love poems. Although the title suggests an aubade (a song sung by lovers who must part at dawn), the poet has actually written a parody making fun of such tender declarations of love. Indeed, this humorous, exuberant poem cheekily scolds the sun for waking Donne and his lover. He is so irritated that he firmly instructs the interfering sun to go off and annoy others.

The opening lines dramatically convey the intimate scene of an irritated lover woken up too soon by a busybody sun. Donne personifies the sun and in a half-serious, petulant tone, he reprimands this 'Busy old fool' for intruding. He does not see why he and his lover should live their lives according to the dictates of the sun: 'Must to thy motions lovers' seasons run?' Throughout this first stanza, **the poet mocks the sun** ('Saucy pedantic wretch') and is highly dismissive of its power. Such lively personification of the sun gives great energy to the poem's opening. Donne goes on to instruct the sun to pester others, repeating the verb 'Go'. As far as he is concerned, lovers should define their own seasons and the sun should do trivial things like 'chide/Late school boys' and other people who have to get up early.

Donne argues that the sun would be better advised to concentrate on sycophantic courtiers and hard-working farmers who are struggling to survive. This is in contrast to the timeless world of true love, which is more important than anything else. Perhaps Donne is protesting too much because he really knows that the sun reminds lovers how their exhilarated state may change over time. However, he concludes confidently with an emphatic rhyme ('clime' and 'time') insisting that **love transcends time**: 'Love, all alike, no season knows nor clime,/Nor hours, days, months, which are the rags of time.'

Mischievously, in stanza two, Donne boasts that he can shut out the power of the sun's rays 'with a wink'. He merely has to close his eyes to 'eclipse and cloud' the sun. But he does not want to be parted from his lover ('would not lose her sight so long') for even that small measure of time. In fact, he believes her beautiful eyes are so bright that they could blind the sun. **In**

JOHN DONNE

a clever conceit, the poet shrinks the huge expanse of the world, its exotic destinations and far-off islands ('both th' Indias') and even the magnificence of the King's court into one little room. He tells the sun that the world's real treasures are contained right there in the bedroom, which is now the centre of the universe, 'All here in one bed lay'. As far as Donne is concerned, his lover is worth more than anything the sun can ever find outside their bedroom. The monosyllabic phrasing asserts that their bed contains the whole world, not only for the lovers but also for the sun. Again, the forceful rhyme ('yesterday' and 'lay') emphasises how love has altered space. For lovers, the universe is contracted into their own enclosed private space: 'All here in one bed lay'.

The third stanza begins with Donne dramatically dismissing the external world, 'Nothing else is'. With typically playful reasoning, he exaggerates the power of love: 'She is all states, and all princes I'. Reality is subverted as real princes are seen as mere actors pretending to be lovers, 'Princes do but play us'. Riches are dismissed as 'alchemy' (or illusion), a poor substitute for true feeling. The poet then realises that the sun – which is a single star – is only half as happy as the lovers who have created their own romantic kingdom. His **tone becomes gentle and more respectful** as he acknowledges that the sun is old, 'Thine age asks ease'. In contrast to the earlier disquiet, the mood has now become much more relaxed and assured.

Donne suggests that since the sun's function is to 'warm the world' and since the lovers encapsulate the whole world, the sun will do his duty if he shines on them. So the poet invites the sun to remain: 'Shine here to us'. **The lovers' bed is the centre of the universe**, their walls its borders. This world of love contains everything of value; it is the only one worth exploring and possessing. The final rhyme ('everywhere' and 'sphere') shows how love overcomes all boundaries with its limitless power. In the end, the sun is seen as a satellite encircling the lovers. 'The Sun Rising' demonstrates many of the qualities of metaphysical poetry. Donne's characteristic use of figurative and rhetorical techniques presents readers with a wonderfully conversational and witty poem, celebrating love and transcending the centuries with its lively energy.

Writing About the Poem

'Donne's original approach to poetry results in lively ideas and ingenious language.' Give your opinion on this statement in relation to the poem 'The Sun Rising'. Use references from the poem to support your views.

Sample Paragraph

It is astonishing to me how Donne in 'The Sun Rising' plays with time, space and location, almost as if none of the physical rules of the world matter. In the early 17th century, the discovery of new lands was the exciting news of the day. Donne uses this contemporary image to great effect. In this unusual love poem, he asks the 'Busy old fool', the sun, to let him know if exotic places like 'both th' Indias of spice and mine' are still where they were when the sun orbited past or whether they now 'lie here with me'. The poet uses this image to show that everything of importance is now contained in the lovers' room. I think this unique idea is wittily expressed by the poet's use of personification of the sun as an interfering intruder. Donne is cleverly showing that love transcends the physical world. This 17th-century poet has transcended time.

> **EXAMINER'S COMMENT**
>
> *As part of a full essay, this is a thoughtful response that attempts to address the question directly, using reference to both content and style. There is also some good personal interaction with the poem and points are clearly expressed throughout. Top-grade standard.*

Class/Homework Exercises

1. 'John Donne's love poetry is dramatic, conversational and intimate.' Is this a valid statement in relation to 'The Sun Rising'? Use quotation from the poem in your response.
2. The effective use of striking rhetorical features – particularly repetition and questions – reinforces Donne's assured tone throughout the poem. Discuss this view with particular reference to 'The Sun Rising'.

Points to Consider

- **Donne celebrates the joys of love and romance.**
- **Poet apostrophises (i.e. addresses the sun in a rhetorical fashion).**
- **Characteristically witty wordplay.**
- **Contrasting tones – playful, loving, comic, dismissive, logical.**
- **Effective developed conceit of the lovers' special world.**
- **Language varies from conversational to dramatic.**

2 Song (Go, And Catch A Falling Star)

JOHN DONNE

Go, and catch a falling star,
    Get with child a mandrake root,
Tell me, where all past years are,
    Or who cleft the Devil's foot,
Teach me to hear mermaids singing,   5
Or to keep off envy's stinging,
      And find
      What wind
Serves to advance an honest mind.

If thou be'est born to strange sights,   10
    Things invisible to see,
Ride ten thousand days and nights,
    Till age snow white hairs on thee,
Thou, when thou return'st, wilt tell me,
All strange wonders that befell thee,   15
      And swear
      No where
Lives a woman true, and fair.

If thou find'st one, let me know,
    Such a pilgrimage were sweet,   20
Yet do not, I would not go,
    Though at next door we might meet,
Though she were true, when you met her,
And last, till you write your letter,
      Yet she   25
      Will be
False, ere I come, to two, or three.

mandrake: a poisonous plant with a forked root.

cleft: split in two.

mermaids singing: when a traveller heard the song of the mermaids, it was an omen of disaster.
envy's stinging: jealous insults and attacks.

be'est born: are destined.

that befell thee: that you experienced.

true, and fair: honest and beautiful.

false: unfaithful.
ere: before.
two, or three: other lovers.

'a falling star'

👤 Personal Response

1. Describe the mood of the first stanza and show how the poet's use of verbs contributes to that mood.
2. Donne uses sound effects throughout the poem – mainly for emphasis. Choose one interesting example and comment briefly on its effectiveness.
3. From reading the poem, what is your initial impression of Donne? Is he a bitter misogynist who has no respect for women? Or is he simply being mischievous? Briefly explain your response.

👁 Critical Literacy

Written by Donne in his youth, when he had seen a good deal of London life (he was a 'great visitor of ladies'), 'Song (Go, And Catch A Falling Star)' is a humorous example of his early work. A woman's faithlessness was a conventional subject of Elizabethan poetry, but Donne's cunning line of argument leaves us wondering. Is he mocking the standard Petrarchan love poem in which a woman is seen as an object of adoration, when he cynically sets out to prove that it is impossible to find a really beautiful and loyal woman?

Stanza one includes a list of sharp commands ('Go', 'Get', 'Tell', 'Teach', 'find') as Donne demands a series of impossible tasks. The comma after 'Go' establishes the curt, almost overbearing tone of the poet. These unachievable tasks range from the magical first line, 'Go, and catch a falling star', to the nightmarish reference to conceiving a child with a poisonous plant. He also wants to know where the past has gone and he wishes to learn how to hear the unworldly music of the 'mermaids singing'. In line 6, Donne returns to the real world, as he seeks to find out how to change human nature so that it will not become jealous or bitter. The poet ends his wish list with another request – that everyone could be totally honest. The regular line length has now shortened, highlighting his frustration. Indeed, Donne's exasperation is vigorously expressed in rhyme ('wind', 'mind') as he struggles to comprehend why life does not encourage honesty. It is typical of his wry humour that his series of impossible demands will lead to his playful views on just **how hard it is to find a beautiful woman who will stay true to her husband**.

The first appearance of emphatic alliteration occurs in the second stanza ('If thou be'est born to strange sights') as the poet introduces an imaginary traveller, one who was destined to see strange and perplexing scenes. The **disquieting world of nightmare fantasy** is continued in the vivid, dramatic details; 'Things invisible', riding 'ten thousand days and nights', returning with hair of snow white, telling tales of 'strange wonders'. Although great distances will have been covered and a long time will have expired, yet the

poet confidently declares that 'No where/Lives a woman true, and fair'. Is Donne serious in these lines? Is he suggesting that ugly women will remain true, perhaps due to a lack of offers?

The conditional word 'If', which began the previous stanza, is also used at the beginning of the final stanza. This device of supposition ('if this were the case, then this follows') is a favourite rhetorical technique used by Donne. For a brief moment, **his tone appears to become more hopeful** when he states that if a perfect woman were discovered ('If thou find'st one, let me know'), then he would go on a 'pilgrimage', a holy journey. He thinks this would be delightful, 'sweet'. But he soon challenges the reader with a swift change of heart as he now decides that it would be better not to know. The stanza ends with Donne petulantly declaring that he would not even go next door to meet such an exceptional woman.

Disillusionment dominates the poem's final lines. The poet asserts that even if the ideal female were found, she would have very likely been unfaithful several times before the poet could have met her. The 'pilgrimage' would have been futile. In Donne's cynical view, there is no one to worship. All beautiful women are unreliable. He uses the recurring pattern of two lines of two words and a three-line rhyme, 'Yet she/Will be/False, ere I come, to two or three', to conclude the poem with a masculine swagger. The theory of the falseness of attractive women has been cleverly proved using the conventions of a type of love poetry which puts women on a pedestal. The heavenly body, 'falling star', has been toppled. Donne's satirical 'song' reflects the underlying theme of many of his other poems in which he blames the apparent wickedness of women for his own pain and heartbreak.

📖 Writing About the Poem

'Donne's changing viewpoint and tone challenge the reader.' Discuss this statement in relation to the poem 'Song (Go, And Catch A Falling Star)'. Refer closely to the text in your answer.

Sample Paragraph

Donne begins 'Song (Go, And Catch A Falling Star)' by setting up expectations of romantic love poetry. He quickly undermines these by the brutal image of the 'mandrake root', a poisonous plant, and the reader is taken into a nightmarish scenario. The poet swaps this surreal scene and expresses disgust at the difficulty of finding 'an honest mind'. Donne uses the device of the traveller, who has seen many 'strange wonders' in far-off places, not to celebrate women but to condemn them. This traveller will 'swear' that 'No where/Lives a woman true, and fair'. The reader is likely to be shocked by this attack. Cruelly, he reinforces his cynical view by stating that even if such a perfect creature was discovered, she would be unfaithful before the traveller could even write a letter informing the poet of her existence, 'False, ere I come, to two, or three'. Donne uses his changing tone and viewpoint to lead the reader through several twists before his final expression of disillusionment.

> **EXAMINER'S COMMENT**
>
> A good focused attempt at addressing a challenging question. References are effectively used to illustrate some of the changing views which make up Donne's argument throughout the poem. The paragraph is also rounded off very well in the final sentence. Top-grade standard.

Class/Homework Exercises

1. 'Donne's love poetry is energetic, intelligent and engaging.' Discuss this statement with reference to 'Song (Go, And Catch A Falling Star)'.
2. In your opinion, is Donne being at all serious in his poem 'Song (Go, And Catch a Falling Star)'? Support your answer with close reference to the text.

Points to Consider

- **Central themes include romantic love and the unreliability of women.**
- **Contrasting tones – humorous, demanding, satirical, loving, cynical.**
- **Effective use of a series of impossible demands.**
- **Characteristic stylistic features – rhetoric, repetition, wit, striking imagery.**

3 The Anniversary

JOHN DONNE

    All kings, and all their favourites,
        All glory of honours, beauties, wits,
The sun itself, which makes times, as they pass,
Is elder by a year now, than it was
When thou and I first one another saw.   5
All other things to their destruction draw,
    Only our love hath no decay;
This, no tomorrow hath, nor yesterday;
Running it never runs from us away,
But truly keeps his first, last, everlasting day.   10

    Two graves must hide thine and my corse;
        If one might, death were no divorce.
Alas, as well as other princes, we
(Who prince enough in one another be)
Must leave at last in death, these eyes and ears,   15
Oft fed with true oaths, and with sweet salt tears;
    But souls where nothing dwells but love
(All other thoughts being inmates) then shall prove
This, or a love increased there above,
When bodies to their graves, souls from their graves remove.   20

    And then we shall be throughly blest,
        But we no more than all the rest;
Here upon earth, we're kings, and none but we
Can be such kings, nor of such subjects be.
Who is so safe as we? where none can do   25
Treason to us, except one of us two.
    True and false fears let us refrain,
Let us love nobly, and live, and add again
Years and years unto years, till we attain
To write threescore; this is the second of our reign.   30

honours: important people of prominence and distinction.
makes times: the sun controls the passing of time.
Is elder: everything in the world is older by a year.

Running it never runs from us away: ongoing love can never cease.

corse: corpse. (In Donne's time, it would have been unacceptable for an unmarried couple to be buried in the same grave.)

sweet salt tears: love can bring both joy and heartbreak.

inmates: temporary occupants.
or a love increased there above: the couple's love will be greater in heaven.

throughly blest: totally blessed.

True and false fears let us refrain: we should put aside both real and imagined misgivings.
the second of our reign: the lovers are now entering the second year of their relationship.

'Who is so safe as we?'

👤 Personal Response

1. What expectations are set up in the opening five lines of this poem? Are they realised or refuted in the remainder of the poem? Refer to the text in your answer.
2. Do you find the ending of the poem convincing or unrealistic? Support your response with close reference to the text.
3. Write a short personal response to this poem, using references to illustrate your views.

👁 Critical Literacy

'The Anniversary' is about a couple celebrating their first year together. Royalty is the underlying conceit of the entire poem, with the speaker addressing his lover as though they were both nobles. Some critics felt that Donne should not irritate women with questions of reason and logic, but should engage their hearts. In fact, he does both. At the age of 27, he fell in love with 16-year-old Anne More. As he was not financially secure, they kept their love and marriage secret. When Donne eventually told her father, he was thrown in prison, and he ended a letter to Anne with the pun, 'John Donne – Anne Donne – Undone'. This type of clever wordplay is a recurring feature of metaphysical poetry.

An anniversary is a useful moment to stand back and reflect. In stanza one, the young lover confidently proclaims that the entire world, 'All kings, and all their favourites … beauties, wits,/The sun itself', is a year older since he and his beloved first met. Everyone and everything on Donne's magnificent list has been changed over time. All splendour fades. The list is not a fanfare, but a requiem, a funeral song. However, in contrast to this 'destruction', the shared love of the young couple escapes: 'Only our love hath no decay'. This short line stands out in defiance of time. The poet's clever paradox (a comparison of opposites) illustrates how their love survives: 'Running it never runs from us away'. The perpetual, unbroken movement is the rhythm and pulsing beat of their constant love. According to Donne, the lovers are at **the centre of the universe, unaffected by time**. The beautifully balanced final line ('But truly keeps his first, last, everlasting day') ends the opening stanza on an assertive note.

However, in stanza two, the poet faces up to life's stark reality and the inevitability of death. He pictures the lovers' bodies lying in separate graves, 'Two graves must hide thine and my corse'. But the couple's love is so strong that even death cannot separate them on a spiritual level. Donne develops the metaphor of royalty to emphasise how their mutual love sets them apart: 'Who prince enough in one another be'. For a moment, the mood is suddenly regretful at the thought of leaving behind love's 'true oaths, and with sweet salt tears'. The argument soon twists as Donne considers how death will free their loving souls from the prison of physical life. **The couple will then be reunited spiritually** 'where nothing dwells but love'. Indeed, they will find in heaven a much greater happiness, 'love increased there above'.

In the third stanza, Donne imagines the afterlife of the sanctified lovers when they will be 'throughly blest'. Yet he realises that they will be no different in heaven than all other lovers who have died – 'But we no more than all the rest'. It is ironic that they will not be as they are on earth, where they are 'kings'. During their lives, the two of them are royalty and subjects at the same time. Their mutual love is beyond deceit ('Treason'). Any harm which can happen to the couple would be self-destructive, so they can love without fear. Donne confidently dismisses whatever anxiety they might feel, whether real or imagined: 'True and false fears let us refrain'. He encourages them to 'love nobly', so they will enjoy a long life and even celebrate their 60th anniversary ('threescore'). Once more, the royal metaphor (suggested by 'nobly' and 'reign') is used to stress the special status of true love. Donne's final tone is optimistic, with its positive message to live in the moment, to love in this world. **The couple can now look forward to celebrating the second year of their relationship**: 'the second of our reign'.

Throughout this **passionate love poem**, the inward-looking nature of young lovers in the excitement of a new romance is beautifully evoked in the conceit of royalty. Love is an exceptional state, an absorbing experience, incapable of being touched by the outside world. But while there is plenty of passion in 'The Anniversary', Donne also gives readers a somewhat superior view of romantic love. The dominant tone throughout is highly assured, 'Only our love hath no decay', yet intimate, 'Who is so safe as we?' Characteristically, the poet's restless mind searches for far-fetched ideas and extravagant images in order to convey the quality of unconditional love. There is much metaphysical wit in Donne's poetry and he was known for his inventive wordplay, such as the oxymoron (the linking of opposite aspects) 'sweet salt tears'.

JOHN DONNE

Writing About the Poem

'Donne's love poetry is lively, inventive and highly compelling.' Discuss this view of the poet's work in relation to the poem 'The Anniversary'. Quote in support of your response.

Sample Paragraph

'The Anniversary' is another of Donne's love poems. It is the celebration of a relationship that is a year old. Donne uses the extended metaphor of royalty to illustrate the special state of the lovers. The opening which begins with the list, 'All kings, and all their favourites,/All glory of honours, beauties' is in the tradition of courtly love. But it is the ending of the poem which is really creative as the poet reassures his loved one: 'Who is so safe as we?' This is also typically imaginative as Donne suggests that they celebrate while they can, 'Here upon earth, we're kings'. Donne's language is energetic, particularly in the paradox, 'Running it never runs from us away'. I thought the unusual idea of movement going nowhere was interesting. The poet uses alliteration, especially the dull 'd' sound in 'destruction draw', to emphasise how everything in the world will change – except for the lovers themselves.

EXAMINER'S COMMENT

As part of a full essay, this is a well-managed paragraph which addresses the question directly and shows good personal interaction with the poem. The focus on Donne's language is clear and supported effectively with suitable reference. Expression is clear, but a little repetitive. Overall, a high-grade standard.

Class/Homework Exercises

1. In your own words, trace the development of the royalty metaphor throughout 'The Anniversary'.
2. Tensions between love's timelessness and the reality of death are central to Donne's poem 'The Anniversary'. To what extent do you agree with this view? Support your response with reference to the text.

Points to Consider

- Donne argues that true love is timeless.
- Presents passionate feelings within a logical context.
- Typical use of a developed conceit comparing the lovers to royalty.
- Contrast between the decaying reality and the lovers' transcendent world.
- Effective use of repetition, paradox and changing moods.

4 Song (Sweetest Love, I Do Not Go)

JOHN DONNE

Sweetest love, I do not go,
    For weariness of thee,
Nor in hope the world can show
    A fitter love for me;
        But since that I   5
Must die at last, 'tis best,
To use myself in jest
    Thus by feigned deaths to die.

Yesternight the sun went hence,
    And yet is here today,   10
He hath no desire nor sense,
    Nor half so short a way:
        Then fear not me,
But believe that I shall make
Speedier journeys, since I take   15
    More wings and spurs than he.

O how feeble is man's power,
    That if good fortune fall,
Cannot add another hour,
    Nor a lost hour recall!   20
        But come bad chance,
And we join to it our strength,
And we teach it art and length,
    Itself o'er us to advance.

When thou sigh'st, thou sigh'st not wind,   25
    But sigh'st my soul away,
When thou weep'st, unkindly kind,
    My life's blood doth decay.
        It cannot be
That thou lov'st me, as thou say'st,   30
If in thine my life thou waste;
    Thou art the best of me.

---

fitter: more appropriate.

in jest: not seriously.

feigned deaths: false deaths (preparations for the actual death which will eventually occur).

hence: from here.

More wings and spurs than he: Donne will return more quickly than the sun.

bad chance: misfortune.

Itself o'er us to advance: we focus on bad times so much that we allow them to almost overwhelm us.

wind: breath.

unkindly kind: her sorrow shows her love, but it also causes him hurt.

Let not thy divining heart
   Forethink me any ill,
Destiny may take thy part,   35
   And may thy fears fulfil;
    But think that we
Are but turn'd aside to sleep;
They who one another keep
   Alive, ne'er parted be.   40

divining: anticipating, foretelling.
Forethink me any ill: do not imagine any harm coming to me.

'Sweetest love'

👤 Personal Response

1. Choose one image from this poem which you consider particularly powerful. Briefly explain its effectiveness.
2. Describe the poet's tone in the first two stanzas. Refer closely to the text in your answer.
3. The final lines of the poem refer to the lovers turning on their sides to sleep. In your view, is this a happy, sad or poignant conclusion to the lovers' dilemma? Briefly explain your response.

👁 Critical Literacy

This song is a simple, eloquent poem on the theme of parting. It is believed that Donne wrote it for his wife before he travelled abroad in 1611. The poet argues that if two people are truly in love, then nothing – including death – can ever separate them. The poem's five stanzas provide a suitable structure for the overwhelming emotion of the scene with its strong rhyme, which forms a pattern throughout. Donne's use of everyday language gives an air of realism to the domestic setting.

Stanza one begins on a tense note, with Donne and his lover engaged in deep conversation about a journey he is planning. His affectionate address, 'Sweetest love', is tender and reassuring as he explains that he is not leaving because he is tired of her, 'For weariness of thee'. Nor does he want to look for something new, 'A fitter love for me'. The tone is serious and shows none of the glittering wit of Donne's other romantic poems, such as 'The Flea'. This makes it much more personal and sincere. Donne then tries to lighten the mood by arguing that **this temporary separation is merely a rehearsal** which will help both his lover and himself to become more accustomed to the inescapable parting of his actual death: 'Thus by feigned deaths to die.'

In the second stanza, Donne offers further assurances by comparing his travels to the movement of the sun across the sky. His own trip abroad will be much shorter than the sun's from dawn to dusk. He flatters his lover by focusing on her attractiveness, saying that he has much more reason than the sun to hurry back to her. **His characteristic use of hyperbole (exaggeration) emphasises just how quickly he will return**: 'I shall make/Speedier journeys'. Donne is keen to express his feelings. Being in love makes him even more powerful than the sun: 'I take/More wings and spurs than he.'

However, in the third stanza, the poet becomes increasingly reflective, widening the argument to discuss how people in general deal with life's good and bad experiences. As far as Donne is concerned, 'good fortune' is taken for granted. But if we are faced with challenging times ('bad chance'), we give in immediately and let it overwhelm us: 'we join to it our strength'.

JOHN DONNE

He is advising his lover to fight misfortune and resist adversity. Otherwise, disappointment will always get the better of the couple, undermining their love: 'Itself o'er us to advance'.

Stanza four is almost entirely focused on Donne's lover, the repetition of 'thou' reflecting his intense feelings for her. His deeply personal tone returns as he describes how close they are. The poet shares every small sadness that she feels. Even the slightest sigh she makes, 'sigh'st my soul away'. When she weeps, she is not being unkind since he understands her unhappiness: 'My life's blood doth decay'. Donne then goes so far as to apparently challenge her love for him: 'It cannot be/That thou lov'st me', accusing her of abandoning him whenever she cries: 'If in thine my life thou waste'. However, **deep down he acknowledges how much he depends on her**: 'Thou art the best of me'. Such an emphatic declaration of love leaves readers feeling that an intensely personal, intimate moment is being witnessed as the two lovers struggle with their overpowering emotions.

Throughout stanza five, the **tone is much more tender**. Donne appeals to his lover, encouraging her not to imagine all the unfortunate things which might happen to him when he is away: 'Forethink me any ill'. In a more light-hearted comment, he warns her against inviting misfortune: 'Destiny may take thy part'. Instead, he coaxes her to think of a beautiful moment in their relationship and suggests that his journey is no more than the parting of a couple as they sleep ('but turn'd aside to sleep'). The poem concludes with this positive image reflecting a secure and stable relationship. The inference is that if his loved one can get used to this parting, then she will be able to rise above death and separation.

✒ Writing About the Poem

'Donne is a highly dramatic poet.' Discuss this statement in relation to the poem, 'Song (Sweetest Love, I Do Not Go)'. Support the points you make with reference to the text.

Sample Paragraph

In 'Song (Sweetest Love, I Do Not Go)', Donne tries to reassure his loved one that his journey away from her is not 'For weariness of thee'. It is a typical lovers' quarrel. The dramatic opening is very realistic. Donne tries to lighten the conflict as he says he might as well practise for death by short separations, 'by feigned deaths to die'. But the fourth stanza is the most powerful in evoking the sheer misery of the girl who is left behind. Using dramatic language he speaks of her sighing, 'When thou weep'st'. He then tries to criticise her for her grief which he says is causing him harm. But then Donne admits the truth, 'Thou art the best of me'.

JOHN DONNE

The short fifth line in each stanza also adds drama, particularly 'Then fear not me'. He is reassuring her that he will return quickly. Finally he reminds her that this separation is just a short night's sleep. After all the drama between the lovers, there is a gentle resolution in the end.

> **EXAMINER'S COMMENT**
> *This high-grade paragraph addresses the question directly and explores key dramatic aspects of the poem both explicitly and implicitly. Expression is varied and well controlled and there is some good personal engagement. Effective use is also made of apt quotation and reference throughout.*

✒ Class/Homework Exercises

1. 'John Donne's poetry is intimate and engaging.' Discuss this statement in relation to 'Song (Sweetest Love, I Do Not Go)'. Support the points you make with reference to the poem.
2. Forceful rhythm is one of Donne's most effective stylistic features. Discuss this view with particular reference to 'Song (Sweetest Love, I Do Not Go)'.

◉ Points to Consider

- **Another of Donne's explorations of ideal love.**
- **Musical sounds, personification, emphatic rhythm, rhyme and repetition.**
- **Language varies – simple, exaggerated, argumentative.**
- **Effective use of contrast.**
- **Ambivalent moods – tender, light-hearted, serious.**

5 A Valediction: Forbidding Mourning

Title: the title comes from the Latin for a farewell message.

As virtuous men pass mildly away,
    And whisper to their souls, to go,
Whilst some of their sad friends do say,
    The breath goes now, and some say, no:

So let us melt, and make no noise,   5
    No tear-floods, nor sigh-tempests move,
'Twere profanation of our joys
    To tell the laity our love.

Moving of th'earth brings harms and fears,
    Men reckon what it did and meant,   10
But trepidation of the spheres
    Though greater far, is innocent.

Dull sublunary lovers' love
    (Whose soul is sense) cannot admit
Absence, because it doth remove   15
    Those things which elemented it.

But we by a love so much refined,
    That our selves know not what it is,
Inter-assured of the mind,
    Care less, eyes, lips, and hands to miss.   20

Our two souls therefore, which are one,
    Though I must go, endure not yet
A breach, but an expansion,
    Like gold to airy thinness beat.

If they be two, they are two so   25
    As stiff twin compasses are two,
Thy soul the fixed foot, makes no show
    To move, but doth, if the other do.

As virtuous men pass mildly: just as good men die peacefully.

melt: dissolve and blend together.

profanation: irreverence, offensiveness.
laity: ordinary people.

reckon what it did and meant: try to understand the significance of the turbulence.
trepidation of the spheres: movement of the planets.

sublunary: undependable; mundane.

elemented: formed.

Inter-assured: trusting.

breach: separation.

twin compasses: instrument for measuring circles.

JOHN DONNE

And though it in the centre sit,
    Yet when the other far doth roam,   30
It leans, and hearkens after it,
    And grows erect, as that comes home.

Such wilt thou be to me, who must
    Like th' other foot, obliquely run;
Thy firmness makes my circle just,   35
    And makes me end, where I begun.

obliquely: curved.
just: exact.

'Thy firmness makes my circle just'

👤 Personal Response

1. Trace Donne's line of argument in the poem 'A Valediction: Forbidding Mourning'. Support your answer with suitable reference.
2. Which comparison appeals most to you in this poem? Briefly explain why.
3. In what way does Donne see the parting of lovers as a positive move? Give reasons for your response using reference from the poem.

 Critical Literacy

'A Valediction: Forbidding Mourning' dates from 1611 when Donne embarked on a long journey to Europe and wrote this special farewell poem for his wife. The poet explores the familiar theme of separation from a loved one, and claims that the relationship between the lovers is such that physical distance cannot part them. Indeed, he argues, being apart actually strengthens their love. Characteristically, Donne breathes new life into this traditional subject by using a series of ingenious metaphors and comparisons. These provide fresh ways of looking at separation which will help the couple to avoid the mourning forbidden by the poem's title.

Stanza one opens on a reflective note. Donne considers how 'sad friends' grieve for those who are dying. The atmosphere is usually sombre but tranquil as loved ones take comfort that 'virtuous' people 'pass mildly away', confident of a spiritual life hereafter. Soft sibilant 's' sounds ('whisper' and 'souls') create this untroubled mood. The separation of body and soul is so gentle that those surrounding the dying are uncertain about whether they are still alive or not. Donne uses breaks in punctuation to suggest this confusion, 'The breath goes now, and some say, no'. This gives way to a metaphor in the second stanza where the poet makes a suggestion to his lover: 'So let us melt, and make no noise'. For Donne, the couple's separation is like a minor death which should also be treated in a dignified and restrained way. **He ridicules people who cannot control their feelings and resort to 'tear-floods' and 'sigh-tempests'**. Such hyperbole (exaggerated speech) was typical of courtly love. The poet emphasises the sacred nature of true love by asserting that it would be almost blasphemous – a 'profanation of our joys' – to let outsiders ('the laity') know about it.

Donne introduces a further conceit in the third stanza when he tells his loved one that earthquakes and similar disturbances – perhaps a hint at her outpourings of grief – only bring 'harms and fears'. However, a mere earthquake is relatively unimportant compared to the movement of the planet, which ordinary people see as presenting no danger. Therefore, the geographical separation which the couple will experience should not be feared. **This astrological analogy** continues into the fourth stanza where the poet speaks disapprovingly of 'Dull sublunary lovers' love'. Unlike the poet and his lover, other couples cannot tolerate being apart because their inferior type of love is dependent on physical contact. As always, Donne interlinks numerous poetic devices. The assonance of the short 'u' sounds in each word of the first line reinforces the concept of dreariness which he associates with shallow relationships. The term 'sublunary' (literally meaning 'under the moon') suggests that all these other lovers are changeable and unreliable just like the variable moon.

JOHN DONNE

Stanza five continues to focus on the superiority of the couple's shared love. This is the reason why Donne forbade mourning in the title. From his viewpoint, their relationship is purified like precious metal. They both know that each is loyal to the other, 'Inter-assured of the mind', because they share this special love. In contrast to ordinary couples, they are not dependent on the actual presence of the loved one, making each of them 'Care less, eyes, lips, and hands to miss'. **Their love is more a union of souls which transcends the physical.** Geographical separation means nothing to two united spirits. The poet's forceful, rhetorical tone is developed in stanza six. Donne argues that since their two souls are 'one', they are not really faced with any 'breach' or division. Indeed, they are experiencing an 'expansion' in much the same way as gold can be stretched to the slender width of paper if it is beaten to 'airy thinness'. Since gold is always associated with beauty and value, this typically inventive simile flatters Donne's lover and celebrates the couple's love.

The final reason for refusing to mourn being separated is presented in stanzas seven and eight when Donne uses compasses as a metaphor to describe the couple's unity. Although lovers retain their souls, they are divided into two parts. When the compasses draw a circle, one point remains stationary in the centre, at a fixed point, which allows the other to complete its circuit. Similarly, if one of the lovers remains at home, it ensures the return of the other. A perfect circle is a symbol of infinity, as there is no apparent beginning or end. This ingenious conceit aptly sums up the couple's spiritual relationship, which is also balanced and mutual. In the final stanzas, their heightened love is seen as serious and beautiful in its simplicity. Yet there is still a human dimension; the fixed foot 'hearkens after' the moving foot. The loved one will always yearn for the one who has gone. Overall, the **poem tenderly comforts both lovers** at this moment of uneasy parting. Donne concludes by offering a firm assurance that the traveller eventually 'comes home'.

> ### ✒ Writing About the Poem
>
> **'Donne's poetry rarely tells us anything new; rather it reminds us of what we know already.' To what extent is this true of 'A Valediction: Forbidding Mourning'? Support your answer with relevant quotation.**

Sample Paragraph

I agree with this view. Donne addresses familiar themes, particularly in his love poetry. However, it is his unique approach which makes him an original poet. He dares to go against conventions and appeals not only to a woman's emotions, but to her intellect through clever comparisons. 'A Valediction: Forbidding Mourning' presents the reader with a sad scene of men accepting death, 'pass mildly away'. The poet is suggesting that this attitude – 'make no noise'– is how he would like himself and his loved one to part, 'So let us melt'. Just as gold expands to 'airy thinness', so their love will bridge the gap of their separation. Finally, Donne compares these two lovers to a mathematical compass, free to move, yet always connected. So the treatment of an ordinary theme – separation – is raised to a new level as readers follow the poet's thought-provoking logic. Donne may not explore new ideas, but he does offer original perspectives.

EXAMINER'S COMMENT

This is a confidently written response to the question and addresses some of Donne's prominent ideas directly. Several suitable references are used effectively to discuss the poet's treatment of recurring themes. Expression is controlled throughout and there is some interesting personal engagement. Impressive top-grade standard.

Class/Homework Exercises

1. 'Donne is an original and thought-provoking poet.' Discuss this statement in relation to the poem, 'A Valediction: Forbidding Mourning'. Use evidence from the poem to support your response.
2. Donne is known for drawing on images from a wide range of sources. To what extent is this true of 'A Valediction: Forbidding Mourning'? Support your answer with reference to the poem.

Points to Consider

- **Donne focuses on the spiritual nature of true love.**
- **Inventive metaphors and extended image patterns illustrate separation.**
- **Effective use of contrast; varying tones – confident, assuring, loving.**
- **Arguments lead to logical conclusion that genuine lovers are never parted.**

6 The Dream

JOHN DONNE

Dear love, for nothing less than thee
Would I have broke this happy dream,
    It was a theme
For reason, much too strong for fantasy.
Therefore thou waked'st me wisely; yet   5
My dream thou brok'st not, but continued'st it.
Thou art so true that thoughts of thee suffice
To make dreams truths, and fables histories;
Enter these arms, for since thou thought'st it best,
Not to dream all my dream, let's act the rest.   10

As lightning, or a taper's light,
Thine eyes, and not thy noise waked me;
    Yet I thought thee
(For thou lovest truth) an angel, at first sight,
But when I saw thou saw'st my heart,   15
And knew'st my thoughts, beyond an angel's art,
When thou knew'st what I dreamt, when thou knew'st when
Excess of joy would wake me, and cam'st then,
I must confess, it could not choose but be
Profane, to think thee anything but thee.   20

Coming and staying showed thee, thee,
But rising makes me doubt, that now,
    Thou art not thou.
That love is weak where fear's as strong as he;
'Tis not all spirit, pure and brave,   25
If mixture it of fear, shame, honour have;
Perchance as torches which must ready be,
Men light and put out, so thou deal'st with me,
Thou cam'st to kindle, goest to come; then I
Will dream that hope again, but else would die.   30

suffice: are enough.
fables histories: stories become true.

taper's light: bright candlelight.

beyond an angel's art: more than an angel.

it could not choose but be: there was no other option.
Profane: disrespectful.

showed thee, thee: revealed your true self.

Perchance as torches which must ready be: worn torches light up more quickly than new ones.
kindle: re-ignite; awaken.
goest to come: you leave in order to return again.

'this happy dream'

👤 Personal Response

1. In your own words, describe Donne's attitude to his lover in the opening stanza.
2. Choose one image from the poem which you consider particularly effective. Briefly explain your choice.
3. Although John Donne enjoys arguing in his love poetry, he treats women as his intellectual equals. Where is this evident in 'The Dream'? Quote in support of your response.

👁 Critical Literacy

John Donne's love poetry reacted against the courtly love tradition of his time. He did not believe in worshipping an aloof, inaccessible figure. Instead, he wanted a real connection with his loved one. This can be clearly seen in 'The Dream', a sensual love poem which plays with ideas of dreams, desire and truth. Like love itself, the woman Donne addresses is praised in exaggerated terms and acclaimed as someone who is above even the level of angels.

At the start of stanza one, Donne is clearly delighted to have been awoken by the same person he was dreaming about. The poet's engaging tone is evident as he sleepily declares, 'Dear love, for nothing less than thee/Would I have broke this happy dream'. There is an unexpected gentleness in these lines. Using this playfully intimate mood, Donne explains that reality (his lover's physical presence) is stronger than fantasy, 'It was a theme/For reason'. The poet congratulates his lover on waking him, 'Therefore thou waked'st me wisely'. He even suggests that she can alter history, 'Thou art so true that thoughts of thee suffice/To make dreams truths'. Donne is implying that women have remarkable power over the perception of reality. **This subtle poem blends dream and reality seamlessly** as the poet declares that his loved one did not ruin his dream, 'My dream thou brok'st not', but by her actual presence, she is continuing it, and so he invites her to 'Enter these arms … let's act the rest'. Donne is clearly not satisfied with any distant adoration of a loved one. Instead, he desires an urgent, passionate connection, 'Not to dream all my dream', but to make his dream come true.

Stanza two begins with a flattering analogy. Donne compares the woman's eyes to a soft light, 'As lightning, or a taper's light,/Thine eyes'. Such characteristic wordplay emphasises her beauty and more than compensates for any interruption which may have disturbed him, 'not thy noise waked me'. For a brief moment, he thought she was an angel, but the bracketed afterthought, '(For thou lovest truth)', removes this romantic poem from the conventional style of Donne's time and gives it a more personal significance. There is no denying the poet's emotional vulnerability. He suddenly realises that his lover 'knew'st my thoughts' – something that makes her more special than any heavenly angel. He imagines that she

knew he was dreaming of her and wanted to play out the dream in reality so that they could share the 'Excess of joy'. The **complicated and challenging argument** continues as Donne confesses that it would be 'Profane' or blasphemous to regard his loved one as anyone but herself. From the poet's viewpoint, their relationship is based on mutual empathy, a sharing of thoughts.

Donne continues to applaud his lover in the opening lines of stanza three. By 'Coming and staying', she has revealed her real character, 'showed thee, thee'. He maintains that when she is with him, she is most like her true self. However, there is an **abrupt change of mood** as she attempts to leave, 'rising makes me doubt'. Donne suddenly criticises his companion for not being truly in love with him, 'that now,/ Thou art not thou'. He challenges her feelings towards him in a finely balanced argument, 'love is weak where fear's as strong as he'. The personification suggests that her fear becomes stronger as her love weakens.

The poet claims that the woman's reluctance to express her love physically is because of various social pressures, especially 'fear, shame, honour'. He bitterly accuses her of taking him for granted, like an old torch. Up until this moment, Donne had been hoping she had come to ignite their love, 'Thou cam'st to kindle'. However, in another startling turn, he uses an oxymoron (a contradictory expression) to reassure himself that his companion only leaves him in order to return, 'goest to come'. She will revisit him and inflame his desires for her even further, just as torches, once lit, are easier to ignite a second time. **The poem ends on an enthusiastic note of expectation**. Donne will 'dream that hope again'. Meantime, he leaves his lover with a parting shot that he 'but else would die' if she does not return to him. Clearly, without the woman of his dreams, he can never be truly satisfied.

✒ Writing About the Poem

'John Donne develops his poetic themes by means of vigorous and surprising arguments.' Discuss this statement in relation to 'The Dream'. Use close reference to the text to support your points.

Sample Paragraph

With an intimate glimpse of the poet in the unguarded moments between sleep and wakefulness, Donne wakes to find his loved one at his side. In an enthusiastic tone, he aims to pursue in real life what he has been dreaming of. He begins with compliments, telling her she is so real that her very presence turns his imaginings to fact, 'Thou art so true'. The poet was so intensely aware of her in his dream that he does not feel that the spell is broken when he wakes, 'My dream thou brok'st not'. His reasoning develops, particularly in the last stanza, he abruptly changes course because she is leaving, accusing her that 'love is weak'. Unexpectedly, the logic takes a different direction as he consoles himself that she 'cam'st to kindle' and she is only going so that she can come again, 'goest to come'. His argument ends optimistically, that he 'Will dream that hope again' – as a result of his dependency on her.

> **EXAMINER'S COMMENT**
>
> *This is a sustained response to a challenging question. There is good engagement with the development of thought in the poem, and supportive reference to the changes in Donne's line of argument. Expression is assured throughout and effective use is made of suitable quotation. Top-grade standard.*

✒ Class/Homework Exercises

1. '"The Dream" is a highly passionate and uninhibited love poem.' To what extent would you agree with this view? Support your answer with reference to the text.
2. Witty wordplay is a recurring feature of John Donne's poetry. In your opinion, is this true of 'The Dream'? Refer closely to the poem in your answer.

⊙ Points to Consider

- **Positive, sensual love poem exploring aspects of dreams, desire and truth.**
- **Simple, conversational language adds immediacy and authenticity.**
- **Varying moods – happiness, misgiving, anticipation.**
- **Mix of serious and light-hearted tones.**
- **Characteristic use of strong rhythm, exaggeration, logical argument.**

7 The Flea

JOHN DONNE

Mark but this flea, and mark in this,
How little that which thou deny'st me is;
Me it suck'd first, and now sucks thee,
And in this flea, our two bloods mingled be;
Thou know'st that this cannot be said   5
A sin, nor shame, nor loss of maidenhead,
    Yet this enjoys before it woo,
        And pampered swells with one blood made of two,
    And this, alas, is more than we would do.

O stay, three lives in one flea spare,   10
Where we almost, yea more than married are.
This flea is you and I, and this
Our marriage bed, and marriage temple is;
Though parents grudge, and you, w'are met,
And cloistered in these living walls of jet.   15
    Though use make you apt to kill me,
        Let not to that self-murder added be,
    And sacrilege, three sins in killing three.

Cruel and sudden, hast thou since
Purpled thy nail, in blood of innocence?   20
Wherein could this flea guilty be,
Except in that drop which it sucked from thee?
Yet thou triumph'st, and say'st that thou
Find'st not thy self, nor me the weaker now.
    'Tis true, then learn how false, fears be;   25
        Just so much honour, when thou yield'st to me,
    Will waste, as this flea's death took life from thee.

Mark: note.

our two bloods mingled be: intimacy between lovers was believed to result in the mingling together of each partner's blood.
maidenhead: virginity.
this enjoys before it woo: the flea achieves what the poet desires, without the trouble of courtship.

cloistered: enclosed.
jet: shiny black.
apt: ready.

sacrilege: destruction of something holy.

sudden: without warning.
Purpled: stained with the blood of the flea.

Yet thou triumph'st: Donne declares that the woman believes she has defeated his argument.

'our two bloods mingled'

👤 Personal Response

1. In your opinion, what is Donne's attitude to love and romance in this poem? Support your answer by close reference to the text.
2. Choose two lines or phrases which you think would have surprised or shocked Donne's readers in the 1600s. Briefly explain your choice in each case.
3. Write your own personal response to the poem, highlighting its impact on you.

👁 Critical Literacy

Donne's humorous and sensual poem makes use of the conceit (extended image) of a flea to explore his relationship with the woman he loves. However, in associating romantic love with a bloodsucking parasite – rather than something of beauty – the poet expresses his own desire for intimacy in an unexpected way. While many of Donne's poems deal with spiritual love between couples, here it is purely physical.

The reader is immediately plunged into a turbulent scene between two lovers in stanza one. The poet addresses an unnamed woman, insisting that she pay close attention to what he is saying. She is denying him something he craves, which is as yet unspecified, but – according to Donne – is trivial, 'How little that which thou deny'st me is'. He then comments on the actions of the flea, 'it suck'd me first, and now sucks thee'. The poet even uses religious imagery ('sin', 'shame') to add weight to his argument that an intimate physical relationship is not wrong. He complains that **the flea has already enjoyed more intimacy than himself with this woman**, even though it has not had to go through the ritual of courtship.

Unlike Donne, the flea is 'pampered' and satisfied. The monosyllabic verb 'swells' dramatically describes the bloating of the insect with the couple's blood. The peevish complaint, 'Yet this enjoys before it woo', highlights just how frustrated Donne feels. **Although he has played the game of love by the rules**, he is a miserable failure. The punctuation breaks before and after 'alas' emphasise how cruelly he believes he is being treated. Is the tone here mock-dramatic, with the use of the regretful 'alas'? If so, the reader can react with amusement. Or is the tone emotional, verging on petulant blackmail? Then the reader might feel anger at the poet's whining, adolescent behaviour.

In stanza two, Donne's argument switches as he asks his lover to respect the flea and what it represents. His pleading tone is evident when he begs for its life to be spared, 'O stay'. Such flamboyant exaggeration strikes a note of humour. The poet presents an elaborate explanation outlining why the flea should be allowed to live. Killing it will result not only in the insect's death, but also the symbolic death of the couple, as their bloods are mingled

in the body of the flea, 'three lives in one flea spare'. Donne maintains that the couple are even closer than if they were joined together in marriage ('yea more than married are') since their bloods have now combined. To the poet, this represents a relationship that is blessed in heaven. He argues that even though there are objections to this sacred union from both his loved one herself and her family, 'Though parents grudge, and you', yet the fact remains that **the lovers are already joined together**, 'cloistered in these living walls of jet'. This striking religious image is typical of Donne, who exaggerates how the flea's glossy, black body contains the couple's unified blood.

Donne develops his argument by referring to a major difficulty in their relationship – the woman's coldness towards him. As far as he is concerned, she takes him for granted, 'Though use make you apt to kill me'. **The tone changes from an almost reflective voice to a more impatient one**. But he continues to persuade the woman, urging her to spare the flea and show her love for him. The 'three lives in one' of the flea (her blood, his and its) is a clear reference to the Christian idea of the Trinity. The flea is seen as their marriage 'temple', which it would be 'sacrilege' to destroy. It's interesting that Donne never lets the reader hear the woman speak, yet from the various twists and turns of his argument, there is a real sense of her presence, and the reader is left in no doubt of her negative reaction to the poet's persistent pleas.

The tone becomes increasingly accusatory in stanza three as Donne reacts to his companion's impulsive killing of the flea, 'Cruel and sudden'. But his real resentment is almost certainly because of the woman's forceful rejection of his advances. Like the unfortunate flea, **he sees himself as a victim of her callous behaviour**. The vivid, colloquial language ('hast thou since/Purpl'd thy nail, in blood of innocence?') seems to have a timeless resonance. For a moment, Donne appears to admit defeat ('Yet thou triumph'st') – but is he lulling his lover into a false sense of security before coming up with yet another argument?

In a final flourish, **the poet insists on having the last word by turning the woman's own resistance against her**. He admits that, of course, she is completely right, ''Tis true'. Neither she nor Donne has lost anything by the flea's death, 'not thy self, nor me the weaker now'. Once again, as in the poem's opening lines, he issues instructions to this alluring woman – 'then learn'. What he wants her to believe is that she will lose almost nothing in yielding to his sexual advances. But readers are still left with an unresolved situation. Will the poet ever convince his beloved to put aside her 'fears'? Or will he be forced to accept that he cannot always get what he desires? What is certain, however, is that during the course of this unusual love poem, Donne's dazzling argument has ingeniously explored some of the age-old questions about the games lovers play.

📝 Writing About the Poem

'John Donne's poems can be described as intimate dramas.' Discuss this statement in relation to 'The Flea', using quotations from the text to support your answer.

Sample Paragraph

Donne's erotic poem opens with an emphatic repetition as he instructs his lover to pay more attention to him – 'How little that which thou deny'st me is'. The seduction scene is highly charged as they disagree about committing to a full sexual relationship. The conflict increases when the poet begs her not to kill the flea – 'O, stay'. Detailed, probing argument is used as Donne points out that this flea 'is you and I', since it contains their mixed blood. The poet's annoyance is suggested in the melodramatic third stanza as he calls his beloved 'Cruel' because she has killed the insect. The drama reaches a high point when he tricks her by suddenly agreeing with her cruel decision to refuse him – 'Yet thou triumph'st'. He ends by then reminding her how little she will have lost if she gives in to his advances. The poem is typical of Donne's exaggerated dramas, filled with striking imagery and characteristic playfulness.

> **EXAMINER'S COMMENT**
>
> *This is a confident top-grade response which addresses the question directly and includes good engagement with the poem. Suitable quotations illustrate key points, highlighting the various references to drama (in this case, a seduction scene involving conflict and melodramatic dialogue). Expression is varied, fluent and very well controlled throughout.*

✒ Class/Homework Exercises

1. Comment on the effectiveness of Donne's use of imagery in his poem 'The Flea'. Support your answer with suitable reference and quotation.
2. In your opinion, does Donne present an effective and convincing argument to his lover in this poem? Support your answer with reference to the text.

⊙ Points to Consider

- **Light-hearted, erotic love poem exploring aspects of desire.**
- **Effective development of witty, provocative imagery based on the central flea conceit.**
- **Use of dramatic, eloquent and precise language.**
- **Typically argumentative and logical.**

8 At the Round Earth's Imagined Corners

JOHN DONNE

At the round earth's imagined corners, blow
Your trumpets, angels, and arise, arise
From death, you numberless infinities
Of souls, and to your scattered bodies go,
All whom the flood did, and fire shall, o'erthrow, 5
All whom war, dearth, age, agues, tyrannies,
Despair, law, chance, hath slain, and you whose eyes
Shall behold God, and never taste death's woe.
But let them sleep, Lord, and me mourn a space;
For, if above all these, my sins abound, 10
'Tis late to ask abundance of thy grace,
When we are there. Here on this lowly ground,
Teach me how to repent; for that's as good
As if thou hadst sealed my pardon, with thy blood.

the round earth's imagined corners: biblical idea of four corners of earth.
Your trumpets: old maps include illustrations of angels blowing trumpets.
All whom the flood did, and fire shall, o'erthrow: God drowned the world in a great flood. Fire will destroy it in the end.
dearth: scarcity, famine.
agues: sickness, disease.
Shall behold God, and never taste death's woe: those people who are still alive on the Last Day will go straight to judgement.
But let them sleep: Donne asks God to postpone Judgement Day.
a space: for a moment.
abundance of thy grace: God's forgiveness.
lowly ground: here on earth.
repent: ask for God's mercy.
As if thou hadst sealed my pardon: Jesus died for people's sins.

'to your scattered bodies go'

👤 Personal Response

1. What picture of the Last Judgement is given in the poem's opening eight lines? Refer to the text in your answer.
2. The poem changes direction in line 9. Describe this change and explain why you think the poet has switched his line of thought. Support your answer with close reference to the text.
3. In your opinion, is Donne fascinated by death? Choose two lines or phrases from the poem which support your view and discuss their impact.

👁 Critical Literacy

John Donne's famous Holy Sonnet, 'At the Round Earth's Imagined Corners', is set against the dramatic backdrop of the Apocalypse, the final destruction of the world, described in the Bible's Book of Revelations. The poem is divided into two parts: the chaotic tumult of Judgement Day in the octet and the quieter, more meditative sestet. What gives this powerful poem its universal significance is that Donne confronts the certainty of death, which all humans face.

Donne presents the reader with a tantalisingly surreal paradox in line 1. Using the traditional expression, 'the round earth's imagined corners', he visualises what will happen when the dead are resurrected and reunited with their spirits. Broad vowel assonance adds to the **magnificent tension of this imagined scene**. The poet's powerful, visual language has cleverly captured a sense of huge expanse. He quickly introduces an urgent tone with the monosyllabic verb 'blow' which teeters at the end of the opening line. Donne is demanding that the angels signal Judgement Day, almost as if it were a race. He imagines them with bright trumpets sounding a triumphant call, just as a fanfare announces the arrival of a king. The sound is so loud and resonant that it immediately wakens the dead. Is this the sign of triumph over death? Donne heightens the drama as he repeats 'arise, arise', insisting that all the dead souls 'go' to their bodies. The run-on lines (enjambment) accelerate with breathless energy as confusion reigns. Spirits rush around trying to find their 'scattered' bodies. Throughout this first quatrain, the forceful end-of-line verbs ('arise', 'go') emphasise this momentous occasion. With characteristic hyperbole, Donne speaks of 'numberless infinities', successfully reinforcing the scale of the overwhelming numbers involved in this frenzy.

In the second quatrain, Donne reflects on how all these people died. The repetition of the phrase, 'All whom', with its monosyllabic broad vowels, signifies the enormity of these events. Ranging over time, the poet considers great natural disasters, 'All whom the flood did' (a reference to the Great Flood described in the Bible). He then imagines the future, 'and fire shall, o'erthrow' (another biblical prophecy about the destruction of the world

JOHN DONNE

by fire). Donne sweeps at breathtaking pace through possible causes of death, such as 'war, dearth, age, agues, tyrannies'. His **pounding rhythm is relentless** as he rushes on through his solemn list: 'Despair, law, chance'. The poet then thinks about everyone who will be alive on the Last Day, those who will 'never taste death's woe'. For Donne, these are the fortunate ones who will go straight to God's judgement, having been spared the ordeal of death. The forceful eight lines with their purposeful, regular rhyme form one overwhelming sentence, concluding with triumph over death.

There is a sudden change of tone in line 9. This dramatic turn (volta) diverts the poem from Donne's insistent demand that the world should end now, and allows readers realise that the apocalypse has not yet happened. Indeed, the poet has been imagining the whole panoramic scene. His enthusiasm for the end of the world evaporates and the earlier impassioned conviction gives way to **a mood of self-doubt and contrition**. But as Donne focuses on his own personal relationship with God, we are left wondering whether his apparent concern for the dead is an act of compassion, or just a selfish request for his own spiritual salvation. At any rate, he realises that he needs time to atone for his own sins, 'and me mourn a space'. Donne becomes acutely aware that he was hasty in calling for the Day of Judgement before knowing if he himself had been forgiven. Now he pleads for more time, begging God to be taught 'how to repent'. He realises that it will be too late to seek forgiveness on Judgement Day, 'to ask abundance of thy grace/When we are there'. His submissive tone is plainly evident in the poignant phrase, 'Here on this lowly ground'.

The sonnet's final lines confirm Donne's belief that Christ's death on the cross brought salvation to the world. This paradox shows that although human beings as a group were redeemed, individuals cannot be saved unless they recognise this sacrifice of 'blood'. An individual act of faith is required. Donne's language is dense and legalistic. This conclusion is a plea for 'pardon', a reprieve. Christ's blood is the seal on the poet's 'pardon'. This poem has moved on considerably from the octet, where Donne confidently urged the angels and the dead to prepare for the end of the world. In the sestet, **he has become unsettled, afraid of the consequences of the Apocalypse for himself**. However, the concluding couplet represents a resolution, since the poet now puts his trust in Christ's salvation. Readers are left with their own questions. Is the poem merely a display of arrogant presumption which ends with a servile plea for forgiveness? Or is it a genuine act of repentance?

✎ Writing About the Poem

Donne's sonnet 'At the Round Earth's Imagined Corners' is a private, personal religious meditation which alienates the modern reader. Discuss this view, supporting your answer with reference to the poem.

Sample Paragraph

All human beings face death. So I do not think Donne's poem 'At the round earth's imagined corners' is all that remote from people today. The difference between the modern reader and Donne is the outdated language used. Biblical references wouldn't be as familiar to today's readers. These describe the angels blowing their trumpets would not be widely known. I think the first eight lines would appeal to the modern reader as the poet shouts 'blow', 'arise', 'go'. I don't think Donne's personal tone in the sestet, 'on this lowly ground', would be familiar today. In some ways, I can relate to Donne's fear of death – which is still the one great unknown. At times of trouble, believers often light candles in hope. Donne's personal hope was for salvation bought by the death of Christ, 'with thy blood'.

EXAMINER'S COMMENT

This is an uneven attempt at a challenging question. While the paragraph touches on some noteworthy points about the poem's archaic expressions and references which might alienate modern readers, it lacks in-depth discussion of Donne's central concern – his own relationship with God. An average mid-grade standard.

Class/Homework Exercises

1. 'A feature of Donne's poetry is that his vocabulary is easy to understand, but his ideas are difficult to follow.' Discuss this statement in relation to the poem 'At the Round Earth's Imagined Corners', quoting in support of your response.
2. Donne is well known for the power of his dramatic imagery. To what extent is this true of 'At the Round Earth's Imagined Corners'? Support your answer with reference to the poem.

Points to Consider

- **Holy Sonnet imagining Judgement Day.**
- **Themes include the poet's intense relationship with God, sin and repentance.**
- **Dramatic language, memorable images, emphatic verbs, rhythm and repetition.**
- **Contrasting moods/atmospheres; effective use of assonant sounds.**

9 Thou Hast Made Me, and Shall Thy Work Decay?

JOHN DONNE

Thou hast made me, and shall thy work decay?
Repair me now, for now mine end doth haste,
I run to death, and death meets me as fast,
And all my pleasures are like yesterday;
I dare not move my dim eyes any way,   5
Despair behind, and death before doth cast
Such terror, and my feeble flesh doth waste
By sin in it, which it towards hell doth weigh.
Only thou art above, and when towards thee
By thy leave I can look, I rise again;   10
But our old subtle foe so tempteth me,
That not one hour myself I can sustain;
Thy grace may wing me to prevent his art,
And thou like adamant draw mine iron heart.

Repair: renew, rescue.
doth: does.

dim: blurred, unseeing.

feeble: weak.

weigh: pull down, think about.

old subtle foe: Satan, the old enemy.

adamant: a naturally occurring magnet or lodestone.
iron: hard, uncompromising.

'like adamant draw mine iron heart'

👤 Personal Response

1. Donne's poem begins on a sharp demanding note. In your opinion, what does the poet mean by the question in line 1?
2. What characteristics of the Devil are implied in the phrase 'old subtle foe'?
3. In your view, is the conclusion of the poem optimistic or pessimistic? Refer closely to the text in your response.

👁 Critical Literacy

The religious poems of John Donne explore the intense spiritual struggle which preoccupied his mind and soul. Sonnets such as 'Thou Hast Made Me, and Shall Thy Work Decay?' are personal dialogues or 'conversations' which show his passionate relationship with God as he privately meditates on the reality of life and death.

Donne begins this poem in a similar way to his love poetry, in mid-action, addressing God directly. His bold question ('Thou hast made me, and shall thy work decay?') manipulatively suggests that God will be unsuccessful in his great work on behalf of sinners if he does not redeem the poet. **Donne's lifelong search for truth is channelled into this simple, dramatic confrontation**. He regards it as a priority that God should forgive him without delay, 'Repair me now', as he is facing imminent death, 'for now mine end doth haste'. Throughout this first quatrain, the poet bluntly admits his spiritual distress. Ironically, while Donne accepts his dependence on God, he uses an authoritative tone in demanding God's immediate help.

The urgency of this impatient request is evident in the personification of death as a familiar figure hurrying towards him, 'I run to death, and death meets me as fast'. **Powerfully monosyllabic language** emphasises the surging movement of this crucial encounter, which is further underlined by the mid-line repetition of 'death'. The running action of two lovers rushing to meet is evoked in this daring image. There is a sense of both intimacy and inevitability as Donne now accepts the chilling realisation that the many sensual delights he once enjoyed are gone: 'And all my pleasures are like yesterday'. Is the remorse of an indulgently sinful life flashing before the eyes of this vulnerable man who is about to die?

In the second quatrain, Donne appears to be haunted by this intense realisation: 'I dare not move my dim eyes any way'. Terrified of looking back at a past that is full of sin, he is equally petrified by the future of certain death and possible damnation. The fragility of his human condition is shown in the adjective 'dim'. He is horrified by the shocking prospect of his decaying body, rotting with sin: 'my feeble flesh doth waste'. An increasing **sense of hopelessness dominates his restless mind**, as Donne imagines his doomed

JOHN DONNE

soul being dragged into eternal punishment, 'towards hell doth weigh'. The mood throughout is fearful and guilt-ridden, focusing on a negative view of man's mortal condition: 'decay', 'dim', 'terror', 'hell'.

However, the sestet signals a change of direction, an acknowledgment that the only hope of salvation is the complete surrender of the poet's strong individual will to the will of God, **an act of submission**. Donne's humble tone is liberating. He asks permission to raise his eyes to God, 'By thy leave I can look'.

Now there is a real possibility of redemption, 'I rise again'. If the poet accepts God's power to forgive, he 'can look' again and focus his 'dim' eyes. The weight of all Donne's sinfulness – which seemed so heavy in the octet – dissolves as he takes a leap of faith towards his Creator. For a moment, the downward spiral of the poem's opening is reversed into an upward movement towards God. Nevertheless, the poet is not quite completely free – since he is so easily tempted by the Devil, 'our old subtle foe'. Donne's use of 'our' suggests his **closeness to God**, in their common struggle against Satan. In eventually coming to terms with his own weakness and constant dependence on God's grace, the poet has found a way to 'sustain' himself.

The rhyming couplet sums up Donne's continuing need of divine power against the Devil's scheming, 'to prevent his art'. God must act on his behalf, so that 'Thy grace may wing me'. It is **God's choice whether Donne is saved or not**. The vision of his immortal soul soaring upwards is graphically conveyed in the verb 'wing'. The sonnet concludes with a typical metaphysical image drawn from science. God is compared to 'adamant', a magnetic stone which can guide ('draw') iron, a symbol of the poet's sinful heart. To his relief, Donne's newly confident faith reassures him that God has the ability to secure his soul with ease. The poet's appealing tone is clearly seen in his reserved form of address to God. This is in sharp contrast to the curt opening question. Throughout these final lines, personal pronouns underline the intimate intensity of the poet's all-consuming relationship with God.

Donne has adapted two sonnet forms for his poem. The basic structure is Petrarchan, divided into the despairing octet and a more hopeful sestet. However, he also uses the compact rhyme scheme of the Shakespearean sonnet.

✒ Writing About the Poem

'The language of Donne's poetry ranges from violence to tenderness, and from the unfamiliar to the paradoxical.' Using close reference to the text, discuss this view in relation to the sonnet 'Thou Hast Made Me, and Shall Thy Work Decay?'

Sample Paragraph

Donne's religious poem, 'Thou Hast Made Me, and Shall Thy Work Decay?' contains both forceful and gentle expressions as he insists, 'Repair me now'. An unexpected image of two lovers rushing to meet describes the terrifying end of life, 'death meets me as fast'. The genuine agony of his position is clear, 'I dare not move my dim eyes any way'. His eyes are closed by sin. For me, the sestet shows a gentler voice as the poet realises that God's grace alone can save him. His tone is softly submissive, 'By thy leave I can look'. The warm, effortless language suggests the possibility of his saved soul which 'may wing' its way to heaven with the power of God. All through this poem, I was impressed by Donne's turbulent yet sensitive expressions which explored a highly dramatic exchange between himself and God.

EXAMINER'S COMMENT

Well-written paragraph which focuses firmly on the poet's style. Effective use is made of a great many accurate quotations to illustrate the variation in tone and range of language evident in the poem. There is also some good personal engagement with the text. Top-grade response.

Class/Homework Exercises

1. 'Donne's religious poetry is both stimulating and challenging.' Discuss this statement in relation to 'Thou Hast Made Me, and Shall Thy Work Decay?' Refer to the poem in your response.
2. 'Many of Donne's poems are noted for their vibrancy of language, urgent tone and inventiveness of metaphor.' In your opinion, is this true of 'Thou Hast Made Me'? Give reasons for your answer, using reference to the text.

Points to Consider

- Themes include Donne's spiritual struggle and his complete dependence on God.
- Varying tones: demanding, persuasive, reliant.
- Use of logic, debate, question-and-answer format.
- Dramatic atmosphere, effective sounds, memorable images.

10 Batter My Heart, Three-Personed God

JOHN DONNE

Batter my heart, three-personed God; for, you
As yet but knock, breathe, shine, and seek to mend;
That I may rise, and stand, o'erthrow me and bend
Your force, to break, blow, burn, and make me new.
I, like an usurped town, to another due,   5
Labour to admit you, but oh, to no end,
Reason your viceroy in me, me should defend,
But is captived, and proves weak or untrue,
Yet dearly I love you, and would be loved fain,
But am betrothed unto your enemy,   10
Divorce me, untie, or break that knot again,
Take me to you, imprison me, for I
Except you enthrall me, never shall be free,
Nor ever chaste, except you ravish me.

Batter: strike, knock down. (Donne wants God to attack his heart as if it were the gates of a fortress town.)
three-personed God: Christianity teaches that God is three separate beings: God the Father, Jesus Christ the Son, and the Holy Spirit.
usurped: occupied, taken over.
viceroy: ruler on God's behalf.

fain: willingly, readily.

betrothed: engaged to be married.
break that knot again: dissolve that marriage union.

enthrall: enslave.

Nor ever chaste, except you ravish me: paradox asserts that true freedom can only be achieved by surrendering.

'Take me to you'

👤 Personal Response

1. 'Donne's poem is an unusual prayer to God.' To what extent do you agree? Consider the poet's use of language and imagery in your response.
2. 'Donne unashamedly thinks of no one but himself.' In your opinion, is this the case in 'Batter My Heart, Three-Personed God'? Give reasons, quoting closely from the poem.
3. 'This sonnet shows a troubled mind in a continuous search for certainty.' To what extent would you agree with this assessment? Refer to the text in your answer.

👁 Critical Literacy

Donne is a poet deeply divided between religious spirituality and a sensual lust for life. In 'Batter My Heart, Three-Personed God', he dares to introduce the powerful, sensuous language of secular love poetry into his treatment of a profoundly religious theme. He claims that he can only overcome his sinful nature if he is forced by God in the most violent ways imaginable.

This sonnet begins with a dramatic exclamation: 'Batter my heart, three-personed God'. The force of this powerful opening line sets a determined tone that is maintained all through the poem. **In this daring image, the poet wants God to attack his heart as if it were the gates of a fortress town.** The fearsome knocking of a battering ram echoes from the heavily stressed verb and pounding rhythm. This was a common metaphor in courtly love poetry to suggest the reluctance of a woman to yield to a lover's advances, but it is a shocking – almost bizarre – conceit when presented in this religious context. This exaggeration is used to highlight how the poet is challenging God to enter his heart, not gently, but aggressively.

The initial commanding tone of the verb 'Batter' with its explosive 'B' sound gives way to a bitter complaint against God's considerate behaviour. In line 2, the poet describes God as a careful craftsman, carrying out superficial repairs to 'mend' Donne's sinful soul. The poet makes use of a forceful paradox, asking God to rebuild him spiritually – 'o'erthrow' me' and 'make me new'. He seems to show neither respect nor humility. Instead, throughout this first quatrain, he is busily putting up a challenge to God. The underlying sense of entitlement is insidious. Donne is convinced that he deserves all God's attention. The tender approach, where the Father knocks, the Son shines and the Holy Spirit breathes, is not sufficient. A series of strong alliterative verbs ('break', 'blow', 'burn') convey the poet's intense emotional conviction. He is pinning all his hopes on divine intervention to rid him of sin.

The second quatrain is dominated by the symbol of a besieged town. Donne sees his helpless soul as 'usurped' from God, its rightful ruler. His greatest

wish now is that God will reclaim what is rightfully his. But who is the real enemy – Satan or Donne himself? **The poet's tone becomes less imperative and more apologetic** as he admits his longing to find God's grace – 'Labour to admit you'. Unfortunately, his own conscience lacks willpower and strength ('Reason' is proving 'weak or untrue') and therefore his sinful soul remains at risk. Ironically, Donne uses the language of unrequited love to express his personal dilemma, caught between life's temptations and spiritual renewal.

The poet's candid admission ('Yet dearly I love you') at the start of the sestet marks a crucial turning-point. Donne exchanges the clever metaphysical comparisons for **a more direct, personal approach**. His open declaration of love for God is reminiscent of the courtly language of romantic poetry as he wistfully requests: 'and would be loved fain'. But the change of tone is short-lived and Donne immediately introduces a new metaphor. He assumes the persona of a 'betrothed' woman, engaged to be married 'unto your enemy' (Satan). The horrifying reality of facing eternal damnation leads him back to the frantic demand that God should do whatever it takes ('Divorce me, untie, or break that knot') in order to rescue his immortal soul. In the midst of this panic, the castle siege metaphor reappears as Donne insists that God 'imprison' him. The initial problem established in the octave is drawing to a solution.

The final rhyming couplet contains a fascinating double paradox. First, Donne states that unless God entices him ('enthrall me'), he will never be free. The second dramatic paradox is even more shocking as he asserts that he can only ever be holy ('chaste') if God will 'ravish' him. He acknowledges his absolute dependence on God to forcibly save him from his own human weakness. Although the word 'ravish' has an obvious violent intent, the tone is soft, almost a whisper, as though Donne deeply relishes the idea of spiritual unity with God. Although he is struggling to define a sacred, spiritual relationship, the language he chooses is the metaphor of brutal, physical love. However, Donne's agonised perseverance ensures that the readers are left in no doubt of the poem's central message: **sinners must first be broken before being made whole again in God's love.**

✒ Writing About the Poem

'Donne is a poet who is full of contradictions.' Discuss this statement in relation to the poem 'Batter My Heart, Three-Personed God'. Refer to the text in your answer.

Sample Paragraph

Donne wants God to save him from himself as if God was somehow physically present. This is the contradiction at the centre of the poem. Donne wants God to 'Batter' the poet into a state of grace. Another inconsistency is that he actually insists that a more forceful approach be taken. For me, the paradox is that the poet must be conquered in order to be made 'new'. Donne complains that his own common sense is actually behaving irrationally. Donne wants to be freed from sin so he can be imprisoned in God's forgiveness. Donne likes the idea of God taking responsibility. As usual, the focus is all about Donne – 'me, me'. This is a contradictory poem, but it has a strong argument to force God to accept the poet's view, even though he is the one who actually needs the favour, and to deliver the poet's solution. Not God's.

EXAMINER'S COMMENT

This lively response touches on interesting aspects of Donne's contradictory views of his complex relationship with God. The discussion is aptly illustrated and includes some good personal engagement. However, expression is note-like and awkward at times (with overuse of 'actually'). Mid-grade response.

Class/Homework Exercises

1. In your view, is 'Batter My Heart, Three-Personed God' a good example of metaphysical poetry? Refer to both content and style in your response, using evidence from the poem to support your opinions.
2. Donne's use of sound effects is a recurring characteristic of his poetry. To what extent is this true of 'Batter My Heart, Three-Personed God'? Support your answer with reference to the poem.

Points to Consider

- **Another highly charged personal address to God.**
- **Dramatic opening, emphatic rhythms, violent/daring imagery.**
- **Varying tones of urgency, desperation, tenderness.**
- **Effective use of alliteration, repetition, paradox.**
- **Sonnet form, demanding first quatrain, apologetic second quatrain, candid sestet, paradoxical rhyming couplet.**

Sample Leaving Cert Questions on John Donne's Poetry

1. 'John Donne's inventive language and imagery often result in startling dramatic moments throughout his poems.' Discuss this statement, with reference to both the themes and language found in the poetry of Donne on your course.
2. Discuss how effectively John Donne makes use of forceful language and rich imagery to create moods that range from joy and hope to sorrow and despair in his poetry. Develop your answer with reference to the poetry of Donne on your course.
3. 'Donne's personal experiences of love – both physical and spiritual – are expressed in a highly distinctive poetic style.' To what extent do you agree with this view? Develop your answer with reference to the poetry of John Donne on your course.

Understanding the Prescribed Poetry Question

Marks are awarded using the PCLM Marking Scheme: P = 15; C = 15; L = 15; M = 5 Total = 50

- **P** (Purpose = 15 marks) refers to the set question and is the launch pad for the answer. This involves engaging with all aspects of the question. Both theme and language must be addressed, although not necessarily equally.
- **C** (Coherence = 15 marks) refers to the organisation of the developed response and the use of accurate, relevant quotation. Paragraphing is essential.
- **L** (Language = 15 marks) refers to the student's skill in controlling language throughout the answer.
- **M** (Mechanics = 5 marks) refers to spelling and grammar.
- Although no specific number of poems is required, students usually discuss at least 3 or 4 in their written responses.
- Aim for at least 800 words, to be completed within 45–50 minutes.

How do I organise my answer?

(Sample question 1)

'John Donne's inventive language and imagery often result in startling dramatic moments throughout his poems.' Discuss this statement, with reference to both the themes and language found in the poetry of Donne on your course.

Sample Plan 1

Intro: *(Stance: agree with viewpoint in question)* Donne startles, provokes and challenges using dramatic scenes, far-fetched imagery, complex metaphors, rigorous argument and clever sound effects in intense scenes of love, parting, seduction and divine judgement.

Point 1: *(Intimate scene explored through conceit and sound effects)* 'The Sun Rising' – exuberant scene of passionate young love captured through extended image which shrinks the expanding newly discovered lands of the globe to the enclosed lovers' bedroom ('This bed thy centre is').

Point 2: *(Lovers' parting produces gripping emotions of sadness and comfort)* 'A Valediction: Forbidding Mourning' – couple's stirring farewell seen as mini-death through mournful sibilance ('sad friends do say,/The breath goes now'). Consolation in striking metaphor of compass celebrating inevitable return ('makes me end, where I begun').

NOTE

In keeping with the PCLM approach, the student has to take a stance by agreeing, disagreeing or partially agreeing that Donne's:

- **inventive language and imagery** (eloquent precision, witty wordplay, inventive metaphors, extended imagery, conceits, humorous exaggeration, intellectual arguments, rhetorical style, language of astrology/law/exploration/science, varied tones – tender, playful, derisive, etc.)

... result in:

- **startling dramatic moments** (joyous moments of love and romance, intimate love scenes, spiritual conflicts between good and evil, Judgement Day, etc.)

Point 3: *(Clever argument and rhetorical language evokes erotic seduction)* 'The Flea' – playful encounter between ardent lover and reluctant mistress uses intellectual and emotional appeals ('This flea is you and I, and this/Our marriage bed'). Melodramatic rhetorical language heightens the pressure on the woman ('Cruel and sudden, hast thou since/Purpled thy nail, in blood of innocence?')

Point 4: *(Chaotic Judgement Day created through innovative sound effects and contrasts)* 'At the Round Earth's Imagined Corners' – dramatic turmoil of divine judgement, urgent repetitive command ('arise, arise') adds to the uproar. Confident tone replaced by submissive plea for salvation expressed in legal language ('As if thou hadst sealed my pardon, with thy blood').

Conclusion: Impact of Donne's original poetic style engages readers. Fresh, energetic use of language creates combative tender and sorrowful scenes of love between man and woman, and man and God.

Sample Paragraph: Point 2

The farewell scene of a departing husband and abandoned wife is presented in a fresh way through Donne's language use throughout 'A Valediction: Forbidding Mourning'. While the sorrow of the occasion is acknowledged as a kind of death by soft sibilance 'Whilst some of their sad friends do say,/The breath goes now', it is the inventive use of the compass metaphor to represent the couple's relationship that is so impressive. This instrument recognises both the individuality of the man and woman as well as the unity of the couple. She is 'the fixed foot' who remains steady and true, 'makes no show/To move', enabling the other foot, the poet, to complete his circuit, 'far doth roam'. The instrument then draws a complete circle, a symbol of unity and infinity, representing Donne's spiritual love, balanced, and intellectual. He concludes with a compliment to his wife, assuring her of his inevitable return, 'Thy firmness makes my circle just, And makes me end, where I begun'.

EXAMINER'S COMMENT

As part of a complete examination essay, this paragraph engages closely with both the question and Donne's poem. Good detailed explanation of the compass metaphor. Expression is clear, varied and well controlled. Excellent use of apt and accurate quotes integrated fluently into the discussion ensure the top-grade standard.

(Sample question 2)

Discuss how effectively John Donne makes use of forceful language and rich imagery to create moods that range from joy and hope to sorrow and despair in his poetry. Develop your answer with reference to the poetry of Donne on your course.

Sample Plan 2

Intro: *(Stance: agree with viewpoint in question)* Donne's poetry ranges from the dizzy heights of young love to the depths of despair at rejection. Religious sonnets range from anguish at his sinfulness to unwavering hope in God's grace to forgive. He uses powerful language, intense imagery, strong conceits, dynamic verbs and inventive syntax.

Point 1: *(Joy of young love expressed through assertive language, paradox and developed metaphor)* 'The Anniversary' – joyous mood of young couple celebrating first year together. Short defiant lines proclaim their never-changing love ('Only our love hath no decay'). Clever paradox ('Running it never runs from us away') details endurance of their feelings.

Point 2: *(Sensual poem uses robust argument and powerful imagery to highlight hope and sorrow of love)* 'The Dream' – rich simile ('As lightning, or a taper's light,/Thine eyes') expresses tender emotion. Sharp mood change at woman's reluctance to submit using image of discarded torch ('light and put out'). Hope re-emerges in concluding paradox ('Thou cam'st to kindle, goest to come').

Point 3: *(Desire and frustration explored through shocking extended comparison and ingenious argument)* 'The Flea' – repetition marks peevish disappointment of rejected lover ('Mark but this flea, and mark in this'). Exaggerated self-pitying tone contrasts flea's success at touching woman to the poet's own failure ('And this, alas, is more than we would do').

Point 4: *(Terror and despair at possible damnation conveyed in intense language)* 'Thou Hast Made Me, And Shall Thy Work Decay?' – terrified by his sinful past, the poet fears to look back at his life ('I dare not move my dim eyes any way'). Alliteration and assonance capture physical decay ('my feeble flesh doth waste'). Stunning simile of naturally occurring magnet portrays hope in God's grace ('thou like adamant draw mine iron heart').

> **NOTE**
> In keeping with the PCLM approach, the student has to explore poems of John Donne on the course that include:
> - **effective use of forceful language and rich imagery** (assertive tones, ingenious arguments appealing to mind and heart, dramatic scenes, clever wordplay, unlikely images, extended metaphors, paradoxes, sensual exaggeration, etc.)
>
> ... that creates:
> - **moods that range from joy and hope to sorrow and despair** (confidence of young lovers, feelings of expectation and disappointment, despair and hope of spiritual salvation, etc.)

Conclusion: Donne startles and coaxes in passionate poems spanning the intensity of young love and sexual experience to extreme frustration. Religious sonnets also range from deep despair at his sinful condition to an overwhelming belief in God's salvation for humanity.

Sample Paragraph: Point 3

'The Flea' explores desire and disappointment through the poet's shocking comparison of a fleabite to the lovers' act of making love. The poet's disappointment at being rejected is forcefully stated through repetition, 'Mark but this flea, and mark in this,/How little that which thou deny'st me is'. Falling into despair, Donne melodramatically declares 'And this, alas, is more than we would do'. The heavily punctuated exaggeration emphasises his mood. He then turns the woman's resistance against her, using a stern tone and more emphatic alliteration, 'learn how false, fears be'. Donne casually dismisses the possible loss to her good name if she gives in to him, 'Just so much honour … Will waste, as this flea's death took life from thee'. Argumentative language recreates an age-old lovers' quarrel, leaving the poet feeling frustrated. Will this woman submit?

> **EXAMINER'S COMMENT**
>
> *Succinct, top-grade paragraph that would make an excellent contribution to a full-length exam essay. Focuses well on the key aspects of the question (forceful language and varying moods). Clear appreciation of Donne's poetic techniques – particularly repetition, tone and argument. Effective textual support throughout. Commentary is clearly expressed and rounded off with a lively conclusion.*

EXAM FOCUS

- As you may not be familiar with some of the poems referred to in the sample plans, substitute poems that you have studied closely.
- Key points about a particular poem can be developed over more than one paragraph.
- Paragraphs may also include cross-referencing and discussion of more than one poem.
- Remember that there is no single 'correct' answer to poetry questions, so always be confident in expressing your own considered response.

Leaving Cert Sample Essay

'Donne's personal experiences of love – both physical and spiritual – are expressed in a highly distinctive poetic style.' To what extent do you agree with this view? Develop your answer with reference to the poetry of John Donne on your course.

Sample Essay

INDICATIVE MATERIAL

- **Donne's personal experiences of love – both physical and spiritual** (desire, frustration, seduction, joy, satisfaction, spiritual salvation, dependence, everlasting love, etc.)

… expressed in:

- **a highly distinctive poetic style** (dramatic rhetorical language, intellectual argument, emotional appeal, intimate tones, vivid imagery, paradox, unusual references, conceits, comparisons, etc.)

1. John Donne is an original poet. He creates intimate yet unusual poetry appealing to his lover's mind as well as feelings in 'The Anniversary' and 'Song (Sweetest Love, I Do Not Go)'. His spiritual poetry is passionate, even using erotic imagery. This is seen in 'Thou Hast Made Me' and 'Batter My Heart, Three-Personed God'. In both his love poetry and his Holy Sonnets, Donne longs for union, either with a lover or God.

2. The love poem, 'The Anniversary', opens with the dramatic claim that nobody escapes 'destruction'. Donne uses emphatic repetition, 'All kings, and all their favourites'. Only the lovers will have an 'everlasting day'. They are unaffected by the cruel passage of time. A stunning paradox, 'Running it never runs from us away', supports the idea of true love's immortality. Donne sets this argument in an intimate moment, the first anniversary of a young couple's love. A rhetorical question asks, 'Who is so safe as we?' He states that the couple must preserve their love as long as they can because 'Here upon earth, we're kings'. He believes that happiness is shared by everyone in heaven, 'we no more than all the rest', so they should enjoy their human love while they can. The logic and self-assured tone are all elements of Donne's unique voice.

3. A couple's separation is presented in 'Song (Sweetest Love, I Do Not Go)'. A personal occasion is established through the sympathetic phrase, 'Sweetest love'. Clever arguments are used to persuade both emotionally and intellectually. Donne tries to convince his sad wife that this parting is a good preparation for him for their inevitable separation at death, 'Thus by feigned deaths to die'. He reminds her that the sun returns every morning, 'yet is here today'. He promises to make even 'Speedier journeys' because, unlike the sun, he has the 'wings and spurs' of his feelings for her to hurry him along. He makes a simple request of his wife, 'think that we/ Are but turned aside to sleep', recalling a beautiful private moment in their relationship. Donne uses an affectionate conversational tone and a rigorous argument to ease this moment of separation. 'The Anniversary' ends with an optimistic image of the lovers' eternal 'reign'.

4. In 'Thou Hast Made Me', the poet issues a forceful challenge to God, 'Repair me now'. The fear of his soul's sinful state is vividly portrayed, 'I dare not move my dim eyes any way'. Powerful sound effects convey his hopelessness, 'Despair behind, and death before'. Alliteration highlights his wickedness, 'feeble flesh', which is about to be dragged down to hell by. Similarly to 'Song', the poet acknowledges his dependence on another, 'not one hour myself I can sustain'. The concluding powerful image from science again ends the poem on a hopeful note, 'thou like adamant draw mine iron heart'. God's forgiveness even to the most hardened sinner who repents is like a powerful magnet pulling the poet to salvation. Donne's personal spiritual struggle is powerfully conveyed through a unique variety of distinctive techniques, including tones (anger, fear and submission), evocative sound effects and scientific imagery.

5. 'Batter My Heart', Three Personed God', is another religious sonnet where Donne demands that God 'Batter' him. This is rather than requesting him to stop sinning by a gentle 'knock'. Again, he takes an unusual aggressive tone, asking God the Father to 'breathe' on him, the Holy Spirit to 'shine' on him and for Jesus Christ to 'seek to mend'. Violent verbs graphically display the aggressive force the sinful poet needs to be renewed, such as 'break', 'blow', 'burn'. A simile is presented of the sinful poet as a 'usurped town', enslaved by another military enemy, a reference to the devil. Military terms and images are used, such as including 'defend', 'captived' showing his hopelessness because 'Reason' has proved 'untrue'. Then Donne compares himself to a married woman, 'betrothed unto your enemy', again the devil reference. Erotic language is used to express the unexpected idea that only being a prisoner of God's will is the only way to be free, 'except you ravish me'.

6. Donne's experience of his love for God is complicated. His comparisons are still seen as shocking. To compare the relationship between himself and God in sexual terms is highly unusual. He is like an unwilling woman forced to marry against her will. Donne suggests that God must act in a similarly violent manner to rescue him from a life of sin and then eternal damnation.

7. The distinct voice of Donne is found in his spiritual poems through the violence of his demanding tones, his unusual comparisons and his passionate sexual references. Readers are drawn into his very personal experiences of love, both romantic and spiritual, through his intimate conversational poetic voice, his confidence and humility, clever comparisons, the violence of his feelings and his witty arguments.

(810 words)

> **EXAMINER'S COMMENT**
> *Focused response with evidence of critical thinking throughout. Points make consistent links back to the task, displaying close engagement with specific poems – both secular and religious. Good illustrations of Donne's characteristic poetic style, including his use of argument, strong tones, imagery and rhetoric. Relevant discussion is developed in structured paragraphs and apt quotations are integrated into the commentary. Expression is clear and impressive, overall, although there is some repetition and awkwardness (e.g. in paragraph 5).*

GRADE: H1
P = 15/15
C = 14/15
L = 13/15
M = 5/5
Total = 47/50

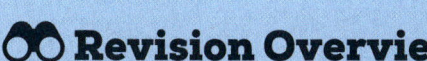

👀 Revision Overview

'The Sun Rising'
Delightful, witty celebration of young love, dismissing external world's importance for the warm interior kingdom of the lovers' bedroom.

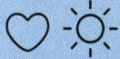

'Song (Go, And Catch A Falling Star)' (OL)
Distinctive love poem, cynically undermining love and fidelity. Donne argues that it is impossible to find a woman who is both faithful and honest.

'The Anniversary'
The lovers' sense of being forever young is central to this beautiful poem celebrating the first anniversary of their passionate relationship.

'Song (Sweetest Love, I Do Not Go)'
Emotional, dramatic poem about a couple's brief separation conveyed through tender appeal and logical argument.

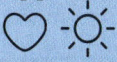

'A Valediction: Forbidding Mourning'
Donne insists that genuine feelings transcend physical distance, comparing the couple's relationship to a spiritual bond between two souls.

'The Dream'
Intimate, sensual poem arguing forcefully for the physical union of the couple's relationship. Passionate and metaphorical language convey the intense feelings Donne has for his lover.

'The Flea' (OL)
Donne's famous poem uses direct language and a comic conceit to play with the idea of sex and seduction.

'At the Round Earth's Imagined Corners'
One of Donne's Holy Sonnets dealing with the subject of death. This dramatic, spiritual poem addresses his personal relationship with God, sin and repentance.

'Thou Hast Made Me, And Shall Thy Work Decay?'
Devotional sonnet examining the poet's deep religious faith. Donne seeks comfort from the only source able to give it – his Creator.

'Batter My Heart, Three-Personed God'
Another of Donne's powerful Holy Sonnets using the sensuous language of romantic poetry to explore sin and spiritual fulfilment.

💬 Last Words

'No man is an island.'
John Donne

'Poetry is not a turning loose of emotion, but an escape from emotion; it is not the expression of personality, but an escape from personality. But, of course, only those who have personality and emotions know what it means to want to escape these things.'
T. S. Eliot

'Rave on, John Donne.'
Van Morrison

 LOVE JOY/HOPE  UNFAITHFULNESS  IMMORTALITY DEATH DESIRE MORTALITY  SALVATION FAITH

T. S. Eliot
1888–1965

'Humankind cannot stand very much reality'

Thomas Stearns Eliot, the American-British poet, playwright and literary critic, was born in St Louis, Missouri in 1888. He was educated at Harvard before settling in England, where he worked as a teacher and publisher. In 1927, Eliot took British citizenship at about the same time he became an Anglican.

T. S. Eliot is one of the most daring innovators of modern literature. Indeed, his experiments in diction, style and versification revitalised English poetry. His collections, from *Prufrock* (1917) to the *Four Quartets* (1943), largely reflect the development of a Christian poet and dramatist.

Eliot's early writing depicts a bleak and barren soullessness, often in spare yet finely crafted modern verse. Much of his work deals with unsettling themes of individual consciousness and spiritual desolation against the decline of civilisation. His poems, which often lack any obvious narrative structure, include numerous cultural allusions.

Although some critics found his poetry esoteric and disconnected, he has been increasingly praised for his originality and is now widely recognised as one of the most significant poetic voices of the 20th century.

An intensely private man, Eliot separated from his first wife in 1933 following an unhappy marriage. He remarried in 1956.

T. S. Eliot received the Nobel Prize for Literature in 1948 and died in London in 1965.

Investigate Further

To find out more about T. S. Eliot, or to hear readings of his poems not already available in your eBook, you could search some useful websites, such as YouTube, BBC Poetry, poetryfoundation.org and poetryarchive.org, or access additional material on this page of your eBook.

Prescribed Poems

T.S. ELIOT

○ **1 'The Love Song of J. Alfred Prufrock'**
Eliot's most famous poem touches on fascinating aspects of human experience. For many people in the 1920s, Prufrock seemed to summarise the uncertainty of the modern individual. He is a man who feels isolated and incapable of decisive action. His poignant monologue is filled with irony since this is not a conventional love song. Prufrock would like to speak about love with a woman, but he does not dare. Hopelessly insecure about rejection and fearful of old age, Prufrock is never able to assert himself by asking the mysterious 'overwhelming question'. **Page 114**

○ **2 'Preludes' (OL)**
Throughout the four sections of this atmospheric poem, Eliot presents a dark vision of the failure of modern secular society, exploring human despair and feelings of failure. Using a stream of consciousness style, the poet reveals a variety of solitary lives that are played out against the backdrop of a dispiriting urban setting. **Page 124**

○ **3 'Aunt Helen' (OL)**
Eliot's unusually accessible poem portrays a prim 'maiden aunt'. Even after her death, there was 'silence in heaven'. The poet's gentle ridicule is directed at the cultural lifelessness and self-satisfaction of Miss Helen Slingsby's sterile lifestyle. **Page 130**

○ **4 from 'The Waste Land': 'II. A Game of Chess'**
Using numerous literary allusions, Eliot focuses on the failure of relationships. In this chilling vision, human interaction is reduced to a set of movements on a chessboard. Characteristically, the poet depicts a false and meaningless world, in keeping with his disillusioned view of modern life. **Page 134**

○ **5 'Journey of the Magi'**
Eliot's version of the three kings who visited the newborn Messiah in Bethlehem is narrated by one of the elderly magi (wise kings). Christ's birth marked the end of their old pagan religion. The painful transition mirrors the poet's own doubts about his spiritual conversion to Christianity. Throughout the poem, Eliot interweaves the real and symbolic journeys of life and death. **Page 141**

○ **6 from 'Landscapes': 'III. Usk'**
This evocative landscape sketch records Eliot's response to the Welsh landscape after a short holiday there. The countryside is associated with the legend of King Arthur. However, the most likely reading of this 11-line poem sees it as a search for religious faith. **Page 147**

○ **7 from 'Landscapes': 'IV. Rannoch, by Glencoe'**
Written after a visit to the Scottish Highlands, Eliot's poem evokes the atmosphere of the remote moor, which provides a compelling backdrop to the poet's message that old conflicts become entrenched in the places where they once occurred. **Page 151**

○ **8 from 'Four Quartets': 'East Coker IV'**
This didactic poem is another illustration of Eliot's critical view of Christianity. He uses the field hospital as a compelling metaphor for the world's suffering patients who are in the hands of Jesus, the 'wounded surgeon'. Striking imagery and thought-provoking paradoxes emphasise the poet's severe view of the Christian experience. **Page 155**

(OL) indicates poems that are also prescribed for the Ordinary Level course.

POETRY FOCUS

1 The Love Song of J. Alfred Prufrock

*S'io credesse che mia risposta fosse
a persona che mai tornasse al mondo,
questa fiamma staria sanza più scosse;
ma però che già mai di questo fondo
non tornò vivo alcun, s'i'odo il vero,
sanza tema d'infamia ti rispondo.*

Let us go then, you and I,
When the evening is spread out against the sky
Like a patient etherised upon a table;
Let us go, through certain half-deserted streets,
The muttering retreats   5
Of restless nights in one-night cheap hotels
And sawdust restaurants with oyster-shells:
Streets that follow like a tedious argument
Of insidious intent
To lead you to an overwhelming question …   10
Oh, do not ask, 'What is it?'
Let us go and make our visit.

In the room the women come and go
Talking of Michelangelo.

The yellow fog that rubs its back upon the window-panes,   15
The yellow smoke that rubs its muzzle on the window-panes,
Licked its tongue into the corners of the evening,
Lingered upon the pools that stand in drains,
Let fall upon its back the soot that falls from chimneys,
Slipped by the terrace, made a sudden leap,   20
And seeing that it was a soft October night,
Curled once about the house, and fell asleep.

And indeed there will be time
For the yellow smoke that slides along the street
Rubbing its back upon the window-panes;   25
There will be time, there will be time
To prepare a face to meet the faces that you meet;
There will be time to murder and create,
And time for all the works and days of hands
That lift and drop a question on your plate;   30

Epigraph: 'If I thought that my response would be to someone who would ever return to earth, this flame would remain without further movement; but as no one has ever returned alive from this depth, if what I hear is true, I can answer you with no fear of disgrace.' This Italian epigraph is taken from Dante's 'Inferno'. The speaker was imprisoned in hell and is filled with hopelessness.

you and I: the public self and the inner man represent Prufrock's divided personality.

etherised upon a table: anaesthetised and unconscious on an operating table.

retreats: places of security.

sawdust restaurants with oyster-shells: cheap restaurants with sawdust on the floor and oyster shells as ashtrays.

insidious intent: deceptive purpose.

Michelangelo: famous Italian Renaissance artist who portrayed heroic figures.

yellow: cowardly; London was also known for its dense fogs.

muzzle: animal's nose and mouth.

And indeed there will be time: biblical reference to each event having a correct time; 'A time to be born, and a time to die' (Book of Ecclesiastes).

T. S. ELIOT

Time for you and time for me,
And time yet for a hundred indecisions,
And for a hundred visions and revisions,
Before the taking of a toast and tea.

   In the room the women come and go
Talking of Michelangelo.

   And indeed there will be time
To wonder, 'Do I dare?' and, 'Do I dare?'
Time to turn back and descend the stair,
With a bald spot in the middle of my hair –
(They will say: 'How his hair is growing thin!')
My morning coat, my collar mounting firmly to the chin,
My necktie rich and modest, but asserted by a simple pin –
(They will say: 'But how his arms and legs are thin!')
Do I dare
Disturb the universe?
In a minute there is time
For decisions and revisions which a minute will reverse.

   For I have known them all already, known them all –
Have known the evenings, mornings, afternoons,
I have measured out my life with coffee spoons;
I know the voices dying with a dying fall
Beneath the music from a farther room.
   So how should I presume?

   And I have known the eyes already, known them all –
The eyes that fix you in a formulated phrase,
And when I am formulated, sprawling on a pin,
When I am pinned and wriggling on the wall,
Then how should I begin
To spit out all the butt-ends of my days and ways?
   And how should I presume?

   And I have known the arms already, known them all –
Arms that are braceleted and white and bare
(But in the lamplight, downed with light brown hair!)
Is it perfume from a dress
That makes me so digress?
Arms that lie along a table, or wrap about a shawl.
   And should I then presume?
   And how should I begin?

. . . . .

morning coat: a formal tailed coat.

dying fall: Shakespearean reference to fading music; 'That strain again, it had a dying fall' (*Twelfth Night*).

formulated phrase: prepared, dismissive expression.

butt-ends: discarded cigarette remains.

digress: stray from the point.

Shall I say, I have gone at dusk through narrow streets   70
And watched the smoke that rises from the pipes
Of lonely men in shirt-sleeves, leaning out of windows? ...

I should have been a pair of ragged claws
Scuttling across the floors of silent seas.

   .   .   .   .   .

And the afternoon, the evening, sleeps so peacefully!   75
Smoothed by long fingers,
Asleep ... tired ... or it malingers,
Stretched on the floor, here beside you and me.
Should I, after tea and cakes and ices,
Have the strength to force the moment to its crisis?   80
But though I have wept and fasted, wept and prayed,
Though I have seen my head (grown slightly bald) brought
  in upon a platter,
I am no prophet – and here's no great matter;
I have seen the moment of my greatness flicker,
And I have seen the eternal Footman hold my coat, and snicker,   85
And in short, I was afraid.

And would it have been worth it, after all,
After the cups, the marmalade, the tea,
Among the porcelain, among some talk of you and me,
Would it have been worth while,   90
To have bitten off the matter with a smile,
To have squeezed the universe into a ball
To roll it towards some overwhelming question,
To say: 'I am Lazarus, come from the dead,
Come back to tell you all, I shall tell you all' –   95
If one, settling a pillow by her head,
  Should say: 'That is not what I meant at all.
  That is not it, at all.'

And would it have been worth it, after all,
Would it have been worth while,   100
After the sunsets and the dooryards and the sprinkled streets,
After the novels, after the teacups, after the skirts that trail along
  the floor –
And this, and so much more? –
It is impossible to say just what I mean!
But as if a magic lantern threw the nerves in patterns
  on a screen: 105
Would it have been worth while

a pair of ragged claws: image of a dismembered crab.

malingers: pretends to be ill.

my head ... upon a platter: biblical reference to John the Baptist, whose head was the price Salome demanded for performing her dance (Matthew).

the eternal Footman: Death.

porcelain: fine chinaware.

squeezed the universe into a ball: literary reference: 'Let us roll all our strength ... into one ball' ('To His Coy Mistress' by Andrew Marvell).
Lazarus: biblical reference to a man Jesus brought back to life.

dooryards: American gardens.

magic lantern: instrument used to project enlarged moving images.

If one, settling a pillow or throwing off a shawl,
And turning toward the window, should say:
   'That is not it at all,
    That is not what I meant, at all.'   110

   .   .   .   .   .

   No! I am not Prince Hamlet, nor was meant to be;
Am an attendant lord, one that will do
To swell a progress, start a scene or two,
Advise the prince; no doubt, an easy tool,
Deferential, glad to be of use,   115
Politic, cautious, and meticulous;
Full of high sentence, but a bit obtuse;
At times, indeed, almost ridiculous –
Almost, at times, the Fool.

   I grow old ... I grow old ...   120
I shall wear the bottoms of my trousers rolled.

   Shall I part my hair behind? Do I dare to eat a peach?
I shall wear white flannel trousers, and walk upon the beach.
I have heard the mermaids singing, each to each.

I do not think that they will sing to me.   125

I have seen them riding seaward on the waves
Combing the white hair of the waves blown back
When the wind blows the water white and black.

We have lingered in the chambers of the sea
By sea-girls wreathed with seaweed red and brown   130
Till human voices wake us, and we drown.

Prince Hamlet: the indecisive hero of Shakespeare's tragic play.

swell a progress: make up part of the crowd.

Deferential: courteous, submissive.
Politic: diplomatic, expedient.
meticulous: scrupulously careful, fussy.
Full of high sentence: speaking in a pompous way (a literary reference to a character in Chaucer's *Canterbury Tales*).
obtuse: dull, insensitive.
Fool: in Shakespearean drama, the court jester or clown often spoke wisely.

I have heard the mermaids singing: literary reference to a poem by John Donne where the mermaids symbolise romance and danger.

👤 Personal Response

1. Eliot once considered 'Prufrock among the Women' as the title for this poem. Would you prefer that title or the present one, 'The Love Song of J. Alfred Prufrock'? Give reasons for your choice.
2. Choose a short section of the poem that you consider particularly rich in sensuous lyrical language. Briefly explain why you found it appealing.
3. Comment briefly on one of the three settings used in this poem: the seedy cityscape, the elegant drawing room and the romantic seashore.

👁 Critical Literacy

'The Love Song of J. Alfred Prufrock' (commonly known as 'Prufrock') was first published in 1915. This period saw Europe lose an entire generation of young men during World War I. The British Empire was breaking up and the certainty of Victorian ideals was still being shaken by the evolutionary theories of Darwin. Society seemed to be in crisis, with signs that cultural and spiritual values were crumbling in the new urban age. Eliot's dramatic monologue traces Prufrock's uneasy stream of consciousness. Through a series of dreamlike scenes, the poem explores the tortured soul of modern man: educated, eloquent, alienated and emotionally paralysed by indecisiveness.

The title immediately raises the question about who is being addressed: possibly the unnamed woman in the poem, or Prufrock himself, or even the reader. What is not in doubt is that the name 'J. Alfred Prufrock' suggests a conceited, pretentious character, one who wishes to be seen as more important than he actually is. The epigraph (from Dante's 'Inferno') makes us think that the love song is not being sung in the real world at all, but in an interior 'Hell' of Prufrock's own making. From the outset, there are signs that the protagonist's torment comes from the division of his own self into a timid public person and a passionate private individual.

This is certainly suggested in the opening section (lines 1–12), where Prufrock proposes setting out on a journey: 'Let us go then, you and I'. The two pronouns might well refer to his divided personality: the reserved, careful outer man and the colourful, emotional inner soul. The initial mood is lethargic. Eliot uses a startling simile to describe the evening sky ('Like a patient etherised upon a table'), emphasising its distant, lifeless quality. Prufrock's own emotional state informs what he sees. There is **an uncomfortable sense of restlessness and dissatisfaction about Prufrock's life**, as though he is struggling with dark secrets. The impersonal streetscape suggests meaningless encounters 'in one-night cheap hotels'. Sea imagery ('oyster-shells') also seems slightly distasteful within the context of the furtive setting. Eliot's unsettling image of the 'half-deserted streets' compared to 'a tedious argument/Of insidious intent' conveys the agitation of modern living. Run-on lines lead Prufrock to

T.S. ELIOT

momentarily think about an undisclosed 'overwhelming question' that is just too unbearable to consider at length.

Lines 13–14 stand alone. The **location has changed to a more sophisticated world** – probably a fashionable social event – where the smart conversation centres on an important sculptor of heroic figures: 'In the room the women come and go/Talking of Michelangelo'. The almost childlike jingling rhythm and rhyme raise the possibility that these cultured socialites are affected and frivolous. But why should Prufrock be intimidated by a group of sophisticated women discussing Renaissance art? Perhaps he fears that if these people are interested in the celebrated artist Michelangelo, they could never relate to somebody as undistinguished as himself. This disquieting feeling of exclusion becomes an increasingly defining characteristic of Prufrock.

In lines 15–22, the scene changes again, moving away from the trivial conversation of the social gathering. Using **a developed metaphor**, Eliot describes the foggy urban district through which Prufrock walks in terms of the sinuous movement of a cat, using sensuous verbs: 'rubs', 'Licked', 'Lingered', 'Slipped', 'Curled' and 'fell asleep'. Images suggesting the sleek movements of the cat combine with soft 'l' and 's' sounds to create a soporific mood. Does the 'yellow fog' convey the blurred vision of humanity in the 20th century?

Prufrock hypnotically repeats the phrase 'there will be time' to adopt a public mask that he can use to 'meet the faces that you meet'. Lines 23–34 convey a feeling of irritation with his surroundings and the people he encounters in public. He seems unnerved by the 'smoke that slides along the street' and his thoughts turn to the stark choices that any individual might face in extreme circumstances, 'to murder and create'. **The pressing rhythm marks Prufrock's growing nervousness** as he looks forward to but also fears meeting with the woman, when he will 'lift and drop a question on your plate'. Anxiously, he delays, hesitating and considering a 'hundred visions and revisions' before concluding with the mock-heroic action of 'the taking of a toast and tea'.

'after tea and cakes and ices'

Lines 35–36 repeat the rhymed couplet, 'In the room the women come and go', further emphasising **the tedium of the women's conversation** as they endlessly discuss the same topic. The refrain might also indicate Prufrock's own inability to join in the social discourse of the elegant drawing room.

POETRY FOCUS

He becomes increasingly more self-conscious in lines 37–48, mainly about his own insecurity ('Do I dare?'). Seemingly obsessed by his ageing appearance, Prufrock speculates about the way other people view him. He particularly **fears hearing the truth**, even about the most trivial matters: 'How his hair is growing thin!' For a moment, he tries to bolster his confidence by relating how carefully he pays attention to the details of his dress: 'My necktie rich and modest, but asserted by a simple pin'. However, the women's gaze seems relentless to Prufrock, who cannot stop imagining their derogatory comments: 'how his arms and legs are thin'. He exaggerates dramatically in the broken line, 'Do I dare/Disturb the universe?' Characteristically, the irony of his pretentious question reflects his self-deprecating humour. But as always, he is tormented by an uncontrollable inadequacy and paralysed by over-thinking. Despite all his self-delusion about future plans, Prufrock does nothing at all but sit and watch as time goes by.

Lines 49–54 present the first of three arguments against asking the 'overwhelming question'. Prufrock is only too aware that his complete lack of confidence stems from the **meaningless life** he leads. Its pointless routine is demonstrated by the repetition of the listless, broad-vowelled phrasing, 'For I have known them all already, known them all'. His earlier apprehension has gradually been replaced by the disillusionment of his wasted years: 'I have measured out my life with coffee spoons'. There is something acutely dismal about the admission of an entirely ineffective existence. Prufrock's social phobias now prevent any type of spontaneity. Feeling so distanced from human contact, he has reached the stage where he is no longer sure about anything, even the right to ask: 'So how should I presume?'

This **sensation of personal failure** increases in lines 55–61. Prufrock is constantly afraid of appearing foolish, which in itself always makes him feel that way. He is terrified of the contemptuous eyes of the women around him, who 'fix you in a formulated phrase'. He feels reduced to an insignificant insect pinned and coldly dissected as if in a laboratory experiment. His pointless lifestyle is further diminished, comparable to an ashtray filled with discarded cigarettes: 'the butt-ends of my days and ways'. Even the forlorn repetition of the question 'And how should I presume?' peters out. For Prufrock, the second argument against addressing the significant question is that he cannot face any further ridicule. It is typical of Eliot's portrayal that while we have sympathy for this pathetic man, we are also irritated by him.

Lines 62–69 reveal the third reason why Prufrock avoids life's most serious questions: he is both **attracted and repulsed** by the physical reality of the women around him. While he admires the perfect ideal of 'Arms that are braceleted and white and bare', he is also put off by the fact that they are 'in the lamplight, downed with light brown hair'. The poet's description of the apparently disembodied woman is impersonal. The sensuous movement of their arms 'that lie along a table, or wrap about a shawl' recalls the feline grace of the yellow fog. Caught between such thoughts of romance and revulsion, Prufrock's dilemma is unresolved. Yet again, he finds himself unable to do anything: 'And how should I begin?'

T. S. ELIOT

This intense sense of helplessness persists throughout lines 70–74. Prufrock rehearses what he might say if forced to make conversation. He wonders whether he might describe the 'narrow streets' he has just passed through and the 'lonely men in shirt-sleeves, leaning out of windows'. But his line of thought diminishes into silence, concluding with an ellipsis. It is as though **he is crushed by all the isolation he sees around him** – a feeling that accurately mirrors his own alienation. As always, in moments of desperate self-loathing, he reverts to using sea imagery: 'I should have been a pair of ragged claws'. Comparing himself to a crab scavenging on the floor of the ocean reduces him even further to an inanimate object, the very opposite of his present excruciating position. The renewed onomatopoeic effect of 'Scuttling' and the hauntingly alliterative 'silent seas' clearly depict this fantastical image of self-disgust.

Prufrock's random reflections continue in lines 75–86, which introduce a soft, trance-like, reflective atmosphere. The afternoon 'sleeps', 'malingers', is 'Stretched on the floor' like the earlier cat-like fog. Not for the first time, he debates whether he can ever have sufficient courage to display his true feelings and desires. For an instant, Prufrock imagines himself as a biblical figure, but soon dismisses this idea, accepting that his personal humiliation is simply ridiculous, especially when compared to such a celebrated martyr as John the Baptist. Arguably, this is the turning point of the poem, marking **the protagonist's stark realisation that his life is essentially insignificant**. His brief 'flicker' of youth and hope has gone. Death is all that lies ahead, personified as a sneering 'eternal Footman' who mocks Prufrock's unproductive past and his fear of the unknown.

Lines 87–98, however, mark yet another of the protagonist's attempts to excuse his failure to take control of his life. Prufrock tries to convince himself that the stylish setting – 'Among the porcelain', a delicate and easily damaged china – inhibits him. In such refined surroundings, an immense effort would be required to express his secret desires openly and squeeze 'the universe into a ball', a self-mocking reference to a poem by Andrew Marvell, who believed in seizing the moment and enjoying life's pleasures. But the **fear of rejection keeps restraining Prufrock**. He has become so self-deluded that he exaggerates his predicament, comparing his task of tackling his questions about the meaning of life to Lazarus coming back from the dead. Tortured by incessant thoughts of failure, he imagines an embarrassing misunderstanding between himself and an unnamed woman who tells him, 'That is not what I meant at all'. Once again, the pained awkwardness of the invented scene stops Prufrock in his tracks.

An edgy mood of growing frustration dominates lines 99–119. The sensuous language and fragmented style become even more evident as Prufrock cries out in exasperation at his inability to communicate: 'It is impossible to say just what I mean!' Almost completely demoralised, he creates an image of his true personality projected onto a screen by a 'magic lantern' for the derision of the woman he wishes to impress. He also admits that **he is no hero** like Prince Hamlet, even though they both share the characteristic of indecisiveness. If anything, Prufrock feels that he is more like the 'attendant lord' Polonius, a relatively minor character who is 'almost ridiculous'. In the end, he accepts that he is much more like 'the Fool' (or court jester), another dramatic stereotype whose quick wit often contained serious criticisms of life's absurdity.

The poem's closing lines (lines 120–131) **show a man anxiously trying to come to terms with ageing and death**: 'I grow old … I grow old'. Having completely failed to confront the 'overwhelming question', the only decision Prufrock will make is about his appearance: 'I shall wear the bottoms of my trousers rolled'. Nonetheless, in this agonising postscript, he indulges in one last flight of fancy set on an idyllic beach.

To the end, however, Eliot seems intent on trivialising the anxieties of a man who knows he is facing death but still cannot 'dare to eat a peach'. Yet, whatever time he has left may not be taken up entirely with mundane considerations. Prufrock can also dream of hearing the seductive 'mermaids singing'. Eliot's mysterious image – possibly symbolising both desire and danger – signals that Prufrock has come close to experiencing something wonderful, yet ultimately unattainable. A single line (the only isolated one in the entire poem) highlights the sad truth for this unfortunate individual: 'I do not think that they will sing to me'.

It could be argued that having the courage to dream is Prufrock's only triumph. Dramatic run-on lines depict a picture of the elusive mermaids through haunting sound effects: 'riding seaward on the waves/Combing the white hair of the waves blown back'. Their ability to enjoy the moment in harmony with their environment is the very antithesis of the neurotic Prufrock. Like so much of this mesmerising poem, **the conclusion is open to various interpretations**. It seems that Prufrock's divided self becomes united in the plural personal pronoun 'We'. He is suddenly awakened from his vision of 'sea-girls'. The heart-rending final line ends Prufrock's tragic fantasy and he is brought back to reality by 'human voices'. With his last words, 'we drown', he invites us into his own private hell. Is Eliot suggesting that all of us are lost in daydreams and desires that we can never realise?

Most critics agree that 'The Love Song of J. Alfred Prufrock' offers **a pessimistic vision of the modern spiritual condition**. The anti-hero of Eliot's ironic love song glimpses redemptive beauty, but settles for a life of indecision and triviality rather than boldly searching for personal fulfilment. This is likely to reflect the poet's own disenchanted outlook on modern secular civilisation, lacking any religious faith or meaningful love, and

paralysed by anxiety. Yet nothing is resolved in this poem. Perhaps it is easier not to ask the 'overwhelming question' about life's meaning after all – particularly if there is no satisfactory answer.

✒ Writing About the Poem

'The sense of isolation and detachment in personal relationships is often evoked in the poetry of T. S. Eliot.' Do you agree with this view? Give reasons for your response, referring to Eliot's poem 'The Love Song of J. Alfred Prufrock'.

Sample Paragraph

'The Love Song of J. Alfred Prufrock' depicts the character of modern man weakened by over-analysis into a state of inaction: 'Do I dare/ Disturb the universe?'. Prufrock is an insecure loner constantly searching for answers. His scattered thoughts wander from the important philosophical questions about life's meaning to the trivial reality of his mundane existence: 'Is it perfume from a dress/That makes me so digress?' The desperate tone of his random question reveals an inner trauma. The tone of self-disgust is conveyed in excruciating detail: 'When I am pinned and wriggling on the wall'. Fear of rejection keeps isolating Prufrock, 'That is not what I meant at all', and prevents him from even making the attempt to communicate.

> **EXAMINER'S COMMENT**
> A well-supported top-grade response that addresses the question directly. Revealing quotes illustrate Prufrock's distressing loneliness effectively and the comments on tone show a good understanding of the poem. Expression is impressive, varied and well controlled throughout.

✎ Class/Homework Exercises

1. 'T. S. Eliot's distinctive poetic voice presents troubled characters in an unsettled world.' Discuss this statement with reference to both the subject matter and style of 'The Love Song of J. Alfred Prufrock'.
2. 'T. S. Eliot explores the disturbing realities of modern life through inventive imagery.' Do you agree with this assessment of his poetry? Write a response, developing your points with suitable reference to the poem 'The Love Song of J. Alfred Prufrock'.

◉ Points to Consider

- **Character of Prufrock – ageing romantic, indecisive, divided self, unheroic.**
- **Inability to articulate shown in digressions, hesitations, mock-heroic tone.**
- **Key themes include human alienation, emotional and spiritual emptiness.**
- **Fragments of sections convey stream of consciousness in this dramatic monologue.**
- **Images of seedy city life, fog/cat, sea; literary, artistic and genteel imagery.**

2 Preludes

Prelude: an introductory event that precedes something longer and more important; a short introductory piece of music.

I

The winter evening settles down
With smell of steaks in passageways.
Six o'clock.
The burnt-out ends of smoky days.
And now a gusty shower wraps   5
The grimy scraps
Of withered leaves about your feet
And newspapers from vacant lots;
The showers beat
On broken blinds and chimney-pots,   10
And at the corner of the street
A lonely cab-horse steams and stamps.

And then the lighting of the lamps.

II

The morning comes to consciousness
Of faint stale smells of beer   15
From the sawdust-trampled street
With all its muddy feet that press
To early coffee-stands.

With the other masquerades
That time resumes,   20
One thinks of all the hands
That are raising dingy shades
In a thousand furnished rooms.

III

You tossed a blanket from the bed,
You lay upon your back, and waited;   25
You dozed, and watched the night revealing
The thousand sordid images
Of which your soul was constituted;
They flickered against the ceiling.
And when all the world came back   30
And the light crept up between the shutters

gusty shower: strong windy rush of rain.

vacant lots: empty or abandoned building sites.

consciousness: awareness.

masquerades: pretences.

dingy shades: soiled window blinds.
furnished rooms: small apartments, often rented for a short time.

sordid: filthy, sleazy.
constituted: brought together, composed.

T.S. ELIOT

And you heard the sparrows in the gutters,
You had such a vision of the street
As the street hardly understands;
Sitting along the bed's edge, where   35
You curled the papers from your hair,   **papers:** small papers used as hair curlers.
Or clasped the yellow soles of feet
In the palms of both soiled hands.

IV

His soul stretched tight across the skies
That fade behind a city block,   40
Or trampled by insistent feet
At four and five and six o'clock;
And short square fingers stuffing pipes,
And evening newspapers, and eyes
Assured of certain certainties,   45   **Assured:** secure, confident.
The conscience of a blackened street
Impatient to assume the world.   **assume:** take responsibility; pretend.

I am moved by fancies that are curled   **fancies:** dreams, fantasies, illusions.
Around these images, and cling:
The notion of some infinitely gentle   50
Infinitely suffering thing.

Wipe your hand across your mouth, and laugh;
The worlds revolve like ancient women
Gathering fuel in vacant lots.

'The conscience of a blackened street'

POETRY FOCUS

👤 Personal Response

1. Based on your reading of Part I of 'Preludes', describe the atmosphere and mood Eliot creates in this opening section. Refer closely to the text in your answer.
2. Choose one interesting image from the poem that you found particularly effective. Briefly explain your choice.
3. Write your own personal response to this poem, referring closely to the text in support of the points you make.

👁 Critical Literacy

'Preludes' was composed between 1910 and 1911 and published in *Prufrock and Other Observations* (1917). Eliot considered these early poems 'the most satisfactory to myself'. Four sections of uneven, irregular verse provide a stream of consciousness, a literal and impressionistic view of various solitary lives as they play out against the backdrop of a seedy urban setting. There is an underlying awareness of the failure of modern secular civilisation throughout the sequence. Each prelude refers to the city as it moves from dusk to morning to night and back to dusk again.

The first prelude begins with vivid personification, 'The winter evening settles down', reminiscent of 'The Love Song of J. Alfred Prufrock'. Eliot blends various sensuous images, imagining the customary end of another unremarkable day. The 'smell of steaks in passageways' exemplifies the monotonous nature of city life and establishes the **dejected tone** of the rest of the poem. Repeated sibilant 's' sounds conjure up the habitual evening rituals of countless urban inhabitants. This is a place of conformity, where both the people and the day itself are exhausted, aptly evoked through the cigarette metaphor: 'burnt-out ends of smoky days'. An unrelenting sense of wasteful neglect and futile living is found everywhere within the dismal urban landscape, with its 'withered leaves' and 'vacant lots'.

Run-on lines mimic the relentless wintry weather while the abrupt rhyming of 'wraps' and 'scraps' suggests the recurring hardships of modern living. The explosive alliteration in lines 9–10, 'showers beat/On broken blinds', forcefully captures the insistent downpour of rain. Eliot presents readers with a range of symbols of alienation and helpless frustration, introducing the 'lonely cab-horse' waiting impatiently at a deserted street corner. Into this **uncomfortable scene of ugly sterility**, a flicker of hope appears in the stand-alone line, 'And then the lighting of the lamps'. Is something about to happen? Will something change? Or is the night closing in?

Eliot opens the second prelude by personifying a new day: 'The morning comes to consciousness'. Ironically, instead of a fresh start, **images of decay**

T. S. ELIOT

and desolation amplify the weariness of modern city living. Precisely descriptive language denotes emptiness, depression and quiet despair, a recurring theme throughout much of Eliot's poetry. This is skilfully evoked through the detail of 'faint stale smells of beer' left over from the previous night's drinking. Under pressure to conform to society's expectations, the anonymous occupants of the 'thousand furnished rooms' continue their daily routines, perhaps to mask their own unhappiness. The headlong rush of everyday life is suggested by the forward movement of run-through lines and the crushing verbs 'trampled' and 'press'.

Within all this urban chaos, individuality is submerged. People slavishly perform the same action at the same time: 'all the hands … raising dingy shades'. The poet clearly regards their routine lifestyles as 'masquerades', a daily pretence. It is as if they are raising a theatrical curtain on their artificial, unreal lives in this **soulless setting**. The rhyme of 'masquerades' and 'shades' reinforces this theme of pretence. By describing the people as mere body parts – 'feet', 'hands' – the individuals are depersonalised.

The third prelude addresses an unnamed woman who is plainly ill at ease: 'You tossed a blanket from the bed'. Eliot's description of her robotic movements develops the growing mood of despair. Indolent verbs describe a restless night: 'lay', 'waited' and 'dozed'. There is a disturbing sense of the woman's personal degeneration, disclosed by flickering patterns – 'The thousand sordid images' of which her soul is composed. Repetition of the conjunction 'And' in lines 30–32 emphasises the monotony of an unfulfilled existence. The morning's intrusion into this bedroom is unwelcome: 'the light crept up between the shutters'. Not unexpectedly, the early morning birdsong ('sparrows in the gutters') only adds to the atmosphere of gloom in this disreputable place. Meanwhile, a somewhat vulnerable and pathetic figure, the woman sits 'along the bed's edge' with her artificially curled hair, 'yellow soles' and 'soiled hands'. Once again, Eliot focuses on the **absence of personal identity**, reducing her to a mere collection of body parts. As morally degraded as her drab environment, she is only capable of a 'vision of the street/As the street hardly understands'.

The poet introduces a surreal image of spiritual torture in the fourth prelude: 'His soul stretched tight across the skies'. The monosyllabic 'tight' is precisely placed in the centre of line 39, suggesting that the tension is so great that it might snap at any moment. It is dusk and the unrelenting march of time is highlighted – 'At four and five and six o'clock' – when people return home from work. The ritual of pipe-filling is conveyed by the close-up image of 'short square fingers stuffing pipes' as the city's male inhabitants seek to relax after a day's toil and begin to read their newspapers. Eliot points out **the irony of their monotonous lives, where they are fed 'certain certainties'**. Does this suggest that these people always accept what they are told? Are they so powerless that they never question anything? Is their environment so 'blackened' that they 'assume the world' and accept it without any real understanding?

Lines 48–51 mark another change of mood to a **dreamlike atmosphere**. For the first time in the poem, a more personal voice emerges: 'I am moved by fancies'. Is this Eliot himself wondering if human life might have some worthwhile significance after all? Does he feel sympathy for all those people who have lost touch with their spiritual selves? Some critics have linked the 'infinitely gentle' reference to the presence of a Christ-like saviour destined to redeem a sinful world. But whatever it is that causes the poet to be 'moved' is wounded: 'Infinitely suffering thing'.

The momentary sense of hopefulness is quickly dismissed in the last three lines. Eliot reverts to cynicism, heralded by the derisive gesture 'Wipe your hand across your mouth', as if a gross appetite has just been satisfied. The vacant lot from the opening section is here again, and now old women are rummaging through the litter of urban desolation. We are left with **a bleak vision of an indifferent universe**.

✒ Writing About the Poem

'T. S. Eliot presents an insightful and downbeat portrayal of the human condition.'
Discuss this statement in relation to the poem 'Preludes', developing your views with suitable reference and quotation.

Sample Paragraph

'Preludes' offers a pessimistic view about the lack of individuality, and the impossibility for spiritual growth in modern society. The poem's mood is depressing, set in the sleaze of a godless urban environment, which reminded me of Prufrock's dismal surroundings. With vivid imagery, Eliot painted a disturbing picture of city life. Nauseating odours ('smell of steaks in passageways'), dirty rooms ('dingy shades') and repugnant characters convey this unglamorous lifestyle. The human condition is described as one of conformity, where everyone is expected to put on an act all the time, whether they are rushing with 'muddy feet that press/To early coffee-stands' or 'raising dingy shades/In a thousand furnished rooms'. No one seems capable of looking upwards to something better. The image of old women hunting for fuel to keep them warm is truly startling.

> **EXAMINER'S COMMENT**
>
> *A very well-focused personal response that tackles this question confidently. The range of accurate quotations are used effectively to support discussion points. Cross-references to other settings in Eliot's work broaden the scope of the answer. The writing is clear, fluent and assured throughout. Top-grade standard.*

T. S. ELIOT

✒ Class/Homework Exercises

1. 'T. S. Eliot believed that human love offered rescue from a lifetime of misery and isolation.' Discuss this view with reference to 'Preludes'.
2. 'Eliot depicts broken individuals and spiritual emptiness through vivid images and arresting sound effects.' To what extent do you agree or disagree with this view of his poetry? Develop your points with reference to the poem 'Preludes'.

⊙ Points to Consider

- Moral decay and isolation of 20th-century life.
- Paralysis of woman and city expressed in use of precise verbs.
- Dramatic journey through the minds and senses, stream of conciousness.
- Olfactory and tactile imagery – the lonely woman, debris of street.
- Use of rhyme to satirise theme of pretence; enjambment conveys movement of people and pressure of time.

3 Aunt Helen

Aunt Helen: a wealthy, unmarried lady who lived in a stylish Boston neighbourhood.

Miss Helen Slingsby was my maiden aunt,
And lived in a small house near a fashionable square
Cared for by servants to the number of four.
Now when she died there was silence in heaven
And silence at her end of the street.   5
The shutters were drawn and the undertaker wiped his feet –
He was aware that this sort of thing had occurred before.
The dogs were handsomely provided for,
But shortly afterwards the parrot died too.
The Dresden clock continued ticking on the mantelpiece,   10
And the footman sat upon the dining-table
Holding the second housemaid on his knees –
Who had always been so careful while her mistress lived.

handsomely provided for: supplying sufficient money to ensure a comfortable life.

Dresden clock: superior china clock from the German town of Dresden.

second housemaid: servant whose duties included cleaning and polishing.

'my maiden aunt'

👤 Personal Response

1. In your opinion, what is the speaker's attitude to Miss Helen Slingsby? Refer to the text in support of your views.
2. Consider the image of the footman and housemaid. How does it contrast with the life Aunt Helen lived? Develop your response with reference to the poem.
3. Based on your reading of the poem, do you think that T. S. Eliot is mocking respectable middle-class society? Briefly explain your response.

👁 Critical Literacy

'Aunt Helen' is included in T. S. Eliot's poetry collection *Prufrock and Other Observations*, published in 1917. The poet paints a satirical portrait of the rigid, conventional society of upper-class Boston in this short piece. What's left unsaid is almost as important as what is said. Boston offended Eliot's sensibilities. He regarded this world as 'quite uncivilised, but refined beyond the point of civilisation'. His critical view of polite society is from an insider's perspective and highlights its tragicomic outcome.

The poem's title, 'Aunt Helen', suggests a close family relationship between the poet and this lady, yet this is immediately dispelled by the formal address in the opening line, 'Miss Helen Slingsby'. Her unmarried status is carefully noted: 'maiden aunt'. This woman lived her life alone without close intimate relationships. Was she too proud to marry? Was she not asked? Her life is described in a three-line sentence that details where she lived. Aunt Helen did not reside in a large house, as Boston society would deem this vulgar and ostentatious. Her home was not on the 'fashionable square', but 'near' it. Such discretion was called for. **She carefully observed all the nuances of the secret codes of her social class.** However, there is no mention of friends. Nobody looks after Helen Slingsby except those she paid: 'servants to the number of four'. Eliot's quaint expression mirrors the old-world aunt and her affected language. Rolling 'r' and 'o' sounds allow the reader to hear the genteel tones of this superior person.

A series of short sentences deal with **the impact of the old lady's death**. The momentous adverb 'Now' in line 4 announces her passing. The poet adopts the persona of a detached observer rather than a regretful nephew, dryly observing that his aunt's death caused 'silence in heaven'. Is the silence indifference on the part of heaven to the death of this self-absorbed lady? Or does the silence suggest hushed awe at the passing of an important individual? We are left to wonder about who, apart from herself, might have regarded Miss Slingsby as a person of note. Eliot humorously concludes that there was 'silence at her end of the street'. Was her death really of sufficient importance to bring the whole street to stillness?

The poet details the correct observance of the expected conventions: 'The shutters were drawn'. However, we are told that the undertaker 'wiped his feet'. Is this a dismissive act? Or is the visitor carefully cleaning his shoes before he enters the house, as the aunt might have demanded? The undertaker's dryly sarcastic attitude ('He was aware that this sort of thing had occurred before') clearly diminishes the aunt's social status. Everyone is equal in death. The tone of the poem so far has been listless and stiff, rather like the passive, submissive woman who bowed to all the strict conventions of her time. The combination of unoriginal rhymes ('before', 'for'), awkward rhythm and uneven lines captures the spirit of Miss Slingsby's stale, inward-looking society. Eliot finds it easy to satirise this cultural lifelessness and the smug righteousness of his aunt's sterile world.

Line 8 **cleverly suggests where the nephew's real interest lay**: 'The dogs were handsomely provided for'. What was left to him is omitted. Is it likely that he was excluded from her will? We also learn that his aunt's parrot died. A pet parrot spends its life imitating its owner. Was this action in sympathy with the elderly lady's passing? Or does it suggest that the aunt's and the parrot's deaths were equally insignificant? Again, the emphasis is on a woman's empty, barren life, which was spent concerned with protocol and etiquette rather than with people.

Eliot reminds us that **everyday life goes on** in the extended line 10: 'The Dresden clock continued ticking on the mantelpiece'. Aunt Helen's fine possessions survived her passing implacably. The poem's somewhat humorous and risqué ending conveys a picture of sound, movement and life ('And the footman sat upon the dining-table/Holding the second housemaid on his knees'), clearly showing that the aunt's distorted sense of values does not survive. The servants ('Who had always been so careful') are finally free of the confines of the aunt's lifeless, artificial world. A new order has been established in the remnants of this proper world. The repeated sibilant 's' mirrors the hushing secrecy upheld while the aunt lived.

In this unusual poem, **Eliot, the dramatist, creates a caricature caught up in her own world from a few detailed images**. He even captures the pompous tones of the aunt in phrases such as 'fashionable square' and 'this sort of thing'. Through the use of a distorted sonnet structure, one line short of the conventional 14-line form, Eliot reflects the failed notions of Aunt Helen's sense of her own importance and grandeur. The random, prosaic rhymes ('four', 'before', 'for') accentuate the dreary tone, leaving readers with an uneasy sense of the old lady's futile existence. Nevertheless, there is an underlying mischief and optimism in the poem's final lines. Now that Miss Slingsby has gone, at least the servants can begin to enjoy life.

✒ Writing About the Poem

'Eliot's poetry unveils a sharply observant picture of ordinary people.' Discuss this statement with reference to 'Aunt Helen'.

Sample Paragraph

Eliot paints a revealing caricature of a lady who is trapped inside a rigid, conservative society. The poet launches a quietly blistering attack on the joyless life of the self-absorbed Miss Slingsby, who required 'servants to the number of four' to look after her in her 'small house near a fashionable square'. Using just a few details, Eliot captures her upper-class voice in the repeated 'r' and 'o' sounds. She is not described, but her possessions are – her 'Dresden clock', her parrot and her dogs. Her real lack of importance is evident in the fact that there was silence in heaven at her passing and the undertaker 'was aware that this sort of thing had occurred before'.

> **EXAMINER'S COMMENT**
> *This well-focused high-grade short paragraph shows a very close reading of the poem. Suitable quotations are effectively used to highlight the poet's portrayal of the central character's lonely life. The fluent, controlled expression is sustained throughout.*

✒ Class/Homework Exercises

1. 'Eliot's poetry is filled with quiet despair.' Discuss this statement in relation to 'Aunt Helen'.
2. 'Eliot explores human activity as habitual and futile through carefully chosen details and an innovative use of form.' Discuss this view of the poetry of T. S. Eliot with reference to the poem 'Aunt Helen'.

◉ Points to Consider

- Self-righteous, emotional and spiritual void.
- Mockery of distorted values of Aunt Helen and servants; appearance is paramount.
- Detached, banal tone, innovative sound effects.
- Imagery of silence, animals, time and servants.
- Unusual structure, effective use of caricature, dead-pan humour.

4 from The Waste Land: II. A Game of Chess

A Game of Chess: Eliot's poem is based on two plays by the Jacobean playwright Thomas Middleton: *A Game of Chess* and *Women Beware Women*. In the second play, a young woman is seduced while her mother-in law unknowingly plays a game of chess with another woman who has facilitated the seduction. Every move in the game of chess represents a stage in the seduction. The audience sees both scenes at once as the action takes place in a gallery above the chess game.

    The Chair she sat in, like a burnished throne,
Glowed on the marble, where the glass
Held up by standards wrought with fruited vines
From which a golden Cupidon peeped out
(Another hid his eyes behind his wing)   5
Doubled the flames of sevenbranched candelabra
Reflecting light upon the table as
The glitter of her jewels rose to meet it,
From satin cases poured in rich profusion.
In vials of ivory and coloured glass   10
Unstoppered, lurked her strange synthetic perfumes,
Unguent, powdered, or liquid – troubled, confused
And drowned the sense in odours; stirred by the air
That freshened from the window, these ascended
In fattening the prolonged candle-flames,   15
Flung their smoke into the laquearia,
Stirring the pattern on the coffered ceiling.
Huge sea-wood fed with copper
Burned green and orange, framed by the coloured stone,
In which sad light a carvèd dolphin swam.   20
Above the antique mantel was displayed
As though a window gave upon the sylvan scene
The change of Philomel, by the barbarous king
So rudely forced; yet there the nightingale
Filled all the desert with inviolable voice   25
And still she cried, and still the world pursues,
'Jug Jug' to dirty ears.
And other withered stumps of time
Were told upon the walls; staring forms
Leaned out, leaning, hushing the room enclosed.   30
Footsteps shuffled on the stair.
Under the firelight, under the brush, her hair
Spread out in fiery points
Glowed into words, then would be savagely still.

The Chair she sat in: a paraphrase of the description of Cleopatra's barge from Shakespeare's play of love and betrayal, *Antony and Cleopatra*: 'The barge she sat in, like a burnished throne/Burned on the water'. Antony decides to marry another woman for political reasons and Cleopatra dies by suicide.
standards: banners, upright supports.
wrought: twisted, formed.
Cupidon: Cupid, the young god of love in classical mythology.
candelabra: large branched candlestick.
vials: small containers.
Unstoppered: opened.
synthetic: artificial, fake.
Unguent: balm, ointment.
laquearia: panelled ceiling, referencing the story of the Queen of Carthage, Dido, and her betrayal by Aeneas in Virgil's famous Latin poem, 'The Aeneid'. The ceiling of the hall in which Dido gave a banquet for Aeneas is described: 'flaming torches hang from the gold-panelled ceiling, and the night is pierced by the flaming lights'.
coffered: decorated with sunken panels.
sylvan scene: a wooded area. In John Milton's great poem 'Paradise Lost', Satan sees a similar scene upon entering the Garden of Eden. Corruption and treachery ensue.
Philomel: an allusion to Ovid's epic poem 'Metamorphoses', which tells the tragic story of Philomel's rape and mutilation by her brother-in-law, Tereus, the King of Thrace. He cut off her tongue to prevent her telling, but she communicated the horrific event to his wife, her sister Procne, by weaving a tapestry. She killed their son and fed him to Tereus in a terrible act of revenge. The gods then turned Philomel into a nightingale and she fills the desert with her song.
inviolable: secure, beyond corruption.
Jug Jug: way of representing birdsong in Elizabethan poetry; also a crude expression for lovemaking.
Glowed into words: reference to Dante's 'Inferno', where the damned souls can only speak through the tip of the flame that engulfs them.

T. S. ELIOT

'My nerves are bad tonight. Yes, bad. Stay with me.   35
Speak to me. Why do you never speak? Speak.
  What are you thinking of? What thinking? What?
I never know what you are thinking. Think.'

 I think we are in rats' alley
Where the dead men lost their bones.   40

'What is that noise?'
          The wind under the door.
'What is that noise now? What is the wind doing?'
          Nothing again nothing.

                    'Do   45
You know nothing? Do you see nothing? Do you remember
Nothing?'

   I remember
Those are pearls that were his eyes.
'Are you alive, or not? Is there nothing in your head?'   50
          But
O O O O that Shakespeherian Rag –
It's so elegant
So intelligent
'What shall I do now? What shall I do?   55
I shall rush out as I am, and walk the street
With my hair down, so. What shall we do tomorrow?
What shall we ever do?'
          The hot water at ten.
And if it rains, a closed car at four.   60
And we shall play a game of chess,
Pressing lidless eyes and waiting for a knock upon the door.

   When Lil's husband got demobbed, I said –
I didn't mince my words, I said to her myself,
HURRY UP PLEASE ITS TIME   65
Now Albert's coming back, make yourself a bit smart.
He'll want to know what you done with that money he gave you
To get yourself some teeth. He did, I was there.
You have them all out, Lil, and get a nice set,
He said, I swear, I can't bear to look at you.   70
And no more can't I, I said, and think of poor Albert,
He's been in the army four years, he wants a good time,
And if you don't give it him, there's others will, I said.
Oh is there, she said. Something o' that, I said.
Then I'll know who to thank, she said, and give me a
  straight look.   75

rats' alley: slang term for World War I trenches.
the dead men lost their bones: soldiers felt great anguish when their fallen comrades were left unburied.
What is that noise?: from the revenge tragedy *The Duchess of Malfi*; the duchess's brother sends madmen to torment her.

Those are pearls that were his eyes: reference to Shakespeare's *The Tempest*, referring to the transformation of the dead into something beautiful and magical.
that Shakespeherian Rag: a popular American tune from *Ziegfeld Follies* (1912).

demobbed: demobilised, retired from the army.
HURRY UP PLEASE ITS TIME: the call of bartenders at closing time in British pubs.

HURRY UP PLEASE ITS TIME
If you don't like it you can get on with it, I said.
Others can pick and choose if you can't.
But if Albert makes off, it won't be for lack of telling.
You ought to be ashamed, I said, to look so antique. 80
(And her only thirty-one.)
I can't help it, she said, pulling a long face,
It's them pills I took, to bring it off, she said.
(She's had five already, and nearly died of young George.)
The chemist said it would be all right, but I've never been
 the same. 85
You *are* a proper fool, I said.
Well, if Albert won't leave you alone, there it is, I said,
What you get married for if you don't want children?
HURRY UP PLEASE ITS TIME
Well, that Sunday Albert was home, they had a hot gammon, 90
And they asked me in to dinner, to get the beauty of it hot –
HURRY UP PLEASE ITS TIME
HURRY UP PLEASE ITS TIME
Goonight Bill. Goonight Lou. Goonight May. Goonight.
Ta ta. Goonight. Goonight. 95
Good night, ladies, good night, sweet ladies, good night,
 good night.

gammon: cured ham.

Good night, ladies: Ophelia's poignant farewell before she dies by suicide in Shakespeare's *Hamlet*. She has been driven mad by the deception and corruption of people around her.

'The Chair she sat in'

👤 Personal Response

1. Choose one image from the poem that you found particularly interesting. Briefly explain your choice.
2. The poet introduces us to various characters whose voices we hear. In your opinion, are they happy or unhappy? Explain your response with reference to the poem.
3. Write your own personal response to the poem, highlighting its impact on you.

👁 Critical Literacy

'A Game of Chess' is the second section in T. S. Eliot's masterpiece, 'The Waste Land'. It was written in 1921, when the poet was recovering from a nervous breakdown in Lausanne, Switzerland. Section II, 'A Game of Chess', explores themes of misdirected love and its destructive consequences. It also examines the insistent march of time and how the past haunts the present. The poem's fragmentary form, irregular punctuation and content respond to the mayhem and devastation caused by World War I. Eliot's many cultural and literary references universalise his themes. This modernist approach in literature also occurred in art with Pablo Picasso and in music with Arnold Schönberg. Such artists struggled to find a voice for this frenetic world of the post-war period. As Eliot's friend, the American poet Ezra Pound, commented, they were attempting to 'make it new'.

The poem presents us with two main scenes, both of which are concerned with deception and betrayal. On an initial reading, there appear to be striking differences between the characters of the first and the second drama in terms of social class, wealth and education. On closer examination, however, interesting similarities emerge. The first half of the poem shows an unnamed, sophisticated woman surrounded by beautiful furnishings – resembling props in a stage play. Eliot's opening line rephrases the account of Cleopatra's arrival on her magnificent barge in Shakespeare's play *Antony and Cleopatra*. The **elaborate language** ('burnished', 'marble', 'wrought') suggests the lavish opulence of the setting. In line 4, the poet describes the mirror decorated with a 'golden Cupidon', like Cleopatra's 'smiling Cupids'. The atmosphere is formal and oppressive. But why is one of the Cupid figurines depicted as hiding 'his eyes behind his wing'? Is there a suggestion of something inappropriate or illicit?

The reference to the 'sevenbranched candelabra' shows Eliot mixing images of the sacred with the profane. God had ordered the Temple of Jerusalem to be furnished with a golden chair and seven ornate candles. The elegant diction is filled with such a 'rich profusion' of lush images that the reader is almost disoriented. However, an **unsettling note** is struck when the woman's 'synthetic perfumes' are described as 'Unstoppered' on her dressing table.

POETRY FOCUS

Something seems wrong and out of control in this apparently luxurious setting. It is likely that the reader becomes 'troubled, confused'. Eliot depicts a stale, stifling atmosphere through the stressed extended sentences of the first nine lines and the evocative assonance of 'Unguent, powdered, or liquid'.

The sumptuously decorated ceiling (the 'laquearia') alludes to the tragic story of the mythical Queen of Carthage. Dido gave a splendid banquet for her lover, Aeneas, who subsequently deserted her. She then threw herself onto a funeral pyre as his ship sailed out of the harbour. Eliot is illustrating how **tragedy and destruction follow misplaced love**. This is an unavoidable reality for the stylish modern woman who is central to the poem's opening section. At every stage, she is viewed in terms of threat and betrayal. With the reference to Philomel (line 23), readers are introduced to another legendary scene of corruption as the seduced heroine, whose tongue was cut off, is eventually changed into a nightingale, allowing her to sing 'with inviolable voice'. Is Eliot himself like the songbird revealing the truth about deception and how it inevitably destroys relationships?

The emphasis on the present tense in line 26 ('still the world pursues') suggests that nothing changes. Beauty and love will always be tainted. The bird's pure song is caught in the Elizabethan 'Jug Jug', yet to 'dirty ears', it has a vulgar sexual meaning.

The disappointments of real life are emphasised. Suddenly, the gaudy decorations are dismissed for what they really are – 'withered stumps of time'. **This is the infertility of the wasteland.** Is Eliot also expressing his cynicism towards those people who possess wonderful works of art but who don't really appreciate them? Is he hinting that the modern world is unaware of its rich cultural inheritance? There is no denying the poet's sharper tone as the earlier longer lines of lavish description now give way to the curt expressions in lines 27–30.

Line 32 focuses on the modern woman, showing her under severe emotional strain while she sits alone. A surreal image, 'her hair/Spread out in fiery points', seems to speak: 'Glowed into words'. This frightening Medusa-like figure appears to be trapped in her own personal hell as she retreats into neurotic silence: 'savagely still'. Anonymous and faceless, she seems to lose control over the safe space of her beautiful dressing room when she hears 'Footsteps shuffled on the stair' – her husband, presumably. She begins to voice her paranoid concerns: 'My nerves are bad tonight'. Her nervous tension is played out in a **staccato rhythm** with the jumpy, erratic repetition of 'Speak', 'What' and 'Think'. Aimless questions and panicky commands show the lack of purpose in her speech. Is Eliot suggesting that she is just like Cleopatra and Dido, an emotional wreck who is depending on the attentions of a man? The man's response is indirect and dismissive, indicating that he thinks but does not voice a reply to the petulant woman.

Caught in his own desperate psychological state, **he is haunted by images of death**: 'I think we are in rats' alley', a reference to World War I trenches. The woman's whining voice intrudes as she wonders, 'What is that noise?' He thinks 'Nothing again nothing' and retreats from the tense questions, blotting out her voice with snippets of Shakespeare and an American hit tune. The syncopated rhythm of ragtime is indicated by the repetition of 'O O O O' and the extra syllable 'he' in 'Shakespeherian' (line 52). Such erratic movement and trite rhyme ('elegant'/'intelligent') reflect the couple's obvious inability to interconnect.

The woman becomes even more hysterical and threatens to 'rush out' and 'walk the street/With my hair down'. Her anxious questioning, 'What shall we ever do?', is characteristic of Eliot's recurring commentary on **the loss of religion and spirituality in modern life**. The sense of meaninglessness is emphasised when the man contemplates the banality of his daily routine. He will rise late, as if to shorten the day, 'hot water at ten' (line 59) before going for a pointless car ride in the rain and playing another dull game of chess. Is he simply waiting, with 'lidless' eyes, for something to happen? Who will make the 'knock upon the door'? Death, perhaps? The boredom and lack of communication of this living hell are enacted by the frightened, loveless woman and the self-centred, nihilistic man.

The second scene opens in a typical working-class British pub (line 63): 'When Lil's husband got demobbed'. A prayer-like mantra of 'I said' breaks up the bar room monologue in which the speaker recalls an earlier dialogue between herself and her friend Lil. The snapshot of post-war British society places ordinary individuals in difficult situations, just like pieces in a game of chess. Marriage between Lil and her husband Albert is reduced to a sexual level. She is advised to 'make yourself a bit smart', otherwise she risks losing her man, who is returning from the war. Albert had given her money to buy false teeth, but she had used it for an abortion: 'She's had five already, and nearly died of young George'. Her relationship is as unsatisfactory as those mentioned in the first section of the poem. **Loneliness and human misery are shared by all social classes.** It is clear from the gossip that the speaker is sympathising with 'poor Albert'. Is this another case of 'Women Beware Women'? Is the speaker taking a perverse delight in Lil's predicament, almost blaming her in advance for what might happen: 'You *are* a proper fool' (line 86)?

The barman's insistent call, 'HURRY UP PLEASE ITS TIME', stresses the sinister absence of hope. Ironically, this urgency is not picked up by any of the other pub characters as they bid each other 'Goonight' (line 95). The bleak ending echoes one of Shakespeare's most unfortunate victims, the naive Ophelia, who dies by suicide, surrounded by heartless manipulation and betrayal. Like so much in the poem, these final lines depict a false and meaningless world, in keeping with Eliot's dark vision of modern life as a wasteland devoid of lasting love or moral values.

✒ Writing About the Poem

'T. S. Eliot's challenging poetic voice makes him inaccessible to the modern reader.' Discuss this view with reference to 'A Game of Chess'.

Sample Paragraph

From my study of 'A Game of Chess', I can understand the criticism of Eliot as a difficult poet. However, I enjoyed his references to Cleopatra, 'The Chair she sat in, like a burnished throne', and to the unfortunate Dido and Philomel. By referring to these mythical women and then comparing them to Lil, the unhappy modern wife, I think Eliot succeeded in exploring sexuality very effectively. All of these women try to defy this cruel world with a determined search for communication: 'Speak to me'. But Tereus cut off Philomel's tongue to prevent her speaking. The self-absorbed modern man also blots out the woman's attempts to connect by responding to her questions with unspoken thoughts: 'we shall play a game of chess'. In my opinion, Eliot is playing a game of chess with his reader as he moves his women, the pawns in this game of love or sex, through their stories.

> **EXAMINER'S COMMENT**
>
> *This is a good top-grade personal response that takes a clear thematic view in support of Eliot's use of cultural and literary allusions. The focus is sustained throughout and aided effectively with accurate quotations. Expression is also varied, fluent and well controlled.*

✏ Class/Homework Exercises

1. 'Eliot's poem "A Game of Chess" moves characters like chess pieces towards destinations they cannot see as they perform in a drama they do not control or understand.' Discuss this statement with reference to the text.
2. 'Eliot often showed people's sense of defeat through the effective use of powerful imagery.' Discuss this view with reference to his poem 'A Game of Chess'.

◎ Points to Consider

- Splendour of the past contrasts sharply with the squalid nature of the present.
- Inhibiting effect of improperly directed love/lust.
- Failure of modern man to get to grips with cultural heritage.
- Past haunts the present, purposelessness in modern life.
- Juxtaposition of cultural imagery and dingy bar culture.
- Effective use of rich allusions.
- Snatches of contrasting dialogue.

5 Journey of the Magi

T. S. ELIOT

Magi: wise men, believed to be kings, who travelled from the East to honour the birth of Jesus in Bethlehem. (Magi is the plural of magus, a wise man.)

'A cold coming we had of it,
Just the worst time of the year
For a journey, and such a long journey:
The ways deep and the weather sharp,
The very dead of winter.'   5
And the camels galled, sore-footed, refractory,
Lying down in the melting snow.
There were times we regretted
The summer palaces on slopes, the terraces,
And the silken girls bringing sherbet.   10
Then the camel men cursing and grumbling
And running away, and wanting their liquor and women,
And the night-fires going out, and the lack of shelters,
And the cities hostile and the towns unfriendly
And the villages dirty and charging high prices: 15
A hard time we had of it.
At the end we preferred to travel all night,
Sleeping in snatches,
With the voices singing in our ears, saying
That this was all folly.   20

   Then at dawn we came down to a temperate valley,
Wet, below the snow line, smelling of vegetation,
With a running stream and a water-mill beating the darkness,
And three trees on the low sky.
And an old white horse galloped away in the meadow.   25
Then we came to a tavern with vine-leaves over the lintel,
Six hands at an open door dicing for pieces of silver,
And feet kicking the empty wine-skins.
But there was no information, so we continued
And arrived at evening, not a moment too soon   30
Finding the place; it was (you may say) satisfactory.

   All this was a long time ago, I remember,
And I would do it again, but set down
This set down
This: were we led all that way for   35
Birth or Death? There was a Birth, certainly,

galled: irritated by the chafing of a saddle.
refractory: difficult to control, unmanageable.

sherbet: sweet fruit juice drink.

folly: foolishness.

three trees on the low sky: the three crosses on Calvary, where Christ was crucified.
old white horse: Christ the conqueror rides on a white horse (according to the Book of Revelations).
lintel: horizontal supporting stone over a doorway.
dicing for pieces of silver: betrayal of Christ by Judas for 30 pieces of silver; soldiers dicing for Christ's clothes at his crucifixion.
wine-skins: wine container made from animal skins.

We had evidence and no doubt. I had seen birth and death,
But had thought they were different; this Birth was
Hard and bitter agony for us, like Death, our death.
We returned to our places, these Kingdoms,   40
But no longer at ease here, in the old dispensation,
With an alien people clutching their gods.
I should be glad of another death.

dispensation: prevailing religion.
clutching: retaining, clinging to.

'and such a long journey'

👤 Personal Response

1. In your opinion, what is the mood of the magi as revealed in lines 19–20?
2. The poem is filled with striking imagery. Choose the image that most appeals to you and briefly explain why you found it interesting.
3. Based on your reading of the poem, what does the speaker mean when he declares: 'I should be glad of another death'? In your response, consider whether he is referring to physical or spiritual death – or both.

👁 Critical Literacy

'Journey of the Magi' was published in 1927 as part of a selection of poems that were to be included later in a series of Christmas cards. T. S. Eliot had converted to Anglicanism in August of that year and had been baptised into his new faith. The poem reflects Eliot's state of mind in transition between his old and new faiths. It fuses past and present as one of the magi, now an old man, recalls his experience of the journey undertaken to witness the birth of Jesus. This dramatic monologue is riddled with ambiguity. Throughout the narrative, Eliot interweaves the real and symbolic journeys of life and death.

The poem recreates the story of the three magi who travelled to Bethlehem from the East to honour the infant Jesus. Eliot's version is based on the gospel of St Matthew and takes the form of a dramatic monologue describing **a painful and life-changing experience**. The opening section (lines 1–20) recounts the arduous journey through the persona of one of the unnamed kings. He is caught between the past and present, no longer at ease in his old world, yet unsure about his new Christian life choice. The narrative tone is tired and unenthusiastic, as though the ageing magus has already told the tale too many times.

Eliot's first five lines are based on a celebrated sermon given by an English clergyman, the Bishop of Winchester, on Christmas Day 1622: 'A cold coming we had of it,/Just the worst time of the year/For a journey'. Such strong **colloquial phrases ground the account of this extraordinary journey in reality**, although the gruelling trek itself was undertaken to find a mystery that was impenetrable to human wisdom. The details of the suffering camels, 'galled, sore-footed, refractory', add to the authenticity of the story.

Lines 8–16 contrast the **world of ease and luxury** that the magi had left behind with the challenging expedition and uncertainty ahead. They had rejected all their earlier comfort and sensuous pleasure: 'The summer palaces on slopes, the terraces,/And the silken girls bringing sherbet'. Frequent pauses in these lines convey the unhurried pace of their former lives. The recurring soft letter 's' floats as effortlessly as the youthful girls, enabling the language to glide by – a stark contrast to the hazardous mountain journey. This harsh trek is vividly captured by the strikingly familiar imagery and run-on lines mimicking the fleeing camel men. Their coarse speech is graphically caught by the emphatic hard 'c' sound and broad assonance in the phrase 'cursing and grumbling'.

Memories tumble from the elderly magus, who reminisces about the various hardships endured: 'And the cities hostile and the towns unfriendly/And the villages dirty and charging high prices'. The impetus of the narrative is driven forward by an insistent rhythm emphasised by the evident repetition of 'And'. A short monosyllabic line curtly sums up his frustration: 'A hard time we had of it'. For the magi, however, there were more serious concerns than the physical discomforts. Along the way, all three kings faced agonising moments of self-doubt: 'voices singing in our ears, saying/That this was all folly'. In many ways, **their difficult experience symbolises every individual's search for spiritual meaning**, particularly Eliot's own painful journey into the Anglican faith.

The poem's second stanza (lines 21–31) describes the arrival of the three wise men. Eliot's version of events is unusual for all the well-known details it omits. There is no talk of a stable or any mention of gold, frankincense and myrrh. Instead, **present and future time blends** as Christ's adult life is predicted. The early morning descent into the 'temperate valley' evokes three significant Christian events: the Nativity, Easter and the Second Coming of Christ. A bewildering range of images follows. Some are positive, such as the 'running stream', 'meadow' and 'vine-leaves', all of which suggest hope, freedom and fruitfulness. However, these are juxtaposed with negative imagery: the winter's 'low sky', the horse 'galloped away', 'feet kicking'.

Ambiguity fills this vivid dream-like state. **Eliot liked to use symbolism to represent philosophical ideas** through simple images. His description of 'three trees on the low sky', for example, implies the spiritual truth of the future (the skies lowered and heaven opened). The trees, of course, are likely representations of the three crosses on Calvary, where Jesus was to be crucified alongside two common criminals. Does the 'old white horse' signify Christ the conqueror? And if so, why is it galloping away? Might the poet be suggesting that true faith is always elusive? Are the 'Six hands ... dicing for pieces of silver' foreshadowing the betrayal of Christ by Judas?

The magi eventually found 'the place' where the new Messiah was born. There is a clear impression of anticlimax: 'it was (you may say) satisfactory'. All of the prophecies had been fulfilled, but there is an edge, an uncertain reticence in tone. The event was no more than adequate or acceptable. The material discomfort of the poem's opening section is replaced by **a growing awareness of a more mysterious discomfort**. Why is the magus so unsure about the importance of what he has witnessed? Undoubtedly, something crucial has happened, but there is a lingering sense of loss. The reader is also left wondering. Why was there no sense of the joyous excitement that is recounted in the Bible at the birth of the infant Jesus?

The final section, lines 32–43, of this typically multi-layered poem conveys the enduring effect that the journey had on the three magi. Emphatic repetition is used to stress that Christ's Nativity must be recorded carefully: 'but set down/This set down/This'. The unusual line placing echoes the breakdown of the old order resulting from this recent momentous event. Eliot highlights **the poem's central paradox**: 'were we led all that way for/Birth or Death?' For the poet, the two experiences are inseparable. The birth of Christ marked the death of all previous religious beliefs. Through the experience of the three kings, Eliot also reveals the trauma of his personal spiritual journey. To an extent, this reflective monologue is that of any individual who has made their choice and achieved belief in the Incarnation, but who is nonetheless linked to the life that Christianity has come to replace.

The poem's conclusion is one of acceptance of a destiny that is the only possible answer, but still seems unbearably painful. The elderly magus admits that he 'should be glad of another death'. After they returned home, the three kings felt 'no longer at ease'. The new order that they witnessed makes them regard 'our places' as full of 'alien people clutching their gods'. The ageing narrator grows to understand that the birth of the Christ child changed everything. He has reached the end of his old pagan life, but despite his acknowledgment of the epiphany, he is still faced with the overwhelming mystery of his new Christian faith. The poem ends on a note of **mystified resignation**, serving as a metaphor for Eliot's own search to find meaning in the modern world.

Writing About the Poem

'Eliot's fondness for using references can make his poetry seem difficult and dense.' Discuss this statement in relation to 'Journey of the Magi'.

Sample Paragraph

I would agree that 'Journey of the Magi' can be demanding, but I did not find it baffling. Eliot explores two journeys simultaneously, that undertaken by the magi to witness the birth of Jesus who was to bring in a new 'dispensation', a new religion. The second journey is Eliot's own spiritual conversion to Anglicanism. He was realising, just as the magi had, that when moving from one faith to another, there is regret for the old familiar ways – 'no longer at ease here'. Both Eliot and the magi found 'an alien people clutching their gods'. I found the poem's content complex, but understandable. Similarly, its many images are by no means

> **EXAMINER'S COMMENT**
>
> *This succinct top-grade paragraph addresses a challenging question effectively. There is a good sense of confident engagement with the poem's central theme. Impressive use is made of relevant quotations and the expression is well controlled throughout.*

obscure. The 'three trees on the low sky' represent the lush vegetation of the 'temperate valley', the promise of heaven. But they also contain a foreshadowing of the crucifixion on Calvary. For me, Eliot's poetry is understandable in its treatment of difficult themes and ingenious in his use of imagery.

✒ Class/Homework Exercises

1. 'Eliot's poetry is modern in outlook yet old in allusions.' Do you agree or disagree with this assessment of his poetry? Develop your response with close reference to the poem.
2. 'Symbolism and dialogue play a large part in Eliot's examination of alienation in his poetry.' Discuss this view with reference to the poem 'Journey of the Magi'.

⊙ Points to Consider

- **Journey symbolising spiritual search.**
- **Alienation, life on the periphery.**
- **Suffering required to enable new birth.**
- **Journey, birth, death and biblical imagery.**
- **Dramatic monologue, natural speech, voice of magus.**
- **Changing tones – critical, regretful, nostalgic, incantatory, anxious, self-pitying.**

6 *from* Landscapes: III. Usk

T. S. ELIOT

Do not suddenly break the branch, or
Hope to find
The white hart behind the white well.
Glance aside, not for lance, do not spell
Old enchantments. Let them sleep.   5
'Gently dip, but not too deep',
Lift your eyes
Where the roads dip and where the roads rise
Seek only there
Where the grey light meets the green air   10
The hermit's chapel, the pilgrim's prayer.

Usk: small town in South Wales located on the river Usk, an ancient crossing point. Caerleon-Upon-Usk is reputed to be the site of the legendary court of King Arthur.
hart: male adult deer, associated with Arthurian legends.
white well: St Cybi's Well was a place of pilgrimage, where the water was reputed to cure various ailments.
Glance aside: have a quick look secretly.
lance: a long spear used by horsemen when jousting in medieval tournaments.
Old enchantments: legends and superstitions.
'Gently dip, but not too deep': do not pry. The quotation comes from an Elizabethan play, *The Old Wives' Tale*, about old superstitions.
Lift your eyes: 'I will lift up mine eyes unto the hills, from whence cometh my help.' (Psalm 21, Old Testament)
hermit's chapel: prayer-room of someone who lives alone for religious reasons.
pilgrim: traveller who goes on a spiritual journey to a holy place.

'The white hart behind the white well'

👤 Personal Response

1. In the poem 'Usk', Eliot uses some effective images to create the atmosphere of the Welsh countryside. Choose one image that you particularly liked and explain its impact.
2. Sound effects, such as alliteration, assonance and rhyme, are used in this brief lyric. In your opinion, what contribution do they make?
3. Did you find the conclusion of the poem satisfactory or not? Give reasons for your view, supporting it with reference to the poem.

👁 Critical Literacy

'Usk' is the third of five short lyrics by Eliot entitled 'Landscapes', published in 1935. Each poem describes a specific place steeped in history. This evocative landscape sketch records Eliot's response to the Welsh landscape after a 10-day holiday spent there. It is the climax of the sequence, representing summer to autumn, symbolising the speaker's search for true tranquillity and spiritual happiness through prayer. The theme of spiritual fulfilment occupies much of Eliot's later poetry.

This is one of Eliot's least well known and most puzzling poems. Typically, it can be seen as a conversation, both with the reader and with the poet himself. To an extent, it is simply a very short landscape or pastoral description of the Welsh countryside around Usk. There was also a pub here called The White Hart Inn and behind it a once-whitewashed well that was so shallow that water was procured by dipping a container in it. However, **Eliot's poem is primarily spiritually instructive**. The ==first line== opens with an abrupt command, 'Do not', rather in the manner of an instruction given to a wayward child. Readers are warned not to seek romantic fantasy in such a landscape. The harsh alliteration ('break the branch') introduces the poet's attitude to 'Old enchantments'. We are strongly advised not to pursue the traditions and superstitions of the past: 'white hart', 'white well', 'lance'. All these symbols figure prominently in the Arthurian legend of the Quest for the Holy Grail. Eliot clearly mocks the medievalism of some of his contemporaries with a self-assured tone suggesting that his advice comes from one who is confident about his own religious faith.

==Line 4== issues another ringing instruction, 'Glance aside', its internal rhyme echoing the medieval word 'lance' and emphasising that the old superstitious beliefs must be avoided: 'Let them sleep'. But ==line 6== introduces a second thought with the quotation, 'Gently dip, but not too deep'. This forms the pivotal point of the poem. The quotation comes from an old Elizabethan play that satirised popular romantic dramas of the time. In the play a mysterious head appears from a well warning not to intrude too closely. As far as the poet is concerned, **legend and tradition are appealing, but should be treated with caution**. In a recording of the poem, Eliot spoke

T. S. ELIOT

this line in a sing-song voice reminiscent of a remembered childhood song. The jaunty rhythm forces readers forward. Is the poet suggesting that our relationship with the landscape should not be escapist or full of romantic fantasy, but should lead us towards the spiritual?

Unlike the restless opening, with its recurring musical effects, the second half of the poem begins with a prayer-like exhortation from the Old Testament: 'Lift your eyes'. The reader is being invited to go on a pilgrimage, a spiritual journey, 'Where the roads dip and where the roads rise', a reference to the smooth rolling countryside of Brecon. The repetition of 'Where' emphasises the need to seek 'The hermit's chapel, the pilgrim's prayer'. But these will only be found 'Where the grey light meets the green air'. This evocative phrase conjures up the misty countryside and green forest, an insubstantial place of light and space. The assertive triple rhyme ('there', 'air', 'prayer') reinforces the sense that the destination is within sight. Is this the symbolic meeting of the two traditions, Arthurian legend and Christianity? While the early section of the poem included repeated punctuation breaks, giving it a disruptive force, the second part flows much more smoothly through several run-on lines. **The poem concludes with a note of hope, firmly rooted in Christian imagery.** Characteristically, Eliot demonstrates his skill at evoking the reverential atmosphere of the 'hermit's chapel'.

The poem's principal tone is one of incantation – 'Hope to find', 'Lift your eyes', 'Seek only there' – which is emphasised by musical sounds and insistent rhyme. Eliot makes good use of both end-rhyme (such as 'well' and 'spell') and internal rhyme ('find', 'behind'). The colours used suggest peace and rejuvenation. White is usually associated with brightness and purity. The 'grey light' hints at the misty past, while 'green' is a natural, soothing shade. **Eliot creates a mysterious, mystical atmosphere** by blending simple images with sibilant sounds.

Some critics have argued that 'Usk' reflects the poet's continuing search for an answer to the 'overwhelming question' first asked in 'The Love Song of J. Alfred Prufrock'. If we accept that **the search for spiritual meaning is central to the poem**, then the chapel of the hermit would seem to represent the pilgrim's destination and the poet's confidence in the 'spell' of Christian faith.

Writing About the Poem

'T. S. Eliot's interest in religion and the spiritual journey people make are important elements in his poetry.' Discuss this statement in relation to his poem 'Usk'.

Sample Paragraph

In 'Usk', readers are instructed to 'Glance aside' and not to become involved with the escapist fantasy of the Arthurian legend of 'white hart' and 'lance'. This is not where to look for spiritual fulfilment. The central quotation from an old play, 'Gently dip, but not too deep', pushes the reader away from the mythological past and instead points the way forward with the following Old Testament command: 'Lift your eyes'. The last four lines of the poem advise that we should look for fulfilment of our spiritual journey by turning to the mysteries of the Christian faith. The poem concludes with two simple symbols of Christianity, the 'hermit's chapel' and the 'pilgrim's prayer'. 'Usk' clearly demonstrates the significance for Eliot of the spiritual journey.

> **EXAMINER'S COMMENT**
>
> *A focused and succinct top-grade paragraph showing close engagement with the text. Suitable quotes are used very effectively to trace the progress of thought through the poem. There are impressive references to key lines which emphasise Eliot's Christian viewpoint.*

Class/Homework Exercises

1. 'T. S. Eliot's presentation of Christianity can be surprisingly positive at times'. To what extent is this the case in the poem 'Usk'?
2. 'Eliot investigates how the present contains the past in fragmented memories, effective imagery and striking sound effects.' Discuss this statement with reference to the poem 'Usk'.

Points to Consider

- Pastoral poem, descriptive and spiritually instructive.
- 'Old enchantments' of Arthurian legend contrasted with spiritual quest.
- Old Testament tone of exhortation, use of imperatives.
- Insistent energy, hopeful note. Evocative sound effects.
- Use of colour suggests peace and energy.

7 *from* Landscapes: IV. Rannoch, by Glencoe

T. S. ELIOT

Here the crow starves, here the patient stag
Breeds for the rifle. Between the soft moor
And the soft sky, scarcely room
To leap or soar. Substance crumbles, in the thin air
Moon cold or moon hot. The road winds in   5
Listlessness of ancient war,
Langour of broken steel,
Clamour of confused wrong, apt
In silence. Memory is strong
Beyond the bone. Pride snapped,   10
Shadow of pride is long, in the long pass
No concurrence of bone.

Rannoch: a moor in the Scottish Highlands, near the valley of Glencoe. It was the location of a terrible battle in 1692 when the Campbell clan massacred the MacDonalds.

Substance: material, solidity.

Listlessness: without energy or enthusiasm.
Langour: tiredness; pain.

Clamour: loud noise, outcry.
apt: appropriate, suitable.

pass: gap, route over mountains.
concurrence: agreement, co-operation.

'Substance crumbles, in the thin air'

👤 Personal Response

1. In your opinion, what do the animal images of the first two lines contribute to the impression of Rannoch being presented by Eliot?
2. Trace how the poet develops his theme that the present is weighed down by the past. Support your answer with suitable quotation from the text.
3. How effective are the poem's sound effects in conveying the atmosphere of Glencoe? Illustrate your response using reference to the text.

👁 Critical Literacy

'Rannoch, by Glencoe' is the fourth poem in T. S. Eliot's five-part series 'Landscapes' (1935). After visiting the Scottish Highlands, he composed this poem evoking the essence of the remote moor in condensed images, and its geography provides a compelling backdrop to the poet's message. Eliot was struck by Rannoch's pervading atmosphere, which he felt was a consequence of a 17th-century battle between two Scottish clans, the Campbells and the MacDonalds. Set during the winter season, this marvellously compressed poem captures the eerie sense of dislocation that is often found on old battlefields.

The opening lines convey an uninviting image of death. Rannoch's barren terrain presents nature at its worst: even 'the crow starves'. The long-suffering deer is fodder for the hunter's 'rifle'. This is a place of brooding menace and extreme harshness, both from nature and from man, captured in the startling death-in-life imagery. Eliot's dismal tone is in keeping with the slow-moving pace. Yet the insistent 's' alliteration hints at the rugged beauty of the bleak surroundings: 'Between the soft moor/And the soft sky'. But **it is a claustrophobic and oppressive place**. The cloudy sky hangs so low above the landscape that there is no room for the stag to leap or the crow to fly. Strangely, the references to softness appear negative, almost tyrannical. Nothing can be relied on in this place – the moon is changeable ('cold' or 'hot') and the rock is being eroded ('Substance crumbles, in the thin air').

Even the lazy description of the winding road in lines 5–6 is misleading. Unlike the routeways symbolising salvation in Eliot's poem 'Usk', there is only 'Listlessness' and 'Languor' here. The countryside is weighed down and **haunted by disturbing memories of the past**, the notorious massacre of 1692. The 'broken steel' of an 'ancient war' still remains in the landscape. This locality is devoid of hope, rooted in the endless cycles of past violence. For Eliot, the silence of the place resonates with memories of the 'Clamour' of warfare, which occurred due to transgressions on both sides ('confused wrong'). The alliterative sharp 'c' effect emphasises the uproar of battle. In the poem's closing lines, Eliot captures the closeness of the past. There is no underlying peace in this land. Instead, disharmony remains between the

bones of the dead enemies. The Scottish hills are darkened by the 'Shadow of pride'. This clearly suggests that the descendants of both clans have never become truly reconciled. The repetition of 'long' (line 11) stresses the brutal consequence of such a terrible event that took place over three centuries ago. In contrast to the hard mountain rock, which can be broken down over time, pride and self-worth do not crumble. Like a shadow blighting the landscape, **memory discourages healing**. This is the stark truth about human pride that Eliot uncovers in the rugged terrain of Rannoch. There is no sign of hope and certainly no religious perspective here.

The poem ends on a discordant note that bristles with tension and the lines run on to finish abruptly: 'Memory is strong/Beyond the bone'. The insistent force of Eliot's monosyllables, 'Pride', 'pass' and 'bone', create a stumbling rhythm. Assonant sounds – particularly the long mournful 'o' in line 12 ('in the long pass/No concurrence of bone') – highlight **the sadness that suffuses the beautiful landscape** damaged for all time by the cruelty of nature and man. Readers are left in no doubt about the poem's central theme – historical events and old conflicts become entrenched in the places where they once occurred.

✒ Writing About the Poem

'Landscape or setting is an important symbol that T. S. Eliot uses to great effect in his poetry.' Discuss this statement in relation to Eliot's poem 'Rannoch, by Glencoe'.

Sample Paragraph

Eliot uses landscape to represent much more than local scenery in 'Rannoch, by Glencoe'. He captures the spirit of Glencoe in dark, vivid imagery associated with death and the winter season: 'the crow starves' and the 'patient stag' destined 'for the rifle'. This cruel place offers no opportunity to escape. Eliot references the battle of 1692, the Massacre of Glencoe, which took place between two rival Scottish clans. I found Eliot's description of the unchanged, winding road revealing, suggesting that there is no hope. Eliot uses landscape to show the outer world's bleak beauty, with its crumbling stone and haunting moonlight. But he also captures the dark workings of the human heart, which won't let go of the past.

EXAMINER'S COMMENT

A very assured top-grade response to the question, tracing the progress of thought in the poem. The connections between past and present are explored effectively, using suitable references and accurate quotations. Expression is clear and coherent throughout.

Class/Homework Exercises

1. 'The poetry of T. S. Eliot is depressing and anguished.' Discuss this statement in relation to 'Rannoch, by Glencoe'. Refer to both the poet's subject matter and style in your response, using suitable quotation from the poem to develop your views.
2. 'In Eliot's poetry, the harshness and beauty of nature is evoked through startling imagery.'
   Discuss this view with reference to the poem 'Rannoch, by Glencoe'.

Points to Consider

- Relation between human beings and nature; old unresolved rivalries.
- Impact of human beings on the natural world – war, erosion, destruction.
- Dysfunctional landscape, discordant poetic structure.
- Closed system of strong memories of confused wrongs.
- Vivid imagery, off-rhyme.

from Four Quartets: East Coker IV

T. S. ELIOT

East Coker: a village in Somerset, near Yeovil. It is Eliot's ancestral home. Family and family history feature in the poem. He had found information on his family from 'Sketch of the Eliot Family', which described how his family had lived in East Coker for 200 years. Andrew Eliot left in 1669, disrupting the family history. Eliot also broke away from his family in America. In the poem, he stresses the need for a journey and the need for inward change.

The wounded surgeon plies the steel
That questions the distempered part;
Beneath the bleeding hands we feel
The sharp compassion of the healer's art
Resolving the enigma of the fever chart. 5

Our only health is the disease
If we obey the dying nurse
Whose constant care is not to please
But to remind of our, and Adam's curse,
And that, to be restored, our sickness must grow worse. 10

The whole earth is our hospital
Endowed by the ruined millionaire,
Wherein, if we do well, we shall
Die of the absolute paternal care
That will not leave us, but prevents us everywhere. 15

The chill ascends from feet to knees,
The fever sings in mental wires.
If to be warmed, then I must freeze
And quake in frigid purgatorial fires
Of which the flame is roses, and the smoke is briars. 20

The dripping blood our only drink,
The bloody flesh our only food:
In spite of which we like to think
That we are sound, substantial flesh and blood –
Again, in spite of that, we call this Friday good. 25

wounded surgeon: Jesus Christ, the Son of God, who suffered for our sins, yet healed humanity.
plies: works steadily using a tool.
steel: scalpel, a knife with a small, sharp blade used by a surgeon.
questions: probes, cross-examines.
distempered: diseased.
bleeding hands: the hands of Jesus were nailed to the Cross.
Resolving: sorting out what man could only 'chart' and observe.
enigma: puzzle, mystery, problem.
dying nurse: the Church.
Adam's curse: original sin. Adam disobeyed the commandment of God and was banished from the Garden of Eden and he and all his descendants were now prone to disease and death.
Endowed: provided, donated.
ruined millionaire: Adam.
paternal care: God's care.
prevents: leads on, stops.

mental wires: mind's torment.

quake: tremble, cower.
frigid: cold, icy.
purgatorial fires: the soul burns in purgatory to be cleansed from sin before ascending to heaven.

substantial: of considerable importance, strongly built.

'the flame is roses'

👤 Personal Response

1. Select one image from the poem that you find particularly unsettling and briefly describe its impact on you.
2. What, in your opinion, is the tone of the poem: devotional, assured, searching, frightened, etc.? Support your views with reference to the poem.
3. Do you consider the final stanza a satisfactory conclusion to the poem? Explain the reasons for your opinion, using reference to the text.

👁 Critical Literacy

'East Coker' forms part of the cycle of four poems titled *Four Quartets*, widely regarded as Eliot's masterpiece. The poems were first published individually with place names as titles: 'Burnt Norton' (1936), 'East Coker' (1940), 'The Dry Salvages' (1941) and 'Little Gidding' (1942). This sequence is loosely based on the four seasons and the four elements. The title, 'Four Quartets', suggests a musical quartet, where themes and images are repeated as the meanings accumulate through the different instrumentation used. Time, experience, purgation, prayer and unity are the themes that are common to each poem.

There is a historical dimension to 'East Coker', as Eliot's ancestor Sir Thomas Elyot was baptised in St Michael's Church in East Coker in 1627. Another ancestor, Andrew Eliot, left East Coker for America in 1669. Eliot visited this

T. S. ELIOT

village in the 1930s and his ashes are buried in the same church with the inscription, 'In my beginning is my end. Of your kindness, pray for the soul of Thomas Stearns Eliot, poet. In my end is my beginning.' Critics have described 'East Coker' as a poem of late summer, earth and faith. It is also seen by some as signifying hope that English communities would survive World War II. The village is an idyll of England at the start of the war. In Eliot's view, the end of all exploring is 'to arrive where we started/And know the place for the first time' ('Little Gidding').

The poem 'East Coker' is divided into five sections. 'East Coker IV' is a formal, elegant section that uses **elaborate paradoxes**. It is full of personal and collective despair paired with the gloom of Good Friday. This religious meditation focuses on the central Christian doctrines of original sin (humanity's state after the fall of Adam), redemption (salvation through the sacrifice of Jesus on the Cross) and atonement (penance undertaken to purge sin). The poem is focused on the magnitude of Christ's death on the Cross as a way of securing salvation for mankind.

Eliot enjoyed the Metaphysical poets, such as Donne, who used intricate comparisons in their work. In this poem, in stanza one, Eliot uses the hospital as a metaphor for the world. The suffering patients are mankind. The 'wounded surgeon' is Jesus Christ, who operates to save sinful/diseased man. Stern love is shown by the surgeon as he skilfully 'plies the steel' to cure the 'distempered part'. He is 'wounded' like Jesus on the Cross. The surgeon's 'bleeding hands' recall how Christ's hands were nailed to the Cross. Through his suffering the puzzle, 'enigma', of sin, denoted by the 'fever chart', is being sorted out, 'Resolving'. This 'sharp compassion' is needed to solve the mystery of our ailing, sinful existence. Metaphysical poetry had a real sense of **argument** running through it, as here: we need to reject the demands of the body and achieve salvation through curing the body's ills. Suffering leads to grace. Eliot saw a close similarity between the poetry of the 17th century and that of the 20th century – both saw the disintegration of old traditions and the arrival of new learning.

In stanza two **the comparison is extended**: 'Our only health is the disease'. This refers to a poem by Andrew Marvell where the soul speaks of being 'Constrained not only to endure/Diseases, but, what's worse, the cure'. According to the poet, we have to do what the 'dying nurse', the Church, says. Its role is 'not to please', but to remind us of our morality. This is a direct consequence of 'our, and Adam's curse'. We have to recognise that **we are sinful and that we need to be redeemed** and then we can be spiritually healthy. This is inspired by 'Dark Night of the Soul' by St John of the Cross, which told of the journey of the soul from its bodily home to its union with God. Purification is needed for spiritual growth.

Stanza three continues the parallel as Adam is described as the 'ruined millionaire': he possessed everything in Paradise, yet threw it all away. God provided the 'whole earth' as a 'hospital' where we can learn the value of suffering and can be cured of our sickness. 'Endowed' suggests something that is gifted or bestowed. Here, it is used paradoxically by Eliot, as **Adam left us with sin, but opened the way for salvation** ('if we do well'). Adam's fall precipitated Christ's sacrifice. One could not have happened without the other. We will be looked after by 'absolute paternal care/That will not leave us'. It 'prevents us everywhere', going before us as spiritual guidance and also stopping us through death.

Rich, sensuous images in **stanza four** describe the fever of sickness: 'The chill ascends from feet to knees'. We feel the icy coldness of death. We experience the shrill sound of mental anguish in the assonance of 'The fever sings in mental wires'. In order to triumph, 'If to be warmed', the individual must suffer, 'freeze/And quake', as the disease of sin is purified through suffering. This results in the experience of **divine love**, 'Of which the flame is roses'. This was the sacrifice of Jesus on the Cross. The 'briars' suggest the crown of thorns placed on Christ's head as he was crucified. The emblems of martyrdom are 'roses' and 'briars'.

The **fifth stanza** concludes with sensational, vivid images of the **Eucharist**. 'The dripping blood' (the wine) and 'The bloody flesh' (the host) form the only sustenance we need for eternal life. Eliot criticises our blindness, 'In spite of which we like to think' that we are whole and complete without this 'sound, substantial flesh and blood'. Nevertheless, he acknowledges that we do realise the value of Jesus' suffering because 'we call this Friday good'.

The **tone** of this poem is one of calm, detached humility. Its **devotional, assured voice** is contained in five stanzas of five lines. Each stanza concludes with a full stop, a complete syntactical unit on its own. The rhyme scheme is regular, *ababb*, *cdcdd*, etc. This polished, formal yet private voice expresses the concerns of an entire generation in the midst of war and doubt.

✒ Writing About the Poem

'T. S. Eliot's poem "East Coker IV" is a bitter poem concluding in resignation.' Discuss this statement, referring to both the content and style of the poem. Develop your response with suitable reference to the text.

T.S. ELIOT

Sample Paragraph

I do not agree that this is a bitter poem. Instead Eliot sets out in a dazzling display of elaborate comparisons the reality of this violent, sinful world which needs healing by the 'wounded surgeon', Jesus Christ. Eliot believed in the Christian doctrine of penance and salvation. In my opinion, that is why he speaks of purging sin and sickness 'in frigid purgatorial fires'. I do not consider that the poem ends in resignation, as there is hope because of Jesus Christ's sacrifice on the Cross which won us our salvation. This is captured in the quite shocking images of the Eucharist's wine and host, 'The dripping blood' and 'The bloody flesh'. Eliot concludes his poem by acknowledging that man does appreciate the sacrifice as 'we call this Friday good', a very positive end note!

EXAMINER'S COMMENT

This is a robust high-grade personal response to the question and presents a number of arguments that show close engagement with the poem. Accurate quotations and contextual references are used effectively throughout.

Class/Homework Exercises

1. '"East Coker IV" is a poem whose lines fail to come to life.' To what extent do you agree or disagree with this view? Develop your response with reference to the poem.
2. 'Eliot surveys the dominant emotion of despair through paradoxical comparisons in his poems.' Discuss this view with reference to 'East Coker IV'.

Points to Consider

- Necessary evil, suffering is redemptive.
- God's caring love.
- Imagery taken from medical world, martyrdom, cross and Eucharist.
- Precise use of language, play of opposites, didactic tone.
- Metaphysical elements – developed argument, paradoxes, conceits and wit.

POETRY FOCUS

Understanding the Prescribed Poetry Question

Marks are awarded using the PCLM Marking Scheme:
P = 15; C = 15; L = 15; M = 5
Total = 50

- **P** (Purpose = 15 marks) refers to the set question and is the launch pad for the answer. This involves engaging with all aspects of the question. Both theme and language must be addressed, although not necessarily equally.
- **C** (Coherence = 15 marks) refers to the organisation of the developed response and the use of accurate, relevant quotation. Paragraphing is essential.
- **L** (Language = 15 marks) refers to the student's skill in controlling language throughout the answer.
- **M** (Mechanics = 5 marks) refers to spelling and grammar.
- Although no specific number of poems is required, students usually discuss at least 3 or 4 in their written responses.
- Aim for at least 800 words, to be completed within 45–50 minutes.

NOTE

In keeping with the PCLM approach, the student has to explore poems of Eliot's on the course that include:

– **serious issues of universal significance** (the search for spiritual fulfilment, transience, personal experience, purification, 20th-century moral decline, estrangement, etc.)

... explored through:

– **a fresh and innovative style** (dramatic monologue, stream of consciousness, fragmentary dialogue, vivid and disturbing imagery, engaging satire, startling contrasts, rich cultural and religious allusions, intense atmospheres, etc.)

Sample Leaving Cert Questions on Eliot's Poetry

1. 'The poetry of T. S. Eliot explores serious issues of universal significance in a fresh and innovative style.' Discuss this statement, developing your answer with suitable reference to the poems by Eliot on your course.
2. 'T. S. Eliot can be a challenging poet to understand, both in terms of language use and central themes.' To what extent do you agree with this statement? Develop your answer with suitable reference to the poems by Eliot that you have studied.
3. 'Eliot's pessimistic vision of life is conveyed in poems that are both interesting and atmospheric.' Discuss this view, developing your answer with suitable reference to the poems by Eliot on your course.

How do I organise my answer?

(Sample question 1)

'The poetry of T. S. Eliot explores serious issues of universal significance in a fresh and innovative style.' Discuss this statement, developing your answer with suitable reference to the poems by Eliot on your course.

Sample Plan 1

Intro: (*Stance: agree with viewpoint in the question*) Eliot's poetry examines serious questions which are important to everyone through an innovative use of descriptive details, discordant poetic structure, cultural and religious allusions and digressions.

Point 1: (*Lack of spirituality – descriptive details*) 'Preludes' provides disturbing examples of a spiritual emptiness in modern society, conveyed by detailed description.

Point 2: (*Destructive experience – dysfunctional landscape, harsh poetic structure*) 'Rannoch, by Glencoe' shows the damaging effect of man on the landscape. Disturbing memories have created a bleak landscape. Abrupt ending and insistent monosyllables emphasise the damage.

Point 3: (*Failure of modern man – rich fragmentary allusions*) 'A Game of Chess' shows man's problems in dealing with his cultural heritage. Fragmentary cultural allusions to Shakespeare and Greek legends show how man struggles to find a voice in today's society.

T. S. ELIOT

Point 4: (*Emotional emptiness – digressions, mock-heroic tone*) 'The Love Song of J. Alfred Prufrock' traces Prufrock's paralysing indecision through random asides about his appearance and a mock-heroic tone as he attempts to come to a decision, 'Shall I part my hair behind?'

Conclusion: Unsettling issues which are both profound and universal are intelligently examined through Eliot's original and challenging poetic style.

Sample Paragraph: Point 1

Lack of a meaningful personal life is a universal theme addressed in 'Preludes'. A woman is described in a series of unattractive body parts, 'yellow soles of feet', 'soiled hands'. This reduction of a human being suggests a spiritual yearning. Her spirit is defeated by constantly moving patterns of 'The thousand sordid images'. The use of the definite article, 'The', suggests that this woman has experienced these shames. Her lack of a name further reduces her to an insignificant status. The verbs 'lay' and 'dozed' create a mood of quiet despair. The woman lacks spiritual vision, even the birds do not fly in the sky but are confined by the 'gutters'. These sleazy descriptions of the woman and her environment convey Eliot's bleak vision of spiritual and moral emptiness.

> **EXAMINER'S COMMENT**
>
> As part of a full essay, this top-grade response shows close engagement with the question and Eliot's poetry. Focused analysis of the poet's fresh writing style in depicting a character who is seeking spiritual fulfilment. Varied, controlled expression and apt quotations add to the quality of the response.

(Sample question 2)

'T. S. Eliot can be a challenging poet to understand, both in terms of language use and central themes.' To what extent do you agree with this statement? Develop your answer with suitable reference to the poems by Eliot that you have studied.

> **NOTE**
>
> In keeping with the PCLM approach, the student has to take a stance by agreeing, disagreeing or partially agreeing that Eliot can be a challenging poet:
>
> – **in terms of language** (innovative poetic style, complex religious references, multi-layered narratives, demanding cultural and literary allusions, shifting moods and atmospheres, etc.)
>
> … and
>
> – **in terms of central themes** (fruitless search for personal and spiritual meaning in life, alienation, insecurity, paralysis, etc.)

Sample Plan 2

Intro: (*Stance – partially agree with viewpoint in question*) Eliot's irregular writing style is interesting – always inviting the reader to explore the possibilities of language. The wide-ranging subject matter can be difficult at times, but it reflects the multi-layered experience in the modern age.

Point 1: (*Meaning of life in secular world – personification, images of decay*) 'Preludes' addresses complex spiritual and philosophical questions, confronting the modern secular world through vivid personification and sordid images of spiritual desolation.

Point 2: (*Lack of personal fulfilment – dramatic vignettes*) Readers are engaged by the dramatic scenes and intriguing atmospheres in 'Prufrock'. In his alienation and insecurity, the unhappy central character raises disturbing questions about contemporary urban society.

Point 3: (*Less challenging content – satire*) Some of the shorter poems, 'Aunt Helen' for example, are more easily understood. This gentle satire is critical of aspects of polite society.

Point 4: (*Religious experience – demanding references*) Cultural allusions and literary references can be difficult, but they enrich our understanding of important themes, such as the Christian experience in 'Journey of the Magi' and 'East Coker IV'.

Conclusion: Eliot's original poetic voice challenges and his thought-provoking poems have much to interest the modern reader in a rapidly changing world.

Sample Paragraph: Point 3

Not all of Eliot's poems are difficult to understand. In 'Aunt Helen', he paints a satirical pen portrait of his 'maiden aunt', a 'fashionable' lady whose fussy ways are seen as quite absurd. The 'silence in heaven' summed her up well. Eliot is daring in ways – especially as he doesn't take death too seriously: 'the undertaker wiped his feet' when he visited, as if Helen would expect good manners even after she had died. This dry ironic humour is also evident where all the aunt's puritanical rules no longer have any effect on the servants who enjoy their new freedom: 'the footman sat upon the dining-table holding the second housemaid on his knees'. The poet's writing is suggestive but down-to-earth and clear. The two servants are lower class, but they are certainly enjoying life – unlike the lonely spinster.

> **EXAMINER'S COMMENT**
>
> *Short and succinct top-grade response to the question. Some good personal engagement with the poem and perceptive discussion of Eliot's satirical approach and use of subtle irony. Points are well supported by apt quotation and the expression is clear throughout.*

EXAM FOCUS

- As you may not be familiar with some of the poems referred to in the sample plans, substitute poems that you have studied closely.
- Key points about a particular poem can be developed over more than one paragraph.
- Paragraphs may also include cross-referencing and discussion of more than one poem.
- Remember that there is no single 'correct' answer to poetry questions, so always be confident in expressing your own considered response.

Leaving Cert Sample Essay

'T. S. Eliot's distinctive poetry is concerned with the search for meaning in an uncertain world.' Develop your response with reference to the poems of Eliot on your course.

Sample Essay

1. Eliot addresses the exploration for life's meaning in several poems I studied, 'Journey of the Magi', 'The Love Song of J. Alfred Prufrock' and 'Preludes'. Eliot's writing style is very distinctive. He uses modern-day language and his poems are often broken into fragments. Revealing contrasts, dramatic imagery and stream of consciousness style are all used in an original way to convey the poet's observations on modern society's faults and failings.

2. A lot of Eliot's poems are concerned with religion and reflect his own spiritual search. 'Journey of the Magi' is a dramatic account of the three kings who visited the infant Jesus in Bethlehem. They seem to symbolise every person who is seeking spiritual or religious meaning in life. But Eliot's approach contrasts to the traditional Bible story. He focuses a lot on the physical hardships the magi faced in 'the very dead of winter'. The elderly king who narrates the story admits 'there were times we regretted' the journey.

3. Powerful sibilant images convey the pleasures and sensual life they had left behind, 'Summer places on the slope', 'silken girls carrying sherbet'. Eliot shows us that Christianity is not an easy religion to follow. The magi describe their destination in Bethlehem – 'Finding the place, it was you may say satisfactory'. The understatement shows the troubled minds of the magi in this clash between their old lives as wealthy pagan kings and a strange new religion.

4. The final lines describe the changing mindset of the magi who are not at all sure about this new Christianity: 'This birth was hard and bitter agony for us just like death'. The journey marked the end of their old easy-going pagan religion. Yet it did not give them a lot of contentment or deep faith in God. The poem has three different storylines – the actual journey of the magi, Eliot's personal journey from doubts about God's existance to Anglican faith and, finally, the journey of any individual in search of religious belief. 'Journey of the Magi' examines the idea that faith can never be free of serious doubt, 'this was all folly'.

5. Eliot's often addresses alienation and powerlessness in a world that is constantly in transition. The absence of any widespread sense of religion in secular 20th-century society is the background to his great poem, 'The Love Song of J. Alfred Prufrock'. The poem's insecure central figure is unable to take control of his life. His need for fulfilment and his anxiety toward watching his time fade away make him a tragic character. Prufrock's fear of rejection stops him from obtaining a lover or any future hopes of happiness. In this dramatic monologue, Prufrock brings us on a journey to meet an unnamed woman. He hopes to ask her 'an overwhelming question'. Possibly to propose marriage.

INDICATIVE MATERIAL

- **Eliot's distinctive poetry:** (original poetic style, powerful imagery, revealing literary allusions, complex cultural references, dramatic use of multiple narrative voices/personae, varied moods – ironic, poignant, weary, satirical, etc.)

... is concerned with:

- **the search for meaning in an uncertain world** (disillusioned vision of urban life in the 20th century, unsettling themes of alienation, failure, spiritual yearning, longing for satisfying personal relationships, etc.)

6. We listen to a lot of Prufrock's random thoughts. He is trying to know himself and make some sense of his unhappy life – 'I have measured out my life with coffee spoons'. This image suggests he has spent a lot of his time in a pointless way. Prufrock questions everything. Eliot breaks up the poem into numerous sub-sections which show his unsettled mind. The stream of consciousness narrative is used to show Prufrock's private anxieties about failing to find a meaningful life. Eliot emphasises his obsession with ageing, 'I grow old, I shall wear the bottoms of my trousers rolled'. He repeatedly voices his fears about making choices, asking himself, 'Do I dare?'

7. Prufrock cannot fully express what he really wants to say, 'It is impossible to say just what I mean!' I found the poem's ending bitter and sad. A haunting image of Prufrock abandoning his secret dreams of finding a girlfriend or wife is described. He imagines being near the ocean and hearing mermaids singing. Unfortunatly he realises, 'I do not think they will sing to me'.

8. 'Preludes' explores the solitary, ordinary lives of unhappy people against the backdrop of a drab run-down modern city. The poet is very effective at creating unsettling moods. Dramatic images of 'grimy scraps of whithered leaves', 'newspapers in vacant lots' and 'broken blinds and chimney-pots' capture the anonymous lives of dingy back-streets. The nameless characters go through daily routines in their own seperate and silent desperation – 'With the other masquerades that time resumes'. The poem's outlook was pessimistic and summed up Eliot's view that a lot of urban life these days can be dreary and dissappointing.

9. Overall, I liked Eliot's distinctive poetry. Individuals seeking meaningful relationships, either human or spiritual, in contrast to the pressures of their day-to-day lives is the main theme of these poems. The dark view of modern life in these poems expresses the unhappiness of people through vivid scenes and memorable characters.

(790 words)

EXAMINER'S COMMENT

Sustained response showing clear engagement with Eliot's poetry. The poems chosen for discussion allowed for well-supported analysis of the question's three elements (distinctive poetry, search for meaning, uncertain world). There are some slight misquotations, some spelling errors ('existance', 'Unfortunatly', 'whithered', 'seperate', 'dissappointing') and overuse of the phrase, 'a lot'. However, expression is generally controlled throughout.

GRADE: H1
P = 15/15
C = 14/15
L = 13/15
M = 4/5
Total = 46/50

👓 Revision Overview

'The Love Song of J. Alfred Prufrock'
Dramatic inner monologue of an indecisive man tormented by feelings of isolation and inadequacy. Central themes include the impact of modern city life on lonely individuals, alienation and fear of death.

'Preludes' (OL)
Complex narrative about the dark and depressing nature of today's urban lifestyle and the uncertain state of the human soul.

'Aunt Helen' (OL)
In this satirical portrayal of a recently deceased woman who appears to have been unloved, Eliot addresses themes of life, death, relationships and solitude.

***from* 'The Waste Land': 'II. A Game of Chess'**
Critical view of today's unfulfilling, shallow world where people are often unable to connect meaningfully with others.

'Journey of the Magi'
Symbolic poem about the pain of spiritual rebirth. Alienation from a meaningless past is another central theme.

***from* 'Landscapes': 'III. Usk'**
Eliot's instructive poem urges people to live a simple life and to continue seeking spiritual fulfilment through prayer.

***from* 'Landscapes': 'IV. Rannoch, by Glencoe'**
Dramatic evocation of Scotland and its tragic history are merged in a haunting landscape.

***from* 'Four Quartets': 'East Coker IV'**
Eliot focuses on man's place in the universe and emphasises the prospect of renewal and spiritual salvation through Christianity.

💬 Last Words

'Although the idea of a life not fully lived is central to his poetry, T. S. Eliot was not the dry old stick of his self-caricature.'
Craig Raine

'As a schoolboy in a Catholic boarding school in Derry, I was daunted by T. S. Eliot and all that he stood for.'
Seamus Heaney

'Genuine poetry can communicate before it is understood.'
T. S. Eliot

RELIGION/SPIRITUALITY | MEANING OF LIFE | MODERN WORLD | ISOLATION | RELATIONSHIPS | HISTORY/MEMORY

Seamus Heaney 1939–2013

'Walk on air against your better judgement.'

Seamus Heaney was born in 1939 in Co. Derry, the eldest of nine children. He was accepted into Queen's University, Belfast in 1957 to study English Language and Literature. Heaney's poetry first came to public attention in the 1960s, when he and a number of other poets, including Michael Longley and Derek Mahon, came to prominence. They all shared the same fate of being born into a society that was deeply divided along religious grounds and was to become immersed in violence, intimidation and sectarianism. In 1966, Heaney's first poetry collection, *Death of a Naturalist*, was published. Throughout the 1970s, he was publishing prolifically and giving public readings. He also wrote several volumes of criticism. Widely regarded as the finest poet of his generation, he was awarded the Nobel Prize for Literature in 1995 'for works of lyrical beauty and ethical depth, which exalt everyday miracles and the living past'. In accepting the award, Heaney stated that his life had been 'a journey into the wideness of language, a journey where each point of arrival … turned out to be a stepping stone rather than a destination'.

Investigate Further

To find out more about Seamus Heaney, or to hear readings of his poems not already available in your eBook, you could search some useful websites, such as YouTube, BBC Poetry, poetryfoundation.org and poetryarchive.org, or access additional material on this page of your eBook.

Prescribed Poems

SEAMUS HEANEY

○ **1 'The Forge'**
At one level, the poem celebrates a traditional craft. However, its central focus is on the mystery and beauty of the creative process itself. **Page 168**

○ **2 'Bogland'**
The poet contrasts the expansive North American grasslands with the narrowly bounded landscape of Ireland's boglands. **Page 172**

○ **3 'The Tollund Man'**
Photographs of the preserved body of an Iron Age man found in the bogs of Denmark prompted Heaney to trace parallels between the imagined circumstances of the Tollund Man's death and more recent violence in Northern Ireland. **Page 176**

○ **4 'Mossbawn: Sunlight'**
This wonderfully atmospheric poem is a nostalgic celebration of the poet's childhood on the family farm in Co. Derry and his close relationship with his aunt. **Page 181**

○ **5 'A Constable Calls' (OL)**
Based on another memory from his boyhood, the poet describes an uneasy encounter when his father was questioned by a local policeman. **Page 185**

○ **6 'The Skunk'**
Sensuous language and an edgy, romantic atmosphere enhance this unusual and playful love poem. **Page 190**

○ **7 'The Harvest Bow'**
A tightly wrought personal poem based on the central image of a decorative 'throwaway love-knot'. The straw bow provides a physical link between Heaney and his father, the present and the past, nature and art. **Page 194**

○ **8 'The Underground' (OL)**
Based on a memory from their honeymoon, the poem explores the enduring love between Heaney and his wife. **Page 198**

○ **9 'Postscript'**
In this short lyric, the poet succeeds in conveying the extraordinary through an everyday experience – the vivid memory of a journey westward to the Co. Clare coastline. **Page 202**

○ **10 'A Call' (OL)**
Another poem dealing with two of Heaney's favourite themes: the father-son relationship and the passing of time. **Page 205**

○ **11 'Tate's Avenue'**
In this beautifully discreet and understated love poem, Heaney recalls three car rugs that mark important stages in the changing relationship between himself and his wife. **Page 209**

○ **12 'The Pitchfork'**
Another typical Heaney poem, celebrating traditional rural life. The poet makes 'a journey back into the heartland of the ordinary', where he is both observer and visionary. **Page 213**

○ **13 'Lightenings viii'**
In his short account of how a mysterious floating air-ship appeared above the monks' oratory at Clonmacnoise monastery, Heaney blurs the lines between reality and illusion and challenges our ideas about life. **Page 217**

(OL) indicates poems that are also prescribed for the Ordinary Level course.

1 The Forge

All I know is a door into the dark.
Outside, old axles and iron hoops rusting;
Inside, the hammered anvil's short-pitched ring,
The unpredictable fantail of sparks
Or hiss when a new shoe toughens in water.   5
The anvil must be somewhere in the centre,
Horned as a unicorn, at one end square,
Set there immoveable: an altar
Where he expends himself in shape and music.
Sometimes, leather-aproned, hairs in his nose,   10
He leans out on the jamb, recalls a clatter
Of hoofs where traffic is flashing in rows;
Then grunts and goes in, with a slam and flick
To beat real iron out, to work the bellows.

Title: the forge refers to a blacksmith's workshop, where iron implements are made and mended. (In the poem, a smith is shaping horseshoes.)

axles: bars or shafts on which wheels rotate.
anvil: iron block that the smith uses as a work surface.

unicorn: mythical animal (usually a white horse) with a spiralled horn growing from its forehead.
expends: burns up, expresses.

jamb: upright door support.

bellows: instrument for drawing air into a fire.

'The unpredictable fantail of sparks'

👤 Personal Response

1. Describe the poet's attitude to the forge. Is he fascinated or fearful, or both? Support your answer with reference to the poem.
2. Based on your study of the poem, what is your impression of the blacksmith?
3. Comment on the effectiveness of the phrase 'The unpredictable fantail of sparks'.

👁 Critical Literacy

'The Forge' comes from Seamus Heaney's second collection, *Door into the Dark*, which was published in 1969. The sonnet form has a clear division of an octave (the first eight lines) and a sestet (the final six lines). While the octave, apart from its initial reference to the narrator, focuses on the inanimate objects and occurrences inside and outside the forge, the sestet describes the blacksmith and his work.

The poem's opening line ('All I know is a door into the dark') is both modest and assured. There is also a **mystical undertone** (a sense of otherworldliness) as Heaney revisits his childhood and his fascination with a local forge. The image, with its negative and mysterious undertones, increases our curiosity and invites us to find out what answers lie beyond. The poet recalls unwanted objects strewn outside, 'old axles and iron hoops rusting'. The irregular rhythm in line 2 suggests the disorder of what has been discarded. He **contrasts** the lifeless exterior scene with the vigorous atmosphere ('the hammered anvil's short-pitched ring') inside the forge. The world outside is decrepit and old, a wasteland, whereas the noisy forge is a place of brilliant sparks where iron is beaten out and renewed.

Heaney's visual and aural images are characteristically striking. His vivid metaphor of 'The unpredictable fantail of sparks' (line 4) lets us see the glorious flurry of changeable flashing light and hear the twang of echoing iron.

Onomatopoeic effects add to our sense of the physical activity taking place as the blacksmith works on a new horseshoe. Suddenly, the incandescent metal begins to 'hiss when a new shoe toughens in water'. The **tone is sympathetic** and attentive as the poet reimagines the smells, sounds and tactile impressions of the blacksmith's workshop.

Lines 6–9 contain the sonnet's central image of the smith's anvil: 'an altar/ Where he expends himself in shape and music'. Interestingly, the transition from the octave to the sestet is a run-on (or enjambment) based on this key metaphor. One effect of this is to enable us to experience the anvil as a **sacred or magical point of transition** between the material and immovable

world of everyday life and the fluid, imaginative world of human consciousness. Heaney stresses the **mystery of the creative process**, associating it with the mythical creature of medieval fiction, 'Horned as a unicorn'. Although the simile seems somewhat strained, the comparison with a legendary beast still serves to highlight the mysterious qualities ('shape and music') of poetry.

The final lines focus on the blacksmith's physical characteristics. **Heaney leaves us with a down-to-earth image of a gruff, hardworking man**, 'leather-aproned, hairs in his nose'. Is the poet suggesting that art – and poetry in particular – is independent of education and social class? Seemingly wary of the world at large, the smith remembers an earlier era of horse-drawn carriages, when his skills were fully appreciated. Contrasting images of 'a clatter/Of hoofs' and modern traffic 'flashing in rows' reflect the changes he has lived through. In the end, he grudgingly accepts that he must return 'into the dark' and resume doing what he does best: 'To beat real iron out, to work the bellows'.

Heaney's poem can immediately be read as an elegy to the past and a lament for the lost tradition of the blacksmith. Readers can also interpret the anvil as a metaphor of an unreachable heritage, a traditional craft made redundant by modernisation. Many critics have seen the blacksmith figure as a **symbol or construction of the role of the poet**, one who opens the 'door into the dark', the creative artist who ritually 'expends himself in shape and music' and who 'grunts' and flicks words and language, forging his poems. As with so much of Heaney's work, the poem shows his ability to cleverly suggest significance by making us wonder.

Writing About the Poem

'Seamus Heaney's imaginative use of descriptive language often adds a mythic quality to his poems.' Discuss this statement with reference to 'The Forge'.

Sample Paragraph

In his nostalgic poem, 'The Forge', the disappearing tradition of the local blacksmith is brought vividly to life. Through dynamic sound effects ('ring', 'hiss') combined with the use of the compound word 'short-pitched', Heaney presents us with a craftsman turning metal into useful farming tools. This blacksmith is given another persona, one of epic quality. He becomes a High Priest at his 'altar', the anvil. We get a sense of legendary times, suggested by the image of the anvil shape, 'Horned as a unicorn'. The poet envisions the craftsman in a mythical role, changing one everyday substance into something special. Like Heaney himself, the priest is involved in the mysterious creative process. The blacksmith is described in detail, 'warts and all'. He stands, 'leather-aproned, hairs in his nose', but he has the ability to control the power of fire. Reality and legend blend seamlessly.

> **EXAMINER'S COMMENT**
>
> This mature top-grade response focuses well on Heaney's powers of description – particularly his use of aural effects. The more challenging aspect of 'mythic qualities' is handled successfully, with clear points linking the anvil and altar. Expression is carefully controlled, using varied sentence lengths and a wide-ranging vocabulary (e.g. 'dynamic', 'persona', 'envisions'). Apt quotations are also used throughout.

SEAMUS HEANEY

✒ Class/Homework Exercises

1. 'Heaney's visual and aural imagery depict a harsh, rural life with lyrical beauty.' Discuss this statement in relation to 'The Forge'.
2. 'Many of Heaney's carefully crafted poems are populated with characters who have made a deep impression on him.' Discuss this view with reference to 'The Forge'.

⊙ Points to Consider

- Lament for and preservation of a traditional craft and rural life.
- Interesting experimental use of structure and rhyme scheme of sonnet form.
- Clever contrasts – exterior/interior, past/present, reality/legend.
- Striking sound effects – onomatopoeia, assonance, sibilant 's'.
- Sensuous visual images and symbols create a powerful sense of time and place.

2 Bogland

for T. P. Flanagan

We have no prairies
To slice a big sun at evening –
Everywhere the eye concedes to
Encroaching horizon,

Is wooed into the cyclops' eye
Of a tarn. Our unfenced country
Is bog that keeps crusting
Between the sights of the sun.

They've taken the skeleton
Of the Great Irish Elk
Out of the peat, set it up,
An astounding crate full of air.

Butter sunk under
More than a hundred years
Was recovered salty and white.
The ground itself is kind, black butter

Melting and opening underfoot,
Missing its last definition
By millions of years.
They'll never dig coal here,

Only the waterlogged trunks
Of great firs, soft as pulp.
Our pioneers keep striking
Inwards and downwards,

Every layer they strip
Seems camped on before.
The bogholes might be Atlantic seepage.
The wet centre is bottomless.

prairies: large open areas of grassland (in North America).

concedes: gives way to; admits defeat.

Encroaching: advancing gradually beyond acceptable limits.

wooed: courted, enticed.

cyclops' eye: in Greek mythology, a race of one-eyed giants.

tarn: small mountain lake.

Great Irish Elk: large northern deer (now extinct) found preserved in Irish bogland.

definition: transformation (into coal).

pioneers: adventurers, explorers.

seepage: the slow escape of liquid through a material.

👤 Personal Response

1. In your opinion, what is Heaney's central theme or point in this poem? Briefly explain your response.
2. How does Heaney employ the senses to allow the reader to share in his experience of the bogland? Refer closely to the poem in your answer.
3. Trace the poet's tone throughout the poem. Comment on where, how and why, in your opinion, the tone changes. Support your views with reference to the text.

👁 Critical Literacy

'Bogland' (1969) is the result of a Hallowe'en holiday Heaney spent with T.P. Flanagan (the artist to whom this poem is dedicated). Flanagan recalls that 'the bogland was burnt the colour of marmalade'. Heaney felt it was 'one of the most important poems' he had written because 'it was something like a symbol. I felt the poem was a promise of something else … it represented a free place for me.' He thought the bogland was a 'landscape that remembered everything that happened in and to it'. Heaney recalled when they were children that they were told 'not to go near the bog because there was no bottom to it'.

The poem is written in seven spare, unrhymed stanzas and uses casual, almost colloquial language. In the opening stanza, a comparison is drawn

'Encroaching horizon,
Is wooed into the cyclops' eye
Of a tarn'

between the American prairies ('We have no prairies') and Ireland's bogs. Heaney said, 'At that time, I had ... been reading about the frontier and the west as an important myth in the American consciousness, so I set up – or rather, laid down – the bog as an answering Irish myth'. The prairie in America represents the vastness of the country, **its unfenced expanse a metaphor for the freedom of its people** to pursue their dreams and express their beliefs. At first, Ireland's bog represents opposite values. It seems narrow, constricting and inward-looking: 'the eye concedes', 'Encroaching horizon', 'cyclops' eye'. In America, the pioneers moved across the country. In Ireland, the pioneers looked 'Inwards and downwards', remembering, almost wallowing in, the past. Is the poet suggesting that Ireland is defined by the layers of its difficult history? Or is each set of pioneers on an adventure, one set discovering new places, the other set rediscovering forgotten places?

Stanza two captures the **bog's fluidity** in the onomatopoeic phrase 'keeps crusting/Between the sights of the sun'. Heaney draws the changing face of the bog, its element of mystery and danger, as it does not always remain exactly the same, but subtly fluctuates. The poet's sense of awe at this place is expressed in stanza three as he recounts the discovery of the Great Irish Elk as 'An astounding crate full of air'. Here the poet is referring to another aspect of the bog – its **ability to preserve the past**.

In stanza four, the bog's capacity to hold and preserve is emphasised when 'Butter sunk under/More than a hundred years' was recovered fit for use, 'salty and white'. This place is 'kind'. Stanza four runs into stanza five in a parallel reference to the bog's fluidity. The bog never becomes hard; 'its last definition' is 'Missing', so it will never yield coal. The squidgy nature of the bog is conveyed in stanza six in the phrase 'soft as pulp'. The phrases of the poem are opening and melting into each other in imitation of the bog. Is this in stark contrast to the hardening prejudices of the two communities in Northern Ireland? **The Irish explore their past**; to them, history is important as they 'keep striking/Inwards and downwards'.

Heaney leaves us with an **open-ended conclusion** in stanza seven. He remembers that the bog 'seemed to have some kind of wind blowing through it that could carry on'. The boglands are feminine, nurturing, welcoming: 'The wet centre is bottomless'. The poet is aware of the depth and complexity of the national consciousness. Should we, like the bog, embrace all aspects of our national identity? Is this how we should carry on? Is there a final truth? Is it unreachable?

✒ Writing About the Poem

'Through the rich musicality of his poetry, Seamus Heaney evokes the difficulty of establishing a national identity.' Discuss this statement with reference to 'Bogland'.

Sample Paragraph

A collective pronoun, 'We', opens 'Bogland'. However, the poet suggests that the Irish define themselves negatively in comparison to America, 'We have no prairies'. While their pioneers move forward in their exploration of new territories, ours dig 'Inwards and downwards'. Yet, through his visual and aural description of the bogland, Heaney succeeds in creating a proud symbol of nationhood. The bog – just like our history – preserves treasures, both natural ('the Great Irish Elk') and manmade. We Irish have a long history. 'Every layer they strip/Seems camped on before'. The bog symbolises a nation in a perpetual state of change. Hard 'k' and 'c' sounds ('keeps crusting') capture the thin surface which breaks to reveal the soft interior of the bog, 'kind black butter'. Run-on lines echo the ever-changing nature of the bog, 'soft as pulp'. History continues forever.

EXAMINER'S COMMENT

A close sensitive analysis of the poem, engaging with the subtle connections between its musical language and the theme of identity. Very good range of informed and incisive points on symbolism, sound effects and run-on lines. Expression is varied and controlled. Excellent use of reference and quotation throughout add to the quality of the discussion in this top-grade response.

✒ Class/Homework Exercises

1. 'Heaney's sensuous imagery often evokes a haunting and dramatic sense of place.' To what extent is this true of 'Bogland'? Support your answer with reference to the poem.
2. 'Through his succinct and exact use of language, Seamus Heaney enables us to make sense of the world and ourselves.' Discuss this view with reference to 'Bogland'.

⊙ Points to Consider

- **Importance of history and identity expressed through the central symbol of bogland.**
- **Free verse, lack of rhyme and rhythm mimic the fluid nature of the bog.**
- **Contrasting tones of insecurity, awe and amazement turn to quiet reflection.**
- **Use of striking sound effects, visual imagery, personification and allusions to myth.**
- **Structure of poem imitates activity of digging – short lines drill down the page, while stacked stanzas reflect the layered nature of the bog.**

3 🔊 The Tollund Man

Title: a reference to the well-preserved body found in 1950 by two turfcutters in Tollund, Denmark. The man had been hanged over 2,000 years earlier. One theory suggested that his death had been part of a ritualistic fertility sacrifice. The Tollund Man's head was put on display in a museum at Aarhus.

I

Some day I will go to Aarhus
To see his peat-brown head,
The mild pods of his eye-lids,
His pointed skin cap.

In the flat country nearby   5
Where they dug him out,
His last gruel of winter seeds
Caked in his stomach,

Naked except for
The cap, noose and girdle,   10
I will stand a long time.
Bridegroom to the goddess,

She tightened her torc on him
And opened her fen,
Those dark juices working   15
Him to a saint's kept body,

Trove of the turfcutters'
Honeycombed workings.
Now his stained face
Reposes at Aarhus.   20

II

I could risk blasphemy,
Consecrate the cauldron bog
Our holy ground and pray
Him to make germinate

The scattered, ambushed   25
Flesh of labourers,
Stockinged corpses
Laid out in the farmyards,

Aarhus: a city in Jutland, Denmark.

pods: dry seeds.

gruel: thin porridge.

girdle: belt.

torc: decorative metal collar.
fen: marsh or wet area.
kept: preserved.

Trove: valuable find.
Honeycombed workings: patterns made by the turfcutters on the peat.

blasphemy: irreverence.
Consecrate: declare sacred.
cauldron bog: basin-shaped bogland (some of which was associated with pagan rituals).
germinate: give new life to.

SEAMUS HEANEY

Tell-tale skin and teeth
Flecking the sleepers   30
Of four young brothers, trailed
For miles along the lines.

        III
Something of his sad freedom
As he rode the tumbril
Should come to me, driving,   35
Saying the names

Tollund, Grauballe, Nebelgard,
Watching the pointing hands
Of country people,
Not knowing their tongue.   40

Out there in Jutland
In the old man-killing parishes
I will feel lost,
Unhappy and at home.

sleepers: wooden beams underneath railway lines.
four young brothers: refers to an infamous atrocity in the 1920s when four Catholic brothers were killed by the police.

tumbril: two-wheeled cart used to carry a condemned person to execution.

Tollund, Grauballe, Nebelgard: places in Jutland.

'Something of his sad freedom'

👤 Personal Response

1. Comment on Heaney's tone in the first three stanzas of the poem.
2. Select one image from the poem that you find startling or disturbing and explain its effectiveness.
3. What is your understanding of the poem's final stanza? Refer closely to the text in your answer.

👁 Critical Literacy

Seamus Heaney was attracted to a book by P. V. Glob, *The Bog People*, which dealt with preserved Iron Age bodies of people who had been ritually killed. It offered him a particular frame of reference or set of symbols he could employ to engage with Ireland's historical conflict. The martyr image of the Tollund Man blended in the poet's mind with photographs of other atrocities, past and present, in the long rites of Irish political struggles. This sad, poignant poem comes from Heaney's third collection, *Wintering Out* (1972).

POETRY FOCUS

Part I opens quietly with the **promise of a pilgrimage**: 'Some day I will go to Aarhus'. The tone is expectant, determined. Yet there is also an element of detachment that is reinforced by the Danish place name, 'Aarhus'. Heaney's placid, almost reverential mood is matched by his economic use of language, dominated by simple monosyllables. The evocative description of the Tollund Man's 'peat-brown head' and 'The mild pods of his eye-lids' conveys a sense of gentleness.

Lines 5–11 focus on the dead man's final hours in a much more realistic way. Heaney suggests that the Tollund Man's own journey begins when 'they dug him out', destroyed and elevated at the same time. The poet's meticulous observations ('His last gruel of winter seeds/Caked in his stomach') emphasise the dead man's **innocent vulnerability**. In the aftermath of a ritualistic hanging, we see him abandoned: 'Naked except for/The cap, noose and girdle'. While the poet identifies himself closely with the victim and makes a respectful promise to 'stand a long time', the action itself is passive.

Heaney imagines the natural boglands as the body of a fertility goddess. The revelation that the sacrificial victim was 'Bridegroom to the goddess' (**line 12**) conveys a more **ominous, forceful tone** as the bleak bog itself is also equated with Ireland, female and overwhelming: 'She tightened her torc on him'. Sensuous and energetic images in **lines 13–16** suggest the physical intimacy of the couple's deadly embrace. The Tollund Man becomes 'a saint's kept body', almost a surrogate Christ, buried underground so that new life would spring up. He is left to chance, 'Trove of the turfcutters', and finally resurrected so that 'his stained face/Reposes at Aarhus'. The delicate blend of sibilance and broad vowel sounds suggest tranquillity and a final peace.

Part II suddenly becomes more emphatic and is filled with references to religion. Heaney addresses the spirit of the Tollund Man, invoking him 'to make germinate' (**line 24**) and give life back to the casualties of more recent violence in Northern Ireland. He acknowledges his own discomfort ('I could risk blasphemy') for suggesting that we should search for an alternative deity or religious symbol to unite people. But although it appears to be in contrast with the earlier violence, the poet's restrained style actually accentuates the horror of one infamous sectarian slaughter ('Of four young brothers'). The callous nature of their deaths – 'trailed/For miles along the lines' – is associated with the repulsive rituals in ancient Jutland. Heaney's **nightmarish images** ('Stockinged corpses') are powerful and create a surreal effect. However, the paradoxical 'survival' and repose of the Tollund Man should, the poet implies, give him the power to raise others.

Part III returns to the mellow beginning, but instead of anticipation, there is sorrow and a sense of isolation. Heaney hopes that the 'sad freedom' (**line 33**) of the Tollund Man 'Should come to me'. Along with religion and a sense of history and myth, evocative language is central to Heaney's poetry,

SEAMUS HEANEY

and here the idea of isolation is brought sharply to the reader through the sense of being 'lost' in a foreign land. Yet ultimately the puzzling nature of exile is realised: the poet feels at home in a state of homelessness, and welcomes the feeling of not belonging to society which he shares with the Tollund Man, who is no longer tied to religious forces. This estrangement from society is emphasised by the list of foreign names ('Tollund, Grauballe, Nebelgard'). **The poem ends on a note of pessimistic resignation** that describes both the familiar sense of isolation and hopelessness Heaney experiences: 'I will feel lost,/Unhappy and at home'.

Heaney's imaginary pilgrimage to Aarhus has led to a **kind of revelation**. By comparing modern Ulster to the 'old man-killing parishes' (line 42) of remote Jutland, the poet places the Northern Irish conflict in a timeless, mythological context. It is as though the only way Heaney can fully express the horrific scenes he has seen in Ireland is to associate them with the exhumed bodies of ancient bog corpses.

✒ Writing About the Poem

'Heaney often addresses the ugliness of human cruelty in subtle poems that are rich in imagery and language use.' Discuss this statement with reference to 'The Tollund Man'.

Sample Paragraph

Throughout 'The Tollund Man', Heaney reflects on the universal experience of human cruelty. He links the ritually murdered body of the Iron Age victim to the executions of 'four young brothers' in the Northern Ireland Troubles. A statement of quiet determination opens the poem, 'Some day I will go to Aarhus', its subtle monosyllables emphasising the poet's resolve. The vulnerability of the victim of Jutland's 'man-killing parishes' is shown in the gentle assonance of the vivid image, 'mild pods of his eye-lids'. The pathetic fate of the victims who were dragged 'miles along lines' is conveyed through the assonance of the letter 'i'. Harsh 't' sounds suggest the suffering of the young men, 'Tell-tale skin and teeth'. Through the meticulous observation of a detached observer, Heaney succeeds in engaging our sympathy for these victims.

> **EXAMINER'S COMMENT**
>
> *This is a first-rate response that shows a very close appreciation of both the poem's subject matter and style. Points are clear, succinct and successfully supported with accurate quotations. The two central elements of the question are addressed, with some particularly incisive commentary on subtle sound effects (e.g. 'subtle monosyllables' and 'gentle assonance'). Expression is also impressive ('the meticulous observation of a detached observer').*

✒ Class/Homework Exercises

1. 'Heaney explores the unpalatable truth of cyclical violence and complicit acceptance through a lyrical examination of the living past.' Discuss this view, supporting your answer with reference to 'The Tollund Man'.
2. 'There is a haunting dreamlike quality to Seamus Heaney's fascination with history and mythology.' Discuss this statement, supporting your answer with reference to 'The Tollund Man'.

⊚ Points to Consider

- Examination of cyclical human violence, vulnerable victims and foreignness.
- Varying tones – resolve, reverence, detachment, uncertainty, despair, empathy.
- Use of similarity and contrast – Tollund Man/four young brothers; colloquial sound patterns; individual human experience/universal experience.
- Lyrical and musical qualities; onomatopoeia, assonance, harsh cacophonous sounds.
- Short lines and fragmented rhythm convey the disturbing reality of death.
- List of foreign place names has intriguing, unsettling effect.

4 Mossbawn: Sunlight

SEAMUS HEANEY

for Mary Heaney

There was a sunlit absence.
The helmeted pump in the yard
heated its iron,
water honeyed

in the slung bucket   5
and the sun stood
like a griddle cooling
against the wall

of each long afternoon.
So, her hands scuffled   10
over the bakeboard,
the reddening stove

sent its plaque of heat
against her where she stood
in a floury apron   15
by the window.

Now she dusts the board
with a goose's wing,
now sits, broad-lapped,
with whitened nails   20

and measling shins:
here is a space
again, the scone rising
to the tick of two clocks.

And here is love   25
like a tinsmith's scoop
sunk past its gleam
in the meal-bin.

Title: Mossbawn was Heaney's birthplace. 'Bawn' refers to the name the English planters gave to their fortified farmhouses. 'Bán' is Gaelic for 'white'. Heaney wonders if the name could be 'white moss' and has commented, 'In the syllables of my home, I see a metaphor of the split culture of Ulster.'

Dedication: the poem is dedicated to the poet's aunt, Mary Heaney, who lived with the family throughout Heaney's childhood. He shared a special relationship with her, 'a woman with a huge well of affection and a very experienced, dry-eyed sense of the world'.

griddle: circular iron plate used for cooking food.

scuffled: moved quickly, making a scraping noise.

plaque: intensity.

measling: red spots on legs made by standing close to heat.

the tick of two clocks: the two time sequences in the poem, past and present.

tinsmith: person who made pots and pans from tin.

meal-bin: a container used to hold flour, etc.

POETRY FOCUS

'to the tick of two clocks'

👤 Personal Response

1. Describe the atmosphere in the poem 'Mossbawn: Sunlight', with particular reference to Heaney's treatment of time.
2. What image of Mary Heaney, the aunt, is drawn? Do you find the picture appealing or unappealing? Quote from the poem in support of your views.
3. Choose one image or phrase from the poem that you found particularly effective, and briefly explain why you found it so.

👁 Critical Literacy

'Sunlight' appeared in the collection *North* (1975) and was the first of two poems under the title 'Mossbawn', the name of Heaney's family home. To the poet, this farm was 'the first place', an idyllic Garden of Eden, full of sunlight and feminine grace, a contrast to the reality of the outside world. At this time, terrible atrocities were being committed in the sectarian struggle taking place in Northern Ireland.

This poem opens with a **vivid, atmospheric portrayal of the silent sunlit yard**, a beautiful, tranquil scene from Heaney's boyhood in the 1940s. The pump marked the centre of this private world, which was untroubled by the activities outside. For the impressionable Heaney growing up, the water pump was a symbol of purity and life. This guardian of domestic life is

described as 'helmeted', a sentry soldier on duty, ready to protect. (The American army had bases in Northern Ireland during the Second World War.) The phrase 'water honeyed' (line 4) emphasises this slender iron idol as an image of deep and hidden goodness, the centre of another world. The poet creates a nostalgic picture of a timeless zone of domestic ritual and human warmth. These were childhood days of golden innocence and security. The repetition of 'h' (in 'helmeted', 'heated' and 'honeyed') portrays the heating process as the reader exhales breath. The sun is described in the striking simile 'like a griddle cooling/against the wall'. This homely image of the iron dish evokes a view of a serene place.

Line 10 moves readers from the place to the person. 'So' introduces us to a **warm, tender portrait of Heaney's beloved Aunt Mary at work.** She is a symbol of the old secure way of life, when a sense of community was firm and traditional rural values were held in high esteem. We are shown the unspectacular routine of work; she 'dusts the board' for baking. We see her domestic skill, her hands 'scuffled' as she kneads the dough. Visual detail paints this picture as if it were a Dutch still life from the artist Vermeer: 'floury apron', 'whitened nails'. The simplicity of this special atmosphere is evident as Heaney acknowledges: 'here is love'. The people in this scene are not glamorous. Realistic details remind us of their ordinariness: 'broad-lapped', 'measling shins'.

The **closing simile** in lines 26–8, 'like a tinsmith's scoop/sunk past its gleam/in the meal-bin', **shows how the ordinary is transformed into the extraordinary** by the power of love. The two time zones of passing time and a timeless moment are held in the alliterative phrase 'the tick of two clocks'. We are invited to listen to the steady rhythm of the repetitive 't'. As the life-giving water lies unseen beneath the cold earth, the aunt's love is hidden, but constant, like the water in the pump. The radiant glow of love is hidden like buried light. The change of tenses at the word 'Now' brings the moment closer as the abstract becomes concrete, and the outside becomes inside. The short four-line stanzas run on, achieving their own energy in this still scene, which reaches its climax in the poignant final stanza.

Writing About the Poem

'Seamus Heaney often uses childhood memories to create sensuous poetry.' Discuss this statement with reference to 'Mossbawn: Sunlight'.

Sample Paragraph

Heaney re-creates his childhood experience through the details of his home life. In recalling his family's farm-yard, the 'helmeted pump' stands as if guarding this special place. Everything Heaney writes appeals to our senses. The steady rhythm, run-on lines and assonance ('slung bucket') create a still painting of a quiet landscape. The cinematic quality zooms to an interior shot of his aunt baking in the kitchen. The poet changes the tense from past to present ('There was', 'here is') while he re-creates the living memory of Mossbawn, which resonates to the sound of the 'tick of two clocks', then and now. Love, in the person of his aunt, fills this timeless place, conveyed in the beautiful simile of the final lines, like the 'tinsmith's scoop/sunk past its gleam/in the meal-bin'.

> **EXAMINER'S COMMENT**
>
> *Succinct top-grade standard that focuses on the effectiveness of Heaney's sensual language. Confidently written and aptly supported by quotations.*

Class/Homework Exercises

1. Seamus Heaney's Nobel Prize for Literature was awarded for 'lyrical beauty ... which brings out the miracles of the ordinary day and the living past'. Discuss this statement using reference to both the content and style of 'Mossbawn: Sunlight'.
2. 'Heaney presents readers with small domestic dramas that explore recurring themes of love and longing in his poems.' Discuss this view with particular reference to 'Mossbawn: Sunlight'.

Points to Consider

- **Recurring themes of love and yearning.**
- **Slow-moving rhythm complements poignant childhood memories.**
- **Evocative tones of fondness, longing and nostalgia.**
- **Exterior scene contrasted with gentle domestic activity within.**
- **Simple language; warm, homely images.**
- **Striking use of personification, simile and evocative sound effects.**

5 🔊 A Constable Calls

SEAMUS HEANEY

His bicycle stood at the window-sill,
The rubber cowl of a mud-splasher
Skirting the front mudguard,
Its fat black handlegrips

Heating in sunlight, the 'spud'   5
Of the dynamo gleaming and cocked back,
The pedal treads hanging relieved
Of the boot of the law.

His cap was upside down
On the floor, next his chair.   10
The line of its pressure ran like a bevel
In his slightly sweating hair.

He had unstrapped
The heavy ledger, and my father
Was making tillage returns   15
In acres, roods, and perches.

Arithmetic and fear.
I sat staring at the polished holster
With its buttoned flap, the braid cord
Looped into the revolver butt.   20

'Any other root crops?
Mangolds? Marrowstems? Anything like that?'
'No.' But was there not a line
Of turnips where the seed ran out

In the potato field? I assumed   25
Small guilts and sat
Imagining the black hole in the barracks.
He stood up, shifted the baton-case

Further round on his belt,
Closed the domesday book,   30
Fitted his cap back with two hands,
And looked at me as he said goodbye.

cowl: covering shaped like a hood.

'spud': potato-like shape.

the boot of the law: heavy footwear of policemen, suggesting power and oppression.

bevel: line on policeman's forehead made by his cap.

ledger: book containing records of farm accounts.
tillage returns: amount harvested from cultivated land.

braid: threads woven into a decorative band.

Mangolds: beets grown for animal feed.
Marrowstems: long, green vegetables.

black hole: small cell in the police station.

domesday book: a survey of all the land in England and its value, ordered by William the Conqueror, the 11th-century English king; also refers to Judgement Day, when all will be brought to account.

POETRY FOCUS

A shadow bobbed in the window.
He was snapping the carrier spring
Over the ledger. His boot pushed off
And the bicycle ticked, ticked, ticked.

35

bobbed: moved up and down.
carrier spring: spiral metal coil on the back of a bike used to secure a bag, etc.

'the boot of the law'

👤 Personal Response

1. How does the poet create an atmosphere of tension in this poem? Support your response with reference to the text.
2. What type of relationship do you think the young boy has with his father? Refer closely to the text in your response.
3. Critics disagree about the ending of the poem. Some find it 'false', others 'stunning'. How would you describe the ending? Give reasons for your response.

👁 Critical Literacy

'A Constable Calls' was written in 1975 and forms the second part of the poem sequence 'Singing School'. The Heaneys were a Catholic family. The constable would have been a member of the Royal Ulster Constabulary (RUC) and probably a Protestant. **This poem illustrates the underlying tensions between the two communities in Northern Ireland.** Heaney's 'country of community ... was a place of division'.

'A Constable Calls' is told from the **viewpoint of a young boy** caught up in the bubbling tensions in Northern Ireland. The conflict erupted into serious violence during the Troubles, usually dated from the late 1960s until the Good Friday Agreement of 1998. The poem explores fear and power from the perspective of the Nationalist community. Catholics did not trust the RUC. In the opening stanzas, crude strength, power and violence are all inherent in the cold, precise language used to describe the constable's bicycle. The 'handlegrips' suggest handcuffs, while the 'cocked back' dynamo hints at a gun ready to be fired, its trigger ready for action. It also signifies confidence and cockiness. The oppression of the local authorities is highlighted in the phrase 'the boot of the law'. Heaney personifies the bicycle, which he describes as being 'relieved' of the pressure of the weight of the constable. This poem was written during the civil rights protest marches, when Nationalists were sometimes treated very severely by the RUC. This is evoked in the assonance of the broad vowels in 'fat black' and the harsh-sounding repetition of 'ck' in the phrase 'cocked back'. Here are the observations of the child of a divided community. The character (and symbolic significance) of the constable is implicit in the description of his bicycle.

In stanzas three to five, Heaney gives us an explicit **description of the constable**. His uniform and equipment are all symbols of power, which the young boy notes in detail: 'the polished holster/With its buttoned flap, the braid cord/Looped into the revolver butt'. This is no friendly community police officer. The repetition of 'his' tells us that the possession of power belongs to him and what he represents. He is not a welcome visitor. His hat lies on the ground. He is not offered refreshment, although he is presumably

thirsty from his work. Even the one human detail ('slightly sweating hair') revolts us. Is he as tense as the Catholic family in this time of sectarian conflict? The print of his great authority is stamped on him like a 'bevel', but does his power weigh heavily on him?

The policeman's function was to oblige the boy's father to give an account of his farm crop returns. Their brief exchange underlines the **tension in this troubled community**. The interrogation by the constable consists of four questions: 'Any other root crops?/Mangolds? Marrowstems? Anything like that?' This is met by the father's short, clipped, monosyllabic reply: 'No'. The encounter is summed up succinctly in the line 'Arithmetic and fear'. In the seventh stanza, the young boy becomes alarmed as he realises that his father has omitted to account for 'a line/Of turnips'. He 'assumed/Small guilts'. His perceived Catholic inferiority is graphically shown in the reference to the 'domesday book', or 'ledger', belonging to the constable. The child imagines a day of reckoning, almost like Judgement Day, when God calls every individual to account for past sins. He fears the immediate punishment of 'the black hole in the barracks', the notorious police cell where offenders were held. This terror of being incarcerated by the law ran deep in the Catholic psyche throughout the Troubles.

In the end, the constable takes his leave (stanzas seven and eight), formally fitting 'his cap back with two hands'. We can empathise with the boy as he 'looked at me'. In the final stanza, the oppressive presence of the visitor ('A shadow') is wryly described as 'bobbed', an ironic reference to the friendly English bobby – which this particular constable was not. The verbs in this stanza continue the underlying ominous mood: 'snapping', 'pushed off'. The **poem concludes** with an intimidating reference to the sound of the departing bicycle as a slowly ticking time bomb: 'And the bicycle ticked, ticked, ticked'. Does this suggest that the tension in this divided community was always on the verge of exploding? Do you consider this an effective image or do you think the symbolism is too obvious?

✒ Writing About the Poem

'Seamus Heaney often presents compelling poetry using autobiographical experience.' Discuss this statement in relation to 'A Constable Calls'.

Sample Paragraph

In 'A Constable Calls', Heaney recalls a tense incident from his childhood during the 1950s. A local policeman calls to interview the boy's father about the taxes due on his farm crops. The focus is placed on the constable's bicycle which 'stood at the window-sill' and then zooms to a

SEAMUS HEANEY

close-up of the 'rubber cowl of a mud-splasher'. This vivid description suggests the repressive power felt by Nationalists. The metaphor, 'the boot of the law', reinforces this impression. Although he is not fully aware of the significance of the encounter, the youthful Heaney experiences a sense of the sectarian world around him. The menacing final line describing the spokes of the bicycle wheels as they 'ticked, ticked, ticked' predicts the terrible violence of bombs that will define Northern Ireland during the so-called Troubles of the 1970s and 80s.

EXAMINER'S COMMENT

A top-grade response, successfully describing the setting for this dramatic confrontation between the constable and Heaney's father. There is a clear explanation of the uneasy atmosphere in which the poet gains an early awareness of sectarian conflict. Supporting quotations are integrated effectively into the commentary and the expression is excellent. The impressive final sentence succinctly sums up the poem's narrative very well.

Class/Homework Exercises

1. 'The question of identity looms large in Seamus Heaney's precisely controlled poetry.' Discuss this statement with reference to 'A Constable Calls'.
2. 'Heaney frequently writes evocative poems that explore the harsh reality of ordinary life.' Discuss this view, referring both to the content and style of 'A Constable Calls'.

Points to Consider

- Key themes include conflict, repressive authority and the loss of innocence.
- Engaging use of first-person narrative and closely observed detail.
- Tension between divided community results in child's discomfort.
- Compelling psychological drama (threat, interrogation, lies, guilt, danger recedes).
- Dynamic cinematic movement (zooms, pans, slow motion, close-up).
- Short snappy lines juxtaposed with flowing lines and run-on quatrains.
- Ominous conclusion.

6 The Skunk

Up, black, striped and damasked like the chasuble
At a funeral mass, the skunk's tail
Paraded the skunk. Night after night
I expected her like a visitor.

The refrigerator whinnied into silence.   5
My desk light softened beyond the verandah.
Small oranges loomed in the orange tree.
I began to be tense as a voyeur.

After eleven years I was composing
Love-letters again, broaching the word 'wife'   10
Like a stored cask, as if its slender vowel
Had mutated into the night earth and air

Of California. The beautiful, useless
Tang of eucalyptus spelt your absence.
The aftermath of a mouthful of wine   15
Was like inhaling you off a cold pillow.

And there she was, the intent and glamorous,
Ordinary, mysterious skunk,
Mythologized, demythologized,
Snuffing the boards five feet beyond me.   20

It all came back to me last night, stirred
By the sootfall of your things at bedtime,
Your head-down, tail-up hunt in a bottom drawer
For the black plunge-line nightdress.

damasked: patterned; rich, heavy fabric.
chasuble: garment worn by a priest saying Mass.

whinnied: sound a horse makes.
verandah: roofed platform along the outside of a house.
voyeur: a person who watches others when they are being intimate.

broaching: raising a subject for discussion.
mutated: changed shape or form.

eucalyptus: tree with scented leaves commonly found in California.
aftermath: consequences of an unpleasant event.

Mythologized: related to or found in myth.

sootfall: soft sound (like soot falling from a chimney).
plunge-line: low-cut.

'the skunk's tail/ Paraded the skunk'

SEAMUS HEANEY

👤 Personal Response

1. In your opinion, how effective is Heaney in creating the particular sense of place in this poem? Refer closely to the text in your answer.
2. The poet compares his wife to a skunk. Does this image work, in your view? Quote from the poem in support of your response.
3. Comment on the poem's dramatic qualities. Refer to setting, characters, action and sense of tension/climax, particularly in the first and last stanzas.

👁 Critical Literacy

'The Skunk' comes from Heaney's 1979 collection, *Field Work*. **The poet called it a 'marriage poem'. While spending an academic year (1971–2) teaching in the USA, he had been reading the work of Robert Lowell, an American poet. Lowell's poem 'Skunk Hour' describes how isolation drives a man to become a voyeur of lovers in cars. Heaney's reaction to his own loneliness is very different; he rediscovers the art of writing love letters to his wife, who is living 6,000 miles away in Ireland. This separation culminated in an intimate, humorous, erotic love poem which speaks volumes for the deep love and trust between husband and wife.**

In the <mark>opening stanza</mark>, we are presented with four words describing the skunk's tail, 'Up, black, striped and damasked'. The punctuation separates the different aspects of the animal's tail for the reader's observation. An unusual simile occurs in <mark>line 1</mark>. In a **playfully irreverent tone**, Heaney likens the skunk's tail to the black and white vestments worn by a priest at a funeral. He then gives us an almost cartoon-like visual image of the animal's tail leading the skunk. The self-importance of the little animal is effectively captured in the verb 'Paraded'. All the ceremony of marching is evoked. The poet eagerly awaits his nightly visitor: 'Night after night/I expected her'. Skunks are small black-and-white striped American mammals, capable of spraying foul-smelling liquid on attackers.

In <mark>stanza two</mark>, the poet's senses are heightened. The verbs 'whinnied', 'softened' and 'loomed' vividly capture the **atmosphere of the soft, exotic California night**. The bright colours of orange and green are associated with the Golden State. The anticipation of stanza one now sharpens: 'I began to be tense'. He regards himself as a 'voyeur', but here there is no sense of violation. He is staring into darkness, getting ready to communicate with his wife. In <mark>stanza three</mark>, the poet, after a break of 11 years, is penning love letters again. In this separation period, he realises how much he misses her. His wife's presence, although she is absent, fills his consciousness. He is totally preoccupied with her. He uses the simile 'Like a stored cask' to show how he values her as something precious. The word 'wife' is savoured like fine wine and his affection is shown in his appreciation of 'its slender vowel',

POETRY FOCUS

which reminds him of her feminine grace. She is present to him in the air he breathes, 'mutated into the night earth and air/Of California'.

Heaney's depth of longing is captured in the **sensuous language** of stanza four. The smell of the eucalyptus 'spelt your absence'. The word 'Tang' precisely notes the penetrating sensation of loneliness. Even a drink of wine, 'a mouthful of wine', does not dull this ache. Instead it intensifies his desire, 'like inhaling you off a cold pillow'. Now, the skunk, long awaited, appears. It is full of contradictions: 'glamorous', 'Ordinary'. We hear in stanza five the sound the little animal makes in the onomatopoeic phrase 'Snuffing the boards'. Only in stanza six is the comparison between the wife and the skunk finally drawn: 'It all came back to me last night'. Heaney imagines himself back home. His wife is rummaging in the bottom drawer for a nightdress. She adopts a slightly comic pose, 'head-down, tail-up', reminding him of the skunk as she 'hunt[s]'. The sibilance of the line 'stirred/By the sootfall of your things' suggests the tender intimacy between the married couple. The word 'sootfall' conveys the gentle rustle of clothes falling. The reader's reaction is also 'stirred' to amused surprise as the realisation dawns that the adjectives 'intent and glamorous,/Ordinary, mysterious ... Mythologized, demythologized' also apply to his wife. A **mature, trusting relationship** exists between the couple.

Longer lines suggest ease. The poet is relaxed and playful, his language conversational and sensuous. All our senses are 'stirred'. The light is romantic ('softened') and the colour black is alluring. The touch of the 'cold pillow' will now be replaced by the warm shared bed. The sounds of California and the couple's bedroom echo: 'Snuffing', 'sootfall'. The 'aftermath of a mouthful of wine' lingers on the tongue. This is something of a rarity, a **successful love poem about marriage**, tender but not cosy, personal but not embarrassingly self-revealing.

Writing About the Poem

'Seamus Heaney makes use of a wide range of striking images to explore experiences of people, places and events.' Discuss this statement in relation to 'The Skunk'.

Sample Paragraph

Heaney writes about subjects that are sometimes tinged with loneliness and often filled with love, as in 'The Skunk'. Through the innovative image of the little nocturnal animal, whose tail paraded, 'Up, black, striped and damasked', he conveys the wonder of married love. It is both mundane and mysterious. The poet is separated from his wife and recalls her presence, 'inhaling you off a cold pillow'. Detailed images connect her to the skunk in the yard outside. He observes the animal's posture, 'head-down, tail-up' and the sultry atmosphere is suddenly replaced by the sensuous 'sootfall of your things'. The close intimacy of the couple is highlighted in the detail of the 'black plunge-line nightdress'. By linking people, places and events, Heaney presents a moment of insight about romantic love.

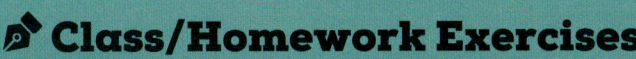
SEAMUS HEANEY

EXAMINER'S COMMENT

A close analysis of the poem, addressing the question with great confidence. Informed and focused discussion – particularly of how the poet uses sensual imagery. Expression is varied ('innovative', 'mundane and mysterious', 'close intimacy') and well controlled. Excellent use of reference and quotation throughout add to the quality of the discussion in this top-grade response.

✒ Class/Homework Exercises

1. 'Relationships, personal or otherwise, lie at the heart of Heaney's most accessible poems.' Discuss this view with reference to the poem, 'The Skunk'.
2. 'Throughout his lyrical poems, Seamus Heaney conjures up a sense of the universal, even when focusing on distinct personal experiences.' Discuss this statement with reference to both the content and style of 'The Skunk'.

⊙ Points to Consider

- Unusual, playful, intimate love poem.
- Range of tones – irreverent, reflective, wistful, emotive.
- Striking visual, aural, tactile imagery.
- Personification and onomatopoeia evoke atmosphere, people and places.
- Disconcerting juxtaposition of past/present, animal/person, loss/love, ordinary/mysterious.
- Contrasting line lengths (brief end-stopped lines, flowing run-on lines and stanzas) create urgency, tension and longing.

7 The Harvest Bow

As you plaited the harvest bow
You implicated the mellowed silence in you
In wheat that does not rust
But brightens as it tightens twist by twist
Into a knowable corona, 5
A throwaway love-knot of straw.

Hands that aged round ashplants and cane sticks
And lapped the spurs on a lifetime of gamecocks
Harked to their gift and worked with fine intent
Until your fingers moved somnambulant: 10
I tell and finger it like braille,
Gleaning the unsaid off the palpable,

And if I spy into its golden loops
I see us walk between the railway slopes
Into an evening of long grass and midges, 15
Blue smoke straight up, old beds and ploughs in hedges,
An auction notice on an outhouse wall –
You with a harvest bow in your lapel,

Me with the fishing rod, already homesick
For the big lift of these evenings, as your stick 20
Whacking the tips off weeds and bushes
Beats out of time, and beats, but flushes
Nothing: that original townland
Still tongue-tied in the straw tied by your hand.

The end of art is peace 25
Could be the motto of this frail device
That I have pinned up on our deal dresser –
Like a drawn snare
Slipped lately by the spirit of the corn
Yet burnished by its passage, and still warm. 30

Title: the harvest bow, an emblem of traditional rural crafts, was made from straw and often worn in the lapel to celebrate the end of harvesting. Sometimes it was given as a love-token or kept in the farmhouse until the next year's harvest.

implicated: intertwined; revealed indirectly.
mellowed: matured, placid.
corona: circle of light, halo.
lapped the spurs: tied the back claws of fighting birds.
gamecocks: male fowl reared to take part in cock-fighting.
Harked: listened, attuned.
somnambulant: automatically, as if sleepwalking.
braille: system of reading by touching raised dots.
Gleaning: gathering, grasping, understanding.
palpable: what can be handled or understood.
midges: small biting insects that usually swarm near water.
flushes: rouses, reveals.
The end of art is peace: art brings contentment (a quotation from the English poet Coventry Patmore, 1823–1896). It was also used by W. B. Yeats.
device: object, artefact.
deal: pine wood.
snare: trap.
burnished: shining.

'A throwaway love-knot of straw'

👤 Personal Response

1. Based on your reading of the poem, what impression do you get of Heaney's father? Refer to the text in your answer.
2. In your view, is the harvest bow a symbol of love? Give reasons for your answer, using reference to the poem.
3. What do you understand by the line 'The end of art is peace'? Briefly explain your answer.

👁 Critical Literacy

'The Harvest Bow' (from the 1972 collection *Field Work*) is a mournful poem in which Heaney pays tribute to his father and the work he did with his hands, weaving a traditional harvest emblem out of stalks of wheat. Remembering his boyhood, watching his father create the corn dolly, he already knew that the moment could not last. The recognition of his father's artistic talents leads the poet to a consideration of his own creative work.

The poem begins with a measured description of Heaney's father as he twists stalks of wheat into decorative love-knots. The delicate phrasing in stanza one ('You implicated the mellowed silence in you') reflects the poet's awareness of how the **harvest bow symbolised the intricate bond between father and son**. The poet conveys a subdued but satisfied mood as another farm year draws to a close. Autumnal images ('wheat that does not rust') add to the sense of accomplishment. Heaney highlights the practised techniques involved in creating this 'throwaway love-knot of straw'. The harvest bow 'brightens as it tightens twist by twist'. Emphatic alliteration and internal rhyme enliven the image, almost becoming a metaphor for the father's expertise. The bow is likened to 'a knowable corona', a reassuring circle of light representing the year's natural cycle.

In stanza two, the intricate beauty of the straw knot prompts Heaney to recall some of the other manual skills his father once demonstrated, 'round ashplants and cane sticks'. He acknowledges the older man's 'gift' of concentration and 'fine intent' as he fashioned the harvest bow ('your fingers moved somnambulant') **without conscious effort towards artistic achievement**. Is Heaney also suggesting that poets should work that way? Carefully handling the bow 'like braille', the poet clearly values it as an expression of undeclared love: 'Gleaning the unsaid off the palpable'.

The pleasurable sentiments of Heaney's childhood memories are realised by the strength of detailed imagery in stanza three: 'I see us walk between the railway slopes'. Such **ordinary scenes are enhanced by sensuous details** of 1940s rural life: 'Blue smoke straight up, old beds and ploughs in hedges'. Many of the sounds have a plaintive, musical quality ('loops', 'slopes', 'midges', 'hedges'). The poet seems haunted by his father's ghost, and the silence that once seemed to define their relationship is now recognised as a secret code of mutual understanding.

Stanza four focuses on the relentless passing of time. The **tone is particularly elegiac** as Heaney recalls his father 'Whacking the tips off weeds' with his stick. In retrospect, he seems to interpret such pointless actions as evidence of how every individual 'Beats out of time' – but to no avail. The poet extends this notion of time's mystery by suggesting that it is through art alone ('the straw tied by your hand') that 'tongue-tied' communities can explore life's wonder.

At the start of stanza five, Heaney tries to make sense of the corn dolly, now a treasured part of his own household 'on our deal dresser'. It mellows in its new setting and gives out heat. While 'the spirit of the corn' may have disappeared from the knot, the power of the poet's imagination can still recreate it there. So rather than being merely a nostalgic recollection of childhood, the poem takes on universal meaning in the intertwining of artistic forces. We are left with a deep sense of lost rural heritage, the unspoken joy of a shared relationship and the rich potential of the poet's art. For Heaney, **artistic achievements produce warm feelings of lasting contentment**. Whatever 'frail device' is created, be it a harvest bow or a formal elegy, '*The end of art is peace*'.

Writing About the Poem

'Heaney makes effective use of striking imagery to explore universal themes of love and loss.' Discuss this statement with reference to 'The Harvest Bow'.

Sample Paragraph

Heaney's poem, 'The Harvest Bow', is a powerful elegy for his father. Its imagery and sound effects describe the traditional straw bow which celebrates the end of the farming year. Remembering this 'frail device' allows Heaney to go back in time like a 'drawn snare', enabling him to re-experience treasured moments. Strong images, broad vowels and enjambment evoke the serene mood, 'I see us walk between the railway slopes'. Poignant memories of childhood are universal and symbolise family love. Heaney's father 'Beats out of time' with his stick, an image that lives forever in his memory. The phrase suggests the bond shared by father and son, but also hints at the sense of loss. For Heaney, the presence of his father lives again in the poet's heart, 'still warm'.

EXAMINER'S COMMENT

This is a sustained top-grade response that shows close engagement with the poem. All the elements of the question (imagery, love and loss, universal significance) are addressed. Relevant quotations – referring to a range of imagery patterns – are used to support discussion points. Expression is well controlled and the critical vocabulary is very impressive.

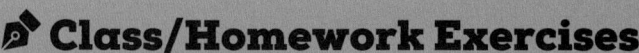

✒ Class/Homework Exercises

1. 'Seamus Heaney frequently uses detailed observation and a lyrical style to explore close family relationships.' Discuss this view with reference to 'The Harvest Bow'.
2. 'Heaney's carefully judged language enables readers to relate to recurring themes that are often grounded in the past.' Discuss this statement with reference to both the subject matter and style of 'The Harvest Bow'.

⊙ Points to Consider

- Elegy directly addresses the poet's father.
- Warm, emotional tone, consoling perfection of the past.
- Similarity drawn between intricate artistry of the bow maker and poet.
- Contrasting aspects of his father – tough, practical, silent, tender, skilled.
- Multiple word meanings, e.g. 'implicate' can mean 'show', 'entrap', or 'include'.
- Clever aural word-play imitates the complexity of the harvest bow.
- Concluding reassuring motto – art confronts every destructive life experience and creates order.

POETRY FOCUS

8 The Underground

There we were in the vaulted tunnel running,
You in your going-away coat speeding ahead
And me, me then like a fleet god gaining
Upon you before you turned to a reed

Or some new white flower japped with crimson   5
As the coat flapped wild and button after button
Sprang off and fell in a trail
Between the Underground and the Albert Hall.

Honeymooning, mooning around, late for the Proms,
Our echoes die in that corridor and now   10
I come as Hansel came on the moonlit stones
Retracing the path back, lifting the buttons

To end up in a draughty lamplit station
After the trains have gone, the wet track
Bared and tensed as I am, all attention   15
For your step following and damned if I look back.

vaulted: domed, arched.
going-away coat: new coat worn by the bride leaving on honeymoon.
fleet: fast; momentary.
reed: slender plant; part of a musical instrument.
japped: tinged, layered.
the Albert Hall: famous London landmark and concert venue.
the Proms: short for Promenade Concerts, a summer season of classical music.
Hansel: fairytale character who, along with his sister Gretel, retraced his way home using a trail of white pebbles.

'Our echoes die in that corridor'

Note: in Greek mythology, Eurydice, the beloved wife of Orpheus, was killed by a venomous snake. Orpheus travelled to the Underworld (Hades) to retrieve her. It was granted that Eurydice could return to the world of the living, but on condition that Orpheus should walk in front of her and not look back until he had reached the upper world. In his anxiety, he broke his promise, and Eurydice vanished again – but this time, for ever.

👤 Personal Response

1. Comment on the atmosphere created in the first two stanzas. Refer to the text in your answer.
2. From your reading of this poem, what do you learn about the relationship between the poet and his wife? Refer to the text in your answer.
3. Write a short personal response to 'The Underground', highlighting the impact it made on you.

👁 Critical Literacy

'The Underground' is the first poem in *Station Island* (1984). It recounts a memory from Heaney's honeymoon when he and his wife (like a modern Orpheus and Eurydice) were rushing through a London Underground Tube station on their way to a BBC Promenade Concert in the Albert Hall. In Dennis O'Driscoll's book *Stepping Stones*, Heaney said, 'In this version of the story, Eurydice and much else gets saved by the sheer cussedness of the poet up ahead just keeping going.'

The poem's title is filled with a sense of threat. Underground journeys are shadowed with a certain menace. Not only is there a mythical association with crossing into the land of the dead, but there is also the actuality of accidents and terrorist outrages. The first stanza of Heaney's personal narrative uses everyday colloquial speech ('There we were in the vaulted tunnel running') to introduce his **dramatic account**. The oppressively 'vaulted' setting and urgent verbs ('speeding', 'gaining') increase this sense of disquiet. For the poet, it is a psychic and mythic underground where he imagines his own heroic quest ('like a fleet god'). What he seems to dread most is the possibility of change and that, like a latter-day Orpheus, he might somehow lose his soulmate.

Cinematic images and run-on lines propel the second stanza forward. This **fast-paced rhythm is in keeping with the restless diction** – 'the coat flapped wild'. The poet's wife is wearing her going-away wedding coat and in the course of her sprint, the buttons start popping off. Internal rhyme adds to the tension; 'japped' and 'flapped' play into each other, giving the impression that whatever is occurring is happening with great intensity.

The poem changes at the beginning of the third stanza and this is evident in the language, which is much more playful, reflecting Heaney's assessment of the occasion in hindsight. He now recognises the youthful insecurity of the time: 'Honeymooning, mooning around'. The reference to the fictional Hansel and Gretel hints at the immaturity of their relationship as newlyweds and emphasises the couple's initial unease. But recalling how he carefully gathered up the buttons, like Hansel returning from the wilderness, **Heaney appears to have now come to terms with his uneasy past**: 'Our echoes die in that corridor'.

This new-found confidence underscores the poet's recollections in the fourth stanza. The action and speed have now ceased. After the uncertainty of the 'draughty lamplit station', he has learned to trust his wife and his own destiny. Unlike Orpheus, the tragic Greek hero, Heaney has emerged from his personal descent into Hades, 'Bared and tense'. Although **he can never forget the desolation of being threatened with loss**, the poet has been well served by the experience, having realised that it will always be him – and not his wife – who will be damned if he dares to look back.

The ending of the poem is characteristically compelling. Commenting on it in *Stepping Stones*, Heaney said, 'But in the end, the "damned if I look back" line takes us well beyond the honeymoon.' Although some critics feel that the final outlook is more regretful, it is difficult to miss the sheer determination that is present in the poem's last line. The **poet's stubborn tone leaves us with overwhelming evidence of his enduring devotion to love**, an emotional commitment which seems to be even more precious with the passing of time.

Writing About the Poem

'Heaney's poetry operates successfully across several levels, dramatically observing and quietly reflecting.' Discuss this statement with reference to 'The Underground'.

Sample Paragraph

'The Underground' is another of Heaney's autobiographical poems in which he gives a dramatic account of a frantic dash by his wife and himself through London's Underground train station. What is interesting is how he interweaves past and present into reality and nightmare throughout the poem. Heaney's observations lead to deep reflection. The poet introduces the Orpheus and Eurydice tale of tragic loss in the Underworld. Suddenly, the personal has become universal. Another cinematic detail – the falling buttons – is associated with the 'moonlit stones' from the fairytale of Hansel and Gretel. Heaney, like Hansel, goes back, 'retracing the path', to find a way forward. The poem's final phrase, 'damned if I look back', also works on two levels. Heaney is determined to put effort into the couple's relationship. The alternative is loss of love – a kind of damnation that he fears.

EXAMINER'S COMMENT

An intelligent top-grade response that addresses both elements of this challenging question. Some focused commentary on dramatic aspects ('frantic dash', 'reality and nightmare', 'cinematic detail'). Apt quotations are successfully integrated into the discussion. Assured vocabulary ('interweaves', 'alternative') is also impressive.

✒ Class/Homework Exercises

1. 'Heaney frequently invokes a vivid range of memories and mythological echoes to reveal intense feelings in his poetry.' Discuss this view with reference to 'The Underground'.
2. 'Heaney's love poems celebrate his subjects warmly, yet realistically, through the use of precise visual imagery and aural detail.' Discuss this statement with reference to both the subject matter and style of 'The Underground'.

⊙ Points to Consider

- Nostalgic love poem of a specific event infused with Greek myth and fairy story.
- Personal narrative using colloquial speech and engaging imagery.
- Dramatic atmosphere, pacy rhythm, dynamic verbs, run-on lines.
- Aural music of internal rhyme and assonance.
- Fear of loss contrasted with the poet's determined commitment to his wife.

9 Postscript

And some time make the time to drive out west
Into County Clare, along the Flaggy Shore,
In September or October, when the wind
And the light are working off each other
So that the ocean on one side is wild   5
With foam and glitter, and inland among stones
The surface of a slate-grey lake is lit
By the earthed lightning of a flock of swans,
Their feathers roughed and ruffling, white on white,
Their fully grown headstrong-looking heads   10
Tucked or cresting or busy underwater.
Useless to think you'll park and capture it
More thoroughly. You are neither here nor there,
A hurry through which known and strange things pass
As big soft buffetings come at the car sideways   15
And catch the heart off guard and blow it open.

the Flaggy Shore: stretch of coastal limestone slabs in the Burren, Co. Clare.

working off: playing against.

cresting: stretching, posing.

buffetings: vibrations, shudderings.

👤 Personal Response

1. Choose one image from the poem that you find particularly effective. Briefly explain your choice.
2. What is your understanding of the poem's final line?
3. In your opinion, is the advice given by Heaney in 'Postscript' relevant to our modern world? Give reasons to support your response.

👁 Critical Literacy

This beautiful pastoral lyric comes at the end of Seamus Heaney's 1996 collection, *The Spirit Level*. The title suggests an afterthought, something that was missed out earlier. As so often in his poetry, Heaney succeeds in conveying the extraordinary by way of an everyday experience – in this case, the vivid memory of a journey westwards. The poem resonates with readers, particularly those who have also shared moments when life caught them by surprise.

Line 1 is relaxed and conversational. The poet invites others (or promises himself, perhaps) to 'make the time to drive out west'. The phrase 'out west' has associations both of adventurous opportunity and dismal failure. By placing 'And' at the start of the poem, Heaney indicates a link with something earlier, some unfinished business. **Keen to ensure that the journey will be worthwhile**, he recommends a definite destination ('the Flaggy Shore') and time ('September or October').

'along the Flaggy Shore'

SEAMUS HEANEY

The untamed beauty of the Co. Clare coastline is described in some detail: 'when the wind/And the light are working off each other' (lines 3–4). The phrase 'working off' is especially striking in conveying the **tension and balance between two of nature's greatest complementary forces: wind and light**. Together, they create an effect that neither could produce singly.

Close awareness of place is a familiar feature of the poet's writing, but in this instance he includes another dimension – the notion of in-betweeness. The road Heaney describes runs between the ocean and an inland lake. Carefully chosen images **contrast** the unruly beauty of the open sea's 'foam and glitter' with the still 'slate-grey lake' (line 7). In both descriptions, the sounds of the words echo their sense precisely.

The introduction of the swans in line 8 brings unexpected drama. Heaney captures their seemingly effortless movement between air and water. The poet's **vigorous skill with language** can be seen in his appreciation of the swans' transforming presence, which he highlights in the extraordinary image of 'earthed lightning'. His expertly crafted sketches are both tactile ('feathers roughed and ruffling') and visual ('white on white'). Tossed by the wind, their neck feathers resemble ruffled collars. To Heaney, these exquisite birds signify an otherworldly force that is rarely earthed or restrained. In response, he is momentarily absorbed by the swans' purposeful gestures and powerful flight.

In line 12, the poet cautiously accepts that such elemental beauty can never be fully grasped: 'Useless to think you'll park and capture it'. Because we are 'neither here nor there', we can only occasionally glimpse 'known and strange things'. Despite this, the poem concludes on a redemptive note, acknowledging those special times when we edge close to the miraculous. These **experiences transcend our mundane lives** and we are shaken by revelation, just as unexpected gusts of winds ('soft buffetings') can rock a car.

Heaney's journey has been both **physical and mystical**. It is brought to a climax in line 16, where it ends in the articulation of an important truth. He has found meaning between the tangible and intangible. The startling possibility of discovering the ephemeral quality of spiritual awareness is unnerving enough to 'catch the heart off guard and blow it open'. The seemingly contradictory elements of comfort and danger add to the intensity of this final image. Heaney has spoken about the illumination he felt during his visit to the Flaggy Shore as a 'glorious exultation of air and sea and swans'. For him, the experience was obviously inspirational, and the poem that it produced might well provide a similar opportunity for readers to experience life beyond the ordinary material world.

Writing About the Poem

'Heaney's work often addresses the wonder of poetic inspiration through the use of carefully chosen images.' Discuss this statement in relation to 'Postscript'.

Sample Paragraph

'Postscript' starts with a casual invitation, 'And some time make the time', building to a crescendo and concluding with a highly charged insight. The poem evokes the creative process of poetry, the ability of language to transport a person to a magical place ('when the wind/And the light are working off each other'). He focuses on nuances of colour ('white on white') and texture ('roughed and ruffling') to capture the enchanting moment. The swans are also carefully noted – their arrogance ('headstrong-looking') and their paddling feet ('busy underwater'). Quietly, the poet cautions readers to appreciate this moment, 'Useless to think you'll park and capture it'. The final explosive line is filled with the emotion of being truly alive. The wind, like the poem itself, triggers uncontrollable emotion.

EXAMINER'S COMMENT

An insightful response to the question. Informed discussion points focused throughout on the theme of the creative process and Heaney's use of language. Good choice of accurate quotations integrated effectively into the commentary. Expression is impressive also: varied sentence length, wide-ranging vocabulary ('crescendo', 'nuances', 'triggers uncontrollable emotion') and good control of syntax. A top-grade standard.

Class/Homework Exercises

1. 'Seamus Heaney's poems are capable of capturing moments of insight in a strikingly memorable fashion.' Discuss this statement with reference to 'Postscript'.
2. 'Heaney evokes the beauty and mystery of Ireland's natural landscape through the precision of his language.' Discuss this view with reference to both the subject matter and style of 'Postscript'.

Points to Consider

- Conversational description of a car drive 'out west' into Co. Clare.
- The poem pays tribute to the sheer power of perception.
- Resonance of memory, contrasting joy at visual experience with sadness at realisation of its transience.
- Vivid visual imagery and subtle sound effects used to convey the scene.
- Cautious, reflective tone contrasts with exhilarating description.

10 A Call

SEAMUS HEANEY

'Hold on,' she said, 'I'll just run out and get him.
The weather here's so good, he took the chance
To do a bit of weeding.'
                      So I saw him
Down on his hands and knees beside the leek rig,   5
Touching, inspecting, separating one
Stalk from the other, gently pulling up
Everything not tapered, frail and leafless,
Pleased to feel each little weed-root break,
But rueful also ...   10
                  Then found myself listening to
The amplified grave ticking of hall clocks
Where the phone lay unattended in a calm
Of mirror glass and sunstruck pendulums ...

And found myself then thinking: if it were nowadays,   15
This is how Death would summon Everyman.

Next thing he spoke and I nearly said I loved him.

tapered: slender; reducing in thickness towards the end.
frail: weak.
rueful: expressing regret.
amplified: increased the strength of the sound.
pendulums: weights that hang from a fixed point and swing freely, used to regulate the mechanism of a clock.
Everyman: character in 15th-century morality plays.

'Pleased to feel each little weed-root break'

POETRY FOCUS

👤 Personal Response

1. How does Heaney dramatise this event? Refer to setting, mood, dialogue, action and climax in your response.
2. Describe the mood of 'A Call'. Does it change during the course of the poem? Support your answer with suitable quotations.
3. One literary critic said that the 'celebration of people and relationships in Heaney's poetry is characterised by honesty and tenderness'. To what extent do you agree or disagree with this view? Refer to the text in your response.

👁 Critical Literacy

'A Call' comes from Heaney's collection *The Spirit Level* (1996) and deals with two of the poet's recurring themes: the father–son relationship and the passing of time. The setting is a routine domestic scene of a mother talking, a father weeding, a son calling. *The Spirit Level* refers to balance, getting the level right, measuring. It also suggests poetry, which is on another plane, free-floating above the confines of the earth. Heaney spoke about this in his Nobel Prize speech, saying 'I am permitting myself the luxury of walking on air'.

This personal narrative opens with a conversational directness, as Heaney is told to 'Hold on'. Heaney has phoned his parents' home and his mother is responding to her son's request to speak with his father. When she puts the receiver down (these were the days of the land line), the poet has time to imagine the old man at work in his garden: 'The weather here's so good, he took the chance/To do a bit of weeding'. The rhythm of colloquial dialogue is realistically caught by the use of everyday expressions and a **simple scene of domesticity is established**. In line 4, the poet becomes the engrossed spectator on the fringes of the scene: 'So I saw him'. The detail of 'Down on his hands and knees beside the leek rig' invites the reader to observe for themselves.

Fragmented description shows the care and skill of the gardener's activity, 'Touching, inspecting, separating', as the father tends his vegetable patch. All farming tradition is associated with decay and growth, and the weakest is usually discarded, 'gently pulling up/Everything not tapered'. The onomatopoeia of the word 'break', with its sharp 'k' sound, suggests the snap of the root as it is pulled from the soil. The father takes pleasure ('Pleased to feel') in his work ('each little weed-root break') but he is, perhaps, regretful too ('rueful') that a form of life is ending, snapped from the nurturing earth.

In line 11, the **visual imagery is replaced by aural effects**. The mood in the deserted hallway indicates a significant change in the tone of the poem. Sounds are 'amplified' due to the subdued atmosphere of the location and Heaney's long wait to hear his father's voice. Time is passing, not just for the

206

SEAMUS HEANEY

weeds but also for the man, measured by the 'grave ticking of hall clocks'. Here the poem begins to move between earthbound reality and airiness. The image of ticking clocks in a sea ('calm') of 'mirror glass and sunstruck pendulums' is almost surreal. Broad vowel sounds create an air of serenity and otherworldliness. The word 'amplified' vividly conveys the echo of the clocks and we can imagine their loud ticking as the sound increases in intensity. The inclusion of the word 'grave' is an obvious reminder that death is edging closer – and not just for the poet's father.

In line 15, Heaney moves from observation to meditation, walking on air, 'And found myself then thinking'. Death is depicted as a personal communication, like a phone call from a loved one. The poet is pushing at the boundaries of what is real. His father, like the weeds, will be uprooted, spirited away to some afterlife. Here Heaney is 'seeing things'; he is mediating between states of awareness. **A keen sense of mortality informs the poem**. The last line stands apart, as Heaney is jolted out of his daydreaming: 'Next thing he spoke'. Family love is an important theme throughout Heaney's poetry. In this case, he considers the deep-rooted closeness of the father–son relationship and we witness the frustrating attempts at communication between them, 'and I nearly said I loved him'. Was it an awareness of his father's mortality which prompted this reaction from the poet? The careful phrasing, relaxed and casual, reflects the powerful love between these silent men and the heart-breaking tension of the impossibility of articulating their feelings. In the poem's poignant conclusion ('Next thing he spoke and I nearly said I loved him'), father and son are both united and separated at the same time.

The title of this poem is intriguing. Apart from referring to a telephone call, it also signals the final summons that 'Everyman' will receive from Death. While the dominant tone of 'A Call' celebrates the poet's father and his regard for nature, there is an underlying elegiac quality that reveals Heaney's deep awareness of mortality and loss.

> ## ✒ Writing About the Poem
> 'Seamus Heaney's poetry engages the reader through his use of striking imagery and thought-provoking themes.' Discuss this statement with reference to 'A Call'.

Sample Paragraph

'A Call', engages readers from the closely observed domestic scene to the dreamlike imagery depicting tender emotion, 'I nearly said I loved him'. We imagine the father working quietly in his garden through a carefully punctuated list of verbs, 'Touching, inspecting, separating'. Heaney also depicts a surreal scene of passing time through the broad vowels of the 'sunstruck pendulums'. His dark humour continues through the image of Death using the telephone to call human beings to the next world. The tender scene gives way to reflections on transience. As often in Heaney's poems, he celebrates life while accepting the reality of death. Through his vivid images, he teaches his readers about the significance of ordinary experiences.

> **EXAMINER'S COMMENT**
>
> An insightful, well-informed response. Engagement with both Heaney's imagery and themes is evident throughout. Perceptive discussion of the poet's recognition of life and death is well supported by apt, accurate quotations. Expression is excellent ('carefully punctuated', 'reflections on transience'). A confident top-grade answer that shows close interaction with the poem.

Class/Homework Exercises

1. 'Seamus Heaney's reflective poetry often reveals moments of sensitivity that can enrich our experience of life.' Discuss this statement with reference to 'A Call'.
2. 'Heaney's lyrical poems go beyond description to disclose rich insights into universal themes.' Discuss this view with reference to both the subject matter and style of 'A Call'.

Points to Consider

- Autobiographical poem expands into profound meditation.
- Colloquial, direct speech is engaging.
- Effective use of carefully observed visual detail.
- Assonance, internal rhyme and alliteration heighten the musicality of the poem.
- Personification adds an ominous note.
- Unusual line breaks highlight the poem's focus on transience.
- Final line poignantly evokes both the communication and the lack of communication between father and son.

11 Tate's Avenue

SEAMUS HEANEY

Not the brown and fawn car rug, that first one
Spread on sand by the sea but breathing land-breaths,
Its vestal folds unfolded, its comfort zone
Edged with a fringe of sepia-coloured wool tails.

Not the one scraggy with crusts and eggshells 5
And olive stones and cheese and salami rinds
Laid out by the torrents of the Guadalquivir
Where we got drunk before the corrida.

Instead, again, it's locked-park Sunday Belfast,
A walled back yard, the dust-bins high and silent 10
As a page is turned, a finger twirls warm hair
And nothing gives on the rug or the ground beneath it.

I lay at my length and felt the lumpy earth,
Keen-sensed more than ever through discomfort,
But never shifted off the plaid square once. 15
When we moved I had your measure and you had mine.

Title: Tate's Avenue is located in South Belfast, a popular student area. Heaney's girlfriend (later his wife) lived there in the late 1960s.

vestal: innocent, untouched (Heaney is comparing the crumpled rug to the modest dresses of vestal virgins in ancient Rome).
sepia-coloured: faded brownish colour; old looking.

Guadalquivir: river in Andalusia, Spain.
corrida: bullfight.

locked-park: Belfast's public parks were closed on Sundays in the 1960s.

plaid: checked, tartan.

'As a page is turned, a finger twirls warm hair'

POETRY FOCUS

👤 Personal Response

1. Comment on the poet's use of sound effects in the first two stanzas.
2. 'I had your measure and you had mine.' Briefly explain what you think Heaney means by this statement.
3. Write your own personal response to the poem.

👁 Critical Literacy

'Tate's Avenue' (from the 2006 collection *District and Circle*) is another celebration of Heaney's love for Marie Devlin. They married in 1965 and lived just off Tate's Avenue in South Belfast during the late 1960s. Here, the poet reviews their relationship by linking three separate occasions involving a collection of car rugs spread on the ground by the couple over the years.

Stanza one invites us to eavesdrop on a seemingly ordinary scene of everyday domesticity. It appears that the poet and his wife have been reminiscing – presumably about their love life over the years. Although the negative opening tone is emphatic ('Not the brown and fawn car rug'), we are left guessing about the exact nature of the couple's discussion. A few tantalising details are given about 'that first' rug, connecting it with an early seaside visit. Heaney can still recall the tension of a time when the couple **were caught between their own desire and strong social restrictions**. He describes the rug in terms of its texture and colours: 'Its vestal folds unfolded' (suggesting their youthful sexuality) contrasting with the 'sepia-coloured wool tails' (symbolising caution and old-fashioned inhibitions). As usual, Heaney's tone is edged with irony as he recalls the 'comfort zone' between himself and Marie.

The repetition of 'Not' at the start of stanza two clearly indicates that the second rug is also rejected, even though it can be traced back to a more exotic Spanish holiday location. Sharp onomatopoeic effects ('scraggy with crusts and eggshells') and the list of Mediterranean foods ('olive stones and cheese and salami rinds') convey **a sense of freedom and indulgence**. Although the couple's hedonistic life is communicated in obviously excessive terms ('Laid out by the torrents of the Guadalquivir'), Heaney's tone is somewhat dismissive. Is he suggesting that their relationship was mostly sensual back then?

'Instead' – the first word in stanza three – signals a turning point in the poet's thinking. Back in his familiar home surroundings, he recalls the rug that mattered most and should answer whatever doubts he had about the past. He has measured the development of their relationship in stages associated with special moments he and Marie shared. The line 'it's locked-park Sunday Belfast' conjures up memories of their early married life in the Tate's Avenue district. The sectarian 1960s was marked by dour

Protestant domination, a time when weekend pleasures were frowned upon and even the public parks were closed. Despite such routine repression and the unromantic setting ('A walled back yard, the dust-bins high and silent'), **the atmosphere is sexually charged.**

Heaney is aware of the scene's **underlying drama**; the seconds tick by 'As a page is turned, a finger twirls warm hair'. The unfaltering nature of the couple's intimacy is evident in the resounding declaration: 'nothing gives on the rug or the ground beneath it'.

This notion of confidence in their relationship is carried through into stanza four and accentuated by the alliterative 'I lay at my length and felt the lumpy earth'. The resolute rhythm is strengthened by the robust adjectival phrase 'Keen-sensed' and the insistent statement: 'But never shifted off the plaid square once'. Heaney builds to a discreet and understated climax in the finely balanced last line: 'When we moved I had your measure and you had mine'. While there are erotic undertones throughout, the poet presents us with restrained realism in place of excessive sensuality. 'Tate's Avenue' is a **beautiful, unembarrassed poem of romantic and sexual love within a committed relationship**. Characteristically, when Heaney touches on personal relationships, he produces the most tender and passionate emotions.

✒ Writing About the Poem

'Seamus Heaney's poetry frequently explores intense relationships in a style that is fresh and innovative.' Discuss this statement with reference to 'Tate's Avenue'.

Sample Paragraph

'Tate's Avenue' is one of Heaney's most romantic poems. The poet traces his relationship with his wife through recalling three rugs that mark stages in their lives together. The breathless nature of courtship is revealed in the colour ('sepia-coloured', reminiscent of an old photo) and texture ('vestal folds unfolded') of the first rug. Yet the strong physical attraction is revealed through sibilance and personification, 'Spread on sand by the sea but breathing land-breaths'. An emphatic 'Not' adds to the drama as the first two rugs are rejected. 'Instead' signals the decision to choose a 'plaid square' to truly sum up their feelings. The poem concludes in a sense of unity between the lovers, 'I had your measure and you had mine'. Overall, restrained, sensuous tension is presented in this lively study of intimacy.

EXAMINER'S COMMENT

An excellent top-grade response that shows a very good understanding of this unusual love poem. Detailed examination of language use (dramatic settings, contrasting atmospheres, energetic imagery and aural effects) is supported by apt and accurate quotations. Expression is also skilfully controlled and the paragraph is well rounded off in the concise final sentence.

Class/Homework Exercises

1. 'Heaney's poetry realistically depicts people and places through carefully chosen language and imagery.' Discuss this view with reference to 'Tate's Avenue'.
2. 'Seamus Heaney's poems are often filled with vivid sensuousness and evocative description.' Discuss this statement with reference to 'Tate's Avenue'.

Points to Consider

- Tender, compelling poem celebrates love in a committed relationship.
- Precise, vibrant details illustrate the various scenes.
- The headlong rush of young love is conveyed in the enjambment of the second quatrain.
- In contrast, the more measured pace of mature love is found in the final stanza.
- Compound words, onomatopoeia, alliteration and assonance create a rich aural texture.
- Compact four-quatrain structure adds to the understated quality of the poem.

12 The Pitchfork

SEAMUS HEANEY

Of all implements, the pitchfork was the one
    That came near to an imagined perfection:
    When he tightened his raised hand and aimed with it,
    It felt like a javelin, accurate and light.

So whether he played the warrior or the athlete   5
    Or worked in earnest in the chaff and sweat,
    He loved its grain of tapering, dark-flecked ash
    Grown satiny from its own natural polish.

Riveted steel, turned timber, burnish, grain,
    Smoothness, straightness, roundness, length and sheen.   10
    Sweat-cured, sharpened, balanced, tested, fitted.
    The springiness, the clip and dart of it.

And then when he thought of probes that reached the farthest,
    He would see the shaft of a pitchfork sailing past
    Evenly, imperturbably through space,   15
    Its prongs starlit and absolutely soundless –

But has learned at last to follow that simple lead
    Past its own aim, out to an other side
    Where perfection – or nearness to it – is imagined
    Not in the aiming but the opening hand.   20

javelin: long spear thrown in a competitive sport; also used as a weapon.

chaff: husks of grain separated from the seed.
grain: wheat.
tapering: reducing in thickness towards one end.

Riveted: fastened.
burnish: the shine on a polished surface.

clip: clasp; smack (colloquial).
dart: follow-on movement; small pointed missile thrown as a weapon.
probes: unmanned, exploratory spacecraft; a small measuring or testing device.
imperturbably: calmly, smoothly; unable to be upset.
prongs: two or more projecting points on a fork.

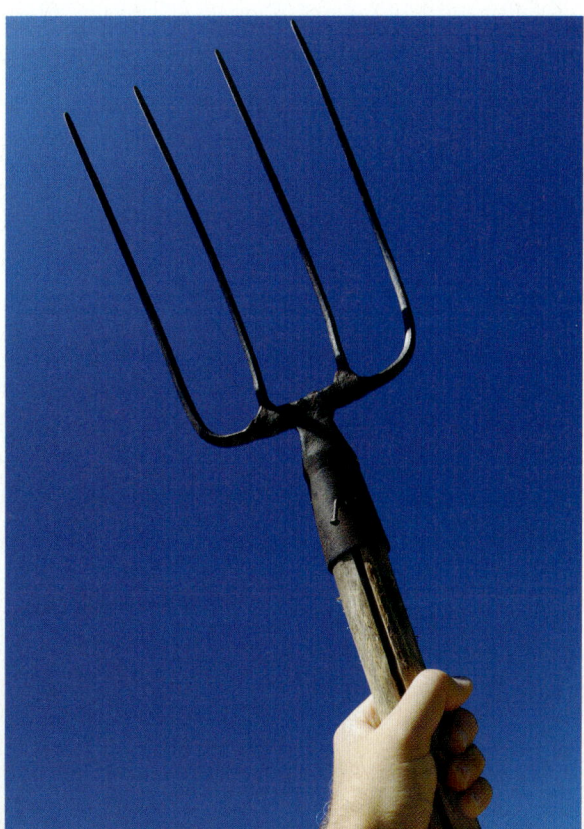

'When he tightened his raised hand and aimed with it'

POETRY FOCUS

👤 Personal Response

1. What is the tone of this poem? Does it change or not? Refer closely to the text in your response.
2. Select one image (or one line) that you find particularly interesting. Briefly explain your choice.
3. What do you think about the ending of this poem? Do you consider it visionary or far-fetched? Give reasons for your answer.

👁 Critical Literacy

'The Pitchfork' was published in Heaney's 1991 collection, *Seeing Things*. These poems turn to the earlier concerns of the poet. Craft and natural skill, the ability to make art out of work, is seen in many of his poems, such as 'The Forge'. Heaney is going back, making 'a journey back into the heartland of the ordinary'. The poet is now both observer and visionary.

In stanza one, Heaney describes a pitchfork, an ordinary farming 'implement'. Through **looking at an ordinary object with intense concentration**, the result is a fresh 'seeing', where the ordinary and mundane become marvellous, 'imagined perfection'. For Heaney, the creative impulse was held in the hand, in the skill of the labourer ('tightened his raised hand and aimed with it'). This skill is similar to the skill of the poet. They both practise and refine their particular ability. The pitchfork is now transformed into a piece of sporting equipment, 'a javelin'. The heaviness of physical work falls away as it becomes 'accurate and light' due to the practised capability of the worker. This is similar to the lightness of being and the **freeing of the poet's spirit** that Heaney allows himself to experience in this collection of poetry.

The worker is described as sometimes playing 'the warrior or the athlete' (stanza two). **Both professions command respect** and both occupations require courage and skill. But the worker's work is also described realistically, 'worked in earnest in the chaff and sweat'. This is heavy manual labour, and Heaney does not shirk from its unpleasant side. However, the worker is not ground down by it because he 'loved' the beauty of the pitchfork. Here we see both the poet and the worker dazzled, as the intent observation of the humble pitchfork unleashes its beauty, its slender 'dark-flecked ash'. The shine of the handle is conveyed in the word 'satiny'. Such tactile language allows the reader to feel the smooth, polished wooden handle. Now three pairs of eyes (the worker's, the poet's and our own) observe the pitchfork.

Close scrutiny of the pitchfork in stanza three continues with a virtuoso display of description, as **each detail is lovingly depicted**, almost like a slow sequence of close-ups in a film. The meeting of the handle and fork is caught

SEAMUS HEANEY

in the phrase 'Riveted steel'. The beauty of the wood is evoked in the alliteration of 'turned timber'. The marvellous qualities of the wood are itemised with growing wonder: its shine ('burnish'), its pattern ('grain'). It is as if the worker and the poet are twirling the pitchfork round as they exclaim over its 'Smoothness, straightness, roundness, length and sheen'. This is more like the description one would give to a work of art or a thoroughbred animal than to a farm implement. The skill that went into the making of the pitchfork is now explored in a list of verbs beginning with the compound word 'Sweat-cured'. This **graphically shows the sheer physical exertion that went into making this instrument**, as it was 'sharpened, balanced, tested, fitted'. The tactile quality of the pitchfork is praised: 'The springiness, the clip and dart of it'. The worker, just like the athlete or warrior, tests his equipment.

In stanza four, the labourer imagines space 'probes' searching the galaxy, 'reached the farthest'. **The long line stretches out in imitation of space**, which pushes out to infinity. The pitchfork now becomes transformed into a spaceship, 'sailing past/Evenly, imperturbably through space'. This ordinary pitchfork now shines like the metal casing of a spaceship, 'starlit', and moves, like the spacecraft, through the vastness of outer space, 'absolutely soundless'.

Stanza five shows the poet becoming a mediator between different states, actual and imagined, ordinary and fantastical. He stands on a threshold, philosophising about the nature of his observation as a familiar thing grows stranger. Together, poet, worker and reader, all follow the line of the pitchfork to 'an other side', a place where 'perfection' is 'imagined'. Perfection does not exist in our world. But it is not the 'tightened' hand, which was 'aiming' at the beginning of the poem, which will achieve this ideal state, but the 'opening hand' of the last stanza. Is the poet suggesting we must be open and ready to receive in order to achieve 'perfection'? Heaney states: '**look at the familiar things you know. Look at them with ... a quality of concentration ... you will be rewarded with insights and visions**.'

✒ Writing About the Poem

'In celebrating traditional rural crafts in his poetry, Heaney reveals his own skills as a master craftsman of the written word.' Discuss this view with reference to 'The Pitchfork'.

Sample Paragraph

'The Pitchfork' is based on a memory of Heaney's father who spent his life working on the family farm in Co. Derry. The poem begins with a dynamic image as Heaney remembers his father holding the fork 'like a javelin'. In his innocent eyes, his father was god-like – 'imagined perfection'. Hard 't' sounds suggest the father's strength in handling the pitchfork with confidence. The sense of deep respect for his father is found in the tone of admiration when Heaney imagines the older man playing 'the warrior or the athlete'. The poet moves from describing the everyday activity of gathering in the hay to a visionary level as the fork hangs in the air, 'starlit and absolutely soundless'. He transforms the implement into a mysterious spacecraft. Through his own precise language skills, Heaney celebrates the working life of the father he idealised.

EXAMINER'S COMMENT

Clear, top-grade response tackling all elements of the question and showing a good understanding of the poem. Impressive awareness of Heaney's expertise with language (particularly imagery, tone and sound effects). Focused quotations are used effectively to support key points and the expression is varied and well controlled.

Class/Homework Exercises

1. 'Seamus Heaney's poetry addresses thought-provoking themes in language that is both realistic and mystical.' Discuss this view with reference to 'The Pitchfork'.
2. 'In Heaney's most compelling poems, ordinary objects are lovingly and exactly described.' Discuss this statement with particular reference to 'The Pitchfork'.

Points to Consider

- Exploration of commitment, craft and creativity.
- Focus on physical details in the first four stanzas.
- Impact of cinematic imagery and energetic rhythm.
- Sudden change of pace and mood in the last stanza.
- Compelling ending reinforces poet's devotion to generosity and acceptance.

13. Lightenings viii

SEAMUS HEANEY

Lightenings: insights, transcendent experiences.

The annals say: when the monks of Clonmacnoise
Were all at prayers inside the oratory
A ship appeared above them in the air.

The anchor dragged along behind so deep
It hooked itself into the altar rails   5
And then, as the big hull rocked to a standstill,

A crewman shinned and grappled down the rope
And struggled to release it. But in vain.
'This man can't bear our life here and will drown,'

The abbot said, 'unless we help him.' So   10
They did, the freed ship sailed, and the man climbed back
Out of the marvellous as he had known it.

annals: monastic records.
Clonmacnoise: established in the 6th century, the monastery at Clonmacnoise was renowned as a centre of scholarship and spirituality.
oratory: place of prayer, small chapel.

shinned: climbed down, clambered.

abbot: head of the monastery.

'Out of the marvellous'

POETRY FOCUS

👤 Personal Response

1. How is the surreal atmosphere conveyed in this poem? Quote in support of your response.
2. Choose one striking image from the poem and comment on its effectiveness.
3. In your view, what does the air-ship symbolise? Refer to the text in your answer.

👁 Critical Literacy

Written in four tercets (three-line stanzas), 'Lightenings viii' (from Seamus Heaney's 1991 collection, *Seeing Things*), tells a legendary story of a miraculous air-ship that once appeared to the monks at Clonmacnoise, Co. Offaly. Heaney has said: 'I was devoted to this poem because the crewman who appears is situated where every poet should be situated: between the ground of everyday experience and the airier realm of an imagined world.'

Heaney's matter-of-fact approach at the start of stanza one leads readers to expect a straightforward retelling of an incident recorded in the 'annals' of the monastery. The story's apparently scholarly source seems highly reliable. While they were at prayers, the monks looked up: 'A ship appeared above them in the air'. We assume that the oratory is open to the sky. The simplicity of the colloquial language, restrained tone and run-through lines all ease us into a **dreamlike world** where anything can happen. But as with all good narratives, the magic ship's sudden appearance raises many questions: Why is it there? Where has it come from? Is this strange story all a dream?

Then out of the air-ship came a massive anchor, which 'dragged along behind so deep' (stanza two) before lodging itself in the altar rails. The poet makes **effective choices in syntax (word order) and punctuation**, e.g. placing 'so deep' at the end of the line helps to emphasise the meaning. The moment when the ship shudders to a halt is skilfully caught in a carefully wrought image: 'as the big hull rocked to a standstill'.

A crewman clambers down the rope to try to release the anchor, but he is unsuccessful. Heaney chooses his words carefully: 'shinned', 'grappled', 'struggled' (stanza three) are all powerful verbs, helping to create a clear picture of the sailor's physical effort. The phrase 'But in vain' is separated from the rest of the line to emphasise the man's hopelessness. The contrasting worlds of magic and reality seem incompatible. Ironically, the story's turning point is the abbot's instant recognition that the **human, earthly atmosphere will be fatal to the visitor**: 'This man can't bear our life here and will drown'.

SEAMUS HEANEY

But a solution is at hand: 'unless we help him' (stanza four). The unconditional generosity of the monks comes naturally to them: 'So/They did'. The word 'So' creates a pause and uncertainty before the prompt, brief opening of the next line: 'They did'. When the anchor is eventually disentangled and 'the freed ship sailed', **the crewman will surely tell his travel companions about the strange beings he encountered** after he 'climbed back out of the marvellous as he had known it'. This last line is somewhat surprising and leaves the reader wondering – marvelling, even.

Heaney's poem certainly raises interesting questions, blurring the lines between reality and illusion, and challenging our ideas about human consciousness. **The story itself can be widely interpreted**. Is the ship a symbol of inspiration while the monks represent commitment and dedication? Presumably, as chroniclers of the annals (preserving texts on paper for posterity), they were not aware of the miracle of their own labours – crossing the barrier from the oral tradition to written records – which was to astonish the world in the forthcoming centuries and help spread human knowledge.

'Lightenings viii' is a beautiful poem that highlights the fact that **the ordinary and the miraculous are categories defined only by human perception**. For many readers, the boat serves as an abstract mirror image, reversing our usual way of seeing things. In Heaney's rich text, we discover that from the outsider's perspective, the truly marvellous consists not of the visionary or mystical experience, but of the seemingly ordinary experience.

✒ Writing About the Poem

'Heaney's evocative language often makes room for everyday miracles and otherworldly wisdom.' Discuss this statement with reference to 'Lightenings viii'.

Sample Paragraph

Heaney's poem 'Lightenings viii' is an account of a surreal experience when the Clonmacnoise monks imagined a ship above them in the sky. Heaney's tone is dreamlike. The long lines and broad vowel sounds suggest an unhurried atmosphere where anything can happen – 'as the big hull rocked to a standstill'. The monks believe that the mysterious sailors have come out 'of the marvellous' – but the stranded sailors see the monks in the same way The poet seems to be saying that everything in life can be viewed as a wonder. The abbot chooses to save the desperate

EXAMINER'S COMMENT

This focused paragraph addresses the question effectively and shows close engagement with the poet's possible themes and language use. Discussion points are clearly expressed and aptly supported. The comments on Heaney's style (dreamlike tone, narrative approach, assonant effects) are particularly impressive. Expression throughout this high-grade response is very well controlled.

crewman – 'This man can't bear our life here and will drown'. For me, this is the poet's central lesson – we should help others when we can. If we do, then our lives will be filled with everyday miracles.

Class/Homework Exercises

1. 'Heaney's poetic world is one of wonder and mystery that is matched by the energy of his language.' Discuss this view with reference to 'Lightenings viii'.
2. 'Many of Seamus Heaney's poems communicate intense observations through thought-provoking images and symbolism.' Discuss this statement with reference to both the subject matter and style of 'Lightenings viii'.

Points to Consider

- Characteristic narrative style and use of colloquial language.
- Dramatic qualities – characters, setting, tension, dialogue, resolution.
- The poem is concerned with visionary experiences, yet rooted in the physical world.
- Effective use of vivid imagery, assonance, powerful verbs.
- Contrasting worlds – mundane monks and magical sailors.

Sample Leaving Cert Questions on Heaney's Poetry

1. Discuss how Heaney uses detailed observation and a reflective tone to address aspects of identity and belonging in his poetry. Develop your response with reference to themes and language evident in the poems by Seamus Heaney on your course.
2. 'Heaney frequently reveals a deep sense of love and loss through the effective use of evocative language in his poetry.' Develop your response with reference to the poems by Seamus Heaney on your course.
3. 'Heaney creates memorable characters, often in dramatic settings, to explore experiences of great emotional intensity.' Develop your response with reference to the poems by Seamus Heaney on your course.

How do I organise my answer?

(Sample question 2)

'Heaney frequently reveals a deep sense of love and loss through the effective use of evocative language in his poetry.' Develop your response with reference to the poems by Seamus Heaney on your course.

Sample Plan 1

Intro: *(Stance: agree with viewpoint in the question)* Heaney's poetry discloses aspects of love and loss in relationships with people, places and culture. Using vivid imagery, mythical reference, colloquial speech, personification and comparisons, the poet invites readers to share these intense experiences.

Point 1: *(Love of home and family – visual and aural imagery)* 'Mossbawn: Sunlight' recreates the rural idyll of Heaney's childhood home through effective similes ('the sun stood/like a griddle cooling'). Detailed visual and aural effects ('floury apron', 'scuffled') paint a picture of Heaney's beloved Aunt Mary at work in the kitchen.

Point 2: *(Loss of love – mythical allusion/dynamic verbs)* 'The Underground' uses the myth of Orpheus and Eurydice to describe the breathless dash of two lovers to a concert in London, widening the appeal from the personal to the universal. Dramatic verbs convey the headlong rush of each lover ('speeding', 'gaining').

Understanding the Prescribed Poetry Question

Marks are awarded using the PCLM Marking Scheme:
P = 15; C = 15; L = 15; M = 5
Total = 50

- **P** (Purpose = 15 marks) refers to the set question and is the launch pad for the answer. This involves engaging with all aspects of the question. Both theme and language must be addressed, although not necessarily equally.
- **C** (Coherence = 15 marks) refers to the organisation of the developed response and the use of accurate, relevant quotation. Paragraphing is essential.
- **L** (Language = 15 marks) refers to the student's skill in controlling language throughout the answer.
- **M** (Mechanics = 5 marks) refers to spelling and grammar.
- Although no specific number of poems is required, students usually discuss at least 3 or 4 in their written responses.
- Aim for at least 800 words, to be completed within 45–50 minutes.

NOTE

In keeping with the PCLM approach, the student has to take a stance by agreeing, disagreeing or partially agreeing that Heaney's:

– **deep sense of love and loss** (love of family, friends, places and people; lost culture, lost love, lost memories, change, etc.)

... is revealed through:

– **effective use of evocative language** (vivid visual/aural imagery, personification, mythical allusions, striking comparisons, dark humour, cinematic detail, colloquial speech, varying tones/atmospheres, innovative poetic structures, etc.)

Point 3: *(Love/passing time – colloquial speech/personification)* 'A Call' details the personal narrative of a phone call home. Colloquial language ('Hold on') sets the mood. Rich vowels recreate the inescapable passage of time ('amplified grave ticking of hall clocks'). Effective personification evokes the universal experience of death ('Death would summon Everyman').

Point 4: *(Vanished memory/change – unusual comparisons, poetic structure)* 'Bogland' is the container of lost memories and culture ('Great Irish Elk', 'Butter sunk'). Aural imagery captures the nature of the ever-changing bog ('Melting and opening'). Poetic structure mirrors act of digging peat.

Conclusion: Heaney offers vivid, evocative descriptions of cherished memories of intense love and loss. The poet's skilful use of language reveals these experiences with exactness.

Sample Paragraph: Point 4

For Heaney, 'Bogland' is the holder of lost memories and culture. These bogs record the transitions in natural history – 'the Great Irish Elk', 'waterlogged trunks'. Long forgotten Celtic traditions are revealed, 'Butter sunk under ... recovered salty and white'. Soft 'm' and 's' sounds suggest the moving, oozing nature of the bog, 'Melting', 'Missing'. Lost history is preserved in the bog, waiting to be discovered, 'Every layer they strip/ Seems camped on before'. Heaney's clever poetic structure is used to mirror the neat piles of turf on the bogland through a series of short lines and stacked stanzas, a nostalgic memory of a lost age. The endless search for the past is conveyed in a tone of longing, 'The wet centre is bottomless'.

> **EXAMINER'S COMMENT**
>
> An insightful response that directly responds to the question and shows excellent understanding of the poem. Heaney's skilful use of sound and structure to express feelings of loss is very well illustrated. Expression throughout is impressive and quotations are carefully integrated into the answer. An assured top-grade standard.

(Sample question 3)

'Heaney creates memorable characters, often in dramatic settings, to explore experiences of great emotional intensity.' Develop your response with reference to the poems by Seamus Heaney on your course.

Sample Plan 2

Intro: *(Stance: agree with viewpoint in the question)* Heaney's autobiographical poems create unforgettable characters in powerful settings. Intense memories of meaningful encounters with people and experiences expressed through visual and aural imagery, contrast, cinematic detail, dark humour and dramatic dialogue.

Point 1: *(Dramatic encounter with RUC policeman – imagery, dialogue)* 'A Constable Calls' recreates an uneasy meeting between the poet's father and an RUC policeman at a time of tense relations between Ulster's two cultures ('the boot of the law'). Terse dialogue ('Any other root crops?') and ominous repetition ('the bicycle ticked, ticked, ticked') capture the oppressive atmosphere.

Point 2: *(Absent wife/exotic location – sensuous imagery/edgy humour)* 'The Skunk' is a playful love poem to his wife using an irreverent image of the pompous little animal ('damasked like the chasuble/At a funeral mass'). Sensuous language conjures up the exotic setting ('Tang of eucalyptus') and desperate longing ('aftermath of a mouthful of wine/Was like inhaling you off a cold pillow').

Point 3: *(Dead father – metaphor, dynamic verbs)* 'The Harvest Bow' brings to life Heaney's reticent father ('tongue-tied') carefully creating the harvest bow ('tightens twist by twist'). Onomatopoeic verbs convey restless energy ('Beats out'). Natural setting reflecting the deep love between father and son nostalgically captured, the memory 'still warm' ('I see us walk').

Point 4: *(Personal relationship – striking contrasts, cinematic detail)* 'Tate's Avenue' describes the evolving relationship between Heaney and his wife through the image of a car rug. Young hedonistic love in an exotic location is shown in the cinematic close-up of a picnic. Mature love ('nothing gives') is sharply contrasted through dour description of the confines ('walled back yard') of a Sunday in Belfast.

NOTE

In keeping with the PCLM approach, the student has to explore poems of Heaney's on the course that include:

– **memorable characters often in dramatic settings** (real people from the poet's past, striking natural landscape, cultural/political tensions in Northern Ireland, etc.)

... to explore:

– **experiences of great emotional intensity** (feelings of love, fear, wonder, etc. heightened by sensuous imagery, vivid details, striking comparisons, energetic sound effects, engaging conversational language, evocative tones, mythical allusions, etc.)

Conclusion: Heaney presents memorable characters in dramatic locations and uses a range of language techniques to investigate experiences of intense emotional depth.

Sample Paragraph: Point 3

In 'The Harvest Bow', Heaney creates a precise description of his father, a reserved Irish farmer ('tongue-tied'). The man's artistic skill in crafting 'A throwaway love-knot of straw' is conveyed through alliteration ('tightened twist by twist'). The harvest bow symbolises the natural bond between father and son. It awakens precious memories of the poet who spies 'into its golden loops'. He remembers their walk in the quiet countryside in the stillness of an Irish evening 'of long grass and midges'. Sensuous sounds suggest the bittersweet sense of past times and the love they once experienced. Heaney's father may be gone but his memory lives 'still warm' in the 'frail device' of the harvest bow 'pinned up' on the poet's kitchen dresser.

> **EXAMINER'S COMMENT**
>
> A successful top-grade paragraph that focuses on both parts of the question (characters in dramatic settings and intense emotion). The response shows a real appreciation of Heaney's poetic techniques, particularly his use of descriptive details and sound effects. Apt quotes are used effectively to support discussion points and there is assured expression throughout.

> **EXAM FOCUS**
> - As you may not be familiar with some of the poems referred to in the sample plans, substitute poems that you have studied closely.
> - Key points about a particular poem can be developed over more than one paragraph.
> - Paragraphs may also include cross-referencing and discussion of more than one poem.
> - Remember that there is no single 'correct' answer to poetry questions, so always be confident in expressing your own considered response.

Leaving Cert Sample Essay

Discuss how Heaney uses detailed observation and a reflective tone to address aspects of identity and belonging in his poetry. Develop your response with reference to the themes and language evident in the poems by Seamus Heaney on your course.

Sample Essay

1. Seamus Heaney, growing up in Co. Derry, inherited a divided identity. He occupied the in-between space of Irish identity resulting from centuries of conflict with England and sectarian disagreement between Protestant and Catholic. 'The Forge' and 'The Pitchfork' are rooted in his rural Irish upbringing. Alienation and conflict are themes explored in 'The Tollund

Man'. Heaney uses precise detailed observation, colloquial language, haunting sound effects, dynamic verbs and inventive contrasts to reveal various aspects of identity.

2. In 'The Forge', Heaney reflects on a disappearing way of life. This scene from his childhood is lovingly recreated from closely observed details. The untidy pile of discarded objects, 'old axles and iron hoops rusting', recalls an earlier time when people depended on horse transport. We get a sense of a very different and simpler way of living among Ireland's farming community. Onomatopoeic verbs, 'short-pitched ring', 'hiss', bring the forge to life and reveal the skill of the blacksmith to 'beat real iron out'. Flashes of light erupt in a forceful image, 'The unpredictable fantail of sparks'. Heaney's aural effects and vivid images emphasise the poet's deep-rooted belonging in this Irish rural society.

3. Heaney also explores his own identity as a poet in this poem. The blacksmith's anvil sits proudly at the centre of the forge, 'Horned as a unicorn'. It seems to possess magical powers that can transform things. The poet, like the blacksmith, makes patterns with words. Each man 'expends himself in shape and music' in a creative act. Heaney is claiming his place in the literary tradition of poetry. The poet is 'immoveable' and like the anvil, he is at home here.

4. 'The Tollund Man' compares ancient and modern conflict. Heaney imagines that 'Some day I will go to Aarhus', the museum in Denmark, to see the remains of the executed Iron Age man. He establishes the man's individuality, using a vivid metaphor to show the victim's gentle innocence, 'The mild pods of his eye-lids'. He enables readers to experience the man's fear as he 'rode the tumbril'. The poet considers the names of the places he might pass on his car journey to Aarhus, 'Tollund, Grauballe', the very same places the Tollund Man passed on his final journey. Both men share a history of experiencing violence in Jutland and Northern Ireland, and 'feel lost' in 'man-killing parishes'.

5. The harsh alliterative phrase, 'tightened her torc on him', highlights the cruelty of the ritual killing, sacrificed to a pagan goddess. Focusing on this victim of the goddess allows Heaney to reflect on the victims of a more recent conflict in Northern Ireland. The reality of sectarian division is conveyed through another jarring alliterative phrase, 'Tell-tale skin and teeth' of four murdered 'young brothers'. The poet compares the Tollund Man's sacrifice for his people to the murdered brothers sacrificed back home. They are hoping their lives might mean something and in the end benefit their local community and country. The experience of the Tollund Man has helped Heaney clarify his own identity. They have both experienced violent pasts. He now feels as 'Unhappy and at home' in the murderous bogs of Jutland as he does in his native Ulster back home.

SEAMUS HEANEY

INDICATIVE MATERIAL

- **Heaney's detailed observation and reflective tone** (descriptive details, vivid sensuous images, aural effects, inventive contrasts, personal narratives, variety of tones – introspective, insightful, elegiac, nostalgic, romantic, inspirational, etc.)

... address:

- **aspects of identity and belonging** (sense of the past, Irish cultural identity and nationalism, landscape and place names, autobiographical focus on real people at home and abroad, etc.)

6. Heaney's vivid memory of his father working the land inspires his poem 'The Pitchfork'. He observes his father working 'in earnest in the chaff and sweat'. The ordinary becomes transformed into the extraordinary, his pitchfork 'imagined perfection'. Once again, Heaney is not only claiming his place in the rural Irish tradition, but his individuality as poet. In this poem, both father and son practise their skill so that their everyday work becomes 'accurate and light'. A close-up image allows us to observe the pitchfork's 'Riveted steel, turned timber, burnish, grain'.

7. Heaney's language also appeals to our sense of touch as he describes the feel of the pitchfork in his father's hand, 'The springiness, the clip and dart of it'. Soft alliteration describes the labourer's dream of 'Its prongs starlit and absolutely soundless'. As he remembers his father quietly working in the field, Heaney reflects on how everyday activities can become mysterious and timeless through the power of the imagination.

8. Identity and belonging are explored by Heaney through reflective reconstructions of rural Irish life, through his detailed observations of people, places and agricultural implements. His identity as poet causes him to understand his place as a native of a divided society. Heaney believed in the power of poetry to know who you are and where you belong.

(745 words)

EXAMINER'S COMMENT

A solid critical response, showing good engagement with Heaney's poetry. Sustained focus on the use of detailed observation and reflection to address aspects of identity. Impressive commentary on stylistic features (sound effects, imagery and tone) in paragraphs 2, 4 and 7. The discussion is supported by accurate quotation ranging over several poems. Points are generally well-developed – although there is some repetition in paragraph 5. Overall, expression is clear (e.g. 'deep-rooted belonging in this Irish rural society', 'The ordinary becomes transformed into the extraordinary') adding to the essay's top-grade standard.

GRADE: H1
P = 15/15
C = 14/15
L = 13/15
M = 5/5
Total = 47/50

👀 Revision Overview

'The Forge'
Sonnet celebrating traditional rural crafts and exploring the mysterious creative process of achieving poetic identity.

'Bogland'
Ireland's boglands function as a metaphor for the poet's search to find his national identity.

'The Tollund Man'
In responding to the violence in Northern Ireland during the 1970s, Heaney draws parallels with earlier victims in Jutland.

'Mossbawn: Sunlight'
Reflective recollection of the poet's childhood and the loving relationship he had with his Aunt Mary.

'A Constable Calls' (OL)
Coming-of-age experience illustrating the divisions between Northern Irish Catholics and the Protestant community.

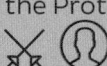

'The Skunk'
In this celebration of enduring love, the poet uses an affectionately teasing tone to express how he feels about his wife.

'The Harvest Bow'
A tender exploration of the father/son relationship and the unspoken understanding between them.

'The Underground' (OL)
Beautiful love poem that draws upon myth to revisit a hectic scene from the poet's honeymoon.

'Postscript'
The poet's description of experiencing transcendent beauty in the natural Irish landscape evokes powerful feelings.

'A Call' (OL)
Elegiac reflection on the passing of time and the poet's complex relationship with his father.

'Tate's Avenue'
Memories of particular places and moods are central to this poem which explores the theme of love in all of its richness.

'The Pitchfork'
Vivid recollection of rural life and the way everyday objects can become more than themselves through the power of the imagination.

'Lightenings viii'
In this curious and thought-provoking poem, Heaney makes room for everyday miracles and otherworldly wisdom.

💬 Last Words

'A poet for whom sound is crucial, who relishes the way words and consonants knock around.'
Tim Nolan

'Heaney has achieved a hard-won clarity of vision.'
Heather Clark

'The best moments are those when your mind seems to implode and words and images rush of their own accord into the vortex.'
Seamus Heaney

 NATURE LOVE IDENTITY CREATIVITY  CONFLICT 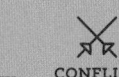 PLACES HISTORY/MEMORY 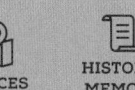 RELATIONSHIPS  WONDER

POETRY FOCUS

Paula Meehan
b. 1955

'When I go into poetry, I go into a kind of dream time.'

Paula Meehan was born in 1955 and spent her early years in Dublin's north inner city. While at secondary school, she wrote lyrics for local bands and began publishing her poems in a young people's magazine. After studying at Trinity College, she travelled round Europe and America before returning to Ireland, where she taught creative writing in universities, prisons and in the wider community. During the mid-1980s, Meehan's first poetry collections, *Return and No Blame* and *Reading the Sky*, were published. However, her work gained broader attention with *The Man who was Marked by Winter* in 1991 and since then her numerous collections have won consistent praise.

Meehan is innovative in experimenting with form, and her poems are haunting in their evocation of Irish places and speech patterns. Many draw their energy from the poet's vivid reminiscences of childhood, family and community. Her poetry also offers a powerful critique of Ireland's recent social history. Paula Meehan's uncompromising engagement with the politics of gender and class, and her love of the natural world, make her one of Ireland's most distinctive and influential voices.

Investigate Further

To find out more about Paula Meehan, or to hear readings of her poems not already available in your eBook, you could search some useful websites, such as YouTube, BBC Poetry, poetryfoundation.org and poetryarchive.org, or access additional material on this page of your eBook.

Prescribed Poems

PAULA MEEHAN

◯ **1 'Buying Winkles' (OL)**
Meehan's childhood memory not only provides a vibrant snapshot of Dublin life in the 1960s, but also evokes the mystery of the act of writing poetry.
Page 230

◯ **2 'The Pattern'**
The poet questions traditional gender roles in this autobiographical poem portraying a heart-rending and conflicted mother–daughter relationship.
Page 234

◯ **3 'The Statue of the Virgin at Granard Speaks'**
Inspired by the death of a fifteen-year-old who gave birth at a Marian shrine in Co. Longford, the poem powerfully challenges aspects of Irish society.
Page 241

◯ **4 'Cora, Auntie'**
In this tender elegy, the poet celebrates the spirit of her vivacious aunt who had emigrated to London for a better life.
Page 247

◯ **5 'The Exact Moment I Became a Poet'**
Meehan recalls a coming-of-age moment from her schooldays when she became aware of social class and the power of language to deprive people of their individual identity.
Page 252

◯ **6 'My Father Perceived as a Vision of St Francis'**
In the unlikely setting of a Dublin suburban garden, the poet's father is suddenly transformed into a saintly vision of natural splendour.
Page 256

◯ **7 'Hearth Lesson' (OL)**
A traumatic family scene from the poet's past teaches her to resist oppression and be true to herself.
Page 260

◯ **8 'Prayer for the Children of Longing' (OL)**
The community of Dublin's north inner city commissioned Meehan to write this empathetic poem in memory of young people who had died from drug abuse.
Page 265

◯ **9 'Death of a Field'**
In this incantatory poem about an open space in suburban Dublin which is about to become a construction site, the poet identifies all the wild herbs that will be displaced.
Page 270

◯ **10 'Them Ducks Died for Ireland'**
Evocative sonnet expressing Meehan's interest in acknowledging the heroism of ordinary lives which go unmentioned in official historical records.
Page 275

(OL) indicates poems that are also prescribed for the Ordinary Level course.

1 Buying Winkles

My mother would spare me sixpence and say,
'Hurry up now and don't be talking to strange
men on the way.' I'd dash from the ghosts
on the stairs where the bulb had blown
out into Gardiner Street, all relief.   5
A bonus if the moon was in the strip of sky
between the tall houses, or stars out,
but even in rain I was happy — the winkles
would be wet and glisten blue like little
night skies themselves. I'd hold the tanner tight   10
and jump every crack in the pavement,
I'd wave up to women at sills or those
lingering in doorways and weave a glad path through
men heading out for the night.

She'd be sitting outside the Rosebowl Bar   15
on an orange-crate, a pram loaded
with pails of winkles before her.
When the bar doors swung open they'd leak
the smell of men together with drink
and I saw light in golden mirrors.   20
I envied each soul in the hot interior.

I'd ask her again to show me the right way
to do *it*. She'd take a pin from her shawl —
'Open the eyelid. So. Stick it in
till you feel a grip, then slither him out.   25
Gently, mind.' The sweetest extra winkle
that brought the sea to me.
'Tell yer Ma I picked them fresh this morning.'

I'd bear the newspaper twists
bulging fat with winkles   30
proudly home, like torches.

'the tall houses'

PAULA MEEHAN

👤 Personal Response

1. How does the poet create a sense of childhood innocence in the opening stanza? Comment on the effect of the tone, rhythm and verbs, using suitable reference to the text.
2. In your opinion, why did the child envy the people who were in the Rosebowl Bar? Briefly explain your response.
3. Do you think Meehan's account of 1960s Dublin life is realistic or is it a sentimental poem that glorifies the old days? Give reasons for your answer, using reference to the text.

👁 Critical Literacy

Memory and continuity are recurring themes in Paula Meehan's work. Her third collection, *The Man who was Marked by Winter* (1991), recalls significant moments from her childhood, several of which combine a wonderful energy with a warm tone. 'Buying Winkles' is not only a vibrant snapshot of Dublin's social history in the early 1960s, it also evokes the mystery and charm of the act of writing poetry.

The poem's opening lines present a tender image of Paula Meehan's early days in Dublin's inner city. She recalls the eager anticipation and excitement of being sent to buy winkles for her mother, who would 'spare me sixpence'. The **close child–mother bond** is highlighted by the verb 'spare', suggesting that she has been specially chosen and trusted with an important task.

This small domestic drama is immediately brought to life with the mother's words of warning: 'don't be talking to strange/men on the way'. The poet recalls her younger self, leaving behind imaginary 'ghosts' on the dark tenement stairs where she lived, to 'dash' along the neighbouring streets on her important errand. Everything delights her on this **magical journey**: 'even in rain I was happy' (line 8).

Closely observed details recreate a vivid picture of **the young girl's zest for life** and its many mysteries. Sibilant 's' sounds used to describe the wet winkles that 'glisten blue like little/night skies' add a tactile quality to the image. Energetic run-on lines emphasise the child's intense feeling of freedom: 'I'd hold the tanner tight/and jump every crack in the pavement'.

A dynamic picture of working-class communal living during the 1960s emerges in this scene, yet history is not entirely romanticised. Despite all the friendliness and good humour, society is shaped by both **poverty and gender roles**. To a great extent, women are shown as being marginalised in this crushingly patriarchal environment. Some are restricted to the shadows, 'at sills', while prostitutes wait patiently, 'lingering in doorways'. Meanwhile, the men are free, 'heading out for the night'.

In line 15, the poet introduces a larger-than-life figure from her past. The winkle-seller is found in her usual location 'outside the Rosebowl Bar'. Using a discarded orange-crate as a makeshift seat, she exhibits her merchandise on an old pram. Equally fascinating is the forbidden male world behind the bar doors where the child would occasionally get an alluring glimpse of 'light in golden mirrors'. Naturally, this only increases her **keen sense of wonder**: 'I envied each soul in the hot interior'.

The evocative description of the winkle-seller's **playful language** is heard as she uses a pin to coax the whelks out of their spiral shells. It conveys the local colour and dialect of the times: 'Stick it in/till you feel a grip, then slither him out./Gently, mind' (lines 24–26). The onomatopoeic verb 'slither' indicates the slow movement and sound of the juicy winkles being de-shelled. Again, there is a suggestion of how the moment was significant in opening up new worlds for Meehan beyond the confines of Dublin, 'The sweetest extra winkle that brought the sea to me'. We are left with the reassurance of the winkle-seller's colloquial voice: 'Tell yer Ma I picked them fresh this morning'.

The poem ends with an engaging picture of the young girl taking the shellfish back home. The concluding lines are short, reflecting the self-assurance she feels after her street adventure: 'I'd bear the newspaper twists/bulging fat with winkles/proudly home, like torches'. The simile is particularly effective in illustrating her innocent **sense of triumph** as she relishes the edgy freedom of the city streets at night. It also suggests that such simple experiences as buying winkles were already lighting the way to her creative future.

✒ Writing About the Poem

'Paula Meehan's poetry often has a powerful dramatic quality which engages readers.' Discuss this view, with reference to 'Buying Winkles'.

Sample Paragraph

'Buying Winkles' is about a time when the poet felt a little bit scared of the adult world. The poem has a number of stand-out characters who appear powerful and intimidating. The poet's mother warns her to avoid 'strange men'. The girl is also slightly afraid of the local women 'lingering in doorways'. The old lady selling winkles really fascinates her. She shows her how to scoop out the shellfish with a clothes pin. She speaks like a true Dub, adding an extra touch of realism. The bar itself is a mystery to the girl who can only dream about what is going on inside what seems like a palace with 'golden mirrors'. The back streets are an exciting setting and I could imagine the night-time atmosphere creating a lot of drama. The central character is the young narrator herself and she is very engaging – particularly at the end when she can't wait to get 'proudly home' with her precious winkles wrapped in newspapers.

PAULA MEEHAN

EXAMINER'S COMMENT

A focused top-grade response that makes good use of accurate quotations integrated well into the commentary. The two elements of the question ('dramatic quality' and 'engages readers') are addressed throughout. Discussion points range across the entire poem, showing close understanding of the text. Expression is also clear, varied and controlled.

✒ Class/Homework Exercises

1. 'Paula Meehan often makes effective use of vivid descriptive details to celebrate ordinary people and everyday Irish life.' Discuss this statement with reference to 'Buying Winkles'.
2. 'Meehan's poetry can be highly emotional, but always manages to avoid sentimentality.' To what extent is this true of 'Buying Winkles'? Develop the points you make with suitable reference to the poem.

◉ Points to Consider

- Enduring impact of family and community, childhood innocence, and the joys of life are central to the poem.
- Other themes include memory, exclusion, creativity and social history.
- Authentic sense of atmosphere, time and place.
- Appealing dramatic elements including characters, storyline and dialogue.
- Contrasting tones: nostalgic, reflective, insightful and celebratory.

2 🔊 The Pattern

Title: a repeated decorative design; a set of instructions; an example for others to follow.

Little has come down to me of hers,
a sewing machine, a wedding band,
a clutch of photos, the sting of her hand
across my face in one of our wars

when we had grown bitter and apart.   5
Some say that's the fate of the eldest daughter.
I wish now she'd lasted till after
I'd grown up. We might have made a new start

as women without tags like *mother*, *wife*,
sister, *daughter*, taken our chances from there.   10
At forty-two she headed for god knows where.
I've never gone back to visit her grave.

*

First she'd scrub the floor with Sunlight soap,
an armreach at a time. When her knees grew sore
she'd break for a cup of tea, then start again   15
at the door with lavender polish. The smell
would percolate back through the flat to us,
her brood banished to the bedroom.

And as she buffed the wax to a high shine
did she catch her own face coming clear?   20
Did she net a glimmer of her true self?
Did her mirror tell her what mine tells me?

I have her shrug and go on
knowing history has brought her to her knees.
She'd call us in and let us skate around   25
in our socks. We'd grow solemn as planets
in an intricate orbit about her.

*

She's bending over crimson cloth,
the younger kids are long in bed.
Late summer, cold enough for a fire,   30
she works by fading light
to remake an old dress for me.
It's first day back at school tomorrow.

*

clutch: handful.

tags: labels, definitions.

Sunlight soap: all-purpose household soap.

percolate: filter gradually.
brood: young family.

buffed: polished.
net a glimmer: catch a trace.

intricate orbit: elaborate circle.

PAULA MEEHAN

'Pure lambswool. Plenty of wear in it yet.
You know I wore this when I went out with your Da. 35
I was supposed to be down in a friend's house,
your Granda caught us at the corner.
He dragged me in by the hair — it was long as yours then —
in front of the whole street.
He called your Da every name under the sun, 40
cornerboy, lout; I needn't tell you
what he called me. He shoved my whole head
under the kitchen tap, took a scrubbing brush
and carbolic soap and in ice-cold water he scrubbed
every spick of lipstick and mascara off my face. 45
Christ but he was a right tyrant, your Granda,
It'll be over my dead body anyone harms a hair of your head.'

*

She must have stayed up half the night
to finish the dress. I found it airing at the fire,
three new copybooks on the table and a bright 50
bronze nib, St Christopher strung on a silver wire,

as if I were embarking on a perilous journey
to uncharted realms. I wore that dress
with little grace. To me it spelt poverty,
the stigma of the second hand. I grew enough to pass 55

it on by Christmas to the next in line. I was sizing
up the world beyond our flat patch by patch
daily after school, and fitting each surprising
city street to city square to diamond. I'd watch

the Liffey for hours pulsing to the sea 60
and the coming and going of ships,
certain that one day it would carry me
to Zanzibar, Bombay, the land of the Ethiops.

*

There's a photo of her taken in the Phoenix Park
alone on a bench surrounded by roses 65
as if she had been born to formal gardens.
She stares out as if unaware
that any human hand held the camera, wrapped
entirely in her own shadow, the world beyond her
already a dream, already lost. She's 70
eight months pregnant. Her last child.

*

lambswool: fine soft wool.

cornerboy: idler.
lout: thug.

carbolic soap: harsh disinfectant soap.

St Christopher: holy medal of the patron saint of travellers.

embarking: setting out.
perilous: dangerous.
uncharted realms: unknown lands.

stigma: shame, disgrace.

pulsing: beating, throbbing.

Zanzibar: island off East Africa.
Bombay: Indian city.
Land of the Ethiops: East African country.

Phoenix Park: public parkland in Dublin.

Her steel needles sparked and clacked,
the only other sound a settling coal
or her sporadic mutter
at a hard part in the pattern. 75
She favoured sensible shades:
Moss Green, Mustard, Beige.

I dreamt a robe of a colour
so pure it became a word.

Sometimes I'd have to kneel 80
an hour before her by the fire,
a skein around my outstretched hands,
while she rolled wool into balls.
If I swam like a kite too high
amongst the shadows on the ceiling 85
or flew like a fish in the pools
of pulsing light, she'd reel me firmly
home, she'd land me at her knees.

Tongues of flame in her dark eyes,
She'd say, 'One of these days I must 90
teach you to follow a pattern.'

clacked: clicked.

sporadic: occasional, random.

skein: loosely coiled length of wool.

kite: light air-borne toy.

reel: roll or wind back.

'a hard part in the pattern'

👤 Personal Response

1. In your opinion, what is the poet's dominant mood in the first three stanzas? Is it confused, bitter, nostalgic, reflective, affirming? Support your answer with reference to the text.
2. Pick two examples of onomatopoeia (words or phrases whose sound echo the meaning) from the poem which you found particularly effective. Briefly explain your choices.
3. Write a short personal response to the poem, outlining the impact it made on you.

👁 Critical Literacy

PAULA MEEHAN

Throughout much of her poetry, Paula Meehan explores the complex reality of her own working-class origins and family relationships. Her 1991 collection, *The Man who was Marked by Winter*, includes candid, deeply personal poems which provide beautiful haunting images of her past. Meehan has spoken of 'going back and taking things from the negative in your life and trying to transform them into … something much more powerful and clear'. 'The Pattern' is an autobiographical series of snapshots portraying a poignant and conflicted mother–daughter relationship.

The poet has only inherited a few modest items from her mother, 'a sewing machine, a wedding band,/a clutch of photos'. Suddenly she thrusts the reader into the furious immediacy of her childhood. The bitter conflict between mother and 'eldest daughter' is vividly conveyed through flowing run-on lines and a sharp onomatopoeic 'sting' of her mother's hand across the poet's face. Wistfully, Meehan reflects on what might have been, had they known each other as adults, unhampered by the restrictive familial labels of '*mother, wife/sister, daughter*' (lines 9–10). The poet records her mother's early death and comments – with droll humour – 'she headed for god knows where'. Their **fractured relationship** is evident in the frank admission, 'I've never gone back to visit her grave'.

Meehan's upbringing in Dublin's inner city is recreated through **dramatic sensory recollections**. Her mother is engaged in routine housework. Soft sibilance recalls the gentle 'Sunlight soap' she used to 'scrub the floor' (line 13). The heady smell of 'lavender polish' filters through the small flat where the 'brood' of children have been confined to the bedroom until the work is complete. Rhetorical questions probe whether the mother has ever recognised her 'true self', her unique identity as a person, in the reflective surfaces. The poet now wonders what her subservient mother might have seen in her reflection. Meehan is keenly aware that Irish society 'brought her to her knees'. Yet she recovers and acknowledges that her childhood was supportive and nurturing. Her pragmatic mother just kept going, allowing the children to skate on the newly polished floor, shining it further with their

stockinged feet. Like satellites, they repeatedly circled her as if orbiting their centre of the universe.

The poet presents another significant episode from the past in line 34. Her mother is busy altering old clothes for her daughter. The **practical maternal voice is heard**, 'Plenty of wear in it yet', while she remakes the crimson dress she wore 'when I went out with your Da'. Suddenly the viciousness of male power in working-class communities erupts. Her mother recollects 'Granda' dragging her home 'by the hair' because she was 'caught' meeting her boyfriend. Harsh 'carbolic soap' with 'ice-cold water' is used to scrub every trace of make-up from her face. Meehan also remembers her mother's angry reaction, swearing to protect her from such male violence, 'It'll be over my dead body anyone harms a hair of your head'. But was this always the case?

However, in lines 48–49, there is further **recognition of her mother's caring nature**, 'She must have stayed up half the night/to finish the dress'. Another list itemises the careful preparation for her daughter's return to school, 'three new copybooks', a 'bright/bronze nib' and a 'St Christopher' medal. The poet believes her mother imagined her going off on 'a perilous journey' of discovery. Despite this, all the loving care is met with petulance from the child who wore the second-hand dress with 'little grace'. Meehan is reminded of the acute shame and 'stigma' of her family's poverty. Run-through lines echo the growing independence of this young girl who looked outwards at a 'world beyond'. She discovers a 'surprising/city street' which fits into a 'city square' and then transforms into a 'diamond' or parallelogram. Is she mirroring her mother's creativity by patterning? Is she making her own unique design?

Hemmed in by disadvantage and gender repression, the poet **desires to escape the oppressive atmosphere of her home**. This is conveyed in the vivid image of the 'pulsing' dynamic flow of the River Liffey with its ever-changing scenes of incoming and departing ships. She tries to escape reality by dreaming of far-off exotic places, the Moorish island of Zanzibar, bustling Bombay and the dramatic landscapes of Ethiopia.

Line 64 brings the reader back to the present, beside the poet while she looks at a photo of her heavily pregnant mother sitting in the Phoenix Park, 'surrounded by roses'. There is a striking contrast between the beauty of the formal gardens and a woman worn out with poverty and constant child-bearing, 'already lost'. Meehan now sees her mother as a victim, someone who never really discovered herself, but sits 'wrapped/entirely in her own shadow'. She only exists in her prescribed place in society, **obscured from her individual identity** as a person in her own right.

PAULA MEEHAN

Vibrant visual and aural imagery in line 72 recreate another episode depicting the mother's creativity, 'Her steel needles sparked and clacked'. But now her voice has dimmed to a 'sporadic mutter' while she tries to negotiate a 'hard part in the pattern'. Once again her daughter dismisses her mother's efforts by ridiculing her colour choices as 'sensible shades'. Two emphatic lines stand alone, however. Her daughter dares to dream of 'a robe of a colour/so pure it became a word'. Unlike her mother, the poet chooses language rather than wool to fashion her dream.

In the final lines, Meehan expresses her feelings about **the effect of her mother's influence**. The daughter is engaged in the mind-numbing activity of holding knitting wool on 'outstretched hands' while her mother rolls the wool into balls. The daunting challenge of longing to escape is captured in the clever swapping of expected verbs, 'swam like a kite', 'flew like a fish'. Meehan's tone is ambiguous as she describes the 'Tongues of flame in her dark eyes'. Beneath the menace and mystery in this powerful image, there is a sense of a manic puppeteer, reeling back the line of the kite to bring her daughter to her proper place within the community, 'at her knees'. Is she repeating the grandfather's tyrannical behaviour, enforcing submission? Is she demanding that her daughter submit to her expected role in Irish patriarchal society?

Interestingly, the poet bears witness to the richness and dignity of her working-class background while refusing to idealise it. We are left to wonder about the extent to which the poet has broken free of 'The Pattern', her mother's legacy. What did she inherit in the end? Was the 'clutch of photos' a loving hug or a devastating embrace? While family tensions have run through the entire poem, Meehan still feels an **intense connection** to her mother, leaving readers to consider the complexity of their troubled relationship.

> **Writing About the Poem**
>
> 'Paula Meehan's poetry is starkly conflicted between her desire to recover the past and her need to move beyond it.' Discuss this view, with reference to 'The Pattern'.

Sample Paragraph

'The Pattern' presents a clear contrast between Meehan's desire to recreate working-class Dublin life in the 1960s while desperately wanting to escape its limitations. Rich imagery recreates this past, 'lavender polish' and 'The smell would percolate', while the children waited for the cleaning of the floor to finish. Meehan appreciates her mother's hopes for her daughter to do well. This is evident in the list of things she buys her for going back to school. Yet in contrast to such concern, violence is used to enforce discipline, the harsh 'sting' of a hand on the young girl's face or the dragging home by the hair. The pattern of society's rules had to be adhered to. Meehan rejects this conformity by dreaming of a 'pulsing' Liffey bringing her to exotic places. She acknowledges her past, but refuses to be 'wrapped' like her mother 'entirely in her own shadow' with no identity except for her oppressed place in the family.

> **EXAMINER'S COMMENT**
>
> *Assured top-grade response that included several focused discussion points based on the poet's successful use of contrast. Good sense of engagement with the text and effective use of apt reference. Accurate quotations well integrated into critical commentary. Clarity and control of varied expression throughout.*

Class/Homework Exercises

1. 'Paula Meehan's poetry presents dramatic and complex perspectives on her Irish working-class background.' Discuss this statement with reference to 'The Pattern'.
2. 'Meehan's reflective poetry candidly explores her Irish identity through stunning aural and visual effects.' To what extent is this true of 'The Pattern'? Develop your answer with suitable textual evidence.

Points to Consider

- **Conflict between warm acknowledgement of Irish working-class past and a more critical adult view of its negative impact.**
- **Other key themes include memory, creativity and identity.**
- **Authentic evocation of character, atmosphere, time and place.**
- **Contrasting tones: nostalgic, reflective, critical, insightful and cynical.**
- **Engaging poetic techniques: visual and aural imagery, contrasts, direct speech.**

3 🔊 The Statue of the Virgin at Granard Speaks

PAULA MEEHAN

It can be bitter here at times like this,
November wind sweeping across the border.
Its seeds of ice would cut you to the quick.
The whole town tucked up safe and dreaming,
even wild things gone to earth, and I   5
stuck up here in this grotto, without as much as
star or planet to ease my vigil.

The howling won't let up. Trees
cavort in agony as if they would be free
and take off — ghost voyagers   10
on the wind that carries intimations
of garrison towns, walled cities, ghetto lanes
where men hunt each other and invoke
the various names of God as blessing
on their death tactics, their night manoeuvres.   15
Closer to home the wind sails over
dying lakes. I hear fish drowning.
I taste the stagnant water mingled
with turf smoke from outlying farms.

They call me Mary — Blessed, Holy, Virgin.   20
They fit me to a myth of a man crucified:
the scourging and the falling, and the falling again,
the thorny crown, the hammer blow of iron
into wrist and ankle, the sacred bleeding heart.
They name me Mother of all this grief   25
though mated to no mortal man.
They kneel before me and their prayers
fly up like sparks from a bonfire
that blaze a moment, then wink out.

It can be lovely here at times. Springtime,   30
early summer. Girls in Communion frocks
pale rivals to the riot in the hedgerows
of cow parsley and haw blossom, the perfume
from every rushy acre that's left for hay
when the light swings longer with the sun's push north.   35

grotto: ornamental religious shrine built into rock.
vigil: night watch.

cavort: twist, shake.
voyagers: travellers, messages.
intimations: suggestions, memories.
garrison towns: places where troops were stationed.
ghetto lanes: backstreet slums.
invoke: pray to.
manoeuvres: movements, plots.

mingled: mixed.

myth of a man crucified: story of Jesus Christ.
scourging: flogging, torture.
thorny crown: Jesus was mocked and a crown of thorns was placed on his head.
sacred bleeding heart: also known as the Sacred Heart. Catholic symbol of Christ's sacrifice and love for humanity.

Communion frocks: white dresses symbolising purity worn at the Holy Communion ceremony.
cow parsley: a wildflower with fern-like leaves and delicate white flowers.

POETRY FOCUS

Or the grace of a midsummer wedding
when the earth herself calls out for coupling
and I would break loose of my stony robes,
pure blue, pure white, as if they had robbed
a child's sky for their colour. My being   40
cries out to be incarnate, incarnate,
maculate and tousled in a honeyed bed.

Even an autumn burial can work its own pageantry.
The hedges heavy with the burden of fruiting
crab, sloe, berry, hip; clouds scud east   45
pear scented, windfalls secret in long
orchard grasses, and some old soul is lowered
to his kin. Death is just another harvest
scripted to the season's play.

But on this All Souls' Night there is   50
no respite from the keening of the wind.
I would not be amazed if every corpse came risen
from the graveyard to join in exaltation with the gale,
a cacophony of bone imploring sky for judgement
and release from being the conscience of the town.   55

On a night like this I remember the child
who came with fifteen summers to her name,
and she lay down alone at my feet
without midwife or doctor or friend to hold her hand
and she pushed her secret out into the night,   60
far from the town tucked up in little scandals,
bargains struck, words broken, prayers, promises,
and though she cried out to me *in extremis*
I did not move,
I didn't lift a finger to help her,   65
I didn't intercede with heaven,
nor whisper the charmed word in God's ear.

On a night like this I number the days to the solstice
and the turn back to the light.
                                O sun,   70
centre of our foolish dance,
burning heart of stone,
molten mother of us all,
hear me and have pity.

---

coupling: physical union, intimacy.

incarnate: alive, embodied.
maculate: flawed, human.

pageantry: spectacle, ceremony.

scud: rush, sail.

keening: wailing, grieving.

exaltation: intense praise.
cacophony: loud outburst.

secret: baby.

in extremis: on the point of death.

intercede: plead.

solstice: year's shortest day.

molten: liquified.

👤 Personal Response

1. Describe the tone of voice in the opening stanza, using close reference to the text.
2. Select one image or phrase from the poem that you find particularly startling or disturbing. Briefly explain your choice.
3. Write a short personal response to the poem, highlighting the overall impact it made on you.

👁 Critical Literacy

PAULA MEEHAN

On 31 January 1984, a fifteen-year-old girl died after giving birth at the hillside grotto on the outskirts of Granard, Co. Longford. Ann Lovett was found by passers-by. Her baby boy also died. Ann had kept the pregnancy hidden from her family, teachers and friends. Meehan is well known as an activist who raises poetry into public consciousness. In this dramatic monologue, she remembers the heartbreak associated with one young woman's tragedy. Set on All Souls' Night, the iconic statue comes alive as the poet assumes the voice of the Blessed Virgin in the grotto recalling the past year. 'The Statue of the Virgin at Granard Speaks' was published in 1991.

The colloquial 'voice' Meehan gives to the iconic statue is out of character with the Blessed Virgin's usual timid image. Mary complains about the 'bitter' cold and northerly winds carrying 'seeds of ice' from which nothing good will grow. She envies 'The whole town tucked up safe' while she is 'stuck up here in this grotto'. Nothing eases her 'vigil'. Her **resentful tone** is evident throughout the opening stanza. There is an emphasis on rejection and alienation. Harsh winter weather is an obvious symbol of cruel times. The isolation of the statue highlights the experience of the young girl who died here and her loneliness in death.

Graphic details of the desolate landscape in stanza two provide a disquieting context for the anguish of the terrible event. Even the trees 'cavort in agony'. Meehan creates **a surreal scene of chaos and suffering**. The windswept branches become 'ghost voyagers', reminders of death elsewhere in Ireland: 'garrison towns, walled cities, ghetto lanes'. Through the statue's 'voice', Meehan expresses contempt for the way murders have sometimes been carried out in the name of religion. She references other dark periods in Irish history – particularly the sectarian conflict in the North where men use 'God as blessing/on their death tactics'. Meanwhile, all around the grotto, the natural world offers further evidence of lifeless images: 'dying lakes', 'stagnant water'.

Stanza three is filled with seething resentment: 'They call me Mary – Blessed, Holy, Virgin'. The insistent repetition creates a religious rhythm. All Mary can do is witness. She 'voices' her disappointment at the way her public

POETRY FOCUS

image has been reduced to a stone statue, a symbolic presence, unable to act. She is primarily associated with her **passive maternal role,** confined to the background in the story of Christ's suffering and death on the cross: 'They fit me to a myth of a man crucified'. She is uneasy with the focus on violence: 'the scourging and the falling'. The Virgin feels distanced from her role as an icon unable to help those who 'kneel before me'. She has no illusions about her own lack of influence, 'their prayers/fly up like sparks'.

Following the graphic description of the crucifixion, an unexpected change of tone occurs in stanza four. Echoing the first line, the poem becomes **more positive and nostalgic**: 'It can be lovely here at times'. The statue goes on to describe the budding greenery surrounding the graveyard. The loveliness of nature is even greater than human beauty: 'Girls in Communion frocks/pale rivals to the riot in the hedgerows'. A series of dynamic images across several run-on lines describe the energy and beauty of springtime: 'the perfume/from every rushy acre'.

The seasonal references continue in stanza five with a particularly vivid description of midsummer, 'when the earth herself calls out for coupling'. For the first time, the statue exchanges her anger with passionate desire. She **yearns for natural physical intimacy,** to 'break loose of my stony robes'. The statue longs to break free, 'to be incarnate, incarnate'. Repetition emphasises her yearning to feel truly alive. In place of Mary's traditional 'immaculate' image, she cries out to be 'maculate and tousled in a honeyed bed'.

Although summer excites the statue the most, she acknowledges the rich pageantry of autumn in stanza six, describing the hedges 'heavy with the burden of fruiting'. But she also **appreciates the realities of life**. In stark contrast to the cheerful images of bright grottos, communion frocks and midsummer weddings, there are images of darkness and pain. Mary is acutely aware of the appropriateness of autumn burial, observing that 'Death is just another harvest/scripted to the season's play'. Dying is part of the cycle of nature too.

Stanza seven takes the reader back to the icy present. It is All Souls' Night and the relentless 'keening' gale returns, bringing more reminders of death. The statue imagines corpses rising from their graves 'to join in exaltation'. The **wild supernatural scene** and disturbing image of the ghosts celebrating death becomes increasingly intense: 'a cacophony of bone'. The dead souls demand 'judgement' and 'release from being the conscience of the town'. It is time for the living to take responsibility for the horrific events that happened here.

The tone in stanza eight alternates between pity and remorse as the statue recalls a young girl ('with fifteen summers to her name') who secretly came to give birth at the grotto. The similarity between the girl's sad

PAULA MEEHAN

history and the story of the Virgin Mary is striking. Both would risk being marginalised by their community, 'the town tucked up in little scandals'. The sense of frustration and guilt is heightened, 'and though she cried out to me *in extremis*/I did not move'. As the forceful voice reaches **a dramatic climax**, short lines intensify the emotional impact: 'I didn't lift a finger to help her,/I didn't intercede with heaven'. The poem's irony is that the Virgin herself is ineffectual. Though the lines are ambiguous as to whether she cannot or will not help the girl, her powerlessness is beyond doubt.

In the final stanza, the statue's monologue becomes a **prayerful lament**. Looking ahead to the winter solstice and turning to pre-Christian pagan values, the speaker appeals directly to nature, addressing the 'molten mother' sun. She describes human existence as 'our foolish dance' and begs for mercy: 'hear me and have pity'. Poignantly, the Virgin herself is now praying for forgiveness. There is little sign, however, of any prospect of a more humanitarian world. Indeed, all that is certain is that the natural cycle of life and death will continue.

From the outset, the statue's disembodied and haunting narration implicates a sense of **communal involvement** based on the repressiveness of Irish society. In voicing such a central Christian icon as the Blessed Virgin, Meehan obviously points to the complicity of organised religion in Ann Lovett's tragedy. In the meantime, the victim herself remains voiceless. While the poet's views are clearly expressed, it is up to individual readers to make up their own minds about the many issues explored in this unsettling, powerful poem.

'It can be bitter here at times'

POETRY FOCUS

✒ Writing About the Poem

'Paula Meehan's deep sense of outrage is often evident in her poetry.' Discuss this view, with reference to 'The Statue of the Virgin at Granard Speaks'.

Sample Paragraph

In 'The Statue of the Virgin', Meehan uses the voice of Our Lady to protest about a schoolgirl who died in childbirth back in 1984. The poet is channelling her own angry feelings through the talking statue. It's clear that religion has not helped the tragic victim. The statue is furious about being left abandoned in the freezing grotto – while the townspeople are 'tucked up safe'. Meehan's frantic tone is really directed at the locals who still go through the motions of praying even though it did the teenager no good whatsoever. Irish people are 'tucked up' in prayers. The phrase is repeated for emphasis. The poet's anger is at its most intense when the statue admits, 'I didn't lift a finger to help her'. Nobody else did either despite our so-called Christian community. Unfortunately, there is no hope at the end of this poem.

EXAMINER'S COMMENT

This clearly focused personal response shows good engagement with both the question and the poem. The focus on the poet's sense of outrage is illustrated effectively and sustained throughout. Valuable use is made of references to tone, repetition and symbolism. Expression is varied and well controlled. Overall, an impressive top-grade standard.

✎ Class/Homework Exercises

1. 'Paula Meehan often makes use of contrasting images of nature that make a powerful impact.' To what extent is this true of 'The Statue of the Virgin at Granard Speaks'? Develop your answer with suitable textual support.
2. 'Meehan's poetry has subversive and feminist qualities that engage readers.' Discuss this view in relation to 'The Statue of the Virgin at Granard Speaks'.

⊙ Points to Consider

- Meehan challenges various aspects of Irish society.
- Themes include religion, nature, inhumanity and the role of women.
- Effective use of dramatic monologue, imagery and irony.
- Varying tones: critical, indignant, compassionate, elegiac and reflective.

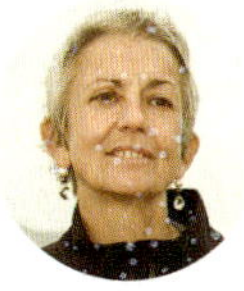

4 Cora, Auntie

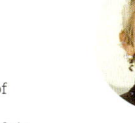

Title: Cora is the name of Meehan's aunt; the Irish form means honest and fair.

Staring Death down
with a bottle of morphine in one hand,
a bottle of Jameson in the other:

laughing at Death —
love unconditional keeping her just this side
of the threshold

as her body withered
and her eyes grew darker and stranger
as her hair grew back after chemo

thick and curly as when she was a girl;
always a girl in her glance
teasing Death — humour a lance

she tilted at Death.
Scourge of Croydon tram drivers and High Street dossers
on her motorised invalid scooter

that last year:
bearing the pain,
not crucifixion but glory

in her voice.
Old skin, bag of bones,
grinning back at the rictus of Death:

always a girl in her name —
Cora, maiden from the Greek Κόρη,
promising blossom, summer, the scent of thyme.

*

Sequin: she is standing on the kitchen table.
She is nearly twenty one.
It is nineteen sixty one.

They are sewing red sequins, the women,
to the hem of her white satin dress
as she moves slowly round and round.

morphine: pain-relieving drug.
Jameson: Irish whiskey.

unconditional: total.

threshold: divide.

chemo: chemotherapy, used to treat cancer.

lance: weapon.

tilted: leaned, attacked.
Scourge: tormentor.
Croydon: suburban area in London.
dossers: homeless people.

crucifixion: agony, execution.

rictus: fixed grimace.

Κόρη: Cora is derived from the Greek word Κόρη (pronounced *kopp*), the goddess Persephone.
thyme: scented herb.

Sequin: small, shiny disc sewn on clothing for decoration.

POETRY FOCUS

Sequins red as berries,
red as the lips of maidens,
red as blood on the snow

in Child's old ballads,   35
as red as this pen
on this white paper

Child's old ballads: traditional British folk songs collected by Francis James Child.

I've snatched from the chaos
to cast these lines
at my own kitchen table —

Cora, Marie, Jacinta, my aunties,   40
Helena, my mother, Mary, my grandmother —
the light of those stars

only reaching me now.
I orbit the table I can barely see over.
I am under it singing.   45

orbit: travel round.

She was weeks from taking the boat to England.
Dust on the mantlepiece,
dust on the cards she left behind:

a black cat swinging in a silver horseshoe,
a giant key to the door,   50
emblems of luck, of access.

emblems: symbols.
access: opportunity.

*

All that year I hunted sequins:
roaming the house I found them
in cracks and crannies,

crannies: small spaces.

in the pillowcase,   55
under the stairs,
in a hole in the lino,

lino: linoleum, floor covering.

in a split in the sofa,
in a tear in the armchair
in the home of the shy mouse.   60

split: rip, slit.

With odd beads and single earrings,
a broken charm bracelet, a glittering pin,
I gathered them into a tin box

charm bracelet: a chain with small jewelled ornaments.

which I open now in memory —
the coinage, the sudden glamour   65
of an emigrant soul.

coinage: currency, invention.
emigrant: person who settles in a foreign country, exile.

'sewing red sequins'

PAULA MEEHAN

👤 Personal Response

1. What impression do you get of Aunt Cora in the opening 16 lines? Comment on the effect of the imagery, tone, verbs and run-on lines, using suitable reference to the text.
2. In your opinion, was Cora an object of admiration or ridicule? Briefly explain your response.
3. In your view, what is the dominant mood in this poem? Happy? Sad? Nostalgic? Celebratory? Briefly explain your response, using reference to the text.

👁 Critical Literacy

Paula Meehan's collection *Painting Rain* (2009) includes poems linking landscape, community and selfhood. She dedicates several to family members. The elegy 'Cora, Auntie' encourages readers to regard the negativity of death not as an end but as a journey towards meaning. The poem also works as a way of re-establishing a lost connection between the past and present. Meehan sees her aunt's red sequins not just as an evocation of memory, but also in terms of feminine interconnection.

The poem's opening lines present a picture of **a vivacious woman**, the poet's aunt Cora, defiantly 'Staring Death down'. The powerful presence of the encroaching end of life is captured in the personification, capitalisation and repetition of the word 'Death'. Despite this, the aunt careers merrily on her 'motorised invalid scooter', clutching a bottle of painkillers in one hand and a bottle of whiskey in the other. Vivid verbs ('laughing', 'teasing') catch the essence of this dynamic character. Yet the poet also acknowledges the realistic details of the ravages of cancer and mortality, 'body withered', 'hair grew back after chemo'. However, it is the **aunt's determined spirit** which predominates, described in the humorous metaphor of a chivalrous knight challenging death with a 'teasing' glance. In her final year, she spins around her adopted home in London, tormenting everyone.

Cora's courage in the face of life's trials is recorded in line 17. She is not broken by suffering, 'crucifixion', but endures, 'bearing the pain'. Meehan's admiration for this display of human spirit is evident in the phrase, 'glory/ in her voice'. Life conspires against the aunt. This is highlighted in the chilling images of the destructive effects of time, 'Old skin, bag of bones'.

Nevertheless, she still dares to grin at the ugly grimace ('rictus') of death. The ominous present then slips into a more optimistic past as the aunt is imagined in all her girlish glory, 'Cora, maiden from the Greek Κόρη' (line 23). Persephone was addressed as Κόρη, the goddess of vegetation and a true nature child. The youthful **Cora also symbolised this abundance of life**, vividly evoked in gentle sibilance and vivid imagery, 'promising blossom, summer, the scent of thyme'.

In line 25, the italicised word '*Sequin*' and its colon suggest that the rest of the poem is an exploration of this tangible aid to memory which links all the women in the poem. Cora is brought to life, 'standing on the kitchen table', slowly twirling around as red sequins are attached to the hem of her white satin dress. Meehan nostalgically recalls the collaborative activity of the women's craft. As a child, she can only sense the complexity of the 'red sequins'. It will be years before she will be able to articulate their significance. However, three similes emphasise their image as folk-tale emblems. The sequins are as 'red as berries', 'the lips of maidens' and 'as blood on the snow'. The vibrant colours also form **a strong connection between women, past and present**, who create order in contrast to 'the chaos' of life. Meehan's fluid poetry flows through time, rather like her free-spirited aunt. The '*Sequin*', fleeting yet twinkling, maintains the female line.

The poet **recalls her female ancestors** like a litany of sacred names, 'Cora, Marie, Jacinta, my aunties,/Helena, my mother, Mary, my grandmother'. She encases these ghost shadows in constellation imagery, 'the light of those stars' (line 42). Their wisdom transcends time and space to become a liberating source of knowledge to her. Once more the poem drifts back into the past, showing the young poet circling her aunt. Line 46 recalls harsh times of enforced emigration from Ireland, 'She was weeks from taking the boat to England'. Home was left behind, gathering 'dust', a sharp reminder of human mortality. Cards wishing the aunt a happy twenty-first birthday, 'a giant key to the door', and good luck, 'a black cat swinging on a silver horseshoe', are all left behind. Cora has crossed the threshold into her new life as an exile in England and won't return.

Line 52 recalls the summer after her aunt had emigrated. In an **act of recollection**, the poet searched the house for the discarded red sequins. Like memories they surfaced in the most unlikely places, 'in cracks and crannies'. The alliterative hard 'c' suggests Meehan's effort in her search for memories. A list of hiding places for the sequins also reminds readers of the harsh effects of time on objects and people, 'a split', 'a tear'. The poet is now aware that she is repeating this action in opening the 'tin box' and by composing an elegy for her beloved aunt. Once again, she discovers the 'glamour' of the alluring Cora who has given her the wealth, 'coinage', of her example on **how to live life with humour and determination**. The emigrant aunt made the transition from her home in Ireland and forged a new life for herself in her adopted London. She has now crossed the threshold between life and death.

Writing About the Poem

'Paula Meehan's poetry often confronts darkness in dynamic language which reveals, questions and heals.' Discuss this view, with reference to 'Cora, Auntie'.

PAULA MEEHAN

Sample Paragraph

In 'Cora, Auntie', Meehan recalls her independent aunt who refused to give up even when faced with serious illness. The verbs 'laughing' and 'teasing' illustrate Cora's upbeat spirit. But the grim reality of old age is acknowledged through powerful images, 'withered body', 'old bag of bones'. Overall, it is the defiant Cora who is most remembered, 'grinning back at the rictus of Death'. Meehan has a close bond with her aunt. This is shown in the link she sees between the sewing of the 'red sequins' for Cora's dress and the poet's creation of her poem in red ink 'on white paper'. Meehan begins to appreciate the lessons of these women from the past who are now distant as 'those stars'. Her precious memories are her wealth or 'coinage', to deal with loss.

EXAMINER'S COMMENT

Focused, confident response to both the task and the poem. Some insightful engagement with the text, backed by supportive commentary – particularly on the effectiveness of imagery and verbs. Points are expressed clearly and quotations are well integrated into the discussion – although there are slight misquotes. Otherwise, a solid high-grade standard.

Class/Homework Exercises

1. 'Paula Meehan makes effective use of language to praise ordinary people and their approach to everyday life.' Discuss this statement with reference to 'Cora, Auntie'.
2. 'Meehan's poetry can be highly dramatic, but always manages to avoid exaggeration.' To what extent is this true of 'Cora, Auntie'? Support the points you make with suitable reference to the poem.

Points to Consider

- The poem's loose structure and time frame reflects the free-spirited aunt.
- Vivid visual imagery provides stark contrast between the ravages of life and the spirited personality of Meehan's aunt.
- Graphic recreation of atmosphere, time and place through the use of specific details.
- Contrasting tones: wistful, reflective, intuitive, triumphant and elegiac.
- Greek mythological reference widens the poem's impact.

5 The Exact Moment I Became a Poet

for Kay Foran

was in 1963 when Miss Shannon
rapping the duster on the easel's peg
half obscured by a cloud of chalk

said *Attend to your books, girls,
or mark my words, you'll end up
in the sewing factory.*

It wasn't just that some of the girls'
mothers worked in the sewing factory
or even that my own aunt did,

and many neighbours, but
that those words 'end up' robbed
the labour of its dignity.

Not that I knew it then,
not in those words — labour, dignity.
That's all back construction,

making sense; allowing also
the teacher was right
and no one knows it like I do myself.

But: I *saw* them: mothers, aunts and neighbours
trussed like chickens
on a conveyor belt,

getting sewn up the way my granny
sewed the sage and onion stuffing
in the birds.

Words could pluck you,
leave you naked,
your lovely shiny feathers all gone.

easel's peg: blackboards supported on wooden frames used in classrooms.

trussed: bound, tied.
conveyor belt: mechanical system for moving goods.

'I *saw* them'

👤 Personal Response

1. What is your impression of the teacher in the poem? Does she mean well in advising her young pupils? Or is she misleading them?
2. In your opinion, what key point is the poet making in the concluding stanza? Refer to the text in your response.
3. Do you think this is an optimistic or pessimistic poem, overall? Briefly explain your response.

👁 Critical Literacy

In 2000, Paula Meehan published her sixth poetry collection, *Dharmakaya*. The word comes from *The Tibetan Book of the Dead* and can be loosely translated as 'Truth-body'. Several of the poems touch on childhood memories, urban poverty, coming of age and self-awareness. 'The Exact Moment I Became a Poet' focuses on familiar themes of social class and oppressive gender relations in Irish society.

The title leads directly into the first stanza where Meehan recalls a significant moment from her childhood when she was eight years old. She sets the scene in an inner-city Dublin national school and recalls Miss Shannon standing at the blackboard. Through 'a cloud of chalk', the poet remembers hearing the teacher's stern advice: '*Attend to your books, girls*'. The use of italics emphasises the **ominous tone**: '*or mark my words, you'll end up/in the sewing factory*'.

For the young pupil, these words represent the beginning of class consciousness and an early sign of a possible future life as a writer. The schoolroom becomes the location where **middle-class values and prejudice are handed down**. Meehan is astounded by what she hears and the expression 'end up' makes an instant impact. The poet's tone wavers between antagonism towards the teacher and natural empathy for the many working women she knew – her aunt, neighbours, friends' mothers. She immediately senses that both the women and their work are being degraded. She describes their labour as being 'robbed' of its dignity in stanza four, reflecting how resentful she feels about the idea that some types of employment are undervalued.

The poet is caught between what she initially sensed as a child about attitudes to different jobs and careers ('Not that I knew it then') and what she eventually came to understand ('back construction') as an adult. She is uncomfortable with the idea that certain occupations are given a social position and that work in a sewing factory was considered inferior in the **class hierarchy**.

Experience has taught Meehan that the 'the teacher was right' about the prejudiced world where academic achievement could directly determine a young person's social position. She is also acutely aware of how education has affected her own life, 'no one knows it like I do myself'. An obvious irony, of course, is that **she herself chose 'books'** and literature as a means of escape from the downgraded world of factories and domesticity.

At the same time, Meehan expresses her solidarity with women who are powerless to change the way Irish society views them. She '*saw*' her local community for what it was and related closely to individual women. Once again, italics highlight how she resists the teacher's middle-class values because she feels they **demean and dehumanise working women** as 'trussed like chickens/on a conveyor belt'. The simile suggests controlled mechanical lives of dreary confinement. This comparison is extended into the two final stanzas as the poet recalls how her granny 'sewed the sage and onion stuffing/in the birds'.

The poem ends with a **rich image about the power of language** to deprive people of their individual identity, 'Words could pluck you,/leave you naked,/your lovely shiny feathers all gone'. Meehan argues that definitions can undervalue individuals, sometimes diminishing them. This is reinforced by the plucked chicken image, adding to the sense of violation and powerlessness. Opposition and resistance are recurring themes in Meehan's poetry. In this case, she challenges class discrimination, restoring dignity to lives that have been overlooked.

While readers may not always agree with the poet about her views on class and gender, there is no denying that poetry has become her way of coming to terms with the past. The memory of an extraordinary school lesson back in 1963 marks a **crucial turning point** that illustrates the origins of a young girl's personal development. Throughout her adult life, Meehan's identity as a poet has never been separated from her self-awareness as a working-class woman.

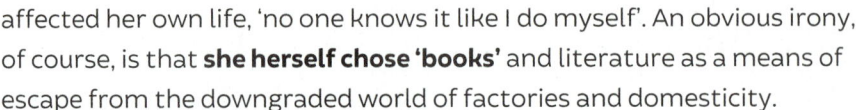

Writing About the Poem

'The effective use of powerful and compassionate language is a recurring feature of Paula Meehan's poetry.' Discuss this view, with reference to 'The Exact Moment I Became a Poet'.

Sample Paragraph

'The exact moment I became a poet' is typical of Paula Meehan. All through, she defends women in jobs who are looked down on. As a young girl, she objects to a teacher saying the factory is somewhere failures 'end up'. The teacher has a position of privilage. She is in authority and this is what Meehan challanges, showing compassion towards ordinary girls. She uses forceful language, saying the privilaged middle class 'robbed the labour of dignity'. Meehan confronts people treating factory-girls as non-human, using a powerful image – 'trussed up like chickens on a conveyor belt'. This idea is repeated when she says nothing has changed. Meehan's tone is challanging all through. The ending image is very forceful – 'words pluck you, leave you naked' and shows sympathy for how women can be unfairly treated.

EXAMINER'S COMMENT

There are several good discussion points here that address the question and focus on language use throughout the poem. Reference to tone, repetition and imagery show reasonably close engagement with the text. Expression is repetitive, however, with some mechanical flaws (e.g. 'privilage', 'challanging') and slight misquotations. A solid middle-grade response.

Class/Homework Exercises

1. 'Paula Meehan's most compelling poems often explore painful memories of childhood.' To what extent is this true of 'The Exact Moment I Became a Poet'? Support the points you make with reference to the text.
2. In your view, how relevant is 'The Exact Moment I Became a Poet' to Ireland today? Develop your answer with reference to the poem.

Points to Consider

- Meehan takes up the struggle for self-definition on behalf of women.
- Themes include work, social class divisions, prejudice and resistance.
- Variety of tones: indignant, empathetic, reflective, impassioned and critical.
- Effective use of direct speech, developed metaphor, imagery and repetition.

6 My Father Perceived as a Vision of St Francis

for Brendan Kennelly

It was the piebald horse in next door's garden
frightened me out of a dream
with her dawn whinny. I was back
in the boxroom of the house,
my brother's room now, 5
full of ties and sweaters and secrets.
Bottles chinked on the doorstep,
the first bus pulled up to the stop.
The rest of the house slept

except for my father. I heard 10
him rake the ash from the grate,
plug in the kettle, hum a snatch of a tune.
Then he unlocked the back door
and stepped out into the garden.

Autumn was nearly done, the first frost 15
whitened the slates of the estate.
He was older than I had reckoned,
his hair completely silver,
and for the first time I saw the stoop
of his shoulder, saw that 20
his leg was stiff. What's he at?
So early and still stars in the west?

They came then: birds
of every size, shape, colour; they came
from the hedges and shrubs, 25
from eaves and garden sheds,
from the industrial estate, outlying fields,
from Dubber Cross they came
and the ditches of the North Road.

The garden was a pandemonium 30
when my father threw up his hands
and tossed the crumbs to the air. The sun

cleared O'Reilly's chimney
and he was suddenly radiant,
a perfect vision of St Francis,   35
made whole, made young again,
in a Finglas garden.

cleared: rose above.
radiant: glowing, transformed.
vision: image, apparition.
whole: complete, unspoiled.
Finglas: Dublin suburb.

PAULA MEEHAN

'a pandemonium'

👤 Personal Response

1. In your view, what was Meehan's attitude towards her father? Does she pity, ridicule or admire the elderly man? Briefly explain your response with reference to the poem.
2. What is your impression of the Dublin suburb of Finglas portrayed in the poem? Support your answer with reference to the text.
3. Meehan's poem is a powerful statement about time and ageing. In your opinion, what is the poet's central theme or message?

👁 Critical Literacy

Paula Meehan creates a loving song of praise and triumph in her observational poem, 'My Father Perceived as a Vision of St Francis', from her 1994 collection *Pillow Talk*. She recounts a story of an overnight stay she made as an adult in the family home in Finglas. Intrigued by her father's early morning rising and activity, she witnessed a man who was transformed.

A striking opening recalls the poet's frightened reaction to a piebald horse in a neighbouring garden. The gentle phrase, 'dawn whinny,' evokes the animal's soft neighing sound. A series of alliterative 'b' sounds ('back', 'boxroom', 'brother's') reinforce the confined sense of her claustrophobic bedroom. Another onomatopoeic sound, 'chinked', announces the early morning arrival of the milkman, delivering bottles of milk. Everyday life is slowly resuming its normal activity. Sibilance

POETRY FOCUS

is used to suggest the quiet household, 'The rest of the house slept' (line 9). One person is already downstairs, however. Meehan describes her father's routine activities. He is busy preparing for the day ahead – clearing the grate, boiling the kettle. The noise of the plug in the electric socket is accompanied by his singing 'a snatch of a tune'. This colloquial phrase roots the family in their Dublin **working-class environment**.

Everything changes when her father crosses the threshold from the mundane domestic interior to the dream-like exterior, and 'stepped out into the garden'. The world of nature is described in line 15. Personification conjures up the changing seasons, 'Autumn was nearly done'. Alliteration suggests the onset of cold, withering winter, 'first frost/whitened'. Suddenly the poet realises that her father has aged more than she had thought. His 'completely silver' hair mirrors the early white frost on the dark roof slates of the housing estate. **The poet's compassionate eye notices the wear and tear of time**. A run-on line suggests the 'stoop/of his shoulder'. Rhetorical questions reflect the poet's fascination as she observes her father closely, 'What's he at?/So early and still stars in the west?'

Line 23 marks a **dramatic development**. A rush of birds replaces the orderly early morning movement. Suddenly, this riotous abundance of nature is on full display. The birds were of 'every size, shape, colour'. They flew in from 'hedges and shrubs', 'garden sheds', 'outlying fields'. The noise in the garden is described as 'pandemonium'. Meehan watches her father greet the dawn with what appears to be his daily ritual of feeding the birds. Raising his arms, he 'tossed the crumbs to the air'.

The old man's gesture is transformative. Amid the commotion of wings moving and the sun rising above a neighbour's chimney, the poet's perception of her father is altered. He had become 'radiant', **ecstatic in his happiness**. In his daughter's estimation, he had replicated the caring action of St Francis of Assisi, the patron saint of animals and the environment. No longer was her father stiff and stooped but vibrant ('young again') in his simple suburban garden. Like the saint, he was 'whole' and at one with nature's creatures.

The poem is firmly anchored in **autobiographical experience**. While Meehan celebrates a local community, she has a heightened awareness of changing times and human mortality. Her sympathetic, intuitive tone recollects and transforms her father. In the vision of the poem's title, he is by no means a stereotypical patriarchal figure, but an iconic nurturing man. For the poet, this simple ritual of her father feeding the birds is a moment of revelation when she unexpectedly sees him in an entirely different light, associating him closely with the sanctity and goodness of the gentle St Francis. The focus on vivid images, small details and the poem's free-flowing form are all in keeping with this eye-opening epiphany.

✍ Writing About the Poem

'Paula Meehan's specific use of language creates a place where private memory and ecology meet.' Discuss this view, with reference to 'My Father Perceived as a Vision of St Francis'.

Sample Paragraph

In 'My Father Perceived as a Vision of St Francis', Meehan uses everyday Dublin speech to create a loving portrait of her father. His recreation as a 'perfect vision of St Francis' is the point where an intimate family memory, mythic story and love for the environment all meet. Onomatopoeia recreates the sleepy housing estate where an ordinary man prepares for a new day. He hums a 'snatch of a tune', the colloquial expression placing her father in his Finglas community. But one simple action transforms him into a symbol of the saint of wildlife and nature, 'my father threw up his hands and tossed the crumbs'. St Francis is often depicted in paintings holding a bird in his hand. Meehan's father is now transfigured, no longer old but 'young again'. He has crossed into a spiritual existence, sharing with Francis an autumnal holy day, 'in a Finglas garden'.

> **EXAMINER'S COMMENT**
> Clear and sustained top-grade response that focuses on the three elements of this challenging question (memory, myth and ecology). The commentary succeeds in tracing the progress of thought in the poem and is rounded off with an impressive overview. Quotations are integrated into the discussion and used effectively to support points.

✒ Class/Homework Exercises

1. 'Paula Meehan places lyrical moments of transcendence into everyday life.' Discuss this statement with reference to 'My Father Perceived as a Vision of St Francis'.
2. 'Meehan's most heart-rending poems highlight the twin themes of love and loss.' To what extent is this true of 'My Father Perceived as a Vision of St Francis'? Support the points you make with suitable reference to the poem.

⊙ Points to Consider

- **Moving tribute expressing enthusiastic praise for the poet's father.**
- **Intriguing parallels between Meehan's father and the Italian saint.**
- **Keen evocation of a particular person, place and time.**
- **Range of tones: wistful, nostalgic, compassionate, illuminating and respectful.**

7 🔊 Hearth Lesson

Title: A hearth is the front area of a fireplace, often associated with home and family.

Either phrase will bring it back —
money to burn, burning a hole in your pocket.

I am crouched by the fire
in the flat in Seán McDermott Street
while Zeus and Hera battle it out: 5

for his every thunderbolt
she had the killing glance;
she'll see his fancyman
and raise him the Cosmo Snooker Hall;
he'll see her 'the only way you get any   10
attention around here is if you neigh';
he'll raise her airs and graces
or the mental state of her siblings,
every last one of them.

I'm net, umpire, and court; most balls   15
are lobbed over my head.
Even then I can judge it's better
than brooding and silence and the particular hell of the unsaid,
of 'tell your mother…' 'ask your father…'.

Even then I can tell it was money,   20
the lack of it day after day,
at the root of the bitter words
but nothing prepared us one teatime
when he handed up his wages.

She straightened each rumpled pound note, then   25
a weariness come suddenly over her,
she threw the lot in the fire.

The flames were blue and pink and green,
A marvellous sight, an alchemical scene.

'It's not enough,' she stated simply.   30
And we all knew it wasn't.

The flames sheered from cinder to chimney breast
like trapped exotic birds;
the shadows jumped floor to ceiling, and she'd
had the last, the astonishing, word.   35

burn: waste.
burning a hole: eager to spend cash.

Zeus and Hera: In Greek mythology, Zeus was king of the gods and had a tempestuous relationship with his wife Hera, goddess of women.
thunderbolt: violent outburst.
fancyman: lover, boyfriend.

neigh: high-pitched cry horses make.
airs and graces: pretentiousness, showing off.
siblings: sisters and brothers.

umpire: adjudicator, referee.
lobbed: hurled.

brooding: sulking.

rumpled: crumpled, creased.
pound note: banknote used in Ireland until 2002.

alchemical: magical, transformative, cathartic.

sheered from cinder to chimney breast: spread upwards.
exotic: strange and colourful.

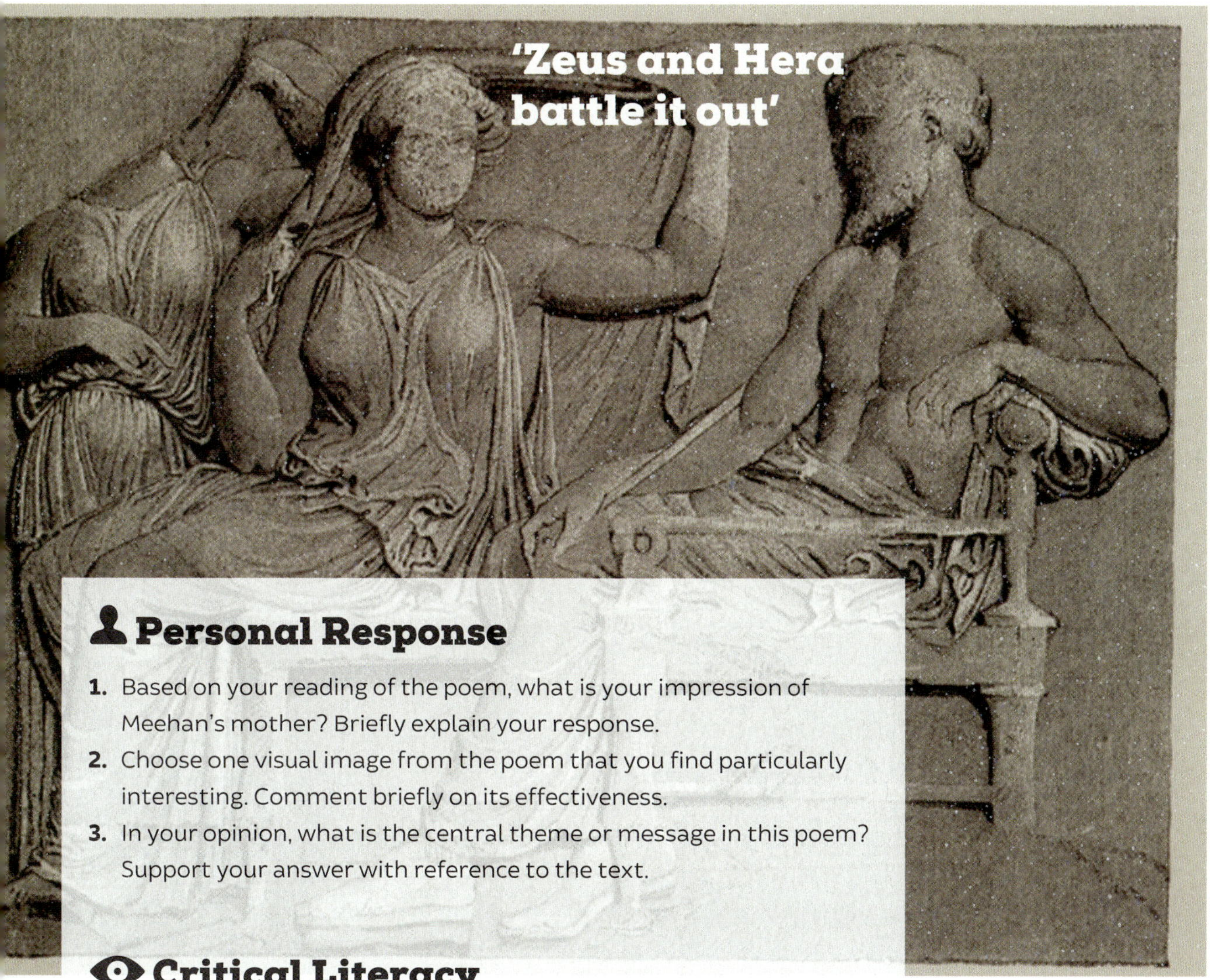

'Zeus and Hera battle it out'

PAULA MEEHAN

👤 Personal Response

1. Based on your reading of the poem, what is your impression of Meehan's mother? Briefly explain your response.
2. Choose one visual image from the poem that you find particularly interesting. Comment briefly on its effectiveness.
3. In your opinion, what is the central theme or message in this poem? Support your answer with reference to the text.

👁 Critical Literacy

Paula Meehan has written many biographical poems mourning the loss of family and remembrances of childhood. Some of these, including 'Hearth Lesson', are found in her 2010 collection *Painting Rain*, and reflect on the politics of the family as a place of unrest. The poet has spoken about her interest in such confessional poetry: 'I wrote what one of my friends calls "the shallow grave poems", excavations of material in my own family life, material that has always disturbed and frightened me'.

The colloquial expressions Meehan quotes in the poem's opening lines trigger stressful childhood memories of family conflict: '*money to burn, burning a hole in your pocket*'. Economic issues were central to the disagreements between her parents. Indeed, the poet is still haunted by the **sarcastic phrases** she remembers from the harsh quarrels between her mother and father. The use of italics emphasises the derisive nature of their rows. Meehan's image of herself as a young child 'crouched by the fire' and already crushed by the tension surrounding her adds poignancy to the unhappy domestic scene.

261 |

POETRY FOCUS

The adult poet finds inspiration in classical references, using Greek mythology to evoke the confrontational mood and her own enduring feelings of hurt. Reflecting on the turbulent relationship between her parents, she imagines this ordinary inner-city Dublin couple into Zeus and Hera. Meehan can now express the **exaggerated perception** she first had when she witnessed her mother and father 'battle it out'. The sadness of their seemingly epic encounters remains, even though the poet has developed a clearer understanding of their lives.

In stanza three, their stormy **marriage is compared to a mock-heroic poker match** between Zeus and his goddess wife. Using an extended metaphor, the poet recollects several dramatic scenes from their vicious exchanges: 'for his every thunderbolt/she had the killing glance'. Card game terminology illustrates how the couple traded spiteful insults. In response to his accusations of unfaithfulness ('she'll see his fancyman'), her mother complains about him wasting time and money on gambling ('raise him the Cosmo Snooker Hall').

Meehan recognises the cynical frustration of a wife who feels unloved because her husband spends so much time betting on horses: 'the only way you get any/attention around here is if you neigh'. As the recriminations continue, the father resorts to sneering. He accuses the poet's mother of putting on 'airs and graces'. Tempers flare and he ends up questioning the sanity of her entire family, 'every last one of them'. **Short lines and brisk rhythms** emphasise the sharp tone of their vindictive dialogue.

Throughout all of this, Meehan is able to cross time and space to re-establish this lost connection with her early home life. We get a poignant sense of the trauma of a child who was powerless to ease the tension. The **tennis metaphor** in stanza four develops the idea that the strained mood was played out like another point-scoring game around her: 'I'm net, umpire and court'. In particular, she remembers experiencing the awkward 'brooding and silence'. Even worse was the 'hell' of being used as a means of communication between her parents, 'tell your mother ...', 'ask your father ...'.

The tone becomes more analytical in stanza five as Meehan acknowledges that poverty was always a factor in the 'bitter' disagreements between her parents: 'Even then I can tell it was money,/the lack of it day after day'. The poet is then reminded of **a defining moment** 'one teatime' when her father 'handed up his wages'. Nothing prepared the family for her mother's extraordinary reaction. Slowly and deliberately, 'she threw the lot in the fire'.

Looking back on this **dramatic event**, the poet remembers the vivid colours of the flames, 'blue and pink and green'. She recalls her mother's weary words, 'It's not enough' – something which she and her siblings instinctively understood at the time, 'we all knew it wasn't'. Indeed, the mother's stark

PAULA MEEHAN

statement captures the hopelessness of someone whose unhappiness is not simply caused by lack of money, but who is disillusioned by a life of quiet desperation.

In the final stanza, Meehan focuses on how inspired she is by her mother's unexpected act of defiance. **Vivid descriptive details** of the burning banknotes create a startling situation that is charged with energy; it is almost surreal. The force of the flames is 'like trapped exotic birds', an evocative simile that reflects the poet's intense awareness of her mother's troubled life. In the end, she is left in awe of a woman who has triumphed by having 'the last, the astonishing, word'.

The concluding lines seem to range over various emotional responses from excitement to empathy and ultimately, admiration. The poet clearly celebrates her mother's courage in challenging a patriarchal world that forces many women to rely on their husbands. Yet there is also a broader appreciation of her parents as two unhappy people who are both victims of their times. Throughout the poem, Meehan's mother has been presented as angry, spirited, unpredictable and enigmatic. However, she has taught her daughter to resist oppression and be true to herself. Is this the crucial lesson Meehan has learned?

✒ Writing About the Poem

'Meehan's attitude to family relationships is often conflicted and unresolved.' To what extent is this the case in 'Hearth Lesson'? Support your answer with reference to the text.

Sample Paragraph

Paula Meehan was born in 1955 and grew up in the inner city before moving to Finglas, a suburb just north of Dublin. Many of her poems deal with family and especially her mother who died in her forties. Meehan had an uneasy relationship with her, but in 'Hearth Lesson', she shows it was complicated. She remembers the rows between her parents – usually over money – the 'lack of it'. Meehan 'crouched by the fire'. Once, her mother was so depressed she threw the weekly pay-packet into the flames. The poet is astonished by such a rebellious thing. She is in shock, but it was 'a marvellous sight'. Basically, Meehan is conflicted. She sees both parents under pressure, but she understands her mother's desperation.

EXAMINER'S COMMENT

Good personal response that engages reasonably well with the question. Time spent on unnecessary biographical details at the start could have been used to examine the poem in greater depth. More discussion about the poet's own relationship with her parents – as the 'umpire' caught up in their rows – would have improved the basic middle-grade standard.

Class/Homework Exercises

1. 'Meehan's carefully chosen language is ideally suited to the disturbing subject matter she often addresses in her poetry.' Discuss this view, with particular reference to 'Hearth Lesson'.
2. 'Readers engage with Paula Meehan's poems because she writes about everyday human experiences that have a universal relevance.' To what extent is this true of 'Hearth Lesson'? Support your answer with reference to the text.

Points to Consider

- **Family life, Irish society and gender roles in the 1960s are all central themes.**
- **Good use of extended metaphors: mythology, poker and tennis.**
- **Variety of tones: nostalgic, realistic, reflective, regretful and admiring.**
- **Effective use of dramatic language, dialogue and vivid imagery.**
- **Interesting, thought-provoking ending.**

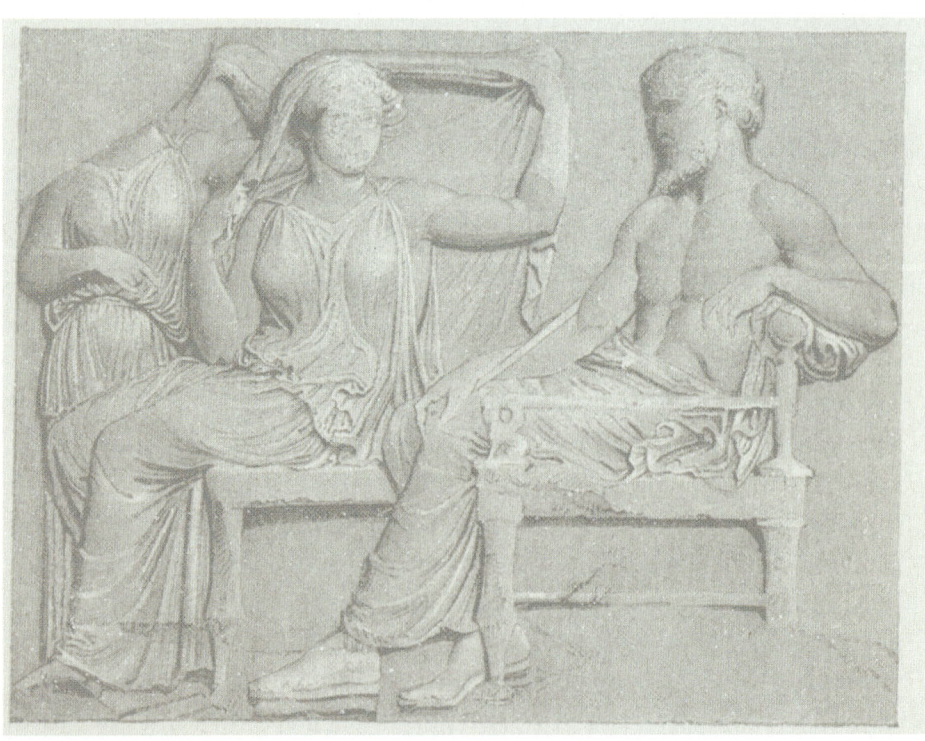

8 Prayer for the Children of Longing

PAULA MEEHAN

A poem commissioned by the community of Dublin's north inner city for the lighting of the Christmas tree in Buckingham Street, to remember their children who died from drug use.

Great tree from the far northern forest
Still rich with the sap of the forest
Here at the heart of winter
Here at the heart of the city

Grant us the clarity of ice   5
The comfort of snow
The cool memory of trees
Grant us the forest's silence
The snow's breathless quiet

For one moment to freeze   10
The scream, the siren, the knock on the door
The needle in its track
The knife in the back

In that silence let us hear
The song of the children of longing   15
In that silence let us catch
The breath of the children of longing

The echo of their voices through the city streets
The streets that defeated them
That brought them to their knees   20
The streets that couldn't shelter them
That spellbound them in alleyways
The streets that blew their minds
That led them astray, out of reach of our saving
The streets that gave them visions and dreams   25
That promised them everything
That delivered nothing

The streets that broke their backs
The streets that we brought them home to

Great tree: large Christmas tree erected annually at Buckingham Street by the community to remember the children's tragic deaths.
sap: liquid energy and strength.

clarity: transparency, intelligibility.

siren: warning alarm on police car or ambulance.

longing: craving, wishing for something, often something unattainable.

spellbound: fascinated, mesmerised.
alleyways: narrow laneways.
astray: off course.

visions: ideas, hallucinations, revelations.

Let their names be the wind through the branches 30
Let their names be the song of the river
Let their names be the holiest prayers

Under the starlight, under the moonlight
In the light of this tree

Here at the heart of winter 35
Here at the heart of the city

'In the light of this tree'

👤 Personal Response

1. Meehan refers to two different locations in the opening nine lines of the poem. Comment on how she establishes these contrasting settings through her choice of poetic techniques (directly addressing the tree, natural imagery, repetition, etc.).
2. Why, in your opinion, is the tone of the poem bitter and accusatory in lines 18–29? Briefly explain your response.
3. Do you regard Meehan's depiction of the tragedy of the young people's deaths from drug use as sentimental or realistic? Give reasons for your answer, using reference to the text.

⊙ Critical Literacy

PAULA MEEHAN

The community of Dublin's north inner city commissioned Paula Meehan to write a poem commemorating young people who had died as a result of a heroin epidemic in the city during the 1980s. Meehan's warm response, published in her collection *Painting Rain* (2009), explores the threads which link trauma, memory, natural imagery and recovery in the form of a spiritual request. The poem also demonstrates Meehan's commitment to her local community and her role as a spokesperson for its residents.

This **tender elegy of love and loss** begins with a direct address to the Christmas tree erected annually by the Buckingham Street community in memory of their children who died from drug abuse. The tree still contains the life-giving 'sap' of the 'far northern forest' where it grew, in contrast to those who have lost their lives so tragically. Meehan's repetition of 'heart' not only refers to the new location of the festive tree in the middle of the city but also to the enduring love within the community. On behalf of the distraught residents of the inner city, she asks for the gifts of the forest – particularly 'the clarity of ice' (line 5), so that families can fully come to terms with the past.

Meehan also asks for the healing of nature, the 'comfort of snow' which blankets everything, beautiful and ugly, in pristine white. She wants its 'breathless quiet' to clear a place where relatives can come together to grieve and understand the terrible events of what happened to all the children they mourn. The verb 'freeze' (line 10) serves as a pivotal point, taking the poem back in time to those raw, cruel memories.

The poet details the **horror of the drug scene** on the city streets in the sibilant spine-chilling 'scream' and the high-pitched sound of the approaching 'siren'. Meehan's unsettling phrase 'the knock on the door' is a poignant reminder of the announcement of yet another heart-rending death when the authorities break the tragic news to anxious parents. In lines 12 and 13, the grim reality of drug use is further conveyed in equally disturbing language ('The needle in its track', 'The knife in the back') adding a devastating impact.

It is in this sacred location, presided over by the Christmas tree, that the poet wants everyone to remember 'the song of the children'. **Their inarticulate cry of 'longing' was ignored** by the busy modern world. Meehan's belief is that these young people were victims of unemployment and poverty, regarded by society as waste material. This lack of a future, of the possibility of love and building a family 'defeated them'. So they disappeared into the oblivion of drugs, 'spellbound them in alleyways', excluded from 'streets that couldn't shelter them' (line 21). The angry tone and striking visual imagery reflect the poet's sense of a whole generation of children who have been failed.

POETRY FOCUS

From Meehan's point of view, the children were led astray, disconnected from their past and families, 'out of reach of our saving'. She acknowledges the wasted potential of these vulnerable young people, who were exploited by drug dealers and a ruthless world which 'gave them visions and dreams' – only to dash them. In turn, the children wandered in the maze of an impersonal society which 'delivered nothing'. The alliterative phrase 'broke their backs' emphasises the pressure which resulted in the fracturing and crushing of the young. However, in line 29, the phrase 'we brought them home' marks a pivotal change as Meehan's bitter, accusatory voice is replaced by a much more sympathetic tone.

The soothing mantra of the final lines references the natural rhythms of the universe, those of 'the wind' and the 'river'. Meehan has used repetition throughout the poem to convey the **sense of a public choral prayer**. The spiritual quality of the conclusion is even more explicit, 'Let their names be the holiest prayers'. The poet restores dignity to a broken community living through the anguish of burying their children. Her powerful voice breaks the silence 'Under the starlight, under the moonlight'. The repetition of 'Here' demonstrates how a special place has been set aside at Christmas to remember, honour and console.

The poem ends as it began, 'at the heart'. With **characteristic compassion,** Meehan has succeeded in changing our perception of the dead children by bringing them home to their families, their community and the natural world. The soft aural effects and flowing lines, without any punctuation, mirror the ceaseless blowing of the wind and the endless movement of the river.

✒ Writing About the Poem

'Paula Meehan's deep sense of anger is often evident in her most compelling poems.' Discuss this view, with reference to 'Prayer for the Children of Longing'.

Sample Paragraph

Paula Meehan's outrage can be felt in 'Prayer for the Children of Longing' when she describes the waste of young lives by modern society. Yet it is the poet's empathetic approach which I remember. This is seen in the image of the 'Great tree' which will bring 'comfort' to heal the grieving families. Run-on lines convey powerful emotion, 'let us hear/The song of the children of longing'. The poem is based on the rhythms of a prayer, 'Grant us', 'Let us'. I felt that it summed up the tragedy of addiction, 'The scream, the siren'. What was interesting to me was that it transformed this violent reality by linking it to the healing beauty of nature, 'the song of the river'. This symbolised that there is more support for young addicts these days. Instead, Meehan restores their self-worth by the final request, 'Let their names be the holiest prayers'. I found calmness in the conclusion, where there was a strong feeling of communal love.

PAULA MEEHAN

EXAMINER'S COMMENT

Good personal engagement with the poem and a clear sustained response to the question. Supportive discussion points made effective reference to the poet's compelling language – including imagery, rhythm and tone. Controlled expression and apt quotations added to the quality of this assured top-grade answer.

Class/Homework Exercises

1. 'Paula Meehan's dynamic, positive poetry depicts the cruelty and deprivation of her working-class background.' Discuss this statement with reference to 'Prayer for the Children of Longing'.
2. 'Meehan's poetry uses effective poetic techniques, such as repetition, sound effects and descriptive detail to convey her themes.' To what extent is this true of 'Prayer for the Children of Longing'? Support the points you make with suitable reference to the poem.

Points to Consider

- **Key themes of loss, alienation, waste, longing and belonging.**
- **Exact visual and aural details contrast the squalid inner city with the cool beauty of nature.**
- **Simple direct language appropriate to the subject matter adds authenticity.**
- **Use of long incantatory lines, prayer-like rhythms and deep spiritual yearning.**
- **Variety of tones: pleading, objective, scathing, reflective and consolatory.**
- **Repetition and lack of punctuation intensify the poem's momentum.**

9 Death of a Field

The field itself is lost the morning it becomes a site
When the Notice goes up: Fingal County Council — 44 units

The memory of the field is lost with the loss of its herbs

Though the woodpigeons in the willow
The finches in what's left of the hawthorn hedge   5
And the wagtail in the elder
Sing on their hungry summer song

The magpies sound like flying castanets

And the memory of the field disappears with its flora:
Who can know the yearning of yarrow   10
Or the plight of the scarlet pimpernel
Whose true colour is orange?

The end of the field is the end of the hidey holes
Where first smokes, first tokes, first gropes
Were had to the scentless mayweed   15

The end of the field as we know it is the start of the estate
The site to be planted with houses each two or three bedroom
Nest of sorrow and chemical, cargo of joy

The end of dandelion is the start of Flash
The end of dock is the start of Pledge   20
The end of teazel is the start of Ariel
The end of primrose is the start of Brillo
The end of thistle is the start of Bounce
The end of sloe is the start of Oxyaction
The end of herb robert is the start of Brasso   25
The end of eyebright is the start of Persil

Who amongst us is able to number the end of grasses
To number the losses of each seeding head?

---

site: land set aside for building.
Notice: official sign, poster.

herbs: plants used for flavouring food or for medicine.

woodpigeons: common garden birds.
willow: willow tree.
finches: small birds.
wagtail: colourful bird.
elder: flowering tree.

castanets: clackers, percussion instruments.

flora: vegetation, plant life.
yarrow: white flowering plant.
plight: predicament.
scarlet pimpernel: plant with brightly coloured flowers.

tokes: cannabis smoking.
mayweed: common summer-flowering wildflower.

cargo: load.

Flash: cleaning product (the first of several listed).
dock: perennial weed.
teazel: tall flowering plant.

sloe: blackthorn.
Oxyaction: popular chemical cleanser.
herb robert: flowering plant with pink flowers.
eyebright: wildflower with small white flowers.

PAULA MEEHAN

                I'll walk out once
Barefoot under the moon to know the field   30
Through the soles of my feet to hear
The myriad leaf lives green and singing   **myriad:** countless.
The million million cycles of being in wing

That — before the field become map memory
In some archive on some architect's screen   35   **archive:** database.
I might possess it or it possess me
Through its night dew, its moon white caul   **caul:** cover.
Its slick and shine and its profligacy   **profligacy:** extravagance.
In every wingbeat in every beat of time   **wingbeat:** motion of a bird's wings in flight.

'the end of grasses'

👤 Personal Response

1. Select one image or line from the poem that you find particularly interesting. Briefly explain your choice.
2. Comment on Meehan's use of repetition throughout the poem. In your view, is it effective or over-done? Give a reason for your answer.
3. Describe the poet's tone throughout lines 29–39. In your opinion, is it angry, reflective, nostalgic or sentimental? Briefly explain your response.

◉ Critical Literacy

This is another of Paula Meehan's signature public poems taken from her 2009 collection *Painting Rain*. It addresses change and loss – particularly nature's losses. 'Death of a Field' is a response to the rampant planning and housing development that characterised much of Celtic Tiger Ireland during the nineties and noughties. Set in a suburban construction site, the poem becomes an elegy for traditional communities during those so-called boom years.

In keeping with the impassioned title, Meehan's opening line reflects her own deep feeling of sorrow. The field is personified and its loss will affect the poet directly. She draws attention to the functional business-like language used on the local planning authority's written 'Notice'. What was once a 'field' is already 'lost' and redefined as a 'site'. A single isolated line emphasises the **irreversible transformation of landscape**: 'The memory of the field is lost with the loss of its herbs'

The poet recognises birds as familiar presences. For the moment, their sounds and rituals are unchanged. The woodpigeons, finches and wagtail all depend for survival on this natural environment where they sing 'their hungry summer song'. Sibilance and soft aural effects ('willow', 'elder') add to the tender elegiac tone. Nature's vibrancy is also acknowledged: 'The magpies sound like flying castanets' (line 8). This vivid simile – referring to exotic Spanish music – highlights Meehan's awareness of the dynamism and excitement of the natural world.

In listing the flora and fauna that will disappear with the housing project, Meehan details the process of both the field's and the humans' loss of memory of this open space. **Rhetorical language** ('Who can know the yearning of yarrow/Or the plight of the scarlet pimpernel') personifies the endangered vegetation. The choice of agonising terms ('yearning' and 'plight') are clearly aimed at appealing to the reader's sympathies.

With inevitable progress and development, the field loses identity. People also lose contact with their personal memories of growing up in the locality. **Nostalgia is tinged with humour** in lines 13 and 14 when the poet reflects on playing childhood games here in 'hidey holes' and later coming-of-age experiences, 'first smokes, first tokes, first gropes'. She also notes the way language changes over time as open space soon becomes an 'estate'.

Oddly, the word 'estate' has connotations with Ireland's grand country houses belonging to the landed gentry during colonial times. However, the end of this field is the start of the modern-day residential estate. Along **with all the new homes come consumer goods** – something else that the poet dislikes. Meehan's thoughts return to what will happen when the earth-moving machines arrive to displace the wild herbs growing here. Her bitterly

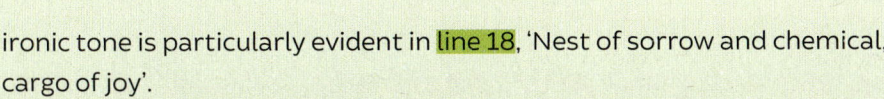

ironic tone is particularly evident in line 18, 'Nest of sorrow and chemical, cargo of joy'.

As the field gives way to concrete, wild plants will disappear – including dandelion, thistle and eyebright. Meehan organises lines 19–26 into a prayer-like mantra through anaphora (repetition at the beginning of successive phrases). She makes **effective use of emphatic contrast**: 'The end of primrose is the start of Brillo', placing the delicate flower beside the rough-sounding scouring pad. A list of nature's losses is compared to leading household brand names, such as Flash, Pledge and Persil. This format allows the poet to highlight aspects of the modern world that she deplores. The rhythmic chanting leads to another rhetorical question warning of future disaster: 'Who amongst us is able to number the end of grasses' (line 27).

For Meehan, nature is mysterious and unknowable. Yet she is determined to create a lasting personal connection with the landscape. She imagines communing with it ('Barefoot under the moon') one last time before it is developed. Her intention is to 'know the field/Through the soles of my feet'. She wants to experience its 'myriad leaf lives', even though this would be like trying to understand creation itself, an experience she describes as the 'million million cycles of being in wing' (line 33). Meehan's **vibrant evocative imagery** creates a haunting sense of the untamed growth and timeless beauty of the natural world.

It could, of course, be argued that the poet is taking an unrealistic approach to an **age-old conflict of interests**. While it's vital to protect natural spaces, housing is a basic human need. In dramatising the battle between nature and urban development, the writing style – particularly the use of repetition – is somewhat laboured and some readers may find the didactic tone heavy-handed at times.

However, the poem's conclusion focuses on Meehan's intimate appreciation of landscape and her acceptance that the field is destined to end up as a 'map memory' in an architect's data bank. This makes her even more determined that readers share her fears about future environmental destruction. The poet's **voice becomes more urgent** as she expresses her heartfelt desire to be at one with nature so that 'I might possess it or it possess me'. In a poignantly beautiful image, she compares the dew-covered field to the 'moon white caul' of a vulnerable new-born child.

By challenging the recklessness of unrestrained capitalism, Meehan wishes to let nature work its magic on her so that she becomes the voice promoting the rich 'profligacy' of nature and the 'slick and shine' of what will soon be absent. Her enthusiasm is evident in the romanticised tone and fast-moving rhythm of the final lines. Having envisaged the transformation of a natural space that she values, Meehan leaves readers with a **thought-provoking elegy** about the destruction of a small ecosystem, a kind of death that signifies a much greater global threat.

Writing About the Poem

'Paula Meehan frequently uses contrast as an effective literary technique to convey key themes in her poetry.' Discuss this statement, with particular reference to 'Death of a Field'.

Sample Paragraph

'Death of a Field' uses contrast to show up the negative effects of house construction. The first example is when the 'field' is described as a 'site'. Meehan repeats two contrasting words, 'end' and 'start', to show up how the change of land use affects nature – 'The end of herb robert is the start of Brasso'. This is part of a whole list of examples where herbs are compared to detergents, like Brillo and Bounce. Even the quiet and harsh sounds are contrasted. This made me think of the link between the field's destruction and the estate's construction. Contrast adds emphasis to the main point that people must pay an extra price for new houses in the loss of the green environment.

EXAMINER'S COMMENT

Some good personal commentary here that engages with the question. Reference to several examples of effective contrast are well supported with accurate quotations. These are integrated into the discussion and show reasonably close engagement with the text. While expression is functional, points are clear. A solid middle-grade response.

Class/Homework Exercises

1. In your opinion, is 'Death of a Field' still relevant to Ireland today? Develop your answer with suitable textual support.
2. 'Many of Meehan's most heartfelt poems are elegies that lament Irish places and culture.' Discuss this view, with particular reference to 'Death of a Field'.

Points to Consider

- Poet addresses the impact of urban development and consumerism on the natural world.
- Contrasting tones: angry, heartfelt, nostalgic, ironic, didactic and anguished.
- Effective use of contrast, personification, onomatopoeia and vivid imagery.
- Rhetorical style: repetition, questions, anaphora, speech rhythms, emotive language, etc.

10. Them Ducks Died for Ireland

PAULA MEEHAN

'*6 of our waterfowl were killed or shot, 7 of the garden seats broken and about 300 shrubs destroyed.*'
Park Superintendent in his report on the damage to
St Stephen's Green sustained during the Easter Rising, 1916

Time slides slowly down the sash window
puddling in light on oaken boards. The Green
is a great lung, exhaling like breath on the pane
the seasons' turn, sunset and moonset, the ebb and flow

of stars. And once made mirror to smoke and fire,   5
a Republic's destiny in a Countess' stride,
the bloodprice both summons and antidote to pride.
When we've licked the wounds of history, wounds of war,

we'll salute the stretcher bearer, the nurse in white,
the ones who pick up the pieces, who endure,   10
who live at the edge, and die there and are known

by this archival footnote read by fading light;
fragile as a breathmark on the windowpane or the gesture
of commemorating heroes in bronze and stone.

'a great lung, exhaling like breath'

POETRY FOCUS

👤 Personal Response

1. How effective is Meehan's use of personification and imagery in the first seven lines of the poem? Refer closely to the text in your answer.
2. Describe the dominant tone throughout this poem. Is it reflective, bitter, respectful, disappointed, ironic? Briefly explain your response.
3. In the sestet (last six lines), Meehan focuses on the untold stories of individuals who do not feature prominently in Irish history. In your view, what is her attitude to these people?

👁 Critical Literacy

Painting Rain **(2009) contains a sequence of sonnets, the 'Six Sycamores'. These were based on the six sycamore trees planted by the original Anglo-Irish leaseholders of the buildings around St Stephen's Green. 'Them Ducks Died for Ireland' is set in the aftermath of the 1916 Easter Rising. Meehan has said: 'I wrote the poem out of a fragment I found in the Architectural Archive, the report of the park superintendent in the clean-up of the Revolution'. The poet has also commented: 'We are now looking back to that initiatory event, the Rising, in a different way, retrieving the stories that were written out of history in the post-revolutionary era. I think this is such a healthy thing to do, to change perspective.'**

The sonnet opens with a sibilant personification of Time, which 'slides slowly' down the windows of the magnificent Georgian mansions encircling St Stephen's Green and ends in a pool of light on their polished hardwood floors, 'oaken boards'. Meehan imagines 'The Green' as 'a great lung', a simple but powerful metaphor reflecting the vitality of the changing seasons. All of nature's mystery and beauty is recorded here: 'sunset and moonset', 'the ebb and flow' of the stars. Long run-on lines add to **the stately, harmonious rhythm** in the first quatrain (four-line section).

A very different image is mirrored in the windows in line 5, 'smoke and fire'. **Revolution, destruction and violence once took hold of the Green** during the struggle to achieve Irish liberty. For Meehan, the Rising was the 'summons and antidote to pride'. Irish freedom fighters fought for the ideal of a politically independent and socially classless society. The Citizen Army had dug defensive trenches in the Green but were fired upon by the British who occupied the upper floors of the nearby Shelbourne Hotel (the 'antidote').

After an innocent civilian was killed, they withdrew to the College of Surgeons. The remarkable Countess Markievicz, 'a Countess' stride', **who was herself a member of the Anglo-Irish Ascendancy**, was one of the senior military leaders involved at the time, calling for the cessation of shooting to allow the ducks to be fed every day.

PAULA MEEHAN

The poet imagines how people attempted to recover from the trauma of battle. Like stricken animals, they 'licked the wounds of history, wounds of war'. **Repetition and alliteration emphasise the suffering** of armed struggle. All the participants had paid the 'bloodprice' (line 7), the Irish and British forces, Dublin's citizens and even the natural inhabitants of the Green, the waterfowl.

The sestet (final six lines) moves beyond the immediate confines of the park as **Meehan personally acknowledges those dealing with the aftermath of conflict**, 'the stretcher bearer, the nurse in white' – those left cleaning up the mess and destruction, who 'pick up the pieces'. They must 'endure' and carry on living 'at the edge', the periphery of history. Their stories are not recorded in the official narrative of important events. They are only discovered by a chance reading of a government document 'by fading light'.

The poem concludes as it began, noting the reflections in the windows. **These unknown characters' beautiful 'fragile' stories disappear** like 'breath on the pane', having been relegated to the footnotes of history books. This is in stark contrast to the 'gesture', the courage and sacrifice of the 'heroes' who are formally memorialised in public statues of 'bronze and stone'.

Meehan expresses her **desire to give voice to unrecorded lives** which remain buried within historical narratives. She has rescued the unknown stories of history from oblivion. In the end, readers are left to reflect on how culture copes with revolutionary change. Were the ideals of the 1916 Rising accomplished? Was an inclusive classless society formed where all are given equal respect?

✒ Writing About the Poem

'Paula Meehan's poetry presents a range of views of Ireland's past.' Discuss this statement, with particular reference to 'Them Ducks Died for Ireland'.

Sample Paragraph

'Them Ducks Died for Ireland' recreates the beauty of St Stephen's Green through personification. 'The Green is a great lung' exhaling breath patterns of the peaceful progress of nature, 'sunset and moonset' onto the Georgian windows surrounding the park. Suddenly the peaceful atmosphere is replaced by the 'smoke and fire' of the Rising. Ireland has had a history of conflict. Meehan also makes the point that the stories of the unknown participants of these momentous events are of equal importance to the more famous 'heroes' commemorated in 'bronze and stone'. The park attendant who fed the birds is recognised in this sonnet. Just as 'The Green' made patterns of nature's beauty on the window panes of great mansions, Meehan breathes the stories of history's unknown men and women, 'the stretcher bearer' and the 'nurse in white'. In this reflective poem, she shows that Ireland's past varied from peaceful to violent and heroic.

> **EXAMINER'S COMMENT**
>
> Focused response engaging with both the task and the poem. Some good illustration of the range of perspectives of St Stephen's Green, supported by accurate reference. Points are expressed clearly and quotations are well integrated into the commentary. Overall, a good top-grade standard.

Class/Homework Exercises

1. 'Paula Meehan's carefully crafted poems offer an insightful vision of Irish history.' Discuss this statement with reference to 'Them Ducks Died for Ireland'.
2. 'Meehan's most memorable poetry can be both compassionate and critical.' To what extent is this true of 'Them Ducks Died for Ireland'? Support the points you make with suitable reference to the text.

Points to Consider

- Various perspectives on places and events – the wonder of nature, the destruction of war, the revision of historical narrative.
- Provocative use of contrast, imaginative use of personification.
- Effective sonnet form – contrasting descriptive quatrains of peace and war followed by sober reflective sestet.
- Interesting rhyme/half rhyme scheme – abba, cddc, efg, efg – adds to poem's musicality.
- Long run-on lines in which spoken rhythms carry meaning across line endings, mirroring breath patterns referenced in poem.

Sample Leaving Cert Questions on Meehan's Poetry

1. 'Some of Meehan's most compelling poems are rooted in community and a sense of place.' To what extent do you agree or disagree with this view? Support your answer with reference to the poetry of Paula Meehan on your course.
2. 'Paula Meehan uses evocative language to create poems that include both personal reflection and public commentary.' Discuss this view, supporting your answer with reference to both the themes and language found in the poetry of Meehan on your course.
3. 'Meehan's distinctive poetic vision often gives voice and dignity to individuals who are marginalised or excluded.' To what extent do you agree or disagree with this statement? Develop your answer with reference to the poetry of Paula Meehan on your course.

How do I organise my answer?

(Sample question 1)

'Some of Meehan's most compelling poems are rooted in community and a sense of place.' To what extent do you agree or disagree with this view? Support your answer with reference to the poetry of Paula Meehan on your course.

Sample Plan 1

Intro: *(Stance: partially agree with viewpoint in question)* Meehan creates captivating poetry clearly established in her Dublin working-class community and environment, but she also encourages readers to look out at the wider world.

Point 1: *(Exact details paint a bleak urban landscape, but also hint at world beyond)* 'Buying Winkles' recalls a drab cityscape transformed by a child's imagination; the moon is a 'bonus', the rain makes the winkles 'glisten blue like little/night skies themselves'. But the outside world is suggested – 'The sweetest extra winkle/that brought the sea to me' – and the child's growing curiosity beyond the limits of the city.

Point 2: *(Colloquialism, vivid visual and aural detail locate the poem in community and place, gesture transforms and transcends)* 'My Father Perceived as a Vision of St Francis' includes details describing an ordinary man in his local environment. A simple transcendent gesture evokes the wider world of the saint.

PAULA MEEHAN

Understanding the Prescribed Poetry Question

Marks are awarded using the PCLM Marking Scheme:
P = 15; C = 15; L = 15; M = 5
Total = 50

- **P** (Purpose = 15 marks) refers to the set question and is the launch pad for the answer. This involves engaging with all aspects of the question. Both theme and language must be addressed, although not necessarily equally.
- **C** (Coherence = 15 marks) refers to the organisation of the developed response and the use of accurate, relevant quotation. Paragraphing is essential.
- **L** (Language = 15 marks) refers to the student's skill in controlling language throughout the answer.
- **M** (Mechanics = 5 marks) refers to spelling and grammar.
- Although no specific number of poems is required, students usually discuss at least 3 or 4 in their written responses.
- Aim for at least 800 words, to be completed within 45–50 minutes.

POETRY FOCUS

NOTE

In keeping with the PCLM approach, the student has to take a stance by agreeing, disagreeing or partially agreeing that Meehan's

– **compelling poems** (intimate personal memories, exact detail, resonant voice full of spiritual energy, intense vision capable of transcending family trauma and celebrating life, engaging colloquial language, vivid imagery, forceful repetition, etc.)

... are:

– **rooted in community and a sense of place** (close awareness of inner-city childhood, perception of Irishness and cultural history, enduring communal identity, place names, collective sense of overcoming hardships, folklore, oral tradition, etc.)

Point 3: *(Colloquial language and details create a local environment, mythological references widen to a universal perspective)* 'Hearth Lesson' uses colloquial expressions to describe a bitter family quarrel. Mythological comparisons in the parody card game between Zeus nd Hera illustrate the age-old struggle between men and women.

Point 4: *(Using rhetoric and private memory, the reader is forced to consider uncontrolled housing development)* 'Death of a Field' uses rhetorical questions, emotive contrasts between plants and products and a litany of repetitive phrases to reflect on the beauty of nature under threat of rampant materialism.

Conclusion: Meehan is a poet of the streets and people of working-class Dublin. She fearlessly confronts the city's tragedies and deprivations through forceful poetry. But she also points the reader to a bigger stage featuring ecology, freedom, transcendence and a universal perspective.

Sample Paragraph: Point 2

In 'My Father Perceived as a Vision of St Francis', Meehan remembers her father as 'a perfect vision'. The scene is an early morning suburb, 'a Finglas garden'. Effective onomatopoeia, 'dawn whinny', 'Bottles chinked' establish the ordinary environment. The colloquial phrase, 'hum a snatch of a tune' places her father in his working-class environment. Suddenly, a transformative gesture of her father who 'tossed the crumbs' for the birds changes the entire scene. Her father has transcended the boundaries of age and environment. He is 'made young again' by repeating the saint's simple act of kindness. This poem broadens its outlook from the local environment to the wider world by showing how a simple act of love can free an ordinary man from the struggle to survive and become 'suddenly radiant'.

EXAMINER'S COMMENT

As part of a full essay, this high-grade paragraph demonstrates close engagement with the poem in addressing the question. Good use of reference and accurate quotation – all skilfully worked into the succinct critical comments. Expression is clear, overall, but could have been a little more varied ('environment' is overused).

| 280

(Sample question 2)

'Paula Meehan uses evocative language to create poems that include both personal reflection and public commentary.' Discuss this view, supporting your answer with reference to both the themes and language found in the poetry of Meehan on your course.

Sample Plan 2

Intro: *(Stance: agree with viewpoint in question)* Meehan's poetry flows from her deep love of people and places. Energetic recollections of childhood, family and environment lead to a robust assessment of Ireland's recent social history. Powerful poems encourage readers to examine attitudes to gender, class, history, ecology, etc.

Point 1: *(Personal horror at event, public criticism)* 'The Statue of the Virgin at Granard Speaks' – dramatic monologue of Mary herself who is ironically ineffective in young girl's hour of need, 'I didn't lift a finger to help her'. Further irony of repressive smug Irish society 'tucked up safe and dreaming'.

Point 2: *(Memories of threatened field, public critique of uncontrolled development)* 'Death of a Field' – nostalgic recollection of teenage years, 'where first smokes, first tokes, first gropes'. Simile conjures memory of dynamic wildlife, 'magpies sound like flying castanets'. Startling list of contrasts emphasises the destruction of the precious ecosystem, 'The end of primrose is the start of Brillo'.

Point 3: *(Personal discovery, public reflection on official historical narrative)* 'Them Ducks Died for Ireland' – reflective sonnet emerges from poet's discovery of footnote in Architectural Archive. Georgian windows reflect changing seasons and scenes of the park. Repetition and alliteration detail the 'bloodprice' of the armed struggle paid not only by the combatants but also by the ordinary people, 'wounds of history, wounds of war'.

Point 4: *(Poet's own experience, public commentary on class division)* 'The Exact Moment I Became a Poet' – personal recollection of incident at school ignites poet's indignation at class prejudice, effective use of teacher's direct speech, 'end up'. Anger at degradation of working women she knew, powerfully captured in extended image of poultry, 'trussed like chickens'.

> **NOTE**
>
> In keeping with the PCLM approach, the student has to explore poems of Meehan's on the course that include:
> - **evocative language** (powerful imagery, colloquial speech, personification, repetition, contrast, irony, evocative tones of compassion, regret, reflection, etc.)
>
> ... to create poems that show:
> - **both personal reflection and public commentary** (warm recollected scenes from Irish working-class community, changing perspectives, intense criticism of patriarchal, materialistic society and the havoc it wreaks on fragile communities and natural environments, etc.)

Conclusion: Meehan's poetry shows empathy for her own people and environment. She is a fearless speaker who searches and defends her childhood and her home. Her evocative poems attack the hypocrisy, uncertainty, materialism and changing identities of a modern world.

Sample Paragraph: Point 4

'The Exact Moment I Became a Poet' comes from a recollection from Meehan's childhood. At eight years of age, she heard her teacher warn the students that if they don't 'Attend' to their lessons they will 'end up' in the sewing factory. Meehan is incensed at the term, 'end up'. She feels that the women she knew are being 'robbed' of their dignity because they are working to support their families. A vibrant simile illustrates the prejudice against these women, 'trussed like chickens on a conveyor belt'. The poet extends the image by declaring that class definitions undervalue and diminish a person, 'Words could pluck you … your lovely shiny feathers all gone'. Meehan's poem publicly expresses her indignation at the insult levelled at her own community in her recollection of this childhood memory.

> **EXAMINER'S COMMENT**
>
> Addresses the question directly and engages well with the text. Further emphasis on the evocative elements (moving atmospheres and tones) would have provided more development. Effective use made of apt reference and relevant quotation. Expression is generally clear and impressive (e.g. 'incensed', 'definitions undervalue and diminish'). Solid high-grade standard.

Leaving Cert Sample Essay

'Meehan's distinctive poetic vision often gives voice and dignity to individuals who are marginalised or excluded.' To what extent do you agree or disagree with this view? Support your answer with reference to the poetry of Paula Meehan on your course.

> **EXAM FOCUS**
>
> - As you may not be familiar with some of the poems referred to in the sample plans, substitute poems that you have studied closely.
> - Key points about a particular poem can be developed over more than one paragraph.
> - Paragraphs may also include cross-referencing and discussion of more than one poem.
> - Remember that there is no single 'correct' answer to poetry questions, so always be confident in expressing your own considered response.

Sample Essay

1. Paula Meehan creates poetry which often results in conversations across time where she re-imagines the past. Using innovative poetic forms, vivid visual detail and colloquial language, Meehan acknowledges the importance of working women, celebrates the vivacity of her emigrant aunt, upholds the dignity of the tragic victims of drug abuse and reinstates the memory of ordinary people who lived on the edge of history.

2. 'Prayer for the Children of Longing' is dedicated to the young people in North Dublin's inner city who died from drug abuse. Meehan's inventive use of incantatory lines without punctuation, propels the poem forward through repetitive phrasing, 'Here at', 'Grant us'. She does not avoid the grim reality of the announcement of a child's death, 'The scream, the siren, the knock on the door'. Incisively, she criticises the pressure of a modern world on an impoverished community through startling personification, 'The streets ... That promised them everything/That delivered them nothing'.

3. Yet her empathetic voice allows these neglected children to be heard at last, 'In that silence let us hear'. Meehan restores their dignity so that their names seem like a litany of 'the holiest prayers'. Her soothing voice consoles their grieving families at the foot of the Christmas tree. For the first time, these children are reclaimed from the statistics in a government report listing the victims of drug abuse. They live again 'Under the starlight, under the moonlight'. Meehan has offered a lifeline to the grieving community by naming a shared loss.

4. 'Cora, Auntie' is another elegy whose run-on lines record the vigour of Meehan's emigrant aunt, 'scourge of Croydon train drivers'. She 'tilted at death' like a chivalrous medieval knight using 'humour' as her 'lance'. Once again, Meehan truthfully visualises the sadness of life, 'her body withered', 'a split', 'a tear'. But by focusing on the rich colours and delicate communal craftwork of the women, 'sewing red sequins', the poet presents her aunt as an impressive extrovert. She stands 'on the kitchen table' in her 'white satin dress' with its sewn border of 'sequins red as berries'.

5. Sensual sibilant details, 'promising blossom, summer, the scent of thyme' convey the aunt's positive energy. Meehan's maternal family line is honoured and the lesson of how to live life, with good humour, is recalled through the symbol of a small frivolous object – the glittering sequin. The poet has 'gathered them 'into a tin box' which she now opens 'in memory' of Cora. This is not just a tribute to Meehan's aunt, but to the countless Irish migrants who had to make new lives for themselves and face untold challenges away from their own families.

6. Another elegy, 'The Pattern', allows Meehan to re-live her personal traumatic childhood memories – particularly the uneasy relationship between herself and her mother. Sharp onomatopoeic details convey the reality, 'the sting of her hand across my face in one of our wars'. As before, the poet candidly acknowledges the harsh life of North Dublin's working-class community during the 1950s. Her mother's voice is heard recalling the rough patriarchal world of the time, 'your Granda caught us at the corner./He dragged me in by the hair'. Meehan is horrified that her mother never truly discovered who she was, 'already lost'. Like so many women, she had been restricted by a male-dominated society and endless child-bearing.

INDICATIVE MATERIAL

- **Meehan's distinctive poetic vision** (probing, recording, empathising, reflecting, transforming, drawing lessons) through visual and aural imagery, contrast, direct speech, mythological reference, personification, innovative poetic structure, etc.
  ... gives voice and dignity to:
- **the marginalised** (by widening the perspective on ordinary lives not included in official historical narrative, e.g. the importance of matriarchal family influence, the courage and resilience of the reluctant emigrant, the exploited victims of drug abuse, etc.)

7. But what is even more shocking is Meehan's revelation that her mother wanted to teach her free-spirited daughter 'to follow a pattern' of conformity just as she had. She will 'reel' her daughter 'home'. The poet refuses to accept such restrictions, however, and will make her own choices in life. Overall, the use of direct speech, onomatopoeia and vivid imagery highlights the oppression of Irish women in unforgiving living conditions during earlier times.

8. The sestet in Meehan's sonnet, 'Them Ducks Died for Ireland', also commemorates the marginalised, those who are not mentioned in the history books. The poet discovers by 'fading light' the Park Superintendent's report of the damage sustained in Stephen's Green during the 1916 Rising. Meehan is inspired to honour those on the periphery of these huge national events, such as 'the stretcher-bearer, the nurse in white'. They are the unnamed people who were left to clear up the destruction of the violent military events of 'smoke and fire'. Using a delicate simile, Meehan emphasises how easily their stories can be lost, 'fragile as a breathmark on the windowpane'. Their small acts of bravery are so quickly erased. At least Meehan's poem will 'salute' these marginalised people and help restore their proper place in the historical records.

9. Paula Meehan is keen to defend the uniqueness and relevance of her Dublin working-class roots. She restores shadows of the past in the elegiac stories about her mother and her aunt. She recovers marginal voices that are usually hidden from history. Meehan's sense of solidarity and compassion is evident in so many of her poems, offering dignity to society's outcasts.

(820 words)

EXAMINER'S COMMENT

A well-sustained and clearly supported response that shows some close engagement with Meehan's poetry. Both elements of the question (poetic vision and acknowledgement of the marginalised) are generally addressed throughout, although a little more on the 'distinctive' element would have been welcome. Good examples of the poet's style illustrated – particularly in paragraphs 5 and 8. The note-like commentary in paragraph 7 could have been more developed, but in referencing all four poems, there is effective use of quotations integrated into the discussion. Overall, a well-written top-grade essay.

GRADE: H1
P = 15/15
C = 13/15
L = 13/15
M = 5/5
Total = 46/50

👓 Revision Overview

'Buying Winkles' (OL)
In this nostalgic poem, the poet creates a vivid sense of an urban working-class community and reflects on a magical journey of discovery.

'The Pattern'
Recalling various scenes in a Dublin flat, Meehan considers a difficult mother-daughter relationship. Many of her poems are informed by the voices of women in her family.

'The Statue of the Virgin at Granard Speaks'
Poignant and dramatic poem in which the self-critical 'voice' of the statue also accuses an entire society that lets young women go to waste.

'Cora, Auntie'
Investigating the lives of her family allows the poet freedom to explore her culture and become reconciled with the past. Here she pays tribute to her aunt's courage and resilience.

'The Exact Moment I Became a Poet'
In this autobiographical poem, Meehan takes up the struggle for self-definition on behalf of women. Challenging class division and prejudice is central to much of her poetry.

'My Father Perceived as a Vision of St Francis'
Set in the poet's family home in Finglas, this moving tribute expresses deep feelings of empathy while conveying an underlying sense of transience and mortality.

'Hearth Lesson' (OL)
Another confessional poem from Meehan's disquieting childhood offers a compelling poetic vision of innocence and newfound determination.

'Prayer for the Children of Longing' (OL)
Empathy and solidarity are recurring features of Meehan's poetry. This prayerful poem for victims of drug abuse explores themes of loss, exploitation and community.

'Death of a Field'
Nature is close to Meehan's heart and many of her poems are environmentalist. This plaintive poem addresses some of the adverse effects of urban development.

'Them Ducks Died for Ireland'
In considering the significance of the Easter Rising, Meehan focuses on what has been officially recorded by history – and what has been left out of history.

💬 Last Words

'I love her verbal energy and the profound compassion that I find in her work. She is a dynamic public advocate for Irish poetry.'
Maureen Kennelly

'Even in the darkness of grief and loss, Paula Meehan celebrates life with a visceral, flaying attention.'
Maura Dooley

'The great thing about poetry is that it's the human voice, the one human voice breaking the silence.'
Paula Meehan

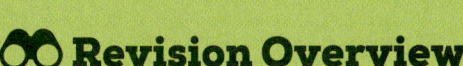
PAULA MEEHAN

 HISTORY/MEMORY   IDENTITY   IRELAND  RELATIONSHIPS  CREATIVITY   LOSS  RELIGION/SPIRITUALITY   LOVE   NATURE   CONFLICT

Eiléan Ní Chuilleanáin
b. 1942

'I chose poetry because it was different.'

Eiléan Ní Chuilleanáin is regarded by many as one of the most important contemporary Irish women poets. Her subject matter ranges from social commentary and considerations of religious issues to quiet, introspective poems about human nature. Ní Chuilleanáin is noted for being mysterious and complex; her poems usually have subtle messages that unfold only through multiple readings. She is well read in history, and a strong sense of connection between past and present characterises her work, in which she often draws interesting parallels between historical events and modern situations. Many of her poems highlight the contrast between fluidity and stillness, life and death, and the undeniable passing of time and humanity's attempts to stop change. She herself has frequently referred to the importance of secrecy in her poetry. Most critics agree that Ní Chuilleanáin's poems resist easy explanations and variously show her interest in explorations of transition, the sacred, women's experience and history.

Investigate Further

To find out more about Eiléan Ní Chuilleanáin, or to hear readings of her poems not already available in your eBook, you could search some useful websites such as YouTube, BBC Poetry, poetryfoundation.org and poetryarchive.org, or access additional material on this page of your eBook.

EILÉAN NÍ CHUILLEANÁIN

Prescribed Poems

○ **1 'Lucina Schynning in Silence of the Nicht'**
While this strangely compelling poem touches on fascinating aspects of Irish history, it is much more than a meditation on past events. **Page 288**

○ **2 'The Second Voyage'**
Transitions are central to Ní Chuilleanáin's poems. Here, she explores the relationship between past and present through the story of Odysseus, who is frustrated by his ocean journeys and decides that his next voyage will be on land. **Page 292**

○ **3 'Deaths and Engines'**
The poet contextualises her experience of death within the setting of another 'burnt-out' ruin, the abandoned wreckage of an aircraft engine. **Page 297**

○ **4 'Street' (OL)**
This typically elusive drama includes various references to Mary Magdalene and the experience of women throughout history. **Page 301**

○ **5 'Fireman's Lift'**
Following her mother's death, the poet used the scene depicted in the painter Correggio's masterpiece, *Assumption of the Virgin*, as the setting for this extraordinary poem. **Page 305**

○ **6 'All for You'**
This multi-layered narrative offers glimpses of salvation and hope. **Page 309**

○ **7 'Following'**
A vividly realised journey by a young girl through a busy Irish fair day invites readers into this mysterious story. **Page 313**

○ **8 'Kilcash'**
This version of the old Irish elegy, *Caoine Cill Chais*, mourns the death of Margaret Butler, Viscountess Iveagh. **Page 318**

○ **9 'Translation'**
Ní Chuilleanáin's poem was read at the reburial ceremony to commemorate Magdalene laundry women from all over Ireland. **Page 323**

○ **10 'The Bend in the Road'**
The poet recalls a journey when a child was suffering from car sickness. For her, the roadside location marks the realisation of time passing. **Page 328**

○ **11 'On Lacking the Killer Instinct'**
The poem intrigues and unsettles from its vivid opening description of a stationary hare – engrossed and 'absorbed'. **Page 333**

○ **12 'To Niall Woods and Xenya Ostrovskaia, married in Dublin on 9 September 2009' (OL)**
This poem, an example of an epithalamium (celebrating the wedding of Eiléan Ní Chuilleanáin's son Niall and his bride, Xenya) is the introductory dedication in her poetry collection *The Sun-fish*. **Page 338**

(OL) indicates poems that are also prescribed for the Ordinary Level course.

1 Lucina Schynning in Silence of the Nicht

Moon shining in silence of the night
The heaven being all full of stars
I was reading my book in a ruin
By a sour candle, without roast meat or music
Strong drink or a shield from the air   5
Blowing in the crazed window, and I felt
Moonlight on my head, clear after three days' rain.

I washed in cold water; it was orange, channelled down bogs
Dipped between cresses.
The bats flew through my room where I slept safely.   10
Sheep stared at me when I woke.

Behind me the waves of darkness lay, the plague
Of mice, plague of beetles
Crawling out of the spines of books,
Plague shadowing pale faces with clay   15
The disease of the moon gone astray.

In the desert I relaxed, amazed
As the mosaic beasts on the chapel floor
When Cromwell had departed, and they saw
The sky growing through the hole in the roof.   20

Sheepdogs embraced me; the grasshopper
Returned with lark and bee.
I looked down between hedges of high thorn and saw
The hare, absorbed, sitting still
In the middle of the track; I heard   25
Again the chirp of the stream running.

Title: Lucina is another name for Diana, the moon goddess. In Roman mythology, Lucina was the goddess of childbirth. Ní Chuilleanáin's title comes from the opening line of 'The Antichrist', a satirical poem by the Scottish poet William Dunbar (c. 1460–1517).

cresses: small strongly flavoured leaves.

plague: curse, diseased group.

spines: inner parts, backs.

astray: off course.

mosaic: mixed, assorted.

Cromwell: Oliver Cromwell (1599–1658), controversial English military and political leader who led an army of invasion in 1649–50, which conquered most of Ireland. Cromwell is still regarded largely as a figure of hatred in the Irish Republic, his name being associated with massacre, religious persecution and mass dispossession of the Catholic community.

chirp: lively sound, twitter.

'shining in silence of the night'

👤 Personal Response

1. How would you describe the atmosphere in the poem's opening stanza? Refer to the text in your answer.
2. Choose one image taken from the natural world that you found particularly interesting. Comment briefly on its effectiveness.
3. Based on your reading of this poem, do you think Ní Chuilleanáin presents a realistic view of Irish history? Give reasons for your response.

👁 Critical Literacy

Eiléan Ní Chuilleanáin takes her title from a Middle Scots poem by William Dunbar. 'Lucina Schynning in Silence of the Nicht' is set in a ruin somewhere in Ireland, after Oliver Cromwell had devastated the country in 1649. However, Ní Chuilleanáin's beautiful and haunting poem is much more than a meditation on an historical event. The poet achieves immediacy by means of a dramatic monologue that recreates the whisperings of desolation in the aftermath of Cromwell's march through Ireland.

As in so many of her poems, Ní Chuilleanáin invites readers into a **strangely compelling setting**. The poet personifies the moon, creating an uneasy atmosphere. Silence enhances the dramatic effect: 'The heaven being all full of stars.' This eerie scene is described in a series of random details. The language – with its archaic Scottish dialect – is note-like and seemingly timeless. There is a notable absence of punctuation and a stilted rhythm as the unknown speaker's voice is introduced: 'I was reading my book in a ruin' (line 3). The series of fragmentary images – 'a sour candle', 'the crazed window' – are immediately unsettling, drawing us back to a darker age in Ireland's troubled history.

Characteristically, Ní Chuilleanáin leaves readers to unravel the poem's veiled meanings and the identity of the dispossessed narrator is never made known. Instead, this forlorn figure 'without roast meat or music' is associated with material and cultural deprivation – **a likely symbol of an oppressed Ireland**? Does the absence of 'Strong drink or a shield' add to the notion of a defeated people? Despite the obvious indications of almost incomprehensible suffering, some respite can still be found: 'I felt/Moonlight on my head, clear after three days' rain' (line 7). This simple image of nature – illuminating and refreshing – suggests comforting signs of recovery.

Ní Chuilleanáin's startling drama moves into the wild Irish landscape: 'I washed in cold water; it was orange.' The sense of native Irish resistance against foreign invasion is clearly evident in the reference to Dutch-born Protestant William of Orange, who defeated the army of Catholic James II at the Battle of the Boyne in 1690. But the poet focuses on the speaker's experience of displacement, illustrating the **alienation which existed within nationalist Ireland**. The narrator, surrounded by animal life and the open sky, becomes an extension of animate and inanimate nature: 'The bats flew through my room … Sheep stared at me' (line 10).

In an increasingly surreal atmosphere, the mood becomes much more disturbed. The poet's apocalyptic dream-vision highlights the 'waves of darkness' in an uninterrupted nightmarish sequence of repulsive images: 'plague/Of mice, plague of beetles/Crawling'. The **emphatic repetition of 'plague' resonates with images of widespread misery, disease and famine**. Nor does the poet ignore the distorted history of Ireland that has resulted from prejudice, propaganda and vested interest 'Crawling out of the spines of books' (line 14). What stands out, however, is Ní Chuilleanáin's ability to suggest distressing glimpses of our island's dark past, poignantly depicted in her heart-rending language describing innocent death: 'Plague shadowing pale faces with clay/The disease of the moon gone astray.'

There is a distinctive change of mood in lines 17–20 as the speaker reflects on the aching aftermath in the period after 'Cromwell had departed'. References to Christian retreat and renewal indicate the **consolation provided by religious faith**: 'In the desert I relaxed, amazed/As the mosaic beasts on the chapel floor'. This sense of wonder through the possibility of spiritual fulfilment is developed in the metaphorical image of 'The sky growing through the hole in the roof'. As always, landscape and nature are features of Ní Chuilleanáin's poem, allowing readers access to her subtle thinking.

In sharp contrast to the earlier trauma, the final tone is remarkably composed and harmonious. The language – which has been somewhat archaic throughout much of the poem – is noticeably biblical: 'Sheepdogs embraced me; the grasshopper/Returned with lark and bee.' **There is an unmistakable sense of survival and newfound confidence** in line 23: 'I looked down between hedges of high thorn.' Ní Chuilleanáin's recognition of 'The hare, absorbed, sitting still' (a cross-reference to her poem 'On Lacking the Killer Instinct') reinforces the feeling of quiet resignation. Is she alluding to the maturity and relative peace of the present Irish state? At any rate, the poem ends on a hopeful note of vigorous resilience, with one of nature's liveliest sounds, 'the chirp of the stream running'.

Throughout this elusive poem, Ní Chuilleanáin has explored fascinating aspects of Irish history – a story that has been often lost in the 'silence of the night'. So much of Ireland's past is marked by exploitation and resistance. The poem has deep undercurrents of countless conflicts springing from both without and within. The moon has long been associated with love, beauty, loneliness, lunacy and death. Some critics have suggested that Ní Chuilleanáin's poem uses the moon to symbolise the struggle of women through the centuries. As usual, readers are free to judge for themselves. However, there is little doubt that 'Lucina Schynning in Silence of the Nicht' presents us with **an intense, self-enclosed world** – but one where the tensions and aspirations of Ireland's complex story are imaginatively explored.

📖 Writing About the Poem

'Eiléan Ní Chuilleanáin's poems offer rich rewards to the perceptive reader.' Discuss this view, with particular reference to 'Lucina Schynning in Silence of the Nicht'.

Sample Paragraph

While I first found Ní Chuilleanáin's poetry quite difficult, I really enjoyed reading 'Lucina Schynning'. The strange title and eerie atmosphere under the moonlight makes us imagine the 'world' of the poem. I found it very dramatic. The narrative voice seemed very traumatised and was convincing as it represented Ireland's troubled history – 'Behind me, waves of darkness'. What I really liked about the poet was that she suggested, rather than explained. The description of Irish people starving was very moving – especially because of the word 'plague'. Ní Chuilleanáin's images of suffering were balanced by the positive ending. The poem asked many questions about how people today look at the past. The poet used many simple nature images such as the hare 'sitting still' and the 'chirp of the stream' to show a present-day Ireland where there is peace – unlike the war-torn past of the history books. Overall, I did enjoy 'Lucina Schynning', as it reminded me that there is still meaning in the beauty of nature.

EXAMINER'S COMMENT

This sensitive reaction to Ní Chuilleanáin's poem reflected on both the subject matter and style of the text using accurate quotations to support the discussion points. The poem's narrative was disclosed by drawing together its significant details. Very impressive vocabulary throughout. A solid high-grade response.

Class/Homework Exercises

1. 'Ní Chuilleanáin's distinctive poetry is filled with subtle messages.' Discuss this statement, with particular reference to 'Lucina Schynning in Silence of the Nicht'.
2. 'Eiléan Ní Chuilleanáin's "Lucina Schynning in Silence of the Nicht" is a highly atmospheric poem that has an elusive dreamlike quality.' To what extent do you agree or disagree with this statement? Support your answer with reference to the poem.

Points to Consider

- **Evocative mid-17th-century Irish setting.**
- **Dramatic monologue form recreates Irish alienation after Cromwell's invasion.**
- **Themes include suffering, loss, human resilience and the celebration of nature.**
- **Effective use of startling imagery, repetition, sibilance and alliteration.**

2 The Second Voyage

Odysseus rested on his oar and saw
The ruffled foreheads of the waves
Crocodiling and mincing past: he rammed
The oar between their jaws and looked down
In the simmering sea where scribbles of weed defined   5
Uncertain depth, and the slim fishes progressed
In fatal formation, and thought
                        If there was a single
Streak of decency in these waves now, they'd be ridged
Pocked and dented with the battering they've had,   10
And we could name them as Adam named the beasts,
Saluting a new one with dismay, or a notorious one
With admiration; they'd notice us passing
And rejoice at our shipwreck, but these
Have less character than sheep and need more patience.   15

I know what I'll do he said;
I'll park my ship in the crook of a long pier
(And I'll take you with me he said to the oar)
I'll face the rising ground and walk away
From tidal waters, up riverbeds   20
Where herons parcel out the miles of stream,
Over gaps in the hills, through warm
Silent valleys, and when I meet a farmer
Bold enough to look me in the eye
With 'where are you off to with that long   25
Winnowing fan over your shoulder?'
There I will stand still
And I'll plant you for a gatepost or a hitching-post
And leave you as a tidemark. I can go back
And organise my house then.   30
                        But the profound
Unfenced valleys of the ocean still held him;
He had only the oar to make them keep their distance;
The sea was still frying under the ship's side.
He considered the water-lilies, and thought about fountains   35
Spraying as wide as willows in empty squares,

The sugarstick of water clattering into the kettle,
The flat lakes bisecting the rushes. He remembered spiders and frogs
Housekeeping at the roadside in brown trickles floored with mud,
Horsetroughs, the black canal, pale swans at dark: 40
His face grew damp with tears that tasted
Like his own sweat or the insults of the sea.

bisecting: cutting through.

EILÉAN NÍ CHUILLEANÁIN

'the simmering sea'

👤 Personal Response

1. From your reading of the first stanza (lines 1–15), describe Odysseus's relationship with the sea. Refer to the text in your response.
2. Select two interesting images from the poem and comment on the effectiveness of each.
3. Write your own personal response to 'The Second Voyage', supporting the points you make with reference to the text.

POETRY FOCUS

👁 Critical Literacy

The relationship between past and present is one of Eiléan Ní Chuilleanáin's recurring themes. In addressing the present within the context of history, she often explores contrasts, such as life and death, motion and stillness, and the inevitable tension between time passing and people's desire to resist change. 'The Second Voyage' refers to the Greek hero Odysseus, whose first epic journey was a relentless battle with the treacherous ocean. But growing frustrated by the endless struggle against nature, he decides that his next voyage will be on land and therefore less demanding.

From the outset, Odysseus is presented as a slightly bemused and ridiculous figure. There is a cartoon-like quality to the exaggerated ocean setting as Ní Chuilleanáin portrays this legendary hero resting on his oar and watching the 'ruffled foreheads of the waves/Crocodiling and mincing past' (line 3). The poet expands this metaphor, describing the waves as great beasts to be challenged: 'he rammed/The oar between their jaws.' **Ní Chuilleanáin's derisive humour mocks the great wanderer's inflated sense of his own masculinity.** But there is no denying that Odysseus is still excited by the 'Uncertain depth' beneath him. For him, anything is possible at sea, where he is truly in his element. The personification is childlike, suggesting his peevish annoyance at being unable to conquer the ocean waves, which don't possess 'a single/Streak of decency' (lines 8–9).

Ní Chuilleanáin's tone is playfully critical. As always, the poet's skill lies in her vigorous images, such as the 'slim fishes' beneath 'scribbles of weeds'. Odysseus's powerful physicality is contrasted with the seemingly pretty waves, which somehow resist the 'battering they've had'. Lording over this surreal scene and filled with disappointment, the egotistical Greek warrior thinks about the Garden of Eden. He is soon envying Adam, who was given God-given control over all living things and had 'named the beasts' of the earth. Completely unaware of the irony of his excessive pride, Odysseus is overwhelmed by self-pity and resorts to ridiculing these foolish waves, which fail to 'rejoice at our shipwreck' (line 14).

Ní Chuilleanáin develops the whimsical drama by letting us hear Odysseus's petulant voice as he prepares to seek recognition onshore. Armed with renewed confidence and his trusty oar – ('I'll take you with me he said to the oar') – he sets out to 'face the rising ground' and seek affirmation far away 'From tidal waters'. But despite the purposeful rhythm and self-assured tone, there is a strong underlying sense that he is deluding himself. The landscape might be serenely beautiful, but it is confined. Unlike the boundless sea, birds define it: 'herons parcel out the miles of stream' (line 21). Yet the brave warrior is eager to boast of his exploits in the outside world and hopes to tell his story to the first farmer he meets who is 'Bold enough to look me in the eye'. **Odysseus even tries to convince himself that**

it is time to put down roots, to plant his oar as 'a gatepost or a hitching-post'. Then he will be ready to return home and 'organise my house'. However, the laboured rhythm and imposing multi-syllabic language convey his half-heartedness about settling down.

Indeed, there are already signs that Odysseus will never surrender the freedom and adventure of dangerous ocean voyages. The powerful oar, which once signified dynamism and exhilaration, is now seen as a decorative symbol of stillness, a 'Winnowing fan'. Unable to deny his true destiny any longer, **he accepts that he cannot ignore his urge to control the sea**: the 'Unfenced valleys of the ocean still held him' (line 32). But his ironic situation remains; while the freedom he yearns for is unattainable on land, he is still unable to conquer the seemingly infinite sea.

The poem's final section is sympathetic to Odysseus's dilemma. Ní Chuilleanáin replaces the pompous first-person pronouns with her own measured narrative account: 'He considered the water-lilies, and thought about fountains' (line 35). The poet makes extensive use of **contrasting water images to highlight land and sea**. Unlike the water 'frying under the ship's side', settled life appears controlled, but unattractive ('Horsetroughs, the black canal'). His uneasy memories of home ('water clattering', 'pale swans at dark') are ominous. For Odysseus, his second excursion into landlocked civilisation offers so little fulfilment that 'His face grew damp with tears'. The hero is forever drawn to that first epic voyage and the wonderful experience of ocean living, with which he is inextricably bound: 'Like his own sweat or the insults of the sea.'

The fluctuating water images – another familiar feature of Eiléan Ní Chuilleanáin's writing – reflect the complex narrative threads throughout the poem. Transitions of various kinds are central to her work. The poet has also been very involved in translating texts, and believes that because of the limits imposed by the translator, the process can never be completely true to the original language. Some literary critics see 'The Second Voyage' as an **extended metaphor exploring how language and culture resist translation**, but like so many of Ní Chuilleanáin's enigmatic poems, the ultimate interpretation is left to individual readers themselves.

✍ Writing About the Poem

'Ní Chuilleanáin's poetry makes effective use of contrasts to illuminate her themes.' Discuss this view, with particular reference to 'The Second Voyage'.

Sample Paragraph

Contrasting themes, such as life and death, permanence and transience, and motion and stillness are all prominent in Ní Chuilleanáin's 'The Second Voyage'. The description of Odysseus who 'rammed' his oar against the waves shows a macho character whose extrovert behaviour could not be more unlike the silent sea which he will never tame. Momentarily, the irritated hero makes up his mind to undertake a new 'voyage' by seeking glory on land. But the reality of settled life disappoints him. Revealing images of fixed landmarks – 'a gatepost', 'tidemark' – all convey the sense of disinterest. Odysseus is immediately aware of the contrasting dynamic qualities of the sea's 'Unfenced valleys'. I found it interesting that the man-made images were all water-based – 'fountains', 'the black canal' – and all lacking the danger of the open sea which Odysseus longs for. Once again, Ní Chuilleanáin succeeds in presenting Odysseus's love-hate obsession with the mysterious ocean.

EXAMINER'S COMMENT

The introductory overview established a very good basis for exploring interesting contrasts within the poem. There is some well-focused personal engagement with the text: 'I found it interesting that the man-made images were all water-based.' Suitable quotations provide valuable support. Diction and expression – in the final sentence, for example – are also excellent. This confident response merits the top grade.

Class/Homework Exercises

1. 'Eiléan Ní Chuilleanáin presents readers with unsettling scenes, both real and otherworldly.' Discuss this statement, with particular reference to 'The Second Voyage'. Refer to the text in your answer.
2. 'In "The Second Voyage", Ní Chuilleanáin addresses the idea of transition and the difficulties associated with change.' Discuss this view, supporting your answer with reference to the poem.

Points to Consider

- Imaginative use of mythic tale of Greek hero.
- Sardonic humour evident in vivid personification of the sea.
- Unsettling scenes, both real and otherworldly.
- Contrasting themes (transience, masculinity, freedom, etc.).
- Vibrant water imagery is a powerful motif.
- Alliteration and sibilance create dynamic sound effects.
- Direct dialogue adds immediacy.

3 Deaths and Engines

EILÉAN NÍ CHUILLEANÁIN

We came down above the houses
In a stiff curve, and
At the edge of Paris airport
Saw an empty tunnel
– The back half of a plane, black   5
On the snow, nobody near it,
Tubular, burnt-out and frozen.

Tubular: cylindrical, tube-shaped.

When we faced again
The snow-white runways in the dark
No sound came over   10
The loudspeakers, except the sighs
Of the lonely pilot.

The cold of metal wings is contagious:

contagious: catching.

Soon you will need wings of your own,
Cornered in the angle where   15
Time and life like a knife and fork
Cross, and the lifeline in your palm
Breaks, and the curve of an aeroplane's track
Meets the straight skyline.

The images of relief: 20
Hospital pyjamas, screens round a bed
A man with a bloody face
Sitting up in bed, conversing cheerfully

conversing: chatting.

Through cut lips:
These will fail you some time.   25

You will find yourself alone
Accelerating down a blind

Accelerating: speeding.

Alley, too late to stop
And know how light your death is;

You will be scattered like wreckage,   30
The pieces every one a different shape
Will spin and lodge in the hearts

lodge: settle.

Of all who love you.

'snow-white runways'

POETRY FOCUS

👤 Personal Response

1. Describe the atmosphere at the airport in lines 1–12. Refer to the text in your response.
2. Based on your reading of lines 13–25, choose one image that you found particularly memorable and comment on its effectiveness.
3. Write your personal response to 'Deaths and Engines', referring closely to the poem in your answer.

👁 Critical Literacy

'Deaths and Engines' addresses Eiléan Ní Chuilleanáin's experience of death – and particularly her father's death – within the setting of another 'burnt-out' ruin: the abandoned wreckage of an aircraft engine. Characteristically, the poet's metaphorical sense is so complete that at times it dominates the poem, constantly inviting readers to tease out meaningful connections within the language.

As with so many of her poems, Ní Chuilleanáin begins mid-narrative – as dreams often do – with an aeroplane coming in to land in Paris. The sense of danger as the plane descends in 'a stiff curve' is typical of the edgy imagery found in stanza one. **The memory immediately suggests a moment of insight – of coming down to earth**: 'We came down above the houses/In a stiff curve.' Details are stark – particularly the absorbing description of the 'empty tunnel' and the peculiar sight of the 'back half of a plane' that has been 'burnt-out and frozen' against the wintry landscape. The contrast of the deserted 'black' wreckage 'On the snow' accentuates the visual effect, adding drama to the memory.

Stanza two emphasises the surreal nature of the hushed 'snow-white runways in the dark'. The poet continues to construct a dreamlike sense of uneasy silence and chilling alienation. The only sounds coming over the loudspeakers are the unsettling 'sighs/Of the lonely pilot'. There is an underlying suggestion of a weary individual – perhaps facing death. This is given a wider relevance by the unnerving opening of stanza three: 'The cold of metal wings is contagious.' For the poet, this insightful moment marks a changing perspective: 'Soon you will need wings of your own.' The 'you' might refer to Ní Chuilleanáin's dying father or the poet herself or possibly the reader. From this point onwards, the metaphor of the wrecked aircraft is central to the fragmentary memories of her father's illness and death. **The poet interweaves two narratives**: the trajectory of the plane as it 'Meets the straight skyline' and the mark of her father's natural life span ('the lifeline in your palm'). Ní Chuilleanáin uses the memorable image of the crossed knife and fork to suggest the inescapable destiny that confronts the dying.

The poet's familiar preoccupations of tension and mystery are even more obvious in stanza four. Disjointed scenes of 'Hospital pyjamas, screens round

a bed' are introduced as 'images of relief'– at least temporarily. **But the prevailing mood is of inevitable death** – 'These will fail you some time'. The poet expresses the final reality of every human being in stanza five: 'You will find yourself alone.' Ní Chuilleanáin conveys the nightmarish realisation of irreversible death through recognisable images of losing control: 'Accelerating down a blind/Alley, too late to stop.' Run-on lines and a persistent rhythm add to the sense of powerlessness. Once again, there are echoes of the 'empty tunnel' and the 'burnt-out' plane. Nevertheless, in imagining her father's final moments, the poet can relate to his experience of dying as a release, so that they both understood 'how light your death is'.

The resigned tone of stanza six reflects Ní Chuilleanáin's deeper understanding of mortality. In celebrating her father's life within a context of enduring love, the poet is able to simultaneously dismantle and preserve the relationship she has had with her father. She returns to the image of the wrecked aeroplane, accepting that in death, 'You will be scattered like wreckage'. However, far from feeling sadness for her father's loss, **Ní Chuilleanáin takes comfort in knowing that he will live 'in the hearts/Of all who love you'**. The sentiment is subdued and poignant, and all the more powerful since it comes from a poet who rarely expresses her feelings directly.

To a great extent, the poem is about families and how they process their personal tragedies. As always, Ní Chuilleanáin's oblique approach is open to many interpretations. But she seems to be suggesting that it takes the sudden shock of death to acknowledge the closeness of relationships in our lives. Typically, in dealing with such emotional subjects as separation, grief and the death of a loved one, **the poet never lapses into sentimentality**. 'Deaths and Engines' was written during the escalation of violence in Northern Ireland, and some critics have understood the poem as a commentary on the human cost of conflict. In the end, readers are left to make up their own minds.

Writing About the Poem

'Ní Chuilleanáin's poems of separation and estrangement transcend the limits of personal experience.' Discuss this view, with particular reference to 'Deaths and Engines'.

Sample Paragraph

One of the most interesting aspects of Ní Chuilleanáin's poetry is her focus on the natural life cycle. Even though she deals with her father's death in 'Deaths and Engines', I found the poem to be more uplifting than depressing. In comparing his death to the wrecked plane, 'burnt-out and frozen', she realises that the wreckage 'Will spin and lodge in the hearts/Of all who love you'. The poem also shows Ní Chuilleanáin stressing the experience of death for every human being: 'You will find yourself alone'. Her message is simple – every individual must face death unaccompanied. In 'Fireman's Lift', for example, she also came to terms with a family death – her mother – by comparing her passing to the Assumption of the Virgin Mary. I believe that such poems transcend the individual and emphasise the naturalness of separation and loss.

> **EXAMINER'S COMMENT**
>
> *This is a well-focused response to the question and shows a close understanding of the poem, particularly in the cross-reference to 'Fireman's Lift'. Accurate quotations are used effectively to support key points. Expression is fluent, varied and clear, with some good personal engagement, such as in the final sentence. A very assured performance securing the highest grade.*

Class/Homework Exercises

1. 'What defines Eiléan Ní Chuilleanáin's poetry is its imaginative power and precision of language.' Discuss this statement, with particular reference to 'Deaths and Engines'.
2. 'In "Deaths and Engines", Ní Chuilleanáin explores aspects of suffering and death by effectively using the metaphor of an aeroplane coming in to land.' Discuss this view, with reference to the poem.

Points to Consider

- **Key themes – memory, family bonds and coming to terms with death.**
- **An underlying sense of tension pervades the poem.**
- **Effective use of metaphor, contrast and repetition throughout.**
- **Positive conclusion: love can transcend death.**

4 Street

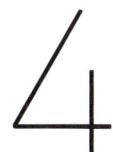

EILÉAN NÍ CHUILLEANÁIN

He fell in love with the butcher's daughter
When he saw her passing by in her white trousers
Dangling a knife on a ring at her belt.
He stared at the dark shining drops on the paving-stones.

One day he followed her   5
Down the slanting lane at the back of the shambles.
A door stood half-open
And the stairs were brushed and clean,
Her shoes paired on the bottom step,
Each tread marked with the red crescent   10
Her bare heels left, fading to faintest at the top.

Dangling: hanging freely, displaying.

shambles: untidy market scene; place of slaughter.

tread: undersole of a shoe; top surface of a step in a staircase.
crescent: half-moon; sickle shape.
fading: dwindling, perishing.
faintest: weakest, exhausted.

'And the stairs were brushed and clean'

POETRY FOCUS

👤 Personal Response

1. Why do you think Ní Chuilleanáin chose to name her poem 'Street' and yet gives the street no name? Give reasons for your response.
2. Which image did you find most intriguing in the poem? Refer closely to the text in your answer.
3. Were you satisfied by the poem's conclusion? Briefly explain your response.

👁 Critical Literacy

'Street' is a short lyric poem from Ní Chuilleanáin's collection *The Magdalene Sermon* (1989). Mary Magdalene was the first person to witness the Resurrection of Christ and these poems reflect on women's religious experiences. The poems also depict edges, borders and crossings between different kinds of worlds as though passing through thresholds and intersections from one realm of experience to another, just as Christ rose from the dead. Characteristically, the poet reveals and conceals women and their strange responsibilities in a graceful, evocative voice.

Ní Chuilleanáin believed in the importance of the ordinary and the domestic as new metaphors for human experience. In the <mark>first section</mark> of the poem, she quietly tells a somewhat unusual tale, giving readers a memorable glimpse into another reality. It is the story of a man falling in love with a woman, 'the butcher's daughter'. Flowing run-on lines depict the rising emotions of the man as he catches sight of her 'in her white trousers'. This colour is often associated with purity and innocence, but it is also the traditional colour butchers wear in their work. **A close-up shot captures a disturbing detail**. 'Dangling' describes the careless movement of the knife as it sways from the 'ring at her belt'. The verb is carefully positioned at the beginning of the line, as it tantalises and entices like a piece of shining jewellery; yet this knife has a deadly purpose. The man is captivated: 'He stared at the dark shining drops on the paving-stones.' Has this knife recently been used? Has blood just been spilled? Is he, as if in a fairy tale, suddenly enthralled by the glittering yet lethal trade of the slaughterer?

In the <mark>second section</mark>, the narrative continues, becoming increasingly menacing: 'One day he followed her.' The assonant 'ow' sound disquietly enhances his journey. Ní Chuilleanáin specialises in the 'poetic of descriptive places'. The man's journey takes him 'Down the slanting lane at the back of the shambles'. **Varying line lengths add to the growing tension**. The adjective 'slanting' suggests a sinister backstreet where everything is oblique, tilted, half-concealed. The 'shambles' is a rough market where meat is carved and animals are slaughtered. To the outside world, it is a place of violence and mayhem. Is Ní Chuilleanáin making a hidden reference to the slaughter of Christ on the cross? 'A door stood half-open'. Does the door

admit or shut out? Is this a symbol of the threshold between life and death which Christ breached? As always, the poet invites the reader to make sense of the clues. A secret is being half-revealed, a mystery is being highlighted. Where does the door lead?

Eiléan Ní Chuilleanáin often peoples her poems with women who studiously attend to their chores. (Mary Magdalene attended to Jesus, washing his feet with her tears and drying them with her hair.) Here 'the stairs were brushed and clean'. Are they awaiting a visit or is this the attention to hygiene which is normal in the butchering trade? This poet's population of silent figures disclose little information. The 'butcher's daughter' had left 'shoes paired on the bottom step'. Yet even this tangible detail reveals only mystery. The full narrative is missing. Is there a suggestion that the man and woman will soon be a pair as well? An inviting flight of stairs leads to all sorts of possibilities. **Ní Chuilleanáin has created a typically ambivalent scenario** filled with underlying danger and excitement. This dreamlike encounter is imbued with an unforgettable atmosphere of edgy anticipation as profound silence echoes.

The poem concludes with a defined image. The girl's 'bare heels' have left traces which become more indistinct as they ascend the stairs. This is emphasised by the alliterative phrase 'fading to faintest'. These are 'marked with the red crescent', like a secret sign beckoning through the enjambed lines. **The mystery resonates**. What really is marked with the bow shapes? The stairs? Her shoes? The heels? Readers are kept wondering. What does the future hold for this couple? Detailed close-ups have been presented, yet there are tantalising gaps in the narrative as we are left like the man who was enticed by the 'Dangling' knife, lured into this ominous atmosphere. As in so many of her elusive dramas, disrupting patterns of communication allows the poet to draw attention to the problem of communication itself. Is this the rounded insight to be glimpsed in the poem?

✒ Writing About the Poem

'Poems of waiting, dramatic and incident-rich, are told quietly by Ní Chuilleanáin.' Discuss this statement in relation to the poem 'Street'.

Sample Paragraph

I felt that the poem 'Street' invited me into its surreal yet tangible world rather like the man is lured by the 'butcher's daughter'. I was caught as if in a dream where details are clearly recognisable, 'the red crescent/her bare heels left', yet their meaning is uncertain. Will the encounter take place between the man and the woman? The reader has been brought like the man on a 'slanting' journey. The full view of the lane was obscured from him, the full story is hidden by the obliqueness of the poem. Yet the atmosphere is unforgettable, the waiting is ominous. The poem disappears at its conclusion as the 'red crescent' marks flow 'fading to faintest'. Suspense and tension reverberate. The reader is led like the man, by sinister signs, a 'door', 'stairs' and footprints as if following a trail in a fairy tale. Yet the poet does not release the dramatic tensions at the poem's conclusion, leaving it in the reader's consciousness.

> **EXAMINER'S COMMENT**
> This response shows a remarkably close reading of the poem, using suitable reference and quotation to address the task in the question throughout. Discussion is coherent and the analysis incisive, especially the point about the dreamlike atmosphere. Expression is also impressive – fluent, varied and well controlled: 'the full story is hidden by the obliqueness of the poem.' Deserves the top grade.

✎ Class/Homework Exercises

1. 'Ní Chuilleanáin's poetry is oblique, yet concrete.' Discuss this statement in relation to 'Street'.
2. 'Ní Chuilleanáin creates an unnerving nightmarish atmosphere in her poem, "Street".' To what extent do you agree with this view? Support your answer with reference to the text.

⊙ Points to Consider

- **Highly dramatic poem filled with suspense and intrigue.**
- **Close-up details create interest.**
- **Run-through lines add a sense of urgency.**
- **Sense of mystery resonates at the end.**

5 Fireman's Lift

EILÉAN NÍ CHUILLEANÁIN

Fireman's Lift: The term refers to a technique commonly used by emergency service workers to carry someone to safety by placing the carried person across the shoulders of the carrier.

I was standing beside you looking up
Through the big tree of the cupola
Where the church splits wide open to admit
Celestial choirs, the fall-out of brightness.

The Virgin was spiralling to heaven, 5
Hauled up in stages. Past mist and shining,
Teams of angelic arms were heaving,
Supporting, crowding her, and we stepped

Back, as the painter longed to
While his arm swept in the large strokes. 10
We saw the work entire, and how the light

Melted and faded bodies so that
Loose feet and elbows and staring eyes
Floated in the wide stone petticoat
Clear and free as weeds. 15

This is what love sees, that angle:
The crick in the branch loaded with fruit,
A jaw defining itself, a shoulder yoked,

The back making itself a roof
The legs a bridge, the hands 20
A crane and a cradle.

Their heads bowed over to reflect on her
Fair face and hair so like their own
As she passed through their hands. We saw them
Lifting her, the pillars of their arms 25

(Her face a capital leaning into an arch)
As the muscles clung and shifted
For a final purchase together
Under her weight as she came to the edge of the cloud.

Parma 1963 – Dublin 1994

cupola: dome-shaped roof.

Celestial: heavenly, divine.

spiralling: whirling, twisting.

crick: arch, strain.
yoked: forced, strained.

capital: upper section of a column supporting a ceiling or arch.

The Assumption of the Virgin: Roman Catholic Church teaching states that the Virgin Mary, having completed the course of her earthly life, was assumed (or elevated) body and soul into heavenly glory. Antonio Allegri da Correggio (1489–1534), usually known as Correggio, was the foremost painter of the Parma school of the Italian Renaissance. One of his best-known works, The *Assumption of the Virgin*, is a fresco which decorates the dome of the Duomo (Cathedral) of Parma, in northern Italy.

'spiralling to heaven'

👤 Personal Response

1. Based on your reading of the poem, comment on the appropriateness of the title, 'Fireman's Lift'.
2. Choose one visual image from the poem which you consider particularly effective. Briefly explain your choice.
3. Write your own short personal response to the poem.

👁 Critical Literacy

This extraordinary poem describes the scene depicted in the painter Correggio's masterpiece, *Assumption of the Virgin*. In 1963 Eiléan Ní Chuilleanáin and her mother had visited Parma Cathedral. Following her mother's death in 1994, the poet used the visit as the setting for 'Fireman's Lift', describing it as a 'cheering-up poem, when my mother was dying because I absolutely knew that she would want me to write a poem about her dying …'

The poem begins with Ní Chuilleanáin's vivid memory of the moment when she and her mother were looking up at Correggio's celebrated ceiling mural. In the opening stanza, she invites readers into the Italian setting: 'I was standing beside you looking up/Through the big tree of the cupola.' There is **an immediate dreamlike sense of intimacy and closeness between mother and daughter**, as though they were both aware that something significant was happening. From the outset, the focus is on the majestic painting's mystery and symbolism, reaching heavenwards to imagined 'Celestial choirs'.

Stanza two emphasises the struggle of the angels to lift Mary into the heavens, and the awkwardness and wonder of being pushed in such a similar manner to birth. We are encouraged to become part of the dynamic scene within the reality of this great spectacle. The dynamic verbs 'spiralling' and 'heaving' suggest **the physical effort involved in raising the Virgin from her earthly life**. Line breaks and frequent commas are used to create a sluggish pace. Ní Chuilleanáin is drawn to the collective energy which becomes a fireman's lift of 'Teams of angelic arms', and the effort to raise Mary 'Past mist and shining' is relentless.

Ní Chuilleanáin then considers the overwhelming effect of Correggio's 'work entire', designed to give the illusion of real and simulated architecture within the painted fresco. This awe-inspiring achievement is reflected in the pulsating run-through rhythms and hushed tones of stanzas three and four. **Dramatic images of the angelic figures and saints assisting Mary's Assumption give expression to the artist's powerful vision**: 'Melted and faded bodies' are intermingled with 'elbows and staring eyes'. Within the dome/petticoat image, Ní Chuilleanáin describes Correggio's Virgin passing into another glorious life. All the time, this vortex of bodies and faces around

her are fully engaged in assisting Mary to reach the waiting Christ.
Stanza five defines an important turning point for the poet, who can now make sense of her mother's death through a fresh understanding of Correggio's perspective: 'This is what love sees, that angle.' **The assured tone marks a coming to terms with deep personal loss**. Ní Chuilleanáin's renewed appreciation of the painting enables her to accept the burden of letting the dead go. Her resignation is evident in the poignant image of a 'branch loaded with fruit', an obvious symbol of the natural cycle.

Stanzas six and seven return to **Correggio's mesmerising skill in his interaction of art and architecture** within the cathedral dome. This intricate collusion is seen in sharper focus, providing a context for Ní Chuilleanáin to reassert her changing relationship with her mother. The restless limbs of the painted angels are in perfect harmony with the great Duomo ceiling: 'The back making itself a roof/The legs a bridge.' This intriguingly harmonious composition merging paint and plaster adds to the urgency of ensuring that the dying soul achieves its ultimate ascension to heaven.

The **final stanzas** observe the figures attending on Mary, 'heads bowed over to reflect on her/Fair face'. Their tenderness is evident in both sound and tone. The poet has said that, on one level, 'Fireman's Lift' is about the nurses who looked after her mother when she was dying. Typically, the poet broadens our understanding of suffering, showing people caring and concerned. The concluding lines, however, acknowledge **the strength of spirit which Ní Chuilleanáin singles out as the hallmark of her mother's life and death**. This is reflected in the purposeful expression on the Virgin's face: 'As the muscles clung and shifted/For a final purchase.' Tactile 'u' sounds ('usc', 'ung', 'urch', etc.) and the drawn-out rhythms emphasise that body goes with soul in the movement across this threshold: 'to the edge of the cloud.'

Death and rebirth are recurring themes in Ní Chuilleanáin's work. But in honouring her mother's life and associating her passing with the Assumption of the Virgin, the poet has brought together Italian art, religion and a deep sense of sorrow. Essentially, however, **'Fireman's Lift' is a moving expression of the poet's enduring love** for her mother. It is not unusual for readers of Ní Chuilleanáin's poetry to encounter beautiful images which leave them searching. Nevertheless, this poem has a universal significance. It is infused with an astounding sense of love, loss and triumph as the ascending figure disappears into the clouds. Poised on the edge of this unknowable boundary, the rest is mystery.

EILÉAN NÍ CHUILLEANÁIN

✒ Writing About the Poem

'For Eiléan Ní Chuilleanáin, boundaries and transitions are central concerns.' Discuss this view with particular reference to 'Fireman's Lift'.

Sample Paragraph

I found 'Fireman's Lift' both puzzling and interesting. Ní Chuilleanáin managed to link her mother's death with the painting *Assumption of the Virgin*. In describing her memory of a visit to Parma Cathedral, the poet seemed to enter the reality of the mural and see her own relationship with her mother in a new way – almost like one of the angels who tries to raise Mary to heaven, 'Teams of angelic arms were heaving'. The transition is shown in terms of brute strength – the Virgin is 'Hauled up in stages'. But the poet also reflects the transition between this life and the next in the optical illusions painted on the dome. Everything appears to be integrated – for example, the hands of angels act as a 'crane and a cradle' supporting Mary. She leans on the 'pillars of their arms'. The poet sees no difference between her own prayers for her mother's soul and the work of the saints who raise the Virgin. To me, Ní Chuilleanáin is absorbed in the art work. I found this typical of her poetry in that she wanders beyond borders.

EXAMINER'S COMMENT

An incisive response which addresses this challenging question directly. There is good personal interaction: 'To me, Ní Chuilleanáin is absorbed in the art work', and effective use of supportive references. Clearly made points explore the poet's emphasis on the blurred lines within the Correggio painting, and between it and Ní Chuilleanáin's own involvement. Such in-depth analysis merits the top grade.

✎ Class/Homework Exercises

1. 'Eiléan Ní Chuilleanáin's poems explore the persistence of memory in a highly distinctive style.' Discuss this statement with particular reference to 'Fireman's Lift'.
2. '"Fireman's Lift" is typical of Ní Chuilleanáin's poems in that it is layered with hidden meaning.' To what extent do you agree with this view? Support your answer with reference to the text.

◎ Points to Consider

- **Characteristic narrative opening recalling a significant memory.**
- **Effective use of run-on lines, symbolism, dramatic images of art and architecture.**
- **Vivid details and powerful verbs suggest physical effort.**
- **Key themes – death, rebirth, family relationships and enduring love.**

6. All for You

EILÉAN NÍ CHUILLEANÁIN

Once beyond the gate of the strange stableyard, we dismount.
The donkey walks on, straight in at a wide door
And sticks his head in a manger.

The great staircase of the hall slouches back,
Sprawling between warm wings. It is for you. 5
As the steps wind and warp
Among the vaults, their thick ribs part; the doors
Of guardroom, chapel, storeroom
Swing wide and the breath of ovens
Flows out, the rage of brushwood, 10
The roots torn out and butchered.

It is for you, the dry fragrance of tea-chests
The tins shining in ranks, the ten-pound jars
Rich with shrivelled fruit. Where better to lie down
And sleep, along the labelled shelves, 15
With the key still in your pocket?

wind: curve, meander.
warp: bend, buckle.
vaults: large rooms often used for storage; chambers beneath a church.
ribs: curved structures that support a vault.
brushwood: undergrowth, small twigs and branches.

'steps wind and warp/ Among the vaults'

👤 Personal Response

1. Would you agree that there is a dramatic trance-like atmosphere in this poem? Support your answer with reference to the text.
2. Choose one particularly vivid image from the poem and briefly explain its effectiveness.
3. Write your own individual response to the poem, referring closely to the text in your answer.

👁 Critical Literacy

'All for You' comes from Eiléan Ní Chuilleanáin's *The Brazen Serpent* (1994). The book's title refers to the biblical story of Moses and the Israelites in the desert. God had become angry with his people, as they had spoken against their leader, Moses, and He let fierce snakes crawl among them and bite them. Moses prayed for the people and God instructed Moses to make a bronze serpent and place it upon a pole in public view. Anyone who was bitten could then look on the brazen snake and they would be cured. This foreshadows the raising onto the cross of Jesus Christ, who died to save sinners. Therefore, God made this sacrifice 'All for You'. Ní Chuilleanáin's collection of poems brings the possibility of hope, of getting through bad times, of being redeemed.

Ní Chuilleanáin **collapses time and distinctions betweeen places** in 'All for You'. Line by line, the reader is drawn into deeper water until the bottom can no longer be touched, a recurring feature of this poet's complex work. The first three lines describe a scene that resonates with detail from the Bible story of the birth of Jesus: 'the strange stableyard', 'The donkey', the 'manger'. Why is the stableyard 'strange'? In the biblical account, Joseph and Mary had to leave their home town and travel to Bethlehem to be listed for a tax census. As is often the case with Ní Chuilleanáin's dramatic presentations, the reader must piece together a bare minimum of narrative sense. However, there is a sense of inevitability about the journey being described.

In lines 4–11, a noticeably different time and space is realised. What follows is **a series of evocative images and metaphors relating to a transitional experience**. Personification brings a staircase vividly to life as it 'slouches back', lolling and slumping – 'Sprawling' almost like a reclining animal as it sits between the 'warm wings' of the hall. Is it ominous or welcoming? It is waiting, as the bronze serpent awaited the Israelites, like a gift 'for you'. Ní Chuilleanáin does not determine the identity of 'you', instead leaving it open to speculation so that 'you' could have a universal application and refer to anyone. Is this gift for all? The poet's descriptive talent engages the reader as the grand staircase is depicted with great clarity, yet its full significance is never defined. Alliteration ('wind and warp') conveys the stairs' sinuous movement, curling like an uncoiling animal through the 'thick ribs' of the intimidating vaults.

The architectural metaphor is a strong element in Ní Chuilleanáin's poetry, which is full of mysterious crannies and alcoves. Could this imposing building be a convent waiting to welcome a young woman as its doors open, revealing the imposing interior of 'guardroom, chapel' and 'storeroom'? The poet's three aunts were nuns and she has commented, 'One is constantly made aware of the fact that the past does not go away, that it is walking around the place causing trouble at every moment.' Is this reference therefore autobiographical or does it encompass a wider significance? Could the staircase lead to salvation and heaven?

A rush of heat from the nearby ovens is suddenly palpable – again conveyed through the poet's effective working of personification: 'the breath of ovens/Flows out.' Ní Chuilleanáin uses a violent image to describe the fierce temperature: 'the rage of brushwood.' This is continued

EILÉAN NÍ CHUILLEANÁIN

in the savagery with which the kindling has been collected: 'roots torn out and butchered.' Is there an echo of the biblical tale of the burning bush from the **Book of Exodus**, where God directed Moses to the Promised Land? This story teaches that we should be able to obey God whenever he calls us. Is the poet also referencing the story of Christ, 'butchered' on the cross for the sins of the world? The forceful rhythm of these dramatic lines creates an intensity, a climax of dread, almost like an ecstatic spiritual experience.

There is a marked **change of tone** in the last five lines. All the tension eases within the ordered space of the building's provisions store. Readers are now immersed in the moment, smelling the 'dry fragrance of tea-chests', observing 'tins shining in ranks, the ten-pound jars'. Repetition of the rich 'r' sound suggests the store's abundance of goods. Yet there is also an unease secreted in this image of confined order. The fruit is 'shrivelled', the fragrance is 'dry'. Is there a life withering, unable to reproduce? Is this another central dimension of religious life? The poem concludes with a rhetorical question intimating that there is nowhere better to take rest, just as Joseph and Mary did long ago in that 'strange stable yard', than here 'along the labelled shelves'. The body's surrender and submission to God's will enables it to act.

Another biblical reference is suggested in the final detail of the 'key still in your pocket'. In Isaiah 33:6, faith is the key to salvation: 'He will be the sure foundation of your times, a rich store of salvation and wisdom and knowledge; the fear of the Lord is the key to this treasure.' Ní Chuilleanáin's poem focuses on the experience of Christian faith as imagined through the imposing challenge and triumph of religious vocations. The 'key' image is typically contradictory – symbolising both confinement and freedom. Is the poet presenting the central paradox of Christian belief? Can the soul's redemption only be achieved through submission to God's will? Characteristically, Ní Chuilleanáin's multi-layered narrative has been subtly woven, offering a glimpse, perhaps, of salvation and hope.

✒ Writing About the Poem

'Eiléan Ní Chuilleanáin's poetry is an unshaped fire demanding to be organised into a sequence of words and images.' Discuss this statement in relation to 'All for You'.

Sample Paragraph

'All for You' is an unsettling poem which springs from the idea of a gift. Like an 'unshaped fire', the poem's religious theme 'Flows out' like the heat from the ovens. I thought the image of the staircase which 'slouches back' was very effective. The image symbolised the ladder of life which Christians must climb to reach salvation. I got the sense of being in a strange building with old-fashioned rooms. The storeroom imagery reflected the enclosed religious world, with 'the dry fragrance' of 'shrivelled fruit'. The sense of order was also present: 'The tins shining in ranks.' The repetition of 'It is for you' suggests a generous God wishing to give a precious gift and what gift could be more important than hope? All the poet's ideas are expressed in patterns of visionary language which can be seen as a powerful 'unshaped fire'.

> **EXAMINER'S COMMENT**
>
> A clear personal response to a challenging question. Key discussion points are very well developed and effectively illustrated. This shows a good understanding of this complex poem – and particularly the poet's use of dense symbols and overlapping images. Expression throughout is confident, fluent and well controlled. An excellent response that deserves the highest grade.

Class/Homework Exercises

1. 'Ní Chuilleanáin's language is subtle and acute enough to undertake its most difficult subject: how we perceive and understand the world.' Discuss this statement in relation to the prescribed work of the poet on your course.
2. '"All for You" illustrates Ní Chuilleanáin's deep interest in the mysteries of Christianity.' To what extent do you agree with this view? Support your answer with reference to the poem.

Points to Consider

- **The poem explores various aspects of choosing the Christian life.**
- **Personification and architectural imagery create a sense of mystery.**
- **Effective use of biblical and religious references.**
- **Descriptive details and provocative images add drama.**

7 Following

EILÉAN NÍ CHUILLEANÁIN

So she follows the trail of her father's coat through the fair
Shouldering past beasts packed solid as books,
And the dealing men nearly as slow to give way –
A block of a belly, a back like a mountain,
A shifting elbow like a plumber's bend –   5
When she catches a glimpse of a shirt-cuff, a handkerchief,
Then the hard brim of his hat, skimming along,

Until she is tracing light footsteps
Across the shivering bog by starlight,
The dead corpse risen from the wakehouse   10
Gliding before her in a white habit.
The ground is forested with gesturing trunks,
Hands of women dragging needles,
Half-choked heads in the water of cuttings,
Mouths that roar like the noise of the fair day.   15

She comes to where he is seated
With whiskey poured out in two glasses
In a library where the light is clean,
His clothes all finely laundered,
Ironed facings and linings.   20
The smooth foxed leaf has been hidden
In a forest of fine shufflings,
The square of white linen
That held three drops
Of her heart's blood is shelved   25
Between the gatherings
That go to make a book –
The crushed flowers among the pages crack
The spine open, push the bindings apart.

POETRY FOCUS

👤 Personal Response

1. Based on your reading of the poem, show how Ní Chuilleanáin conjures up the atmosphere of an Irish fair day. Refer closely to the text in your response.
2. In your opinion, how many settings are there in this poem? Which one did you prefer? Give reasons for your choice, quoting to support your answer.
3. Choose one vivid image from the third stanza of the poem and briefly explain its effectiveness.

'And the dealing men nearly as slow to give way'

👁 Critical Literacy

Eiléan Ní Chuilleanáin often assumes a storytelling role in her poems as she relates memories from the past. She readjusts the perspective of readers by taking us into the lives of ordinary people who literally and physically made history. In her collection *The Brazen Serpent*, Ní Chuilleanáin highlights family and women as makers of history. She hints at the untold through her use of characters, silences and secrets. These confidential witnesses, like the poet herself, reconstruct subtle revelations of family unease and discontentment. Female imagery expresses what is silenced. The poet frequently explores religious themes as well as death and rebirth. Quietly and precisely, she offers us the comfort that the past does not go away.

In the opening section, the poet begins her story in her usual oblique, non-confessional style, yet deeply engages the reader despite her seeming

EILÉAN NÍ CHUILLEANÁIN

detachment. A vividly realised journey by a girl through the hurly-burly of an Irish fair day catapults the reader into the story. She is trying to follow her father through the dense crowds: 'the trail of her father's coat through the fair.' Long run-on lines and broad vowels convey the difficulty of negotiating the route as she attempts to push past 'beasts packed as solid as books'. This unusual simile illustrates the tightly packed rows of animals. Nor could she easily make her way through the dealers, men caught up in the very serious business of buying and selling, making a deal. Their thick-set bodies, bulky like their animals, are described through a tumbling list of similes and metaphors to highlight their immobile weight: 'A block of a belly, a back like a mountain.' A 'shifting elbow' is like the measure used in plumbing. All these images reinforce the **tough, masculine world of the fair**. Ní Chuilleanáin has pushed the reader, through her unwavering gaze, into the poem's self-enclosed world.

Suddenly, in line 6, the girl catches a glimpse of her father. This is shown by a list of his clothing: 'a shirt-cuff, a handkerchief,/Then the hard brim of his hat.' His progress is swift and effortless. He moves as swiftly as the punctuation (a series of fast-moving commas) accelerates the motion of the line. Sharp contrast in the verbs used to describe the progress of the girl and her father **highlight their different rates of success in moving through the fair**. The girl is struggling, 'Shouldering past', while the father moves with ease, 'skimming along'. Is Ní Chuilleanáin suggesting that a woman finds it difficult to negotiate a man's world? The poet has hypnotically caught the excitement as well as the danger of the fair day.

Distance and time blur in the second section. Ní Chuilleanáin shifts the scene and time frame from the noise and physical bulk of the fair to the '**shivering bog**'. Personification and slender vowels effectively convey the cold 'starlight' scene she is revisiting, 'tracing light footsteps', mapping faint prints. **A surreal, nightmarish world is presented**, as 'The dead corpse risen from the wakehouse' appears 'before her in a white habit'. Whose corpse is this? The effortless sense of 'Gliding' suggests the agile movement of the father. Momentarily, the packed animals of the fair have given way to the ground 'forested with gesturing trunks'. Now the heavy trees are highlighting her way, she will ultimately follow her father into death. Thin waving rushes are evocatively described as 'Hands of women dragging needles'. Their slow cumbersome movement is presented in visionary terms. Is this a reference to the story from the Bible when the Pharaoh of Egypt decreed that because of the increasing numbers of Israelites, all first-born boys were to be drowned in the River Nile? Are these the half-choked heads? Is this the wail of Israelite women and children as they cry and 'roar' like the beasts in the fair, aware of their fate? Or is it a reference to the subordination of women as they work?

In the poem's concluding section, the girl meets her father in a much more hospitable setting with 'whiskey poured out in two glasses', 'His clothes all

finely laundered'. Within these domestic interiors of the poet's imagination lies the remote **possibility of utopia**. The 'square of white linen', redolent of the survivor's suffering, shrunk and stained by the body's signifiers of hurt, becomes a relic of love and loss. Ní Chuilleanáin has commented, 'A relic is something you enclose, and then you enclose the reliquary in something else. In the *The Book of Kells* exhibition, the book satchel is in leather, which is meant to protect, and there is a shrine which in turn is meant to protect the book.' A relic is associated with people seeking comfort in difficult times. The past is beautifully evoked in the phrase 'The smooth foxed leaf has been hidden', with its haunting image of time-stained pages. Inside the book are 'crushed flowers', reminders that love was violated, yet something of it remains.

These memories have tremendous power; they 'crack' and push apart as if being reborn. Living and dead touch each other through such memories. The dust and noise of the cattle market, the cold starry bog have all evaporated to be replaced by this interior where the 'light is clean', making it easy to see. Comfort and hope are being offered as the poem suggests that the past is not dead.

✒ Writing About the Poem

'Ní Chuilleanáin's poems explore how the most basic legends – family stories – fragment and alter in each individual's memory.' Discuss this statement with particular reference to the poem 'Following'.

Sample Paragraph

Ní Chuilleanáin's poem, 'Following', dredges up Irish family stories (the fair day, a wake, women sewing) and rearranges them, as cards are moved in 'shufflings'. This reconstructs and transforms the past so that we can see and understand from a new perspective. We are brought as followers, just like the girl in the fair, on a journey to discover that the past is not dead, but resonates through the present by means of relics, 'The square of white linen'. The title suggests that we are all following one another through life, like the girl and the father in the fair. In the masculine world of the fair, 'beasts packed solid as books' the girl found it hard to negotiate her way. The poet has identified the difficult role women have in life, 'dragging needles', employed in domestic drudgery. These women are unable to express their concerns, 'Half-choked'. The legends become 'crushed flowers' yet the poet suggests

> **EXAMINER'S COMMENT**
> *This is a very impressive response which deserves the highest grade. The focus throughout is firmly placed on addressing the various parts of the question. Quotations are integrated effectively and the answer ranges widely from the title to the individual stories and the imagery used in conveying the narratives. Language is carefully controlled to express points clearly, e.g. 'This reconstructs and transforms the past so that we can see and understand from a new perspective'.*

that they can 'crack' open the book in which they are enclosed. I felt that she was communicating the message of hope that the past does not stay in the past. Our memories do not remain 'shelved' but live again in the present.

EILÉAN NÍ CHUILLEANÁIN

✒ Class/Homework Exercises

1. 'The mysterious writing style of Ní Chuilleanáin allows the reader to explore the poems on many levels, each tracking a different aspect of the cycle of life.' Discuss this statement in relation to the prescribed poems of this poet on your course.
2. 'Ní Chuilleanáin's unsettling poetic voice can often seem deceptively simple.' Discuss this statement with particular reference to the poem 'Following'. Support your answer with reference to the text.

⊙ Points to Consider

- The poet assumes a familiar story-telling role in this mystery tale.
- Themes include Irish identity and the power of memory.
- Effective use of commas, dashes and run-on lines.
- Prominent sound effects (alliteration and assonance) add emphasis.

Kilcash

From the Irish, c. 1800

Title: Eiléan Ní Chuilleanáin's translation of the early 19th-century ballad *Caoine Cill Chais* (The Lament for Kilcash), an anonymous lament that the castle of Cill Chais stood empty, its woods cut down and all its old grandeur disappeared. Kilcash was one of the great houses of a branch of the Butler family near Clonmel, Co. Tipperary, until well into the 18th century. Ní Chuilleanáin's poem encompasses several generations of the Butler family, but the presiding spirit is that of Margaret Butler, Viscountess Iveagh (who died in 1744).

What will we do now for timber
With the last of the woods laid low —
No word of Kilcash nor its household,
Their bell is silenced now,
Where the lady lived with such honour,   5
No woman so heaped with praise,
Earls came across oceans to see her
And heard the sweet words of Mass.

It's the cause of my long affliction
To see your neat gates knocked down,   10
The long walks affording no shade now
And the avenue overgrown,
The fine house that kept out the weather,
Its people depressed and tamed;
And their names with the faithful departed,   15
The Bishop and Lady Iveagh!

The geese and the ducks' commotion,
The eagle's shout, are no more,
The roar of the bees gone silent,
Their wax and their honey store   20
Deserted. Now at evening
The musical birds are stilled
And the cuckoo is dumb in the treetops
That sang lullaby to the world.

Even the deer and the hunters   25
That follow the mountain way
Look down upon us with pity,
The house that was famed in its day;
The smooth wide lawn is all broken,
No shelter from wind and rain;   30
The paddock has turned to a dairy
Where the fine creatures grazed.

the last of the woods: a reference to the mass clearance of native Irish forests by plantation settlers to create agricultural land and to fuel the colonial economy. The woodlands belonging to the Butlers of Kilcash were sold in 1797 and 1801.
the lady: Margaret Butler, Viscountess Iveagh, a staunch Catholic (d. 1744).
The Bishop: Catholic clergy – including Lady Iveagh's brother-in-law – were often given shelter in Kilcash.
commotion: noise, clamour.
lullaby: soothing song.
paddock: enclosure.

EILÉAN NÍ CHUILLEANÁIN

Mist hangs low on the branches
No sunlight can sweep aside,
Darkness falls among daylight 35
And the streams are all run dry;
No hazel, no holly or berry,
Bare naked rocks and cold;
The forest park is leafless
And all the game gone wild. 40

And now the worst of our troubles:
She has followed the prince of the Gaels —
He has borne off the gentle maiden,
Summoned to France and to Spain.
Her company laments her 45
That she fed with silver and gold:
One who never preyed on the people
But was the poor souls' friend.

My prayer to Mary and Jesus
She may come safe home to us here 50
To dancing and rejoicing
To fiddling and bonfire
That our ancestors' house will rise up,
Kilcash built up anew
And from now to the end of the story 55
May it never again be laid low.

prince of the Gaels: probably a reference to the 18th Earl of Ormonde.
the gentle maiden: Countess of Ormonde, wife of the 18th Earl.

preyed: harmed, took advantage of.

'affording no shade now'

👤 Personal Response

1. From your reading of the poem, what is your impression of Lady Iveagh? Refer to the text in your answer.
2. Choose one interesting image from 'Kilcash' that you consider particularly effective. Give reasons to explain why this image appealed to you.
3. Write your own individual response to the poem, referring closely to the text in your answer.

👁 Critical Literacy

'Kilcash' comes from Eiléan Ní Chuilleanáin's *The Girl Who Married the Reindeer* (2001). Many of the poems in this collection deal with outsiders and the dispossessed. Kilcash was the great house of one of the branches of the Butler family near Clonmel, Co. Tipperary, until the 18th century. The Butlers were Catholic landed gentry who had come to Ireland as part of an Anglo-Norman invasion during the 12th century and had taken over vast amounts of land. Over time, the family became absorbed into Irish ways. Ní Chuilleanáin's version of the traditional Irish elegy, *Caoine Cill Chais*, mourns the death of Margaret Butler, Viscountess Iveagh.

Stanza one opens with a plaintive voice lamenting 'What will we do now for timber'. The ballad was originally composed in the early 1800s following the demise of the Butlers of Kilcash and the eventual clearing of the family's extensive woodlands, which had supplied timber for local people. **The early tone typifies the entire poem's sense of hopelessness now that the woods are 'laid low'.** The systematic felling of trees is symbolic of the decline of this aristocratic Catholic family. Following colonisation, the Irish were consigned to nature as a symbol of their barbarity. In some British circles, they were referred to as the 'natural wild Irish' because the country's remote boglands and forests offered shelter to Irish rebels. The poem emphasises the uneasy silence around Kilcash and the speaker pays extravagant tribute to 'the lady' of the house, who is immediately associated with Ireland's Catholic resistance: 'Earls came across oceans to see her.'

As always, Ní Chuilleanáin's approach is layered, recognising the genuine feelings of loss while suggesting a misplaced dependence on all those who exploited the native population. For the most part, however, the poem's anonymous narrator appears to express the desolation ('long affliction') felt by the impoverished and leaderless Irish of the time. There is no shortage of evidence to illustrate what has happened to the 'fine house'. Throughout stanzas two and three, broad assonant sounds add to the maudlin sentiments. The **'neat gates knocked down' and the 'avenue overgrown' reflect the dramatic turnaround in fortunes**. But is Ní Chuilleanáin's translation of the old song also unearthing an underlying sense of delight in the sudden fall of the mighty? There is 'no shade now' for the once-powerful gentry or for the impoverished community. Many of the references to the

EILÉAN NÍ CHUILLEANÁIN

'stilled' birds and animals can also be seen as both a loss and a possible release from an unhappy phase of oppression and dependence.

Images of hardship taken from nature dominate stanzas four and five. The abandoned peasants are depicted as pitiable. The atmosphere becomes increasingly disturbing as the natural world order is transformed: 'Darkness falls among daylight/And the streams are all run dry.' **As in so many other Irish legends, the landscape reflects the terms of the Butlers' exile: 'The forest park is leafless.'** Negative language patterns – 'No sunlight', 'No hazel, no holly' – highlight the sense of intense grief resulting from abandonment. Relentlessly, the regular lines and ponderous rhythm work together to create a monotonous trance-like effect. The extravagant praise for 'the gentle maiden' (probably a reference to the wife of the 18th Earl) dominates stanza six. As a representative of the Butler dynasty, her absence is seen as 'the worst of our troubles' and she is glorified as someone 'who never preyed on the people' despite her privileged lifestyle.

The prayer-like tone of the final stanza is in keeping with the deep yearning for a return to the old ways in Kilcash. The Catholic allusion also reinforces the central importance of religion in expressing political and cultural identity. In wishing to restore the former Gaelic order, the speaker imagines lively scenes of communal celebration: 'fiddling and bonfire.' **The aspiration that the castle will be 'built up anew' offers a clear symbol of recovery.** This rallying call is in keeping with traditional laments and is characteristic of the poet's sympathies for the oppressed. Ní Chuilleanáin has retained the rhetorical style of Gaelic poetry throughout, revealing the experience of isolated communities through numerous images of restless desolation and uncomfortable silences.

'Kilcash' marks a significant transition in Irish history. As the old native aristocracy suffered military and political defeat and, in many cases, exile, the world order that had supported the bardic poets disappeared. In these circumstances, it is hardly surprising that much Irish poetry of this period laments these changes and the poet's plight. However, **Ní Chuilleanáin's translation of the old ballad differs from other versions in being more ambivalent towards Viscountess Iveagh and what she represented**. Is the poem a poignant expression of loss and a genuine tribute to those landlords who were seen as humane? Does the poet satirise the subservient native Irish who had been conditioned to accept some convenient generosity from the Catholic gentry? To what extent did the original lament present a romantic distortion of Ireland's history? Readers are left to decide for themselves.

🗎 Writing About the Poem

'Eiléan Ní Chuilleanáin's poems retain the power to connect past and present in ways that never cease to fascinate.' Discuss this statement, with particular reference to 'Kilcash'.

Sample Paragraph

On a first reading, I thought that 'Kilcash' was a simple version of the old ballad, *Caoine Cill Chais*. After studying the poem, however, I feel that Ní Chuilleanáin has raised many interesting questions about Irish history. The opening lament of the peasants seems self-pitying – 'What will we do now for timber'. The compliments paid to Lady Iveagh focus on her Catholic faith and support for Gaelic culture – 'Earls came across oceans to see her'. As a young person looking back on this period of upheaval, I could appreciate the way impoverished Irish people had become dependent on the Catholic gentry as symbols of freedom. The poem repeatedly places 'the lady' as the embodiment of hope – 'the poor souls' friend'. The main insight I gained from the poem was that colonisation – whether by Catholic or Protestant landlords – had broken the Irish spirit. Ní Chuilleanáin manages to link past and present, broadening our view of the complex relationships between powerful interests and a conquered population.

EXAMINER'S COMMENT

An assured personal response, focused throughout and well illustrated with suitable quotations. The paragraph carefully highlights Ní Chuilleanáin's exploration of the plight of the native Irish community in various ways: 'impoverished Irish people had become dependent on the Catholic gentry'. Points are clearly expressed throughout in this excellent, top-grade answer.

Class/Homework Exercises

1. 'Ní Chuilleanáin's distinctive poetic world provides an accessible platform for marginalised voices.' Discuss this view, with particular reference to 'Kilcash'.
2. 'While Eiléan Ní Chuilleanáin's poems often deal with complex themes, they have an enigmatic quality that engages readers.' To what extent is this true of 'Kilcash'? Support your answer with close reference to the poem.

Points to Consider

- **Traditional lament for Catholic aristocracy raises questions about Ireland's past.**
- **Desolate landscape and negative language reflect the mood of hopelessness.**
- **Regular rhythm; the prayer-like tone and stark images emphasise the atmosphere.**
- **Ambivalent ending intrigues readers about the poet's own viewpoint.**

9 Translation

EILÉAN NÍ CHUILLEANÁIN

for the reburial of the Magdalenes

The soil frayed and sifted evens the score —
There are women here from every county,
Just as there were in the laundry.

White light blinded and bleached out
The high relief of a glance, where steam danced   5
Around stone drains and giggled and slipped across water.

Assist them now, ridges under the veil, shifting,
Searching for their parents, their names,
The edges of words grinding against nature,

As if, when water sank between the rotten teeth   10
Of soap, and every grasp seemed melted, one voice
Had begun, rising above the shuffle and hum

Until every pocket in her skull blared with the note —
Allow us now to hear it, sharp as an infant's cry
While the grass takes root, while the steam rises: 15

>   Washed clean of idiom · the baked crust
>   Of words that made my temporary name ·
>   A parasite that grew in me · that spell
>   Lifted · I lie in earth sifted to dust ·
>   Let the bunched keys I bore slacken and fall ·   20
>   I rise and forget · a cloud over my time.

Subtitle: The Magdalenes refers to Irish women, particularly unmarried mothers, who were separated from their children and forced to work in convent laundries. Inmates were required to undertake hard physical labour, including washing and needlework. They also endured a daily regime that included long periods of prayer and enforced silence. In Ireland, such institutions were known as Magdalene laundries. It has been estimated that up to 30,000 women passed through such laundries in Ireland, the last one of which (in Waterford) closed on 25 September 1996.
frayed: ragged.
sifted: sorted, examined.
the laundry: clothes-washing area.

blared: rang out, resounded.

idiom: language, misinterpretation.

parasite: bloodsucker.

👤 Personal Response

1. Comment on the effectiveness of the poem's title, 'Translation', in relation to the themes that Ní Chuilleanáin addresses in the poem.
2. Choose one image from the poem that you found particularly interesting. Briefly explain your choice.
3. How does the poem make you feel? Give reasons for your response, supporting the points you make with reference to the text.

POETRY FOCUS

'Washed clean of idiom'

👁 Critical Literacy

During the early 1990s, the remains of more than 150 women were discovered at several Dublin religious institutions as the properties were being excavated. The bones, from women buried over a very long period, were cremated and reburied in Glasnevin Cemetery. Eiléan Ní Chuilleanáin's poem was read at the reburial ceremony to commemorate Magdalene laundry women from all over Ireland. 'Translation' links the writer's work with the belated acknowledgement, in the late 20th century, of the stolen lives and hidden deaths of generations of Irishwomen incarcerated in Magdalene convents.

The poem begins with a macabre description of the Glasnevin grave where the reburial is taking place: 'The soil frayed and sifted evens the score.' Ní Chuilleanáin expresses the feelings of the mourners ('here from every county') who are **united by a shared sense of injustice**. This dramatic ceremony represents a formal acknowledgement of a dark period in Ireland's social history. Lines 4–5 take readers back in time behind convent walls, imagining the grim laundry rooms in which the Magdelene women worked: 'White light blinded and bleached out/The high relief of a glance.'

EILÉAN NÍ CHUILLEANÁIN

The poet's delicate and precise language contrasts the grinding oppression of routine manual labour with the young women's natural playfulness. **Their stolen youth and lost gaiety are poignantly conveyed through familiar images of the laundry**, 'where steam danced/Around stone drains and giggled and slipped across water' (lines 5–6). Vigorous verbs and a jaunty rhythm add emphasis to the sad irony of their broken lives. The relentless scrubbing was intended to wash away the women's sins. However, no matter how much the women washed, they were considered dirty and sinful throughout their lives.

All through the poem, Ní Chuilleanáin focuses on the importance of words and naming as though she herself is aiming to make sense of the shocking Magdalene story. But how is she to respond to the women who have come to the graveyard, 'Searching for their parents, their names'? Typically, the language is dense and multi-layered. In death, these former laundry workers are mere 'ridges under the veil' of the anonymous earth. The metaphor in line 7 also evokes images of the stern Magdalene nuns. **Ní Chuilleanáin sees all these women as victims of less enlightened times**, ironically recalled in the prayer-like note of invocation: 'Assist them now.'

The poem's title becomes clear as we recognise **Ní Chuilleanáin's intention to communicate ('translate') decades of silence into meaningful expression on behalf of the Magdalene laundry inmates**. Their relentless efforts to eventually become a 'voice' is compared to the almost impossible challenge of 'rising above the shuffle and hum' within the noisy laundry itself. In line 9, Ní Chuilleanáin visualises the women setting 'The edges of words grinding against nature' until their misrepresentation is overcome as it is turned to dust along with their bodies.

From line 13, much of the **focus is placed on exploring the experience of one of the nuns who managed the laundries**. As the true history emerges, she is also being cleansed of 'the baked crust/Of words that made my temporary name'. The 'temporary name' is her name in religion; that is, the saint's name she chose on entering strict convent life, which, as Ní Chuilleanáin notes, involved relinquishing her previous identity as an individual. She too has been exploited and the poet's generous tone reflects an understanding of this woman, who is caught between conflicting influences of duty, care, indoctrination and doubt, 'Until every pocket in her skull blared'. The evocative reference to the 'infant's cry' echoes the enduring sense of loss felt by young mothers who were forced to give up their babies shortly after birth.

In the poem's final lines, we hear the voice of a convent reverend mother, whose role is defined by 'the bunched keys I bore'. The reburial ceremony has also cleansed her from 'that spell' which maintained the cruel system she once served. Almost overwhelmed, she now recognises the 'parasite' power 'that grew in me' and only now can the keys she carries, an obvious symbol of her role as gaoler, 'slacken and fall'. **Bleak, disturbing images and broken**

rhythms have an unnerving, timeless effect. This woman's punitive authority over others has haunted her beyond the grave.

In the end, Ní Chuilleanáin's measured and balanced approach shows genuine compassion for all institutionalised victims, drawing together the countless young women and those in charge in their common confinement. In addition to their time spent in convents, they are now reunited, sifting the earth that they have all become. **The tragic legacy of these institutions involves women at many levels.** Nevertheless, the poem itself is a faithful translation, as these victims have been raised from their graves by the poet's response to their collective dead voice. Ní Chuilleanáin relates their compelling story to 'Allow us now to hear it'. She also tenderly acknowledges the complete silencing of the Irish Magdalenes as they did their enforced and, in some cases, lifelong penance.

Although Eiléan Ní Chuilleanáin's mournful 'translation' reveals glimpses of their true history, **none of these Magdalene women can ever be given back the lives they had before they entered the laundries**. The poem stops short of pretending to even the score in terms of power between those in authority and the totally subservient and permanently disgraced women under their control. At best, their small voices rise up together like 'steam' and form a 'cloud over my time' (line 21). This metaphor of the cloud can be construed as a shadow of shame over Irish society, but it can also be seen as a warning that the cycle of abuse is likely to be repeated.

✒ Writing About the Poem

'Ní Chuilleanáin's poems address important aspects of women's experiences in an insightful fashion.' Discuss this view, with particular reference to 'Translation'.

Sample Paragraph

I would agree that 'Translation' deals with an issue which is important to Irish women. The scandal of the unfortunate girls in Magdalene convents deserves to be publicised. Ní Chuilleanáin's poem gave me a deeper understanding of their story. The reburial service was attended by relatives 'from every county', suggesting the scale of the mistreatment. The details of the cold laundries – where 'White light blinded' seemed a subtle way of symbolising the misguided actions of those religious orders who punished young girls. I admired the poet's fair treatment of those nuns who are also presented as being imprisoned. The last stanza was revealing as it envisaged one cruel nun who was still confused by her part in the cruelty. The poet makes it clear that she was a product of an oppressive Catholic Ireland. 'Translation' succeeds in explaining the true story of the Magdalene women. It is powerful because Ní Chuilleanáin avoids being over-emotional. Her quiet tone conveys sadness for this dreadful period which still lingers like 'a cloud over my time'.

EXAMINER'S COMMENT

This top-grade response shows a clear understanding of Ní Chuilleanáin's considered approach to her theme, empathising with both those imprisoned and those in charge. Short quotations are well integrated while discussion points are clear and coherent, ranging over much of the poem. There is also some good personal interaction, including the final sentence. An excellent standard.

Class/Homework Exercises

1. 'Eiléan Ní Chuilleanáin's poetry offers a variety of interesting perspectives that vividly convey themes of universal relevance.' Discuss this statement with particular reference to 'Translation'.
2. 'In her poem "Translation", Ní Chuilleanáin's poetic voice is both critical and compassionate.' Discuss this statement with particular reference to the text.

Points to Consider

- The poet addresses aspects of the Magdalene laundries scandal.
- Several changes and translations are explored in the poem.
- Sensuous imagery evokes the harsh atmosphere in the laundry.
- Effective use of sound, contrast, mood and viewpoint throughout.

10. The Bend in the Road

This is the place where the child
Felt sick in the car and they pulled over
And waited in the shadow of a house.
A tall tree like a cat's tail waited too.
They opened the windows and breathed   5
Easily, while nothing moved. Then he was better.

Over twelve years it has become the place
Where you were sick one day on the way to the lake.
You are taller now than us.
The tree is taller, the house is quite covered in   10
With green creeper, and the bend
In the road is as silent as ever it was on that day.

Piled high, wrapped lightly, like the one cumulus cloud
In a perfect sky, softly packed like the air,
Is all that went on in those years, the absences,   15
The faces never long absent from thought,
The bodies alive then and the airy space they took up
When we saw them wrapped and sealed by sickness
Guessing the piled weight of sleep
We knew they could not carry for long;   20
This is the place of their presence: in the tree, in the air.

creeper: climbing plant.

cumulus: rounded, fluffy.

'This is the place'

👤 Personal Response

1. 'The importance of memory is a key theme in many of Ní Chuilleanáin's poems.' To what extent is this true of 'The Bend in the Road'? Briefly explain your answer.
2. Choose one image from 'The Bend in the Road' that you consider effective. Give reasons why this image appealed to you.
3. How would you describe the poem's conclusion? Is it mysterious? Hopeful? Comforting? Bitter? Briefly explain your response.

👁 Critical Literacy

'The Bend in the Road' is part of Eiléan Ní Chuilleanáin's poetry collection *The Girl Who Married the Reindeer*. In many of these poems, the autobiographical becomes transformed as Ní Chuilleanáin takes a moment in time and fills it with arresting images, exact description, stillness and secrecy, linking together selected memories from various times and places. This poem's title suggests that the road will go on even though it is not visible at the moment.

Stanza one opens with Ní Chuilleanáin pointing to the exact place where 'the child/Felt sick in the car and they pulled over'. The memory of such a familiar occurrence is given significance by the use of the demonstrative pronoun, 'This'. Run-on lines catch the flurry of activity as concerned adults attend to the sick child. Everything is still as they 'waited' for the sickness to pass. This suspended moment resonates as they linger 'in the shadow of a house'. **For a split second, an ominous – almost surreal – atmosphere begins to develop.** The poet introduces a slightly sinister simile, 'A tall tree like a cat's tail', peeking in from the world of fairy tale. Then the tree is personified: it 'waited too' as people and landscape merge in the moment of hush. Suddenly, a simple action ('They opened the windows') relieves the tension and everyone 'breathed/Easily'. The position of the adverb at the beginning of the line captures the relief at the recovery of the child. Yet the stationary atmosphere remained: 'while nothing moved.' However, the routine narrative of everyday life quickly resumes: 'Then he was better.'

In the second stanza, this roadside location takes on the shared resonance of memory: 'Over twelve years.' Readers are left imagining how the adults and child, when passing 'the place', would point it out as 'Where you were sick one day on the way to the lake'. The length of the line mirrors the long car journey. There is a sense of time being concentrated. Ní Chuilleanáin marvels at how the child has grown to adulthood: 'You are taller now than us.' The place has also changed – and even the tree is 'taller'. Assonance pinpoints how the nearby house is becoming yet more mysterious, 'quite covered in/With green creeper'. The insidious 'ee' sound mimics the silent takeover of the house by nature, as it recedes more and more into the shadows. Nature is alive. Creepings and rustlings stir, dispersing solidity and sureness. The poet cleverly places the line as if on a bend at the turn of a line: 'the bend/In the road is as silent as ever it was on that day.' Everything seems focused on the serenity of the place. **A bend in a road prevents us seeing what is coming next. Is this an obvious symbol of the human experience?** No one knows what lies ahead. The tone of this reflective stanza is introspective as Ní Chuilleanáin considers the undeniable passing of time and the human condition.

In the final stanza, memory and place interplay with other recollections. The poet's attention turns towards the sky, which she imagines 'Piled high' with past experiences. A lifetime's memories now tower 'like the one cumulus cloud/In a perfect sky'. The alliteration of the hard 'c' successfully captures the billowing cloud as it sails through the sky. **Similarly, the recollections of 'all that went on in those years' heave and surge as they drift through the poet's consciousness.** Naturally, they flow from the exact description of 'the bend/In the road'. They are now visible as feelings of loss expand into the present: 'The faces never long absent from thought.' Ní Chuilleanáin had lost not only her father and mother, but also her sister. But she remembers them **similarly** as they were, 'bodies alive then and the airy space they took up', just as the cloud in the sky. Poignantly, the poet also recalls them in their final sickness, 'wrapped and sealed by sickness', as if they had been parcelled for dispatch away from the ordinary routine of life by the ordeal of suffering.

EILÉAN NÍ CHUILLEANÁIN

However, the harsh reality of sickness and old age is also recognised: 'We knew they could not carry for long.' Just as the cloud grows bigger as it absorbs moisture, finally dissolving into rain, so did the poet's loved ones buckle beneath the weight of their illness, under the 'piled weight of sleep'. **Ní Chuilleanáin finds constant reminders of her family's past in the natural world.** She uses a simple image of cloud-like shapes of pillows and bed-covers as they surrender to sickness. Characteristically, the thinking within the poem has progressed considerably. The poet has widened its scope, its spatial dimension, to include those external experiences to which she so eloquently pays witness. Indeed, the poem now stands as a monument to silence and time, absence and presence, past and present. The moment of stillness is evoked. This roadside location takes on a special importance. It marks the place where lost family members now reside. Ní Chuilleanáin's alliterative language is emphatic: 'This is the place of their presence.' They belong 'in the tree, in the air'. As in so many of her poems, Ní Chuilleanáin honours the invisible, unseen presence of other thoughts and feelings that – just like the bend in the road – lie waiting in silence to be discovered and brought to life again.

✒ Writing About the Poem

'Eiléan Ní Chuilleanáin's poetry illuminates moments of perception in exact description.' Discuss this view in relation to 'The Bend in the Road'. Use suitable reference and quotation to support the points you make.

Sample Paragraph

'The Bend in the Road' is filled with accurate description. The opening lines pinpoint the exact place where 'the child/Felt sick in the car'. The conversational language, 'They opened the windows', 'Then he was better', brings me into this precise moment. I experience the tree, as if a child, through the almost cartoon-like simile, 'A tall tree like a cat's tail'. Yet, an otherworldly experience is present as personification transforms the tree into a living being; it 'waited too'. The place has become a metaphor for the reality of being human. The poet suddenly realises that the child has now grown into a man, 'You are taller than us now'. Another layer is added with the perception that the place has become filled with the 'presence' of those 'faces never long absent from thought'. I now began to understand that in a single moment, the distinctions between life and death, being and memory,

> **EXAMINER'S COMMENT**
>
> This is a top-grade personal response that addresses the poet's interest in transience and memory. Apt, accurate quotes provide good support for developed discussion points which range effectively through the poem. There is some highly impressive focus on aspects of the poet's distinctive style. Expression is also excellent throughout, e.g. 'The place has become a metaphor for the reality of being human'.

POETRY FOCUS

all become blurred. Through precise description, this poet transports readers into an understanding that many experiences, 'all that went on in those years', can be savoured in various forms, 'softly packed like the air'.

✒ Class/Homework Exercises

1. 'Space in Ní Chuilleanáin's poetry is used as an expression of one's experience of the world and is a metaphor for the linking together of self and the world.' Discuss this statement, with particular reference to 'The Bend in the Road'.
2. 'The evocative power of a specific location is central to Ní Chuilleanáin's "The Bend in the Road".' Discuss this view, supporting your answer with reference to the poem.

◉ Points to Consider

- Key themes include memory, family, transience, loss and grief.
- Symbolism used throughout the poem to suggest meaning.
- Effective use of assonance and alliteration to create atmosphere.
- Recurring references to sickness add unity to the poem.

11 On Lacking the Killer Instinct

EILÉAN NÍ CHUILLEANÁIN

One hare, absorbed, sitting still,
Right in the grassy middle of the track,
I met when I fled up into the hills, that time
My father was dying in a hospital —
I see her suddenly again, borne back   5
By the morning paper's prize photograph:
Two greyhounds tumbling over, absurdly gross,
While the hare shoots off to the left, her bright eye
Full not only of speed and fear
But surely in the moment a glad power,   10

Like my father's, running from a lorry-load of soldiers
In nineteen twenty-one, nineteen years old, never
Such gladness, he said, cornering in the narrow road
Between high hedges, in summer dusk.
                              The hare   15
Like him should never have been coursed,
But, clever, she gets off; another day
She'll fool the stupid dogs, double back
On her own scent, downhill, and choose her time
To spring away out of the frame, all while   20
The pack is labouring up.
                       The lorry was growling
And he was clever, he saw a house
And risked an open kitchen door. The soldiers
Found six people in a country kitchen, one   25
Drying his face, dazed-looking, the towel
Half covering his face. The lorry left,
The people let him sleep there, he came out
Into a blissful dawn. Should he have chanced that door?
If the sheltering house had been burned down, what good   30
Could all his bright running have done
For those that harboured him?
                          And I should not
Have run away, but I went back to the city
Next morning, washed in brown bog water, and   35
I thought about the hare, in her hour of ease.

hare: mammal resembling a large rabbit.
absorbed: engrossed, immersed, preoccupied.

absurdly: ridiculously, nonsensically.
gross: disgusting, outrageous.

coursed: hunted with greyhounds.

frame: picture, enclosure.
labouring: moving with difficulty.

👤 Personal Response

1. Who, in your opinion, lacked the killer instinct in this poem? Was it the hare, the soldiers, the greyhounds, the father, the poet? Refer closely to the text in your response.
2. The poet alters time and place frequently in this poem. With the aid of quotations, trace these changes as the poem develops.
3. Did you find the poem's conclusion satisfying or mystifying? Give reasons for your response, referring closely to the text.

👁 Critical Literacy

'On Lacking the Killer Instinct' is part of Eiléan Ní Chuilleanáin's *The Sun-fish* collection. Sunfish get their name from their habit of basking on the water's surface. Ní Chuilleanáin often presents daily life with a sense of mystery and otherworldliness as the poems move between various realms of experience. Each scene lies open to another version of the narrative. She blurs the distance between past and present in this three-part poem. History, which is something of an Irish obsession, always informs the present. This poet discovers and remembers. As she herself has said, 'In order for the poem to get written, something has to happen.'

The title of the poem immediately intrigues and unsettles. The <mark>opening lines</mark> focus on a stationary hare, silent, engrossed, 'absorbed', at rest. It is a vivid picture. Why is this hare preoccupied? The sibilant alliterative phrase, 'sitting still', captures the motionless animal in 'the grassy middle of the track'. This **naturalistic setting** and image is brought into high resolution as the poet recounts that her own journey 'up into the hills' led her to meet this creature. Ní Chuilleanáin juxtaposes the stillness of the wild hare with her own headlong flight from the awful reality, 'that time/My father was dying in a hospital'. In describing this terrible experience, her tone is remarkably controlled – detached, yet compassionate.

Another narrative thread is introduced in <mark>line 6</mark> when the poet recalls 'the morning paper's prize photograph'. Here the predators are presented as ungainly, almost comical characters incapable of purposeful action: 'Two greyhounds tumbling over, absurdly gross.' The broad vowels and repetition

'While the hare shoots off to the left'

EILÉAN NÍ CHUILLEANÁIN

of 'r' highlight the hounds' unattractively large appearance. Irish coursing is a competitive sport where dogs are tested on their ability to run and overtake the hare, turning it without capturing it. It is often regarded as a cruel activity that causes pain and suffering to the pursued creature. From the start of the poem, **readers are left wondering who exactly lacks the killer instinct**. Do the dogs not have the urge to pounce and kill? Has the hare got the killer instinct, running for its life, showing the strong will to survive against all odds? The rapid run-on lines mimic the speed and agility of the hare exulting in 'glad power'.

In line 11, the **reader is taken into another realm** – a common feature of Ní Chuilleanáin's interconnected narratives. In this case, she recalls another pursuit. Her father was a combatant in the Irish Civil War in 1922 and was on the run. Like the hare, he fled, 'cornering in the narrow road/Between high hedges, in summer dusk'. Both are linked through 'gladness' as they exult in their capacity to outrun their pursuers. For her father, this was a 'lorry-load of soldiers' – the compound word emphasising the unequal odds against which the poet's father struggled. This is similar to the hare's predicament against the 'Two greyhounds'. The precise placing of 'The hare' tucked away at the end of line 15 suggests the animal's escape. Ní Chuilleanáin comments that neither the hare nor her father should ever have 'been coursed'. She is happy to think that on some other occasion, the hare is likely to outwit the 'stupid dogs' and will 'spring away out of the frame', nimbly escaping her pursuers. In Irish coursing, the hare is not run on open land but in a secure enclosure over a set distance. The heavy, panting exertions of the pursuing dogs is illustrated in the run-through line, 'all while/The pack is labouring up'.

Ní Chuilleanáin returns to her father's story in line 22, imagining a moment of danger from his time as a fugitive. The scene is dominated by the threatening sound of a lorry, 'growling' like a pursuing hound. The repetition of the adjective 'clever' links her father and the hare as he too made his escape. Intent on surviving, 'he saw a house/And risked an open kitchen door'. **The enemy soldiers go through the motions of pursuit cursorily, seemingly lacking the killer instinct** when they 'Found six people in a country kitchen'. Ní Chuilleanáin is characteristically ambivalent about why the rebels were not challenged, reminding us of the contradictory attitudes among the various combatants of the Civil War.

For whatever reason, the fugitives ('one/Drying his face, dazed-looking') were not arrested and their deception worked. The poet's father is allowed refuge: 'The people let him sleep there.' Throughout Ireland's troubled history, there were 'safe houses' that sheltered those on the run. In her mind's eye, the poet pictures her father emerging in triumph the next day 'Into a blissful dawn' (line 29). In a **series of questions**, she considers his crucial decision to stand his ground and feign innocence. In retrospect, anything might have happened to affect the outcome at 'the sheltering house'.

Ní Chuilleanáin emphasises how chance has played such a significant role – not just in her father's life, but in Ireland's history.

The poet concludes by returning to the opening scene. Having observed the hare and remembered her father's encounter during the Civil War, she now realises that she should never have run away from her dying father. Her decision to return is seen as a mature one – almost like a religious ritual in which the poet cleanses herself, 'washed in brown bog water'. Is this a form of absolution to remove her guilt for running away? Typically, she uses this unifying symbol to gently draw the poem's three narratives together. After the common experience of the turbulence of the run, all three (the hare, the father and the poet herself) have entered a new state of being – calm composure. Ní Chuilleanáin reflects on 'the hare, in her hour of ease', the soft monosyllabic final word gently conveying a sense of peace and reconciliation. The poem closes as it began, with the **beautiful silent image of the hare**, self-possessed and serene after all the turmoil of the chase.

🖋 Writing About the Poem

'Eiléan Ní Chuilleanáin is a quiet, introspective, enigmatic poet.' Discuss this statement with particular reference to 'On Lacking the Killer Instinct'.

Sample Paragraph

'On Lacking the Killer Instinct' moved effortlessly, mysteriously weaving three different narratives: the story of the hare, the history of Ní Chuilleanáin's father's escape in 1921 and her own flight from the city. She celebrates resilience, the hare's 'bright eye' is full of 'a glad power'. Similarly, her father exulted in his cleverness, as he out-manoeuvred the 'lorry-load of soldiers'. The poet also faced up to death and 'went back to the city'. Her impressionistic style is similar to watching a photograph as it slowly develops before our eyes. The reader is effortlessly guided through different times and places as the focus of the poet's gaze shifts from the hunt of the hare in coursing to the hunt of her father in the Civil War. She then quietly reflects on her own flight and concludes that running does not solve problems, 'what good/Could all his bright running have done'. In the end, this poet poses questions that resonate. Does she too lack the killer instinct? The word 'ease' suggests that staying calm is more effective than running. Is the killer instinct worth having? This introspective poet leaves us with an image of stillness to think about.

EXAMINER'S COMMENT

This insightful paragraph offers a very clear and focused response to a testing question. Interesting critical discussion – aptly illustrated by accurate quotations – ranges widely, tracing the subtle development of the poem's various narrative threads. Impressive use of language throughout adds clarity to the key points. The questions posed towards the end round off the discussion effectively in this excellent top-grade answer.

✒ Class/Homework Exercises

1. 'Eiléan Ní Chuilleanáin's poems elude categories and invite and challenge the reader in equal measure.' Discuss this statement with particular reference to 'On Lacking the Killer Instinct'.
2. 'Ní Chuilleanáin is capable of blending multiple narratives with great skill in her poetry.' To what extent is this the case in 'On Lacking the Killer Instinct'? Support your answer with reference to the poem.

⊙ Points to Consider

- Interwoven stories: hunting the hare, her father's death and Ireland's Civil War.
- Effective use of rhythm and contrast – movement and stillness.
- Subtle blending of past and present, time and place.
- Alliterative and sibilant sound effects echo related ideas throughout.

12. To Niall Woods and Xenya Ostrovskaia, married in Dublin on 9 September 2009

When you look out across the fields
And you both see the same star
Pitching its tent on the point of the steeple —
That is the time to set out on your journey,
With half a loaf and your mother's blessing.   5

Leave behind the places that you knew:
All that you leave behind you will find once more,
You will find it in the stories;
The sleeping beauty in her high tower
With her talking cat asleep   10
Solid beside her feet — you will see her again.

When the cat wakes up he will speak in Irish and Russian
And every night he will tell you a different tale
About the firebird that stole the golden apples,
Gone every morning out of the emperor's garden,   15
And about the King of Ireland's Son and the Enchanter's Daughter.

The story the cat does not know is the Book of Ruth
And I have no time to tell you how she fared
When she went out at night and she was afraid,
In the beginning of the barley harvest,   20
Or how she trusted to strangers and stood by her word:

You will have to trust me, she lived happily ever after.

Title: An epithalamium is a poem (or song) in celebration of a wedding. Eiléan Ní Chuilleanáin has included this poem (to her son Niall and his bride, Xenya) as the introductory dedication in her poetry collection *The Sun-fish*.

sleeping beauty: European fairy tale from 'La Belle au bois dormant' ('Beauty of the Sleeping Wood') by Charles Perrault and 'Dornröschen' ('Little Briar Rose') by the Brothers Grimm.

the firebird: Russian fairy tale; 'Tsarevitch Ivan, the Fire Bird and the Gray Wolf' by Alexander Afanasyev.
the King of Ireland's Son: Irish fairy tale; 'The King of Ireland's Son' by Padraic Colum.
Book of Ruth: religious story from the Old Testament.

Or how she trusted to strangers: In the Bible story, Boaz owned the field Ruth harvested. He was a relative of the family and by law could 'redeem' her if he married her now that she was a widow. He wished to do so because he admired how she had stood by her mother-in-law, 'For wherever you go, I will go'.

'the firebird that stole the golden apples'

👤 Personal Response

1. Do you think the references to fairy tales are appropriate on the occasion of Eiléan Ní Chuilleanáin's son's marriage? Give one reason for your answer.
2. In your opinion, what is the dominant tone of voice in the poem? Is it one of warning, reassurance, hope, consolation? Briefly explain your response with reference to the poem.
3. Write your own short personal response to the poem, highlighting the impact it made on you.

👁 Critical Literacy

'I write poems that mean a lot to me' (Eiléan Ní Chuilleanáin). This particular poem is dedicated to her son, Niall, and his new bride, Xenya, on the happy occasion of their marriage. Folklore is central to this poet's work. Her mother, Eilís Dillon, was a famous writer of children's stories. Fairy tales allow Ní Chuilleanáin the opportunity to approach a subject from an oblique, non-confessional perspective. It gives distance. Story-tellers rarely comment on or explain what happens. They simply tell the tale. In this poem, Ní Chuilleanáin refers to folklore and a well-known Bible story as she addresses the young couple.

The **first stanza** opens with **warm advice** from a loving mother as she gives the young man leave to set out on his own journey through life with his new partner. Run-on lines contain a beautiful, romantic image of a harmonious vision: 'you both see the same star.' Personification and alliteration bring this natural image to radiant life, 'Pitching its tent on the point of the steeple', suggesting the new home which the young couple are about to set up for themselves. **Ní Chuilleanáin's gaze is one of relentless clarity and attentiveness.** She illuminates details. She also counsels that it is the right time to go, 'to set out on your journey' when you are prepared ('With half a loaf') and with good wishes ('and your mother's blessing'). She combines colloquial and fairy tale language. The tone is warm, but also pragmatic – offering practical advice to the newlyweds to make the most of whatever they have to start with: 'half a loaf is better than none.'

Stanza two begins with the imperative warning: 'Leave behind.' The mother is advising the couple to forget 'the places that you knew'. Is 'places' a metaphor for their actual homes or their cultural environments? Or does it refer to values the young people hold sacred? She consoles them that past experiences can still be found 'in the stories'. Ní Chuilleanáin now weaves an intricate web of such stories from many different sources. The first tale is that of 'sleeping beauty in her high tower'. This classic folk story involves a beautiful princess, enchantment, and a handsome prince who has to brave the obstacles of tall trees that surround the castle and its sleeping princess.

POETRY FOCUS

Is Ní Chuilleanáin illustrating that the path to true love is filled with difficulties and that only the brave will be successful? The extended run-on lines suggest the hundred years' sleep of the spellbound princess, who can only be awakened by a kiss. The poet also makes use of another familiar element of fairy tales – talking animals. In this case, the 'talking cat' probably refers to Irish folklore, and the King of Cats, a renowned teller of tales. Ní Chuilleanáin is able to link the basic characteristics of the animal with human behaviour. The cat slumbers with the princess, 'Solid', stable and dependable, beside her feet. Despite the poet's realism, however, this fairy tale allusion is primarily optimistic.

In stanza three, Ní Chuilleanáin imagines the cat awakening and telling stories in both 'Irish and Russian', a likely reference to the young couple's **two cultural backgrounds**. The poet has said that in her work she is trying 'to suggest, to phrase, to find a way to make it possible for somebody to pick up certain suggestions ... They might not be seeing what I am seeing.' The poet continues to set her personal wishes for Niall and Xenya within the context of folktales, turning to the Russian tradition: 'Tsarevitch, the Fire Bird and the Gray Wolf.' Again, the hero of this story is on a challenging mission, as he attempts to catch the 'firebird that stole the golden apples ... out of the emperor's garden'. The assonance of the broad vowel 'o' emphasises the exasperation of the repeated theft. As always in folklore, courage and determination are required before the hero can overcome many ordeals and find true happiness.

Ní Chuilleanáin introduces the Irish tradition with the story of the King of Ireland's son, who must pluck three hairs from the Enchanter's beard in order to save his own life. On his quest, he gains the hand of Fedelma, the Enchanter's youngest daughter. But he falls asleep and loses her to the King of the Land of Mist. **Is the poet simply advising her son and daughter-in-law that love must be cherished and never taken for granted?** Throughout the poem, she draws heavily on stories where heroes have to fight for what they believe in. All of these tales convey the same central meaning – that lasting love has to be won through daring, determination and sacrifice.

In the playful link into stanza four, Ní Chuilleanáin remarks that 'the story the cat does not know is the Book of Ruth'. This final story is not from the world of folklore, but from the Bible (although the poet has commented that 'a lot of religious narrative is very folkloric'). The Book of Ruth teaches that **genuine love can require uncompromising sacrifice**, and that such unselfish love will be well rewarded. This particular tale of inclusivity shows two different cultures coming together. The Israelites (sons of Naomi) marry women from the Moab tribe, one of whom is Ruth. She embraces Naomi's people, land, culture and God. This is very pertinent to the newly married couple, as they are also from different lands and cultures. Not surprisingly, the biblical tale is one of loving kindness – but it also includes a realistic message. After her husband's death, Ruth chooses to stay with her

EILÉAN NÍ CHUILLEANÁIN

mother-in-law and undertakes the backbreaking farm work of gleaning to support the family. This involves lifting the grain and stalks left behind after the harvesting of barley. The metaphor of the harvest is another reminder that married couples will reap what they sow, depending on the effort and commitment made to their relationship.

The poem's last line is placed apart to emphasise its significance. Ní Chuilleanáin tells the newlyweds that they 'will have to trust me' – presumably just as Ruth trusted her mother-in-law, Naomi. For doing this, she was rewarded with living 'happily ever after', as in the best tales. The poet's quietly light-hearted approach, however, does not lessen her own deeply felt hopes for Niall and Xenya. **All the stories she has used are concerned with the essential qualities of a loving relationship** – and share a common thread of courage, faithfulness and honesty as the couple journey to a happy future. Tales and dreams are the shadow-truths that will endure. Ní Chuilleanáin's final tone is clearly sincere, upbeat and forward-looking.

✒ Writing About the Poem

'The imagination is not the refuge but the true site of authority.' Comment on this statement in relation to the poem 'To Niall Woods and Xenya Ostrovskaia, married in Dublin on 9 September 2009'.

Sample Paragraph

I feel that Ní Chuilleanáin's poem has subtle messages which only become clear after several readings. I think the poet is counselling her son and his new bride, Xenya, that stories, 'the imagination' are where truth, 'the true site of authority' lies. The stories she chooses, 'sleeping beauty in her high tower', 'the firebird that stole the golden apples' and the 'King of Ireland's Son and the Enchanter's Daughter' all suggest that perseverance and sincerity win the day. Nothing worthwhile is won easily. I thought the inclusion of the story of Ruth was very apt as it involved two cultures which is relevant to the couple's Irish and Russian origins. People in this new era will have to 'trust' strangers. I understood that Ní Chuilleanáin is showing that no matter where these imaginative tales come from, Europe, Russia, Ireland or the Bible, obstacles have to be overcome in life through determination. I thought the poet was clever because by putting this insight into the realm of a fairy story, it does not sound like preaching which the young couple might resent, yet the message rings true through time from this 'site of authority', the kingdom of storytelling.

EXAMINER'S COMMENT

A sustained personal response showing genuine engagement with the poem. The focused opening tackles the discussion question directly. This is followed by several clear points, e.g. 'perseverance and sincerity win the day', 'Nothing worthwhile is won easily', 'obstacles have to be overcome', tracing the development of thought throughout the poem. Accurate quotations and clear expression ensure the highest grade.

Class/Homework Exercises

1. What impression of Ní Chuilleanáin do you get from reading 'To Niall Woods and Xenya Ostrovskaia, married in Dublin on 9 September 2009'? Write at least one paragraph in response, illustrating your views with reference to the text of the poem.
2. 'Ní Chuilleanáin's poems are often seen as challenging, but ultimately rewarding.' To what extent is this true of 'To Niall Woods and Xenia Ostrovskaia, married in Dublin on 9 September 2009'? Support your answer with reference to the poem.

Points to Consider

- The advice to the young couple is couched in the language of a fairy tale.
- Recurring references to Bible stories and legends.
- Effective use of personification, alliteration and sibilance.
- Ending is sincere, sympathetic and optimistic.

Sample Leaving Cert Questions on Ní Chuilleanáin's Poetry

1. 'Eiléan Ní Chuilleanáin's captivating stories explore significant issues for modern-day Ireland, in an intriguing and attractive style.' Discuss this statement, developing your response with reference to the themes and language evident in the poems by Ní Chuilleanáin on your course.
2. 'Ní Chuilleanáin's multi-layered poems invite readers into a variety of settings and enhance our understanding of the world around us.' Discuss this view, developing your response with reference to the poems by Eiléan Ní Chuilleanáin on your course.
3. 'Eiléan Ní Chuilleanáin's thought-provoking subject matter and distinctive poetic style can sometimes prove challenging.' Discuss this statement, developing your response with reference to the themes and language evident in the poems by Ní Chuilleanáin on your course.

Understanding the Prescribed Poetry Question

Marks are awarded using the PCLM Marking Scheme: P = 15; C = 15; L = 15; M = 5 Total = 50

- **P** (Purpose = 15 marks) refers to the set question and is the launch pad for the answer. This involves engaging with all aspects of the question. Both theme and language must be addressed, although not necessarily equally.
- **C** (Coherence = 15 marks) refers to the organisation of the developed response and the use of accurate, relevant quotation. Paragraphing is essential.
- **L** (Language = 15 marks) refers to the student's skill in controlling language throughout the answer.
- **M** (Mechanics = 5 marks) refers to spelling and grammar.
- Although no specific number of poems is required, students usually discuss at least 3 or 4 in their written responses.
- Aim for at least 800 words, to be completed within 45–50 minutes.

How do I organise my answer?

(Sample question 2)

'Ní Chuilleanáin's multi-layered poems invite readers into a variety of settings and enhance our understanding of the world around us.' Discuss this view, developing your response with reference to the poems by Eiléan Ní Chuilleanáin on your course.

Sample Plan 1

Intro: *(Stance: agree with viewpoint in the question)* Ní Chuilleanáin's innovative poetry challenges with a vast canvas of people, places, voices, times and images. Weaving fragmentary narratives, she propels readers into a greater awareness of the world. She focuses on death, communication, memory, sacrifice and salvation.

Point 1: *(Blended stories – memory and death)* 'Deaths and Engines' uses surreal tactile imagery to link two stories, a plane crash and her father's death. Both share the nightmarish event of losing control ('too late to stop'). Acceptance of powerlessness of individual in difficult times.

NOTE

In keeping with the PCLM approach, the student has to take a stance by agreeing, disagreeing or partially agreeing that Ní Chuilleanáin's:

- **multi-layered poems** (complexities of life and relationships, the continuous past, Irish phenomena, historical and mythical references, mystical experiences, etc.)

... invite readers into a:

- **variety of settings** (changing locations, Ireland past and present, altered landscapes, collapse of time and place, etc.)
- **enhance our understanding of the world** (power of memory, new awareness, importance of communication and responsibility, possibility of spiritual redemption, etc.)

Point 2: *(Ambivalent detailed scenario – lack of communication/comprehension)* 'Street' entices reader and would-be lover into an altered world. Cinematic close-up ('white trousers/Dangling a knife on a ring at her belt') reveals uncertain atmosphere. Dreamlike encounter draws attention to gaps in communication and comprehension.

Point 3: *(Altered landscapes – power of memory)* 'Following' details changing settings; dust and noise of cattle mart ('beasts packed solid'), cold bog ('shivering bog by starlight'). Memory does not remain 'shelved' but will 'crack' so dead and living can reconnect through relics ('crushed flowers').

Point 4: *(Complex themes – sacrifice/reward)* 'All for You' reveals tremendous sacrifice of nun's celibate religious life through personification of architectural detail, staircase ('Sprawling') and orderly provision store ('tins shining in ranks'). Submission to God's will 'key' to salvation.

Conclusion: Ní Chuilleanáin's poems offer elusive visions and subtle messages. Breaking down barriers between shifting realms, fragmented narratives open doors into multiple worlds and experiences. Challenging perspectives from which to view our own world.

Sample Paragraph: Point 4

Strange hypnotic images from convent life appear in Ní Chuilleanáin's poem 'All for You'. The writhing 'staircase of the hall', described as 'Sprawling', seems both welcoming and threatening. The poet refers to the bible story of the serpent that Moses constructed to gain salvation from God for his people. The harsh staircase of life must also be climbed to gain salvation. The nun's choice of a confined celibate life is suggested by slender assonant sounds, 'The tins shine in ranks … Rich with shrivelled fruit'. A violent image, 'rage of brushwood', reveals the intensity of the nun's vocation and also echoes another bible story – about the burning bush. The 'key' representing both confinement and freedom shows the paradox of Christian faith. Redemption can only be achieved through submission to God's will. This complex and challenging poem moves through various settings, focusing mainly on the Christian belief of salvation through surrender to God.

EXAMINER'S COMMENT

As part of a full essay, this is a strong, top-grade paragraph showing clear engagement with the poem. The discussion points relating to Ní Chuilleanáin's dense imagery and sound effects are particularly impressive. Accurate supportive quotations are effectively worked into the critical analysis. Language use is also excellent throughout.

(Sample question 3)

'Eiléan Ní Chuilleanáin's thought-provoking subject matter and distinctive poetic style can sometimes prove challenging.' Discuss this statement, developing your response with reference to the themes and language evident in the poems by Ní Chuilleanáin on your course.

NOTE

In keeping with the PCLM approach, the student has to take a stance by agreeing, disagreeing or partially agreeing with the statement that:

- **Ní Chuilleanáin's poems are thought-provoking** (complex history of Ireland, exploiter/exploited, love, loss, death, women's experiences, religious life, celebration of nature, impact of change, etc.)

... written in a:

- **distinctive style** (layered narratives, dense dreamlike imagery, wide-ranging references, dramatic personification, etc.)

- **can prove challenging** (demanding themes, elusive characters, obscure, ambivalent settings, complex ideas, etc.)

Sample Plan 2

Intro: *(Stance: agree with viewpoint in the question)* Ní Chuilleanáin addresses universal concerns of exploiter and exploited and disturbing contrasts between the past and present. Poems challenge the reader to wonder and reflect. Unique style interweaves narratives, using layered fragments of powerful visual and aural imagery.

Point 1: *(Exploiter/exploited – dramatic contrasts)* 'Lucina Schynning in Silence of the Nicht' suggests material and cultural deprivation ('without roast meat or music'). Repulsive imagery traces the devastation left by Cromwell ('plague'). Contrasting positive sense of resilience expressed in animal imagery ('chirp of the stream running').

Point 2: *(Landlord/tenant – translation of traditional Irish lament)* 'Kilcash' explores impact of change on Irish society past and present ('What will we do now'). Only solution offered is the restoration of the big house 'Kilcash'. Ambivalent attitude of poet – is this a genuine tribute to humane landlords or a satire on subservience of Irish?

Point 3: *(Past/present – sardonic humour)* 'The Second Voyage' describes mythic tale of the Greek hero, Odysseus, battling with the treacherous ocean ('simmering sea'). Mockery of inflated sense of masculine power ('rammed/The oar'). Enigmatic poem poses the question whether recollected memory captivates more than routine present experience.

Point 4: *(Offender/victim – detailed imagery)* 'Translation' offers perceptive account of wrongs inflicted on Irish women in Magdalene laundries. Sensuous imagery captures the harsh atmosphere in the laundry. Inclusion of authority figure as victim challenges modern readers' perceptions.

Conclusion: Ní Chuilleanáin investigates universal themes of oppressor and oppressed, using Irish history's troubled backstory. Mythic references explore man's frustration with what he possesses and challenge us to re-examine our own views.

Sample Paragraph: Point 4

'Translation' offers an intriguing account of a very dark period in Irish history. Ní Chuilleanáin focuses on the terrible oppression of the laundry's young women – something that should never be repeated or forgotten. The poem made me think about their loss of youth and happiness. The bleak atmosphere – 'light blinded' – is poignantly contrasted with their natural playfulness, suggested by the lively image, 'steam danced/Around stone drains and giggled'. The poet also notes the nun's loss of identity, 'my temporary name'. Both the girls' lives and hers have been 'bleached out'. Fortunately, her rule over the girls is now gone, 'the bunched keys I bore slacken'. I found it interesting that a shame still hangs over the nun, 'a cloud over my time'. The inclusion of Magdalene victims and authority figures, such as the nun, as equal victims of a less tolerant time is likely to be challenged by many people today.

EXAMINER'S COMMENT

Good personal response demonstrating close engagement with the poem. As part of a full essay, it shows an appreciation of Ní Chuilleanáin's thought-provoking presentation of victims. Critical commentary is well supported by suitable quotation and some awareness of poetic techniques, including evocative imagery and atmosphere. Expression is assured throughout this successful high-grade paragraph.

EXAM FOCUS

- As you may not be familiar with some of the poems referred to in the sample plans, substitute poems that you have studied closely.
- Key points about a particular poem can be developed over more than one paragraph.
- Paragraphs may also include cross-referencing and discussion of more than one poem.
- Remember that there is no single 'correct' answer to poetry questions, so always be confident in expressing your own considered response.

Leaving Cert Sample Essay

'Eiléan Ní Chuilleanáin's captivating stories explore significant issues for modern-day Ireland, in an intriguing and attractive style.' Discuss this statement, developing your response with reference to the themes and language evident in the poems by Ní Chuilleanáin on your course.

Sample Essay

1. Eiléan Ní Chuilleanáin's poems engage readers with stories, in a variety of settings. These intimate narratives are often blended to include universal issues that are relevant to today's Ireland. Her vibrant imagery and range of interesting references produce fascinating and mysterious poems.

2. 'The Bend in the Road' takes a familiar family event, a child who once 'felt sick in the car' on a quiet country road. The poem involves readers through the use of personification from the slightly sinister world of fairy tales, 'A tall tree like a cat's tail'. Ní Chuilleanáin reminds us of the universal truth that life does not permit us to see into the future. This is important for everyone in modern Ireland – we cannot take anything for granted as everything can change in an instant. By combining different narratives, the poet shows how the past can sometimes be found in the present. 'Piled high' clouds remind her of lost loved ones. In their final days they were 'wrapped and sealed by sickness', like parcels about to be dispatched. In this compelling poem, an ordinary family story is transformed into an engaging reflection on love and memory through layers of vivid imagery.

3. Another harsh truth, the death of the poet's mother, is addressed in 'Fireman's Lift'. The poem is set inside Parma Cathedral in northern Italy. The close relationship between mother and daughter is vividly captured, 'I was standing beside you looking up'. Strong verbs, such as 'spiralling' and 'heaving', describe what is depicted in the religious artwork – the huge effort of the angels lifting Mary into the glory of heaven. The image of the angels acting as 'A crane and a cradle' for Mary reminds the poet of the nurses, 'heads bowed', who looked after her mother during her illness. It is time for her mother, like the Virgin, to go 'spiralling to heaven'. For Ní Chuilleanáin, this represents an acceptance of loss. The poem is a powerful lesson for modern Ireland to accept what cannot be changed.

4. The relevance of history is a theme in 'On Lacking the Killer Instinct'. Ní Chuilleanáin recalls her father's escape from the Black and Tans. This is when in 1921 British military soldiers hunted down her father. But he escaped by hiding in a safe house. Sibilant sounds show his relief as he escaped 'into a blissful dawn'. The poet also tries escaping when she 'fled up into the hills' at a tough time in her own past when her father was dying in hospital. There she met 'one hare' which also like her father had been hunted, 'coursed'. Through these interwoven stories, Ní Chuilleanáin teaches us a valuable lesson for life. We can't always 'run away' from difficulties but must stand our ground like her father and the hare experienced in an 'hour of ease'.

INDICATIVE MATERIAL

- **Ní Chuilleanáin's captivating stories** (engaging recollections from her past, family relationships, stories about Ireland's complex history, compelling accounts of women's experience, universal folktales and myths, spiritual life, etc.)

... explore:

- **significant issues for modern-day Ireland** (relevance of myth and history, the enduring need for compassion, importance of the feminine perspective, universal themes, e.g. love, loss, memory, death, afterlife, etc.)

- **intriguing and attractive style** (vivid imagery, layered quality of the work, reference/allusions, choice of settings and moods: surreal/suggestive/evocative/obscure/mysterious, etc.)

POETRY FOCUS

5. 'To Niall Woods and Xenya Ostrovskaia' closely links two folktales. The Russian 'firebird' story and the Irish tale of 'the Enchanter's Daughter' are used to honour the two distinct cultures of the newly-married couple. Ní Chuilleanáin engages readers with the frustration felt by the hero on his mission to capture the thieving firebird. This is done through broad assonance sounds, 'stole the golden apples'. She is reminding the young couple that courage and determination are required if true happiness is to be achieved. The Irish tale recounts how love must never be taken for granted. The King of Ireland's son lost the Enchanter's Daughter because he fell asleep. Once again, these stories emphasise the importance of determination and sacrifice, making them relevant to qualities that Irish people now need more than ever.

6. 'Translation' is based on the Magdalene convents' scandal. The poem addresses an issue that is important to every Irish person. Without becoming angry or over-emotional, Ní Chuilleanáin makes the point that abuse of any individual is wrong. The dramatic description of the infamous laundries – places where 'white light blinded' the unfortunate victims – sums up the tragic events of a once shameful Ireland and teaches the lesson that such cruelty should ever happen again. Ní Chuilleanáin is respectful towards those nuns who were also victims of an oppressive religious system that was supported by the state. Like the young girls who were so mistreated, some of these nuns were also imprisoned, even losing their own names and identities by taking the names of saints.

7. Ní Chuilleanáin's poetry isn't always easy to understand, but memory and reflection are central to many of the poems on our course. There is often a dream-like quality which allows readers to take their own meaning – particularly from the open-ended poems that leave us asking questions. I enjoyed Ní Chuilleanáin's lyrical poetry which included stories from her family life. These were thought-provoking and often illustrated important issues about love, loss and endurance.

(800 words)

> **EXAMINER'S COMMENT**
>
> *This solid top-grade response addresses the question's three key elements (the poet's stories, issues and style), although a little more focus on relevance to today's Ireland would have been welcome. The short introductory paragraph gives a clear overview that shows good engagement with Ní Chuilleanáin's poems. Effective use is made of reference to support perceptive discussion. The importance of interwoven narratives and sound effects is illustrated – particularly in paragraphs 3 and 5. Apart from some awkwardness in paragraph 4, expression is generally well controlled throughout this impressive essay.*

GRADE: H1
P = 15/15
C = 13/15
L = 13/15
M = 5/5
Total = 46/50

 Revision Overview

'Lucina Schynning in Silence of the Nicht'
Powerful monologue addresses themes of exploitation, loss and resistance.

'The Second Voyage'
Dramatic presentation of theme of transience. Innovative use of mythical Greek hero's love/hate relationship with the sea.

'Deaths and Engines'
Themes of memory, loss and death. Blending of two narratives (plane and father's death).

'Street' (OL)
Intriguing oblique narrative of falling in love. Central puzzling enigma.

'Fireman's Lift'
Vivid memory poem explores themes of death, regeneration and love.

'All for You'
Intricately layered broken narrative depicts theme of transience through analysis of the challenges and rewards of religious life.

'Following'
Themes of power, of memory and unjust balance of power through metaphor of journey.

'Kilcash'
Translation of Irish lament addresses theme of impact of change on Irish society, past and present.

'Translation'
Belated acknowledgment of wrongs perpetrated on Irish women in Magdalene laundries.

'The Bend in the Road'
Blended autobiographical events express transience and loss. The continuing existence of memory is acknowledged and honoured.

'On Lacking the Killer Instinct'
Interwoven introspective narratives bridge past and present. Enigmatic examination of theme of powerful and powerless, through illustrations of hunter and hunted.

'To Niall Woods and Xenya Ostrovskaia, married in Dublin 9 September 2009' (OL)
Celebratory epithalamium blends folk tales and biblical stories. Theme of sacrifice needed for success.

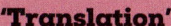 Last Words

'There is something second-sighted about Eiléan Ní Chuilleanáin's work. Her poems see things anew, in a rinsed and dreamstruck light.'
Seamus Heaney

'Ní Chuilleanáin's eccentric poems uncover hidden dramas in many guises, and she continually holds us captive by her luminous voice.'
Molly Bendall

'Inspiration comes from everywhere, from the places I go and the things I do. I never write unless I have an idea that seems really interesting to me.'
Eiléan Ní Chuilleanáin

EILÉAN NÍ CHUILLEANÁIN

 SUFFERING   HISTORY/MEMORY   TIME   DEATH   LOVE  RELATIONSHIPS 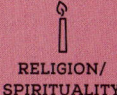 RELIGION/SPIRITUALITY   STRENGTH

POETRY FOCUS

Tracy K. Smith
b. 1972

'You want a poem to unsettle something'

Tracy K. Smith was born on 16 April 1972 in Massachusetts and grew up in California. She became interested in writing and poetry early in life, reading Emily Dickinson and Mark Twain in elementary school. Dickinson's poems in particular struck her as working like 'magic'. Smith studied at Harvard University, where Seamus Heaney was one of her teachers. The work of Elizabeth Bishop and Rita Dove also became significant influences.

Her poetry is lyrical and political – combining honesty, imagination and compassion as she explores issues of desire, loss and the African-American experience. While she shows her wonder in the world, she never retreats from its injustices. Reflections on race and slavery surface throughout her poems.

Smith is the author of several prize-winning collections, including *Life on Mars*, which won the 2012 Pulitzer Prize. She also served as the 22nd United States Poet Laureate from 2017 to 2019.

Smith's poetry retains a close awareness of how individual lives are embedded in wider society. Her signature poetic voice, whether in elegy or praise or outrage, insists upon vibrancy and hope – particularly in moments of grief and empathy.

Investigate Further

To find out more about Tracy K. Smith, or to hear readings of her poems not already available in your eBook, you could search some useful websites, such as YouTube, BBC Poetry, poetryfoundation.org and poetryarchive.org, or access additional material on this page of your eBook.

Prescribed Poems

Note that Smith uses American spellings in her work.

○ 1 'Joy'
Smith's intimate memory poem in tribute to her late mother confronts the significance of death and asks readers to review their own beliefs about the possibility of an afterlife.
Page 352

○ 2 'Dominion over the Beasts of the Earth'
A series of vivid memories about the excitement and uncertainty of young love addresses universal themes of desire, personal choices and coming of age.
Page 357

○ 3 'The Searchers' (OL)
Based on a Hollywood movie about a white girl brought up by Native Americans, the poem reflects on issues of identity, race and belonging.
Page 364

○ 4 'Letter to a Photojournalist Going-In'
Smith describes the reality of being a war photojournalist and considers the wider impact of the photographer's work – particularly its effect on his personal relationships.
Page 369

○ 5 'The Universe is a House Party'
In this imaginative and thought-provoking exploration of modern life, the poet contrasts the limits of human comprehension with the vast, mysterious universe.
Page 374

○ 6 'The Museum of Obsolescence'
Smith imagines a public gallery in the distant future. The building displays forgotten and useless artefacts from the human species' time on planet Earth.
Page 379

○ 7 'Don't You Wonder, Sometimes?'
While processing the sorrow she feels after her father's death, the poet combines references to pop culture and science fiction to reflect on people's place in the universe.
Page 384

○ 8 'It's Not' (OL)
In this moving elegy in tribute to her father, the poet examines some of the mysteries of science and explores crucial questions about life and death.
Page 391

○ 9 'The Universe as Primal Scream'
Hearing the screams of young children leads to a meditation on the limited nature of human life, the universe, death and the hereafter.
Page 395

○ 10 'The Greatest Personal Privation' (OL)
Powerful poem in which Smith imagines the voices of two mid-19th-century African-American slaves and urges readers to question governments and challenge injustice.
Page 401

○ 11 'I am 60 odd years of age'
(*from* 'I Will Tell You the Truth About This, I Will Tell You All About It')
The compelling voices of African-American Civil War soldiers and their families challenge racism, awakening awareness of and compassion for forgotten people.
Page 407

○ 12 'Ghazal'
In declaring her support for those whose voices cry out for justice, Smith confronts both historical discrimination and ongoing inequality that have made an impact on the African-American identity.
Page 414

(OL) indicates poems that are also prescribed for the Ordinary Level course.

POETRY FOCUS

1 Joy

In memoriam KMS 1936–1994

Imagining yourself a girl again,
You ask me to prepare a simple meal
Of dumplings and kale.

The body is memory.
You are nine years old,   5
Playing hospital with your sisters.

These will be my medicine,
You tell them, taking a handful
Of the raisins that you love.

They've made the room dark   10
And covered you with a quilt,
Though this is the South in summer.

The body is appetite.
You savor the kale,
Trusting this one need.   15

But the body is cautious,
Does not want more
Than it wants. Soon

There will be a traffic
Of transparent tubes, striking   20
Their compromise with the body.

When you close your eyes,
I know you are listening
To a dark chamber

Around a chord of light.   25
I know you are deciding
That the body's a question:

What do you believe in?

Dedication: Kathryn M. Smith, the poet's mother.

Imagining: picturing.
dumplings: savoury filled balls of dough.
kale: leafy green vegetable.

memory: recollection, retention, celebration.

quilt: bedspread, duvet.

appetite: hunger, desire.
savor: enjoy.

cautious: wary, restrained.

traffic: flow, to-ing and fro-ing.
transparent: clear.
compromise: agreement.

chamber: bedroom, space.

chord: harmony.

question: point at issue.

believe in: understand about life, rely on.

TRACY K. SMITH

👤 Personal Response

1. Based on the evidence of the poem, briefly describe your impression of the poet's mother.
2. Throughout the poem, Smith describes the body in various ways, using metaphors and images. Choose one image or metaphor which you found particularly interesting. What did it reveal to you about the body's ability?
3. In your opinion, what is the meaning of the concluding question? Is the tone demanding or pleading? Briefly explain your response.

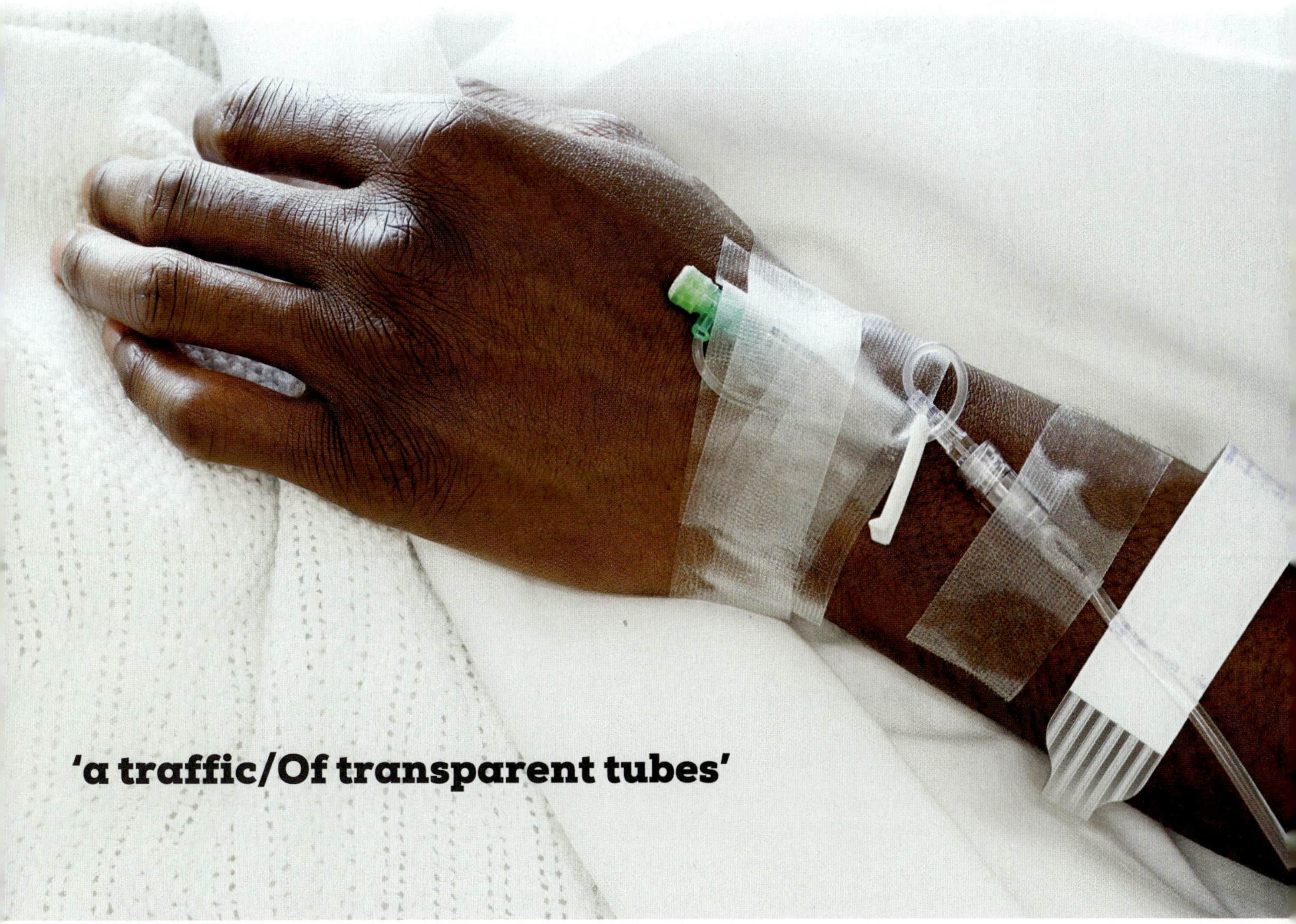

'a traffic/Of transparent tubes'

👁 Critical Literacy

'Joy' forms Part III of Tracy K. Smith's debut collection, *The Body's Question*. The poem is one of several elegies written in response to her mother's death from cancer in 1994. After graduating from Harvard, the poet returned home; 'I knew I needed to go home and be with my mom because she was coming to the end'. This intimate memory poem makes Smith's mother seem radiant and special. In this tender elegy, the body itself becomes a question and puzzle.

POETRY FOCUS

From the outset, Smith confronts the **challenging themes of loss, grief and identity** using plain-spoken, precise description. Her terminally ill mother visualises herself as a young 'girl again'. She asks her daughter to make her a 'simple meal' of filled dough and green vegetables, 'dumplings and kale' (line 3). This occasion hints at Christ's Last Supper which he shared with his disciples shortly before his death.

Smith's mother, a schoolteacher from Alabama, was **a devout Christian** who believed that God created the world and that a person can attain salvation after death through faith in Jesus Christ. Smith wrote: 'The black church was part of my parents' lives … The role of that institution lay in erecting hope and structure and the sense that there is justice … something larger that's watching and keeping tabs'.

The emphatic metaphor 'The body is memory' (line 4) suggests that **the human body stores a memory bank** of echoes from the past. Often, very ill people in their final days recollect and revert back to happier times, 'You are nine years old'. A cherished moment with her sisters is recalled, 'Playing hospital'. Time and identity shapeshift as the mother's confident young voice is heard, '*These will be my medicine*' (line 7), announcing that the 'raisins' would cure her. Is Smith imagining all this? Or is the mother actually recounting this precious memory to her daughter?

In line 10, the poem slips back to the present. Smith's **straightforward description** of the grim reality of her mother's final days replaces the nostalgic memory of childhood. Carers darken the room and place a soft covering on the sick woman. Hard consonants ('c', 'k' and 'q') ominously foreshadow her impending death, vividly contrasting with the soft sibilance of the alliterative phrase describing the sultry weather, 'this is the South in summer'.

Another powerful metaphor, 'The body is appetite' (line 13), suggests not only the body's capacity for taste and hunger but also its **desire and longing**. Again, the daughter attentively watches her mother enjoying her food, 'You savor the kale'. Smith's mother is calmly and resolutely resigned to her destiny. Her faith gives her the power to believe that her illness is part of God's plan for her. The poet understands how her mother is putting her trust into a satisfaction of her senses and she also becomes aware that the body is 'cautious'. Although her mother relishes her meal, her body still warns against over-indulging, 'Does not want more/Than it wants' (lines 17–18).

Run-on lines reflect a **sudden flurry of medical activity**. The hard sound of the alliterative phrase, 'traffic/Of transparent tubes', (lines 19–20), graphically conveys the intrusive medical procedures now being carried out on the poet's dying mother, enabling her to survive a little longer, 'striking/

Their compromise with the body'. But despite this agreement, the violent verb 'striking' implies an attack on the body as well as an acceptance of a situation that is unwanted.

TRACY K. SMITH

Line 22 poignantly notes the mother's final moments as her senses shut down and she withdraws from this world, 'When you close your eyes'. Smith's deep sense of empathy is emphasised in the repeated phrase, 'I know'. Richly nuanced metaphors fill this personal moment with **universal significance**. The private darkened bedroom hints at the oncoming final obscurity of death. Yet there is also the suggestion of greater light on the outside. Is the mother now viewing life through a clearer lens at the moment of death?

The 'chord of light' (line 25) is a reminder of the **biblical sense of redemption** sung about so often in the church which Smith's mother regularly attended. The image also pays homage to an alternative viewpoint, her father's scientific understanding of the universe. The poet wonders about her mother's level of awareness at this crucial time. Is she now experiencing things in a new way? Is she experiencing joy?

The poem closes with Smith's firm belief that her mother has decided 'the body's a question'. After nine carefully arranged three-line stanzas, a single stand-alone line emerges to ask a final question, 'What do you believe in?' – leaving readers with an open-ended conclusion. **Smith has said that 'poems live in questions'**. To whom is this particular question posed? Does the query refer to a spiritual or scientific understanding of the world? Is the mother trying to gently guide her daughter or is she challenging her? She herself did not fully share her mother's deep religious beliefs. 'I have a lot of ambivalence to it ... I like a lot of the mystery but not the language' (TKS).

Or is Smith interrogating the reader? **The poem resists closure**, weaving instead a continuous present, rejecting the notion of tying everything up neatly. 'I realised I didn't know how to solve the problem – just dwell upon it, live in it, make it present, and speak to it ... the most honest stance you can take is that of questioning' (TKS).

All through the poem, Smith **freezes time into a lyrical, light-filled memory space**, a sharp contrast to the darkened bedroom. This allows readers a period to question the significance of death and to review their own beliefs about the possibility of an afterlife.

POETRY FOCUS

✒ Writing About the Poem

'Tracy K. Smith's most dramatic poetry is often written as a response to her personal doubts.' Discuss this view with reference to her poem 'Joy'.

Sample Paragraph

'Joy' is presented as an important moment between a loving daughter and her dying mother. The scene is set in several locations, beginning with the joyful childhood setting of her mother 'Playing hospital' and a pretend happy outcome of a cure with 'raisins'. But a more harrowing setting is the darkened room from which there is no escape. The image of a 'traffic of transparent tubes' invading the mother's body is highly dramatic. The location is a reality apart from earthly experience where Smith imagines a 'chord of light' almost like an ascension into heaven for the deeply religious mother. But Smith does not share her mother's faith. The peaceful mood is challenged by the question, 'What do you believe in?' Dramatically, both the poet and readers are left wondering about what happens after death.

> **EXAMINER'S COMMENT**
>
> An assured top-grade response that includes some perceptive engagement with the poem. The consideration of relevant dramatic aspects (such as setting, imagery and tension) is impressive. Points are expressed clearly and aptly supported with reference and quotation.

✎ Class/Homework Exercises

1. 'Tracy K. Smith often explores issues of loss and identity'. Discuss this view with reference to her poem 'Joy'.
2. 'The effective use of powerful language and imagery is a recurring feature of Smith's poetry.' To what extent is this true of 'Joy'?

◉ Points to Consider

- Moving elegy in tribute to the poet's mother.
- Smith uses different locations in her exploration of the mystery of life and death.
- Stylistic features include striking imagery, metaphor and interesting poetic structure.
- Effective juxtaposition of religious and scientific imagery to explore the unknowable.
- Varied tones: elegiac, nostalgic, mournful, hopeful and questioning.

2 Dominion over the Beasts of the Earth

TRACY K. SMITH

Title: According to the Bible, God gave humans dominion or power over all other creatures.

... and whatsoever Adam called every living creature, that was the name thereof.
— *Genesis 2:19*

Last night it was Mauricio again,
At the hacienda they say
He and Veronica bought together.
Dark rooms. Floors lain
With exquisite dust. We ran   5
Back and forth, opening
All the sturdy doors, giddy
As kid goats that have learned
To dance on two hooves.
Breath after breath charging   10
In and out. Heavy, heavy,
And then weightless, moving
With the prescience of light.

*Hazlo que te da
La puta gana*. He said it   15
Over and over. Mauricio –
Enormous Mauricio
With the drunken legs
And hands as large
And white as magnolias –   20
What would've really happened
If we'd done it that night
In your neighborhood
At the end of the world?
What would we have changed,   25
Splayed together on that
Rotten mattress
While the buses slept
And the papers curled
Around themselves,   30
Cradling their news?

hacienda: ranch, large estate.

lain: covered.

exquisite: delicate, beautiful.

sturdy: strong, solid.
kid: young goat (less than one year).
hooves: hard covering of the end of a goat's feet.

prescience: foresight, insight.

Hazlo ... gana: Do whatever the hell you want.

magnolias: large white flowers.

Splayed: spread out.

POETRY FOCUS

I want to speak now
To the ones I've said
Meant nothing,
And I want to call them all   35
Mauricio.

Mauricio at 13 with skin
Like sunset over the Pacific.
Boy on the cusp, on a bicycle
On the porch my father put up.   40
Did I stare at my lap,
Wishing myself someone else?
Kathy, with the wild limbs,
A fast girl with bracelets
That made music on her wrists?   45
And the starlings perched
In rafters – did I invent them?
Tell me, Mauricio, at that age
What does a boy carry with him?

Years later you were tall,   50
A teacher, a spool
That would not stay wound.
When I burned our letters,
Ordinary moths swarmed my eyes.

I almost even want to speak   55
To that Mauricio
Who lay awake one whole summer,
Weak with anger, behind me.
Who finally drove off,
Windows obscured by an army   60
Of striped shirts, but even now
Tries to climb back
Along the frayed thread of dreams.
He stood up to fight once
In a crowded room, insisting   65
I was his wife. I couldn't laugh
Until I made sure the ring
That married me to the right person
(Two sizes too loose)
Was still on my finger.   70

Pacific: Pacific Ocean.
cusp: point of transition.
lap: knees and thighs.
fast: experienced, confident.
starlings: small garden birds.
rafters: wooden roof beams.
spool: small reel for holding thread.
wound: stored in place.
moths swarmed: insects clouded.
obscured: hidden, masked.
frayed: worn, unravelled.

'the hacienda'

A Note on the Title

The title of the poem is taken from the first book of the Hebrew Bible and the Christian Old Testament. The book gives an account of the creation of the world and the early history of humanity. It states that human beings are superior to all other living creatures. God brought the animals to man, allowing him to name them, enabling man to be part of creation in a caretaking or stewardship role. But rights and power come with responsibility.

Tracy K. Smith had a devoutly Baptist religious upbringing and attended Bible classes. As a young woman, she was very aware of the Old Testament emphasis on how Christians are expected to resist uncontrolled sexual desires.

The creatures in the Bible story are symbolic of the lower animal nature within humans. God expected people to exercise dominion (or control) over themselves, over their passions and desires. In 'Dominion over the Beasts of the Earth', Smith explores adolescence and emerging adulthood.

👤 Personal Response

1. Briefly describe the atmosphere Smith creates in the poem's opening stanza. Is it exciting? Dreamlike? Ecstatic? Menacing? Refer to the text in your answer.
2. In your opinion, how effective is Smith at creating a vivid sense of place in this poem? Refer to the text in your response.
3. Write your own short response to the poem, focusing on the impact it made on you.

👁 Critical Literacy

'Dominion over the Beasts of the Earth' comes from Tracy K. Smith's *The Body's Question* (2003). This debut collection included many love poems and memory poems that were confessional or sensual in tone. The poet has said that these early poems allowed her 'to tell stories that weren't necessarily my own stories, and to let pieces of myself come into those other stories'.

The title of the poem (a quotation from the Book of Genesis) states that humans are superior to all other living creatures. Smith had a devoutly Baptist religious upbringing and attended Bible classes. As a young woman, she was very aware of the Old Testament emphasis on how Christians are expected to resist uncontrolled sexual desires. In 'Dominion over the Beasts of the Earth', she explores female sensuality and the sometimes turbulent transition from childhood to adulthood.

In the **opening lines**, Smith invites readers to share a vivid teenage memory of a warm sultry night in Mexico. The speaker recalls spending time in a run-down hacienda with Mauricio, with whom she was infatuated. While the exotic setting and staccato rhythms ('We ran/Back and forth') emphasise **a sense of daring excitement**, the reference to 'Dark rooms' suggests the unreliability of memories. The vibrant simile in **lines 7–8** highlights the young couple's passionate feelings as they rushed around, feeling as 'giddy/As kid goats'.

This **atmosphere of new-found freedom** and a feeling of being almost out of control continues in **line 10**: 'Breath after breath charging'. The speaker imagines having a light-headed awareness of her 'weightless' body. She shifts her attention back to Mauricio, who urged her to do whatever she wanted. The focus is on her recollection of his physical attractiveness, his 'Enormous' physique and large hands, 'white as magnolias'.

She wonders about how close they were to becoming lovers at that moment – and how their lives might have been affected: 'What would we have changed' (**line 25**). But her **fascination with this coming-of-age moment**

TRACY K. SMITH

remains – even though she is still unsure about its true significance. The speaker recalls details of the scene where her 'world' might have been transformed. Images of the 'Rotten mattress' and discarded newspapers suggest that the encounter with Mauricio was really an unromantic, sleazy experience.

In looking back on turning points during her emerging adulthood, **the speaker broadens her approach** by wondering about all of the other boys she remembers: 'the ones I've said/Meant nothing'. In a reflective mood and with characteristic humour, she chooses to forget their individual personalities and 'call them all/Mauricio' (lines 35–36). This might also be a subtle reference to man's 'naming' of the animals, an empowering act given to him by God. Is the poet now exercising her power over her memories, obliterating their unique identities by calling them all the same name?

In contrast to the earlier uncertainty and unresolved questions about adolescent development, the **mood becomes much more nostalgic**. The portrayal of 'Mauricio at 13' – whose skin was like 'sunset over the Pacific' – celebrates the beauty and potential of youth. In retrospect, the speaker acknowledges that he was 'on the cusp', poised on the threshold between innocence and maturity. She also recalls her awkwardness and lack of confidence during her early teenage years: 'Wishing myself someone else' (line 42).

The speaker confesses that she envied another 'fast' girl, 'Kathy, with the wild limbs', who seemed more assured and was popular with boys. But she begins to challenge her own random recollections – of Kathy's 'bracelets/ That made music on her wrists' and an image of roosting starlings. The **lingering uncertainty about memories of the past** – 'did I invent them?' (line 47) – leads her to think more deeply about the experiences of other young people ('What does a boy carry with him?'), particularly Mauricio's feelings at the time.

The final section of the poem moves forward in time and recalls a later stage in the speaker's relationship with Mauricio. His **edgy, unpredictable character** is suggested by the metaphor comparing him to a spool of thread that 'would not stay wound' (line 52). Despite her lasting feelings for him, it became clear that they had no future together. For her, destroying old love letters was an emotional experience ('moths swarmed my eyes') and she remembers him with tenderness.

Indeed, the speaker acknowledges that she is still haunted by casual memories of Mauricio and of what might have been. Another **evocative metaphor** ('the frayed thread of dreams') reflects fondly on the joys and disappointments of young love, a reminder of the previous description of Mauricio as a 'spool'. In Genesis, God decided that it was not good for man

to be alone and he created a female companion for him. However, in Mauricio's case, young love was not to be.

In the closing lines, **Smith presents readers with several questions** surrounding the intriguing detail of the wedding band 'Two sizes too loose' for her. Was Mauricio too domineering? He once stood up in a 'crowded room, insisting/I was his wife'. Does this suggest that he assumed the God-given right of 'naming'? Did the speaker need more space and freedom in their relationship?

Yet she still acknowledges just how close she came to marrying Mauricio – even though he wasn't 'the right person' for her. The mood is one of resignation, concluding without judgement or blame – and takes on a more universal significance. In the end, Smith's **bittersweet tone of young love** acts as a kind of confessional for every human who has had similar experiences.

🖋 Writing About the Poem

'Tracy K. Smith's sensual poems often explore universal themes of desire and longing.' To what extent is this true of her poem 'Dominion over the Beasts of the Earth'? Develop your answer with reference to the text.

Sample Paragraph

'Dominion over the Beasts of the Earth' has relevance to most young people. Nearly all teenagers experience love – or at least infatuation. Smith describes her obsessive feelings for Mauricio and their sweaty nights full of desire in 'dark rooms' in Mexico. The couple are almost out of control as they rush around an empty hacienda, 'giddy as kid goats'. This sensual image really showed the power of physical attraction. As an adult, she later thinks back to their carefree love and how unsure she was about starting a relationship with him, 'What would've really happened?' Coming-of-age moments like this are normal and the poet still doesn't seem totally sure that she made the right choice – even though she was happy to marry someone else. Many adults would have doubts about choices they made in their teens.

EXAMINER'S COMMENT

Good top-grade response that traced the progress of thought in the poem and tackled the question's basic elements ('sensual', 'desire' and 'universal'). Varied expression and clear, well-written points, supported by relevant reference and quotation throughout.

TRACY K. SMITH

✏ Class/Homework Exercises

1. 'Tracy K. Smith is a natural storyteller who loves to explore how a person can respond in intimate situations.' Discuss this statement, developing your answer with reference to 'Dominion over the Beasts of the Earth'.
2. 'There is often a haunting, dream-like quality to Smith's fascination with the past.' To what extent do you agree with this view? Develop your answer with reference to 'Dominion over the Beasts of the Earth'.

◉ Points to Consider

- Personal subject matter confronting the theme of emerging adulthood.
- Sub-themes include making choices, destiny and the unreliability of memory.
- Dramatic language and scenes are enlivened by the Mexican setting and culture.
- Changing moods and tones – nostalgic, erotic, reflective, compassionate.
- Effective use of descriptive detail, metaphors, rhythm and rhetorical questions.

3 The Searchers

after the film by John Ford

He wants to kill her for surviving,
For the language she spits,
The way she runs, clutching
Her skirt as if life pools there.

Instead he grabs her, puts her　　　　5
On his saddle, rides back
Into town where faces
She barely remembers

Smile into her fear
With questions and the wish,　　　　10
The impossible wish, to forget.
What does living do to any of us?

And why do we grip it, hang on
As if it's the ribs of a horse
Past commanding? A beast　　　　15
That big could wreck us easily,

Could rise up on two legs,
Or kick its back end up
And send us soaring.
We might land, any moment,　　　　20

Like cheap toys. There's always
A chimney burning in the mind,
A porch where the rocker still rocks,
Though empty. Why

Do we insist our lives are ours?　　　　25
Look at the frontier. It didn't resist.
Gave anyone the chance
To plant shrubs, dig wells.

Watched, not really concerned
With whether it belonged　　　　30
To him or to him. Either way
The land went on living,

Dying. What else could it choose?

👤 Personal Response

1. Based on the evidence of the poem, briefly describe the dilemma facing the young abducted girl.
2. Select one line or image from the poem that you find particularly interesting. Briefly explain your choice.
3. In your opinion, what is the tone of the poem's conclusion? Briefly explain your response.

👁 Critical Literacy

'The Searchers' comes from Tracy K. Smith's second poetry collection, *Duende*, published in 2007. The title refers to a mischievous house spirit. In her book, the poet includes a comment from the Spanish writer Federico García Lorca, 'The *duende* does not come at all unless he sees that death is possible.' Smith often explores themes of loss, desire, identity with quiet relentless focus. This poem springs from a controversial dramatic scene in a famous Western movie and widens out into a reflection on identity, ownership and attitude to life.

The title of the poem 'The Searchers' and its dedication is a reference to John Ford's melancholic Western about an obsessive quest. Twelve-year-old Debbie, niece of the central character, Ethan Edwards (played by John Wayne), is kidnapped by Native Americans from the Comanche tribe who have lured the men from the homestead with a cattle raid. The Comanche

TRACY K. SMITH

'He wants to kill her for surviving'

POETRY FOCUS

murder Debbie's family and burn their home. Edwards, a world-weary Confederate veteran, spends five years hunting down the tribe who hold the girl. He attempts to shoot her, but fails. This complex character can be viewed as an anti-hero.

Edwards has a **fanatical hatred towards interracial mixing**. Line 1 bluntly states, 'He wants to kill her for surviving'. The first stanza of this lyric shows the situation from Edwards' perspective. He is appalled that his niece now speaks Comanche, revealed by the ugly monosyllabic verb 'spits'. He is shocked that she does not want to be rescued, but runs away 'clutching' her native skirt. Has this young woman decided that her life is now with the Comanche? The evocative verb 'pools' suggests that her new life has merged with the tribe. By running away from her 'rescuer', is she desperately trying to take ownership of her own destiny?

The emphatic adverb 'Instead' in line 5 indicates that Edwards is now deciding his niece's fate. He takes control through a quick series of actions, powerfully portrayed by aggressive monosyllabic verbs, 'grabs', 'puts'. He then 'rides back' to take her home. But is he making a mistake? Can what has happened to the girl be erased? Run-on lines and stanzas capture the **confused response** of the young woman, suddenly catapulted back into a past 'She barely remembers'.

While she is met with well-meaning kindness from the inhabitants of this unfamiliar white world, displayed by their 'Smile', she is also confronted by their inquisitiveness. They bombard her with 'questions'. They also pressure her with an 'impossible' demand, the 'wish' that she should move on from her ordeal and her life with the Comanches. The definite article suggests that it is more their wish than the girl's that she should 'forget' her time among the Native American tribe. The adjective 'impossible' and the repetition of 'wish' point out the futility of this desire to wipe out what occurred (line 11). **The past cannot be erased**.

In lines 13–15, Smith uses the evocative Wild West simile of a rider on an untamed horse to reveal how desperately humans cling to life. The rider cannot rule the horse's spirit, just as the events that occur in life are not always controlled by humans, despite their best efforts. **Ironically, it is people who are at the mercy of fate**. The rider risks serious injury by insisting on mastering a wild horse. The harsh-sounding verb 'wreck' suggests both the horse's and life's potential to hurt. Smith extends the metaphor of the untamed horse rearing up on its hind legs or flicking up its back end to dislodge its rider. This vividly displays the ups and downs of life which are often left 'soaring' beyond control. Hissing sibilance and the elongated sound of the verb in line 19 emphasise how those who sought to control are sometimes placed in an uncontrollable situation, and sent flying helplessly through the air.

TRACY K. SMITH

The unpredictable situation continues in line 20, 'We might land, any moment'. Both the rider and the individual's irrelevance and unimportance in life's bigger scheme is sharply conveyed in the simile 'Like cheap toys'. Although colourful, they are worthless and easily broken. The poet now presents the reader with two well-known domestic images from life on the frontier, the cosy fire in the homestead and the rocking chair on the porch. But **these exist only in memory**, 'in the mind' (line 22). The stark adjective 'empty' confronts readers with the inescapable truth: that particular time is past. There is now no one there.

A run-on rhetorical question addresses the reader, 'Why/Do we insist our lives are ours?' Human beings cannot control or take possession of something which they are unable to manage. This is rather like the rescuer who will 'insist' on saving someone who does not wish to be rescued. The poet offers us advice in line 26: 'Look at the frontier' as a guide. Careful rhyme, 'insist'/'resist', exposes a startling contrast. **People display a closed attitude to life in comparison to the open frontier landscape which accepts all** and 'Gave anyone the chance'. Homely images ('plant shrubs, dig wells') reflect the lives of the early settlers, illustrating the opportunity to survive and prosper.

Smith personifies the landscape which 'Watched' (line 29), placing it in the role of observer. Unlike humans, who are active participants seeking to control and own, the vast Western frontier stands aloof, 'not really concerned/With whether it belonged/To him or to him'. Run-on lines emphasise the indifferent attitude of this harshly beautiful, open place, 'Either way'. The **concluding stand-alone line accentuates the natural inescapable progression of life towards 'Dying'**. The poem ends with a fatalist rhetorical question, 'What else could it choose?'

This poignant lyric weaves questions about identity and belonging. The overall **tone is darkly meditative**. Should we indulge a nostalgic longing for home and family and the past? Does an anti-hero act out of vengeance or a commitment to honour and decency? Do the very qualities which form the anti-hero make him an outcast in society? The question posed by Smith is whether the displaced, marginalised young victim of abuse should embrace life, adapting to uncontrollable circumstances, or refuse to change and give in to death.

POETRY FOCUS

✍ Writing About the Poem

Discuss how Tracy K. Smith makes effective use of a variety of characters, often in dramatic settings, to probe various personal issues. Develop your response with reference to 'The Searchers'.

Sample Paragraph

'The Searchers' opens with an intense scene from John Ford's film. Set in the American Wild West, the story is about an obsessive search for a kidnapped girl. Smith uses this drama to explore personal identity and choices. The landscape is personified – like another character. This land is open to everybody, 'Gave anyone the chance'. In contrast, the uncle, the film's anti-hero, searching for the girl, is determined that his personal view of life should triumph. Violent verbs, such as 'grabs', highlight his attempts to control others. Smith raises issues about individual rights. Two central characters dominate, the traditional male and the personified Wild West. The first is opposed to change, the second welcoming and inclusive. The conflict between them really made me think about power and powerlessness.

EXAMINER'S COMMENT

Clearly written top-grade response that engages with the key aspects of the question. Effective discussion points focus on identity and opposing attitudes to life. Good use of relevant reference and quotation throughout.

🖋 Class/Homework Exercises

1. 'Tracy K. Smith often explores complex issues of identity and belonging.' Discuss this view with reference to her poem 'The Searchers'.
2. 'The effective use of evocative imagery is a recurring feature of Smith's poetry.' To what extent is this true of 'The Searchers'?

⊙ Points to Consider

- Poignant exploration of loss, revenge, obsession, racism and acceptance.
- Features of style include rhetorical questions, cinematic scenes, irony, personification and contrast.
- Effective extended metaphor – bucking bronco suggesting life's ungovernable events.
- Extensive use of run-on lines to indicate life's unpredictability and the inviting landscape.
- Varied tones: dark, honest, nostalgic, reflective, chilling, questioning.

4 Letter to a Photojournalist Going-In

TRACY K. SMITH

You go to the pain. City after city. Borders
Where they peer into your eyes as if to erase you.   **erase:** delete, remove.

You go by bus or truck, days at a time, just taking it
When they throw you in a room or kick at your gut,   **gut:** stomach.

Taking it when a strong fist hammers person after person   5
A little deeper into the ground. Your camera blinks:

Soldiers smoking between rounds. Bodies   **rounds:** firing weapons.
Blown open like curtains. In the neighborhoods,

Boys brandish plastic guns with TV bravado. Men   **brandish:** display.
Ask you to look them in the face and say who's right.   10   **bravado:** machismo, showing off.

At night you sleep, playing it all back in reverse:

The dance of wind in a valley of dirt. Rugs and tools,
All the junk that rises up, resurrected, then disappears   **resurrected:** revitalised.

Into newly formed windows and walls. People
Close their mouths and run backwards out of frame.   15

Up late, your voice fits my ear like a secret.
But who can hear two things at once?

Errant stars flare, shatter. A whistle, then the indescribable thud   **Errant:** stray.
Of an era spilling its matter into the night. Who can say the word *love*   **era:** time.

When everything – everything – pushes back with the promise   20
To grind itself to dust?   **grind:** turn.

          And what if there's no dignity to what we do,
None at all? If our work – what you see, what I say – is nothing

But a way to kid ourselves into thinking we might last? If trust is just   **kid:** fool.
Another human trick that'll lick its lips and laugh as it backs away?   25

Sometimes I think you're right, wanting to lose everything and wander
Like a blind king. Wanting to squeeze a lifetime between your hands

369

And press it into a single flimsy frame. Will you take it to your lips
Like the body of a woman, something to love in passing,

Or set it down, free finally, empty as the camera,   30
Which we all know is just a hollow box, mechanized to obey?

Sometimes I want my heart to beat like yours: from the outside in,
A locket stuffed with faces that refuse to be named. For time

To land at my feet like a grenade.

flimsy: light.

mechanized: set.

locket: pendant that holds a small photo.

grenade: bomb thrown by hand.

'Boys brandish plastic guns'

👤 Personal Response

1. Choose one image from the poem that, in your opinion, conveys the reality of what happens in conflict areas. Comment briefly on the effectiveness of the image.
2. Briefly describe the poem's dramatic qualities. You might refer to some of the following: setting, characters, tension, vivid language.
3. Outline your own immediate thoughts and feelings in response to the poem.

◉ Critical Literacy

TRACY K. SMITH

Tracy K. Smith has always been drawn to questions about what it means to survive, to endure. 'Letter to a Photojournalist Going-In' (taken from her 2007 collection, *Duende*) paints a poignant scenario of war documented by embedded photojournalists. The poem is divided into two halves, 17 shorter lines and 17 longer lines. The first half describes the day-to-day reality of being a war photographer. In the more reflective second half, Smith addresses issues around the wider impact of the photojournalist's work and its impact on his personal relationships.

The letter-writer (the speaker) addresses the photojournalist directly in the poem's opening line: 'You go to the pain. City after city'. The images are like 'snapshots' recording the tragedy and suffering ('pain') that he photographs in war zones. Brisk **staccato (or jerky) rhythm gives an impression of breathlessness**. We can imagine the everyday dangers faced by working journalists, who are often viewed as intrusive outsiders in places of conflict – especially at border checkpoints where suspicious guards 'peer into your eyes'.

This could be the frightful experience of any war correspondent who is **resigned to endure almost anything as part of the job**. Smith focuses on the predictable risks experienced 'days at a time'. The emphasis is on 'taking it', putting up with whatever brutality occurs, 'When they throw you in a room or kick at your gut'. The phrase 'taking it' also suggests a deepening awareness by visiting reporters who suddenly take in and understand **the dehumanising effects of war**. Their shock and disbelief is conveyed through personification: 'Your camera blinks'.

Lines 7–9 include several **graphic images** of soldiers and victims. The poet's unflinching picture of routine atrocities when bodies are 'Blown open like curtains' is **both horrifying and surreal**. The simile emphasises how images of war can open a window to what is happening outside in the real world. Smith's sense of hopelessness is evident in the association of violence with impressionable young boys who 'brandish plastic guns with TV bravado' (line 9).

Photojournalists have often recorded images of innocent children playing war games they have learned from what they have witnessed directly. But in referencing how television can glamourise violence, the poet raises a **disturbing question about the bigger gun culture in society**. Smith has always encouraged readers to think seriously about complex issues, such as the connection between masculine culture, violence and moral confusion: 'Men/Ask you to look them in the face and say who's right'.

POETRY FOCUS

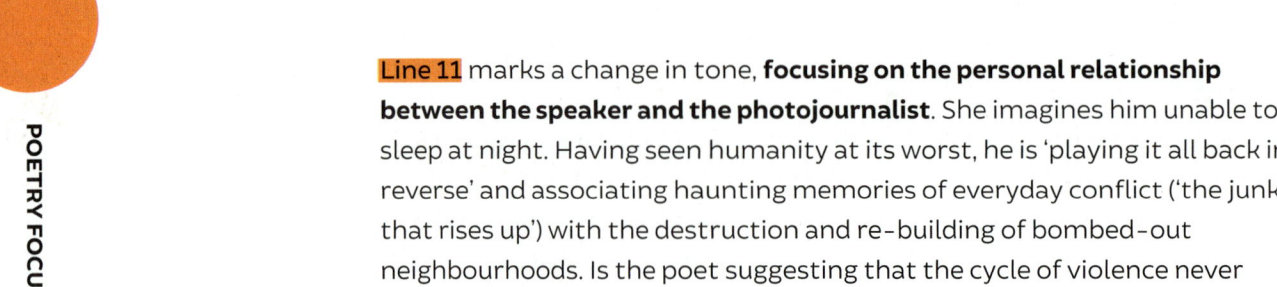

Line 11 marks a change in tone, **focusing on the personal relationship between the speaker and the photojournalist**. She imagines him unable to sleep at night. Having seen humanity at its worst, he is 'playing it all back in reverse' and associating haunting memories of everyday conflict ('the junk that rises up') with the destruction and re-building of bombed-out neighbourhoods. Is the poet suggesting that the cycle of violence never ends? As always, she voices her greatest concern for ordinary 'People' who are powerless, the fearful who 'run backwards out of frame'.

The intimate moment between the speaker and journalist (lines 16–17) recalls a phone call between them and the mysterious question: 'who can hear two things at once?' She is **reflecting on her love for a photojournalist** who chooses to risk his life and finding it difficult to understand his true feelings. Glimpses of chaos and destruction ('stars flare, shatter') associate battle scenes with their emotional lives. Are the dehumanising consequences of his job as a war correspondent likely to destroy their relationship – 'Who can say the word *love*'?

The final section of the poem centres mainly on **the pressures that threaten their relationship**. Poignant, long-lined couplets are filled with disquieting visions of conflict and inevitable death where everything is destined to 'grind itself to dust' (line 21). The speaker is overwhelmed by doubts, questioning their commitment to love each other and fearing that they are trying to 'kid ourselves into thinking we might last'. Once again, she wonders if she can rely on her lover and whether he is more devoted to his adventurous work to ever be 'free finally' of the camera. Does she see the camera as another dangerous weapon coming between them?

The poem's uneasy **ending develops this battle-weary view of romantic love**. The speaker realises that the photojournalist's experiences of war force him to suppress his emotions. But she seems unsure about what she herself wants. There are times when she wants to be like her lover and escape reality by hiding her feelings, so that her heart can 'beat like yours: from the outside in' (line 32). The concluding tone is particularly ominous, reflecting her dreadful fear of a future that will 'land at my feet like a grenade'.

The searing simile of an unexploded bomb highlights the lingering tension in the couple's complex relationship. Smith leaves readers in no doubt that **war can make victims of many people** – and not just individuals who, like the journalist, are directly caught up in the turmoil of conflict.

TRACY K. SMITH

✒ Writing About the Poem

'In many of her poems, Tracy K. Smith intertwines stories, often linking personal and public experiences.' Discuss this statement in relation to 'Letter to a Photojournalist Going-In'.

Sample Paragraph

'Letter to a Photojournalist' is mainly about the dangerous work of a reporter in parts of the world where wars are taking place. But it's also linked in with a love story. Smith's violent images show the horror of war through the journalist's eyes, 'kick you', 'bodies are blown up like curtains'. He has nightmares 'playing it all back'. But there is another tragic story because his job also affects the poet. Stray bombs could put an end to her partner and their relationship in a flash. The couple's love is over-shadowed by his job as a war correspondent. Smith's personal relationship is always under threat and she has doubts about her love for him, 'At times I think you're right, wanting to lose everything'. Both storylines are closely linked throughout this sad poem.

EXAMINER'S COMMENT

Good high-grade response showing a clear understanding of the two narrative strands in the poem and the overlap between public and private experiences. Critical comments are clearly expressed and supported by relevant reference (although there are some slight misquotations).

✏ Class/Homework Exercises

1. 'Smith's compelling poems often raise questions about the complexity of human relationships.' Discuss this view with reference to 'Letter to a Photojournalist Going-In'.
2. 'Powerful and dramatic imagery is a recurring feature of Tracy K. Smith's most intense poetry.' To what extent is this true of 'Letter to a Photojournalist Going-In'?

⊙ Points to Consider

- Insightful exploration of the photojournalist's experience.
- Themes include conflict, male violence, personal relationships.
- Striking images of conflict – both public and personal.
- Effective use of questions, tension, varied sentence length.
- Contrasting tones – empathic, reflective, self-doubting, anxious.

5 The Universe is a House Party

The universe is expanding. Look: postcards
And panties, bottles with lipstick on the rim,

Orphan socks and napkins dried into knots.
Quickly, wordlessly, all of it whisked into file

With radio waves from a generation ago   5
Drifting to the edge of what doesn't end,

Like the air inside a balloon. Is it bright?
Will our eyes crimp shut? Is it molten, atomic,

A conflagration of suns? It sounds like the kind of party
Your neighbors forget to invite you to: bass throbbing   10

Through walls, and everyone thudding around drunk
On the roof. We grind lenses to an impossible strength,

Point them toward the future, and dream of beings
We'll welcome with indefatigable hospitality:

How marvelous you've come! We won't flinch   15
At the pinprick mouths, the nubbin limbs. We'll rise,

Gracile, robust. *Mi casa es su casa.* Never more sincere.
Seeing us, they'll know exactly what we mean.

Of course, it's ours. If it's anyone's, it's ours.

TRACY K. SMITH

A Note on the Title

The poem's title, 'The Universe is a House Party' is a metaphor. Smith believes that metaphors allow a person to depart from their normal literal self. They distort our sense of the way the world works so that it can be viewed from another angle. Throughout the 1970s, America was gripped by a craze for all things Martian.

The title of Smith's poetry collection *Life on Mars* was taken from the song 'Life on Mars?' from David Bowie's pop album *Hunky Dory* (1971). Smith uses science fiction as a means of asking ourselves questions. What characterises our views of ourselves? Are they true? Have we a false opinion of our own importance in the grand scheme of things? Are we prepared to admit that we don't know everything?

👤 Personal Response

1. Based on the evidence of the poem, briefly describe your impression of the universe.
2. The poet includes two phrases in italics which are used by humans greeting the aliens. Do you think Smith is being sarcastic when she imagines this meeting? Give a reason for your response.
3. In your opinion, what is the tone of the poem's concluding line? Is it positive or negative? Briefly explain your response.

👁 Critical Literacy

Tracy K. Smith's third poetry collection, *Life on Mars* (2011), includes the poem, 'The Universe is a House Party'. This book won the Pulitzer Prize in 2012. With wry humour, Smith not only explores a supernatural universe beyond what can be known, but from that future vantage point, she looks back to explore modern life. The limits of human comprehension are contrasted sharply with the vast, mysterious universe.

A short, emphatic statement dramatically opens the poem, 'The universe is expanding'. Smith was very close to her father, an engineer on the Hubble Space Telescope, named after the astronomer Edwin Hubble.

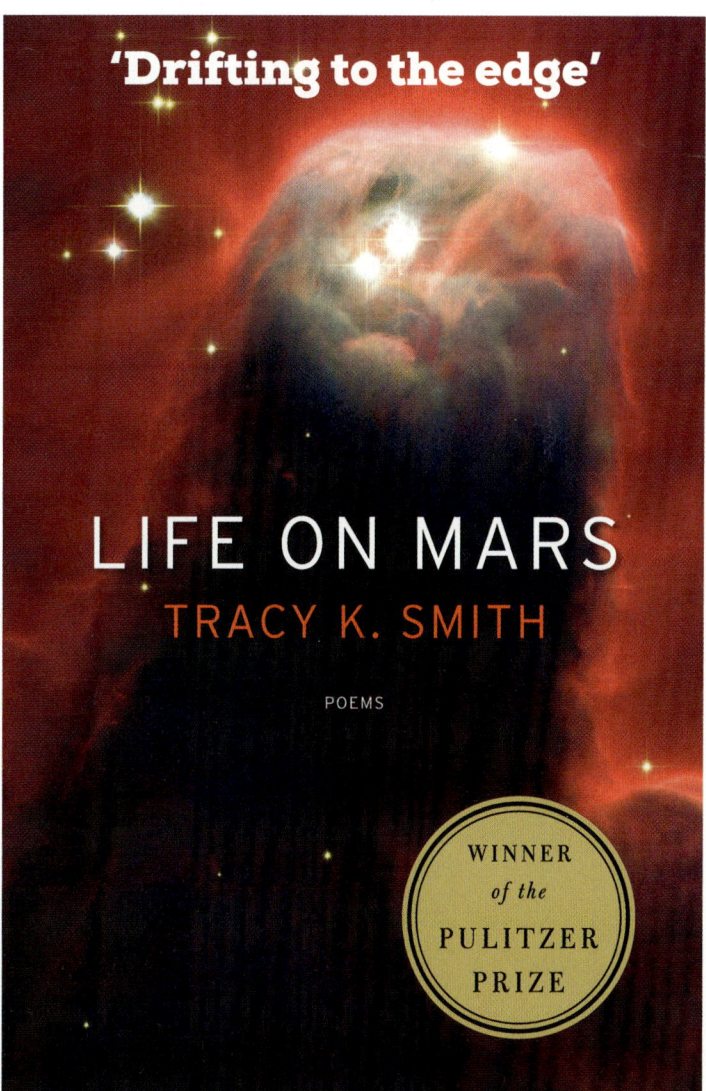

The front cover of *Life on Mars* shows a dramatic picture from the Hubble Space Telescope of Cone Nebula, a pillar of dust and gas, more than 2,500 light years from Earth.

POETRY FOCUS

During the 1920s, Hubble had made an astonishing discovery that the universe was not static, as had been believed earlier. He found that it had been growing since its beginning with the Big Bang, over 13 billion years ago. The universe is expanding into itself as the familiar analogy of rising bread dough in the oven illustrates. The galaxies of stars (like the raisins in the dough) are retreating from each other as the universe expands. But just as the raisins remain in the dough, the stars continue to exist in space. This is the **mysterious nature** of the universe.

An insistent command verb, 'Look', in line 1, draws attention to the present. A party's debris-strewn aftermath is vividly highlighted in explosive alliteration and run-on lines, 'postcards/And panties'. Sharply focused cinematic close-ups, 'bottles with lipstick on the rim,/Orphan socks' suggest **a hedonistic lifestyle**. The poet views today's human race as specks in the future's rear-view mirror. Swiftly moving punctuation underlines the busybody humans sweeping the mess into order to the background sound of the radio.

The discovery of 'radio waves' by Hertz in 1880 allowed sound to be transmitted and formed our modern communication system. But radio waves are also transmitted from objects in space to our telescopes, informing us of what is present in space, but which we cannot see. These radio waves travel for ever within the infinite universe, 'to the edge of what doesn't end'. There is a striking contrast between the purposeful human action, 'whisked' in line 4 and the aimless action of **the eternal universe**, 'Drifting'. This also hints at the weightlessness experienced in space, when objects are free from Earth's gravitational pull.

In line 7, Smith compares the radio waves to the air moving around the interior empty space within a balloon. Follow-up **staccato questions** examine the nature of the universe. She wonders if it glows brilliantly, perhaps from the light of the stars? Will it be too much for humans to bear, causing our eyes to 'crimp shut' against the glare? Is it a boiling, fragmentary blaze ('molten', 'atomic', 'conflagration')? According to the Big Bang theory, our universe began as an extremely hot, dense state which later underwent colossal rapid expansion.

The poem turns to modern-day life in line 9 when Smith compares the universe to a noisy house party. The scene is described in terms of sound, a subtle reference to our knowledge of what space contains being comprehended through 'radio waves' on our telescopes. **Onomatopoeic verbs**, 'throbbing', 'thudding', vividly enact the hectic party atmosphere heard 'Through walls'. But a more disquieting tone is struck with the observation that 'Your neighbors forget to invite you'. Is mankind relegated to being a mere listener who is always excluded from the universe's party?

TRACY K. SMITH

Once again, Smith is examining our confusing, question-riddled relationship with the universe.

Line 12 again references the purposeful action of the humans who pulverise glass, 'grind lenses', to make telescopes to peer into space, to seek to know the unknowable. Poet and astronomer are both trying to further understand the immensity of the universe, 'Point them toward the future'. At this point, **the poem changes dramatically**, becoming a surreal 'dream' where 'beings' suddenly arrive on Earth from space.

The poet imagines people greeting the aliens with 'indefatigable hospitality', almost a relentless or perhaps even forced welcome. An italicised phrase suggests the interchange, '*How marvelous you've come!*' The humans have adopted the role of welcoming hosts. Yet another **unsettling note** is struck, however, by the humans' description of these 'beings'. While they promise not to recoil, 'flinch', their focus is negatively fixated on the strange appearance of the visitors who have 'pinprick mouths' and stunted limbs, 'nubbin limbs'. Slender assonance underlines the aliens' disturbing presence.

Line 16 again stresses the human race's sense of self-importance. Smith emphatically states that humanity will 'rise' to the occasion, nimbly, 'Gracile', and firmly, 'robust'. Another italic phrase is used to show the emphatic welcome offered to the alien visitors, '*Mi casa es su casa*' (My house is your house). But are people speaking from the heart, 'Never more sincere'? The poem shifts focus again, as we look at ourselves from the aliens' perspective with the ironic phrase, 'they'll know exactly what we mean'. Are the humans being hospitable or presumptuous? After nine carefully ordered couplets a stand-alone line suggests a shocking possibility, a new perspective. Are human beings really assuming that the universe belongs solely to them, 'Of course, it's ours', line 19. Readers are left wondering who is the host of the universe's house party. And who are the guests?

✎ Writing About the Poem

To what extent is your response to Smith's poetry heightened by her use of both provocative and evocative imagery? Develop your answer with reference to her poem 'The Universe is a House Party'.

Sample Paragraph

'The Universe is a House Party' left me thinking how people can give a wrong impression of what they are truly like. Provocative images describe the chaos after a party and suggest a wild lifestyle, 'postcards and panties'. Alliteration adds to the self-indulgent mood. I got a sense of human superiority in their reaction to the alien 'beings'. Although humans seem 'indefatigable' in their welcome, it is their negative focus on the creatures' appearance that is emphasised. This is seen in the offensive images, 'pinprick mouths', 'nubbin limbs'. In contrast, powerful sci-fi images highlight the mystery of space. It sends 'radio waves' from unseen objects travelling 'to the edge of what doesn't end'. The mix of disturbing modern images and haunting science fiction imagery helped me reflect on people's desire to control the universe.

> **EXAMINER'S COMMENT**
>
> *Good personal top-grade response that focuses on the main aspects of the question and engages closely with the poem. Effective discussion of contrasting images and their effectiveness. Relevant supportive reference and quotation throughout.*

✒ Class/Homework Exercises

1. 'Tracy K. Smith often explores issues of acceptance and rejection'. Discuss this view with reference to her poem 'The Universe is a House Party'.
2. 'The effective use of sound effects is a recurring feature of Smith's poetry.' To what extent is this true of 'The Universe is a House Party'? Develop your answer with reference to the poem.

⊙ Points to Consider

- **Thought-provoking exploration of modern life through insightful observation and imaginative perspective.**
- **Revealing contrasts between vast, mysterious universe and narrow and sometimes vacuous human existence.**
- **Stylistic features include irony, pertinent questions and distinctive imagery.**
- **Effective use of metaphor: the image of space to explore contemporary human existence.**
- **Use of present tense adds immediacy and collective pronouns strengthen engagement with the reader.**

6 The Museum of Obsolescence

TRACY K. SMITH

So much we once coveted. So much
That would have saved us, but lived,

Instead, its own quick span, returning
To uselessness with the mute acquiescence

Of shed skin. It watches us watch it: 5
Our faulty eyes, our telltale heat, hearts

Ticking through our shirts. We're here
To titter at gimcracks, the naïve tools,

The replicas of replicas stacked like bricks.
There's green money, and oil in drums. 10

Pots of honey pilfered from a tomb. Books
Recounting the wars, maps of fizzled stars.

In the south wing, there's a small room
Where a living man sits on display. Ask,

And he'll describe the old beliefs. If you 15
Laugh, he'll lower his head to his hands

And sigh. When he dies, they'll replace him
With a video looping on *ad infinitum*.

Special installations come and go. 'Love'
Was up for a season, followed by 'Illness', 20

Concepts difficult to grasp. The last thing you see
(After a mirror – someone's idea of a joke?)

Is an image of the old planet taken from space.
Outside, vendors hawk t-shirts, three for eight.

POETRY FOCUS

👤 Personal Response

1. Describe the poet's mood in lines 1–4. Is it sad? Cynical? Humorous? Hopeful? Briefly explain your response, using reference to the text.
2. Select one image or line from the poem that you find particularly interesting. Briefly explain your choice.
3. In your opinion, what is the central theme or message in this poem? Refer to the text in your response.

'maps of fizzled stars'

👁 Critical Literacy

Tracy K. Smith's 2011 collection, *Life on Mars*, includes several poems that consider the future of humanity. The poet uses the image of outer space to allow her to explore the even bigger concept of life's meaning. Readers are presented with a dystopian future commenting on a dystopian present. Smith writes of stars and oceans, a futuristic planet and the universal sense of loss. 'The Museum of Obsolescence' imagines a public gallery far into the future. The building is full of forgotten and useless artefacts from the human species' time on Earth.

In the poem's opening lines, Smith envisions a time when generations to come will look back on all the things we thought were essential. Biblical language ('we once coveted') suggests that people today are greedy and

TRACY K. SMITH

obsessed with material possessions. Yet the sad truth is that all of our **greed and wishful thinking have failed us**. Ironically, everything that we hoped 'would have saved us' became outdated and inadequate after lasting for just a 'quick span'.

The graphic metaphor in lines 4–5 compares the museum's exhibits to a body that is slowly but naturally decaying 'with the mute acquiescence/Of shed skin'. A poignant sense of the inevitable cycle of change is evident in the **gentle sounds and elegiac tone**. Smith's poetic voice has the soft sibilant hush of someone almost whispering. Is she saddened by the excessive trust placed in technology that quickly becomes outmoded? Does she feel sympathy for her fellow human beings? Or is she critical of them?

We are invited on a tour of the gallery, but line 5 **personifies the museum: 'It watches us watch it'**. The poet takes a quirky approach, asking us to reflect more closely on our own lives. If we take time to consider ourselves as the exhibits, what do our various moods and feelings ('telltale heat, hearts') reveal about us? Do we have a 'faulty' view of the world? Is Smith focusing on what really defines us as people? Have we been mistaken about the importance of emotions? Are human feelings also destined to become obsolete?

For visitors to this futuristic museum, **our world will simply be a passing attraction**. The poet imagines tourists being entertained by the technology we have today and ridiculing our 'naïve tools' (line 8). She reminds us of the lack of innovation ('replicas of replicas') associated with modern mass consumerism. The simile 'stacked like bricks' adds to the sense of sameness. Smith's catalogue of obsolescence includes 'green money, and oil in drums' (line 10), vivid images of a capitalist world. She is in no doubt that our present economic system will ultimately be looked upon as primitive – and not least because our consumerist system has led to planetary devastation.

The poem's central viewpoint is emphasised in lines 11–12. Everything in **the universe will keep changing**, regardless of successive human civilisations. Images of out-dated paraphernalia, 'honey pilfered from a tomb' and 'Books/Recounting the wars', are reminders that history shows there is no escape from destruction and death. The onomatopoeic adjective 'fizzled' suggests a light being extinguished. All things will pass and even the stars will eventually burn out.

Perhaps the poem's most haunting scene is found in line 14: 'a living man sits on display'. The idea that human beings as we know them are becoming an endangered species reflects **Smith's deep sense of tragedy as well as her dark humour**. Although the man can answer questions about the 'old beliefs', he is often mocked and put to shame. In the dehumanised sci-fi world of the future, he will soon be replaced by a machine, 'a video looping on *ad infinitum*' (line 18), perpetual motion going nowhere.

POETRY FOCUS

The dystopian vision intensifies in the closing lines. The poet imagines future generations laughing at many of our current beliefs and values, even consigning key aspects of what makes us human, such as 'Love' and 'Illness', to the museum. The desire to love or to be sympathetic to others is in stark contrast to the material things on display. However, she sees the **tragic irony** of the entire museum. The mirror seems to be 'someone's idea of a joke' (line 22). Through our reflections in the mirror, we now become part of the exhibits in the museum of obsolescence. It's a cruel joke, of course, since it shows us our real selves in light of our own insignificance.

The final exhibit item before the exit is 'an image of the old planet taken from space' (line 23). This is a reproduction of one of the first photographs of the whole Earth, taken from space. Does this bittersweet relic of a bygone era lament a lost connection to Earth as a natural home for the human race? Throughout the poem, Smith has questioned the usefulness of human knowledge and emphasised **our small place in the universe**.

Meanwhile, certain aspects of human nature don't seem to change and commercial life goes on. Outside the museum building, street vendors 'hawk t-shirts', making a living by selling history. The trashy T-shirts are not much different from the old photograph of planet Earth. As she **looks ahead to a time when human individuality has become obsolete**, readers are left wondering if we are rapidly losing an entire shared world. Smith's concluding tone is obviously cynical. But is she also being realistic?

Writing About the Poem

Comment on Smith's use of effective irony throughout this poem. Refer closely to the text in your response.

Sample Paragraph

'The Museum of Obsolescence' is set long after people have abandoned Planet Earth. Human life has evolved and the museum amuses future visitors. They 'titter' at the 'naïve tools' we once thought were so advanced. It's ironic that we always think of ourselves as so developed when everything becomes obsolete so quickly. In space we are insignificant. Smith's tone is gentle, yet she seems really troubled that people are destined be replaced by machines. A 'living man' is on display, but is of little interest. It's just like nowadays, when sightseers make a quick visit to Pompeii to check out life back in AD 79. The irony is most effective when Smith describes special 'installations' including 'Love'. Even people's feelings have died out – something I found really shocking.

EXAMINER'S COMMENT

Good personal response that includes some insightful engagement with the poem. Clear discussion of irony is supported with relevant reference and integrated quotations. A slightly more developed point about the irony of the poet's gentle tone would have improved the answer. Expression is lively and coherent throughout. Overall, a solid high-grade standard.

TRACY K. SMITH

✒ Class/Homework Exercises

1. 'Tracy K. Smith emphasises the importance of the imagination to raise questions about our lives.' To what extent is this true of 'The Museum of Obsolescence'? Develop your answer with reference to the poem.
2. 'Smith's poems often include strange and disturbing imagery to convey thought-provoking insights.' Discuss this view with reference to 'The Museum of Obsolescence'.

⊙ Points to Consider

- Themes include transience, dehumanisation, loss and human destiny.
- Poet illustrates the significance of the imagination in addressing life's mysteries.
- Effective use of vivid imagery, haunting atmosphere, irony and sound effects.
- Variety of tones: regretful, cynical, reflective, ironic, nostalgic and elegiac.

7 Don't You Wonder, Sometimes?

Title: from David Bowie's song 'Sound and Vision'.

1.

After dark, stars glisten like ice, and the distance they span
Hides something elemental. Not God, exactly. More like
Some thin-hipped glittering Bowie-being – a Starman
Or cosmic ace hovering, swaying, aching to make us see.
And what would we do, you and I, if we could know for sure   5

That someone was there squinting through the dust,
Saying nothing is lost, that everything lives on waiting only
To be wanted back badly enough? Would you go then,
Even for a few nights, into that other life where you
And that first she loved, blind to the future once, and happy?   10

Would I put on my coat and return to the kitchen where my
Mother and father sit waiting, dinner keeping warm on the stove?
Bowie will never die. Nothing will come for him in his sleep
Or charging through his veins. And he'll never grow old,
Just like the woman you lost, who will always be dark-haired   15

And flush-faced, running toward an electronic screen
That clocks the minutes, the miles left to go. Just like the life
In which I'm forever a child looking out my window at the night sky
Thinking one day I'll touch the world with bare hands
Even if it burns.   20

2.

He leaves no tracks. Slips past, quick as a cat. That's Bowie
For you: the Pope of Pop, coy as Christ. Like a play
Within a play, he's trademarked twice. The hours

Plink past like water from a window A/C. We sweat it out,
Teach ourselves to wait. Silently, lazily, collapse happens.   25
But not for Bowie. He cocks his head, grins that wicked grin.

Time never stops, but does it end? And how many lives
Before take-off, before we find ourselves
Beyond ourselves, all glam-glow, all twinkle and gold?

The future isn't what it used to be. Even Bowie thirsts   30
For something good and cold. Jets blink across the sky
Like migratory souls.

elemental: fundamental, essential.
Bowie: influential pop artist.
Starman: alien creature.
cosmic ace: space champion.

squinting: peering.

Pope: supreme leader.
coy: shy, flirtatious.
trademarked: branded.

A/C: air conditioner.

glam: glamorous.

migratory souls: travelling spirits.

TRACY K. SMITH

3.

Bowie is among us. Right here
In New York City. In a baseball cap
And expensive jeans. Ducking into   35
A deli. Flashing all those teeth
At the doorman on his way back up.
Or he's hailing a taxi on Lafayette
As the sky clouds over at dusk.
He's in no rush. Doesn't feel   40
The way you'd think he feels.
Doesn't strut or gloat. Tells jokes.

I've lived here all these years
And never seen him. Like not knowing
A comet from a shooting star.   45
But I'll bet he burns bright,
Dragging a tail of white-hot matter
The way some of us track tissue
Back from the toilet stall. He's got
The whole world under his foot,   50
And we are small alongside,
Though there are occasions

When a man his size can meet
Your eyes for just a blip of time
And send a thought like SHINE   55
SHINE SHINE SHINE SHINE
Straight to your mind. Bowie,
I want to believe you. Want to feel
Your will like the wind before rain.
The kind everything simply obeys,   60
Swept up in that hypnotic dance
As if something with the power to do so
Had looked its way and said:
    Go ahead.

deli: food shop.

Lafayette: a major street in Lower Manhattan, New York City.

strut or gloat: show off.

comet: icy body orbiting the sun.
shooting star: meteor.

track: trail.

blip: fleeting moment.

hypnotic: spellbinding.

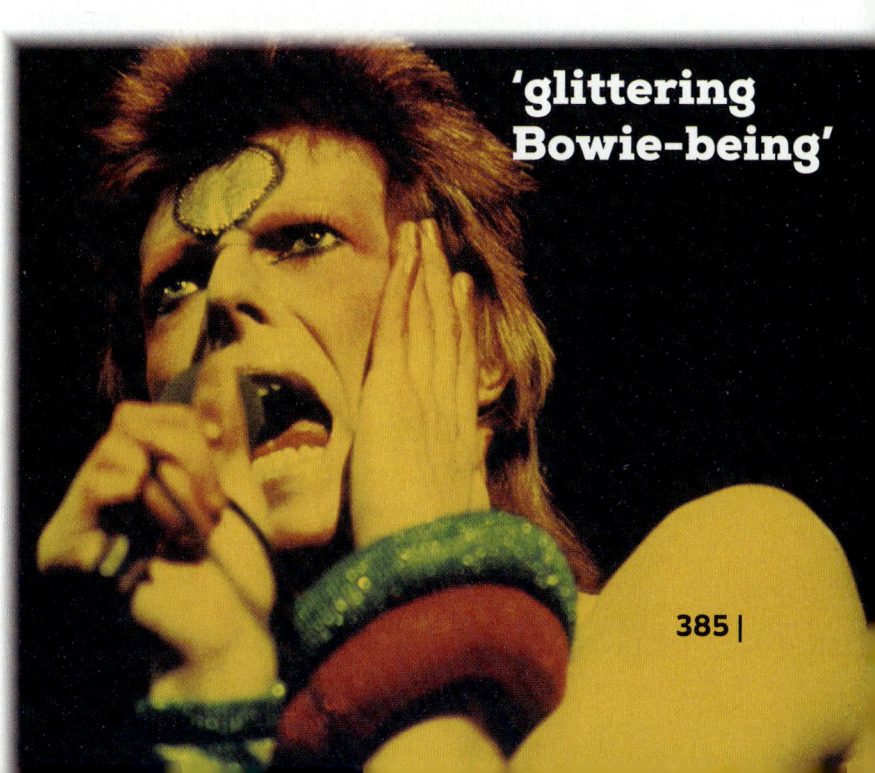

'glittering Bowie-being'

POETRY FOCUS

👤 Personal Response

1. Briefly outline one key question that Tracy K. Smith is exploring and wondering about in her poem 'Don't You Wonder, Sometimes?'
2. Smith uses alliteration extensively in her poem. Choose one example which appealed to you and explain how alliteration is effectively used to convey the poet's ideas.
3. Based on your reading of the poem, what is meant by the concluding italicised phrase, '*Go ahead*'? Briefly explain your response.

👁 Critical Literacy

Tracy K. Smith's poetry often addresses the reality of the human condition, including change and our place in the universe. 'Don't You Wonder, Sometimes?' is taken from her collection *Life on Mars* **(2011). Smith's father grew up in pre-civil rights Alabama and subsequently worked as an engineer developing the Hubble Telescope. The poet uses his career to illustrate the collection's central metaphor – outer space as a vast, unknowable infinity. She alters the punctuation of Bowie's song 'Life on Mars?' to make it into a statement rather than a question. Is she asserting that there is hope for a better future? The poet combines pop culture, anecdote and science fiction while working the grief she feels after her father's death into otherworldliness in the three-part poem.**

Section 1 of the poem focuses on visions of the future and meditations on outer space. The poem's title comes from the song 'Sound and Vision' by the English musician David Bowie – 'Don't you wonder sometimes/'Bout sound and vision?' – his casual reference to how we primarily experience our reality through hearing and seeing. The poet diverts the reader's eye towards the heavens with the declaration that **something fundamental, 'elemental', is hidden among the stars**. Sibilance and slender vowel sounds in the simile 'stars glisten like ice' softly hint at another reality. Broad assonance ('distance'/'span'/'elemental') suggests the vast expanse and mystery of space.

The notion of hope after 'dark' times begins to emerge: it's 'Not God, exactly' (line 2). **This symbol of eternity takes the form of Bowie's persona Ziggy Stardust**, an alien rock star who looked partly male and partly female. The androgynous messenger was sent to save the world from an impending apocalypse through rock 'n' roll. Compound words, slender vowels and explosive alliteration, 'Some thin-hipped glittering Bowie-being', capture the outlandish appearance of this unique creature in the high-heeled boots and extravagant make-up and costumes of the 1970s glam rock era. The verbs 'hovering, swaying' and a series of run-on lines suggest a character not subject to Earth's limitations. He is longing, 'aching', to share his message, 'make us see'.

| 386

TRACY K. SMITH

Just as Bowie used the Ziggy persona to examine the rock star culture he uneasily occupied, Smith uses Bowie for a similar function, to analyse and comment on human life here on Earth. In line 5, she addresses readers directly: 'And what would we do, you and I'. The tone is intimate, revealing uncertainty when faced with this strange event, 'That someone was there squinting through the dust'. Bowie's Starman offers **the wonderful reassurance that 'nothing is lost'**.

Bowie and the Starman show us the power of the imagination. **By going into the world of science fiction, the poet helps us to escape our mortal world.** We are given the opportunity to reconsider time. A note of hesitancy creeps in when the poet asks 'Would you go' back to a previous 'happy' time even if you would be 'blind', because the future would be unknown. The poet turns the question on herself, 'Would I' return to the secure, comfortable past to sit again with her mother and father at the dining table? The homely visual detail, 'dinner keeping warm on the stove' (line 12) evokes an idyllic family scene.

A short emphatic statement, 'Bowie will never die', interrupts the uncertain, nostalgic mood. The poet sees God in him just as the child saw God in the Starman waiting in the sky, a powerful sign of hope. The wry allusion to Bowie's everlasting youth, 'he'll never grow old', conjures up **the star's mystifying ability to reinvent his image**. He escapes mortality by continually changing, 'Nothing will come for him'.

Bowie's mute presence overhead encourages Smith to articulate the grief animating the poem. His chameleon style, pop idol, glam artist, actor, transcends the limitations of this earthly world and his creativity will endure. **A modern vision of death and eternity emerges.** For the poet, life can be reclaimed through memory and positive acceptance.

Compound words accentuate how her father will remember her deceased mother in her prime, 'dark-haired', 'flush-faced', even though time's clock ticks on, 'the minutes, the miles left to go'. **The poet has returned to the innocent perspective of a child**, just as in Bowie's album, 'I'm forever a child looking out my window', believing everything is possible. 'I'll touch the world with bare hands/Even if it burns' (lines 19–20).

Smith continues to weave **references to sci-fi, popular culture and space** throughout the poem's second section. It begins by conveying Bowie's ability to transcend the limitations of Earth, revealed through short sentences, 'He leaves no tracks. Slips past'. The paradox of his public and private personae is embodied in the conflicting alliterative phrases, 'Pope of Pop, coy as Christ'. Both confer a religious aura on the star, referencing his flamboyant appearance similar to the pomp and ceremony of the Church and his contrasting demure private attitude, comparable to the modesty of Jesus.

POETRY FOCUS

Bowie has admitted that **he adopted multiple personae** because he was extremely shy. This ambivalence is his intellectual property, 'trademarked twice', because both opposing roles are being played out at the same time, 'Like a play/Within a play'. Time's ongoing momentum is caught in the contemporary detail of the air-conditioning unit, 'The hours/Plink past like water from a window A/C' (lines 23–24). The run-on line and alliteration underline the relentless forward movement of time.

Resigned acceptance of the human condition is described in terms of the discomfort of a hot day, 'We sweat it out'. The inevitable end comes for everyone, described in the present tense, 'collapse happens'. But Bowie rises above it all through his carefree, humorous attitude, 'He cocks his head, grins that wicked grin', a heavenly being not subject to Earth's constraints.

An **unanswerable riddle** is posed in line 27: 'Time never stops, but does it end?' Humans vainly seek the unknowable for solace. A follow-up question asks: 'how many lives' must we live before we 'take-off' into another sphere, 'find ourselves/Beyond ourselves'. Bowie's flashy rock persona is evoked in the shimmering phrase, 'all glam-glow, all twinkle and gold' to suggest existence in this other dimension. The language of science fiction and glam rock are intertwined to imagine this new form of being.

In line 30, Smith paraphrases the French poet Paul Valéry's observation, 'The future isn't what it used to be'. She herself can only guess as to what the new future will be. The modern world is assuming the shape of humankind's mind – unstable and volatile. 'Even Bowie thirsts/For something good and cold'. His song that inspired the poem's title was written at a time when he had decided to live healthily after a period of drug addiction.

The onomatopoeic verb 'blink' captures the fleeting quality of time as everything moves and changes – both 'Jets' and 'migratory souls'. The poet suggests that **wondering about life on other planets is similar to wondering about the afterlife**, attempting to gain an insight into the intangible. Smith's search for spiritual reassurance is central to the poem and she considers Bowie's mythical Starman as the cosmic answer to this elemental need.

Section 3 shifts perspective and presents Bowie as an average person, the celebrity who walks among us, 'Right here/In New York City', lines 33–34. The reality of modern urban life is detailed in casual language and abbreviations, 'Ducking into/A deli', 'hailing a taxi'. But the otherworldliness of the 'star' is suggested by the celluloid imagery, 'Flashing all those teeth'. The real Bowie lacks ego, 'Doesn't strut or gloat' (line 42). He has a sense of humour, 'Tells jokes'.

Ironically, his alter ego, Ziggy Stardust, falls from grace because he gave in to his own inflated sense of self-importance. The poet confesses that she has

TRACY K. SMITH

'never seen' Bowie, likening it to a lack of knowledge about the difference between a 'comet' which circles the sun, and a 'shooting star' which enters Earth's atmosphere. Both have bright trails in the sky, but only the shooting star comes to Earth, like Bowie, 'among us'. Alliteration and details from the language of space suggest **Bowie's explosive, charismatic personality**, 'But I'll bet he burns bright,/Dragging a tail of white-hot matter' (lines 46–47).

The poet humorously deflates the elevated image of the shooting star by linking it with the banal simile of humans walking from a toilet with a piece of toilet paper stuck to a shoe, two very different trails. Bowie's **star status as a rock god** is accentuated, 'He's got/The whole world under his foot'. Ordinary people are 'small alongside'.

In an enactment of the famous biblical scene when God touches man to inspire him, the poet imagines Bowie meeting 'Your eyes' to motivate and convey a sense of what might be possible. The brief encounter is described in the onomatopoeia of 'a blip of time' (line 54). Capital letters and repetition underline this **special message** to 'SHINE', to twinkle, to be the best that we can be. This advice has been sent without sound and vision, 'Straight to your mind', in a scene reminiscent of a science fiction movie.

The poet's act of faith in Bowie ('I want to believe you') means abandoning self-determination and surrendering to 'Your will', to the elemental pull of this charismatic being, in the same way as the wind is driven before a rainstorm. **Everything 'simply obeys' this primary force of nature.** Everyone is 'Swept up in that hypnotic dance', spellbound because a powerful entity had encouraged and given permission, '*Go ahead*', so that humans can wonder, re-imagine reality and travel into the unknown.

✒ Writing About the Poem

'Tracy K. Smith effectively blends the language of science fiction and pop culture to convey her questions about the limitations of life on Earth.' Discuss this view with reference to her poem 'Don't You Wonder, Sometimes?'

Sample Paragraph

The poem's intimate title, from Bowie's Ziggy Stardust album sets the surreal tone for Smith's gentle questioning of the reality of human life. Like the Starman, she encourages us to look towards the heavens for another take on reality. She successfully combines sci-fi and pop by presenting Bowie's glam rock creation as a godlike presence to transcend our limited lives on Earth. After 'take-off' from Earth, it's 'all

EXAMINER'S COMMENT
Assured top-grade response that addresses the key aspects of a challenging question. Effective critical discussion demonstrates close engagement with the poem. Excellent use of relevant reference and direct quotation throughout.

twinkle and gold'. Smith compares him to a 'shooting star', almost from another world. Bowie bypasses time, so 'nothing is lost'. His cosmic image is mesmerising 'thin-hipped glittering Bowie-being', 'coy as Christ'. While humans struggle with grief and loss, Bowie is the source of energy which has the 'power' to inspire, 'Go ahead'.

✒ Class/Homework Exercises

1. 'Tracy K. Smith often challenges accepted perspectives of loss and grief.' Discuss this view with reference to her poem 'Don't You Wonder, Sometimes?'
2. 'The effective use of sound effects (sibilance, alliteration, assonance, etc.) is a recurring feature of Smith's poetry.' To what extent is this true of 'Don't You Wonder, Sometimes?'

◉ Points to Consider

- **Smith juxtaposes surreal features from the world of science fiction and pop to question accepted limitations of human life.**
- **Stylistic features include free verse, aural and visual imagery, irony, first-person viewpoint and inclusive personal address to reader.**
- **Balance of extraordinary subject matter with accessible language.**
- **Varied moods: confessional, analytical, imaginative, humorous, optimistic.**

8 It's Not

for Jean

That death was thinking of you or me
Or our family, or the woman
Our father would abandon when he died.
Death was thinking what it owed him:
His ride beyond the body, its garments,   5

Beyond the taxes that swarm each year,
The car and its fuel injection, the fruit trees
Heavy in his garden. Death led him past
The aisles of tools, the freezer lined with meat,
The television saying over and over *Seek*   10

And ye shall find. So why do we insist
He has vanished, that death ran off with our
Everything worth having? Why not that he was
Swimming only through this life – his slow,
Graceful crawl, shoulders rippling,   15

Legs slicing away at the waves, gliding
Further into what life itself denies?
He is only gone so far as we can tell. Though
When I try, I see the white cloud of his hair
In the distance like an eternity.   20

Dedication: the dedication is to Smith's sister, who looked after their mother in her final years.

abandon: leave, forsake.

garments: clothes.

aisles: lines, rows.

Seek/And ye shall find: biblical proverb.

rippling: moving.

gliding: floating.

eternity: infinity, for ever.

'the white cloud of his hair'

👤 Personal Response

1. Based on the evidence of the poem, briefly describe your impression of Tracy K. Smith's father.
2. Smith personifies death throughout the poem. Does this add to the sense that death is something to be feared? Or is it a natural part of life? Give a reason for your response.
3. In your opinion, what is the tone of the poem's two concluding lines? Is it positive or negative? Briefly explain your response.

👁 Critical Literacy

Tracy K. Smith frequently addresses themes of loss, grief and memory in her work. 'It's Not' was published in her 2011 collection, *Life on Mars*. Some critics have viewed the book as a work of mourning for her father, an engineer who worked on developing the Hubble Space Telescope. He died in 2008. Smith has said that many of the poems became a way to wrestle with her sorrow and create a satisfying sense of where her father's spirit resided.

The poem's **title** is part of the first sentence, which ends in **line 3**. Death is personified as a powerful force which acts independently, regardless of what sadness it causes. Smith's **tone of resentment** is evident in describing the impact of her father's death on 'our family'. The poet highlights how people are shocked by bereavement and often struggle to cope with it. Smith recalls the devastating effect of death and separation. The underlying sense of her own personal feelings of betrayal is also apparent. How dare death and time erode the world that she had become used to?

As Smith reflects on her perception of her father's life, **she considers his passing as a natural progression** beyond the control of every human, 'Death was thinking what it owed him'. The intensity of his spiritual journey through life and death into the unknown is suggested by the dynamic phrase, 'ride beyond the body' (**line 5**).

With a touch of **wry humour**, the poet notes that dying finally freed her father from his routine concerns and irritations, such as 'the taxes that swarm each year' (**line 6**). There is an evocative feeling of celebrating key aspects of his vibrant character through a series of everyday images she associates with him. She recalls some of his wide-ranging interests from technology ('fuel injection', 'tools') to gardening ('fruit trees').

Smith draws interesting parallels between her own efforts to accept her father's death and his work as an engineer on the Hubble Telescope. Father and daughter have much in common. He wondered about whether or not there was life on other planets while she now wonders about the possibility of an afterlife. The biblical quotation, '*Seek/And ye shall find*' (**lines 10–11**) is

TRACY K. SMITH

an ironic reference to their shared inquiring minds. **Is Smith questioning religion?** Does it really provide her with meaningful answers?

Although she understands the sad reality that her father has died, **the poet challenges the view that earthly life is the end**. She still feels cheated by death, which 'ran off' with 'Everything worth having'. Refusing to believe that he 'has vanished', she imagines his athletic body 'Swimming only through this life' (line 14). The metaphor is extended to reflect a loving recollection of her father's qualities, such as his simple dignity ('Graceful crawl') and physical strength ('shoulders rippling').

The vigorous language in line 16 emphasises his determination: 'Legs slicing away at the waves'. But while she accepts the inevitability of death, **Smith converts her mourning into something redemptive**. The poet senses that her father spent his entire life 'gliding' into the unknowable afterlife. She experiences both the thrill and terror of thinking about the cycle of life. The interplay between what she now feels and what she can remember – between love and loss – adds a tender energy to the poem.

The final lines are a reminder that Smith thinks about her father in galactic dimensions. Does this make him less significant? Or does it associate him with a greater universal power? The poet acknowledges the limitations of human knowledge about a possible spiritual existence after death. But for her, **space is a symbol of the unknowable**: 'He is only gone so far as we can tell' (line 18).

She turns her eyes to the stars in search of perspective and consolation, seeing 'the white cloud of his hair' (line 19). This vivid metaphor expresses her hope that his life hasn't ceased, but merely changed – and he is somewhere 'In the distance like an eternity'. In this beautiful sequence, her reflections seem filled with the love of a child for a parent. **Smith converts her own experience into a universal one**, allowing readers to identify the pervasive sense of grief and longing in the poem. The conclusion offers a kind of acceptance mingled with philosophy – life and death are part of a natural progression.

This elegy alternates cosmic context and personal focus. Both in life and in death, the poet's parents gave her a sense of anchoring. It is especially poignant because she seems to imply that her father has gone to a perfect heaven that is also a part of the universe. She has said: 'We all have our own language for what we've lived and what loss feels like.' Imagining the afterlife through the metaphor of outer space helped Smith come to terms with loved ones who had died. Yet **mystery remains** alongside her deep yearning to connect with her father.

Writing About the Poem

'Tracy K. Smith's most compelling poetry is often written as a response to her personal uncertainties.' Discuss this view with reference to her poem 'It's Not'.

Sample Paragraph

'It's Not' is filled with very compelling questions about how the poet deals with her dad dying and leaving this world. Smith isn't sure about how she feels, except she resents losing him to 'Death' which she looks on as a thief in the night who 'ran off' with him. She wonders if dying is really the end. Has he totally 'vanished' forever? The poem is extremely sad but has a reassuring ending. I found it very compelling that she believes her father 'is only gone as far as we can tell'. In a strange way, she solves her own worries, because she ends up thinking of her dad in the next world with his soul returning to nature like a cloud 'in the distance like an eternity'.

EXAMINER'S COMMENT

This succinct response addresses the question directly, engages with the text and makes effective use of supportive quotes worked into the commentary. Expression is slightly repetitive and points are reasonably clear, but could have been developed more. A solid middle-grade standard.

Class/Homework Exercises

1. 'Tracy K. Smith often explores issues of loss and mystery.' Discuss this view with reference to her poem 'It's Not'.
2. 'The effective use of vivid imagery is a recurring feature of Smith's poetry.' To what extent is this true of 'It's Not'?

Points to Consider

- Moving elegy in tribute to the poet's father.
- Smith juxtaposes some of the mysteries of science with the major questions of life.
- Stylistic features include irony, personification and striking imagery.
- Effective use of metaphor: the image of space to explore the unknowable.
- Varied tones: elegiac, mournful, exhilarated and questioning.

9 The Universe as Primal Scream

TRACY K. SMITH

Title: all matter and energy as first sound.

5pm on the nose. They open their mouths
And it rolls out: high, shrill and metallic.
First the boy, then his sister. Occasionally,
They both let loose at once, and I think
Of putting on my shoes to go up and see   5
Whether it is merely an experiment
Their parents have been conducting
Upon the good crystal, which must surely
Lie shattered to dust on the floor.

Maybe the mother is still proud   10
Of the four pink lungs she nursed
To such might. Perhaps, if they hit
The magic decibel, the whole building
Will lift-off, and we'll ride to glory
Like Elijah. If this is it – if this is what   15
Their cries are cocked toward – let the sky
Pass from blue, to red, to molten gold,
To black. Let the heaven we inherit approach.

Whether it is our dead in Old Testament robes,
Or a door opening onto the roiling infinity of space.   20
Whether it will bend down to greet us like a father,
Or swallow us like a furnace. I'm ready
To meet what refuses to let us keep anything
For long. What teases us with blessings,
Bends us with grief. Wizard, thief, the great   25
Wind rushing to knock our mirrors to the floor,
To sweep our short lives clean. How mean

Our racket seems beside it. My stereo on shuffle.
The neighbor chopping onions through a wall.
All of it just a hiccough against what may never   30
Come for us. And the kids upstairs still at it,
Screaming like the Dawn of Man, as if something
They have no name for has begun to insist
Upon being born.

metallic: harsh, clanging.

good crystal: fine glassware.

decibel: high-pitched volume.

Elijah: biblical prophet, miracle worker.
cocked: pointed.
molten: melted.
inherit: are due to receive.

Old Testament robes: pre-Christian clothes.
roiling: boiling, churning.
furnace: incinerator.

mean: cruel, miserable.

racket: noise, uproar.
stereo: record player.
shuffle: random selection.
hiccough: slip-up, hiccup.

Dawn of Man: beginning of human life.

POETRY FOCUS

👤 Personal Response

1. Describe the mood and atmosphere created by the poet in the opening stanza.
2. Comment briefly on the impact of Smith's sound effects (alliteration, assonance, onomatopoeia, internal rhyme) in the poem.
3. In your opinion, what is the tone of the poem's conclusion? Is it positive or negative? Briefly explain your response.

👁 Critical Literacy

'The Universe as Primal Scream' was published in Tracy K. Smith's third poetry collection, the Pulitzer Prize-winning *Life on Mars* (2011). This selection of poems searches for a viewpoint and sense of peace while elegising her beloved father, an engineer who worked on the development of the Hubble Telescope. A broad spectrum of modern experience is addressed, including pop culture, astronomy, physics, science and religion. The poet also explores human pain, loss, forgiveness and otherworldliness. Her father was obsessed by the idea of space as the final frontier and Smith brings readers on a cinematic journey to the ends of the galaxy, then reels back, frame by frame, until she focuses on the reality of life on Earth, noisy children in an upstairs apartment.

The title is **an interesting simile**, 'The Universe as Primal Scream'. The Big Bang theory is the astronomers' explanation for the creation of the universe. At a particular time in the remote past, all matter was created with a giant explosion. A primal scream is a release of intense frustration and anger that can help people to resolve psychological issues by allowing them to express their emotions in a safe environment. Smith uses her poem to explore the universe through the screams of two young children who live above her in an apartment block.

Stanza 1 opens with a private interior scene, a portrayal of screaming children and the speaker's curiosity about what is happening in the upstairs apartment. A curt colloquial expression, '5pm on the nose' (line 1) pinpoints the exact time the yelling begins. This is similar to the specific moment identified when the universe was created by the Big Bang. **The ear-piercing sound suggests a parallel between the birth of a child and the creation of the world.** The use of the present tense, 'They open', and broad assonance, 'rolls out', conveys the overwhelming nature of the noise. High-pitched screeches echo in the slender assonance ('shrill', 'metallic'). The drawn-out racket is mimicked through lengthening the 'o' and 'a' vowels with a double 'l' sound ('roll', 'metallic'). This exceptionally loud noise seems to reach right into the poet's mind, arousing the need to find out what is going on. The primal instinct has spurred a rational response.

TRACY K. SMITH

The beginning of creation is now evolving with the introduction of the cognitive self, 'I think' (line 4). Smith contrasts the over-emotional squealing children with the mature adult ascending to a higher plane of being, 'go up and see'. The speaker self-consciously dresses ('putting on my shoes') to go out in public, just as Adam and Eve clothed themselves when they became self-aware in the Garden of Eden. She **humorously wonders** why the children are allowed to make such a galactic commotion before offering a sarcastic suggestion that their parents must be conducting 'an experiment'.

'high, shrill and metallic'

This places the parents in the elevated role of scientists testing truth. Will their children's shrieks shatter 'the good crystal'? Fortunately, sound vibrations only break the finest leaded crystal. This scientific allusion gives way to a biblical allusion, 'Lie shattered to dust', reminiscent of the phrase 'For you are dust, and unto dust you shall return' (Genesis). The first stanza concludes with the **circular motion of the universe – creation, evolution and death**. The stanza's short opening sentences represent the beginning of creation while the more complex structure ('Occasionally ... on the floor' in lines 3–9) indicates the evolution of the rational thought process in humans.

Exasperated by the continuing din, **the speaker resorts to hyperbole**. In the second stanza, she proposes that 'Maybe' the mother is pleased that she has produced 'four pink lungs' of 'such might'. Run-on lines expose humanity's self-congratulatory sense of its own importance. The poet believes that

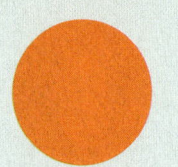

humans are taking credit for what some other power created. She theorises, 'Perhaps', if the children strike the 'magic decibel', the precise volume, something extraordinary might occur. The speaker imagines this sound propelling the whole apartment building to 'lift-off' like a space rocket soaring into the sky. Like Elijah in the biblical story, she visualises ascending to heaven, a riotous 'ride to glory' (line 14).

The tone suddenly becomes resigned, 'If this is it'. Harsh alliteration introduces a warlike attitude ('cries', 'cocked'), a possible reference to the **two differing opinions on the origin of the universe, one scientific, the other religious**, each introduced by the phrase 'let the'. The changing colours of the sky (line 17) introduce the Doppler effect of the Big Bang theory. The wave frequency changes; red signifies a longer wavelength while blue indicates a shorter one. Black refers to the dark matter and energy thought to make up 95 per cent of the universe. The poet's deceased mother was devoutly Christian and the stanza concludes with the calm acceptance of religious faith, 'Let the heaven we inherit approach'. The wild flurry of noisy activity has been stilled.

In stanza 3, **two opposing viewpoints of the apocalypse** further explore the idea of heaven and how we will be greeted in the afterlife. The poet alternates between the traditional soothing view of heaven, 'our dead in Old Testament robes' (line 19) and a terrifying scientific dystopia, 'the roiling infinity of space'. The serene biblical scene, 'bend down to greet us like a father', is vividly contrasted with the seething turbulence of the black hole of infinity. A petrifying simile, 'swallow us like a furnace' (line 22), implies the utter annihilation of the human being. But the speaker is determined to challenge the threat and is 'ready/To meet' whatever is ahead. She also accuses this power of depriving humans of what they cherish, 'refuses to let us keep anything/For long'.

The **memory of Smith's late father is now subtly introduced**. Negative verbs ('teases', 'Bends') indicate the harshness of this mysterious power which governs human life and death. The speaker calls it a 'Wizard' (line 25), an enchanter who plays tricks. It is a 'thief' who steals from humanity. It is also seen as an uncontrollable elemental force, 'the great/Wind', its strength highlighted by the run-on line. This destructive energy eliminates the self-reflective minds of humans, 'knock our mirrors'. Smith illustrates the finite nature of human existence in the visual image, 'sweep our short lives clean'. The stanza's momentum is halted while readers consider how cruel this spiteful force is in clearing away human existence. As the poem slips into the final stanza, we are left with a sense of how inferior and squalid people's lives are in contrast to the almighty universal power.

TRACY K. SMITH

The fourth stanza echoes the circular motion of the first, returning to the opening picture of noisy children and the familiar 'racket' of everyday life (line 28). Ordinary pictures of the meaningless activities of human existence reinforce **how puny and insignificant our lives are in contrast to the immense roar of the universe**. Readers are jolted back to the present through commonplace imagery, 'The neighbor chopping onions' and 'My stereo on shuffle'. Even the random selection of music suggests the lack of order in real life.

From Smith's viewpoint, **every human being is shuffled by an incomprehensible power** with no apparent order or reason. People stumble closer to their graves unaware that they approach an inscrutable void. For the poet, humankind is a mere 'hiccough' (line 30), a technical hitch, an interruption in the grand and unknowable scheme of things.

The poem ends as it began with screaming children, 'the kids upstairs still at it'. A tone of weary exasperation notes that people have always cried out – since the beginning of creation, 'like the Dawn of Man' (line 32). The noise heralds the arrival of something new and strange and nameless. The shortest stanza in the poem implies an unfinished work. **Is the speaker suggesting that human life ends incomplete**, cut short by inevitable but unpredictable death?

Throughout the poem, free verse, enjambment, prose-like expression and an absence of rhyme all permit a wide-ranging exploration of the limited nature of human life. **This central theme is supported by the poem's structure**. The four-part shape is contained neatly in four stanzas: a specific incident (children screaming), the relationship of the incident to humanity, then to the entire universe, before finally returning to the initial incident. The neat order of a row of nine-line stanzas is disturbed by the final short seven-line stanza, signifying a life randomly torn apart. Is this a reference to the poet's attitude to her father's death? Does human life have any significant meaning?

✍ Writing About the Poem

Based on your reading of 'The Universe as Primal Scream', to what extent is your emotional response to the poem heightened by Smith's use of both calm and disturbing imagery? Develop your answer with reference to the text.

Sample Paragraph

Biblical and scientific imagery increased my feelings of confusion in this exploration of the universe and human existence in 'The Universe as Primal Scream'. Although Smith includes joyous details such as Elijah being swept to heaven in a whirlwind, a 'ride to glory' and a gentle religious scene, 'bend down like a father', the main message is that God causes grief and pain. She calls this almighty power a 'thief' who 'teases us'. She accuses this divine force of being 'mean' to humanity because it removes what is most loved. Smith's scientific imagery is even more terrifying. She paints a horrifying scene of being 'swallowed' in a 'roiling infinity of space'. The poem concluded with a short stanza, suggesting life cut short by 'the great wind'. I found these contrasting images very unsettling.

> **EXAMINER'S COMMENT**
>
> *Clearly written top-grade personal response that addresses the question directly and engages closely with the poem. Effective discussion points focus on how Smith's themes are illustrated through contrasting images. Good use of relevant reference and quotation throughout.*

Class/Homework Exercises

1. 'In Tracy K. Smith's poetry, personal anecdote and philosophical questioning are blended to examine the strangeness of contemporary life.' To what extent is this true of 'The Universe as Primal Scream'?
2. 'Smith is well known for the power and energy of her dramatic language.' Discuss this view with reference to her poem 'The Universe as Primal Scream'.

Points to Consider

- Challenging perspectives on human existence and the meaning of life.
- Other themes include God, the universe, loss, death and the hereafter.
- Blend of visual, biblical and scientific imagery.
- Effective use of sounds, contrast and repetition.
- Incomplete poetic structure mirrors the theme of life randomly cut short.
- Ordinary language balances extraordinary subject matter.
- Varied tones: wry humour, exasperation, determination, grief, questioning.

10 The Greatest Personal Privation

TRACY K. SMITH

Title: Mary Jones complained of privation (deprivation and hardship).

The greatest personal privation I have had to endure has been the want of either Patience or Phoebe – tell them I am never, if life is spared us, to be without both of them again.
– Letter from Mary Jones to Elizabeth Jones Maxwell regarding two of her slaves, 30 August 1849

1.

It is a painful and harassing business
Belonging to her. We have had trouble enough,
Have no comfort or confidence in them,

And they appear unhappy themselves, no doubt
From the trouble they have occasioned.   5
They could dispose of the whole family

Without consulting us – Father, Mother,
Every good cook, washer, and seamstress
Subject to sale. I believe Good shall be

Glad if we may have hope of the loss of trouble.   10
I remain in glad conscience, at peace with God
And the world! I have prayed for those people

Many, many, very many times.

2.

Much as I should miss Mother,
I have had trouble enough   15
And wish no more to be
Only waiting to be sent
Home in peace with God.

3.

In every probability
We may yet discover   20

harassing: annoying.
Belonging: being owned, enslaved.

occasioned: caused.

seamstress: woman whose job is sewing.

glad: happy, clear.

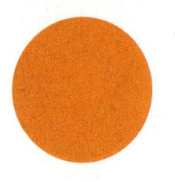

POETRY FOCUS

The whole country
Will not come back

From the sale of parent
And child. So far

As I can see, the loss   25
Is great and increasing.

I know they have desired
We should not know

What was for our own good,
But we cannot be all the cause   30

Of all that has been done.

          4.
We wish to act. We may yet.
But we have to learn what their

Character and moral conduct   **moral conduct:** behaviour.
Will present. We have it in   35

Contemplation to wait and see.   **Contemplation:** mind.
If good, we shall be glad; if

Evil, then we must meet evil
As best we can.

          5.
Father, mother, son, daughter, man.   40
And if that family is sold:
                  Please –
We cannot –
        Please –
               We have got to –   45
Please –
        The children –
Mother and Father and husband and –
All of you –
            All –   50
                  I have no more –
How soon and unexpectedly cut off
Many, many, very many times.

A Note on Erasure Poetry

TRACY K. SMITH

An erasure poem takes a pre-existing text and makes a poem by *erasing* or removing some of the words. It is sometimes referred to as 'found', 'redacted' or 'blackout' poetry.

Erasure poems are created from any source, including novels, published poems, letters, political publications or newspaper articles. The remaining text can then be framed into lines and/or stanzas on the page as a new poem.

Tracy K. Smith uses erasure poetry to allow those she wishes to honour, and sometimes challenge, to speak for themselves. She reveals the text beneath the text by listening closely to hidden voices. The poems address some of the most troubling events in history and often give voice to the oppressed or marginalised.

The title of Smith's poetry collection *Wade in Water* comes from an African-American spiritual hymn, 'Wade in the water/God's gonna trouble the water'. Many of the poems are rooted in questioning US history and identity through collective reckoning and empathy. The poet has commented: 'You want a poem to unsettle something.'

'Subject for sale'

POETRY FOCUS

👤 Personal Response

1. Based on the short extract from the letter in the poem's subtitle, briefly describe your impression of Mary Jones.
2. Repetition is used throughout the poem. Select one example and comment on its effectiveness.
3. In your opinion, what is Smith's key message or viewpoint in this poem? Briefly explain your response.

👁 Critical Literacy

Tracy K. Smith's 2018 collection, *Wade in the Water*, includes this erasure poem, drawn directly from letters between white slave-owners Charles Colcock Jones and his wife, written in the mid-19th century. On one occasion, when she was away from home, Mary Jones wrote about how much she missed the services of two slaves, a mother and daughter. The poem opens with a quote from one of her letters. She considers herself deprived and helpless without them. The poem centres on the slaves' reaction to the news of their upcoming sale. It is a poignant commentary on the violence done to black Americans.

In the **opening section**, Smith inverts the letter-writer's views by turning Jones's own words against her. The great **irony**, of course, is that her self-pitying letter shows no regard for the people enslaved by Jones herself and her family. Instead, the sentimental tone and exaggerated description of her 'greatest personal privation' reinforces Smith's point about the obvious racial injustice involved.

The **dual perspective** is evident in everything that is said. Using the mid-19th-century language from the Jones family's letters, Smith imagines the voices of Patience and Phoebe – and of countless other families who were held in bondage. For them, the reality of 'Belonging' is what is 'painful and harassing'. The quietly insistent tone makes it clear that what is unacceptable today is the idea of any human being ever 'Belonging' to another.

Readers get a glimpse of the mercilessness of routine plantation life where slaves who had been accused of causing 'trouble' were 'Subject to sale'. However, the generosity of those who suffered enslavement is highlighted in the simple expression of forgiveness, 'I have prayed for those people'. The **emphatic commentary**, 'Many, many, very many times' (**line 13**) reminds us of how long the injustice of slavery endured.

In the short **second section**, we hear the voice of a daughter who has experienced 'trouble enough' and now seems defeated by a life of oppression. Although distressed about being separated from her mother,

TRACY K. SMITH

her **religious faith offers consolation** and she hopes to find 'peace with God'. The subdued tone and slow-moving pace add to the powerful impact of her poignant prayer.

Section 3 presents a devastating portrait of American history. Smith recalls the human cost of historical racism directly in a series of **carefully controlled couplets**. The short lines emphasise her considered view of the legacy of slavery: 'The whole country/Will not come back/From the sale of parent/And child'. The sparse diction and simple syntax are compelling.

Smith examines the injustice – at both a political and a personal level – with sharp insight. She **invites her readers to face up to the racist** past when generations of African Americans were deprived of determining 'What was for our own good'. We are challenged to question the 'cause/Of all that has been done'.

As the poem progresses, it turns from a reflective probing of historical injustice to a more determined desire 'to act'. Section 4 focuses on the need for a communal response, reflected in the repetition of the personal pronoun, 'We'. The haunting **voices of Patience and Phoebe transcend time**, appealing for justice from the people in power who control their lives. But Smith is not particularly confident of social progress and is realistic enough to admit that 'we must meet evil/As best we can'.

The dramatic final section is much more urgent in tone. An agonising chorus of desperate voices call injustice and its perpetrators to account. The fragmented phrasing and use of unfinished sentences filled with cries of '*Please*' have **a timeless quality** – spelling out the experience of enslaved families over generations. The insistent repetition of the pronoun '*We*' emphasises the power of community and elevates compassion as a liberating force.

Smith's use of italics and dashes adds to the tension, highlighting the continuing gap between the ideal of universal human rights and the ongoing discrimination against African Americans. The poem's **frantic rhythm** builds to a high point in line 51: '*I have no more*'. Is Smith overwhelmed by her country's history? Or is she still hopeful that despite the failures to eradicate oppression in the past, the world must continue to fight against injustice?

The haunting refrain of 'Many, many, very many times' (line 53) leaves readers in no doubt that lack of freedom and widespread inequality are still found worldwide. In moments like this, the poet's example in creating a spiritual hymn to America's forgotten people makes the point that there is still an ever-increasing amount of work to do.

The poem is a compelling response to the original letter from which it is derived. Smith's choice of **the erasure form works well** because she is

primarily highlighting how the truth was erased for centuries. The poet inverts this original erasure of the appalling reality of countless people who were denied the most basic human rights, allowing us to understand the present through the past.

✍ Writing About the Poem

'Tracy K. Smith uses a range of compelling voices to communicate disturbing aspects of American life.' Discuss this view with reference to 'The Greatest Personal Privation'.

Sample Paragraph

The title quotes a letter from a white woman who owned a plantation in the American South. Although she kept slaves, she had two favourites and depended on them. Her voice is full of self-pity which actually makes the point that she feels no guilt. It's not always clear who is actually speaking in this poem, but it's mainly the two slaves, 'We have had trouble enough'. I actually believe they represent every person deprived of freedom either during times of slavery or in the present day. The poem's last lines involve mixed voices chanting the need for an end to racism. The one voice behind all of these is, of course, the actual poet herself. Tracy Smith's tone is angry and persuasive, 'We wish to act', 'We have got to' – and this has a very disturbing impact.

> **EXAMINER'S COMMENT**
> *Confident response that includes some insightful engagement with the poem. Points are expressed clearly – particularly the idea of Smith's own governing voice throughout. Apart from some repetitive expression ('actually'), this is a solid high-grade standard.*

✒ Class/Homework Exercises

1. 'Tracy K. Smith's poems often combine deep compassion with an insistence on hope.' To what extent is this the case in 'The Greatest Personal Privation'? Develop your response with reference to the poem.
2. 'Smith makes effective use of various tones and moods to illustrate her thematic concerns.' Discuss this statement with reference to 'The Greatest Personal Privation'.

◉ Points to Consider

- **Erasure form weaves together past and present, personal and political.**
- **Effective stylistic features include irony, repetition and a range of speakers.**
- **Contrasting tones: sympathetic, didactic, dramatic and questioning.**
- **Smith urges readers to question governments and challenge injustice and lack of freedom.**

11 I am 60 odd years of age

TRACY K. SMITH

Note: Smith did not initially give the poem a title. This emphasised the lack of identity of African-American soldiers.

(from 'I Will Tell You the Truth About This, I Will Tell You All About It')

I am 60 odd years of age –

I am 62 years of age next month –

I am about 65 years of age –

I reckon I am about 67 years old –

I am about 68 years of age –   5

I am on the rise of 80 years of age –

I am 89 years old –

I am 94 years of age –

I don't know my exact age –

I am the claimant in this case. I have testified before you   10
two different times before –

claimant: applicant.

I filed my claim I think first about 12 years ago –

filed: put on record.

I am now an applicant for a pension,
because I understand
that all soldiers are entitled to a pension –   15

applicant: person applying.
entitled: eligible, due.

I claim pension under the general law
on account of disease of eyes
as a result of smallpox
contracted in service –

general: usual, universal.
smallpox: viral disease.
contracted: caught.

The varicose veins came on both my legs   20
soon after the war and the sores were there
when I first put in my claim –

varicose: swollen, twisted.

I claim pension for rheumatism
and got my toe broke and I was struck
in the side with the breech of a gun   25
breaking my ribs –

rheumatism: chronic pain.
breech: rear barrel.

POETRY FOCUS

I was a man stout and healthy
over 27 years of age when I enlisted –   **enlisted:** joined the army.

When I enlisted I had a little mustache,
and some chin whiskers –   30

I was a green boy right off the farm and did   **green:** inexperienced.
just what I was told to do –

When I went to enlist the recruiting officer   **enlist:** sign up as a soldier.
said to me, your name is John Wilson.
I said, no, my name is Robert Harrison,   35
but he put me down as John Wilson. I was
known while in service by that name –   **in service:** in the army.

I cannot read nor write, and I do not know
how my name was spelled when I enlisted
nor do I know how it is spelled now   40
I always signed my name while in the army
by making my mark   **making my mark:** signing using X.
I know my name by sound –   **by sound:** by hearing.

My mother said after my discharge that the reason   **discharge:** release.
the officer put my name down as John Wilson   45
was he could draw my bounty –   **bounty:** cash payment.

I am the son of Solomon and Lucinda Sibley –

I am the only living child of Dennis Campbell –

My father was George Jourdan and my mother was Millie Jourdan –

My mother told me that John Barnett was my father –   50

My mother was Mary Eliza Jackson and my father Reuben Jackson –

My name on the roll was Frank Nunn. No sir,   **roll:** official register.
it was not Frank Nearn –

My full name is Dick Lewis Barnett.
I am the applicant for pension   55
on account of having served
under the name Lewis Smith
which was the name I wore before
the days of slavery were over –

My correct name is Hiram Kirkland.   60
Some persons call me Harry and others call me Henry,
but neither is my correct name.

| 408

A Note on Erasure Poetry

TRACY K. SMITH

An erasure poem takes a pre-existing text and makes a poem by erasing or removing some of the words. It is sometimes referred to as 'found', 'redacted' or 'blackout' poetry.

Erasure poems are created from any source, including novels, published poems, letters, political publications or newspaper articles. The remaining text can then be framed into lines and/or stanzas on the page as a new poem.

Tracy K. Smith uses erasure poetry to allow those she wishes to honour, and sometimes challenge, to speak for themselves. She reveals the text beneath the text by listening closely to hidden voices. The poems address some of the most troubling events in history and often give voice to the oppressed or marginalised.

Smith's collection *Wade in Water* includes extracts from letters by African Americans who served in the American Civil War and their surviving relatives. These soldiers and their families speak on their own behalf. They tell of tragedies on and off the battlefield, ask for news of loved ones, and beg President Lincoln for help and the payment of pensions due.

'all soldiers are entitled to a pension'

POETRY FOCUS

👤 Personal Response

1. Based on the evidence of the poem, what is your understanding of the treatment of the African-American soldiers who served in the Civil War?
2. Choose one image from the poem that you find shocking or disturbing. Comment briefly on its effectiveness.
3. In your opinion, what is the tone of the poem's three concluding lines? Is it positive or negative? Briefly explain your response.

👁 Critical Literacy

Tracy K. Smith's fourth volume of poetry, *Wade in the Water* (2018), examines racial and environmental injustice. Named after a popular slave spiritual, this collection is a spiritual hymn to America's forgotten people. Split into four chapters, each carrying a number rather than a title, the chapters resemble self-contained movements in a piece of music. They invite readers to interact and interpret. The various voices, identified and unidentified, create a communal chorus enabling negative realities to be confronted in a positive way. 'I am 60 odd years of age' forms part of Chapter II, which contains agonising near-verbatim letters and statements of African-American Civil War soldiers and their families.

The poet has commented: '*A lot of the blacks who fought in the Civil War while enslaved and who were emancipated didn't have birth certificates; they didn't have marriage licenses; they often changed their names once they were given a say in the matter. And then the government said to them: we can't pay you your pension, because how can you prove to us that you are you?*' (From 'A Conversation with Tracy K. Smith' – *The Adroit Journal*, Issue 22.)

'I am 60 odd years of age' is an extract from 'I Will Tell You the Truth About This, I Will Tell You All About It'. Smith researched the US Bureau of Pensions files and she **fills the poem with fragments** from African-American Civil War soldiers' pension applications. These are accentuated by the use of italics to remind readers that they are the person's actual words. Ironically, the poet uses these official records to reveal the soldiers' lack of recognition in society's formal records of its citizens' lives. The war was fought primarily over the issue of slavery. Smith brings to life the encounters between these soldiers and the system in which they live.

The poem begins in a shy, self-effacing manner, 'I am 60 odd years of age –'. Many speakers **introduce themselves in anonymous phrases** that trail off with a dash. Are these dashes pleading or threatening? The hesitant echoes of these voices register uncertainty regarding their precise age, 'about 65', 'I don't know my exact age' (line 9). Many African-American soldiers were never issued with birth certificates and official records did not list their existence. Is this a symptom of how society viewed these people?

TRACY K. SMITH

Their **unwavering perseverance in pursuing their entitlement** to a pension is evident in lines 10–12: 'I have testified before you/two different times before', 'I filed my claim I think first about 12 years ago'. The authority of this army of living ghosts is heightened by the use of formal legal language, such as 'claimant' and 'testified'. It is also suggested by the repetition and capitalisation of the first-person singular pronoun, 'I'. The deep pride of these people is unmistakable in their claim for what they are due for their service to the country, 'all soldiers are entitled to a pension' line 15. Their voices combine to cast light on the shadows of history which have obscured their story.

A list of specific injuries sustained while 'in service' begins to illuminate these people as unique individuals. One suffered 'disease of eyes/as a result of smallpox' (lines 17–18). Another claimant described how 'varicose veins came on both my legs/soon after the war'. The violent brutality of conflict is conveyed in the explosive alliterative phrase 'breech of a gun/breaking my ribs'. This carefully collated **collage of archival fragments** has a hypnotic effect. Everyone mentioned is given dignity by being allocated a specific place in the widely spaced poem's canvas. It records their distinguishing characteristics, 'a man stout and healthy', 'I had a little mustache' (line 29). Smith weaves memorable images together with compassion as if making a hand-stitched quilt from treasured fragments of cloth.

One **individual story is developed**, inviting readers further into the narrative and so into their own humanity. The arrogance of a recruiting officer is exposed in his insistence that the young enlistee, the 'green boy', should be recorded by a new name. Despite the young man's protest, 'he put me down as John Wilson' (line 36). Does the officer have so little regard for the new black recruit that he will register him any way he chooses? Or is there a more sinister motive to his action? The vulnerability of the young soldier is evident in his timid disclosure that he did 'just what I was told to do'.

At the time of the American Civil War (1860–1865), it was illegal in some states to teach slaves basic literacy. In line 38, a young soldier admits that he 'cannot read nor write'. During his time in the army, he signed his name simply by placing an X ('making my mark'). The soft alliterative phrase foreshadows how easily he could be deceived since he only knew his name 'by sound'. The mother of this 'green boy' exposes the ulterior motives of the recruiting officer's act of renaming her son. The fraud was carried out to steal the young man's initial enlistment payment or 'bounty' (line 46). **Run-on lines accentuate the overwhelming rush of frustration** felt because he could not prove who he was and that he had served his country.

In the final section, Smith emphasises the **importance of one's name to establish identity and status**. Speakers are no longer anonymous, contrasting with those referenced at the beginning of the poem. Instead,

the individual is firmly placed within a particular family, 'I am the son of Solomon and Lucinda Sibley' (line 47). The tone here is much more self-assured. These overlooked people are now being treated with due respect. Some have married parents, 'My father was George Jourdan and my mother was Millie Jourdan'. Others have not, 'My mother told me that John Barnett was my father'. The first-person singular pronoun 'I' is replaced by the possessive adjective 'My', indicating that the person's place in society is now reclaimed.

A brief exchange between a claimant and an official illustrates the ongoing battle for recognition: 'My name on the roll was Frank Nunn. No sir,/it was not Frank Nearn' (lines 52–53). The struggle for reclamation of identity is detailed in the fragment from Dick Lewis Barnett who served 'under the name Lewis Smith', his slave name. The verb 'wore' suggests that this slave name was a cloak which hid the soldier's true identity. However, **the poem concludes on a dignified note, establishing one person's 'correct name'**. The two anglicised names sometimes given to Kirkland, 'Henry' and 'Harry', are now set aside and his proper forename, 'Hiram', is finally placed on record (line 60). This biblical name means 'exalted brother'.

In this **poignant erasure poem**, the voices of forgotten people have now asserted their individuality and reinstated their rightful place in history. With characteristic compassion, Smith has stirred things up by making visible the words of the forgotten African-American soldiers who served in the Civil War. The cumulative effect of their simple statements is unexpectedly powerful, a litany of wrongs crying out for redress. The poet is drawing back the curtains to reveal America's historical racism. Her poems, like the great spirituals, witness, protect and raise the roof, because they contribute to the national dialogue.

✒ Writing About the Poem

'Tracy K. Smith's fearless exploration of history constructs a powerful account of misidentifying and discrimination.' Discuss this view with reference to 'I am 60 odd years of age'.

TRACY K. SMITH

Sample Paragraph

'I am 60 odd years of age' is a collection of extracts from the pension applications of African-American soldiers after the Civil War. Smith builds a powerful poem by using these forgotten voices. The poet fearlessly insists on identifying particular soldiers by describing their injuries, 'smallpox', 'rheumatism'. These young black recruits are presented as individuals in both appearance, 'chin whiskers' and personality, 'a green boy'. Smith exposes official misidentification and exploitation, 'he put me down as John Wilson'. She details how the true identity of slaves was hidden by the assumed names they 'wore'. By recording their proper names, 'My correct name is Hiram Kirkland', Smith has challenged historical injustice and corrected the official records.

> **EXAMINER'S COMMENT**
>
> *This is a solid top-grade response that addresses the question and engages intelligently with the poem. Good critical commentary is supported by apt reference and accurate quotation. Points are clearly expressed throughout.*

Class/Homework Exercises

1. 'Tracy K. Smith often confronts issues of loss and wrong-doing.' Discuss this view with reference to her poem 'I am 60 odd years of age'.
2. 'In "I am 60 odd years of age", the structure of the poem increases the strength of Smith's central message.' To what extent do you agree or disagree? Explore some of the following in your response: the use of italicised fragments, dashes, line spacing, repetition, contrast, run-on lines, etc.

Points to Consider

- **Powerful combination of fragmentary voices from US Bureau of Pensions archives.**
- **Smith awakens reader's awareness of and compassion for forgotten people and their story through the mix of many voices.**
- **Stylistic features include specific details, repetition, contrast, colloquial speech, legal language.**
- **Effective use of alliteration, dashes, replacement of first-person singular pronoun with possessive adjective.**
- **Varied tones: timid, steadfast, moral, demanding, authoritative, moving.**

12 Ghazal

The sky is a dry pitiless white. The wide rows stretch on into
  death.
Like famished birds, my hands strip each stalk of its stolen
  crop: our name.   **famished:** starved.

History is a ship forever setting sail. On either shore: mountains
  of men,
Oceans of bone, an engine whose teeth shred all that is not
  our name.   **shred:** cut.

Can you imagine what will sound from us, what we'll rend and
  claim   5   **rend:** rip up.
When we find ourselves alone with all we've ever sought: our
  name?   **sought:** wanted.

Or perhaps what we seek lives outside of speech, like a tribe
  of goats
On a mountain above a lake, whose hooves nick away at rock.
  Our name   **nick:** scratch.

Is blown from tree to tree, scattered by the breeze. Who am I
  to say what,
In that marriage, is lost? For all I know, the grass has caught
  our name.   10

Having risen from moan to growl, growl to a hound's low bray,   **bray:** cry.
The voices catch. No priest, no sinner has yet been taught
  our name.

Will it thunder up, the call of time? Or lie quiet as bedrock
  beneath
Our feet? Our name our name our name our fraught,   **fraught:** tense,
  fraught name.   oppressed.

A Note on Ghazal Poems

'Ghazal' (often pronounced 'guzzle') means 'the cry of a gazelle when it is cornered by a hunter'. This Arabic form of poetry originated in the 7th century and was made up of a minimum of five couplets (two-line sections).

These short poems have an intricate rhyme scheme and every couplet ends with the same word or phrase (known as the radif). Traditionally, ghazals told stories and were sung by musicians. Popular themes included longing, love, sadness and mysticism.

In this poem, Tracy K. Smith concludes each couplet with the phrase, 'our name', referring to the identity and human rights denied to generations of African Americans.

👤 Personal Response

1. Comment briefly on the effectiveness of the imagery in the poem's opening couplet.
2. In your opinion, what does the poet mean when she says: 'History is a ship forever setting sail'?
3. How does the poem make you feel? In your opinion, is it hopeful or despondent? Briefly explain your response, using reference to the text.

'scattered by the breeze'

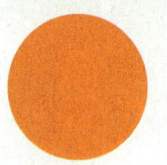

POETRY FOCUS

◉ Critical Literacy

In her 2018 collection, *Wade in the Water*, Tracy K. Smith reflects on her own racial identity. An awareness of history and her relationship to it also runs throughout the book. 'Wade in the Water' comes from an African-American spiritual which emphasises faith in God during harsh times. It also references how slaves sought to escape captivity by going into water to evade the dogs which were unleashed to hunt them down. 'Ghazal' laments the historical and current traumas that have impacted the African-American 'name'. The poet chose 'our name' as the repeated phrase at the end of each couplet, concluding with a haunting chant for the loss of what has been stolen.

The poem's **opening lines** present a dystopian scene: 'The sky is a dry pitiless white' that stretches 'into death'. Graphic images of decay suggest a future of inescapable hopelessness. This treacherous landscape is arid and lifeless, reflecting the dark parts of America's troubled past. Smith uses this **harrowing setting** to guide readers towards an understanding of the injustice of denying people their identity.

She focuses on the African-American experience, emphasising the basic human rights 'stolen' from successive generations of enslaved plantation workers: 'Like famished birds, my hands strip each stalk'. The **harsh simile highlights their suffering** in being deprived of the freedom they were due, their 'name'.

All through the poem, the long-dead voices of every individual wronged by inequality and neglect call across the centuries across a chasm of suffering. Their **anguished cries** appeal not only to the humanity of those who had none to give, but to those of us alive today who long to express our sympathy.

The despondent mood eases in **line 3** as **Smith reflects on the possibility of change**: 'History is a ship forever setting sail'. She develops the metaphor, charting the waters of the past to illuminate contemporary culture. But while the poet retains some confidence and can almost believe that all is not lost, she still sees American history as male-dominated and an abuse of privilege.

For Smith, **the truth about racism has been erased** by 'mountains of men' and 'Oceans of bone' (**line 4**). These startling images refer to the deaths of thousands of black people down through the centuries. Acutely conscious that the reality of slavery and oppression has been generally 'shredded' from history, she repeats the phrase, 'our name', including their countless individual voices and reclaiming their true story. Smith's poems witness and protest.

She brings great sensitivity to the poem, leading us deeper into other people's lives – and ultimately into our own humanity. She is a curious poet, and her inquisitive nature reflects this thoughtfulness. Smith also believes in the **power of imagination** as a way of sustaining the hope that subjugated people would eventually be free. The rhetorical question posed in lines 5–6 looks ahead to a more optimistic future for black America: 'Can you imagine what will sound from us, what we'll rend and claim'. The poet urges readers to foresee the swelling power that all excluded people have sought and fought for: their 'name'. In giving voice to the voiceless, her resolute vision is both challenging and uplifting.

Line 7 focuses on the difficulty of responding effectively to racial prejudice: 'perhaps what we seek lives outside of speech'. This is an important reminder to any human struggling with how to release emotion. During the period when this poem was written, the names of brutally murdered African Americans began to symbolise the greater injustice their deaths were part of. Those names in turn found their way into public street protests demanding change. The past is pressing up against the present. However, Smith is **realistic about the slow pace of progress**, signified in the timeless image of mountain goats 'whose hooves nick away at rock'. She is the poetic caretaker who calls for collective reckoning and collective empathy.

While being personally uncertain of a way to break the circle of injustice, Smith examines American history with an incisive, yet positive, honesty. In that portrait, she includes the images of her ancestors, those who have come before her. Although 'scattered by the breeze', there is still the possibility that 'the grass has caught our name' (line 10). Despite her abhorrence of the past and society's sins against marginalised people, **the poet's personal compassion remains intact**, even as she questions its power to change anything for the better.

The pattern of animal imagery in line 11 is evocative and resonant, bringing to mind different responses to racial oppression, from endurance to anger and ultimately to a sense of redemption: 'Having risen from moan to growl, growl to a hound's low bray'. Smith is a recorder of destructive realities. **She places herself within the collective movement in support of human rights** – where the 'voices catch'. Such unity of purpose offers the most likely reason to be guardedly hopeful – even though 'No priest, no sinner has yet been taught our name'.

History is never finished, never finite. By posing questions about social justice, the poet asks readers to become involved, to hear the 'sound' that will either 'thunder up' or 'lie quiet as bedrock'. Her concluding tone is both urgent and determined. She asks us to keep reflecting on the African-American past, 'our fraught, fraught name'. Repetition emphasises her deep-rooted sense of loss, lending poignancy to these final lines. As in so many of her most compelling poems, Smith declares her **solidarity with those who are abandoned by history** and unites herself with the voices who

TRACY K. SMITH

cry out for justice. She believes that 'we are accountable to each other'. Tracy K. Smith has commented that 'poems pull me out of my own perspective ... and challenge our assumptions of the world'.

✒ Writing About the Poem

'In her most humane poems, Tracy K. Smith shows a tremendous range that often blends disturbing reflective passages with cautious hope.' Discuss this view, with reference to 'Ghazal'.

Sample Paragraph

'Ghazal' reflects on discrimination against black people going right back to the slave trade. Tracy Smith has a conscience about the prejudice of those 'pitiless' times. She uses disturbing images of cruelty and starvation to show this – 'famished birds', 'oceans of bone'. She also asks questions about whether or not racism is ending – 'Who am I to say'. Yet Smith has not given up. She dares to dream of restoring human rights to victims of racist abuse – their good 'name' – by saying that protests are growing worldwide – 'the voices catch'. This is a more confident point of view. Her own views seem to range over the issue of racism – reflecting different attitudes. She concludes that universal human rights – 'our name' – will 'thunder up'. I think this is quietly hopeful.

> **EXAMINER'S COMMENT**
>
> *Confident top-grade response that addressed the question's three basic elements ('humane', 'reflective' and 'hope'). Some effective discussion of disturbing images and their impact. Relevant supportive reference and apt quotation throughout.*

✏ Class/Homework Exercises

1. 'Tracy K. Smith often uses effective poetic techniques, such as descriptive detail and repetition, to convey key thematic concerns in her work.' Discuss this statement, with particular reference to 'Ghazal'.
2. 'In her poem "Ghazal", Tracy K. Smith surveys African-American history with an incisively critical mind, but without resorting to bitterness or sentimentality.' To what extent do you agree with this statement? Refer to the text in your response.

◎ Points to Consider

- Perceptive and insightful consideration of racism and injustice.
- Startling images and descriptive details are evocative and resonant.
- Effective use of repetition – 'our name' reinforces the poem's central theme.
- Variety of moods and tones: open-ended conclusion.

Sample Leaving Cert Questions on Smith's Poetry

1. 'Smith makes effective use of language to address universal themes of love, loss and identity.' To what extent do you agree with this statement? Develop your answer with reference to the poetry of Tracy K. Smith on your course.
2. 'In presenting an evocative voice for victims of racism and injustice, Smith makes compelling connections between the current state of American culture and its history.' To what extent do you agree with this view? Develop your answer with reference to the poetry of Tracy K. Smith on your course.
3. Discuss how Smith effectively uses a variety of characters, often in dramatic settings, to probe both personal issues and wider public concerns in her poems. Develop your response with reference to the poetry of Tracy K. Smith on your course.

Understanding the Prescribed Poetry Question

Marks are awarded using the PCLM Marking Scheme:
P = 15; C = 15; L = 15; M = 5
Total = 50

- **P** (Purpose = 15 marks) refers to the set question and is the launch pad for the answer. This involves engaging with all of the question. Both theme and language must be addressed, although not necessarily equally.
- **C** (Coherence = 15 marks) refers to the organisation of the developed response and the use of accurate, relevant quotation. Paragraphing is essential.
- **L** (Language = 15 marks) refers to the student's skill in controlling language throughout the answer.
- **M** (Mechanics = 5 marks) refers to spelling and grammar.
- Although no specific number of poems is required, students usually discuss at least 3 or 4 in their written responses.
- Aim for at least 800 words, to be completed within 45–50 minutes.

How do I organise my answer?

(Sample question 1)

'Smith makes effective use of language to address universal themes of love, loss and identity.' To what extent do you agree with this statement? Develop your answer with reference to the poetry of Tracy K. Smith on your course.

Sample Plan 1

Intro: (*Stance: agree with viewpoint in the question*) Smith's poetry is distinguished by her position as witness and recorder. Universal themes include first love, loss of loved ones and self-identity. Varied settings, clever contrasts, interesting use of poetic structure, resonant sound effects and repetition create a powerful examination of this subject matter.

Point 1: (*Loss/racism – poetic structure and aural imagery*) 'Ghazal' repeats key words to emphasise the African-American experience of loss of identity and human rights. Onomatopoeic animal sounds capture the rising confidence of oppressed people. Hopeful conclusion reclaims identity.

POETRY FOCUS

> **NOTE**
>
> In keeping with the PCLM approach, the student has to take a stance by agreeing, disagreeing or partially agreeing that Smith:
>
> – **makes effective use of language** (vivid imagery, striking contrasts, dramatic language, dialogue, varied settings, evocative sound effects, rhetorical questions, direct address to reader, open-ended conclusions, range of moods and tones, etc.)
>
> ... to address:
>
> – **universal themes of love, loss and identity** (love of parents/community, loss of loved ones, choices, transition to adulthood, sense of self, awareness of recurring racism and injustice, mysteries of human existence, fascination with the cycle of life and death, etc.)

Point 2: *(Lost love/unreliable memory – exotic setting/religious references)* 'Dominion over the Beasts of the Earth' uses the vivid sensuality of a Mexican setting to emphasise the heady experience of first love. Colloquial Spanish expressions bring to life the young character of Mauricio. Vivid metaphor, 'frayed thread of dreams', expresses unreliability of memory. Bittersweet confessional of lost love.

Point 3: *(Limitations of human life – clever contrast of science fiction/pop culture)* 'Don't you Wonder, Sometimes?' showcases charismatic pop icon David Bowie to explore the inevitable transcendence of earthly limitations. Mystery of space suggested by broad assonant sounds and soft sibilance, 'stars glisten like ice'. Optimistic ending urges 'Go ahead'.

Point 4: *(Loss of mother – varied settings, powerful metaphors)* 'Joy' is a tender elegy contrasting Smith's mother as carefree child and terminally ill patient. Powerful metaphors, 'The body is memory', 'The body is appetite', explore the physical body's purpose. Vivid symbol, 'a dark chamber around a chord of light' exposes a new reality. Inconclusive and challenging ending: 'What do you believe in?'

Conclusion: Smith's poetry 'speaks to life'. Her carefully crafted poems and sympathetic viewpoint provide consolation to universal concerns about love, loss and identity.

Sample Paragraph: Point 1

Tracy K. Smith's choice of the traditional form of poetry, 'Ghazal', allows her to explore the Afro-American experience. She highlights the loss of human rights and identity. The repeated phrase, 'our name', is like a mantra at the end of each stanza, leading to the heart-breaking final 'our fraught, fraught name'. Compelling animal sounds, such as 'moan', 'growl' and 'low bray', convey the rising tension of an oppressed people. We can sense the sorrow, anger and hunt for recognition. The final line's repetition leaves us in no doubt that reclamation of identity and equal rights is happening and will go on being heard.

> **EXAMINER'S COMMENT**
>
> *As part of a more developed response to the poem, this is a clearly written top-grade standard. Insightful points succinctly address the question through focusing on the poet's use of repetition and sound effects. Some good close engagement with the text and the supportive quotation is effective.*

(Sample question 3)

Discuss how Smith effectively uses a variety of characters, often in dramatic settings, to probe both personal and wider public concerns in her poems. Develop your response with reference to the poetry of Tracy K. Smith on your course.

NOTE

In keeping with the PCLM approach, the student has to explore poems of Smith's on the course that include:

- **a variety of characters, often in dramatic settings** (real people from poet's personal life, oppressed African-American communities, real and imaginary figures in futuristic and dangerous settings, cinematic scenes, pop icons from surreal fantasy, etc.)

... to probe:

- **personal issues** (identity, loss, conflicted views, search for meaning in life, etc.) **and wider public concerns in her poems** (racial injustice, use and abuse of power, etc.)

TRACY K. SMITH

Sample Plan 2

Intro: (*Stance: agree with viewpoint in the question*) Smith's poetry creates unforgettable characters in a variety of settings in order to examine personal matters of identity, first love, power and oppression.

Point 1: (*Power – film scene of rescue in Wild West setting*) 'The Searchers' explores male power and female acquiescence/identity through dramatic rescue scene of an abducted girl. Wild West setting exposes not only the dangers of the frontier but also its healing capacity.

Point 2: (*Repression – chorus of voices from aftermath of American Civil War*) 'I am 60 odd years of age' is a collage of archival fragments from pension applications of African-American soldiers. The poignant setting for those attempting to reclaim what is due to them exposes corruption of power and an extinction of identity.

Point 3: (*Young love – vibrant characters in exotic location*) 'Dominion over the Beasts of the Earth' vividly evokes a sultry Mexican setting and the experience of first love with the charismatic character of Mauricio. Male dominance and female identity are questioned.

Point 4: (*Meaning of existence – glamorous pop icon in fantasy setting*) 'Don't You Wonder, Sometimes?' presents David Bowie's mesmerising persona, Ziggy Stardust, as a channel through which to escape the sorrow of this mundane earthly world.

Conclusion: Both private issues and public concerns are explored by Smith through vivid portrayals in a wide variety of settings, including the unpredictable Wild West, the poignant aftermath of the Civil War, the heat of Mexico and the surreal world of science fiction.

Sample Paragraph: Point 1

'The Searchers', focuses on a dramatic scene of the rescue of an abducted girl by a former Confederate soldier. He is furious that the girl has survived and has adapted Comanche customs, so he 'wants to kill her'. Aggressive verbs show the patriarchal power of this angry man – 'grab', 'puts'. His old-fashioned attitude about how things should be is contrasted with the wide-open landscape which accepts everyone, 'Gave anyone the chance'. The Wild West shows us how to exist, by not being concerned with control and ownership, 'With whether it belonged to him or to him'. The poet is saying that this ex-soldier was wrong to condemn the girl for 'surviving' the landscape.

> **EXAMINER'S COMMENT**
>
> Engages quite well with a challenging question – although the 'public concerns' element could be more clearly developed. Some perceptive analysis of dramatic tension through reference to contrasts and language use, e.g. 'Aggressive verbs show the patriarchal power'. Good high-grade standard as part of a full essay response.

> **EXAM FOCUS**
> - As you may not be familiar with some of the poems referred to in the sample plans, substitute poems that you have studied closely.
> - Key points about a particular poem can be developed over more than one paragraph.
> - Paragraphs may also include cross-referencing and discussion of more than one poem.
> - Remember that there is no single 'correct' answer to poetry questions, so always be confident in expressing your own considered response.

Leaving Cert Sample Essay

Discuss how effectively, in your opinion, Tracy K. Smith uses a range of stylistic features to convey both the overwhelming compassion and deep-rooted anger in her work. Develop your response with reference to the poems by Smith on your course.

Sample Essay

1. Tracy K. Smith's poems clearly show her personal sympathy for human beings and her deep outrage at injustice both in today's world and in the past. Her powerful imagery and emotive tones really involve readers and appeal to their dislike of prejudice. She repeatedly explores universal themes, such as grief, racism and the mystery of life. Anger and compassion can sometimes be found in the same poem.

2. Smith's compassion for the forgotten truth about the African-American Civil War soldiers is central to her poem, 'I am 60 odd years of age'. Actual extracts from letters written by the black troops and their families over 160 years ago show them begging the authorities for basic pension rights due to all veterans. Italics are used to emphasise their authentic words,

which adds to the anger and compassion Smith obviously feels. Smith also uses dashes to reinforce how lacking in confidence the soldiers were, 'I am about 65 years of age –' and the chorus of voices shows Smith's compassion for these victims of racism. The tragic reality was that some of these unfortunate people were not even given a birth certificate to record that they even existed. As one soldier wrote, 'I don't know my exact age'.

3. Smith tells the story of an innocent volunteer, a 'green boy', who had been a former slave who was always happy to do 'just what I was told to do'. He became the victim of a dishonest army officer who registered the soldier as 'John Wilson' so he could cheat him out of his bounty. The young soldier's signature was just a 'mark' that could be easily forged. Smith's rage is clear in her quiet tone as she reminds us that at this time slaves were often forbidden to read or write. This clearly illustrates both her tender compassion for these soldiers and her outrage at how they were mistreated.

4. 'Ghazal' also deals with the oppression of African-Americans whose basic human rights were 'stolen' by white plantation owners. Smith details the brutal mistreatment of slaves, comparing them to 'famished birds'. This graphic image clearly emphasises the suffering of countless people who were robbed of freedom and their rights as humans, their 'name'. The poet's voice is compassionate throughout. Smith uses another disturbing image, 'oceans of bone', to describe the thousands of black people trafficked from Africa during the 1900s. Her frustration and anger is a reaction to the fact that the full truth about what happened has been 'shredded' from the history books.

5. In 'The Universe as Primal Scream', Smith clearly shows her empathy for anyone struggling to come to terms with the cycle of life and death. She feels angry at the powerlessness of ordinary people to control their own destiny. She lashes out at nature or God or whatever force 'steals' loved ones from their families in death. Her sympathy for those left grieving is seen in the homely image, 'sweep all our short lives clean'. Smith believes that humans cannot find any real answers to the mysteries of creation – either in religion or in science. She is clearly resentful that man's so-called understanding is just an illusion and that every life is cut short by 'the great wind'.

6. Smith also uses disturbing images effectively to convey her sympathy for victims of conflict. In 'Letter to a Photojournalist Going-In', she emphasises the terrible suffering that news photographers witness. Soldiers and civilians are 'blown open like curtains'. Sometimes the journalist can also be arrested and beaten, 'they throw you into a room

TRACY K. SMITH

INDICATIVE MATERIAL

- **Smith is/is not effective in using stylistic features:** (striking imagery – Western, scientific, space, pop culture, etc. – dramatic settings, metaphor, personification, contrasts, accessible language, universal themes, colloquial speech, repetition, run-through lines, unusual structures, evocative/provocative tones – ironic, dark, honest, nostalgic, questioning, hesitant, reflective, etc.)
- **to convey both compassion and anger** (empathy for oppressed people, concern for victims of violence, anger about historical racism, deep resentment of injustice, awareness of the desire for acceptance, shared understanding of the mystery of the universe and human existence, etc.)

or kick at your gut'. We are given an insight into the intense dangers some of these reporters face, 'you go to the pain'.

7. Smith's despair is also clearly seen in her description of the effects of war on local children who imitate the violence of the adult world around them. Innocent kids show off by playing war games as if violence is a good thing, 'brandishing their plastic guns with TV bravado'. But the poet has sympathy for other victims of conflict apart from those who are directly involved.

8. The letter writer in the poem worries about the effect on her personal relationship with the photojournalist. She wonders if the awful scenes he has witnessed have caused him to hide his own feelings. The trauma of war seems to be destroying their relationship, turning it onto another battleground. Once again, Smith's imagery is effective in conveying her compassion. The writer ends her letter with a dark image suggesting that the couple's future is in great danger, imagining it 'landing at my feet like a grenade'.

9. Overall, I found Smith's poetry to be very effective. Her imagery and strong tones express her feelings about issues, such as racism. She has a strong social conscience and calls out injustice and oppression in many of her poems.

(805 words)

EXAMINER'S COMMENT

Good solid response that stays focused on how stylistic features convey anger and compassion in Smith's poetry. Most discussion points are developed reasonably well, particularly on the use of imagery (paragraphs 2, 3 and 8). Good use is made of relevant supportive reference. There are slight misquotes, some weaknesses in the notelike expression and the adverb, 'clearly', is over-used.

GRADE: H1
P = 15/15
C = 13/15
L = 13/15
M = 5/5
Total = 46/50

👀 Revision Overview

'Joy'
Tender elegy for Smith's mother addressing universal themes of identity, grief, death and life's great mysteries.

'Dominion over the Beasts of the Earth'
Enlivened by the dramatic Mexican setting, this nostalgic poem reflects on the uneasy transition from childhood to adulthood.

'The Searchers' (OL)
Smith uses the John Ford Western to explore the concept of home while raising questions about memory and how we relate to past experiences.

'Letter to a Photojournalist Going-In'
Perceptive reflection on how war makes victims of many people – and not just those directly caught up in conflict.

'The Universe is a House Party'
In comparing the universe to a noisy party, Smith uses science fiction to investigate the significance of the human race.

'The Museum of Obsolescence'
The image of outer space allows Smith to explore life's meaning and imagine the possibility of human beings eventually becoming obsolete.

'Don't You Wonder, Sometimes?'
Outer space as a vast, unknowable infinity and the enduring presence of David Bowie allow the poet to articulate underlying feelings of grief.

'It's Not' (OL)
In a poem written after her father's death, Smith expresses a deep yearning to connect with his spirit while wrestling with the mystery of an afterlife.

'The Universe as Primal Scream'
Reflective poem focusing on the challenge of making sense of everyday life, loss, the universe, and human existence.

'The Greatest Personal Privation' (OL)
Smith's compelling commentary on the history of slavery in America is central to this poignant erasure poem.

'I am 60 odd years of age'
Disadvantaged African-American Civil War soldiers ask President Lincoln for due recognition and equal pension rights.

'Ghazal'
Another searing indictment exposing the historical denial of basic human rights to generations of African Americans.

💬 Last Words

'Smith is a storyteller who loves to explore how the body can respond to a lover, to family, and to history.'
Hilton Als

'A truly exceptional poet, with an eye for the arresting image.'
Paul Muldoon

'Poetry invites us to listen to other voices.'
Tracy K. Smith

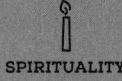 SPIRITUALITY
 LOSS
 IDENTITY
 RELATIONSHIPS
 WONDER
 HISTORY/MEMORY
 CONFLICT
 MEANING OF LIFE
INJUSTICE

TRACY K. SMITH

W. B. Yeats
1865–1939

'I have spread my dreams under your feet ...'

William Butler Yeats was born in Dublin in 1865. The son of a well-known Irish painter, John Butler Yeats, he spent much of his childhood in Co. Sligo. As a young writer, Yeats became involved with the Celtic Revival, a movement against the cultural influences of English rule in Ireland that sought to promote the spirit of our native heritage. His writing drew extensively from Irish mythology and folklore. Another great influence was the Irish revolutionary Maud Gonne, a woman as famous for her passionate nationalist politics as for her beauty. She rejected Yeats, who eventually married another woman, Georgie Hyde Lees. However, Maud Gonne remained a powerful figure in Yeats's writing. Over the years, Yeats became deeply involved in Irish politics and despite Ireland's independence from England, his work reflected a pessimism about the political situation here. He also had a lifelong interest in mysticism and the occult. Appointed a senator of the Irish Free State in 1922, he is remembered as an important cultural leader, as a major playwright (he was one of the founders of Dublin's Abbey Theatre) and as one of the greatest 20th-century poets. Yeats was awarded the Nobel Prize in 1923 and died in 1939 at the age of 73.

Investigate Further

To find out more about W. B. Yeats, or to hear readings of his poems, you could do a search of some of the useful websites available such as YouTube, BBC Poetry, poetryfoundation.org and poetryarchive.org, or access additional material on this page of your eBook.

Prescribed Poems

○ **1 'The Lake Isle of Innisfree' (OL)**
Written when Yeats lived in London and was homesick for Ireland, the poem celebrates the simple joys of nature and the search for peace. **Page 428**

○ **2 'September 1913'**
In this nostalgic poem, Yeats contrasts the disillusionment he feels about the Ireland of his own day with the romanticised past. **Page 431**

○ **3 'The Wild Swans at Coole' (OL)**
Based on the symbolism of the swans, Yeats reviews his own emotional state. He reflects on deeply personal concerns: love, ageing and the loss of poetic inspiration. **Page 435**

○ **4 'An Irish Airman Foresees His Death' (OL)**
This war poem is written as a monologue in the 'voice' of Yeats's friend, Major Robert Gregory. Its themes include heroism, nationalism and the youthful desire for excitement. **Page 439**

○ **5 'Easter, 1916'**
Yeats explores a variety of questions and issues provoked by the 1916 Rising. In re-evaluating his personal views, he struggles to balance heroic achievement with the tragic loss of life. **Page 443**

○ **6 'The Second Coming'**
The poem addresses the chaos brought about by violence and political change. Having witnessed war in Europe, Yeats feared that civilisation would break down completely. **Page 448**

○ **7 'Sailing to Byzantium'**
Yeats's wide-ranging themes (including old age, transience, death, immortality and art) are all associated with the importance of finding spiritual fulfilment. **Page 452**

○ **8 *from* 'Meditations in Time of Civil War': 'The Stare's Nest by My Window'**
Written in response to the Irish Civil War, the poem tries to balance the destruction caused by conflict with the regenerative power of nature. **Page 457**

○ **9 'In Memory of Eva Gore-Booth and Con Markiewicz'**
Yeats's tribute to the Gore-Booth sisters is a lament for lost youth and beauty. He also reflects on the decline of the Anglo-Irish Ascendancy. **Page 461**

○ **10 'Swift's Epitaph'**
In this short translation from the original Latin inscription commemorating Jonathan Swift, Yeats honours a courageous writer who also came from the Anglo-Irish tradition. **Page 465**

○ **11 'An Acre of Grass'**
Yeats refuses to grow old quietly. Instead, he takes inspiration from William Blake and Michelangelo to continue using his creative talents in search of truth. **Page 468**

○ **12 *from* 'Under Ben Bulben'**
Written shortly before his death, the poem is often seen as Yeats's last will and testament. It includes a summary of his beliefs and ends with the poet's own epitaph. **Page 471**

○ **13 'Politics'**
A short satirical poem in which Yeats rejects political activity, preferring romantic love. **Page 475**

(OL) indicates poems that are also prescribed for the Ordinary Level course.

1 The Lake Isle of Innisfree

I will arise and go now, and go to Innisfree,
And a small cabin build there, of clay and wattles made:
Nine bean-rows will I have there, a hive for the honey-bee,
And live alone in the bee-loud glade.

And I shall have some peace there, for peace comes dropping slow,   5
Dropping from the veils of the morning to where the cricket sings;
There midnight's all a glimmer, and noon a purple glow,
And evening full of the linnet's wings.

I will arise and go now, for always night and day
I hear lake water lapping with low sounds by the shore;   10
While I stand on the roadway, or on the pavements grey,
I hear it in the deep heart's core.

Innisfree: island of heather.
clay and wattles: mud and rods were used to build small houses.
midnight's all a glimmer: stars are shining very brightly in the countryside.
linnet: songbird.
lapping: gentle sounds made by water at the edge of a shore.
heart's core: essential part; the centre of the poet's being.

'lake water lapping'

W. B. YEATS

👤 Personal Response

1. This appealing poem explores the dream of escaping to find a peaceful paradise. Comment on Yeats's use of imagery to describe this ideal place.
2. What does the poem reveal to you about Yeats's own state of mind? Use reference to the text in your response.
3. The third stanza uses stirring sound effects (alliteration, broad vowel sounds, regular rhyme and rhythm) to conjure up Innisfree. Comment on one aural effect which you found interesting.

👁 Critical Literacy

'The Lake Isle of Innisfree' was written in 1890. Yeats was in London, looking in a shop window at a little toy fountain. He was feeling very homesick. He said the sound of the 'tinkle of water' reminded him of 'lake water'. He was longing to escape from the grind of everyday life and he wrote an 'old daydream of mine'.

This timeless poem has long been a favourite with exiles everywhere, as it **expresses a longing for a place of deep peace**. The poet's decision to go is unannounced in solemn biblical language, suggesting a carefully thought-out choice. Then the poet describes the idyllic life of self-sufficiency: 'Nine bean-rows' and 'a hive for the honey-bee'. These details give the poem a timeless quality as the poet lives 'alone in the bee-loud glade'.

Stanza two describes Innisfree so vividly that the future tense of 'I will arise' slips gently into the present tense: 'There midnight's all a glimmer'. Repetition ('peace', 'dropping') lulls readers into this tranquil place. Beautiful imagery brings us through the day, from the gentle white mists of the morning that lie like carelessly thrown veils over the lake to the blazing purple of the heather under the midday sun. The starry night, which can only be seen in the clear skies of the countryside, is vividly described as 'midnight's all a glimmer', with slender vowel sounds suggesting the sharp light of the stars. The soft 'l', 'm' and 'p' sounds in this stanza create a gentle and magical mood.

The third stanza repeats the opening, giving the air of a solemn ritual taking place. The **verbal music** in this stanza is striking, as the broad vowel sounds slow down the line 'I hear lake water lapping with low sounds by the shore', emphasising peace and tranquility. Notice how the alliteration of 'l' and the assonance of 'o' recreate the serenity of the scene. The only **contemporary detail** in the poem is 'pavements grey', suggesting the relentless concrete of the city. The exile's awareness of what he loves is eloquently expressed as he declares he hears the sound 'in the deep heart's core'. The monosyllabic ending drums home his deep longing for this place. The harmony of this peaceful island is reinforced by the regularity of the end rhyme (abab) and the four even beats in every fourth line.

✒ Writing About the Poem

'W. B. Yeats writes dramatic poetry that addresses the human desire for harmony and fulfilment.' Discuss this statement with reference to 'The Lake Isle of Innisfree'.

Sample Paragraph

'The Lake Isle of Innisfree', depicts a tranquil refuge from modern living. A dramatic opening, 'I will arise and go now, and go to Innisfree', declares his intention in a tone heightened by the repetition of the single syllable verb. In this idyllic place, time stands still. The steady end-rhyme ('Innisfree', 'honey-bee') and broad vowel sounds ('alone in the bee-loud glade') convey an alluring vision of tranquillity. The hypnotic description suggests quietness. The alliteration and assonance ('lake water lapping with low sounds by the shore') enables us to experience this calm atmosphere, even though Yeats is stranded on the 'pavements grey'. The poet's dream is universal, because we all long for peace. In the end, Yeats succeeds in instilling this vision 'in the deep heart's core'.

> **EXAMINER'S COMMENT**
> This is a focused top-grade response that addresses the question effectively and shows good engagement with the poem. Ideas are considered closely, clearly expressed and aptly supported by accurate quotes. The sustained focus on sound effects is particularly impressive. Language use throughout is well controlled, with phrases such as 'intensely hypnotic' conveying the poet's dramatic style.

✏ Class/Homework Exercises

1. 'Yeats is a perceptive and subtle poet, both in terms of his universal themes and his lyrical style'. Discuss this view with reference to 'The Lake Isle of Innisfree'.
2. 'Yeats's poems are often defined by a tension between the real world in which the poet lives and an ideal world that he imagines.' Discuss this view with reference to 'The Lake Isle of Innisfree'.

⊙ Points to Consider

- Poetic vision of longing and desire for utopian escape.
- Formal opening and repetition give the sense of a solemn ritual.
- Romantic details and sensual images place the poem out of time while concrete description produces a realistic experience for the reader.
- Verbal music (assonance, alliteration, onomatopoeia) heightens the reader's involvement.
- Traditional rhyming structure and the steady beats of the concluding line of each quatrain add a sense of stability and security.

2 September 1913

What need you, being come to sense,
But fumble in a greasy till
And add the halfpence to the pence
And prayer to shivering prayer, until
You have dried the marrow from the bone? 5
For men were born to pray and save:
Romantic Ireland's dead and gone,
It's with O'Leary in the grave.

Yet they were of a different kind,
The names that stilled your childish play, 10
They have gone about the world like wind,
But little time had they to pray
For whom the hangman's rope was spun,
And what, God help us, could they save?
Romantic Ireland's dead and gone, 15
It's with O'Leary in the grave.

Was it for this the wild geese spread
The grey wing upon every tide;
For this that all that blood was shed,
For this Edward Fitzgerald died, 20
And Robert Emmet and Wolfe Tone,
All that delirium of the brave?
Romantic Ireland's dead and gone,
It's with O'Leary in the grave.

Yet could we turn the years again, 25
And call those exiles as they were
In all their loneliness and pain,
You'd cry, 'Some woman's yellow hair
Has maddened every mother's son':
They weighed so lightly what they gave. 30
But let them be, they're dead and gone,
They're with O'Leary in the grave.

you: merchants and business people.

O'Leary: John O'Leary, Fenian leader, one of Yeats's heroes.

they: the selfless Irish patriots.

the wild geese: Irish independence soldiers forced into exile in Europe after 1690.

Edward Fitzgerald: 18th-century Irish aristocrat and revolutionary.
Robert Emmet and Wolfe Tone: Irish rebel leaders. Emmet was hanged in 1803. Tone died by suicide in prison after being sentenced to death in 1798.

'Romantic Ireland's dead and gone'

Personal Response

1. Comment on the effectiveness of the images used in the first five lines of the poem.
2. How would you describe the tone of this poem? Is it bitter, sad, ironic, angry, etc.? Refer closely to the text in your answer.
3. In the final stanza, Yeats changes the refrain, cautioning the middle class not to judge the heroes. Why, in your opinion, does Yeats offer this warning? Support your views with reference to the poem.

Critical Literacy

'September 1913' is typical of Yeats's hard-hitting political poems. Both the content and tone are harsh as the poet airs his views on public issues, contrasting the idealism of Ireland's heroic past with a materialistic, uncultured present.

This poem is set against two events which **exposed anti-culturalism** and grasping commercialism in contemporary Ireland. Dublin Corporation refused to house paintings donated by Hugh Lane to the Irish people; and 1913 was the year of a general strike and lockout of the workers in Dublin who mostly lived in poverty in run-down tenements.

The first stanza begins with a derisive **attack on a materialistic society** that Yeats sees as being both greedy and hypocritical. Ireland's middle classes are preoccupied with making money and with slavish religious devotion. The rhetorical opening is sharply sarcastic, as the poet depicts the petty, penny-pinching shopkeepers who 'fumble in a greasy till'. Yeats's tone is as angry as it is ironic: 'For men were born to pray and save'. Images of the dried bone and 'shivering prayer' are equally forceful – the poor are exploited by ruthless employers and a domineering Church. This disturbing picture leads the poet to regret the loss of 'Romantic Ireland' in the concluding refrain.

Stanza two develops the contrast between past and present as Yeats considers the **heroism and generosity of an earlier era**. Ireland's patriots – 'names that stilled' earlier generations of children – could hardly have been more unlike the present middle class. Yeats clearly relates to the self-sacrifice of idealistic Irish freedom fighters: 'And what, God help us, could they save?' These contemptuous words echo the fearful prayers referred to at the start of the poem. The heroes of the past were so selfless that they did not even concern themselves with saving their own lives.

The wistful and nostalgic tone of stanza three is evident in the rhetorical question about all those Irish soldiers who had been exiled in the late 17th century. Yeats's high regard for these men is evoked by comparing them to

'wild geese', a wistful metaphor reflecting their nobility. Yet the poet's admiration for past idealism is diminished by the fact that **such heroic dedication was all for nothing**. The repetition of 'for this' hammers home Yeats's contempt for the pious materialists of his own imperfect age. In listing a roll of honour, he singles out the most impressive patriots of his own class, the Anglo-Irish Ascendancy. For the poet, Fitzgerald, Emmet and Tone are among the most admirable Irishmen. In using the phrase 'All that delirium of the brave', Yeats suggests that their passionate dedication to Irish freedom bordered on a frenzied or misplaced sense of daring in the eyes of the materialists.

This romanticised appreciation continues into the final stanza, where the poet imagines the 'loneliness and pain' of the heroic dead. His empathy towards them is underpinned by an **even more vicious portrayal of the new middle class**. He argues that the establishment figures of his own time would be unable to comprehend anything about the passionate values and dreams of 'Romantic Ireland'. At best, they would be confused by the ludicrous self-sacrifice of the past. At worst, the present generation would accuse the patriots of being insane or of trying to impress friends or lovers. Perhaps Yeats is illustrating the cynical thinking of his time, when many politicians courted national popularity. 'Some woman's yellow hair' might well refer to the traditional symbol of Ireland as a beautiful woman.

The poet's disgust on behalf of the patriots is rounded off in the last two lines: 'But let them be, they're dead and gone'. The refrain has been changed slightly, adding further emphasis and a **sense of finality**. After reading this savage satire, we are left with a deep sense of Yeats's bitter disillusionment towards his contemporaries. The extreme feelings expressed in the poem offer a dispirited vision of an unworthy country. Some critics have accused Yeats of over-romanticising the past. Whether or not this is true, the poem challenges us to examine the present values of modern Ireland, our understanding of Irish history and the meaning of heroism.

Writing About the Poem

'W. B. Yeats often makes uses of contrasting images of self-interest and selflessness to communicate powerful feelings.' Discuss this statement in relation to 'September 1913'.

Sample Paragraph

Contrast plays a central role in 'September 1913'. The poem's angry opening lines are aimed at the merchants who 'fumble in a greasy till'. Their behaviour is reflected by vivid imagery. These individuals exploit ordinary people and could not be more unlike the Irish patriots –

'names that stilled your childish play'. Yeats also uses the beautiful image of the wild geese spreading 'the grey wing upon every tide' to describe the flight of Irish soldiers who refused to accept colonial rule. The imagery is taken from the world of nature and makes us aware of Yeats's high opinion of those heroes. The poet's feeling is evident in his violent description of the materialistic society of his own time – especially those who have 'dried the marrow from the bone'. Stark contrasts carry the argument throughout the poem and leave a deep impression on readers.

> **EXAMINER'S COMMENT**
>
> Well-focused on how the poet's imagery patterns convey deeply felt views. This top-grade response is also effectively supported by suitable reference and accurate quotation. Informed discussion covers a range of contrasting images (such as greed, natural beauty and violence). There is evidence throughout of close interaction with the poem. Expression is controlled, and the paragraph is rounded off with a succinct concluding sentence.

✒ Class/Homework Exercises

1. 'W. B. Yeats manages to create a series of powerfully compelling moods throughout "September 1913".' Discuss this statement with reference to both the subject matter and style of the poem.
2. 'Yeats frequently addresses political themes in poems that are filled with tension and drama.' Discuss this view with reference to 'September 1913'.

⊙ Points to Consider

- **Central contrast between the materialistic present and the romanticised past.**
- **The heroic patriots were idealistic, unlike the self-serving middle classes of 1913.**
- **Various tones: disillusionment, irony, admiration, resignation.**
- **Effective use of repetition, vivid imagery, colloquial language.**
- **Refrain emphasises Yeats's deep sense of disenchantment with Ireland's cynical establishment.**

3 The Wild Swans at Coole

W. B. YEATS

The trees are in their autumn beauty,
The woodland paths are dry,
Under the October twilight the water
Mirrors a still sky;
Upon the brimming water among the stones   5
Are nine-and-fifty swans.

The nineteenth autumn has come upon me
Since I first made my count;
I saw, before I had well finished,
All suddenly mount   10
And scatter wheeling in great broken rings
Upon their clamorous wings.

I have looked upon those brilliant creatures,
And now my heart is sore.
All's changed since I, hearing at twilight,   15
The first time on this shore,
The bell-beat of their wings above my head,
Trod with a lighter tread.

Unwearied still, lover by lover,
They paddle in the cold   20
Companionable streams or climb the air;
Their hearts have not grown old;
Passion or conquest, wander where they will,
Attend upon them still.

But now they drift on the still water,   25
Mysterious, beautiful;
Among what rushes will they build,
By what lake's edge or pool
Delight men's eyes when I awake some day
To find they have flown away?   30

brimming: filled to the very top or edge.

clamorous: loud, confused noise.

Trod ... tread: walked lightly; carefree.

lover by lover: swans mate for life; this highlights Yeats's loneliness.

Companionable: friendly.

Attend upon them still: waits on them yet.

'The bell-beat of their wings'

👤 Personal Response

1. Why do you think the poet chose the season of autumn as his setting? What changes occur at this time of year? Where are these referred to in the poem?
2. In your opinion, what are the main contrasts between the swans and the poet? Describe two, using close reference to the text.
3. What do you think the final stanza means? Consider the phrase 'I awake'. What does the poet awake from?

👁 Critical Literacy

'The Wild Swans at Coole' was written in 1916. Yeats loved spending time in the West of Ireland, especially at Coole, the home of Lady Gregory, his friend and patron. He was 51 when he wrote this poem, which contrasts the swans' beauty and apparent immortality with Yeats's ageing, mortal self.

The poem opens with a tranquil, serene scene of **autumnal beauty** in the park of Lady Gregory's home in Galway. This romantic image is described in great detail: the 'woodland paths are dry'. It is evening, 'October twilight'. The water is 'brimming'. The swans are carefully counted, 'nine-and-fifty'. The use of the soft letters 'l', 'm' and 's' emphasise the calm of the scene in stanza one.

In stanza two, the poem moves to the personal as he recalls that it is nineteen years since he first counted the swans. The word 'count' links the two stanzas. The poet's counting is interrupted as these mysterious creatures all suddenly rise into the sky. Run-through lines suggest the flowing movement of the rising swans. Strong verbs ('mount', 'scatter') reinforce this natural action. The great beating wings of the swans are captured in the onomatopoeic 'clamorous wings'. They are independent and refuse to be restrained. The ring is a symbol of eternity. The swans are making the same patterns as they have always made; they are unchanging.

Stanza two is linked to stanza three by the phrases 'I saw' and 'I have looked'. Now the poet tells us his 'heart is sore'. He has taken stock and is **dissatisfied with his emotional situation**. He is fifty-one, alone and unmarried and concerned that his poetic powers are lessening: '**All's changed**'. All humans want things to remain as they are, but life is full of change. He has lost the great love of his life, the beautiful Irish activist Maud Gonne. He also laments the loss of his youth, when he 'Trod with a lighter tread'. Nineteen years earlier, he was much more carefree. The noise of the beating wings of the swans is effectively captured in the compound word 'bell-beat'. The alliterative 'b' reinforces the steady, flapping sound. The poet is using his intense personal experiences to express universal truths.

The swans in stanza four are **symbols of eternity**, ageless, 'Unwearied still'. They are united, 'lover by lover'. They experience life together ('Companionable streams'), not on their own, like the poet. He envies them their defiance of time: 'Their hearts have not grown old'. They do what they want, when they want. They are full of 'Passion or conquest'. By contrast, he is indirectly telling us, he feels old and worn out. The **spiral imagery** of the 'great broken rings' is reminiscent of the spirals seen in ancient carvings representing eternity. Yeats believed there was a cyclical pattern behind all things. The swans can live in two elements, water and air, thus linking these elements together. They are living, vital, immortal, unlike their surroundings. The trees are yellowing ('autumn beauty') and the dry 'woodland paths' suggest the lack of creative force which the poet is experiencing. Yeats is heartbroken and weary. Only the swans transcend time.

Stanza five explores a **philosophy of life**, linked to the previous stanza by the repetition of 'still'. The swans have returned to the water, 'Mysterious, beautiful'. The poem ends on a speculative note as the poet asks where they will 'Delight men's eyes'. Is he referring to the fact that **they will continue to be a source of pleasure to someone else** long after he is dead? The swans appear immortal, a continuing source of happiness as they practise their patterns, whereas the poet is not able to continue improving his own writing, as he is mortal. The poet is slipping into the cruel season of winter while the swans infinitely 'drift on the still water'.

✒ Writing About the Poem

'W. B. Yeats makes effective use of rich, dramatic symbols to address themes of transience and mortality.' Discuss this view with reference to 'The Wild Swans at Coole'.

Sample Paragraph

Two contrasting symbols are used in 'The Wild Swans at Coole'. The swans represent youthful passion while autumn symbolises the sadness of ageing. Yeats is presenting the view that life is fragile. The swans epitomise unchanging nature. The poet's confession, 'my heart is sore', engages the reader in accepting the profound truth that humanity cannot conquer time. Unlike the poet, the swans 'drift on the still water', but they are not subject to time's powers. Yeats is connected to the decay of autumn, 'October twilight' where 'woodland paths are dry', all of which signify advancing age. In considering these symbols, Yeats is led to ask a penetrating question about the transience of beauty and creative energy, 'when I awake some day/ To find

EXAMINER'S COMMENT

A perceptive top-grade response to the question. Informed discussion based on the poet's awareness of key symbols (the swans and the natural world). Effective supporting reference and accurate quotations throughout. Expression is also very good ('accepting the profound truth', 'penetrating question') and the paragraph is rounded off with an impressive personal comment.

they have flown away? 'I particularly liked the final rhyme which trails off into the distance – just like the 'brilliant creatures'.

Class/Homework Exercises

1. 'W. B. Yeats frequently uses personal aspects of his own life to evocatively explore universal truths.' Discuss this view with reference to 'The Wild Swans at Coole'.
2. 'Yeats often draws on the beauty and stillness of the natural world to convey a deep sense of loss.' Discuss this statement with reference to 'The Wild Swans at Coole'.

Points to Consider

- Intense personal meditation on the search for lasting beauty in a transient world.
- Sad tone reflects concerns about ageing, romantic rejection, political upheaval, fading creativity.
- Slow rhythm conveys the poet's meditative mood.
- Vivid visual descriptive details portray places and creatures.
- Dynamic verbs, compound words and onomatopoeia capture the energy of the swans.
- Use of contrast highlights the gap between mortality and eternity.
- Poem ends on an optimistic note.

4 An Irish Airman Foresees His Death

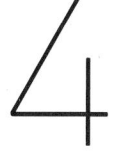

Title: the Irish airman in this poem is Major Robert Gregory (1881–1918), son of Yeats's close friend Lady Gregory. He was shot down and killed while on service in northern Italy.

W. B. YEATS

I know that I shall meet my fate
Somewhere among the clouds above;
Those that I fight I do not hate,
Those that I guard I do not love;
My country is Kiltartan Cross,   5
My countrymen Kiltartan's poor,
No likely end could bring them loss
Or leave them happier than before.
Nor law, nor duty bade me fight,
Nor public men, nor cheering crowds,   10
A lonely impulse of delight
Drove to this tumult in the clouds;
I balanced all, brought all to mind,
The years to come seemed waste of breath,
A waste of breath the years behind   15
In balance with this life, this death.

Those that I fight: the Germans.
Those that I guard: Allied countries, such as England and France.
Kiltartan: townland near the Gregory estate in Co. Galway.
likely end: outcome.

tumult: turmoil; confusion.

'I balanced all'

👤 Personal Response

1. 'This poem is not just an elegy or lament in memory of the dead airman. It is also an insight into the excitement of warfare.' Write your response to this statement, using close reference to the text.
2. Repetition is used throughout the poem. Does it suggest Gregory's boredom with everyday life? Or his unstoppable drive for adventure? Refer closely to the poem in your response.
3. In your opinion, what is the central or dominant mood in the poem? Refer to the text in your answer.

👁 Critical Literacy

Thousands of Irishmen fought and died in the British armed forces during World War I. Robert Gregory was killed in Italy at the age of 37. The airman's death had a lasting effect on Yeats, who wrote several poems about him.

Is it right to assume anything about young men who fight for their country? Why do they enlist? Do they always know what they are fighting for? In this poem, Yeats expresses what he believes is the airman's viewpoint as he comes face to face with death. This **fatalistic attitude** is established in the emphatic opening line. The poem's title also leads us to believe that the speaker has an intuitive sense that his death is about to happen. But despite this premonition, he seems strangely resigned to risking his life.

In lines 3-4, he makes it clear that he neither hates his German enemies nor loves the British and their allies. His thoughts are with the people he knows best back in Kiltartan, Co. Galway. Major Gregory recognises the irony of their detachment from the war. The ordinary people of his homeland are unlikely to be affected at all by whatever happens on the killing fields of mainland Europe. Does he feel that he is abandoning his fellow countrymen? What is the dominant tone of lines 7–8? Is there an underlying bitterness?

In line 9, the speaker takes time to reflect on why he joined the air force and immediately dismisses the obvious reasons of conscription ('law') or patriotism ('duty'). As a volunteer, Gregory is more openly cynical of the 'public men' and 'cheering crowds' he mentions in line 10. Like many in the military who have experienced the realities of warfare, **he is suspicious of hollow patriotism** and has no time for political leaders and popular adulation. So why did Robert Gregory choose to endanger his life by going to war? The answer lies in the key comments 'A lonely impulse of delight' (line 11) and 'I balanced all' (line 13). The first phrase is paradoxical. The airman experiences not just the excitement, but also the isolation of flying. At the same time, his 'impulse' to enlist as a fighter pilot reflects both his **desire for adventure** as well as his regret.

The last four lines explain the real reason behind his decision. It was neither rash nor emotional, but simply a question of balance. Having examined his life closely, Gregory has chosen the heroism of a self-sacrificing death. It is as though he only feels truly alive during the 'tumult' of battle. Yeats's language is particularly evocative at this point. Awesome air battles are effectively echoed in such dynamic phrasing as 'impulse of delight' and 'tumult in the clouds'. This **sense of freedom and power** is repeatedly contrasted with the dreary and predictable security of life away from the war – dismissed out of hand as a 'waste of breath'. From the airman's perspective, as a man of action, dying in battle is in keeping with 'this life' that he has chosen. Such a death would be his final adventurous exploit.

Some commentators have criticised Yeats's poem for glorifying war and pointless risk-taking. Others have suggested that the poet successfully highlights Anglo-Irish attitudes, neither exclusively Irish nor English. The poet certainly raises interesting questions about national identity and ways of thinking about war. However, in writing an elegy for Robert Gregory, he emphasises the **airman's daring solitude**. Perhaps this same thrill lies at the heart of other important choices in life, including the creative activity of artists. Is there a sense that the poet and the pilot are alike, both of them taking calculated risks in what they do?

Writing About the Poem

'Some of Yeats's most poignant poems have a tragic vision, a sense that life is meaningless and has to be endured.' Discuss this view, with particular reference to 'An Irish Airman Foresees His Death'.

Sample Paragraph

The title suggests tragedy. However, the 'Irish Airman' is courageous in the face of danger. Although the word 'fate' suggests an inevitable destiny, the poem is dominated by a mood of resignation. The calm tone – 'I know that I shall meet my fate' – and slow rhythm is like a chant or a prayer. While the pilot is realistic about his chances in war, he seems to have distanced himself from everything. He admits the truth about his passion for adventure – 'A lonely impulse of delight' – and this might signify that he views life as beyond his control. The ending is pessimistic, and he repeats the phrase 'waste of breath' to emphasise the absurdity of life. Overall, the speaker is caught between realism and pessimism. The subtle concluding line sums this up – 'In balance with this life, this death' – and leaves a sense of his tragic dilemma.

EXAMINER'S COMMENT

An insightful, focused response to the question. Perceptive discussion engages with the airman's fatalistic attitude. Apt, accurate quotations are integrated effectively into the commentary. Expression is well controlled and vocabulary is also impressive ('inevitable destiny', 'sheer absurdity of life', 'subtle concluding line'). A solid, top-grade standard.

✒ Class/Homework Exercises

1. 'W. B. Yeats's evocative poems can raise interesting questions about national identity.' Discuss this statement with reference to 'An Irish Airman Foresees His Death'.
2. 'Yeats's most compelling poetry often explores fatalistic themes.' Discuss this view with reference to 'An Irish Airman Foresees His Death'.

⊙ Points to Consider

- Yeats adopts the persona of Major Robert Gregory, who died in 1918.
- Dramatic monologue form engages the sympathy of readers.
- Contrasting attitudes and tones: passion, detachment, resignation, courage, joy, loneliness.
- Effective use of repetition, rhyme and contrast.

5 Easter, 1916

W. B. YEATS

Title: on 24 April 1916, Easter Monday, about 700 Irish Republicans took over several key buildings in Dublin. These included the Four Courts, Bolands Mills, the Royal College of Surgeons and the General Post Office. The rebellion lasted six days and was followed by the execution of its leaders. The Rising was a pivotal event in modern Irish history.
them: the rebels involved in the Rising.

I have met them at close of day
Coming with vivid faces
From counter or desk among grey
Eighteenth-century houses.
I have passed with a nod of the head   5
Or polite meaningless words,
Or have lingered awhile and said
Polite meaningless words,
And thought before I had done
Of a mocking tale or a gibe   10
To please a companion
Around the fire at the club,
Being certain that they and I
But lived where motley is worn:
All changed, changed utterly: 15
A terrible beauty is born.

That woman's days were spent
In ignorant good-will,
Her nights in argument
Until her voice grew shrill.   20
What voice more sweet than hers
When, young and beautiful,
She rode to harriers?
This man had kept a school
And rode our wingèd horse;   25
This other his helper and friend
Was coming into his force;
He might have won fame in the end,
So sensitive his nature seemed,
So daring and sweet his thought.   30
This other man I had dreamed
A drunken, vainglorious lout.
He had done most bitter wrong
To some who are near my heart,
Yet I number him in the song;   35
He, too, has resigned his part
In the casual comedy;
He, too, has been changed in his turn,
Transformed utterly:
A terrible beauty is born.   40

motley: ridiculous clothing.

That woman: Countess Markievicz, friend of Yeats and a committed nationalist.

This man: Padraig Pearse, poet and teacher, was shot as a leader of the Rising.
wingèd horse: Pegasus, the mythical white horse that flies across the sky, was a symbol of poetic inspiration.
This other: Thomas MacDonagh, writer and teacher, executed in 1916.

This other man: Major John MacBride was also executed for his part in the rebellion. He was the husband of Maud Gonne.
most bitter wrong: there were recurring rumours that MacBride had mistreated Maud Gonne.

Hearts with one purpose alone
Through summer and winter seem
Enchanted to a stone
To trouble the living stream.
The horse that comes from the road,   45
The rider, the birds that range
From cloud to tumbling cloud,
Minute by minute they change;
A shadow of cloud on the stream
Changes minute by minute;   50
A horse-hoof slides on the brim,
And a horse plashes within it;
The long-legged moor-hens dive,
And hens to moor-cocks call;
Minute by minute they live: 55
The stone's in the midst of all.

Too long a sacrifice
Can make a stone of the heart.
O when may it suffice?
That is Heaven's part, our part   60
To murmur name upon name,
As a mother names her child
When sleep at last has come
On limbs that had run wild.
What is it but nightfall?   65
No, no, not night but death;
Was it needless death after all?
For England may keep faith
For all that is done and said.
We know their dream; enough   70
To know they dreamed and are dead;
And what if excess of love
Bewildered them till they died?
I write it out in a verse –
MacDonagh and MacBride   75
And Connolly and Pearse
Now and in time to be,
Wherever green is worn,
Are changed, changed utterly:
A terrible beauty is born.   80

needless death: Yeats asks if the Rising was a waste of life, since the British were already considering independence for Ireland.

Connolly: trade union leader and revolutionary, executed in 1916.

W. B. YEATS

👤 Personal Response

1. Describe the atmosphere in the opening stanza of the poem. Refer closely to the text in your answer.
2. 'Easter, 1916' has many striking images. Choose two that you find particularly interesting and briefly explain their effectiveness.
3. On balance, does Yeats approve or disapprove of the Easter Rising? Refer to the text in your answer.

👁 Critical Literacy

Yeats, who was in London at the time of the Rising, had mixed feelings about what had happened. He was clearly fascinated but also troubled by this heroic and yet in some ways pointless sacrifice. He did not publish the poem until 1920.

In the opening stanza, Yeats recalls how he used to meet some of the people who were later involved in the Easter Rising. He was unimpressed by their 'vivid faces' and he remembers routinely dismissing them with 'Polite meaningless words'. His admission that he **misjudged these insignificant Republicans** as subjects for 'a mocking tale or a gibe' among his clever friends is a reminder of his derisive attitude in 'September 1913'. Before 1916, Yeats had considered Ireland a ridiculous place, a circus 'where motley is worn'. But the poet confesses that the Rising transformed everything – including his own condescending apathy. In the stanza's final lines, Yeats introduces what becomes an ambivalent refrain ending in 'A terrible beauty is born'.

This sense of shock and the need to completely re-evaluate his views is developed in stanza two. The poet singles out individual martyrs killed or imprisoned for their activities, among them his close friend Countess Markievicz. He also mentions Major John MacBride, husband of Maud Gonne, who had refused Yeats's proposal of marriage. Although he had always considered MacBride little more

'changed utterly'

445

POETRY FOCUS

than a 'drunken, vainglorious lout', Yeats now acknowledges that he too has been distinguished by his bravery and heroism. The poet wonders about the usefulness of all the passion that sparked the rebels to make such a bold move, but his emphasis is on the fact that **the people as well as the whole atmosphere have changed**. Even MacBride, whom he held in utter contempt, has grown in stature.

In stanza three, Yeats takes powerful images from nature and uses them to explore the meaning of Irish heroism. The metaphor of the stubborn stone in the stream might represent the defiance of the revolutionaries towards all the forces around them. **The poet evokes the constant energy and dynamism of the natural world**, focusing on the changes that happen 'minute by minute'. Image after dazzling image conjure up a vivid picture of unpredictable movement and seasonal regeneration (as 'hens to moor-cocks call') and skies change 'From cloud to tumbling cloud'. For the poet, the Rising presented many contradictions, as he weighs the success of the revolt against the shocking costs. In contrasting the inflexibility of the revolutionaries with the 'living stream', he **indicates a reluctant admiration for the rebels' dedication**. Does Yeats suggest that the rebels risked the loss of their own humanity, allowing their hearts to harden to stone? Or is he also thinking of Maud Gonne and blaming her cold-hearted rejection of him on her fanatical political views?

In the final stanza, the poet returns to the metaphor of the unmoving stone in a flowing stream to warn of the dangers of fanaticism. The rhetorical questions about the significance of the rebellion reveal his **continuing struggle to understand** what happened. Then he asks the single most important question about the Rising: 'Was it needless death after all', particularly as 'England may keep faith' and allow Ireland its independence, all of which would prompt a more disturbing conclusion, i.e. that the insurgents died in vain.

Yeats quickly abandons essentially unanswerable questions about the value of the Irish struggle for freedom. Instead, he simply pays tribute to the fallen patriots by naming them tenderly, 'As a mother names her child'. The final assertive lines commemorate the 1916 leaders in dramatic style. Setting aside his earlier ambivalence, Yeats acknowledges that these patriots died for their dreams. The hushed tone is reverential, almost sacred. The rebels have been transformed into martyrs who will be remembered for their selfless heroism 'Wherever green is worn'. The insistent final refrain has a stirring and increasingly disquieting quality. The poem's central paradox, 'A terrible beauty is born', concludes that **all the heroic achievements of the 1916 Rising were at the tragic expense of human life**.

✒ Writing About the Poem

'W. B. Yeats's public poetry responds to particular situations in terms that can often seem unclear and contradictory.' Discuss this view with reference to both the subject matter and style of 'Easter, 1916'.

Sample Paragraph

Yeats admired, yet was troubled by the 1916 Rising. The sound of the resonating refrain, 'All changed, changed utterly', adds a solemn note. Yet Yeats also honestly debates the wisdom of the uprising, asking 'Was it needless death after all?' The image of the heart as a stone reflects the poet's own torn emotions because it not only suggests the fierce determination of those rebels involved, but also underlines the inflexibility of their thinking. The poem concludes with a list of the rebel leaders and the realisation that the implacable stone in the midst of the 'living stream' does change the flow. These famous Irish names had changed history. The paradoxical statement, 'A terrible beauty is born', reflects the poet's admiration of the rebels' sacrifice and also his shocked reaction to the events they unleashed.

> **EXAMINER'S COMMENT**
> A focused, top-grade response that addresses the question directly. The commentary throughout shows a very good understanding of Yeats's divided views. Points are aptly supported with accurate quotation. Some perceptive discussion regarding the poet's use of the stone symbol to illustrate his appreciation of how the 1916 Rising had changed Irish history. Expression ('resonating', 'inflexibility', 'implacable') is also impressive.

✐ Class/Homework Exercises

1. 'W. B. Yeats explores complex political themes in richly energetic language.' Discuss this statement with reference to 'Easter, 1916'.
2. 'Yeats honestly reflects on change and immortality in his dynamic, lyrical poetry.' Discuss this view with reference to 'Easter, 1916'.

⊙ Points to Consider

- Deeply felt elegy commemorating a controversial historical event.
- Effective contrast of formal structure with colloquial language.
- Ambivalent attitudes of admiration and shock.
- Formal rhyme scheme, rhythmic phrases, economy of language.
- Symbolism, repetition, antithesis and paradox all convey the poet's contradictory views.
- Thrilling refrain resonates with the consequence of change.

6 The Second Coming

Turning and turning in the widening gyre
The falcon cannot hear the falconer;
Things fall apart; the centre cannot hold;
Mere anarchy is loosed upon the world,
The blood-dimmed tide is loosed, and everywhere   5
The ceremony of innocence is drowned;
The best lack all conviction, while the worst
Are full of passionate intensity.

Surely some revelation is at hand;
Surely the Second Coming is at hand.   10
The Second Coming! Hardly are those words out
When a vast image out of *Spiritus Mundi*
Troubles my sight: somewhere in sands of the desert
A shape with lion body and the head of a man,
A gaze blank and pitiless as the sun,   15
Is moving its slow thighs, while all about it
Reel shadows of the indignant desert birds.
The darkness drops again; but now I know
That twenty centuries of stony sleep
Were vexed to nightmare by a rocking cradle,   20
And what rough beast, its hour come round at last,
Slouches towards Bethlehem to be born?

Title: a reference to the Bible. It is from Matthew and speaks of Christ's return to reward the good.

in the widening gyre: Yeats regarded a cycle of history as a gyre. He visualised these cycles as interconnecting cones that moved in a circular motion, widening outwards until they could not widen any further, then a new gyre or cone formed from the centre of the circle created. This spun in the opposite direction to the original cone. The Christian era was coming to a close and a new, disturbed time was coming into view. In summary, the gyre is a symbol of constant change.
falcon: a bird of prey, trained to hunt by the aristocracy.
falconer: the trainer of the falcon. If the bird flies too far away, it cannot be directed.
Mere: nothing more than; only.
anarchy: lack of government or order. Yeats believed that bloodshed and a worship of bloodshed were the end of an historical era.
blood-dimmed: made dark with blood.
Spiritus Mundi: Spirit of the World, the collective soul of the world.
lion body and the head of a man: famous statue in Egypt; an enigmatic person.
desert birds: birds of prey.
twenty centuries: Yeats believed that two thousand years was the length of a period in history.
vexed: annoyed; distressed.
rocking cradle: coming of the infant Jesus.
rough beast: the Antichrist.
Bethlehem: birthplace of Christ. It is usually associated with peace and innocence, and it is terrifying that the beast is going to be born there. The spiral has reversed its spinning. A savage god is coming.

'lion body and the head of a man'

👤 Personal Response

1. In your opinion, what is the central mood in the opening stanza? Anxiety? Confusion? Fear? Support your views with reference to the text.
2. Yeats uses symbols to express some of his most profound ideas. What symbols in this poem appeal to you? Use reference to the text in your response.
3. 'Yeats is yearning for order, and fearing anarchy.' Discuss two ways in which the poem illustrates this statement. Support your answer with reference to the text.

👁 Critical Literacy

'The Second Coming' is a terrifying, apocalyptic poem written in January 1919 against a background of the disintegration of three great European empires at the end of World War I and the catastrophic War of Independence in Ireland. These were bloody times. Yeats yearned for order and feared anarchy.

Sparked off by both disgust at what was happening in Europe as well as his interest in the occult, Yeats explores, in stanza one, what he perceives to be the failure at the heart of society: 'Things fall apart'. In his opinion, **the whole world was disintegrating** into a bloody, chaotic mess. This break-up of civilisation is described in metaphorical language. For Yeats, the 'gyre' is a symbol representing an era. He believed that contrary expanding and contracting forces influence people and cultures and that the Christian era was nearing its end. The failure of the old world order is conveyed through hunting imagery, 'The falcon cannot hear the falconer'. We have lost touch with Christ, just as the falcon loses touch with the falconer as he swings into ever-increasing circles. This bird was trained to fly in circles to catch its prey. The circular imagery, with the repetitive '-ing', describes the continuous, swirling movement. Civilisation is also 'Turning and turning in the widening gyre' as it buckles and fragments.

The **tension** is reflected in a list of contrasts: 'centre' and 'fall apart', 'falcon' and 'falconer', 'lack all conviction' and 'intensity', 'innocence' and 'anarchy'. The strain is too much: 'the centre cannot hold'. The verbs also graphically describe this chaotic world: 'Turning and turning', 'loosed', 'drowned', 'fall apart'. Humans are changing amidst the chaos: 'innocence is drowned'. **Anarchy** is described in terms of a great tidal wave, 'the blood-dimmed tide', which sweeps everything before it. The compound word reinforces the overwhelming nature of the water. Yeats feels that the 'best', the leaders and thinkers, have no energy; they are indifferent and 'lack all conviction'. On the other hand, the 'worst', the cynics and fanatics, are consumed with hatred and violence, 'full of passionate intensity'.

Disillusioned, Yeats thinks **a new order has to be emerging**. He imagines a Second Coming. He repeats the word 'Surely' in a tone of both belief and fear in stanza two. The Second Coming is usually thought of as a time when Christ will return to reward the good, but the image Yeats presents us with is terrifying. **A blank, pitiless creature emerges.** It is straight from the Book of Revelations: 'And I saw a beast rising out of the sea'. This was regarded as a sign that the end of the world was near. Such an unnatural hybrid of human and animal is the Antichrist, the opposite force of the gentle infant Jesus who signalled the beginning of the end of the pagan era. The 'gaze blank' suggests its lack of intelligence. The phrase 'pitiless as the sun' tells us the creature has no empathy or compassion. It 'Slouches'. It is a brutish, graceless monstrosity.

The **hostile environment** is a nightmare scenario of blazing desert sun, shifting sands and circling predatory birds. The verbs suggest everything is out of focus: 'Reel', 'rocking', 'Slouches'. 'The darkness drops again' shows how disorder, disconnectedness and the 'widening gyre' have brought us to nihilism. This seems to be a prophetic statement, as fascism was to sweep the world in the mid-20th century. Then Yeats has a moment of epiphany: 'but now I know'. Other eras have been destroyed before. The baby in the 'rocking cradle' created an upheaval that resulted in the end of 'twenty centuries of stony sleep'.

Yeats believed that a **cycle of history** lasted two thousand years in a single evolution of birth, growth, decline and death. All change causes upheaval. The Christian era, with its qualities of innocence, order, maternal love and goodness, is at an end. The new era of the 'rough beast' is about to start. It is pitiless, destructive, violent and murderous. This new era has already begun: 'its hour come round at last'. It is a savage god who is coming, uninvited. The spiral has reversed its motion and is now spinning in the opposite direction. The lack of end rhyme mirrors a world of chaos. Yeats looks back over thousands of years. We are given a thrilling and terrifying prospect from a vast perspective of millennia.

✒ Writing About the Poem

'Yeats frequently uses powerful and disturbing imagery to express a dark vision of the future.' Discuss this view with reference to 'The Second Coming'.

Sample Paragraph

The themes of stability and chaos are central to 'The Second Coming'. From the opening line, 'Turning and turning in the widening gyre', Yeats presents the disturbing image of the falcon spinning out of control. The sense of disintegration continues and the language becomes more violent – 'The blood-dimmed tide is loosed'. Dramatic details create a dark vision of life – 'anarchy is loosed'. There is irony in the poet's prophecy of a new saviour ('The Second Coming'). Unlike the first Christian Messiah, the next one will be a 'rough beast' bringing unknown horrors – 'A shape with lion body'. Yeats believed that Christianity was about to be replaced by a world where evil would triumph. The image of the sinister beast, with its 'gaze blank and pitiless as the sun' was particularly chilling.

EXAMINER'S COMMENT

A clear, insightful response to the question. Informed points focused directly on how Yeats's imagery conveyed his pessimistic prophecy. Good choice of accurate quotations provide support throughout. Expression is impressive also: varied sentence length, wide-ranging vocabulary ('sense of disintegration') and good control of syntax. A top-grade standard.

Class/Homework Exercises

1. 'W. B. Yeats's political poems are remarkable for their forceful language and sensuous imagery.' Discuss this statement with reference to 'The Second Coming'.
2. 'Yeats often presents a dramatic tension between order and disorder.' Discuss this view with reference to 'The Second Coming'.

Points to Consider

- **The poem's title has obvious biblical associations.**
- **Scenes of anarchy and disorder lead to an apocalyptical vision of the future.**
- **Variety of tones/moods: foreboding, disillusionment, fear, despair.**
- **Effective use of contrast, dramatic imagery, symbols, striking comparisons.**

7 Sailing to Byzantium

Title: for Yeats, this voyage would be one taken to find perfection. This country only exists in the mind. It is an ideal. The original old city of Byzantium was famous as a centre of religion, art and architecture.

I

That is no country for old men. The young
In one another's arms, birds in the trees,
– Those dying generations – at their song,
The salmon-falls, the mackerel-crowded seas,
Fish, flesh, or fowl, commend all summer long   5
Whatever is begotten, born, and dies.
Caught in that sensual music all neglect
Monuments of unageing intellect.

That: Ireland – all who live there are subject to ageing, decay and death.

dying generations: opposites are linked to show that in the midst of life is death.

sensual music: the young are living life to the full through their senses and are neglecting the inner spiritual life of the soul.

II

An aged man is but a paltry thing,
A tattered coat upon a stick, unless   10
Soul clap its hands and sing, and louder sing
For every tatter in its mortal dress,
Nor is there singing school but studying
Monuments of its own magnificence;
And therefore I have sailed the seas and come   15
To the holy city of Byzantium.

paltry thing: worthless, of no importance. Old age is not valued in Ireland.
tattered coat: an old man is as worthless as a scarecrow.
unless/Soul clap its hands and sing: man can only break free if he allows his spirit the freedom to express itself.
Nor is there … own magnificence: all schools of art should study the discipline they teach, while the soul should study the immortal art of previous generations.

III

O sages standing in God's holy fire
As in the gold mosaic of a wall,
Come from the holy fire, perne in a gyre,
And be the singing-masters of my soul.   20
Consume my heart away; sick with desire
And fastened to a dying animal
It knows not what it is; and gather me
Into the artifice of eternity.

O sages: wise men, cleansed by the holy fire of God.
Come … artifice of eternity: Yeats asks the sages to teach him the wonders of Byzantium and gather his soul into the perfection of art.
perne in a gyre: spinning; turning very fast.
fastened to a dying animal: the soul trapped in a decaying body.

IV

Once out of nature I shall never take   25
My bodily form from any natural thing,
But such a form as Grecian goldsmiths make
Of hammered gold and gold enamelling
To keep a drowsy Emperor awake;
Or set upon a golden bough to sing   30
To lords and ladies of Byzantium
Of what is past, or passing, or to come.

past, or passing, or to come: in eternity, the golden bird sings of transience (passing time).

'the holy city of Byzantium'

👤 Personal Response

1. This poem tries to offer a form of escape from old age. Does it succeed? Write a paragraph in response, with support from the text.
2. Why are the 'Monuments of unageing intellect' of such importance to the poet? What does this imply about Yeats's Ireland?
3. The poem is defiant in its exploration of eternity. Discuss, using reference or quotation.

👁 Critical Literacy

'Sailing to Byzantium' confronts the universal issue of old age. There is no easy solution to this problem. Yeats found the idea of advancing age repulsive and he longed to escape. Here he imagines an ideal place, Byzantium, which allowed all to enjoy eternal works of art. He celebrates what humanity can create and he bitterly condemns the mortality to which man is subject.

POETRY FOCUS

Yeats wrote, 'When Irishmen were illuminating the Book of Kells … Byzantium was the centre of European civilization … so I symbolise the search for the spiritual life by a journey to that city.'

The poet declares the theme in the first stanza as he confidently declaims that the world of the senses is not for the old – they must seek another way which is timeless, **a life of the spirit and intellect**. The word 'That' tells us he is looking back, as he has already started his journey. But he is looking back wistfully at the world of the lovers ('The young/In one another's arms') and the world of teeming nature ('The salmon-falls, the mackerel-crowded seas'). The compound words emphasise the dynamism and fertility of the life of the senses, even though he admits the flaw in this wonderful life of plenty is mortality ('Those dying generations'). The life of the senses and nature is governed by the harsh cycle of procreation, life and death.

The poet asserts in the second stanza that **what gives meaning to a person is the soul**, 'unless/Soul clap its hands and sing'. Otherwise an elderly man is worthless, 'a paltry thing'. We are given a chilling image of the thin, wasting frame of an old man as a scarecrow in tattered clothes. In contrast, we are shown the wonders of the intellect as the poet tells us that all schools of art study what they compose, what they produce – 'Monuments of unageing intellect'. These works of art are timeless; unlike the body, they are not subject to decay. Thus, music schools study great music and art schools study great paintings. The life of the intellect and spirit must take priority over the life of the senses. Yeats will no longer listen to the 'sensual music' that is appropriate only for the young, but will study the carefully composed 'music' of classic art.

In Byzantium, the buildings had beautiful mosaics, pictures made with little tiles and inlaid with gold. One of these had a picture of martyrs being burned. Yeats addresses these wise men ('sages') in stanza three. He wants them to whirl through time ('perne in a gyre') and come to **teach his soul how to 'sing'**, how to live the life of the spirit. His soul craves this ('sick with desire'), **but it is trapped in the decaying, mortal body** ('fastened to a dying animal'). This is a horrendous image of old age. The soul has lost its identity: 'It knows not what it is'.

He pleads to be saved from this using two interesting verbs, 'Consume' and 'gather'. Both suggest a desire to be taken away. A fire consumes what is put into it and changes the form of the substance. Yeats wants a new body. He pleads to be embraced like a child coming home: 'gather me'. But where will he go? He will journey into the cold world of art, 'the artifice of eternity'. 'Artifice' refers to the skill of those who have created the greatest works of art, but it also means artificial, not real. Is the poet suggesting that eternity also has a flaw?

The **fourth stanza** starts confidently as Yeats declares that 'Once out of nature', he will be transformed into the ageless perfect work of art, the **golden bird**. This is the new body for his soul. Now he will sing to the court. But is the court listening? The word 'drowsy' suggests not. Isn't he singing about transience, the passing of time: 'what is past, or passing, or to come'? Has this any relevance in eternity? Is there a perfect solution to the dilemma of old age?

Yeats raises these questions for our consideration. He has explored this problem by contrasting the abundant life of the young with the 'tattered coat' of old age. He has shown us the golden bird of immortality in opposition to the 'dying animal' of the decaying body. The poet has lulled us with end-rhymes and half-rhymes. He has used groups of threes – 'Fish, flesh, or fowl', 'begotten, born, and dies', 'past, or passing, or to come' – to argue his case. At the end of the poem, do we feel that Yeats genuinely longs for the warm, teeming life of the senses with all its imperfections, rather than the cold, disinterested world of the 'artifice of eternity'?

Writing About the Poem

'W. B. Yeats frequently uses vigorous language to denounce transience and old age.' Discuss this view with reference to 'Sailing to Byzantium'.

Sample Paragraph

In 'Sailing to Byzantium', Yeats confronts old age. A grotesque image of an old man as a scarecrow, 'A tattered coat upon a stick', is presented. The figure is unable to move, graphically illustrating age. The vivid adjective 'tattered' suggests the physical wear and tear elderly people endure. Yeats longed to escape this fate, through a passionate appeal to the 'sages' to 'Consume my heart away'. Thinking of time's decay, he is 'sick with desire' just as in his poem, 'The Wild Swans at Coole' – 'And now my heart is sore'. So Yeats decides to shed the 'dying animal' of his ageing body and change into a golden bird, a precious, immortal work of art. Ironically, the bird's function is reduced to keeping a 'drowsy Emperor awake' while, like the scarecrow, it is 'set upon a golden bough'. I feel that it is the allure of 'The young/In one another's arms' that Yeats really craves. His rich dynamic description of youth is achieved through compound words ('salmon-falls') and alliteration, 'Fish, flesh, fowl'. He longs to be young again.

EXAMINER'S COMMENT

A successful top-grade response that focuses on both aspects of the question. Points are developed and aptly illustrated with accurate quotation. Impressive discussion regarding the poet's robust, vigorous style ('graphically illustrating', 'passionate appeal', 'rich dynamic description'). Some insightful personal response and cross-referencing show close engagement with Yeats's poems. Expression throughout is very well controlled.

✒ Class/Homework Exercises

1. 'Yeats's search for truth serves to highlight the intense fury and disillusionment expressed in his poetry.' Discuss this view with reference to 'Sailing to Byzantium'.
2. 'W. B. Yeats makes effective use of imagery and symbolism to communicate thought-provoking insights about life.' Discuss this statement with reference to 'Sailing to Byzantium'.

⊙ Points to Consider

- **Central themes include transience, old age and the timeless world of art.**
- **Rich symbols, metaphors, imagery and similes communicate the complexity of humans' struggle with transience and decay.**
- **Balance, contrast and paradox reveal the complexity of the problem of old age.**
- **Compound words, onomatopoeia, intriguing use of verbs lend energy and passion to the argument.**

8 *from* Meditations in Time of Civil War: The Stare's Nest by My Window

The bees build in the crevices
Of loosening masonry, and there
The mother birds bring grubs and flies.
My wall is loosening; honey-bees,
Come build in the empty house of the stare.   5

We are closed in, and the key is turned
On our uncertainty; somewhere
A man is killed, or a house burned,
Yet no clear fact to be discerned:
Come build in the empty house of the stare.   10

A barricade of stone or of wood;
Some fourteen days of civil war;
Last night they trundled down the road
That dead young soldier in his blood:
Come build in the empty house of the stare.   15

We had fed the heart on fantasies,
The heart's grown brutal from the fare;
More substance in our enmities
Than in our love; O honey-bees,
Come build in the empty house of the stare.   20

Title: stare is another name for the starling, a bird with distinctive dark brown or greenish-black feathers.

grubs: larvae of insects.

civil war: the Irish Civil War (1922–1923) between Republicans, who fought for full independence, and supporters of the Anglo-Irish Treaty.
trundled: rolled.

fare: diet (of dreams).

enmities: disputes; hatred.

'days of civil war'

POETRY FOCUS

👤 Personal Response

1. Comment on how Yeats creates an atmosphere of concern and insecurity in stanzas two and three.
2. In your opinion, how effective is the symbol of the bees as a civilising force amid all the destruction of war? Support your answer with close reference to the poem.
3. How would you describe the dominant mood of the poem? Is it positive or negative? Refer closely to the text in your answer.

👁 Critical Literacy

The Irish Civil War prompted Yeats to consider the brutality and insecurity caused by conflict. It also made him reflect on his own identity as part of the Anglo-Irish Ascendancy. The poet wrote elsewhere that he had been shocked and depressed by the fighting during the first months of hostilities, yet he was determined not to grow bitter or to lose sight of the beauty of nature. He wrote this poem after seeing a stare building its nest in a hole beside his window.

Much of the poem is dominated by the images of building and collapse. Stanza one introduces this tension between creativity ('bees build') and disintegration ('loosening'). In responding to the bitter civil war, Yeats finds suitable **symbols in the nurturing natural world** to express his own hopes. Addressing the bees, he asks that they 'build in the empty house of the stare'. He is desperately conscious of the political vacuum presently being filled by bloodshed. His desperate cry for help seems heartfelt in tone. There is also a possibility that the poet is addressing himself – he will have to revise his own attitudes to the changing political realities caused by the war.

In stanza two, Yeats expresses a sense of being **threatened by the conflict** around him: 'We are closed in'. The use of the plural pronoun suggests a community under siege. He is fearful of the future: 'our uncertainty'. Is the poet reflecting on the threat to his own immediate household or to the once-powerful Anglo-Irish ruling class? The constant rumours of everyday violence are highlighted in the stark descriptions: 'A man is killed, or a house burned'. Such occurrences seem almost routine in the grim reality of war.

Stanza three opens with a **haunting image**, the 'barricade of stone', an enduring symbol of division and hostility. The vehemence and inhumanity of the times is driven home by the stark report of soldiers who 'trundled down the road' and left one 'dead young soldier in his blood'. Such atrocities add greater depth to the plaintive refrain for regeneration: 'Come build in the empty house of the stare'.

In the final stanza, Yeats faces up to the root causes of war: 'We had fed the heart on fantasies'. Dreams of achieving independence have led to even greater hatred ('enmities') and intransigence than could have been imagined. It is a tragic irony that the Irish nation has become more divided than ever before. The poet seems despairing as he accepts the failure represented by civil conflict: 'The heart's grown brutal'. It is as though he is reprimanding himself for daring to imagine a brave new world. His **final plea for healing** and reconstruction is strengthened by an emphatic 'O' to show Yeats's depth of feeling: 'O honey-bees,/Come build in the empty house of the stare'.

✒ Writing About the Poem

'Yeats's poetic vision is one of darkness and disappointment, balanced by moments of insight and optimism.' Discuss this view with reference to 'The Stare's Nest by My Window' *from* 'Meditations in Time of Civil War'.

Sample Paragraph

In 'The Stare's Nest by My Window', Yeats reveals his views on the Irish Civil War. Throughout the poem, there are recurring images of destruction. Observing the bees outside his window, he is surprised to see something purposeful going on within the 'loosening masonry'. Although the crumbling building suggests the break-up of the Irish nation, there is also an ironic recognition of something new happening. This is typical of the poet's ambivalent attitude – similar to his view of Easter 1916 as a 'terrible beauty'. The positive image of the bees is symbolic of recovery from the conflict. The poet's use of symbolism contrasts the two forces of devastation and regeneration when he urges the bees to 'build in the empty house'. However, there are several dark images that show the poet's realism, e.g. the 'house burned' and the tragic life of the 'young soldier in his blood'. These are stark reminders of human loss – the reality of conflict. But in the end, Yeats seems to argue that we can learn from nature. He hopes that just as the birds take care of their young, Ireland will recover from warfare.

EXAMINER'S COMMENT

A well-written top-grade response. Informed discussion focused throughout on the balance between Yeats's positive and negative attitudes. Accurate quotations provided good support. Cross-referencing shows engagement with the poet's complex views. Expression throughout is very well controlled ('recurring images', 'ironic recognition', 'stark reminders of human loss').

Class/Homework Exercises

1. 'W. B. Yeats often uses startling language and imagery to raise key questions about Irish nationalism.' Discuss this statement, referring both to the subject matter and style of 'The Stare's Nest by My Window'.
2. 'Yeats's poems frequently address serious issues in a fresh and accessible style.' Discuss this view with reference to 'The Stare's Nest by My Window'.

Points to Consider

- Another of Yeats's political poems expressing his personal views on Irish history.
- Central themes: Civil War violence and destruction; the natural world.
- Effective use of repetition, varying tones (dismay, hopelessness, acceptance, yearning).
- Contrasting images of destruction ('loosening masonry') and renewal ('bees build').

9 In Memory of Eva Gore-Booth and Con Markiewicz

W. B. YEATS

The light of evening, Lissadell,
Great windows open to the south,
Two girls in silk kimonos, both
Beautiful, one a gazelle.
But a raving autumn shears   5
Blossom from the summer's wreath;
The older is condemned to death,
Pardoned, drags out lonely years
Conspiring among the ignorant.
I know not what the younger dreams –   10
Some vague Utopia – and she seems,
When withered old and skeleton-gaunt,
An image of such politics.
Many a time I think to seek
One or the other out and speak   15
Of that old Georgian mansion, mix
Pictures of the mind, recall
That table and the talk of youth,
Two girls in silk kimonos, both
Beautiful, one a gazelle.   20

Dear shadows, now you know it all,
All the folly of a fight
With a common wrong or right.
The innocent and the beautiful
Have no enemy but time;   25
Arise and bid me strike a match
And strike another till time catch;
Should the conflagration climb,
Run till all the sages know.
We the great gazebo built,   30
They convicted us of guilt;
Bid me strike a match and blow.

Lissadell: the Gore-Booth family home in Co. Sligo.
kimonos: traditional Japanese robes.
gazelle: graceful antelope.
shears: cuts.

Conspiring: plotting; scheming.

Utopia: a perfect world.

folly: foolishness.

conflagration: blazing inferno.
sages: philosophers.
gazebo: ornamental summer house, sometimes seen as a sign of extravagance.

'that old Georgian mansion'

👤 Personal Response

1. What mood does Yeats create in the first four lines of the poem? Explain how he achieves this mood.
2. Would you agree that this is a poem of contrasts? How does Yeats use contrasts to express his thoughts and feelings? Support your points with relevant reference.
3. What picture of Yeats himself emerges from this poem? Use close reference to the text to support the points you make.

👁 Critical Literacy

Yeats wrote this poem about the two Gore-Booth sisters shortly after their deaths. He was 62 at the time. Eva was a noted campaigner for women's rights and Constance was a revolutionary who took part in the 1916 Rising. She later became the first woman elected to the British House of Commons at Westminster. The poet had once been fascinated by their youthful grace and beauty, but he became increasingly opposed to their political activism. Although the poem is a memorial to the two women, it also reveals Yeats's own views about the changes that had occurred in Ireland over his lifetime.

Stanza one begins on a nostalgic note, with Yeats recalling a magical summer's evening in the company of the Gore-Booth sisters. The details he remembers suggest a **world of elegance and privilege** in the girls' family home, Lissadell House, overlooking Sligo Bay. 'Great windows' are a reminder of the grandeur to be found in the Anglo-Irish 'Big House'. Eva and Constance are portrayed as being delicately beautiful, their elusive femininity indicated by the exotic 'silk kimonos' they wear. The poet compares one of the girls to 'a gazelle', stylishly poised and graceful.

The abrupt contrast of mood in line 5 disrupts the tranquil scene. Yeats considers the harsh effects of time and how it changes everything. He describes autumn (personified as an overenthusiastic gardener) as 'raving' and uncontrollable. The metaphor illustrates the way **time destroys** ('shears') the simple perfection of youth ('Blossom'). Typically, Yeats chooses images from the natural world to express his own retrospective outlook.

In lines 7–13, the poet shows his **deep contempt** for the involvement of both the Gore-Booth sisters in revolutionary politics. As far as Yeats is concerned, their activism 'among the ignorant' was a great mistake. These beautiful young women wasted their lives for a 'vague Utopia'. The graphic image of one of the girls growing 'withered old and skeleton-gaunt' is also used to symbolise the unattractive political developments of the era. Repulsed by the idea, Yeats retreats into the more sophisticated world of Lissadell's 'old Georgian mansion'.

The second stanza is in marked contrast to the first. Yeats addresses the spirits ('shadows') of Eva and Constance. The tone of voice is unclear. It appears to be compassionate, but there is an undertone of weariness as well. He goes on to scold the two women for wasting their lives on 'folly'. Yeats seems angry that their innocence and beauty have been sacrificed for nothing. It is as though he feels **they have betrayed both their own femininity and their social class**. If they had only known it, their one and only enemy was time.

In the final lines of the poem, Yeats dramatises his feelings by turning all his **resentment against time** itself. He associates the failed lives of the women with the decay of the Anglo-Irish Ascendancy. The energetic rhythm and repetition reflect his fury as he imagines striking match after match ('And strike another till time catch') and is consumed in a great 'conflagration'. The poet imagines that the significance of this inferno will eventually be understood by those who are wise, the 'sages'. In the last sentence, Yeats considers how 'They' (the enemies of the Anglo-Irish Ascendancy) hastened the end of a grand cultural era in Ireland. The 'great gazebo' is a symbol of the fine houses and gracious living that were slowly disappearing. The poem ends on a defiant note ('Bid me strike a match and blow'), with Yeats inviting the ghosts of Eva and Constance to help him resist the devastating effects of time.

✒ Writing About the Poem

'Many of Yeats's most evocative poems lament the loss of youth and beauty.' Discuss this view with reference to 'In Memory of Eva Gore-Booth and Con Markiewicz'.

Sample Paragraph

'In Memory of Eva Gore-Booth and Con Markiewicz' is largely focused on time as a destructive force. Yeats begins by describing the aristocratic sisters as 'Two girls in silk kimonos', the gentle sibilant sounds suggesting their elegance. The poem is really an elegy for the past and Yeats's nostalgic portrayal of the time he shared with the young women at Lissadell is filled with regret. The tone becomes more wistful as he remembers summer evenings 'and the talk of youth'. Yeats illustrates the effects of age when he contrasts the girls in their graceful refinement in their later years – 'withered old and skeleton-gaunt'. The image is startling, evidence of how he views the ravages of time. It is all the more shocking when compared with the delicate kimonos – symbols of lost beauty.

EXAMINER'S COMMENT

A well-focused top-grade standard which directly addresses the question. Good discussion of the poem's mood of regret ('nostalgic portrayal', 'tone becomes more wistful'). Excellent use of contrasting images to illustrate the poet's theme. The references and quotes are carefully chosen and show clear engagement with the poem. Expression is also impressive.

Class/Homework Exercises

1. 'W. B. Yeats makes effective use of contrasting moods and atmospheres to express his strongly held ideas and heartfelt feelings.' Discuss this statement with reference to 'In Memory of Eva Gore-Booth and Con Markiewicz'.
2. 'Yeats frequently combines both a sensitive romantic nature and a fiercely critical voice.' Discuss this view with reference to both to the subject matter and style of 'In Memory of Eva Gore-Booth and Con Markiewicz'.

Points to Consider

- Elegy for a lost world of great beauty, style and sophistication.
- The poem reveals Yeats's own attitudes to the two sisters.
- Life's transience sharply contrasted with the longevity of art.
- Various tones: nostalgic, reflective, scornful, critical.
- Striking imagery of light and shade and seasonal change.

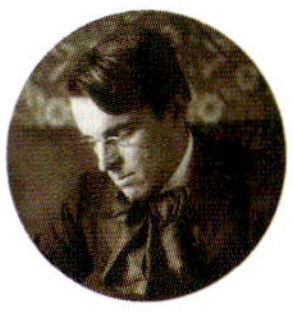

10 Swift's Epitaph

Swift has sailed into his rest;
Savage indignation there
Cannot lacerate his breast.
Imitate him if you dare,
World-besotted traveller; he
Served human liberty.

Title: Jonathan Swift, satirist and clergyman, author of *Gulliver's Travels* and dean of St Patrick's Cathedral. The original inscription in Latin is on his memorial in the cathedral. Yeats liked to spend time there.
Epitaph: inscription for a tomb or memorial.

his rest: suggestion of afterlife; death is not an end.
Savage indignation: the driving force of Swift's satirical work. He believed in a society where wrong was punished and good rewarded.
lacerate: cut; tear.
World-besotted: obsessed with travelling or with material concerns rather than spiritual matters.
he/Served human liberty: Yeats believed Swift served the liberty of the intellect, not liberty for the common people. Yeats associated democracy with organised mobs of ignorant people.

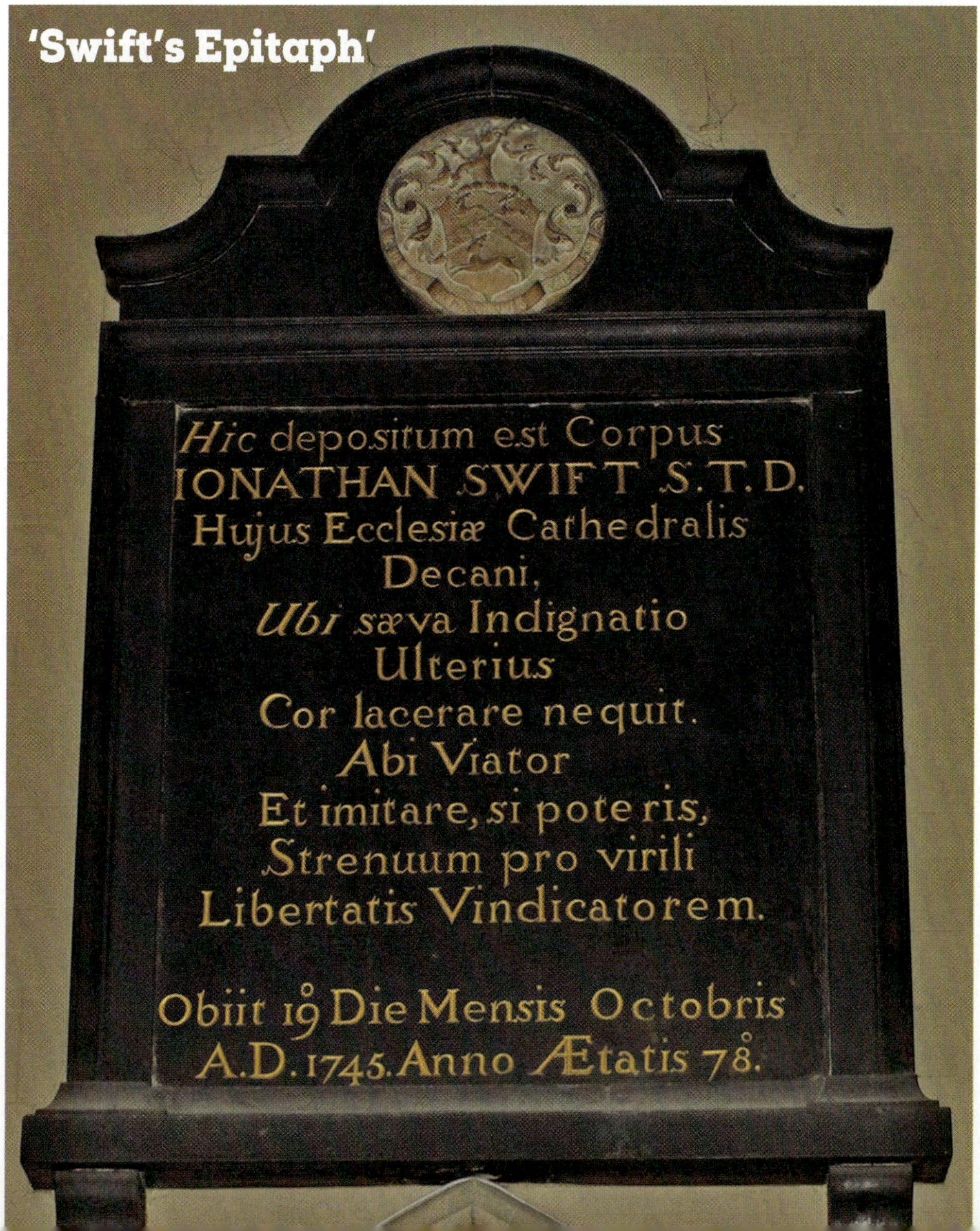

👤 Personal Response

1. How would you describe the tone of this poem?
2. Comment on the poet's use of the verb 'lacerate'. What do you think Yeats is trying to convey?

👁 Critical Literacy

'Swift's Epitaph' is a translation from the original Latin epitaph composed by Swift for himself. Yeats adds a new first line to the original. He regarded this epitaph as the 'greatest … in history'.

W. B. Yeats admired Swift, who was proud and solitary and belonged to the Anglo-Irish tradition, as did Yeats himself. He regarded the Anglo-Irish as superior. He once said, 'We have created most of the modern literature of this country. We have created the best of its political intelligence.' Yeats's additional first line to the epitaph conveys a dignified sailing into the spiritual afterlife by the deceased Swift. The rest of the poem is a **translation** from the Latin original. Swift is now free from all the negative reactions he was subjected to when alive: 'Savage indignation there/Cannot lacerate his breast.' Swift's self-portrait conveys the impression of a man of fierce **independence and pride**. 'Imitate him if you dare' is the challenge thrown down like a gauntlet to the reader to try to be like him. 'World-besotted traveller' can be read as a man who has travelled extensively in his imagination as well as in reality. His contribution to humanity is summed up in the final sentence: 'he/Served human liberty'. **He freed the artist** from the masses so that the artist could 'make liberty visible'. The tone of this short, compressed poem is proud and defiant, like Swift.

✒ Writing About the Poem

'W. B. Yeats frequently confronts the painful reality of death in fierce, challenging poetry.' Discuss this view with particular reference to 'Swift's Epitaph'.

Sample Paragraph

Yeats wrote two epitaphs – his own in 'Under Ben Bulben' and this translation of Swift's. Both show a disregard for life as a permanent end in itself. Yeats reveals a fearless, confident Swift departing this life for the next in the sibilant line, 'Swift has sailed into his rest'. The metaphor highlights the natural progression of the soul returning to its eternal rest. Death is a reality of life's circle. Swift's 'Savage indignation' was directed at the two great evils of society, starvation and emigration. But 'there', in paradise, he is able to leave aside his life's work and all the criticism he received. The verb 'lacerate' suggests the public backlash he suffered as a result. Yeats challenges readers, asking if we are brave enough to stand up (like Swift) for what is right, 'Imitate him if you dare'.

EXAMINER'S COMMENT

A top-grade response that shows good engagement with Yeats's poetry. This focused paragraph examines the poet's philosophy in some detail – and particularly his belief that what matters is the legacy an individual leaves behind after death. Several excellent discussion points are effectively supported with suitable quotation and there is fluent control of language throughout.

✒ Class/Homework Exercises

1. 'Yeats uses dramatic and forceful language to express his passionate views on ageing and the passing of time.' Discuss this statement with reference to 'Swift's Epitaph'.
2. 'W. B. Yeats often chooses confrontation when exploring universal themes in thought-provoking poetry.' Discuss this view with reference to 'Swift's Epitaph'.

⊙ Points to Consider

- The satirist Jonathan Swift made a strong impact on Yeats's imagination.
- Sibilant metaphor of sailing suggests the ease of passage from this life to the next.
- Emphatic language highlights Swift's efforts to improve the human condition and the resulting response.
- Poem offers a direct provocative challenge to readers.

11 An Acre of Grass

Picture and book remain,
An acre of green grass
For air and exercise,
Now strength and body goes;
Midnight, an old house   5
Where nothing stirs but a mouse.

My temptation is quiet.
Here at life's end
Neither loose imagination,
Nor the mill of the mind   10
Consuming its rag and bone,
Can make the truth known.

Grant me an old man's frenzy,
Myself must I remake
Till I am Timon and Lear   15
Or that William Blake
Who beat upon the wall
Till Truth obeyed his call;

A mind Michael Angelo knew
That can pierce the clouds,   20
Or inspired by frenzy
Shake the dead in their shrouds;
Forgotten else by mankind,
An old man's eagle mind.

acre: the secluded garden of Yeats's home, where he spent his final years.

an old house: the house was in Rathfarnham, Co. Dublin.

loose imagination: vague, unfocused ideas.

frenzy: wildly excited state.

Timon and Lear: two of Shakespeare's elderly tragic heroes, both of whom raged against the world.
William Blake: English visionary poet and painter (1757–1827).

Michael Angelo: Michelangelo, Italian Renaissance artist (1475–1564).

shrouds: burial garments.

'An acre of green grass'

👤 Personal Response

1. How does Yeats create a mood of calm and serenity in the opening stanza?
2. Briefly explain the change of tone in stanza three.

👁 Critical Literacy

Written in 1936 when Yeats was 71, the poet expresses his resentment towards ageing gracefully. Instead, he will dedicate himself to seeking wisdom through frenzied creativity. People sometimes take a narrow view of the elderly and consider them completely redundant. In Yeats's case, he is determined not to let old age crush his spirit.

Stanza one paints a picture of retirement as a surrender to death. Yeats's life has been reduced to suit his basic needs. 'Picture and book' might refer to the poet's memories. Physically weak, he feels like a prisoner whose enclosed garden area is for 'air and exercise'. There is an underlying **feeling of alienation and inactivity**: 'nothing stirs'.

In stanza two, the poet says that it would be easy to give in to the stereotypical image of placid contentment: 'My temptation is quiet', especially since old age ('life's end') has weakened his creative powers. **Yeats admits that his 'loose imagination' is not as sharp as it was when he was in his prime.** He no longer finds immediate inspiration ('truth') in everyday experiences, which he compares to life's 'rag and bone'.

The third stanza opens on a much more dramatic and forceful note as the poet confronts his fears: 'Grant me an old man's frenzy'. Yeats's personal prayer is totally lacking in meekness. Instead, he urges himself to focus enthusiastically on his own creative purpose – 'frenzy'. **He pledges to 'remake' himself** in the image of such heroic figures as Timon, Lear and William Blake. The passionate tone and run-on lines add to his sense of commitment to his art.

In stanza four, Yeats develops **his spirited pursuit of meaningful old age** by reflecting on 'A mind Michael Angelo knew'. The poet is stimulated and encouraged to follow the great artist's example and 'pierce the clouds'. The image suggests the daring power of imagination to lift the spirit in the search for truth and beauty. The final lines build to a climax as Yeats imagines the joys of 'An old man's eagle mind'. Such intense creativity can 'Shake the dead' and allow the poet to continue experiencing life to its fullest.

🖋 Writing About the Poem

'W. B. Yeats uses powerful language and imagery to express his personal views.' Discuss this statement with reference to 'An Acre of Grass'.

Sample Paragraph

Yeats takes a highly unusual approach to ageing in 'An Acre of Grass'. To begin with, his subdued tone suggests that he is happy in his quiet 'acre of green grass'. Everything seems organised, yet a little too organised for his liking. In the first few lines, we see someone close to second childhood, engrossed in his 'Picture and book'. Acutely aware of his years, he resents being at 'life's end'. Clearly, he yearns for renewed energy and inspiration. His forceful language emerges in the second half of the poem when he demands 'an old man's frenzy'. His need to be creative again is illustrated by the references to Lear (the tragic king in Shakespeare's play who fought to the bitter end) and to William Blake and Michelangelo. Like them, Yeats wants to live a productive life – with an 'eagle mind'. The dramatic metaphor typifies his startling imagery. In these final lines, his tone is defiant.

EXAMINER'S COMMENT

There is some good discussion in this paragraph and a clear sense of engagement. Informed points focused on the subdued tone and irony in the early stanzas. Accurate quotations are integrated effectively into the commentary. Expression is impressive also: varied sentence length, ranging vocabulary ('yearns for renewed energy and inspiration', 'dramatic metaphor typifies his startling imagery') and good control of syntax. A top-grade standard.

✒ Class/Homework Exercises

1. 'Some of Yeats's most thought-provoking poems combine his personal concerns with public issues.' Discuss this view with reference to 'An Acre of Grass'.
2. 'Yeats uses simple and direct language in exploring his concerns about ageing and death.' Discuss this statement with reference to 'An Acre of Grass'.

⊙ Points to Consider

- **Confessional poem addresses familiar themes of old age and artistic revitalisation.**
- **Striking contrast between his initial acceptance of age and his final determination to renew himself.**
- **Effective use of imagery to show that the house has also been engulfed by old age.**
- **References to Blake, Timon of Athens and King Lear focus on Yeats's desired poetic frenzy.**

12 from Under Ben Bulben

W. B. YEATS

V

Irish poets, learn your trade,
Sing whatever is well made,
Scorn the sort now growing up
All out of shape from toe to top,
Their unremembering hearts and heads   5
Base-born products of base beds.
Sing the peasantry, and then
Hard-riding country gentlemen,
The holiness of monks, and after
Porter-drinkers' randy laughter;   10
Sing the lords and ladies gay
That were beaten into the clay
Through seven heroic centuries;
Cast your mind on other days
That we in coming days may be   15
Still the indomitable Irishry.

VI

Under bare Ben Bulben's head
In Drumcliff churchyard Yeats is laid,
An ancestor was rector there
Long years ago, a church stands near,   20
By the road an ancient cross.
No marble, no conventional phrase;
On limestone quarried near the spot
By his command these words are cut:
    Cast a cold eye   25
    On life, on death.
    Horseman, pass by!

whatever is well made: great art.

base: low; unworthy.

indomitable: invincible; unbeatable.

Under bare Ben Bulben's head: defiant symbol of the famous mountain.

ancestor: the poet's great-grandfather.

Horseman: possibly a symbolic figure from local folklore; or possibly any passer-by.

'Under bare Ben Bulben's head'

👤 Personal Response

1. Comment on the tone used by Yeats in giving advice to other writers. Refer to the text in your answer.
2. From your reading of the poem, explain the kind of 'Irishry' that Yeats wishes to see celebrated in poetry. Support the points you make with reference or quotation.
3. Describe the mood of Drumcliff churchyard as visualised by the poet. Use close reference to the text to show how Yeats uses language to create this mood.

👁 Critical Literacy

This was one of Yeats's last poems. Sections V and VI of the elegy sum up his personal views on the future of Irish poetry and also include the enigmatic epitaph he composed for his own gravestone. Using art as a gateway to spiritual fulfilment is characteristic of the poet.

Section V is a hard-hitting address by Yeats to his contemporaries and all the poets who will come after him. He encourages them to set the highest 'well-made' standards for their work. His uncompromisingly negative view of contemporary writing ('out of shape from toe to top') is quickly clarified. The reason why modern literature is in such a state of confusion is that the poets' 'unremembering hearts and heads' **have lost touch with tradition**. The formality and discipline of great classic poetry have been replaced by unstructured writing and free verse. The authoritative tone becomes even more scathing as Yeats rebukes the inferiority of his peers as 'Base-born products'.

It is not only intellectual artistic tradition that the poet admires; he finds another valuable tradition in the legends and myths of old Ireland. Yeats urges his fellow writers to 'Sing the peasantry'. But he also advises them to **absorb other cultural traditions**. Here he includes the 'Hard-riding country gentlemen' of his own Anglo-Irish class and the 'holiness of monks' – those who seek truth through ascetic or spiritual means. Even the more sensuous 'randy laughter' of 'Porter-drinkers' can be inspirational. For Yeats, the peasant and aristocratic traditions are equally worth celebrating. Irish history is marked by a combination of joy, heroism, defeat and resilience. Yet despite (or perhaps because of) his harsh criticism of the present generation, there is little doubt about the poet's passionate desire to encourage new writing that would reflect the true greatness of 'indomitable Irishry'.

Section VI is a great deal less confident. Writing in the third person, Yeats describes his final resting place in Drumcliff. The voice is **detached and dignified**. Using a series of unadorned images, he takes us to the simple churchyard at the foot of Ben Bulben. The mountain stands as a proud symbol of how our unchanging silent origins outlive human tragedy. It is to

his Irish roots that the poet ultimately wants to return. His wishes are modest but curt – 'No marble'. Keen to avoid the well-worn headstone inscriptions, Yeats provides his own incisive epitaph. The three short lines are enigmatic and balance opposing views, typical of so much of his poetry. The poet's last warning ('Cast a cold eye') reminds us to live measured lives based on a realistic understanding of the cycle of life and death. The beautiful Christian setting, subdued tone and measured rhythm all contribute to the quiet dignity of Yeats's final farewell.

Writing About the Poem

'W. B. Yeats's inspired poetry gives expression to the spirit of a whole nation through his distinctive style.' Discuss this view with reference to 'Under Ben Bulben'.

Sample Paragraph

'Under Ben Bulben' addresses themes close to Yeats's heart – the perfection of art, Irish nationalism and the reality of death. The poet's views are expressed in an imperative voice: 'Irish poets, learn your trade'. Yeats believed in traditional verse, spending hours shaping a poem. He is bitterly opposed to the free verse of contemporary poets, 'Scorn the sort now growing up/All out of shape from toe to top'. His use of enjambed lines and the inverted phrase ('toe to top') mimics the ugliness of modern poetry. He also makes being Irish something to be desired, a race, undefeated after years of oppression, 'Still the indomitable Irishry', even inventing a new word to express our unique culture. The modern poets he is addressing are urged to remember this, 'Cast your minds on other days'. Yeats's poetry practises what he preaches, presenting a 'well-made' poem with a vision of what it means to be Irish.

EXAMINER'S COMMENT

A top-grade response that explores Yeats's writing style alongside the central theme of Irishness. Points are aptly illustrated with accurate quotation. Some impressive discussion regarding the poet's critical tone in mocking aspects of contemporary poetry. Expression throughout is clear and well controlled.

Class/Homework Exercises

1. 'W. B. Yeats has remarked that his poetry is generally written out of despair.' Discuss this statement, referring to both the subject matter and style of 'Under Ben Bulben'.
2. 'Yeats's forceful language and vivid imagery convey his intense vision of life and death.' Discuss this view with reference to 'Under Ben Bulben'.

⊙ Points to Consider

- **Self-epitaph achieving his aim 'to hammer my thoughts into unity'.**
- **Formal vision of integrated spiritual reality, natural cycle of life and death.**
- **Revitalised use of traditional rhyme scheme and metered poetry (strict four-beat rhythm).**
- **Use of colloquial language. Short lines give a modern quality to the poem.**
- **Distinctive poetic voice, authoritative, compelling, direct and exhilarating.**

13 Politics

Title: winning and using power to govern society.

'In our time the destiny of man presents its meanings in political terms.'
Thomas Mann

Thomas Mann was a German novelist who argued that the future of humanity is determined by states and governments.

How can I, that girl standing there,
My attention fix
On Roman or on Russian
Or on Spanish politics?
Yet here's a travelled man that knows   5
What he talks about,
And there's a politician
That has read and thought,
And maybe what they say is true
Of war and war's alarms,   10
But O that I were young again
And held her in my arms!

On Roman or on Russian/ Or on Spanish politics: a reference to the political upheavals of Europe in the 1930s.

'O that I were young again'

POETRY FOCUS

👤 Personal Response

1. This poem suggests that politics is not important. Does the poet convince you? Write a paragraph in response, with reference to the text.
2. Where does the language used in the poem convey a sense of deep longing? Comment briefly on the effectiveness of this.

👁 Critical Literacy

'Politics' is a satire written in 1939, when Yeats was 73, in response to a magazine article. He said it was based on 'a moment of meditation'.

A **satire** uses ridicule to expose foolishness. A magazine article praised Yeats for his 'public' work. The poet was delighted with this word, as one of his aims had always been to 'move the common people'. However, the article went on to say that Yeats should have used this 'public' voice to address public issues such as politics. Yeats disagreed, as he had always regarded politics as dishonest and superficial. He thought professional politicians manipulated through 'false news'. This is evident from the ironic comment, 'And maybe what they say is true'. Here we see the poet's indifference to these matters.

This poem addresses **real truths**, the proper material for poems, the universal experience of **human relationships**, not the infinite abstractions that occupied politicians ('war and war's alarms'). Big public events, Yeats is suggesting, are not as important as love. The girl in the poem is more important than all the politics in the world: 'How can I ... My attention fix/ On Roman or on Russian/Or on Spanish politics'? So Yeats is overthrowing the epigraph at the beginning of the poem, in which the novelist Thomas Mann states that people should be concerned with political matters. Politics is the winning and using of power to govern the state. Yeats is adopting the persona of the distracted lover who is unable to focus on the tangled web of European politics in the 1930s. This poem was to be placed in his last poetry collection, almost like a farewell, as he states again that what he desires is youth and love.

But this poem can also give another view. Is the 'she' in the poem Ireland? Yeats had addressed public issues in poems such as 'Easter, 1916' and 'September 1913' and he was already a senator in the Irish government. As usual, he leaves us with questions as he draws us through this deceptively simple poem with its **ever-changing tones** that range from the questioning opening to mockery, doubt and finally longing. The **steady rhyme** (the second line rhymes with the fourth and so on) drives the poem forward to its emphatic **closing wish**, the cry of an old man who wishes to recapture his youth and lost love.

Writing About the Poem

'Yeats's final poems are particularly poignant because all that matters to him is youth and love.' Discuss this view with reference to 'Politics'.

Sample Paragraph

It's thought that 'Politics' is Yeats's last poem – and it expresses his belief in the importance of emotions over everything else. Although written in 1938 when Europe was edging towards war, the poet is unable to focus on public affairs – 'Roman or on Russian/Or on Spanish politics'. Instead, he is more interested in a beautiful girl who is nearby. His tone is tender – 'O that I were young again/ And held her in my arms'. As in 'Sailing to Byzantium', he is well aware of the impossibility of reversing time – and that is what makes the poem so moving. The exclamation 'O' is all the more touching because the poet understands how hopeless his desires are. For me, this bittersweet realisation makes 'Politics' one of Yeats's most poignant poems.

> **EXAMINER'S COMMENT**
>
> *An insightful high-grade response that engages loosely with the poem. Points are clearly focused on Yeats's reluctant acceptance that youth and love can only be memories. Good focus on the poet's mood and tone ('tender', 'touching', 'bittersweet'). The cross-reference broadens the discussion and expression is well controlled throughout.*

Class/Homework Exercises

1. 'W. B. Yeats frequently writes simple but beautiful poems that have universal significance.' Discuss this statement with reference to 'Politics'.
2. 'Despite his intense disappointment with reality, Yeats can often find hope in his imagination.' Discuss this view with reference to 'Politics'.

Points to Consider

- Central focus on the poet's nostalgia for his younger days.
- Yeats is preoccupied with private human interaction rather than public or political situations.
- The poet expresses little optimism or even interest in the future.
- Various tones: reflective, sceptical, ironic, nostalgic, resigned.
- Effective use of contrasts: intellect and emotion, age and youth, male and female.

POETRY FOCUS

Understanding the Prescribed Poetry Question

Marks are awarded using the PCLM Marking Scheme:
P = 15; C = 15; L = 15; M = 5
Total = 50

- **P** (Purpose = 15 marks) refers to the set question and is the launch pad for the answer. This involves engaging with all aspects of the question. Both theme and language must be addressed, although not necessarily equally.
- **C** (Coherence = 15 marks) refers to the organisation of the developed response and the use of accurate, relevant quotation. Paragraphing is essential.
- **L** (Language = 15 marks) refers to the student's skill in controlling language throughout the answer.
- **M** (Mechanics = 5 marks) refers to spelling and grammar.
- Although no specific number of poems is required, students usually discuss at least 3 or 4 in their written responses.
- Aim for at least 800 words, to be completed within 45–50 minutes.

NOTE

In keeping with the PCLM approach, the student has to take a stance by agreeing, disagreeing or partially agreeing with the statement:
- **Yeats's reflective poetry** (conflict, disappointment, loss, mortality, ageing, escape, perfection of art, immortality, eternity, etc.)
... is defined through:
- **the tension between idealism and reality** (contrasting imagery, compelling symbols, dramatic language, powerful rhetoric, intense paradoxes, conflicting moods and tones, etc.)

Sample Leaving Cert Questions on Yeats's Poetry

1. 'W. B. Yeats's reflective poetry is defined largely by the tension between his search for an ideal world and the failure to escape reality.' To what extent do you agree or disagree with this statement? In developing your answer, discuss both the themes and poetic language of the poetry of W. B. Yeats on your course.
2. 'Yeats's poetry can sometimes seem obscure and challenging, but his powerful language has enduring appeal.' Discuss this view, developing your answer with reference to both the themes and poetic style of the poetry of W. B. Yeats on your course.
3. From your study of the poetry of W. B. Yeats on your course, select the poems that, in your opinion, best demonstrate his effective use of rich symbolism and vivid imagery to explore a range of poetic themes. Justify your response, developing your answer with reference to the poetry of W. B. Yeats on your course.

How do I organise my answer?

(Sample question 1)

'W. B. Yeats's reflective poetry is defined largely by the tension between his search for an ideal world and the failure to escape reality.' To what extent do you agree or disagree with this statement? In developing your answer, discuss both the themes and poetic language of the poetry of W. B. Yeats on your course.

Sample Plan 1

Intro: (*Stance: agree with viewpoint in the question*) Yeats's poetry is distinguished by a powerful strain between his pursuit of an ideal state and the inability to flee the harsh reality of everyday life. Effective use of forceful imagery, dramatic language and a variety of compelling tones.

Point 1: (*Elegy – world of beauty and grace/ugly reality – contrast*) 'In Memory of Eva Gore-Booth and Con Markiewicz' nostalgically recalls an elegant world, juxtaposing it against the ravages of time. Contemptuous tone conveys Yeats's resentment at real life choices made by Gore-Booth sisters ('gazelle' transforms into 'skeleton-gaunt').

Point 2: (*Confession – ageing/renewal – vivid imagery, allusions*) 'An Acre of Grass' presents Yeats's resentful attitude to the reality of ageing ('Now

strength and body goes'). He yearns for the artistic world ('an old man's frenzy'). Startling imagery captures the poet's intense desire for artistic activity and productivity ('Shake the dead in their shrouds').

Point 3: (*Self-epitaph – inferior modern literature/perfection of classical literature – imperative, contrast*) from 'Under Ben Bulben' contrasts ugliness of modern verse ('Base-born products') with perfection of heroic couplets ('learn your trade,/Sing whatever is well made').

Point 4: (*Satire – ageing/renewal – contrasts*) 'Politics' ironically comments on reality of politicians' false promises ('And maybe what they say is true') with his deeply held belief in the power of the emotions ('O that I were young again/And held her in my arms').

Conclusion: Yeats frequently reveals his inner struggle in confronting human realities. He creates poetry bringing his ideal world to life to enable us to see beyond what meets the eye while acknowledging but never fully accepting the harsh truths of everyday experience.

Sample Paragraph: Point 2

'An Acre of Grass' is Yeats's confession that he refuses to grow old gracefully. While he acknowledges the reality that he is 'Here at life's end', he despises old age's inactivity, 'nothing stirs'. Instead, he desires 'an old man's frenzy'. Yeats's internal struggle with the reality of ageing causes him to turn to his great role models. These include characters from Shakespeare, 'Timon and Lear', who challenged this unjust world. His desperate tone is evident in his prayer for help, 'Grant me'. But the poet is determined to continue with his artistic pursuits, despite his acknowledgement that his 'loose imagination' no longer finds inspiration in the dull 'rag and bone' of 'everyday routine'. Dramatic verbs ('pierce', 'inspired') describe the creative vigour of this 'old man's eagle mind'. His tone reflects his inner conflict.

> **EXAMINER'S COMMENT**
> Sustained top-grade response that addresses the question. Analytical points show a clear understanding of the poem. There is close engagement with the text, particularly in the discussion of how the poet's turmoil is conveyed through vivid imagery, intense tones and contrasts. Impressive expression throughout and excellent use of supportive quotes.

(Sample question 2)

'Yeats's poetry can sometimes seem obscure and challenging, but his powerful language has enduring appeal.' Discuss this view, developing your answer with reference to both the themes and poetic style of the poetry of W. B. Yeats on your course.

Sample Plan 2

Intro: (*Stance: partially agree with viewpoint in the question*) Yeats forces readers to consider challenging concepts – transience, creativity, the

POETRY FOCUS

NOTE

In keeping with the PCLM approach, the student has to take a stance by agreeing and/or disagreeing that Yeats's poetry can sometimes seem
- **obscure and challenging** (complex philosophical themes – materialism/idealism, ageing/regeneration, nature/mysticism, art/beauty, political conflict/patriotism, unclear references/allusions, etc.)

... but there is enduring appeal in:
- **powerful language** (evocative imagery, startling sound effects, dramatic verbs, striking comparisons, engaging tones, compelling rhythms, etc.)

breakdown of civilisation, political change, heroism, the immortality of art. His powerful language has enduring appeal – forceful metaphors, vivid images and symbols, dramatic quality, repetition.

Point 1: (*Apocalyptic vision – chilling imagery, foreboding tone*) 'The Second Coming' presents compelling imagery – a falcon spiralling out of control ('turning and turning'). Interesting biblical imagery ('rough beast') lends authority and dramatic verbs emphasise the turbulent mood.

Point 2: (*Transience/eternity – absorbing symbols, compound words*) 'Sailing to Byzantium' tackles the eternal problem of mortality/immortality. Vigorous phrases ('salmon-falls', 'mackerel-crowded') evoke fertility. Poet regards ageing man as worthless ('paltry thing') presenting a haunting image of frailty and decay ('dying animal'). Using emphatic language, Yeats addresses this stimulating theme.

Point 3: (*Destruction/nurturing – rich metaphor, repetition, contrasts*) 'The Stare's Nest by My Window' from 'Meditations in Time of Civil War' introduces nature's regenerative power ('bees build') to expose the horrific damage wreaked by conflict ('A man is killed, or a house burned'). Repetitive image of political vacuum ('empty house of the stare') contrasted with maternal nurturing ('mother birds bring grubs and flies').

Point 4: (*Provocative challenge – sibilant language, defiant tone*) 'Swift's Epitaph' opens with an evocative metaphor describing Swift's death ('sailed into his rest'). This serene image contrasts with reality of hostile reaction ('Savage indignation') to Swift's efforts for improving humanity.

Conclusion: Yeats defiantly confronts his readers with challenging but clearly defined themes, including the future, transience and conflict. Attractive writing style, inspiring visual and aural effects, innovative language and a rich variety of tones all excite the reader.

Sample Paragraph: Point 1

'The Second Coming' presents another challenging idea – the apocalyptic vision of society's collapse. This is seen in the image of the falcon spiralling out of control, 'Turning and turning and in the widening gyre'. Yeats believes that fanatics are taking control, 'the worst/Are full of passionate intensity'. Although he presents us with a disturbing image of humanity's spirit rising in a shocking 'Second Coming', he vividly describes it – 'blank and pitiless as the sun'. As always, the poet's alliteration, 'darkness drops', strikes a foreboding note. Vigorous visual imagery, 'blood-dimmed tide', reinforces the hectic scene. For Yeats, the era of innocence and order symbolised by the 'rocking cradle' in Bethlehem is disappearing. In its place, is a new era where a savage god will be 'moving its slow thighs'. A difficult subject is brought to life by the power of the poet's language.

EXAMINER'S COMMENT

Perceptive analysis of Yeats's powerful and appealing writing style in exploring provocative themes. Accurate references and supportive quotations are effectively integrated into the discussion. Impressive focus on some of the poem's rich imagery. Overall, a confidently written top-grade response, showing close engagement with both the poet's subject matter and style.

Leaving Cert Sample Essay

'W. B. Yeats makes effective use of rich symbolism and vivid imagery to explore a range of poetic themes.' Discuss this statement, developing your answer with reference to both the themes and poetic style of the poetry of W. B. Yeats on your course.

EXAM FOCUS

- As you may not be familiar with some of the poems referred to in the sample plans, substitute poems that you have studied closely.
- Key points about a particular poem can be developed over more than one paragraph.
- Paragraphs may also include cross-referencing and discussion of more than one poem.
- Remember that there is no single 'correct' answer to poetry questions, so always be confident in expressing your own considered response.

Sample Essay

1. The passing of time, political change and the search for spiritual meaning are recurring themes in Yeats's poetry. He is often angry about ageing and the limits of human existence. He offers his personal opinions on public and universal themes in poems such as 'The Lake Isle of Innisfree', 'September 1913', 'The Wild Swans at Coole' and 'Easter, 1916'. Yeats communicates his views in a powerful display of vibrant symbolism and vivid imagery.

2. In 'The Lake Isle of Innisfree', Yeats addresses a personal yet public theme, the longing of exiled emigrants to return to the peace of their homeland. Beautiful images describe the idyllic existence on Innisfree. The intensity of noonday heat on the heather is suggested by the broad-vowelled phrase 'purple glow'. The serenity of this magical place is evoked through slow broad vowels, alliterative 'l' sounds and onomatopoeia, 'I hear lake water lapping with low sounds by the shore'. This hypnotic vision – and Yeats's deep sense of longing – is interrupted by the startling reality of impersonal urban life, 'I stand on the roadway, or on the pavements grey'. Insistent monosyllable sounds emphasise the poet's deep desire to escape, 'I hear it in the deep heart's core'.

3. 'The Wild Swans at Coole' uses equally contrasting images. The swans are a powerful symbol of youthful vigour. Alliteration and onomatopoeia convey the dynamism of the noisy swans 'wheeling in great broken rings'. The swans' strong relationship, 'Lover by lover', is noted. Swans usually mate for life. This serene image is interrupted, as in the previous poem, with the bitter reality of Yeats's personal anguish. Unlike these 'brilliant creatures', he is ageing. He has been disappointed in life, 'now my heart is sore'. Yet, it is the dream which lingers in the reader's mind due to the poet's technical brilliance. The swans 'still drift on the still water,/ Mysterious, beautiful'. Yeats, again has combined personal and universal concerns, lost love and transience in haunting language.

4. In contrast to such lyrical beauty, the political poem, 'September 1913', attacks Irish citizens who focus on materialistic gain. Their attitude to religion is also mocked – they count 'prayer to shivering prayer'. Yeats was furious at the Dublin merchant classes of early-20th-century Dublin who refused to fund the Hugh Lane Gallery and who were partly

POETRY FOCUS

INDICATIVE MATERIAL

- **Yeats's effective use of rich symbolism and vivid imagery** (powerful metaphors, colourful similes, vibrant descriptive details, striking references and allusions, lively aural imagery, etc.)

  … that explore:

- **a range of poetic themes** (public and private, reality/escape, transience/immortality, exhilaration/tragedy of conflict, materialistic present/romanticised past, creativity, culture, etc.)

responsible for the trade union lockout. In contrast, Yeats communicates the idealistic dream which these merchants do not understand. He reminds them that there were once patriotic heroes who 'stilled your childish play'. The price they paid was the 'hangman's rope' or exile from their homeland, 'The grey wing upon every tide'. Yeats has taken a local conflict and given it a global application through powerful visual and aural imagery.

5. 'Easter, 1916' is another political poem highlighting Yeats's feelings. He is condescending towards those who fought for Irish freedom. He is barely civil, exchanging 'polite meaningless words' with them. The poet thought of Ireland as a land of fools who wore the clothes of clowns, 'where motley is worn'. Yet another paradox, 'A terrible beauty', acknowledges the pain and suffering of the rebels of 1916. Their devotion to a cause made their hearts 'Enchanted to a stone'. Yeats believed that dedication to an ideal resulted in men losing their humanity. This is indeed 'terrible'. However, their devotion also made it 'beautiful'.

6. Yeats addresses the conflict between mortality and immortality in 'Sailing to Byzantium'. The poet belittles an old man through the use of the telling symbol, 'at tattered coat upon a stick'. Alienated from a youthful Ireland, described in dynamic images, 'salmon-falls', 'mackerel-crowded seas', he lists the inescapable cycle of life, 'begotten, born, and dies'. He will fight against old age through art. Yeats rejects the decaying mortal body, 'A dying animal', and decides to become a golden bird 'set upon a golden bough' to continue his trade as poet, singing of 'what is past or passing or to come'. But this time the dream does not work. The Emperor is 'drowsy', inattentive. Byzantium, this mythical symbol of 'artifice' does not satisfy. Instead, it is the realistic image of the 'young/in one another's arms' which lingers in the reader's mind. The poet poses the problem of mortality and immortality and leaves it to the reader to consider.

7. Yeats repeatedly considers public and private themes, including escape, transience, conflict and death. These are carefully shaped, resulting in poems that echo 'like a ringing bell' due to forceful symbolism and compelling imagery.

(760 words)

EXAMINER'S COMMENT

Following the clear introduction, this focused top-grade response engages enthusiastically with both the question and selected illustrative poems. Some excellent critical discussion of the visual and aural imagery in 'The Lake Isle of Innisfree' and 'The Wild Swans at Coole'. While there was impressive focus on symbolism in 'Sailing to Byzantium', this element of the question might also have been developed more in paragraphs 4 and 5. Overall, confident expression and effective use of suitable quotation throughout contribute much to this highly commendable essay.

GRADE: H1
P = 15/15
C = 13/15
L = 15/15
M = 5/5
Total = 48/50

W. B. YEATS

👓 Revision Overview

'The Lake Isle of Innisfree' (OL)
In this beautiful poem, filled with sensual images, Yeats dreams of escaping the modern world to find peace in the countryside.

'September 1913'
Disenchanted with materialism, Yeats contrasts Ireland's past with the self-serving values of modern society.

'The Wild Swans at Coole' (OL)
A persistent sense of failure and regret underlies this poem in which Yeats explores the transience of human life.

'An Irish Airman Foresees His Death' (OL)
In this presentation of the power of the human spirit, Yeats addresses Irish national identity.

'Easter, 1916'
The force of political passion is central to this poem in which Yeats expresses his conflicted emotions regarding the Easter Rising.

'The Second Coming'
Yeats's longing for order leads him to envision some sort of Second Coming. This was traditionally associated with the return of Christ to Earth.

'Sailing to Byzantium'
Yeats yearns for meaning in this complex poem which addresses the reality of ageing.

'The Stare's Nest by My Window'
Yeats returns to the subject of moral and social collapse, and the search for renewal. The desire for freedom is central to the poem.

'In Memory of Eva Gore-Booth and Con Markiewicz'
Yeats laments time's effects on beauty and youthful idealism. The poem also considers the contribution that artists make to society.

'Swift's Epitaph'
Yeats's high regard for Swift can be seen as part of his commitment to Anglo-Irish cultural politics.

'An Acre of Grass'
Another confessional poem. The loss of poetic vision makes Yeats long for insight into the mystery of life and death.

***from* 'Under Ben Bulben'**
Facing death, Yeats embraces the spiritual world of eternity. He urges Irish poets to share his vision for fulfilment through art.

'Politics'
In this nostalgic poem, Yeats acknowledges human weakness. He believed love is more important than politics in shaping destiny.

💬 Last Words

'Yeats's poetry is simple and eloquent to the heart.'
Robert Louis Stevenson

'He had this marvellous gift of beating the scrap metal of the day-to-day life into a ringing bell.'
Seamus Heaney

'All that is beautiful in art is laboured over.'
W. B. Yeats

 CREATIVITY  TRANSIENCE MEANING OF LIFE LOVE IRELAND NATURE HISTORY/MEMORY LONGING ART HEROISM

POETRY FOCUS

The Unseen Poem

'Students should be able ... to read poetry conscious of its specific mode of using language as an artistic medium.'
(DES English Syllabus, 4.5.1)

Note that responding to the unseen poem is an exercise in aesthetic reading. It is especially important, in assessing the responses of the candidates, to guard against the temptation to assume a 'correct' reading of the poem.

Reward the candidates' awareness of the patterned nature of the language of poetry, its imagery, its sensuous qualities, and its suggestiveness.

SEC Marking Scheme

In the Unseen Poem 20-mark question, you will have 20 minutes to read and respond to a short poem that you are unlikely to have already studied. Targeted reading is essential. **Read over the questions** first to focus your thoughts and feelings.

In your **first reading** of the poem:
- Aim to get an initial sense of what the poet is saying and think about why the poet is writing about that particular subject.
- What is happening? Who is involved? Is there a sense of place and atmosphere?
- Underline interesting words or phrases that catch your attention. Avoid wasting time worrying about any words that you don't understand. Instead, **focus on what makes sense** to you.

Read through the poem **a second time**:
- Who is speaking in the poem? Is it the poet or another character?
- Is the poet describing a scene?
- Or remembering an experience?
- What point is the poet making?
- What do you notice about the poet's language use?
- How does the poem make you feel?
- Did it make you wonder? Trust your own reaction.

Check the **'Glossary of Common Literary Terms'** on GillExplore.ie.

- **Theme** (the central idea or message in a poem. There may be more than one theme)
- **Imagery** (includes similes, metaphors, symbols and personification)
- **Sound (aural) effects** – often referred to as onomatopoeia (includes alliteration, assonance, sibilance, rhyme and repetition)
- **Tone** (nostalgic, happy, sad, reflective, angry, optimistic, etc.)
- **Mood** (atmosphere can be relaxed, mysterious, poignant, uneasy, etc.)
- **Rhythm** (the pace or movement of lines, similar to the musical 'beat' of a song. Rhythm often reflects mood and can be slow, regular, rapid, uneven, etc.)
- **Language** (the poet's choice and order of words, including imagery and poetic devices)
- **Style** (the use of language. Poets choose various techniques, such as imagery, tone, etc. to convey meaning and emotion)
- **Lyric** (poem that expresses the poet's thoughts and feelings. Lyric poems are often short and sometimes resemble a song in form or style)
- **Rhyme** (the occurrence of the same or similar sounds – usually at the end of a line. Rhyme often adds emphasis)
- **Stanza** (two or more lines of poetry that together form a section of a poem)
- **Persona** (the speaker or 'voice' in the poem. This may or may not be the poet)
- **Personification** where the poet gives a human quality to something which is not human. Bishop's 'The Fish' uses personification to show empathy towards the writhing fish, 'A five-haired beard of wisdom/trailing from his aching jaw')
- **Enjambment** (when a line doesn't have punctuation at the end. The resulting run-on lines usually add emphasis)
- **Irony** (where there is another meaning to what is stated, e.g. Eliot's 'The Love Song of J. Alfred Prufrock' is really about a frustrated man who will never find love)
- **Emotive language** (when language and imagery affect the reader's feelings e.g. 'The streets that couldn't shelter them' in Meehan's poem, 'Prayer for the Children of Longing')
- **Contrasts** (contrasting themes, tones and images emphasise differences and similarities, e.g. in 'The Universe as Primal Scream', Smith contrasts the insignificance of human life compared to the universe)
- **Structure and layout** (a poem can often be identified by its structure or shape. Donne's religious sonnets consist of fourteen lines. The first eight lines are called the octave and often describe a problem or challenge. The next six lines are called the sestet and present a response to the octave)

> **REMEMBER!**
> 'This section [Unseen Poetry] was often not answered, resulting in a loss of 20 marks. Omitting questions or parts of questions has a deleterious effect and is often due to poor time management.'
> **Chief Examiner's Report**

POETRY FOCUS

Unseen Poem – Practice 1

Read the following poem by Alan Bold and answer **either** Question 1 **or** Question 2 which follow.

1 Autumn

Autumn arrives
Like an experienced robber
Grabbing the green stuff
Then cunningly covering his tracks
With a deep multitude
Of colourful distractions.
And the wind,
The wind is his accomplice
Putting an air of chaos
Into the careful diversions
So branches shake
And dead leaves are suddenly blown
In the faces of inquisitive strangers.
The theft chills the world,
Changes the temper of the earth
Till the normally placid sky
Glows red with a quiet rage.

Alan Bold

1. **(a)** What do you learn about the poet's attitude to autumn in the above poem? Support your answer with reference to the poem. (10)
   (b) Identify two images from the poem that make an impact on you and give reasons for your choice. (10)

   OR

2. Discuss the appeal of this poem, commenting on its theme, tone and the poet's use of language and imagery. Support your answer with reference to the poem. (20)

Sample Answer 1

Q1. (a) (Poet's attitude to autumn)
(Basic response)

The poet's attitude to autumn is not good at all because he calls autumn an experienced robber which is a negative thing. Alan does not compare the beauty in which nature is full of descriptive scenery of leaves falling in countryside areas. I think he's wrong about autumn to call it a theif in the night because this is not the whole picture at all and he only sees the negative side like storms and trees shaking. There is another story to the beauty of autumn's nature other than the dead leaves which are a reminder of death which is a totally negative side. Alan has a pesimmistic attitude and this is too narrow to be true to life.

EXAMINER'S COMMENT
- Makes one valid point about negativity.
- Little development or use of reference.
- No focus on the varied aspects of autumn.
- Expression is awkward and repetitive.
- Incorrect spellings ('theif', 'pesimmistic').

Marks awarded: 3/10

Sample Answer 2

Q1. (a) (Poet's attitude to autumn)
(Top-grade response)

Alan Bold has a very playful outlook towards the season of autumn. In comparing it to a cunning 'experienced' robber who sneaks in every year to steal 'the green stuff' that grows in summer, he seems fascinated by the way nature changes so secretively. Bold develops the metaphor throughout the poem, closely observing how the wind (autumn's 'accomplice') creates chaos, tossing colourful leaves across the ground. Autumn is depicted as a powerful natural force which not only changes the landscape, but also affects how people feel. This is evident in the poem's final lines where he suggests that autumn marks the transition into winter and is a reminder that nature can be destructive – and even something to be feared. The poet's overall attitude is that the season of autumn warns human beings about our fragile relationship with the natural world.

EXAMINER'S COMMENT
- Insightful answer that engages closely with the poem.
- Interesting final point about nature's destructive power.
- Good use made of supportive quotations throughout.
- Varied sentence length, fluent expression.
- Grammar and spellings are excellent.

Marks awarded: 10/10

Sample Answer 3

Q1. (b) (Two images that make an impact)
(Basic response)

'the faces of inquisitive strangers' This is the first image that makes an impact on me and my reasons for my choice is that it is just as it would happen in reality when people are in parks. This when we see the leaves are blown around into your face during October. If people have young children with them they never stop asking questions about the weather and everything.

'normally placid sky' The second image from the poem that made an impact on me and my reason for my choice is because this is that it is pure Irish weather in which the clouds are grey. It is usually about to rain in Ireland just like the calm before the storm. It does not exactly stay placid for long in this country. This image is detailed and true to life.

> **EXAMINER'S COMMENT**
> - Little engagement with the poem's language.
> - Limited point about the realism of both images.
> - Needs more developed discussion.
> - Drifted into general commentary.
> - Repetitive, flawed expression throughout.
>
> Marks awarded: 4/10

Sample Answer 4

Q1. (b) (Two images that make an impact)
(Top-grade response)

I thought the 'experienced robber' image was powerful. The simile suggests that autumn is sly – disturbing the peace of summer. Bold cleverly develops the comparison, emphasising the criminal image of the season, with associated words, such as 'covering his tracks' and 'cunningly'. The effect is playful – autumn is fooling everyone into a false sense of security by disguising the changes that are happening to the climate. This lively colourful season is not to be fully trusted.

In a second striking image, the poet personifies the wind, describing it as autumn's 'accomplice' in creating widespread havoc. It creates an air of chaos – literally. This gives nature a human characteristic, which only strengthens its awesome power. The wind shows autumn to be even more terrifying because something so strong is merely its accomplice.

> **EXAMINER'S COMMENT**
> - Perceptive analysis of the poet's inventive language.
> - Good understanding of the extended metaphor.
> - Effective use of apt textual reference.
> - Excellent expression throughout.
>
> Marks awarded: 9/10

Unseen Poem – Practice 2

Read the following poem by Grace Nichols and answer **either** Question 1 **or** Question 2 which follow.

2 Roller-Skaters

Flying by
on the winged-wheels
of their heels

Two teenage earthbirds
zig-zagging
down the street

Rising
unfeathered –
in sudden air-leap

Defying law
death and gravity
as they do a wheely

Landing back
in the smooth swoop
of youth

And faces gaping
gawking, impressed
and unimpressed

Only mother watches – heartbeat in her mouth

Grace Nichols

POETRY FOCUS

1. **(a)** What do you think the poet is saying about the relationships between parents and their children in 'Roller-Skaters'? Support your answer with reference to the poem. (10)

   (b) Identify two images from the poem that make an impact on you and give reasons for your choice. (10)

   OR

2. Discuss the language, including the imagery, used by the poet throughout this poem. Make detailed reference to the poem in support of your answer. (20)

Sample Answer 1

Q2. (Poet's language use)
(Basic response)

The poet's language including the imagry used by the poet is very detailed. It shows a street where roller skaters are taking place. The details show they are brave doing the wheely and zig zags as they are actually risking their lives for the sport they love. I myself have mixed feelings about the imagry because it shows how they jump in amazing tricks. Like leaps but on the other hand their mother is afraid that he will be hurt. The language describes the danger.

People out in the street are looking at the image of these skaters. This is an image of risking life or just to show off to attract attention. The images make me think of the danger involved behind the first impressions of an exciting sport that attracts kids in every city. At the start it is very exciting because no one is injured so far but as Grace protrays the skaters more in a detailed way the language becomes more dangerous for example when she says there is a risk of death during the wheely. No wonder the mother watching has an image of her heart in her mouth because it is a dangerous situation and she is not too impressed.

EXAMINER'S COMMENT

- Makes some points about detailed description.
- Little development or use of close reference to language.
- Minimal focus on the effectiveness of imagery.
- Expression is awkward and repetitive at times.
- Mechanical errors ('imagry', 'protrays').

Marks awarded: 6/20

Sample Answer 2

Q2. (Poet's language use)
(Top-grade response)

Vivid imagery and energetic language are key features in this poem. Nichols describes the roller skaters 'Flying by' and having 'winged-wheels'. Both descriptions are metaphors as the skaters are not actually 'flying' nor do they have real 'wings'. The poem can be seen as one developed metaphor that suggests the breakneck actions of the skaters. Short lines and dynamic verbs, such as 'zig-zagging' suggest their speed.

The skaters are compared to 'earthbirds' which is very effective. I can imagine that they will take off into the air at any minute. Later on, they are described as 'unfeathered', which links back to the same idea that they are defying 'death and gravity'. Towards the end, the poet mentions the 'smooth sweep of youth' and suggests that the skaters are enjoying their freedom.

The poem's rhythm is lively throughout and not interrupted by punctuation. This highlights the reckless moves the skaters make. Run-on lines create a sense of continuous movement. Sound effects play a huge part. There is a pattern of slender vowels – e.g. 'winged-wheels' – in the opening lines which increases the pace. The alliteration suggests the repeated actions of the skaters.

The layout is arranged in a series of short lines and this highlights the skaters' lively movement. The final separate line cleverly suggests how the mother is outside of the action and can only watch from a distance as her child takes risks.

> **EXAMINER'S COMMENT**
> - Focused on the effectiveness of language throughout.
> - Ranges over various aspects, including imagery and sound.
> - Well-developed discussion of the bird metaphor.
> - Insightful comments on rhythm and structure.
> - Good expression (although 'suggests' is overused).
> Marks awarded: 18/20

> **REMEMBER!**
> There is no single 'correct' reading of the poem. Respond to the poem honestly. How does it make you feel? Trust your own reaction.

Unseen Poem – Practice 3

Read the following poem by David Harmer and answer **either** Question 1 **or** Question 2 which follow.

At Cider Mill Farm

I remember my uncle's farm
Still in mid-summer
Heat hazing the air above the red roof tops
Some cattle sheds, a couple of stables
Clustered round a small yard
Lying under the hills that stretched their long back
Through three counties.

I rolled with the dogs
Among the hay bales
Stacked high in the barn he built himself
During a storm one autumn evening
Tunnelled for treasure or jumped with a scream
From a pirate ship's mast into the straw
Burrowed for gold and found he'd buried
Three battered Ford cars deep in the hay.

He drove an old tractor that sweated oil
In long black streaks down the rusty orange
It chugged and whirred, coughed into life
Each day as he clattered across the cattle grids
I remember one night my cousin and I
Dragging back cows from over the common
We prodded them homeward through the rain
And then drank tea from huge tin mugs
Feeling like farmers.

He's gone now, he sold it
But I have been back for one last look
To the twist in the lane that borders the stream
Where Mary, Ruth and I once waded
Water sloshing over our wellies
And I showed my own children my uncle's farm
The barn still leaning over the straw
With for all I know three battered Ford cars
Still buried beneath it.

David Harmer

1. **(a)** What is your impression of the poet's experiences on the farm in 'At Cider Hill Farm'? Support your answer with reference to the poem. (10)
   (b) Select two images from the poem that appeal to you and give reasons for your choice. (10)

   OR

2. Discuss the language used by the poet, commenting on imagery, tone and sound effects. Support your answer with reference to the poem. (20)

Sample Answer 1

Q1. (a) (Poet's experiences on the farm)
(Basic response)

My impression of David Harmer is he remembers spending happy times on his holidays in cider mill farm. It belonged to his uncle who was the farm owner during his childhood, so he would have been there in the holidays. He had happy experiences splashing in the river and messing with the dogs but his best experience is of the one time he drank tea from the mugs belonging to the proper farmers after working with the cattle one evening. But the boy was dissapointed after the farm was sold, any child would naturally suffer from dissapointment by loosing their freedom. Up to then the farm life was very appealing, a good break away from school during the holidays.

EXAMINER'S COMMENT
- Some references to the poet's happy experiences.
- These could have been more effectively supported by quotes.
- Lacks discussion on stylistic features, e.g. nostalgic tone.
- Capital letter errors and misspellings ('dissapointed', 'loosing').
Marks awarded: 4/10

Sample Answer 2

Q1. (a) (Poet's experiences on the farm)
(Top-grade response)

Harmer's reminiscences are of exciting childhood days on his uncle's farm. From the start, his tone is nostalgic, 'Heat hazing the air above the red roof tops'. The vowel sounds and gentle alliteration emphasise the poet's happy memories of far-off times. The images of rural scenes show the impact that the countryside 'under the hills' had on him. I think it's almost as if the changing seasons matched the change in the poet's life as he grew up. The mood is enthusiastic, however. The boy's sense of adventure is seen when exploring new sensations among the farm animals, 'We prodded them homeward through the rain'. He seems fascinated by the 'rusty orange' tractor – 'It chugged and whirred'. As a child, he delighted in creating his own world. It's clear that the time on the farm was important, so much so that he wants to pass on his memories to his own children.

EXAMINER'S COMMENT
- Intuitive response focusing on the poet's idyllic childhood.
- Good range of discussion points.
- Well-supported by suitable quotations.
- Effective reference to imagery, tone and sound effects.
- Confident expression and excellent mechanics.
Marks awarded: 10/10

Sample Answer 3

Q1. (b) (Two appealing images)
(Basic response)

The first appealing image is of 'one night dragging cows' because this shows cows don't hurry and have to be prodded with sticks. They nearly have to get dragged along as the image says, so this is the reason why this is a good image as it really shows farmers totally have their hands full trying to get animals to go anywhere. The next image is 'three battered Ford cars'. This is the second appealing image of cars rusting in a field. This can be seen in parts of the country where cars are dumped and they are a complete and total eyesore to the public who have to look at them. So in one way this is not appealing as an image because some people just dump rubbish anywhere.

> **EXAMINER'S COMMENT**
> - Slight points that need to be much more developed.
> - Drifts into irrelevant general commentary.
> - No attempt to examine the effectiveness of the language.
> - Repetitive expression lacks fluency.
>
> Marks awarded: 3/10

Sample Answer 4

Q1. (b) (Two appealing images)
(Top-grade response)

There are many appealing images in this poem. I liked the ones that focused on the poet's carefree childhood, such as 'Heat hazing the air above the red roof tops'. The summer setting has strong associations with warmth and happiness. The poet remembers the haze of bright sunlight and the vivid red colours of the farm buildings. This vibrant imagery suggests an exaggerated childlike memory which is reinforced by the 'h' and 'r' alliteration. The line has a dreamlike quality, suggesting the wonder of the experience. Some of the feelings the poet recalls are reinforced by sound images, for example, 'Water sloshing over our wellies'. The onomatopoeic effect of 'sloshing' echoes the squelching noises made by the children as they splashed through the water. This all contributes to the upbeat mood of the poem. Harmer is re-living a moment when he was totally happy-go-lucky on his uncle's farm.

> **EXAMINER'S COMMENT**
> - Perceptive analysis of visual and aural imagery.
> - Well-developed discussion examining language closely.
> - Points supported by relevant textual reference.
> - Excellent expression and varied vocabulary throughout.
>
> Marks awarded: 10/10

Unseen Poem – Practice 4

Read the following poem by Rosita Boland and answer **either** Question 1 **or** Question 2 which follow.

4 Lipstick

Home from work one evening
I switched the radio on as usual,
chose a knife and started to slice
red peppers, scallions, wild mushrooms.

I started listening to a programme about Iran.
After the Shah fled, Revolutionary Guards
patrolled the streets of Teheran
looking for stray hairs, exposed ankles
and other signs of female disrespect.

The programme ended.
I was left standing in my kitchen
looking at the chopped vegetables on the table;
the scarlet circles of the peppers
delicate mouths, scattered at random.

When they discovered a woman wearing lipstick
they razor-bladed it off:
replaced one red gash with another.

Rosita Boland

POETRY FOCUS

> 1. (a) What do you learn about the kind of person the poet is from reading this poem? Explain your answer with reference to the poem. (10)
>
> (b) Identify a mood or feeling evoked in 'Lipstick' and explain how the poet creates this mood or feeling. Support your answer with reference to the poem. (10)
>
> OR
>
> 2. What impact did this poem make on you? Refer closely to the text in discussing its theme, tone and the poet's use of language and imagery. (20)

Sample Answer 1

Q2. (Impact of the poem)
(Basic response)

This was a hard to understand poem about a worker who comes home to make a meal. But she starts to listen to the news about what is happening in the war. I think she imagines the soilders running wild attacking people. One soilder uses a knife and attacks an innocent woman who is just dressed up and wearing lipstick which is her basic human right and just out for the evening. This guard should of known better. This is the part of the poem that made the most impact on me personally.

This is the theme of war and the tone of this poem is showing what happens on the back streets in some parts of the world. If your not doing harm you should be left in peace. There is a big difference between the image of the innocent woman out to enjoy herself on a night out as she is intitled and the angry language of the soilder who attacks her for no reason. Unfortunately it is not a state of peace everywhere else which is the main impact of the poem.

EXAMINER'S COMMENT

- *Makes one reasonable point about the impact of violence.*
- *Only slight engagement with the poem.*
- *No convincing analysis of the poet's language use.*
- *Expression could have been much more controlled.*
- *Mechanical errors ('soilder', 'intitled', 'should of', 'your').*
Marks awarded: 6/20

Sample Answer 2

Q2. (Impact of the poem)
(Top-grade response)

Although the language is simple in this poem, it actually makes the point that routine violence against women is still common in some societies. This makes a greater impact as the poem develops because the poet's tone is almost relaxed in the first stanza – 'I switched the radio on as usual'. The programme is truly shocking. Boland points out the stark difference between what we take for granted as normality here at home and the grotesque reality of life in conflict areas, such as the Middle East.

The vivid image of the attack on the civilian is horrific. The poet creates a dramatic effect by contrasting the girl's beauty and the brutal violence she experiences. The guard's vicious action is foreshadowed by the earlier image of the poet herself using a kitchen knife to slice vegetables. I can relate to her sense of revulsion as she imagines the Iranian policeman's use of a razor blade to replace 'one red gash with another'.

The quiet tone of the final stanza reflects her sense of failure, 'left standing there in my kitchen'. Vivid images of the half-chopped vegetables, particularly the 'scarlet circles of the peppers', are closely associated with the 'Delicate mouths' of vulnerable women who suffer vicious abuse and injustice.

EXAMINER'S COMMENT

- Convincing personal response to the question.
- Points are clear, incisive and aptly supported.
- Links theme and stylistic features very well.
- Perceptive analysis of tone, imagery and contrast.
- Excellent expression, fluent and varied.

Marks awarded: 20/20

REMEMBER!

Avoid wasting time worrying about any words in an Unseen Poem that you don't understand. Instead, focus on what makes sense to you.

Unseen Poem Revision Points

- **Study the wording of questions** to identify the task that you have to do.
- Express your **key points** clearly.
- Include **supportive reference or quotation** (correctly punctuated).
- Refer to both the poet's **style** (how the poem is written) as well as the **themes** (what the poet is writing about).
- **Select interesting phrases** that give you an opportunity to discuss subject matter and use of language.
- **Avoid summaries** that simply repeat the text of the poem.
- **Engage with the poem** by responding genuinely to what the poet has written.

Unseen Poem – Practice 5

Read the following poem by Pat Boran and answer **either** Question 1 **or** Question 2 which follow. (Allow 20 minutes to complete the answer.)

5 Stalled Train

In the listening carriage, someone's
phone cries out for help: A student frisks himself,
a woman weighs her handbag
then stares into space. Our train
is going nowhere, stalled here
so long now the cattle in this field
have dared come right up close
to chew and gaze. We tell ourselves
that somewhere down the line
things we cannot understand
are surely taking place — the future
almost within reach — and into each
small telephone that rings
or shudders now, like doubt,
we commit (if still in whispers)
our hopes and fears,
our last known whereabouts.

Pat Boran

1. **(a)** In your opinion, is the dominant mood in the poem positive or negative? Explain your answer with reference to the poem. (10)
   (b) Identify two images from the poem that you find interesting and give reasons for your choice. (10)

   OR

2. Discuss the impact of this poem, with reference to its theme and the poet's use of language and imagery. Refer closely to the text in support of your answer. (20)

PROMPT!
- *Think about the poet's attitude to modern life.*
- *Imagery is vivid, graphic, cinematic.*
- *Surreal, mysterious, dream-like atmosphere.*
- *Effective use of personification and symbols.*
- *Final lines are disturbing.*
- *Poem raises many interesting questions.*